PLAYFAIR
CRICKET ANNUAL 2002

55th edition

EDITED BY ~~BI~~ ~~L~~

PREFACE

Australians almost totally dominated the 2001 English season. Such was the extent of the dazzling array of talent in Steve Waugh's touring team that selecting their man of the series must have been one of the most difficult tasks to have confronted any adjudicator. With Damian Martyn and the Waugh twins contributing a brace of hundreds apiece, Glenn McGrath and Shane Warne sharing 63 wickets and Adam Gilchrist playing two match-turning innings, the decision must have been exceptionally close. The prize eventually went to McGrath whose tally of victims exceeded that of Warne by just one. His steep bounce and unerring accuracy probed the technical and mental skills of every English batsman and he now ranks with the greatest new-ball operators of the last fifty years. Michael Atherton, whose shy twirl of the bat as he left the international stage at The Oval provided the summer's most poignant memory, can confirm that status.

One innings dominates my recall of that Ashes rubber but that was played against McGrath at Headingley when acting captain Gilchrist set England the task of scoring 315 runs from 110 overs. On only one occasion, at Melbourne in 1928-29, had England achieved a fourth innings target in excess of 300. In scoring his undefeated 173 off 227 balls, Mark Butcher played one of the finest hands ever seen in Test cricket and against one of its strongest attacks supported by an exceptional combination. He began the season struggling for selection in Surrey's first eleven but he ended it with the highest aggregate (456 runs) of the series. So fickle is form. If *Playfair* had established a Cricketer of the Season Award he would certainly have been my choice.

Three other Aussies, Michael Hussey, Darren Lehmann and Ian Harvey, dominated the county scene. Northamptonshire's scorer, Tony Kingston, rated Hussey's balance and footwork as the most impressive of all his county's post-war batsmen. His undefeated 329 established a Northants record and he became the first to score 2000 first-class runs since 1995. Lehmann made a massive contribution to Yorkshire's first Championship title since 1968 and his 252 set a new record for a Roses Match innings. Harvey's 61-ball century won the coveted Walter Lawrence Trophy for the fastest first-class hundred of the season. Martin Bicknell enjoyed the most notable summer by a home player and came close to an England recall by scoring 748 runs, including his maiden hundred, and taking 72 wickets.

Now we welcome the Sri Lankan and Indian teams and look forward to another packed international and domestic season. So congested is it that the final Test will start at the latest date since the very first one in 1880. A streamlined elite of umpires and referees will now supervise all Tests. Hopefully the increased scope of their training and liaison will inspire new confidence and better behaviour from the players.

Such is the marvel of modern technology that I have been able instantly to relay copy and scan proofs of this edition from the other side of the globe during a brief gap in England's international schedule. Chris Leggett's expertise and enthusiasm at Letterpart has made this possible. Special thanks are also due to Jo Roberts-Miller of Headline for much fine-tuning and for overseeing this edition's final stages.

Once again *Playfair* is greatly indebted to the county clubs' administrators, scorers and statisticians, to Alan Fordham and Andrew Smith (ECB), and to many overseas correspondents. We wish David Armstrong, long the tireless secretary of the MCCA, a happy retirement. Philip Bailey, Ric Finlay, David Fitzgerald, David Mitchell and Debbie Frindall have all made notable contributions. Thanks are also due to Juliet and Brian Kirke for turning part of their spectacular Marlborough Sounds home into a nocturnal office.

BILL FRINDALL
Karaka Point, New Zealand
11 March 2002

ENGLAND v SRI LANKA

SERIES RECORDS

1981-82 to 2000-01

HIGHEST INNINGS TOTALS

England	in England	445		The Oval	1998
	in Sri Lanka	387		Kandy	2000-01
Sri Lanka	in England	591		The Oval	1998
	in Sri Lanka	470-5d		Galle	2000-01

LOWEST INNINGS TOTALS

England	in England	181		The Oval	1998
	in Sri Lanka	189		Galle	2000-01
Sri Lanka	in England	194		Lord's	1988
	in Sri Lanka	81		Colombo (SSC)	2000-01
HIGHEST MATCH AGGREGATE		1254 for 30 wickets		The Oval	1998
LOWEST MATCH AGGREGATE		645 for 36 wickets		Colombo (SSC)	2000-01

HIGHEST INDIVIDUAL INNINGS

England	in England	174	G.A.Gooch	Lord's	1991
	in Sri Lanka	128	R.A.Smith	Colombo (SSC)	1992-93
Sri Lanka	in England	213	S.T.Jayasuriya	The Oval	1998
	in Sri Lanka	201*	M.S.Atapattu	Galle	2000-01

HIGHEST AGGREGATE OF RUNS IN A SERIES

England	in England	212	(av 106.00)	G.A.Gooch	1991
	in Sri Lanka	269	(av 67.25)	G.P.Thorpe	2000-01
Sri Lanka	in England	237	(av 237.00)	S.T.Jayasuriya	1998
	in Sri Lanka	262	(av 52.40)	D.P.M.deS.Jayawardena	2000-01

RECORD WICKET PARTNERSHIPS – ENGLAND

1st	101	M.A.Atherton (44)/M.E.Trescothick (57)	Galle	2000-01
2nd	139	G.A.Gooch (174)/A.J.Stewart (43)	Lord's	1991
3rd	167	N.Hussain (109)/G.P.Thorpe (59)	Kandy	2000-01
4th	128	G.A.Hick (107)/J.P.Crawley (156*)	The Oval	1998
5th	86	G.P.Thorpe (113*)/M.P.Vaughan (26)	Colombo (SSC)	2000-01
6th	87	A.J.Lamb (107)/R.M.Ellison (41)	Lord's	1984
	87	A.J.Stewart (54)/C.White (39)	Kandy	2000-01
7th	63	A.J.Stewart (113*)/R.C.Russell (17)	Lord's	1991
8th	28	G.P.Thorpe (113*)/R.D.B.Croft (16)	Colombo (SSC)	2000-01
9th	37	P.J.Newport (26)/N.A.Foster (14*)	Lord's	1988
10th	89	J.P.Crawley (156*)/A.R.C.Fraser (32)	The Oval	1998

RECORD WICKET PARTNERSHIPS – SRI LANKA

1st	99	R.S.Mahanama (64)/U.C.Hathurusinghe (59)	Colombo (SSC)	1992-93
2nd	92	M.S.Atapattu (201*)/K.Sangakkara (58)	Galle	2000-01
3rd	243	S.T.Jayasuriya (213)/P.A.de Silva (152)	The Oval	1998
4th	148	S.Wettimuny (190)/A.Ranatunga (84)	Lord's	1984

5th	150	S.Wettimuny (190)/L.R.D.Mendis (111)	Lord's	1984
6th	138	S.A.R.Silva (102*)/L.R.D.Mendis (94)	Lord's	1984
7th	93	K.Sangakkara (95)/H.D.P.K.Dharmasena (54)	Kandy	2000-01
8th	53	H.D.P.K.Dharmasena (54)/W.P.U.C.J.Vaas (36)	Kandy	2000-01
9th	83	H.P.Tillekeratne (93*)/M.Muralitharan (19)	Colombo (SSC)	1992-93
10th	64	J.R.Ratnayeke (59*)/G.F.Labrooy (42)	Lord's	1988

BEST INNINGS BOWLING ANALYSIS

England	in England	7- 70	P.A.J.DeFreitas	Lord's	1991
	in Sri Lanka	6- 33	J.E.Emburey	Colombo (PSS)	1981-82
Sri Lanka	in England	9- 65	M.Muralitharan	The Oval	1998
	in Sri Lanka	6- 73	W.P.U.C.J.Vaas	Colombo (SSC)	2000-01

BEST MATCH BOWLING ANALYSIS

England	in England	8-115	P.A.J.DeFreitas	Lord's	1991
	in Sri Lanka	8- 95	D.L.Underwood	Colombo (PSS)	1981-82
Sri Lanka	in England	16-220	M.Muralitharan	The Oval	1998
	in Sri Lanka	8- 94	S.T.Jayasuriya	Galle	2000-01

HIGHEST WICKET AGGREGATE IN A SERIES

England	in England	8	(av 14.37)	P.A.J.DeFreitas	1991
	in Sri Lanka	14	(av 19.57)	D.Gough	2000-01
Sri Lanka	in England	16	(av 13.75)	M.Muralitharan	1998
	in Sri Lanka	16	(av 14.75)	S.T.Jayasuriya	2000-01
		16	(av 15.25)	W.P.U.C.J.Vaas	2000-01

RESULTS SUMMARY
ENGLAND v SRI LANKA – IN ENGLAND

| | Tests | Series | | | Lord's | | | Oval | | |
		E	SL	D	E	SL	D	E	SL	D
1984	1	–	–	1	–	–	1	–	–	–
1988	1	1	–	–	1	–	–	–	–	–
1991	1	1	–	–	1	–	–	–	–	–
1998	1	–	1	–	–	–	–	–	1	–
	4	2	1	1	2	–	1	–	1	–

ENGLAND v SRI LANKA – IN SRI LANKA

| | Tests | Series | | | Colombo (PSS) | | | Colombo (SSC) | | | Galle | | | Kandy | | |
		E	SL	D	E	SL	D	E	SL	D	E	SL	D	E	SL	D
1981-82	1	1	–	–	1	–	–	–	–	–	–	–	–	–	–	–
1992-93	1	–	1	–	–	–	–	–	1	–	–	–	–	–	–	–
2000-01	3	2	1	–	–	–	–	1	–	–	1	–	1	1	–
	5	3	2	–	1	–	–	1	1	–	1	–	1	1	–
Totals	9	5	3	1												

SRI LANKA REGISTER

Sri Lanka's touring team had not been selected at the time of going to press. Career statistics are to 11 March 2002. See page 11 for key to abbreviations.

ARNOLD, Russel Premakumaran, b Colombo 25 Oct 73. LHB, OB. F-c debut 1993-94. Nondescripts. **Tests:** 37 (1996-97 to 2001-02); HS 123 v P (Lahore) 1998-99; BB 3-76 v SA (Cape Town) 2000-01. **LOI:** 72 (1997-98 to 2001-02); HS 103 v Z (Bulawayo) 1999-00; BB 2-12 v Z (Colombo) 2001-02. HS (f-c) 217* Nondescripts v Moors (Colombo) 1995-96. BB (f-c) 7-84.

ATAPATTU, Marvin Samson (Ananda C), b Kalutara 22 Nov 1970. 5'9". RHB, LB. F-c debut 1988-89. Sinhalese. **Tests:** 55 (1990-91 to 2001-02); HS 223 v Z (Kandy) 1997-98; BB 1-9. **LOI:** 143 (1990-91 to 2001-02, 1 as captain); HS 132* v E (Lord's) 1998. HS (f-c) 253* Sinhalese v Galle (Colombo) 1995-96. BB (f-c) 3-19.

CHANDANA, Umagiliya Durage **Upul**, b Galle 5 Jul 1972. RHB, LB. F-c debut 1991-92. Tamil Union. **Tests:** 6 (1998-99 to 2001-02); HS 92 v Z (Galle) 2001-02; BB 6-179 v P (Dhaka) 1998-99 – on debut. **LOI:** 81 (1993-94 to 2001-02); HS 50 v E (Melbourne) 1998-99; BB 4-31 v Z (Colombo) 1997-98. HS (f-c) 194. BB (f-c) 7-80.

De SILVA, Pinnaduwage **Aravinda**, b Colombo 17 Oct 1965. 5'3½". RHB, OB. F-c debut 1983-84. Nondescripts. Kent 1995; cap 1995. Auckland. *Wisden* 1995. **Tests:** 89 (1984 to 2000-01, 6 as captain); HS 267 v NZ (Wellington) 1990-91; BB 3-30 v NZ (Colombo) 1997-98. **LOI:** 275 (1983-84 to 2000-01, 18 as captain); HS 145 v K (Kandy) 1995-96; BB 4-45 v P (Paarl) 1997-98. HS (f-c) 267 (*see Tests*). BB (f-c) 7-24 Nondescripts v Panadura (Panadura) 1994-95.

DHARMASENA, Handunnettige Deepthi Priyantha **Kumar**, b Colombo 24 Apr 1971. 5'11". RHB, OB. F-c debut 1988-89. Bloomfield. Moratuwa. Nondescripts. **Tests:** 25 (1993-94 to 2000-01); HS 62* v P (Sialkot) 1995-96; BB 6-72 v NZ (Galle) 1997-98. **LOI:** 123 (1994-95 to 2001-02); HS 69* v SA (Lahore) 1997-98; BB 4-37 v SA (Port Elizabeth) 1994-95. HS (f-c) 157. BB (f-c) 7-30.

DILSHAN, Tuwan Mohamed (*changed forenames to Tillakaratne Mudiyanselage* after converting to Buddhism), b Kalutara 14 Oct 1976. RHB, WK. F-c debut 1993-94. Bloomfield. Kalutara. Sebastianites. Singha. **Tests:** 10 (1999-00 to 2000-01); HS 163* v Z (Harare) 1999-00. **LOI:** 14 (1999-00 to 2000-01); HS 53 v Z (Harare) 1999-00. HS (f-c) 194. BB (f-c) 3-40.

FERNANDO, Conganige Randhi **Dilhara**, b Colombo 19 Jul 1979. RHB, RFM. F-c debut 1997-98. Sinhalese. **Tests:** 9 (1999-00 to 2001); HS 5* (twice); BB 5-42 v I (Galle) 2001. **LOI:** 19 (2000-01 to 2001-02); HS 12* v SA (Bloemfontein) 2000-01; BB 3-43 v P (Sharjah) 2001-02. HS (f-c) 42. BB (f-c) 6-29.

FERNANDO, Thudellage **Charitha** Buddika, b Panadura 22 Aug 1980. RHB, RFM. F-c debut 1999-00. Panadura. **Tests:** 5 (2001-02); HS 45 v Z (Kandy) 2001-02; BB 4-27 v Z (Kandy) 2001-02. **LOI:** 5 (2001-02); HS 3; BB 5-67 v Z (Sharjah) 2001-02 – on debut. HS (f-c) 81. BB (f-c) 6-39.

JAYASURIYA, Sanath Teran (St Servatius C), b Matara 30 Jun 1969. 5'6". LHB, SLA. F-c debut 1988-89. Colombo. Bloomfield. *Wisden* 1996. **Tests:** 70 (1990-91 to 2001-02, 32 as captain); HS 340 v I (Colombo) 1997-98; BB 5-43 v Z (Galle) 2001-02. **LOI:** 252 (1989-90 to 2001-02, 69 as captain); HS 189 v I (Sharjah) 2000-01; BB 6-29 v E (Moratuwa) 1992-93. Scored fastest LOI fifty (17 balls) v P (Singapore) 1995-96. HS (f-c) 340 (*see Tests*). BB (f-c) 5-43 (*see Tests*).

JAYAWARDENA, Denagamage Proboth **Mahela** DeSilva (Nalanda C), b Colombo 27 May 1977. 5'9". RHB, RM. F-c debut 1995-96. Sinhalese. **Tests:** 41 (1997-98 to 2001-02); HS 242 v I (Colombo) 1998-99; BB 2-32 v P (Galle) 2000-01. **LOI:** 94 (1997-98 to 2001-02, 1 as captain); HS 128 v I (Sharjah) 2000-02; BB 2-56 v K (Southampton) 1999. HS (f-c) 242 (*see Tests*). BB (f-c) 5-72.

KALUWITHARANA, Romesh Shantha (St Sebastian's C), b Colombo 24 Nov 1969. 5'4½". RHB, WK. F-c debut 1988-89. Colts. Galle. Sebastianites. **Tests:** 40 (1992-93 to 2000-01); HS 132* v A (Colombo) 1992-93 – on debut. **LOI:** 170 (1990-91 to 2001-02); HS 102* v E (Colombo) 2000-01. HS (f-c) 179.

LIYANAGE, Dulip Kapila, b Kalutara 6 Jun 1972. LHB, RMF. F-c debut 1991-92. Colts. **Tests:** 9 (1992-93 to 2001); HS 23 v I (Lucknow) 1993-94; BB 4-56 v A (Moratuwa) 1992-93. **LOI:** 16 (1992-93 to 2001-02); HS 43 v WI (P-o-S) 1996-97; BB 3-49 v P (Sharjah) 1993-94. HS (f-c) 108*. BB (f-c) 6-20.

MURALITHARAN, Muthiah (St Anthony's C), b Kandy 17 Apr 1972. 5'5". RHB, OB. F-c debut 1989-90. Tamil Union. Lancashire 1999 (taking 7-44 and 7-73 v Warwks at Southport on debut), 2001; cap 1999. *Wisden* 1998. **Tests:** 73 (1992-93 to 2001-02); HS 67 v I (Kandy) 2001-02; BB 9-51 v Z (Kandy) 2001-02. **LOI:** 183 (1993-94 to 2001-02); HS 18 v E (Lord's) 1998; BB 7-30 v I (Sharjah) 2000-01. HS (f-c) 67 (*see Tests*). 50 wkts (2+3); most – 66 (1996-97; 1999 – in 7 CC matches). BB 9-51 (*see Tests*).

SAMARAWEERA, Thilan Thusara, b Colombo 22 Sep 1976. RHB, OB. F-c debut 1995-96. Colts. Sinhalese. **Tests:** 9 (2001 to 2001-02); HS 123* v Z (Colombo) 2001-02; BB 1-7; scored 103* v I (Colombo) on debut. **LOI:** 8 (1998-99 to 2000-01); HS 27 v NZ (Sharjah) 2000-01; BB 3-34 v E (Sydney) 1998-99. HS (f-c) 123* (*see Tests*). BB (f-c) 6-55.

SANGAKKARA, Kumar, b Colombo 27 Oct 1977. LHB, WK. F-c debut 1997-98. Nondescripts. **Tests:** 20 (2000-01 to 2001-02); HS 230 v P (Lahore) 2001-02. **LOI:** 40 (2000-01 to 2001-02); HS 85 v SA (Galle) 2000-01. HS (f-c) 230 (*see Tests*).

TILLEKERATNE, Hashan Prasantha (D.S.Senanayake C), b Colombo 14 Jul 1967. 5'6". LHB, OB, occ WK. F-c debut 1984-85. Nondescripts. **Tests:** 67 (1989-90 to 2001-02, 1 as captain); 204* v Z (Colombo) 2001-02. **LOI:** 186 (1986-87 to 1999); HS 104 v WI (Bombay) 1993-94; BB 1-3. HS (f-c) 204* (*see Tests*). BB (f-c) 4-37.

VAAS, Warnakulasooriya Patabendige Ushantha **Chaminda** Joseph, b Mattumagala 27 Jan 1974. LHB, LFM. F-c debut 1990-91. Colts. **Tests:** 59 (1994-95 to 2001-02); HS 74* v Z (Colombo) 2001-02; BB 7-71 (14-191 match) v WI (Colombo) 2001-02. **LOI:** 175 (1993-94 to 2001-02); HS 50* v P (Sharjah) 2000-01; BB 8-19 v Z (Colombo) 2001-02; hat-trick v Z (Colombo) 2001-02. HS (f-c) 74* (*see Tests*). BB (f-c) 7-71 (*see Tests*).

WICKREMASINGHE, Gallage Pramodya, b Matara 14 Aug 1971. RHB, RMF. F-c debut 1988-89. Burgher. Sinhalese. **Tests:** 40 (1991-92 to 2000-01); HS 51 v SA (Cape Town) 1997-98; BB 6-60 v Z (Bulawayo) 1999-00. **LOI:** 132 (1990-91 to 2000-01); HS 32 v SA (Bloemfontein) 2000-01. BB 4-48 v P (Jamshedpur) 1998-99. HS (f-c) 76*. BB (f-c) 10-41 Sinhalese v Kalutara (Colombo) 1991-92.

ZOYSA, Demuni **Nuwan** Tharanga, b Colombo 13 May 1978. LHB, LFM. F-c debut 1996-97. Sinhalese. **Tests:** 22 (1996-97 to 2001-02); HS 26 v P (Rawalpindi) 1999-00; BB 4-76 v SA (Pretoria) 2000-01; hat-trick v Z (Harare) 1999-00. **LOI:** 57 (1996-97 to 2000-01); HS 32 v NZ (Christchurch) 2000-01; BB 4-28 v NZ (Wellington) 2000-01. HS (f-c) 60*. BB (f-c) 7-58.

ENGLAND v INDIA

SERIES RECORDS
1932 to 2001-02

HIGHEST INNINGS TOTALS

England	in England	653-4d	Lord's	1990
	in India	652-7d	Madras	1984-85
India	in England	606-9d	The Oval	1990
	in India	591	Bombay	1992-93

LOWEST INNINGS TOTALS

England	in England	101	The Oval	1971
	in India	102	Bombay	1981-82
India	in England	42	Lord's	1974
	in India	83	Madras	1976-77

HIGHEST MATCH AGGREGATE   1614 for 30 wickets   Manchester   1990
LOWEST MATCH AGGREGATE   482 for 31 wickets   Lord's   1936

HIGHEST INDIVIDUAL INNINGS

England	in England	333	G.A.Gooch	Lord's	1990
	in India	207	M.W.Gatting	Madras	1984-85
India	in England	221	S.M.Gavaskar	The Oval	1979
	in India	224	V.G.Kambli	Bombay	1992-93

HIGHEST AGGREGATE OF RUNS IN A SERIES

England	in England	752	(av 125.33)	G.A.Gooch	1990
	in India	594	(av 99.00)	K.F.Barrington	1961-62
India	in England	542	(av 77.42)	S.M.Gavaskar	1979
	in India	586	(av 83.71)	V.L.Manjrekar	1961-62

RECORD WICKET PARTNERSHIPS – ENGLAND

1st	225	G.A.Gooch (116)/M.A.Atherton (131)	Manchester	1990
2nd	241	G.Fowler (201)/M.W.Gatting (207)	Madras	1984-85
3rd	308	G.A.Gooch (333)/A.J.Lamb (139)	Lord's	1990
4th	266	W.R.Hammond (217)/T.S.Worthington (128)	The Oval	1936
5th	254	K.W.R.Fletcher (113)/A.W.Greig (148)	Bombay	1972-73
6th	171	I.T.Botham (114)/R.W.Taylor (43)	Bombay	1979-80
7th	125	D.W.Randall (126)/P.H.Edmonds (64)	Lord's	1982
8th	168	R.Illingworth (107)/P.Lever (88*)	Manchester	1971
9th	83	K.W.R.Fletcher (97*)/N.Gifford (19)	Madras	1972-73
10th	70	P.J.W.Allott (41*)/R.G.D.Willis (28)	Lord's	1982

RECORD WICKET PARTNERSHIPS – INDIA

1st	213	S.M.Gavaskar (221)/C.P.S.Chauhan (80)	The Oval	1979
2nd	192	F.M.Engineer (121)/A.L.Wadekar (87)	Bombay	1972-73
3rd	316	G.R.Viswanath (222)/Yashpal Sharma (140)	Madras	1981-82
4th	222	V.S.Hazare (89)/V.L.Manjrekar (133)	Leeds	1952
5th	214	M.Azharuddin (110)/R.J.Shastri (111)	Calcutta	1984-85
6th	130	S.M.H.Kirmani (43)/Kapil Dev (97)	The Oval	1982
7th	235	R.J.Shastri (142)/S.M.H.Kirmani (102)	Bombay	1984-85
8th	128	R.J.Shastri (93)/S.M.H.Kirmani (67)	Delhi	1981-82

9th	104	R.J.Shastri (93)/Madan Lal (44)	Delhi 1981-82
10th	51	R.G.Nadkarni (43*)/B.S.Chandrasekhar (16)	Calcutta 1963-64
	51	S.M.H.Kirmani (75)/C.Sharma (17*)	Madras 1984-85

BEST INNINGS BOWLING ANALYSIS

England	in England	8-31	F.S.Trueman	Manchester	1952
	in India	7-46	J.K.Lever	Delhi	1976-77
India	in England	6-35	L.Amar Singh	Lord's	1936
	in India	8-55	M.H.Mankad	Madras	1951-52

BEST MATCH BOWLING ANALYSIS

England	in England	11-93	A.V.Bedser	Manchester	1946
	in India	13-106	I.T.Botham	Bombay	1979-80
India	in England	10-188	C.Sharma	Birmingham	1986
	in India	12-108	M.H.Mankad	Madras	1951-52

HIGHEST AGGREGATE OF WICKETS IN A SERIES

England	in England	29	(av 13.31)	F.S.Trueman	1952
	in India	29	(av 17.55)	D.L.Underwood	1976-77
India	in England	17	(av 34.64)	S.P.Gupte	1959
	in India	35	(av 18.91)	B.S.Chandrasekhar	1972-73

RESULTS SUMMARY
ENGLAND v INDIA – IN ENGLAND

	Tests	Series E	I	D	Lord's E	I	D	Manchester E	I	D	The Oval E	I	D	Leeds E	I	D	Nottingham E	I	D	Birmingham E	I	D
1932	1	1	-	-	1	-	-															
1936	3	2	-	1	1	-	-	-	-	1	1	-	-									
1946	3	1	-	2	1	-	-	-	-	1	-	-	1									
1952	4	3	-	1	1	-	-	1	-	-	-	-	1	1	-	-						
1959	5	5	-	-	1	-	-	1	-	-	1	-	-	1	-	-	1	-	-			
1967	3	3	-	-	1	-	-							1	-	-				1	-	-
1971	3	-	1	2	-	-	1	-	-	1	-	1	-									
1974	3	3	-	-	1	-	-	1	-	-										1	-	-
1979	4	1	-	3	-	-	1				-	-	1	-	-	1				1	-	-
1982	3	1	-	2	1	-	-	-	-	1	-	-	1									
1986	3	-	2	1	-	1	-							-	1	-				-	-	1
1990	3	1	-	2	1	-	-	-	-	1	-	-	1									
1996	3	1	-	2	-	-	1										-	-	1	1	-	-
	41	22	3	16	9	1	3	3	-	5	2	1	5	3	1	1	1	-	1	4	-	1

ENGLAND v INDIA – IN INDIA

	Tests	Series E	I	D	Bombay E	I	D	Calcutta E	I	D	Madras E	I	D	Delhi E	I	D	Kanpur E	I	D	Bangalore E	I	D	Chandigarh E	I	D	Ahmedabad E	I	D
1933-34	3	2	-	1	1	-	-	-	-	1	1	-	-															
1951-52	5	1	1	3	-	-	1	-	-	1	-	1	-	-	-	1	1	-	-									
1961-62	5	-	2	3	-	-	1	-	1	-	-	1	-	-	-	1	-	-	1									
1963-64	5	-	-	5	-	-	1	-	-	1	-	-	1	-	-	1	-	-	1									
1972-73	5	1	2	2	-	-	1	-	1	-	-	1	-	1	-	-	-	-	1									
1976-77	5	3	1	1	-	-	1	1	-	-	1	-	-	1	-	-				-	1	-						
1979-80	1	1	-	-	1	-	-																					
1981-82	6	-	1	5	-	1	-	-	-	1	-	-	1	-	-	1	-	-	1	-	-	1						
1984-85	5	2	1	2	-	1	-	-	-	1	1	-	-	1	-	-	-	-	1									
1992-93	3	-	3	-	-	1	-	-	1	-	-	1	-															
2001-02	3	-	1	2																-	-	1	-	1	-	-	-	1
	46	10	12	24	2	3	5	1	3	5	3	4	2	3	-	4	1	-	5	-	1	2	-	1	-	-	-	1
Totals	87	32	15	40																								

8

INDIA REGISTER

India's touring team had not been selected at the time of going to press. Career statistics are to 5 March 2002. See page 11 for key to abbreviations.

AGARKAR, Ajit Bhalchandra, b Bombay 4 Dec 1977. RHB, RMF. F-c debut (Bombay) 1996-97. **Tests:** 11 (1998-99 to 2001-02); HS 41* v SA (Bombay) 1999-2000; 5 successive ducks in Australia 1999-2000; BB 3-43 v A (Adelaide) 1999-2000. **LOI:** 88 (1997-98 to 2001-02); HS 67* v Z (Rajkot) 2000-01; BB 4-25 v Z (Kanpur) 2000-01. HS (f-c) 109* India A v Peshawar (Peshawar) 1997-98. BB (f-c) 6-72 India A v Pakistan A (Karachi) 1997-98.

BANGAR, Sanjay Bapusaheb, b Beed, Maharashtra 11 Oct 1972. RHB, RMF. F-c debut (Railways) 1993-94. **Tests:** 3 (2001-02); HS 100* v Z (Nagpur) 2001-02. **LOI:** 2 (2001-02); HS 1; BB 2-42 v Z (Faridabad) 2001-02. HS (f-c) 212 Railways v Tamil Nadu (Delhi) 2001-02. BB (f-c) 5-17.

DAS, Shiv Sunder, b Bhubaneshwar 5 Nov 1977. RHB, RM. F-c debut (Orissa) 1993-94. **Tests:** 18 (2000-01 to 2001-02); HS 110 v Z (Nagpur) 2000-01. **LOI:** 3 (2001-02); HS 5*. HS (f-c) 253 Orissa v Bengal (Baripada) 2001-02. BB (f-c) 1-0.

DASGUPTA, Deep, b Calcutta 7 June 1977. RHB, WK. F-c debut (Bengal) 1998-99. **Tests:** 7 (2001-02); HS 100 v E (Chandigarh) 2001-02. **LOI:** 5 (2001-02); HS 24* v K (Bloemfontein) 2001-02. HS (f-c) 137 Bengal v Orissa (Baripada) 2001-02.

DRAVID, Rahul (St Joseph's HS; Bangalore U), b Indore 11 Jan 1973. 5'11½". RHB, OB, WK. F-c debut (Karnataka) 1990-91. Kent 2000; cap 2000. *Wisden* 1999. **Tests:** 55 (1996 to 2001-02); HS 200* v Z (Delhi) 2000-01. **LOI:** 164 (1995-96 to 2000-01, 2 as captain); HS 153 v NZ (Hyderabad) 1999-00; BB 2-43 v SA (Cochin) 1999-00. 1000 runs (1+2); most – 1264 (1997-98). HS (f-c) 215 Karnataka v Uttar Pradesh (Bangalore) 1997-98. BB (f-c) 2-16 Kent v Surrey (Oval) 2000.

GANGULY, Sourav Chandidas (St Xavier's Collegiate S), b Calcutta 8 Jul 1972. Brother of Snehasish C. Ganguly (Bengal 1986-87 to 1996-97). 5'11". LHB, RM. F-c debut (Bengal) 1989-90. Lancashire 2000. **Tests:** 53 (1996 to 2001-02, 18 as captain); HS 173 v SL (Bombay) 1997-98; BB 3-28 v A (Calcutta) 1997-98. **LOI:** 187 (1991-92 to 2001-02, 58 as captain); HS 183 v SL (Taunton) 1999; BB 5-16 v P (Toronto) 1997-98. HS (f-c) 200* Bengal v Tripura (Calcutta) 1993-94 and 200* Bengal v Bihar (Calcutta) 1994-95. BB (f-c) 6-46 Bengal v Orissa (Calcutta) 2000-01.

HARBHAJAN SINGH, b Jullundur 3 Jul 1980. RHB, OB. F-c debut (Punjab) 1997-98. **Tests:** 22 (1997-98 to 2001-02); HS 66 v Z (Bulawayo) 2001; BB 8-84 (15-217 match) v A (Madras) 2000-01. Took 28 wickets, including a hat-trick, in 2 Tests v Australia 2000-01. **LOI:** 41 (1997-98 to 2001-02); HS 46 v A (Vishakapatnam) 2000-01; BB 5-43 v E (Bombay) 2001-02. HS (f-c) 84 Punjab v Haryana (Amritsar) 2000-01. BB (f-c) 8-84 (15-217 match) (*see Tests*).

KHAN, Zaheer, b Shrirampur, Maharashtra 7 Oct 1978. RHB, LFM. F-c debut (Baroda) 1999-00. **Tests:** 11 (2000-01 to 2001-02); HS 45 v SL (Colombo) 2001; BB 4-76 v SL (Kandy) 2001. **LOI:** 30 (2000-01 to 2001-02); HS 32* v Z (Jodhpur) 2000-01; BB 4-42 v Z (Sharjah) 2000-01. HS (f-c) 48 Baroda v Maharashtra (Poona) 1999-2000. BB (f-c) 6-25 Baroda v Punjab (Baroda) 2001-02.

KAIF, Mohammad, b Allahabad 1 Dec 1980. RHB, OB. F-c debut (Uttar Pradesh) 1997-98. **Tests:** 4 (1999-00 to 2001-02); HS 37 v SL (Galle) 2001-02. **LOI:** 4 (2001-02); HS 46 v E (Delhi) 2001-02. HS (f-c) 119*. BB (f-c) 3-4.

KUMBLE, Anil (National HS; R.V. Engineering C, Bangalore), b Bangalore 17 Oct 1970. 6'1½". RHB, LB. F-c debut (Karnataka) 1989-90. Northamptonshire 1995 (cap 1995). Leicestershire 2000; cap 2000. *Wisden* 1995. **Tests:** 68 (1990 to 2001-02); HS 88 v SA (Calcutta) 1996-97; BB 10-74 (14-149 match) v P (Delhi) 1998-99 (second-best innings analysis in Test cricket). **LOI:** 222 (1989-90 to 2001-02, 1 as captain); HS 26 v A (Perth) 1999-00; BB 6-12 v WI (Calcutta) 1993-94. HS (f-c) 154* Karnataka v Kerala (Bijapur) 1991-92. 50 wkts (1+1) inc 100 (1): 105 (1995). BB (f-c) 10-74 (*see Tests*).

LAXMAN, Vangipurappu Venkata Sai (**'VVS'**), b Hyderabad 1 Nov 1974. RHB, OB. F-c debut (Hyderabad) 1992-93. *Wisden* 2001. **Tests:** 30 (1996-97 to 2001-02); HS 281 v A (Calcutta) 2000-01. **LOI:** 33 (1997-98 to 2001-02); HS 101 v A (Margoa) 2000-01. HS (f-c) 353 Hyderabad v Karnataka (Bangalore) 1999-2000. BB (f-c) 3-11 Hyderabad v Railways (Delhi) 1999-2000.

MONGIA, Dinesh, b Chandigarh 17 Apr 1977. LHB, SLA. Debut (Punjab) 1995-96. **LOI:** 11 (2000-01 to 2001-02); HS 71 v E (Calcutta) 2001-02. HS (f-c) 308* Punjab v Jammu & Kashmir (Jullundur) 2000-01. BB (f-c) 1-0.

RATRA, Ajay, b Faridabad 13 Dec 1981. RHB, WK. F-c debut (Haryana) 1998-99. **LOI:** 7 (2001-02); HS 30 v E (Calcutta) 2001-02. HS (f-c) 77.

SARANDEEP SINGH, b Amritsar 21 Oct 1979. RHB, OB. F-c debut (Punjab) 1998-99. **Tests:** 2 (2000-01 to 2001-02); HS 4; BB 4-136 v Z (Nagpur) 2000-01 – on debut. **LOI:** 1 (2001-02); HS 6*. HS (f-c) 57. BB (f-c) 6-38.

SEHWAG, Virender, b Delhi 20 Oct 1978. RHB, OB. F-c debut (Delhi) 1997-98. **Tests:** 5 (2001-02); HS 105 v SA (Bloemfontein) 2001-02 – on debut. **LOI:** 28 (1998-99 to 2001-02); HS 100 v NZ (Colombo) 2001; BB 3-59 v A (Bangalore) 2000-01. HS (f-c) 274 N Zone v S Zone (Agartala) 1999-2000. BB (f-c) 4-32 N Zone v S Zone (Bombay) 1998-99.

SIDDIQUI, Iqbal Rashid, b Aurangabad 26 Dec 1974. RHB, RMF. F-c debut (Maharashtra) 1992-93. **Tests:** 1 (2001-02); HS 24 and BB 1-32 v E (Chandigarh) 2001-02 – on debut. HS (f-c) 116. BB (f-c) 8-72 Maharashtra v Saurashtra (Poona) 1999-00.

SRINATH, Javagal, b Mysore 31 Aug 1969. 6'3". RHB, RFM. F-c debut (Karnataka) 1989-90. Gloucestershire 1995; cap 1995. **Tests:** 59 (1991-92 to 2001-02); HS 76 v NZ (Hamilton) 1998-99; BB 8-86 (13-132 match) v P (Calcutta) 1998-99. **LOI:** 204 (1991-92 to 2001-02); HS 53 v SA (Rajkot) 1996-97; BB 5-23 v B (Dhaka) 1997-98. HS (f-c) 76 (*see Tests*). 50 wkts (1): 87 (1995). BB (f-c) 9-76 (13-150 match) Glos v Glam (Abergavenny) 1995.

TENDULKAR, Sachin Ramesh (Sharadashram Vidyamandir; Kirti C, Bombay), b Bombay 24 Apr 1973. 5'5". RHB, RM/LB. F-c debut (Bombay) 1988-89 (scoring 100* v Gujarat when record 15yr 232d). Yorkshire 1992; cap 1992. **Tests:** 91 (1989-90 to 2001-02, 25 as captain); HS 217 v NZ (Ahmedabad) 1999-2000; BB 3-10 v SA (Bombay) 1999-2000. **LOI:** 286 (1989-90 to 2001-02, 73 as captain); HS 186* v NZ (Hyderabad) 1999-00; BB 5-32 v A (Cochin) 1997-98. Holds record LOI aggregates of runs (11069) and hundreds (31). HS (f-c) 233* Bombay v Tamil Nadu (Bombay) 1999-2000. BB (f-c) 3-10 (*see Tests*). Scored 326* for Sharadashram Vidyamandir (English) v St Xavier's HS in Bombay in 1987-88, adding 664 unbroken for the 3rd wicket with Vinod Kambli (world record partnership for any wicket).

YOHANNAN, Tinu, b Quilon 18 Feb 1979. RHB, RFM. F-c debut (Kerala) 1999-00. First Kerala Test cricketer. RHB, RFM. **Tests:** 2 (2001-02); HS 3*; BB 2-56 v E (Chandigarh) 2001-02 – on debut; took wicket of M.A.Butcher with his fourth ball in Tests. HS (f-c) 21*. BB (f-c) 6-117.

THE FIRST-CLASS COUNTIES REGISTER, RECORDS AND 2001 AVERAGES

Career statistics are to 5 March 2002 and include all England's winter tours

ABBREVIATIONS – General

*	not out/unbroken partnership	l-o	limited-overs
b	born	LOI	Limited-Overs Internationals
BB	Best innings bowling analysis	Tests	Official Test Matches
Cap	Awarded 1st XI County Cap	Tours	Overseas tours involving first-class
f-c	first-class		appearances
HS	Highest Score		

Awards

BHC	Benson and Hedges Cup 'Gold' Award
CGT	Gillette Cup/NatWest/Cheltenham & Gloucester Trophy Match Award
Wisden 2001	One of *Wisden Cricketers' Almanack's* Five Cricketers of 2001
YC 2001	Cricket Writers' Club Young Cricketer of 2001

ECB Competitions

BHC	Benson & Hedges Cup
CC	County Championship
CGT	Cheltenham & Gloucester Trophy
NL	NU National League (1999-2001)
SL	Sunday League (1969-98)

Overseas Competitions

BHS	Benson & Hedges Night Series (SA)
FAI	Federated Automobile Insce Cup (A)
MM	Mercantile Mutual Cup (A)
RSB	Red Stripe Bowl (WI)
SBC	Standard Bank Cup (SA)
SST	Shell/Sandals Trophy (WI)
WT	Wills Trophy (I)

Education

BHS	Boys' High School
C	College
CFE	College of Further Education
CHE	College of Higher Education
CS	Comprehensive School
GS	Grammar School
HS	High School
IHE	Institute of Higher Education
RGS	Royal Grammar School
S	School
SFC	Sixth Form College
SM	Secondary Modern School
SS	Secondary School
TC	Technical College
T(H)S	Technical (High) School
U	University
UMIST	University of Manchester Institute of Science and Technology
UWIC	University of Wales Institute, Cardiff

Playing Categories

LBG	Bowls right-arm leg-breaks and googlies
LF	Bowls left-arm fast
LFM	Bowls left-arm fast-medium
LHB	Bats left-handed
LM	Bowls left-arm medium pace
LMF	Bowls left-arm medium fast
OB	Bowls right-arm off-breaks
RF	Bowls right-arm fast
RFM	Bowls right-arm fast-medium
RHB	Bats right-handed
RM	Bowls right-arm medium pace
RMF	Bowls right-arm medium-fast
RSM	Bowls right-arm slow-medium
SLA	Bowls left-arm leg-breaks
SLC	Bowls left-arm 'Chinamen'
WK	Wicket-keeper

Teams (see also p 113)

ACT	Australian Capital Territory
B	Bangladesh
CD	Central Districts
DHR	D.H.Robins' XI
EP	Eastern Province
GW	Griqualand West
K	Kenya
NSW	New South Wales
NT	Northern Transvaal
(O)FS	(Orange) Free State
PIA	Pakistan International Airlines
Q	Queensland
RW	Rest of the World XI
SAB	South African Breweries XI
SAU	South African Universities
WA	Western Australia
WP	Western Province

DERBYSHIRE

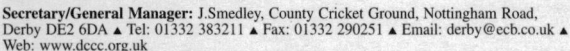

Formation of Present Club: 4 November 1870
Colours: Chocolate, Amber and Pale Blue
Badge: Rose and Crown
County Champions: (1) 1936
Gillette/NatWest/C & G Trophy Winners: (1) 1981
Benson and Hedges Cup Winners: (1) 1993
NU National League (Div 1) Winners: (0); best – 8th (Div 2) 1999
Sunday League Winners: (1) 1990
Match Awards: CGT 46; BHC 71

Secretary/General Manager: J.Smedley, County Cricket Ground, Nottingham Road, Derby DE2 6DA ▲ Tel: 01332 383211 ▲ Fax: 01332 290251 ▲ Email: derby@ecb.co.uk ▲ Web: www.dccc.org.uk

Captain: D.G.Cork. **Vice-Captain:** T.A.Munton. **Overseas Player:** M.J.Di Venuto.
2002 Beneficiary: K.M.Krikken. **Scorer:** J.M.Brown.

ALDRED, Paul (Lady Manner's S, Bakewell), b Chellaston 4 Feb 1969. 5'10". RHB, RM. Debut 1995; cap 1999. Cheshire 1994. HS 83 v Hants (Chesterfield) 1997. 50 wkts (1): 50 (1999). BB 7-101 (13-184 match) v Lancs (Derby) 1999. LO HS 39* v Surrey (Derby) 1999 (NL). LO BB 4-30 v Lincs (Lincoln) 1997 (NWT).

BAILEY, Robert John (Biddulph HS), b Biddulph, Staffs 28 Oct 1963. 6'3". RHB, OB. Northamptonshire 1982-99; cap 1985; benefit 1993; captain 1996-97. Derbyshire debut/cap 2000. Staffordshire 1980. YC 1984. **Tests:** 4 (1988 to 1989-90); HS 43 v WI (Oval) 1988. **LOI:** 4 (1984-85 to 1989-90); HS 43* v SL (Oval) 1988. Tours: SA 1991-92 (Nh); WI 1989-90; Z 1994-95 (Nh). 1000 runs (13); most – 1987 (1990). HS 224* Nh v Glam (Swansea) 1986. De HS 136* v Worcs (Derby) 2001. BB 5-54 Nh v Notts (Northampton) 1993. De BB 2-17 v Hants (Derby) 2001. Awards: CGT 7; BHC 9. LO HS 153* Nh v Pak A (Northampton) 1997. LO BB 5-45 v Durham (Chester-le-St) 2000 (BHC).

BASSANO, Christopher Warwick Godfrey (Grey S, Port Elizabeth; Launceston Church GS; Tasmania U, Hobart), b East London, SA 11 Sep 1975. 6'2". ECB qualified – British passport; son of the late B.S.Bassano (cricket writer, historian and broadcaster). RHB, LB. Debut 2001. First to score 100 in each innings on Championship debut – 186* and 106 v Glos (Derby) 2001. HS 186* (*see above*). BB – . LO HS 45 v Sussex (Arundel) 2001 (NL).

CORK, Dominic Gerald (St Joseph's C, Stoke-on-Trent; Newcastle CFE), b Newcastle-under-Lyme, Staffs 7 Aug 1971. 6'2". RHB, RFM. Debut 1990; cap 1993; captain 1998 to date; benefit 2001. *Wisden* 1995. Staffordshire 1989-90. **ECB contract 2001. Tests:** 34 (1995 to 2001); HS 59 v NZ (Auckland) 1996-97; BB 7-43 v WI (Lord's) 1995 – on debut (record England analysis by Test match debutant); hat-trick v WI (Manchester) 1995 – the first in Test history to occur in the opening over of a day's play. **LOI:** 30 (1992 to 2001); HS 31* v NZ (Napier) 1996-97; BB 3-27 v WI (Lord's) 1995. Tours: A 1992-93 (Eng A), 1998-99; SA 1993-94 (Eng A), 1995-96; WI 1991-92 (Eng A); NZ 1996-97; I 1994-95 (Eng A); P 2000-01 (*part*). 1000 runs (1). HS 200* v Durham (Derby) 2000. 50 wkts (5); most – 90 (1995). BB 9-43 (13-93 match) v Northants (Derby) 1995. Took 8-53 before lunch on his 20th birthday v Essex (Derby) 1991. 2 hat-tricks: 1994 and 1995 (*see Tests*). Awards: CGT 4; BHC 4. LO HS 93 v Derbys CB (Derby) 2000 (NWT). LO BB 6-21 v Glam (Chesterfield) 1997 (BHC).

DEAN, Kevin James (Leek HS; Leek CFE), b Derby 16 Oct 1975. 6'5". LHB, LMF. Debut 1996. Cap 1998. HS 27* v SA (Derby) 1998. CC HS 25* v Essex (Derby) 1998. 50 wkts (1): 74 (1998). BB 8-52 v Kent (Canterbury) 2000. 2 hat-tricks (1998, 2000). Award: CGT 1. LO HS 16* v Glam (Cardiff) 1998 (SL). LO BB 5-32 v Glos (Derby) 1996 (SL).

Di VENUTO, Michael James (St Virgil's C; Hobart), b Hobart, Australia 12 Dec 1973. 6'0". LHB, RM/LB. Tasmania 1991-92 to date. Sussex 1999; cap 1999. Derbyshire debut/cap 2000. **LOI** (A): 9 (1996-97 to 1997-98); HS 89 v SA (Jo'burg) 1996-97. Tours: Z 1995-96 (Tas); Sc/Ire 1998 (Aus A). 1000 runs (2): most – 1082 (2001). HS 189 Tas v WA (Perth) 1997-98. De HS 165 v Notts (Nottingham) 2001. BB (Tas) 1-0. UK BB (Sx) 1-3. De BB 1-16. Awards: CGT 1; BHC 1. LO HS 173* v Derbys CB (Derby) 2000 (NWT). LO BB (Tas) 1-10 (MM).

DOWMAN, Mathew Peter (St Hugh's CS; Grantham C), b Grantham, Lincs 10 May 1974. 5'10". LHB, RMF. Nottinghamshire 1994-99; cap 1998. Derbyshire debut/cap 2000. Scored 267 for England YC v WI YC (Hove) 1993 – record score in youth 'Tests'. 1000 runs (1): 1091 (1997). HS 149 Nt v Leics (Leicester) 1997. De HS 145* v P (Derby) 2001. BB 3-10 Nt v Pak A (Nottingham) 1997. CC BB 2-10 Nt v Kent (Canterbury) 1998. De BB 2-46 v Durham (Darlington) 2000. Awards: BHC 2. LO HS 92 Nt v Northants (Nottingham) 1997 (BHC). LO BB 3-21 Nt v Worcs (Nottingham) 1996 (BHC).

DUMELOW, Nathan Robert Charles (Foremark Hall S; Denstone C), b Derby 30 Apr 1981. 5'9". RHB, OB. Debut 2001. HS 61 and CC BB 4-103 v Middx (Southgate) 2001. BB 4-81 v P (Derby) 2001. LO HS 33 v Lancs (Manchester) 2001 (NL). LO BB 3-32 v Middx (Derby) 2001 (NL).

‡**GAIT, Andrew** Ian (Kearnsley C; UNISA), b Bulawayo, Rhodesia 19 Dec 1978. ECB qualified – British/EU passport. RHB. Free State 1998-99 to 2000-01. HS 112 FS v Border (Bloemfontein) 2000-01. LO HS 138* FS v GW (Bloemfontein) 2000-01.

‡**GUNTER, Neil** Edward Lloyd, Basingstoke, Hants 12 May 1981. LHB, RFM. Berkshire 2000-01. Staff 2002 – awaiting f-c debut. LO HS (Berks) 5 (CGT).

‡**HEWSON, Dominic** Robert (Cheltenham C; West of England U), b Cheltenham, Glos 3 Oct 1974. 5'8". RHB, occ RM. Gloucestershire 1996-2001. HS 168 v Derbys (Bristol) 2001. BB (Gs) 1-7. LO HS 64 Gs v SL A (Cheltenham) 1999.

‡**KERR, Jason** Ian Douglas (Withins HS; Bolton C), b Bolton, Lancs 7 Apr 1974. 6'2". RHB, RMF. Somerset 1993-2001; cap 2001. HS 80 Sm v WI (Taunton) 1995. CC HS 68* Sm v Derbys (Taunton) 1996. BB 7-23 Sm v Leics (Taunton) 1999. Hat-trick 2000. LO HS 56 Sm v Middx (Southgate) 1999 (NL). LO BB 4-28 Sm v Hants (Basingstoke) 1997 (SL).

KHAN, Rawait Mahmood (Moseley S; Solihull SFC), b Birmingham 5 Mar 1982. Elder brother of Z.M.Khan (Derbyshire 2000). 5'10". RHB, OB. Debut 2001. HS 13 v Glos (Bristol) 2001 – on debut. LO HS 29 Derbys CB v Glos CB (Heanor) 2000 (NWT).

KRIKKEN, Karl Matthew (Rivington & Blackrod HS & SFC), b Bolton, Lancs 9 Apr 1969. Son of B.E.Krikken (Lancs and Worcs 1966-69). 5'9". RHB, WK. GW 1988-89. Derbyshire debut 1989; cap 1992; benefit 2002. HS 104 v Lancs (Manchester) 1996. BB 1-54. LO HS 55 v Kent (Derby) 1996 (NWT).

LUNGLEY, Tom (St John Houghton SS; SE Derbyshire C), b Derby 25 Jul 1979. 6'1". LHB, RM. Debut 2000. HS 47 and CC BB 3-89 v Warwks (Derby) 2001. BB 3-10 (6-41 match) v CU (Cambridge) 2000 – on debut. LO HS 45 v Essex (Chelmsford) 2001 (NL). LO BB 4-28 v Essex (Derby) 2001 (NL).

MUNTON, Timothy Alan (Sarson HS; King Edward VII Upper S, Melton Mowbray), b Melton Mowbray, Leics 30 Jul 1965. 6'6". RHB, RMF. Warwickshire 1985-99; cap 1989; captain 1997 (no appearances – back injury); benefit 1998. Derbyshire debut/cap 2000. *Wisden* 1994. **Tests**: 2 (1992); HS 25* v P (Manchester) 1992; BB 2-22 v P (Leeds) 1992. Tours: SA 1992-93 (Wa); WI 1991-92 (Eng A); P 1990-91 (Eng A), 1995-96 (Eng A – *part*); SL 1990-91 (Eng A); Z 1993-94 (Wa). HS 54* Wa v Worcs (Worcester) 1996. De HS 52 v Durham (Darlington) 2000. 50 wkts (6); most – 81 (1994). BB 8-89 (11-128 match) Wa v Middx (Birmingham) 1991. De BB 7-34 v Surrey (Derby) 2000. Hat-trick (Wa) 1999. Awards: CGT 2; BHC 1. LO HS 18 v Essex (Chelmsford) 2000 (NL). LO BB 5-23 Wa v Glos (Moreton-in-M) 1990 (SL).

PYEMONT, James Patrick (Tonbridge S; Trinity Hall, Cambridge), b Eastbourne, Sussex 10 Apr 1978. Son of C.P.Pyemont (Cambridge U 1967; cricket and hockey blue). 6'0". RHB, OB. Sussex 1997 – no CC appearances. Cambridge U 1998-99; blue 1998-99. Derbyshire debut 1999 (dismissed first ball in both innings – first instance by Derbyshire player). British U 2000-01; captain 2001. HS 124 CU v OU (Lord's) 2000. De HS 40 v Hants (Southampton) 2000. BB 4-101 CU v OU (Cambridge) 2001. LO HS 50 v Hants (Southampton) 2000 (NL).

SELWOOD, Steven Andrew (Mill Hill S; Albany C, Loughborough U), b Barnet, Herts 24 Nov 1979. Son of T.Selwood (Middlesex and C Districts 1966-73). 6'0". LHB, SLA. Debut 2001. HS 18 v Glos (Bristol) 2001 – on debut. LO HS 37 v Essex (Chelmsford) 2001 (NL).

STUBBINGS, Stephen David (Frankston HS, Aus; Swinburne U, Aus), b Huddersfield, Yorks 31 Mar 1978. 6'3". LHB, OB. Debut 1997. Cap 2001. 1000 (1): 1047 (2001). HS 135* v Kent (Canterbury) 2000. LO HS 96* v Sussex (Derby) 2001 (NL).

SUTTON, Luke David (Millfield S; Durham U), b Keynsham, Somerset 4 Oct 1976. 5'11". RHB, WK. Somerset 1997-98. Derbyshire debut 2000. HS 140* (carried bat) v Sussex (Derby) 2001. LO HS 60 Brit U v Kent (Oxford) 1998 (BHC).

WELCH, Graeme (Hetton CS), b Durham City 21 Mar 1972. 5'11½". RHB, RM. Warwickshire 1994-2000; cap 1997. Derbyshire debut/cap 2001. Tour: SA 1994-95 (Wa). HS 84* Wa v Notts (Birmingham) 1994. De HS 64 v Warwks (Birmingham) 2001. 50 wkts (1): 65 (1997). BB 6-30 v Durham (Chester-le-St) 2001. Award: BHC 1. LO HS 71 Wa v Kent (Maidstone) 1999 (NL). LO BB 5-22 v Glam (Derby) 2001 (NL).

WHARTON, Lian James (Ecclesbourne S; Malkworth C), b Holbrook 21 Feb 1977. 5'9". LHB, SLA. Debut 2000. HS 13* v Warwks (Derby) 2001. BB 5-96 (9-179 match) v WI (Derby) 2000. CC BB 2-74 v Sussex (Arundel) 2001. LO HS 9* (NL). LO BB 3-23 v Durham (Chester-le-St) 2001 (NL).

RELEASED/RETIRED
(Having made a first-class County appearance in 2001)

EDWARDS, Alexander David (Imberhorne CS, E Grinstead; Loughborough U), b Cuckfield, Sussex 2 Aug 1975. 6'0". RHB, RFM. Combined U 1995. Sussex 1995-99. Middlesex staff 2000 – no f-c appearances. Derbyshire 2001 (1 match). HS 23 v Hants (Southampton) 2001. BB 5-34 Sx v Pak A (Hove) 1997. CC BB 4-94 Sx v Surrey (Hove) 1997. LO HS 43 Sx v Essex (Hove) 1998 (BHC). LO BB 3-34 Sx v Notts (Nottingham) 1998 (SL).

KHAN, Wasim Gulzar (Small Heath CS; Josiah Mason SFC, Erdington), b Birmingham 26 Feb 1971. 6'1". LHB, LB. Warwickshire 1995-97. Sussex 1998-2000. Derbyshire 2001 (1 match). HS 181 Wa v Hants (Southampton) 1995. De HS 1. LO HS 33 Sx v Glam (Hove) 1998 (BHC) and 33 Sx v Warwks (Hove) 1998 (SL). LO BB 1-7 (NL).

ILLINGWORTH, Richard Keith (Salts GS), b Bradford, Yorks 23 Aug 1963. 5'11". RHB, SLA. Worcestershire 1982-2000; cap 1986; benefit 1997. Natal 1988-89. Derbyshire 2001. **Tests:** 9 (1991 to 1995-96); HS 28 v SA (Pt Elizabeth) 1995-96; BB 4-96 v WI (Nottingham) 1995. Took wicket of P.V.Simmons with his first ball in Tests – v WI (Nottingham) 1991. **LOI:** 25 (1991 to 1995-96); HS 14 v P (Melbourne) 1991-92; BB 3-33 v Z (Albury) 1991-92. Tours: SA 1995-96; NZ 1991-92; P 1990-91 (Eng A); SL 1990-91 (Eng A); Z 1989-90 (Eng A), 1990-91 (Wo), 1993-94 (Wo), 1996-97 (Wo). HS 120* Wo v Warwks (Worcester) 1987 – as night-watchman. Scored 106 for England A v Z (Harare) 1989-90 – also as night-watchman. De HS 61* v Hants (Derby) 2001. 50 wkts (5); most – 75 (1990). BB 7-50 Wo v OU (Oxford) 1985. CC BB 7-79 Wo v Hants (Southampton) 1997. De BB 4-37 v Middx (Derby) 2001. LO HS 36* Wo v Kent (Worcester) 1990 (BHC). LO BB 5-24 Wo v Somerset (Worcester) 1983 (SL).   **RELEASED/RETIRED** continued on p 19

DERBYSHIRE 2001

RESULTS SUMMARY

	Place	Won	Lost	Tied	Drew	No Result
County Championship (2nd Division)	9th	1	9		6	
All First-Class Matches		1	9		7	
C & G Trophy	3rd Round					
Benson & Hedges Cup	6th in North Group					
NU National League (2nd Division)	9th	4	12			

COUNTY CHAMPIONSHIP AVERAGES

BATTING AND FIELDING

Cap		M	I	NO	HS	Runs	Avge	100	50	Ct/St
–	C.W.G.Bassano	7	12	2	186*	493	49.30	2	2	4
2000	M.J.Di Venuto	14	25	1	165	1082	45.08	4	5	15
1993	D.G.Cork	3	4	–	128	163	40.75	1	–	3
2001	S.D.Stubbings	16	29	–	127	1024	35.31	3	6	4
–	L.D.Sutton	14	25	3	140*	628	28.54	2	1	9
–	N.R.C.Dumelow	8	14	1	61	298	22.92	–	2	1
1992	K.M.Krikken	13	23	4	93*	425	22.36	–	3	33/1
2000	R.J.Bailey	14	25	1	136*	515	21.45	1	2	8
2001	G.Welch	16	29	2	64	511	18.92	–	1	3
–	T.Lungley	5	10	4	47	108	18.00	–	–	–
–	R.K.Illingworth	5	8	1	61*	125	17.85	–	1	–
2000	M.P.Dowman	13	24	–	50	386	16.08	–	1	4
2000	T.A.Munton	9	13	1	50	145	12.08	–	1	2
1998	K.J.Dean	8	12	2	23	117	11.70	–	–	2
–	S.A.Selwood	2	4	–	18	43	10.75	–	–	1
1999	P.Aldred	8	13	1	35	120	10.00	–	–	5
–	T.M.Smith	5	9	1	19	65	8.12	–	–	4
–	L.J.Wharton	10	17	9	13*	29	3.62	–	–	1

Also batted: A.D.Edwards (1 match) 4*, 23; R.M.Khan (1) 13, 5; W.G.Khan (1) 1; A.R.K.Pierson (1) 9, 1* (1 ct); S.P.Titchard (2) 37, 39, 5.

BOWLING

	O	M	R	W	Avge	Best	5wI	10wM
K.J.Dean	250.5	58	888	34	26.11	6- 73	2	1
R.K.Illingworth	126.4	39	316	10	31.60	4- 37	–	–
T.A.Munton	242.1	61	659	19	34.68	5- 85	1	–
G.Welch	502.3	108	1631	44	37.06	6- 30	3	–
P.Aldred	189.3	30	742	13	57.07	3-102	–	–
N.R.C.Dumelow	158.5	28	632	10	63.20	4-103	–	–

Also bowled:

	O	M	R	W	Avge	Best	5wI	10wM
R.J.Bailey	76.3	17	245	7	35.00	2- 17	–	–
T.M.Smith	70.3	11	319	7	45.57	4- 61	–	–
D.G.Cork	90.2	18	290	6	48.33	4-122	–	–
T.Lungley	97.1	12	449	9	49.88	3- 89	–	–
L.J.Wharton	206.3	56	600	8	75.00	2- 74	–	–

C.W.G.Bassano 2-0-11-0; M.J.Di Venuto 30-2-124-1; M.P.Dowman 10-3-53-0; A.D.Edwards 13-3-40-0; K.M.Krikken 7-0-27-0; A.R.K.Pierson 10-0-28-0; S.D.Stubbings 4-0-36-0.

The First-Class Averages (pp 113-126) give the records of Derbyshire players in all first-class county matches (Derbyshire's other opponents being the Pakistanis), with the exception of J.P.Pyemont, whose only first-class appearances were in University matches, and:
  D.G.Cork 4-6-0-128-205-34.16-1-0-5ct. 111.2-24-334-6-55.66-4/122.

DERBYSHIRE RECORDS

FIRST-CLASS CRICKET

Highest Total	For 645		v	Hampshire	Derby	1898
	V 662		by	Yorkshire	Chesterfield	1898
Lowest Total	For 16		v	Notts	Nottingham	1879
	V 23		by	Hampshire	Burton upon T	1958
Highest Innings	For 274	G.A.Davidson	v	Lancashire	Manchester	1896
	V 343*	P.A.Perrin	for	Essex	Chesterfield	1904

Highest Partnership for each Wicket

1st	322	H.Storer/J.Bowden	v	Essex	Derby	1929
2nd	417	K.J.Barnett/T.A.Tweats	v	Yorkshire	Derby	1997
3rd	316*	A.S.Rollins/K.J.Barnett	v	Leics	Leicester	1997
4th	328	P.Vaulkhard/D.Smith	v	Notts	Nottingham	1946
5th	302*†	J.E.Morris/D.G.Cork	v	Glos	Cheltenham	1993
6th	212	G.M.Lee/T.S.Worthington	v	Essex	Chesterfield	1932
7th	258	M.P.Dowman/D.G.Cork	v	Durham	Derby	2000
8th	198	K.M.Krikken/D.G.Cork	v	Lancashire	Manchester	1996
9th	283	A.Warren/J.Chapman	v	Warwicks	Blackwell	1910
10th	132	A.Hill/M.Jean-Jacques	v	Yorkshire	Sheffield	1986

† 346 runs were added for this wicket in two separate partnerships

Best Bowling	For 10- 40	W.Bestwick	v	Glamorgan	Cardiff	1921
(Innings)	V 10- 45	R.L.Johnson	for	Middlesex	Derby	1994
Best Bowling	For 17-103	W.Mycroft	v	Hampshire	Southampton	1876
(Match)	V 16-101	G.Giffen	for	Australians	Derby	1886

Most Runs – Season	2165	D.B.Carr	(av 48.11)		1959
Most Runs – Career	23854	K.J.Barnett	(av 41.12)		1979-98
Most 100s – Season	8	P.N.Kirsten			1982
Most 100s – Career	53	K.J.Barnett			1979-98
Most Wkts – Season	168	T.B.Mitchell	(av 19.55)		1935
Most Wkts – Career	1670	H.L.Jackson	(av 17.11)		1947-63
Most Career W-K Dismissals	1304	R.W.Taylor	(1157 ct; 147 st)		1961-84
Most Career Catches in the Field	563	D.C.Morgan			1950-69

LIMITED-OVERS CRICKET

Highest Total	NWT	365-3	v	Cornwall	Derby	1986
	BHC	366-4	v	Combined U	Oxford	1991
	NL	292-9	v	Worcs	Knypersley	1985
Lowest Total	NWT	79	v	Surrey	The Oval	1967
	BHC	98	v	Worcs	Derby	1994
	NL	61	v	Hampshire	Portsmouth	1990
Highest Innings	NWT	173*	M.J.Di Venuto	v	Derbys CB	Derby	2000
	BHC	142	D.M.Jones	v	Minor C	Derby	1996
	NL	141*	C.J.Adams	v	Kent	Chesterfield	1992
Best Bowling	NWT	8-21	M.A.Holding	v	Sussex	Hove	1988
	BHC	6-33	E.J.Barlow	v	Glos	Bristol	1978
	NL	6- 7	M.Hendrick	v	Notts	Nottingham	1972

DURHAM

Formation of Present Club: 10 May 1882
Colours: Navy Blue, Yellow and Maroon
Badge: Coat of Arms of the County of Durham
County Champions: (0) 8th 1999, 8th (Div 1) 2000
Gillette/NatWest/C & G Trophy Winners: (0); best – quarter-finalist 1992, 2001
Benson and Hedges Cup Winners: (0); best – quarter-finalist 1998, 2000, 2001
NU National League (Div 1) Winners: (0); best – 2nd (Div 2) 2001
Sunday League Winners: (0); best – 7th 1993
Match Awards: CGT 22; BHC 18

Chief Executive: D.Harker, County Ground, Riverside, Chester-le-Street, Co Durham DH3 3QR ▲ Tel: 0191 387 1717 ▲ Fax: 0191 387 1616 ▲ Email: marketing@durham-ccc.org.uk ▲ Web: www.durham-ccc.org.uk

Captain: J.J.B.Lewis. **Vice-Captain:** No appointment. **Overseas Player:** M.L.Love.
2002 Beneficiary: None. **Scorer:** B.Hunt. ‡ New registration
Durham initially awarded caps immediately their players joined the staff but revised this policy in 1998 and now cap players on merit, past 'awards' having been nullified.

BRIDGE, Graeme David (Southmoor S, Sunderland), b Sunderland 4 Sep 1980. 5'8". RHB, SLA. Debut 1999. HS 39* and BB 6-84 v Hants (Chester-le-St) 2001. Award: CGT 1. LO HS 15 Durham CB v Glos (Chester-le-St) 1999 (NWT). LO BB 3-44 v Glos (Bristol) 2001 (CGT).

BRINKLEY, James Edward (Marist C, Canberra, Aus; Trinity C, Perth, Aus; Manchester Metropolitan U), b Helensburgh, Scotland 13 Mar 1974. 6'3". RHB, RFM. Worcestershire 1993-94 (Z tour) to 1995. Matabeleland 1994-95. Essex (one SL appearance) 1998. Scotland 1998-2000. Herefordshire 2000. Durham debut 2001. **LOI** (Scot): 5 (1999); HS 23 v A (Worcester) 1999 – on debut; BB 1-29. Tour: Z 1993-94 (Wo). HS 65 v Hants (Chester-le-St) 2001. BB 6-14 v Derbys (Chester-le-St) 2001. LO HS 30* Scot v Yorks (Linlithgow) 1998 (BHC). LO BB 3-55 Scot v NZ (Kuala Lumpur) 1998-99.

BROWN, Simon John Emmerson (Boldon CS; S Tyneside Marine & TC), b Cleadon 29 Jun 1969. 6'3". RHB, LFM. Northamptonshire 1987-90. Durham debut 1992; captain 1996 (*part*); cap 1998; benefit 2001. **Tests:** 1 (1996); HS 10* and BB 1-60 v P (Lord's) 1996. HS 69 v Leics (Durham) 1994. 50 wkts (7); most – 79 (1996). BB 7-51 v Lancs (Chester-le-St) 2000. Awards: CGT 1; BHC 1. LO HS 18 v Derbys (Derby) 1996 (SL). LO BB 6-30 v Northants (Chester-le-St) 1997 (BHC).

COLLINGWOOD, Paul David (Blackfyne CS; Derwentside C), b Shotley Bridge 26 May 1976. 5'11". RHB, RMF. Debut 1996 v Northants (Chester-le-St) taking wicket of D.J.Capel with his first ball before scoring 91 and 16; cap 1998. **LOI:** 18 (2001 to 2001-02); HS 77 v Z (Bulawayo) 2000-01; BB 4-38 v NZ (Napier) 2001-02. 100: 1; 1108 (2001). HS 153 v Warwks (Birmingham) 2001. BB 3-7 v Glam (Cardiff) 1999. Awards: BHC 3. LO HS 95* v Leics (Chester-le-St) 2001 (BHC). LO BB 4-31 v Yorks (Chester-le-St) 2000 (BHC).

DALEY, James Arthur (Hetton CS), b Sunderland 24 Sep 1973. 5'10". RHB, RM. Debut 1992; cap 1999. MCC YC. HS 159* v Hants (Portsmouth) 1994. BB 1-12. LO HS 105 v Surrey (Oval) 2000 (NL).

DAVIES, Anthony Mark (Northfield CS, Billingham), b Stockton-on-Tees 4 Oct 1980. 6'2". RHB, RM. Development-contracted former Durham Academy player awaiting f-c debut. LO HS 10 v Glam (Chester-le-St) 2001. LO BB 4-13 v Sussex (Chester-le-St) 2001.

GOUGH, Michael Andrew (English Martyrs CS; Hartlepool SFC), b Hartlepool 18 Dec 1979. Son of M.P.Gough (Durham 1974-77). 6'5". RHB, OB. Debut 1998. Tours (Eng A): NZ 1999-00; B 1999-00. HS 123 v CU (Cambridge) 1998. CC HS 79 v Glos (Gloucester) 2001. BB 5-66 V Middx (Chester-le-St) 2001. LO HS 58 v Yorks (Leeds) 2001 (BHC). LO BB 3-36 v Glos (Bristol) 2001 (BHC).

HARMISON, Stephen James (Ashington HS), b Ashington, Northumb 23 Oct 1978. 6'4". RHB, RF. Debut 1996; cap 1999. Northumberland 1996. Tours (Eng A): SA 1998-99; Z 1998-99. HS 36 v Kent (Canterbury) 1998. 50 wkts (2); most – 64 (1999). BB 6-111 v Sussex (Chester-le-St) 2001. LO HS 11* v Glam (Chester-le-St) 2001 (NL). LO BB 4-43 v Glam (Cardiff) 2001 (NL).

HATCH, Nicholas Guy (Barnard Castle S; Hull U), b Darlington 21 Apr 1979. 6'7". RHB, RMF. Debut 2001. HS 24 v Sussex (Chester-le-St) 2001. BB 3-42 v Hants (Southampton) 2001. LO HS 8* (NL). LO BB 3-26 v Glam (Chester-le-St) 2001 (NL).

HUNTER, Ian David (Fyndoune Community C, Sacriston; Durham New C), b Durham City 11 Sep 1979. 6'1". RHB, RMF. Debut 2000. HS 63 v Leics (Chester-le-St) 2000 – on debut. BB 4-55 v Warwks (Birmingham) 2001. LO HS 21 v Hants (Southampton) 2001 (NL). LO BB 4-29 v Essex (Ilford) 2000 (NL).

KILLEEN, Neil (Greencroft CS; Derwentside C; Teesside U), b Shotley Bridge 17 Oct 1975. 6'2". RHB, RFM. Debut 1995; cap 1999. HS 48 v Somerset (Chester-le-St) 1995. 50 wkts (1): 58 (1999). BB 7-85 v Leics (Leicester) 1999. Award: BHC 1. LO HS 32 v Middx (Lord's) 1996 (SL). LO BB 6-31 v Derbys (Derby) 2000 (NL).

LAW, Danny Richard (Steyning GS), b Lambeth, London 15 Jul 1975. 6'5". RHB, RFM. Sussex 1993-96; cap 1996. Essex 1997-2000. Durham debut/cap 2001. HS 115 Sx v Young A (Hove) 1995. Du HS 103 v Hants (Chester-le-St) 2001. BB 6-53 v Hants (Southampton) 2001. Hat-trick (Ex) 1998. LO HS 82 Ex v Durham (Chelmsford) 1997 (SL). LO BB 3-26 Ex v Leics (Leicester) 1999 (NL).

LEWIS, Jonathan James Benjamin (King Edward VI S, Chelmsford; Roehampton IHE), b Isleworth, Middx 21 May 1970. 5'9½". RHB, RSM. Essex 1990-96; cap 1994. scored 116* on debut v Surrey (Oval). Durham debut 1997; cap 1998; captain 2000 (*part*) to date. 1000 runs (3); most – 1252 (1997). HS 210* v OU (Oxford) 1997 – on Du debut. CC HS 160* v Derbys (Chester-le-St) 1997. BB 1-73. Award: BHC 1. LO HS 102 v Glos (Cheltenham) 1997 (NL).

LOVE, Martin Lloyd (Toowoomba GS; Queensland U), b Mundubbera, Queensland, Australia 30 Mar 1974. 6'1". RHB, OB. Queensland 1992-93 to date. Durham debut/cap 2001. Tour: E 1995 (Young A). 1000 (1+1): most – 1364 (2001). HS 228 Q v NSW (Brisbane) 1999-00. Du HS 149* v Notts (Chester-le-St) 2001. BB 1-5 (Q). LO HS 124 Q v WA (Brisbane) 2000-01 (MM).

‡**MANN, Christopher** (Boldon CS; South Tyneside C), b South Shields 14 Apr 1981. 5'11". RHB, RM. Former Durham Academy. Staff 2002 – awaiting f-c debut. LO HS (Durham CB) 7 (CGT).

‡**MUCHALL, Gordon** James (Durham S), b Newcastle upon Tyne, Northumb 2 Nov 1982. 6'0". RHB, RM. Northumberland 2001. England U-19 and former Durham Academy player. Staff 2002 – awaiting f-c debut. LO HS 19 Durham CB v Bucks (Beaconsfield) 2001 (CGT).

‡**MUSTARD, Philip** (Usworth CS), b Sunderland 8 Oct 1982. 5'11". LHB, WK. Former Durham Academy. Staff 2002 – awaiting f-c debut. LO HS (Durham CB) 8 (NWT).

PATTISON, Ian (Seaham CS), b Ryhope, Sunderland 5 May 1982. 5'11". RHB, RM. Development-contracted former Durham Academy player – awaiting f-c debut. LO HS 48* and LO BB 1-25 Durham CB v Leics CB (Gateshead) 2000 (NWT).

PENG GILLENDER, Nicky (Newcastle upon Tyne RGS), b Newcastle upon Tyne, Northumb 18 Sep 1982. 6'2". RHB, OB. Debut 2000. Cap 2001. Eng U-19 captain. HS 101 v Middx (Chester-le-St) 2001. Scored 98 v Surrey (Chester-le-St) on debut. Award: CGT 1. LO HS 121 v Worcs (Worcester) 2001 (NL).

PHILLIPS, Nicholas Charles (Wm Parker S, Hastings), b Pembury, Kent 10 May 1974. 5'10½". RHB, OB. Sussex 1993-97. Durham debut 1998; cap 2001. HS 53 Sx v Young A (Hove) 1995. CC HS 52 Sx v Lancs (Lytham) 1995. Du HS 42 v Glos (Cheltenham) 1999. BB 6-97 (12-268 match) v Glam (Cardiff) 1999. Award: CGT 1. LO HS 38* Sx v Essex (Chelmsford) 1996 (SL). LO BB 4-13 v Derbys (Chester-le-St) 1999 (NL).

PRATT, Andrew (Willington Parkside CS; Durham New C), b Helmington Row, Crook 4 Mar 1975. Elder brother of G.J.Pratt. 6'0". LHB, WK. Debut 1997. Cap 2001. MCC YC. HS 68* v Derbys (Chester-le-St) 2001. LO HS 86 v Derbys (Chester-le-St) 2001 (NL).

PRATT, Gary Joseph (Willington Parkside CS), b Bishop Auckland 22 Dec 1981. Younger brother of A.Pratt. 5'11". LHB, OB. Debut 2000. HS 37 v Worcs (Chester-le-St) 2001. LO HS 32 Durham CB v Bucks (Beaconsfield) 2001 (CGT).

SCOTT, Gary Michael (Hetton CS), b Sunderland 21 Jul 1984. 6'0". RHB, OB. Debut 2001 – youngest Durham f-c debutant (17y 19d). HS 25 v Derbys (Chester-le-St) 2001 – on debut. LO HS 20 and LO BB 2-32 Durham CB v Bucks (Beaconsfield) 2001 (CGT).

SYMINGTON, Marc Joseph (St Michaels S, Billingham; Stockton SFC), b Newcastle upon Tyne, Northumb 10 Jan 1980. 5'8". RHB, RM. Debut 1998. No appearances 2001. HS 36 v Yorks (Chester-le-St) 2000. BB 3-55 v Derbys (Derby) 1998. LO HS 16 v Derbys (Darlington) 2000 (NL). LO BB 1-15 (NL).

‡**THORPE, Ashley** Michael (High Street Senior HS, Western Australia), b Kiama, NSW, Australia 2 Apr 1975. 5'11". LHB, RM. ECB qualified by residence. LHB, RM. Staff 2002 – awaiting f-c debut.

RELEASED/RETIRED
(Having made a first-class County appearance in 2001)

SPEAK, Nicholas Jason (Parrs Wood HS, Manchester; Didsbury SFC), b Manchester 21 Nov 1966. 6'0". RHB, LB. Lancashire 1986-87 to 1996; cap 1992. Durham 1997-2001; cap 1998; captain 2000 (*part*). Tours (La): WI 1986-87, 1995-96. 1000 runs (3); most – 1892 (1992). HS 232 La v Leics (Leicester) 1992. Du HS 124* v CU (Cambridge) 1997. BB 1-0. Awards: BHC 2. LO HS 102* La v Yorks (Leeds) 1992 (SL).

SPEIGHT, Martin Peter (Hurstpierpoint C; Durham U), b Walsall, Staffs 24 Oct 1967. 5'9". RHB, WK. Sussex 1986-96; cap 1991. Wellington 1989-90 to 1992-93. Durham 1997-2001; cap 1998. 1000 runs (3); most – 1375 (1990). HS 184 Sx v Notts (Eastbourne) 1993. Du HS 97* v Hants (Southampton) 1998 and 97* v Glam (Cardiff) 1999. BB 1-2. Awards: BHC 2. LO HS 126 Sx v Somerset (Taunton) 1993 (SL).

DERBYSHIRE – RELEASED/RETIRED (continued from p 14)
(Having made a first-class County appearance in 2001)

PIERSON, Adrian Roger Kirshaw (Kent C, Canterbury; Hatfield Poly), b Enfield, Middx 21 Jul 1963. 6'4". RHB, OB. Warwickshire 1985-91. Leicestershire 1993-97; cap 1995. Somerset 1998-2000. Derbyshire 2001. Cambridgeshire 1992. MCC YC. Tour (Le): SA 1996-97. HS 108* Sm v Sussex (Hove) 1998. De HS 9. 50 wkts (1): 69 (1995). BB 8-42 Le v Warwks (Birmingham) 1994. Awards: CGT 1; BHC 1. LO HS 31* Sm v Northants (Northampton) 2000 (NL). LO BB 5-36 Le v Derbys (Leicester) 1995 (SL). Appointed 2nd XI coach.

SMITH, Trevor Mark (Friesland CS, Sandiacre; Broxtowe CFE, Chilwell), b Derby 18 Jan 1977. 6'3". LHB, RFM. Derbyshire 1997-2001. HS 53* v Lancs (Derby) 2000. BB 6-32 v Essex (Derby) 1998. LO HS 27 v Leics (Leicester) 2001 (BHC). LO BB 4-38 v Somerset (Derby) 1999 (NL).

TITCHARD, Stephen Paul (Lymm County HS; Priestley C), b Warrington 17 Dec 1967. 6'3". RHB, RM. Lancashire 1990-98; cap 1996. Derbyshire 1999-2001. HS 163 La v Essex (Chelmsford) 1996. De HS 141* v Kent (Canterbury) 2000. BB (La) 1-11 (*twice*). Award: CGT 1. LO HS 96 La v Essex (Chelmsford) 1994 (SL). LO BB (De) 1-19 (SL).

Z.M.Khan, A.J.Marsh and B.L.Spendlove left the staff having made no f-c appearances in 2001.

DURHAM 2001

RESULTS SUMMARY

	Place	Won	Lost	Tied	Drew	No Result
County Championship (2nd Division)	8th	3	6		7	
All First-Class Matches		3	6		8	
C & G Trophy	Quarter-Finalist					
Benson & Hedges Cup	Quarter-Finalist					
NU National League (2nd Division)	2nd	9	4			3

COUNTY CHAMPIONSHIP AVERAGES

BATTING AND FIELDING

Cap		M	I	NO	HS	Runs	Avge	100	50	Ct/St
2001	M.L.Love	15	29	2	149*	1364	50.51	1	13	21
1998	P.D.Collingwood	22	23	3	153	978	48.90	2	6	10
1998	J.J.B.Lewis	16	31	–	129	890	28.70	2	3	6
2001	N.Peng	12	22	2	101	551	27.55	1	3	6
2001	D.R.Law	15	26	1	103	586	23.44	1	1	10
1998	M.P.Speight	7	14	2	67*	281	23.41	–	1	1
1998	S.J.E.Brown	4	5	2	29	64	21.33	–	–	1
1999	J.A.Daley	8	15	–	89	300	20.00	–	1	1
2001	A.Pratt	16	28	4	68*	476	19.83	–	3	49/7
–	M.A.Gough	12	22	–	79	428	19.45	–	1	8
–	I.D.Hunter	8	14	3	37	199	18.09	–	–	4
–	N.G.Hatch	9	16	8	24	129	16.12	–	–	1
–	G.J.Pratt	2	4	–	37	53	13.25	–	–	1
2001	N.C.Phillips	7	11	4	30	87	12.42	–	–	6
–	G.D.Bridge	7	13	2	39*	125	11.36	–	–	5
–	J.E.Brinkley	9	13	2	65	111	10.09	–	1	.4
1999	S.J.Harmison	11	14	4	27	97	9.70	–	–	–

Also batted: N.Killeen (3 matches – cap 1999) 5, 0, 1; G.M.Scott (1) 8, 25 (1 ct); N.J.Speak (2 – cap 1998) 41, 2, 7.

BOWLING

	O	M	R	W	Avge	Best	5wI	10wM
J.E.Brinkley	207.1	49	629	30	20.96	6- 14	2	–
G.D.Bridge	172	48	413	18	22.94	6- 84	1	–
S.J.E.Brown	115	29	333	14	23.78	6- 70	1	–
D.R.Law	339.1	69	1070	40	26.75	6- 53	3	–
N.G.Hatch	248.4	43	867	26	33.34	3- 42	–	–
M.A.Gough	150	31	434	13	33.38	5- 66	1	–
S.J.Harmison	397.5	76	1228	34	36.11	6-111	2	–
N.C.Phillips	285.5	60	939	23	40.82	5- 64	1	–
I.D.Hunter	181.3	27	700	16	43.75	4- 55	–	–

Also bowled:

N.Killeen	72	22	194	7	27.71	3- 35	–	–
P.D.Collingwood	154	41	463	7	66.14	2- 22	–	–

G.M.Scott 3-1-11-0.

The First-Class Averages (pp 113-126) give the records of Durham players in all first-class county matches (Durham's other opponents being Durham University).

DURHAM RECORDS

FIRST-CLASS CRICKET

Highest Total	For 625-6d		v	Derbyshire	Chesterfield	1994
	V 810-4d		by	Warwicks	Birmingham	1994
Lowest Total	For 67		v	Middlesex	Lord's	1996
	V 67		by	Durham UCCE	Chester-le-St[2]	2001
Highest Innings	For 210*	J.J.B.Lewis	v	Oxford U	Oxford	1997
	V 501*	B.C.Lara	for	Warwicks	Birmingham	1994

Highest Partnership for each Wicket

1st	334*	S.Hutton/M.A.Roseberry	v	Oxford U	Oxford	1996
2nd	258	J.J.B.Lewis/M.L.Love	v	Notts	Chester-le-St[2]	2001
3rd	205	G.Fowler/S.Hutton	v	Yorkshire	Leeds	1993
4th	204	J.J.B.Lewis/J.Boiling	v	Derbyshire	Chester-le-St[2]	1997
5th	185	P.W.G.Parker/J.A.Daley	v	Warwicks	Darlington	1993
6th	193	D.C.Boon/P.D.Collingwood	v	Warwicks	Birmingham	1998
7th	127	D.R.Law/J.E.Brinkley	v	Hants	Chester-le-St[2]	2001
8th	134	A.C.Cummins/D.A.Graveney	v	Warwicks	Birmingham	1994
9th	127	D.G.C.Ligertwood/S.J.E.Brown	v	Surrey	Stockton	1996
10th	103	M.M.Betts/D.M.Cox	v	Sussex	Hove	1996

Best Bowling	For 9- 64	M.M.Betts	v	Northants	Northampton	1997
(Innings)	V 8- 22	D.Follett	for	Middlesex	Lord's	1996
Best Bowling	For 14-177	A.Walker	v	Essex	Chelmsford	1995
(Match)	V 12- 68	J.N.B.Bovill	for	Hampshire	Stockton	1995

Most Runs – Season	1536	W.Larkins	(av 37.46)		1992
Most Runs – Career	5670	J.E.Morris	(av 32.77)		1994-99
Most 100s – Season	4	D.M.Jones			1992
	4	W.Larkins			1992
	4	J.E.Morris			1994
Most 100s – Career	14	J.E.Morris			1994-99
Most Wkts – Season	77	S.J.E.Brown	(av 25.87)		1992
Most Wkts – Career	516	S.J.E.Brown	(av 28.29)		1992-2001
Most Career W-K Dismissals	195	M.P.Speight	(190 ct; 5 st)		1997-2001
Most Career Catches in the Field	87	P.D.Collingwood			1996-2001

LIMITED-OVERS CRICKET

Highest Total	NWT	326-4		v	Herefords	Chester-le-St[2]	1995
	BHC	287-5		v	Leics	Leicester	1996
	NL	281-2		v	Derbyshire	Durham	1993
Lowest Total	NWT	82		v	Worcs	Chester-le-St[1]	1968
	BHC	133		v	Glos	Bristol	2001
	NL	99		v	Warwicks	Birmingham	1996
Highest Innings	NWT	125	S.Hutton	v	Herefords	Chester-le-St[2]	1995
	BHC	145	J.E.Morris	v	Leics	Leicester	1996
	NL	131*	W.Larkins	v	Hampshire	Portsmouth	1994
Best Bowling	NWT	7-32	S.P.Davis	v	Lancashire	Chester-le-St[1]	1983
	BHC	6-30	S.J.E.Brown	v	Northants	Chester-le-St[2]	1997
	NL	6-31	N.Killeen	v	Derbyshire	Derby	2000

[1] Chester-le-Street CC (Ropery Lane)　[2] Riverside Ground

ESSEX

Formation of Present Club: 14 January 1876
Colours: Blue, Gold and Red
Badge: Three Seaxes above Scroll bearing 'Essex'
County Champions: (6) 1979, 1983, 1984, 1986, 1991, 1992
Gillette/NatWest/C & G Trophy Winners: (2) 1985, 1997
Benson and Hedges Cup Winners: (2) 1979, 1998
NU National League (Div 1) Winners: (0); best – 9th 1999
Sunday League Winners: (3) 1981, 1984, 1985
Match Awards: CGT 49; BHC 85

Chief Executive: D.E.East, County Ground, New Writtle Street, Chelmsford CM2 0PG ▲ Tel: 01245 252420 ▲ Fax: 01245 254030 ▲ Email: administration.essex@ecb.co.uk ▲ Web: www.essexcricket.org.uk

Club Captain: N.Hussain. **1st XI Captain:** R.C.Irani. **Vice-Captain:** No appointment. **Overseas Player:** A.Flower. **2002 Beneficiary:** M.C.Ilott. **Scorer:** D.J.Norris. ‡ New registration

BISHOP, Justin Edward (Bury St Edmunds County Upper S; Durham U), b Bury St Edmunds, Suffolk 4 Jan 1982. 6'0". LHB, LMF. Debut 1999. Awaiting CC debut. No f-c appearances 2000. HS 18 v Somerset (Chelmsford) 2001. BB 5-148 v Leics (Chelmsford) 2001. LO HS 16* v Hants (Colchester) 2000 (NL). LO BB 3-33 v Worcs (Worcester) 2001 (NL).

‡BOPARA, Ravinder Singh, b Forest Gate 4 May 1985. RHB. Staff 2002 – awaiting f-c debut. LO HS (Essex CB) 1 (CGT).

‡CLARKE, Andrew John (St Martin's S, Hutton), b Brentwood 9 Nov 1975. LHB, RM. MCC YC. Staff 2002 – awaiting f-c debut. LO HS 9 (CGT). LO BB 2-39 v Worcs (Chelmsford) 2001 (NL).

CLINTON, Richard Selvey (Colfes S), b Sidcup, Kent 1 Sep 1981. Son of G.S.Clinton (Kent and Surrey 1974-90). 6'3". LHB, RM. Kent staff 1999-2000 – no f-c appearances. Essex debut 2001. HS 58* v Surrey (Ilford) 2001 – on debut. BB 2-30 v A (Chelmsford) 2001. CC BB – . LO HS 56 v Durham (Ilford) 2001 (NL). LO BB – .

COWAN, Ashley Preston (Framlingham C), b Hitchin, Herts 7 May 1975. 6'4". RHB, RFM. Debut 1995; cap 1997. Cambridgeshire 1993. Tour: WI 1997-98. HS 94 v Leics (Leicester) 1998. 50 wkts (1): 52 (1997). BB 6-47 v Glam (Cardiff) 1999. Hat-trick 1996. Award: BHC 1. LO HS 45 v Middx (Chelmsford) 2001 (BHC). LO BB 5-14 v Middx (Southgate) 2001 (NL).

‡DAKIN, Jonathan Michael (King Edward VII S, Johannesburg) b Hitchin, Herts 28 Feb 1973. 6'4". LHB, RM. Leicestershire 1993-2001; cap 2000. Tour (Le): SA 1996-97. HS 190 Le v Northants (Northampton) 1997. BB 4-27 Le v Worcester (Worcester) 1999. Awards: CGT 1; BHC 1. LO HS 179 Le v Wales MC (Swansea) 2001 (CGT). LO BB 5-30 Le v Kent (Leicester) 1999 (NL).

‡FLOWER, Andrew (Wainona HS, Harare), b Cape Town, SA 28 Apr 1968. 5'10". Elder brother of G.W.Flower (Zimbabwe). LHB, WK, occ RM. Mashonaland 1986-87 to date. MCC 1996-99. *Wisden* 2001. **Tests** (Z): 61 (1992-93 to 2001-02, 20 as captain); HS 232* v I (Nagpur) 2000-01. **LOI** (Z): 191 (1991-92 to 2001-02, 52 as captain); HS 142* v E (Harare) 2001-02; scored 115 v SL (New Plymouth) on debut. Tours (Z) (C=captain): E 2000C; SA 1999-00; WI 1999-00C; NZ 1995-96C, 1997-98, 2000-01; I 1992-93, 2000-01, 2001-02; P 1993-94C, 1996-97, 1998-99; SL 1996-97, 1997-98, 2001-02; B 2001-02. HS 232* (*see* TESTS). BB 1-1. LO HS 142* (*see* LOI).

22

FOSTER, James Savin (Forest S, Snaresbrook; Collingwood C, Durham U), b Whipps Cross 15 Apr 1980. 6'0". RHB, WK. British U 2000. Essex debut 2000; cap 2001. Durham UCCE 2001. British U 2001. **Tests**: 3 (2001-02); HS 48 v I (Bangalore) 2001-02. **LOI**: 11 (2001-02); HS 13 v I (Bombay) 2001-02. Tours: WI 2000-01 (Eng A); NZ 2001-02; I 2001-02. HS 103 DU v Worcs (Worcester) 2001. Ex HS 79 v Northants (Northampton) 2001. LO HS 56* v Sussex (Hove) 2001 (NL).

GRANT, Joseph Benjamin (Petersvale All-Age S, Jamaica), b White House, Jamaica 17 Dec 1967. 5'11". RHB, RFM. Jamaica 1990-91 to 1995-96. Essex debut 2001. Cambridgeshire 2001. HS 36* Jamaica v Guyana (Albion) 1994-95. Ex HS 1*. BB 3-43 Jamaica v Trinidad (Kingston) 1994-95. Ex BB 3-81 v Yorks (Scarborough) 2001. LO HS 14 Jamaica v Trinidad (Port-of-Spain) 1991-92 (GG). LO BB 3-10 Jamaica v Trinidad (Kingston) 1990-91 (GG).

GRAYSON, Adrian Paul (Bedale CS), b Ripon, Yorks 31 Mar 1971. 6'1". RHB, SLA. Yorkshire 1990-95. Essex debut/cap 1996. **LOI**: 2 (2000-01 to 2001-02); HS 6 and BB 3-40 v Z (Bulawayo) 2001-02. Tour: SA 1991-92 (Y). 1000 runs (4); most – 1275 (2001). HS 189 v Glam (Chelmsford) 2001. BB 5-20 v Yorks (Scarborough) 2001. Award: BHC 1. LO HS 82* v Worcs (Chelmsford) 1997 (NWT). LO BB 4-25 Y v Glam (Cardiff) 1994 (SL).

‡HABIB, Aftab (Millfield S; Taunton S), b Reading, Berkshire 7 Feb 1972. Cousin of Zahid Sadiq (Surrey and Derbys 1988-90). 5'11". RHB, RMF. Middlesex 1992 (one match). Leicestershire 1995-2001; cap 1998. **Tests**: 2 (1999); HS 19 v NZ (Lord's) 1999. Tours (Eng A): WI 2000-01 (*part*); NZ 1999-00; B 1999-00. 1000 runs (2); most – 1055 (1999). HS 215 Le v Worcs (Leicester) 1996. Award: BHC 1. LO HS 111 Le v Durham (Chester-le-St) 1997 (BHC). LO BB 2-5 Le v Ire (Dublin) 1999.

HUSSAIN, Nasser (Forest S, Snaresbrook; Durham U), b Madras, India 28 Mar 1968. Son of J.Hussain (Madras 1966-67); brother of M.Hussain (Worcs 1985). 5'11". RHB, LB. Debut 1987; cap 1989; captain 1999; club captain 2000 to date; benefit 1999. YC 1989. OBE 2002. **ECB contracts 2000, 2001. Tests**: 66 (1989-90 to 2001-02, 27 as captain); HS 207 v A (Birmingham) 1997. **LOI**: 65 (1989-90 to 2001-02, 33 as captain); HS 95 v B (Nairobi) 2000-01. Tours (C=captain): A 1998-99; SA 1999-00C; WI 1989-90, 1991-92 (Eng A), 1993-94, 1997-98; NZ 1996-97, 2001-02C; I 2001-02C; P 1990-91 (Eng A), 1995-96C (Eng A), 2000-01C; SL 1990-91 (Eng A), 2000-01C; Z 1996-97. 1000 runs (5); most – 1854 (1995). HS 207 (*see Tests*). Ex HS 197 v Surrey (Oval) 1990. BB 1-38. Awards: CGT 3; BHC 3. LO HS 118 Comb U v Somerset (Taunton) 1989 (BHC).

HYAM, Barry James (Havering SFC; Westminster C), b Romford 9 Sep 1975. RHB, WK. Debut 1993; cap 1999. MCC YC. HS 63 v Glam (Chelmsford) 2001. LO HS 37 v Leics (Leicester) 1999 (NL).

ILOTT, Mark Christopher (Francis Combe SMS, Garston), b Watford, Herts 27 Aug 1970. 6'0½". LHB, LFM. Debut 1988; cap 1993; benefit 2002. Hertfordshire 1987-88 (at 16, the youngest to represent that county). **Tests**: 5 (1993 to 1995-96); HS 15 v A (Oval) 1993; BB 3-48 v SA (Durban) 1995-96. Tours: A 1992-93 (Eng A); SA 1993-94 (Eng A), 1995-96; I 1994-95 (Eng A – *part*); SL 1990-91 (Eng A). HS 60 Eng A v Warwks (Birmingham) 1995. Ex HS 58 v Worcs (Worcester) 1996. 50 wkts (6); most – 78 (1995). BB 9-19 (14-105 match; inc hat-trick – all lbw) v Northants (Luton) 1995. Hat-trick 1995. Awards: BHC 2. LO HS 56* v Sussex (Hove) 1995 (SL). LO BB 5-21 v Scot (Forfar) 1993 (BHC).

IRANI, Ronald Charles (Smithills CS, Bolton), b Leigh, Lancs 26 Oct 1971. 6'3". RHB, RMF. Lancashire 1990-93. Essex debut/cap 1994; captain 2000 to date. **Tests**: 3 (1996 to 1999); HS 41 v I (Lord's) 1996; BB 1-22. Took wicket of M.Azharuddin with his fifth ball in Test cricket. **LOI**: 10 (1996 to 1996-97); HS 45* v P (Birmingham) 1996; BB 1-23. Tours: NZ 1996-97, 1999-00 (Eng A); P 1995-96 (Eng A). HS 168* v Glam (Cardiff) 2000. 50 wkts (1): 51 (1999). BB 6-79 v Lancs (Colchester) 2001. Awards: CGT 4; BHC 2. LO HS 124 v Durham (Chelmsford) 1996 (NWT). LO BB 5-33 v Hants (Southampton) 1999 (NL).

JEFFERSON, William Ingleby (Beeston Hall S, Norfolk; Oundle S; St Hild & St Bede C, Durham U), b Derby 25 Oct 1979. Son of R.I.Jefferson (Cambridge U and Surrey 1961-66); grandson of J.Jefferson (Army 1919, Comb Services 1922). 6'9½". RHB, RMF. British U 2000-01. Essex debut 2000. Durham UCCE 2001. Scored 50 and 65 in first two l-o innings. HS 69 v Leics (Leicester) 2001. LO HS 65 v Glam (Southend) 2000.

McGARRY, Andrew Charles (King Edward VI GS, Chelmsford; SE Essex C of Arts & Technology, Southend), b Basildon 8 Nov 1981. 6'5". RHB, RFM. Debut 1999. HS 4*. BB 3-29 v Worcs (Chelmsford) 2000. LO HS 1 (NL). LO BB 2-20 v Surrey (Colchester) 2000 (NL).

‡**MIDDLEBROOK, James** Daniel (Pudsey Crawshaw S), b Leeds, Yorks 13 May 1977. 6'1". RHB, OB. Yorkshire 1998-2001. HS 84 Y v Essex (Chelmsford) 2001. BB 6-82 (10-170 match) Y v Hants (Southampton) 2000 – including 4 wkts in 5 balls. LO HS 15* Y v Sussex (Scarborough) 2000 (NL). LO BB 3-16 Y v Glos (Leeds) 2000 (NL).

NAPIER, Graham Richard (The Gilberd S, Colchester), b Colchester 6 Jan 1980. 5'9½". RHB, RM. Debut 1997. HS 104 v CU (Cambridge) 2001. CC HS 56 v Somerset (Chelmsford) 2001. BB 3-55 v Leics (Chelmsford) 2001. Award: CGT 1. LO HS 79 Essex CB v Lancs CB (Chelmsford) 2000 (NWT). LO BB 6-29 v Worcs (Chelmsford) 2001 (NL).

PETTINI, Mark Lewis (Comberton Village C; Hills Road SFC, Cambridge), b Brighton, Sussex 7 Aug 1983. RHB, RM. 5'10". Debut 2001. HS 41 v Yorks (Scarborough) 2001 – on debut. LO HS 14 v Worcs (Worcester) 2001 (NL).

PHILLIPS, Timothy James (Felsted S; St Hild & St Bede C, Durham U), b Cambridge 13 Mar 1981. 6'1". LHB, SLA. Debut 1999. Durham UCCE 2001. HS 27 v Leics (Chelmsford) 2001. BB 4-42 v SLA (Chelmsford) 1999 – on debut. CC BB 1-66. LO HS 2 (NL). LO BB 2-56 v Hants (Southend) 1999 (NL).

ROBINSON, Darren David John (Tabor HS, Braintree; Chelmsford CFE), b Braintree 2 Mar 1973. 5'10½". RHB, RMF. Debut 1993; cap 1997. HS 200 v NZ (Chelmsford) 1999. CC HS 148 v Worcs (Chelmsford) 1997. Awards: BHC 2. LO HS 137* v Sussex (Hove) 1998 (BHC). LO BB 1-7 (SL).

SHARIF, Zoheb Khalid (Warwick S; Chigwell S; Coopers Co & Coborn S), b Leytonstone 22 Feb 1983. LHB, LB. 5'10". Debut 2001. HS 15 v Yorks (Scarborough) 2001 – on debut.

STEPHENSON, John Patrick (Felsted S; Durham U), b Stebbing 14 Mar 1965. 6'1". RHB, RM. Essex 1985-94; cap 1989. Hampshire 1995-2001; cap 1995; captain 1996-97; benefit 2001. Boland 1988-89. **Tests:** 1 (1989); HS 25 v A (Oval) 1989. Tours: WI 1991-92 (Eng A); Z 1989-90 (Eng A). 1000 runs (9); most – 1887 (1990). HS 202* v Somerset (Bath) 1990. BB 7-51 H v Middx (Lord's) 1995. Ex BB 6-54 v Notts (Colchester) 1992. Awards: CGT 1; BHC 5. LO HS 142 v Warwks (Birmingham) 1991 (BHC). LO BB 6-33 H v Worcs (Southampton) 1997 (SL).

RELEASED/RETIRED
(Having made a first-class County appearance in 2001)

ANDERSON, R.S.G. – see NORTHAMPTONSHIRE.

DAVIES, Michael Kenton (Loughborough GS; Loughborough U), b Ashby-de-la-Zouch, Leics 17 Jul 1976. 6'0". RHB, SLA. Northamptonshire 1997-2000. Essex 2001. British U 1998. Tours (Eng A): NZ 1999-00; B 1999-00. HS 32* Nh v Durham (Northampton) 1999. Ex HS 10* v Somerset (Chelmsford) 2001. BB 6-49 Nh v Hants (Northampton) 1999. Ex BB 3-121 v Lancs (Manchester) 2001. LO HS (Nh) 4 (NL). LO BB 3-11 Brit U v Somerset (Taunton) 1998 (BHC).

LAW, S.G. – see LANCASHIRE.

MASON, Timothy James (Brookvale HS, Leicester; Denstone C), b Leicester 12 Apr 1975. 5'8". RHB, OB. Leicestershire 1994-99. Essex 2000-01. HS 52* v Glam (Cardiff) 2000. BB 5-40 v CU (Cambridge) 2001. CC BB 3-32 Le v Worcs (Worcester) 1999. LO HS 36 Le v Yorks (Leicester) 1997 (NWT). LO BB 4-12 Le v Essex (Leicester) 1998 (SL).

PETERS, S.D. – see WORCESTERSHIRE   RELEASED/RETIRED continued on p 29

ESSEX 2001

RESULTS SUMMARY

	Place	Won	Lost	Tied	Drew	No Result
County Championship (1st Division)	9th	2	7		7	
All First-Class Matches		3	7		8	
C & G Trophy	4th Round					
Benson & Hedges Cup	5th in South Group					
NU National League (2nd Division)	7th	5	9	1		1

COUNTY CHAMPIONSHIP AVERAGES

BATTING AND FIELDING

Cap		M	I	NO	HS	Runs	Avge	100	50	Ct/St
1996	S.G.Law	13	23	3	153	1311	65.55	4	8	18
1996	A.P.Grayson	14	27	3	189	1148	47.83	5	1	6
1997	D.D.J.Robinson	16	29	2	118*	812	30.07	2	4	10
1994	R.C.Irani	16	28	2	119	761	29.26	1	6	4
–	G.R.Napier	8	14	–	56	343	24.50	–	1	3
–	R.S.Clinton	7	14	1	58*	283	21.76	–	1	2
–	S.D.Peters	14	25	3	56*	464	21.09	–	1	3
2001	J.S.Foster	11	19	–	79	388	20.42	–	2	20/4
1999	B.J.Hyam	5	8	1	63	131	18.71	–	1	15
1993	M.C.Ilott	8	11	1	34	179	17.90	–	–	4
–	T.J.Mason	2	4	1	41*	46	15.33	–	–	–
–	R.S.G.Anderson	7	10	–	45	148	14.80	–	–	2
1997	A.P.Cowan	14	23	2	68	310	14.76	–	1	8
–	T.J.Phillips	3	5	–	27	63	12.60	–	–	–
1991	P.M.Such	13	19	9	25	117	11.70	–	–	7
1986	P.J.Prichard	6	10	–	34	90	9.00	–	–	1
–	J.E.Bishop	7	11	2	18	74	8.22	–	–	–
–	M.K.Davies	2	4	1	10*	22	7.33	–	–	–
–	A.C.McGarry	5	7	5	4*	5	2.50	–	–	1

Also batted (1 match each): J.B.Grant 1*; N.Hussain (cap 1989) 15, 34; W.I.Jefferson 69;
M.L.Pettini 1, 41 (1 ct); Z.K.Sharif 15, 2 (1 ct).

BOWLING

	O	M	R	W	Avge	Best	5wI	10wM
R.S.G.Anderson	217.1	51	665	29	22.93	5- 50	2	–
M.C.Ilott	229	47	728	23	31.65	5- 85	1	–
R.C.Irani	346.5	94	1029	32	32.15	6- 79	3	–
J.E.Bishop	191	34	765	21	36.42	5-148	1	–
A.P.Cowan	442.5	97	1475	32	46.09	3- 64	–	–
P.M.Such	353	74	1107	17	65.11	4- 81	–	–

Also bowled:

	O	M	R	W	Avge	Best	5wI	10wM
A.C.McGarry	118	17	430	9	47.77	3- 77		
G.R.Napier	88.1	14	390	8	48.75	3- 55		
A.P.Grayson	136	19	493	9	54.77	5- 20	1	

R.S.Clinton 1-1-0-0; M.K.Davies 38-4-141-3; J.B.Grant 19-0-101-3; T.J.Mason 14-5-40-0;
T.J.Phillips 62-7-261-1; Z.K.Sharif 2-0-23-0.

The First-Class Averages (pp 113-126) give the records of Essex players in all first-class county matches (Essex's other opponents being the Australians and Cambridge University), with the exception of W.I.Jefferson and T.J.Phillips, whose full county figures are as above, and:
N.Hussain 2-3-0-34-65-21.66-0-0-0ct. 1-0-1-0.
J.S.Foster 12-20-0-79-462-23.10-0-3-24ct, 6st. 2-0-6-0.

ESSEX RECORDS

FIRST-CLASS CRICKET

Highest Total	For	761-6d		v	Leics	Chelmsford	1990
	V	803-4d		by	Kent	Brentwood	1934
Lowest Total	For	30		v	Yorkshire	Leyton	1901
	V	14		by	Surrey	Chelmsford	1983
Highest Innings	For	343*	P.A.Perrin	v	Derbyshire	Chesterfield	1904
	V	332	W.H.Ashdown	for	Kent	Brentwood	1934

Highest Partnership for each Wicket

1st	316	G.A.Gooch/P.J.Prichard	v	Kent	Chelmsford	1994
2nd	403	G.A.Gooch/P.J.Prichard	v	Leics	Chelmsford	1990
3rd	347*	M.E.Waugh/N.Hussain	v	Lancashire	Ilford	1992
4th	314	Salim Malik/N.Hussain	v	Surrey	The Oval	1991
5th	316	N.Hussain/M.A.Garnham	v	Leics	Leicester	1991
6th	206	J.W.H.T.Douglas/J.O'Connor	v	Glos	Cheltenham	1923
	206	B.R.Knight/R.A.G.Luckin	v	Middlesex	Brentwood	1962
7th	261	J.W.H.T.Douglas/J.Freeman	v	Lancashire	Leyton	1914
8th	263	D.R.Wilcox/R.M.Taylor	v	Warwicks	Southend	1946
9th	251	J.W.H.T.Douglas/S.N.Hare	v	Derbyshire	Leyton	1921
10th	218	F.H.Vigar/T.P.B.Smith	v	Derbyshire	Chesterfield	1947

Best Bowling	For	10- 32	H.Pickett	v	Leics	Leyton	1895
(Innings)	V	10- 40	E.G.Dennett	for	Glos	Bristol	1906
Best Bowling	For	17-119	W.Mead	v	Hampshire	Southampton	1895
(Match)	V	17- 56	C.W.L.Parker	for	Glos	Gloucester	1925

Most Runs – Season	2559	G.A.Gooch	(av 67.34)	1984
Most Runs – Career	30701	G.A.Gooch	(av 51.77)	1973-97
Most 100s – Season	9	J.O'Connor		1929, 1934
	9	D.J.Insole		1955
Most 100s – Career	94	G.A.Gooch		1973-97
Most Wkts – Season	172	T.P.B.Smith	(av 27.13)	1947
Most Wkts – Career	1610	T.P.B.Smith	(av 26.68)	1929-51
Most Career W-K Dismissals	1231	B.Taylor	(1040 ct; 191 st)	1949-73
Most Career Catches in the Field	519	K.W.R.Fletcher		1962-88

LIMITED-OVERS CRICKET

Highest Total	NWT	386-5		v	Wiltshire	Chelmsford	1988
	BHC	388-7		v	Scotland	Chelmsford	1992
	NL	310-5		v	Glamorgan	Southend	1983
Lowest Total	NWT	57		v	Lancashire	Lord's	1996
	BHC	61		v	Lancashire	Chelmsford	1992
	NL	69		v	Derbyshire	Chesterfield	1974
Highest Innings	NWT	144	G.A.Gooch	v	Hampshire	Chelmsford	1990
	BHC	198*	G.A.Gooch	v	Sussex	Hove	1982
	NL	176	G.A.Gooch	v	Glamorgan	Southend	1983
Best Bowling	NWT	5- 8	J.K.Lever	v	Middlesex	Westcliff	1972
		5- 8	G.A.Gooch	v	Cheshire	Chester	1995
	BHC	5-13	J.K.Lever	v	Middlesex	Lord's	1985
	NL	8-26	K.D.Boyce	v	Lancashire	Manchester	1971

GLAMORGAN

Formation of Present Club: 6 July 1888
Colours: Blue and Gold
Badge: Gold Daffodil
County Champions: (3) 1948, 1969, 1997
Gillette/NatWest/C & G Trophy Winners: (0); best – finalists 1977
Benson and Hedges Cup Winners: (0); best – finalists 2000
NU National League (Div 1) Winners: (0); best – 1st (Div 2) 2001
Sunday League Winners: (1) 1993
Match Awards: CGT 43; BHC 56

Chief Executive: M.J.Fatkin, Sophia Gardens, Cardiff, CF1 9XR ▲ Tel: 029 2040 9380 ▲ Fax: 029 2040 9390 ▲ Email: glam@ecb.co.uk ▲ Web: www.glamorgancricket.com

Captain: S.P.James. **Vice-Captain:** R.D.B.Croft. **Overseas Player:** tba.
2002 Beneficiary: A.Dale. **Scorer:** G.N.Lewis. ‡ New registration

‡**BUKHARI, Syed** Muhammad Ali, b Pakistan 8 Nov 1973. Nephew of Taslim Arif (Pakistan 1979-80 to 1980-81). RHB, LFM. Staff 2002 – awaiting f-c debut.

CHERRY, Daniel David (Tonbridge S; U of Wales, Swansea), b Newport, Gwent 7 Feb 1980. 5'9". LHB, RM. Debut 1998. No f-c appearances since 1999. HS 11 v Derbys (Cardiff) 1998 – on debut.

COSKER, Dean Andrew (Millfield S), b Weymouth, Dorset 7 Jan 1978. 5'11". RHB, SLA. Debut 1996; cap 2000. Tours (Eng A): SA 1998-99, SL 1997-98; Z 1998-99, K 1997-98. HS 49 v Sussex (Cardiff) 1999. BB 6-140 v Lancs (Colwyn Bay) 1998. LO HS 27* v Somerset (Taunton) 1999 (NL). LO BB 3-18 v Warwks (Birmingham) 1998 (SL).

CROFT, Robert Damien Bale (St John Lloyd Catholic CS, Llanelli; Neath Tertiary C; W Glam IHE), b Morriston 25 May 1970. 5'10½". RHB, OB. Debut 1989; cap 1992; benefit 2000. **Tests:** 21 (1996 to 2001); HS 37* v SA (Manchester) 1998; BB 5-95 v NZ (Christchurch) 1996-97. **LOI:** 50 (1996 to 2001); HS 32 v SL (Perth) 1998-99; BB 3-51 v SA (Oval) 1998. Tours: A 1998-99; SA 1993-94 (Eng A), 1995-96 (Gm); WI 1991-92 (Eng A), 1997-98; NZ 1996-97; SL 2000-01; Z 1990-91 (Gm), 1994-95 (Gm), 1996-97. HS 143 v Somerset (Taunton) 1995. 50 wkts (5); most – 76 (1996). BB 8-66 (14-169 match) v Warwks (Swansea) 1992. Awards: CGT 1; BHC 2. LO HS 114* v Middx (Cardiff) 2001 (NL). LO BB 6-20 v Worcs (Cardiff) 1994 (SL).

DALE, Adrian (Chepstow CS; Swansea U), b Germiston, SA 24 Oct 1968 (to UK at 6 mths). 5'11½". RHB, RM. Debut 1989; cap 1992; benefit 2002. Tours (Gm): SA 1993-94 (Eng A), 1995-96; Z 1990-91, 1994-95. 1000 runs (4); most – 1472 (1993). HS 214* v Middx (Cardiff) 1993. BB 6-18 v Warwks (Cardiff) 1993. Awards: CGT 2; BHC 3. LO HS 110 v Lincs (Swansea) 1994 (NWT). LO BB 6-22 v Durham (Colwyn Bay) 1993 (SL).

DAVIES, Andrew Philip (Dwr-y-Felin CS; Christ C, Brecon), b Neath 7 Nov 1976. 5'11". LHB, RMF. Debut 1995. Wales (MC). No appearances 2000. HS 40 v Essex (Cardiff) 2001. BB 3-76 v Surrey (Oval) 2001. LO HS 24 v Sussex (Hove) 2001 (NL). LO BB 5-39 v Essex (Cardiff) 2001 (NL).

EVANS, Alun Wyn (Fishguard HS; Neath Tertiary C), b Glanamman, Dyfed 20 Aug 1975. 5'8". RHB, RM. Debut 1996 v OU (Oxford), scoring 66* and 71*. MCC YC. HS 125 v CU (Cambridge) 1998. CC HS 88* v Durham (Cardiff) 1999. LO HS 108 v Derbys (Cardiff) 1999 (NL).

‡**EVISON, Tomos** David, Bangor 17 Dec 1983. LHB, SLA. Staff 2002 – awaiting f-c debut.

HARRISON, David Stuart (W Monmouth CS; Usk C, Pontypool), b Newport, Gwent 30 Jul 1981. Son of S.C.Harrison (Glamorgan 1971-77). 6'4". RHB, RM. Glamorgan debut 1999. HS 27 v Glos (Bristol) 2000. BB 1-15 (not CC). LO HS 5* (NL).

HEMP, David Lloyd (Olchfa CS; Millfield S; W Glamorgan C; Birmingham U), b Hamilton, Bermuda 8 Nov 1970. UK resident since 1976. 6'0". LHB, RM. Glamorgan 1991-96; cap 1994. Warwickshire 1997-2001; cap 1997. Wales (MC) 1992-94. Tours: SA 1995-96 (Gm); I 1994-95 (Eng A); Z 1994-95 (Gm). 1000 runs (3); most – 1452 (1994). HS 186* Wa v Worcs (Birmingham) 2001. Gm HS 157 Gm v Glos (Abergavenny) 1995. BB 3-23 v SA A (Cardiff) 1996. CC BB 2-29 Wa v Glos (Birmingham) 2000. Awards: CGT 4; BHC 2. LO HS 121 v Comb U (Cardiff) 1995 (BHC). LO BB 4-32 Wa v Minor C (Lakenham) 1998 (BHC).

HUGHES, Jonathan (Coed-y-Land CS, Pontypridd), b Pontypridd 30 Jun 1981. 5'10". RHB, RM. Debut 2001. MCC YC. HS 49 v Surrey (Cardiff) 2001 – on debut.

JAMES, Stephen Peter (Monmouth S; University C, Swansea; Hughes Hall, Cambridge), b Lydney, Glos 7 Sep 1967. 6'0". RHB. Debut 1985; cap 1992; captain 2001 to date; benefit 2001. Cambridge U 1989-90; blue 1989-90. Mashonaland 1993-94 to 1994-95. Tests: 2 (1998); HS 36 v SL (Oval) 1998. Tours: SA 1995-96 (Gm); SL 1997-98; Z 1990-91 (Gm); K 1997-98. 1000 runs (8); most – 1775 (1997). HS 309* v Sussex (Colwyn Bay) 2000. Awards: CGT 3; BHC 2. LO HS 135 v Comb U (Cardiff) 1992 (BHC).

JONES, Simon Philip (Coedcae CS; Millfield S), b Swansea 25 Dec 1978. Son of I.J.Jones (Glamorgan and England 1960-68). 6'3½". LHB, RF. Debut 1998. HS 46 v Yorks (Scarborough) 2001. BB 5-31 v Sussex (Cardiff) 1999. LO HS 12* and BB 1-39 v Notts (Nottingham) 1999 (NL).

MAYNARD, Matthew Peter (David Hughes S, Anglesey), b Oldham, Lancs 21 Mar 1966. 5'10½". RHB, RM. Debut 1985 v Yorks (Swansea), scoring 102 out of 117 in 87 min, reaching 100 with 3 sixes off successive balls; cap 1987; captain 1996-2000; benefit 1996. *Wisden* 1997. N Districts 1990-91 to 1991-92. Otago 1996-97 to 1997-98. YC 1988. Tests: 4 (1988 to 1993-94); HS 35 v WI (Kingston) 1993-94. LOI: 14 (1993-94 to 2000); HS 41 v P (Manchester) 1996. Tours: SA 1989-90 (Eng XI), 1995-96 (Gm – captain); WI 1993-94; Z 1994-95 (Gm). 1000 runs (11); most – 1803 (1991). HS 243 v Hants (Southampton) 1991. BB 3-21 v OU (Oxford) 1987. CC BB 1-3. Awards: CGT 4; BHC 9. LO HS 151* v Durham (Darlington) 1991 (NWT) and 151* v Middx (Lord's) 1996 (BHC). LO BB 1-13 (NL).

NEWELL, Keith (Ifield Community C), b Crawley, Sussex 25 Mar 1972. Brother of M.Newell (Sussex 1996-98). 6'0". RHB, RM. Sussex 1995-98. Matabeleland 1995-96. Glamorgan debut 1999. HS 135 Sx v WI (Hove) 1995. Gm HS 103 v Northants (Northampton) 2001. CC HS 112 and BB 4-61 Sx v Kent (Horsham) 1997. Gm BB 2-15 v Worcs (Worcester) 1999. Award: CGT 1. LO HS 129 v Dorset (Bournemouth) 2000 (NWT). LO BB 5-33 Sx v Worcs (Worcester) 1998 (SL).

PARKIN, Owen Thomas (Bournemouth GS; Bath U), b Coventry, Warwks 24 Sep 1972. 6'2". RHB, RFM. Dorset 1992. Debut 1994. HS 24* v Essex (Chelmsford) 1998. BB 5-24 v Somerset (Cardiff) 1998. LO HS 8 (BHC). LO BB 5-28 v Sussex (Hove) 1996 (SL).

POWELL, Michael John (Crickhowell SS; Pontypool CFE), b Abergavenny 3 Feb 1977. 6'1". RHB, RSM. Debut 1997 scoring 200* v OU (Oxford); cap 2000. 1000 runs (1): 1060 (1999). HS 200* (*see above*). CC HS 164 v Notts (Colwyn Bay) 1999. BB 2-39 v OU (Oxford) 1999. CC BB – . LO HS 86 v Middx (Cardiff) 2000 (NL).

SHAW, Adrian David (Llangatwg CS; Neath Tertiary C), b Neath 17 Feb 1972. 5'11". RHB, WK. Wales (MC) 1990-92. Debut 1994; cap 1999. HS 140 v OU (Oxford) 1999. CC HS 88* v Glos (Cardiff) 2000. LO HS 48 v Glos (Swansea) 1997 (SL).

SMITH, LLOYD Alexander (Millfield S), b Cardiff 8 Nov 1983. RHB, RM. Staff 2002 – awaiting f-c debut.

THOMAS, Ian James (Bedwas CS; Bassaleg CS; UWIC), b Newport, Gwent 9 May 1979. 5'11". LHB, OB. Debut 2000. Wales MC. HS 82 v Essex (Southend) 2000 – on debut. LO HS 53 v Derbys (Cardiff) 2001 (NL).

THOMAS, Stuart Darren (Graig CS, Llanelli; Neath Tertiary C), b Morriston 25 Jan 1975. 6'0". LHB, RFM. Debut v Derbys (Chesterfield) 1992, taking 5-80 when aged 17yr 217d; cap 1997. Tours (Eng A): SA 1995-96 (Gm), 1998-99; NZ 1999-00; Z 1994-95 (Gm), 1998-99. HS 138 v Essex (Chelmsford) 2001. 50 wkts (4); most – 71 (1998). BB 8-50 Eng A v Zim A (Harare) 1998-99 – record Eng A analysis. CC BB 5-24 v Sussex (Swansea) 1997. Award: BHC 1. LO HS 40 v Hants CB (Southampton) 1999 (NWT). LO BB 7-16 v Surrey (Swansea) 1998 (SL).

WALLACE, Mark Alexander (Crickhowell HS), b Abergavenny, Gwent 19 Nov 1981. 5'9". LHB, WK. Debut 1999. HS 80* v Kent (Maidstone) 2001. LO HS 8* (NL).

WATKINS, Ryan Edward (Cross Keys TC), b Abergavenny 9 Jun 1983. LHB, RM. Staff 2002 – awaiting f-c debut.

WHARF, Alexander George (Buttershaw Upper S; Thomas Danby C), b Bradford, Yorks 4 Jun 1975. 6'5". RHB, RMF. Yorkshire 1994-97. Nottinghamshire 1998-99. Glamorgan debut 2000, scoring 100* v OU (Oxford); cap 2000. HS 101* v Northants (Northampton) 2000. BB 5-63 v Yorks (Swansea) 2001. LO HS 38* Nt v Surrey (Nottingham) 1999 (NL). LO BB 4-29 Y v Notts (Leeds) 1996 (BHC).

RELEASED/RETIRED
(Having made a first-class County appearance in 2001)

MAHER, James Patrick (St Augustine's C, Cairns), b Innisfail, Queensland, Australia 27 Feb 1974. LHB, RM. Queensland 1993-94 to date. Glamorgan 2001; cap 2001. **LOI** (A): 2 (1997-98); HS 13 v SA (Perth) 1997-98. 1000 (1+1); most – 1142 (2000-01). HS 217 v Essex (Cardiff) 2001. BB 3-11 Q v WA (Perth) 1995-96. LO HS 142* v Glos (Bristol) 2001 (BHC). LO BB 2-43 Q v WA (Perth) 1995-96.

WATKIN, Steven Llewellyn (Cymer Afan CS; Swansea CFE; S Glamorgan IHE), b Maesteg 15 Sep 1964. 6'3". RHB, RMF. Glamorgan 1986-2001; cap 1989; benefit 1998. *Wisden* 1993. **Tests**: 3 (1991 to 1993); HS 13 and BB 4-65 v A (Oval) 1993. **LOI**: 4 (1993-94); HS 4; BB 4-49 v WI (Kingston) 1993-94. Tours: SA 1995-96 (Gm); WI 1991-92 (Eng A), 1993-94; P 1990-91 (Eng A); Z 1989-90 (Eng A), 1990-91 (Gm), 1994-95 (Gm). HS 51 v Glos (Cardiff) 2000. 50 wkts (9); most – 94 (1989). BB 8-59 v Warwks (Birmingham) 1988. Awards: CGT 1; BHC 2. LO HS 31* v Derbys (Checkley) 1991 (NWT). LO BB 5-23 v Warwks (Birmingham) 1990 (SL).

A.J.Davies left the staff having made no f-c appearances in 2001.

ESSEX – RELEASED/RETIRED (continued from p 24)
(Having made a first-class County appearance in 2001)

PRICHARD, Paul John (Brentwood County HS), b Billericay 7 Jan 1965. 5'10". RHB, RSM. Essex 1984-2001; cap 1986; captain 1995-98; benefit 1996. Tour (Eng A): A 1992-93. 1000 runs (8); most – 1485 (1992). HS 245 v Leics (Chelmsford) 1990. BB 1-28. Awards: CGT 1; BHC 4. LO HS 114 v Somerset (Chelmsford) 1997 (BHC).

SUCH, Peter Mark (Harry Carlton CS, East Leake, Notts), b Helensburgh, Dunbartonshire 12 Jun 1964. 5'11". RHB, OB. Nottinghamshire 1982-86. Leicestershire 1987-89. Essex 1990-2001; cap 1991; benefit 2001. **Tests**: 11 (1993 to 1999); HS 14* and BB 6-67 v A (Manchester) 1993 – on debut. Tours: A 1992-93 (Eng A), 1998-99; SA 1993-94 (Eng A). HS 54 v Worcs (Chelmsford) 1993 and 54 v Notts (Chelmsford) 1996. 50 wkts (6); most – 82 (1996). BB 8-93 (11-160 match) v Hants (Colchester) 1995. LO HS 19* v Notts (Ilford) 1994 (SL). LO BB 5-29 v Glam (Cardiff) 1997 (SL).

GLAMORGAN 2001

RESULTS SUMMARY

	Place	Won	Lost	Tied	Drew	No Result
County Championship (1st Division)	8th	2	5		8	1
All First-Class Matches		2	5		8	1
C & G Trophy	4th Round					
Benson & Hedges Cup	6th in Mid/West/Wales Group					
NU National League (2nd Division)	1st	11	3			2

COUNTY CHAMPIONSHIP AVERAGES

BATTING AND FIELDING

Cap		M	I	NO	HS	Runs	Avge	100	50	Ct/St
2001	J.P.Maher	14	23	2	217	1133	53.95	4	3	13
1992	A.Dale	15	23	3	204	1026	51.30	3	4	9
1992	S.P.James	9	15	3	156	568	47.33	1	4	5
–	K.Newell	7	11	2	103	296	32.88	1	1	5
1992	R.D.B.Croft	9	13	2	93	350	31.81	–	3	6
1987	M.P.Maynard	13	20	–	145	621	31.05	1	3	6
2000	M.J.Powell	15	25	2	108	681	29.60	2	4	12
1997	S.D.Thomas	15	21	2	138	562	29.57	1	4	5
1999	A.D.Shaw	5	6	1	62	143	28.60	–	1	11
	M.A.Wallace	10	16	3	80*	290	22.30	–	2	27/1
2000	A.G.Wharf	5	4	1	31	59	19.66	–	–	1
–	I.J.Thomas	6	11	1	59	194	19.40	–	1	2
1989	S.L.Watkin	15	17	7	38	188	18.80	–	–	5
2000	D.A.Cosker	11	15	4	35	175	15.90	–	–	10
–	A.P.Davies	4	7	1	40	85	14.16	–	–	2
–	S.P.Jones	8	11	1	46	83	8.30	–	–	–

Also batted: A.W.Evans (2 matches) 8, 5, 41 (1 ct); J.Hughes (1) 38, 49; O.T.Parkin (1) 0 (1 ct).

BOWLING

	O	M	R	W	Avge	Best	5wI	10wM
A.G.Wharf	127.4	19	448	14	32.00	5-63	1	–
S.L.Watkin	472.4	113	1400	43	32.55	6-67	1	–
R.D.B.Croft	325.3	86	917	23	39.86	5-95	2	1
D.A.Cosker	423.5	84	1390	33	42.12	4-48	–	–
S.D.Thomas	420.1	56	1668	33	50.54	4-54	–	–
S.P.Jones	198.2	29	887	17	52.17	3-36	–	–

Also bowled:

A.P.Davies	86	16	341	9	37.88	3-76	–	–
A.Dale	117	25	410	7	58.57	3-34	–	–

A.W.Evans 1-0-2-0; J.P.Maher 21-3-88-0; M.P.Maynard 1-1-0-0; K.Newell 13-0-48-0; O.T.Parkin 44-4-176-4; I.J.Thomas 3-1-2-0.

Glamorgan played no first-class fixtures outside the County Championship in 2001. The First-Class Averages (pp 113-126) give the records of Glamorgan players in all first-class county matches, with the exception of R.D.B.Croft whose full county figures are as above.

GLAMORGAN RECORDS

FIRST-CLASS CRICKET

Highest Total	For 718-3d		v	Sussex	Colwyn Bay	2000
	V 712		by	Northants	Northampton	1998
Lowest Total	For 22		v	Lancashire	Liverpool	1924
	V 33		by	Leics	Ebbw Vale	1965
Highest Innings	For 309*	S.P.James	v	Sussex	Colwyn Bay	2000
	V 322*	M.B.Loye	for	Northants	Northampton	1998

Highest Partnership for each Wicket

1st	374	M.T.G.Elliott/S.P.James	v	Sussex	Colwyn Bay	2000
2nd	249	S.P.James/H.Morris	v	Oxford U	Oxford	1987
3rd	313	D.E.Davies/W.E.Jones	v	Essex	Brentwood	1948
4th	425*	A.Dale/I.V.A.Richards	v	Middlesex	Cardiff	1993
5th	264	M.Robinson/S.W.Montgomery	v	Hampshire	Bournemouth	1949
6th	230	W.E.Jones/B.L.Muncer	v	Worcs	Worcester	1953
7th	211	P.A.Cottey/O.D.Gibson	v	Leics	Swansea	1996
8th	202	D.Davies/J.J.Hills	v	Sussex	Eastbourne	1928
9th	203*	J.J.Hills/J.C.Clay	v	Worcs	Swansea	1929
10th	143	T.Davies/S.A.B.Daniels	v	Glos	Swansea	1982

Best Bowling	For	10- 51	J.Mercer	v	Worcs	Worcester	1936
(Innings)	V	10- 18	G.Geary	for	Leics	Pontypridd	1929
Best Bowling	For	17-212	J.C.Clay	v	Worcs	Swansea	1937
(Match)	V	16- 96	G.Geary	for	Leics	Pontypridd	1929

Most Runs – Season	2276	H.Morris	(av 55.51)	1990
Most Runs – Career	34056	A.Jones	(av 33.03)	1957-83
Most 100s – Season	10	H.Morris		1990
Most 100s – Career	52	A.Jones		1957-83
	52	H.Morris		1981-97
Most Wkts – Season	176	J.C.Clay	(av 17.34)	1937
Most Wkts – Career	2174	D.J.Shepherd	(av 20.95)	1950-72
Most Career W-K Dismissals	933	E.W.Jones	(840 ct: 93 st)	1961-83
Most Career Catches in the Field	656	P.M.Walker		1956-72

LIMITED-OVERS CRICKET

Highest Total	NWT	373-7		v	Beds	Cardiff	1998
	BHC	318-3		v	Combined U	Cardiff	1995
	NL	305-6		v	Worcs	Cardiff	2001
Lowest Total	NWT	76		v	Northants	Northampton	1968
	BHC	68		v	Lancashire	Manchester	1973
	NL	42		v	Derbyshire	Swansea	1979
Highest Innings	NWT	162*	I.V.A.Richards	v	Oxfordshire	Swansea	1993
	BHC	151*	M.P.Maynard	v	Middlesex	Lord's	1996
	NL	155*	J.H.Kallis	v	Surrey	Pontypridd	1999
Best Bowling	NWT	5-13	R.J.Shastri	v	Scotland	Edinburgh	1988
	BHC	6-20	S.D.Thomas	v	Combined U	Cardiff	1995
	NL	7-16	S.D.Thomas	v	Surrey	Swansea	1998

GLOUCESTERSHIRE

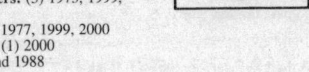

Formation of Present Club: 1871
Colours: Blue, Gold, Brown, Silver, Green and Red
Badge: Coat of Arms of the City and County of Bristol
County Champions (since 1890): (0); best – 2nd 1930, 1931, 1947, 1959, 1969, 1986
Gillette/NatWest/C & G Trophy Winners: (3) 1973, 1999, 2000
Benson and Hedges Cup Winners: (3) 1977, 1999, 2000
NU National League (Div 1) Winners: (1) 2000
Sunday League Winners: (0); best – 2nd 1988
Match Awards: CGT 53; BHC 68

Chief Executive: T.Richardson, County Ground, Nevil Road, Bristol BS7 9EJ ▲ Tel: 0117 910 8000 ▲ Fax: 0117 924 1193 ▲ Email: info@glosccc.co.uk ▲ Web: www.glosccc.co.uk

Captain: M.W.Alleyne. **Vice-Captain:** T.H.C.Hancock. **Overseas Player:** I.J.Harvey.
2002 Beneficiary: M.C.J.Ball. **Scorer:** K.T.Gerrish. ‡ New registration

ALLEYNE, Mark Wayne (Harrison C, Barbados; Cardinal Pole S, London E9; Haringey Cricket C), b Tottenham, London 23 May 1968. 5'10". RHB, RM. Debut 1986; cap 1990; captain 1997 to date; benefit 1999. *Wisden* 2000. **LOI:** 10 (1998-99 to 2000-01); HS 53 v SA (E London) 1999-00; BB 3-27 v SL (Sydney) 1998-99. Tours (Eng A) (C=captain): WI 2000-01C; NZ 1999-00C; SL 1986-87 (Gs), 1992-93 (Gs); B 1999-00C. 1000 runs (6); most – 1189 (1998). HS 256 v Northants (Northampton) 1990. 50 wkts (1): 54 (1996). BB 6-49 v Middx (Lord's) 2000. Awards: CGT 3; BHC 3. LO HS 134* v Leics (Bristol) 1992 (SL). LO BB 5-27 v Comb U (Bristol) 1988 (BHC).

AVERIS, James Maxwell Michael (Cathedral S, Bristol; Portsmouth U; St Cross C, Oxford), b Bristol 28 May 1974. 5'11". RHB, RMF. Oxford U 1997; blue 1997; rugby blue 1996-97. Gloucestershire debut 1997; cap 2001. HS 42 OU v Durham (Oxford) 1997 – on debut. Gs HS 25* v Glam (Cardiff) 2000. BB 5-52 v Middx (Lord's) 2001. Award: BHC 1. LO HS 23* v Lancs (Manchester) 2000 (NL). LO BB 5-20 v Northants (Northampton) 2000 (NL).

BALL, Martyn Charles John (King Edmund SS; Bath CFE), b Bristol 26 Apr 1970. 5'8". RHB, OB. Debut 1988; cap 1996; benefit 2002. Tours: 1 2001-02; SL 1992-93 (Gs). HS 71 v Notts (Bristol) 1993. BB 8-46 (14-169 match) v Somerset (Taunton) 1993. Award: CGT 1. LO HS 51 v SL A (Cheltenham) 1999. LO BB 5-42 v Yorks (Cheltenham) 1999 (NL).

BARNETT, Kim John (Leek HS), b Stoke-on-Trent, Staffs 17 Jul 1960. 6'1". RHB, RM/LB. Derbyshire 1979-98; cap 1982; captain 1983-95; benefit 1992. Boland 1982-83 to 1987-88. Staffordshire 1976. Gloucestershire debut/cap 1999. *Wisden* 1988. **Tests:** 4 (1988 to 1989); HS 80 v A (Leeds) 1989. **LOI:** 1 (1988); HS 84 v SL (Oval) 1988. Tours: SA 1989-90 (Eng XI); NZ 1979-80 (DHR); SL 1985-86 (Eng B). 1000 runs (16); most – 1734 (1984). HS 239* De v Leics (Leicester) 1988. Gs HS 125 v Kent (Canterbury) 1999. BB 6-28 De v Glam (Chesterfield) 1991. Gs BB 2-52 v Worcs (Cheltenham) 1999. Awards: CGT 6; BHC 12. LO HS 136 English XI v SA (Jo'burg) 1989-90. LO BB 6-24 De v Cumb (Kendal) 1984 (NWT).

BRESSINGTON, Alastair Nigel (Marling GS, Stroud; UWIC), b Downend, Bristol 28 Nov 1979. 6'1". LHB, RMF. Debut 2000. HS 17* v Hants (Cheltenham) 2001. BB 4-36 v Glam (Bristol) 2000 – on debut. LO HS 54 Glos CB v Yorks CB (Cheltenham) 1999 (NWT). LO BB 3-21 Glos CB v Notts CB (Cheltenham) 2000 (NWT).

‡**FISHER, Ian** Douglas (Beckfoot GS, Bingley; Thomas Danby C, Leeds), b Bradford, Yorks 31 Mar 1976. 5'10½". LHB, SLA. Yorkshire 1995-96 (Y in Zim) to 2001. Tour: Z 1995-96 (Y). HS 68* Y v Somerset (Taunton) 2000. BB 5-35 Y v Mashonaland Inv XI (Harare) 1995-96 – on debut. CC BB 5-73 Y v Essex (Chelmsford) 1999. LO HS 20 and LO BB 3-20 Y v Somerset (Scarborough) 2000 (NL).

GANNON, Benjamin Ward (Dragon S, Oxford; Abingdon S; Cheltenham & Gloucester CHE), b Oxford 5 Sep 1975. 6'3". RHB, RMF. Debut 1999. Herefordshire 1996. HS 28 v Essex (Colchester) 2000. BB 6-80 v Glam (Cardiff) 1999 – on debut. LO HS 2. LO BB 2-29 v SL A (Cheltenham) 1999.

GIDMAN, Alex Peter Richard (Wycliffe C), b High Wycombe, Bucks 22 Jun 1981. 6'3". RHB, RM. Awaiting f-c debut. LO HS 23 and LO BB 1-43 Glos CB v Yorks CB (Bristol) 2001 (CGT).

HANCOCK, Timothy Harold Coulter (St Edward's S, Oxford; Henley C), b Reading, Berks 20 Apr 1972. 5'10". RHB, RM. Debut 1991; cap 1998. Oxfordshire 1990. Tour: SL 1992-93 (Gs). 1000 runs (1): 1227 (1998). HS 220* v Notts (Nottingham) 1998. BB 3-5 v Essex (Colchester) 1998. Awards: CGT 3. LO HS 110 v Northants (Bristol) 2000 (NWT). LO BB 6-58 v Scot (Bristol) 1997 (NWT).

HARDINGES, Mark Andrew (Malvern C; Bath U), b Gloucester 5 Feb 1978. 6'1". RHB, RMF. Debut 1999. British U 2000. HS 22 v Notts (Nottingham) 2001. BB 2-16 v Essex (Bristol) 2000. LO HS 65 v Notts (Nottingham) 2001 (NL). LO BB 2-50 v SL A (Cheltenham) 1999.

HARVEY, Ian Joseph (Wonthaggi TC), b Wonthaggi, Victoria, Australia 10 Apr 1972. 5'10". RHB, RMF. Victoria 1993-94 to date. Gloucestershire debut/cap 1999. **LOI** (A): 38 (1997-98 to 2001-02); HS 47* v WI (Sydney) 2000-01; BB 4-28 v Z (Melbourne) 2000-01. Tour: NZ 1994-95 (Aus Academy). HS 136 Vic v S Aus (Melbourne) 1995-96. Gs HS 150* v Middx (Lord's) 2001. BB 7-44 Vic v S Aus (Melbourne) 1996-97. Gs BB 6-19 (10-32 match) v Sussex (Hove) 2000. Hat-trick (Victoria) 2001-02. Awards: CGT 1; BHC 2. LO HS 92 v Worcs (Bristol) 2001 (BHC). LO BB 5-19 v Northants (Bristol) 2000 (NL).

LEWIS, Jonathan (Churchfields S, Swindon; Swindon C), b Aylesbury, Bucks 26 Aug 1975. 6'2". RHB, RMF. Debut 1995; cap 1998. Wiltshire 1993. Northamptonshire staff 1994. Tour: WI 2000-01 (Eng A). HS 62 v Worcs (Cheltenham) 1999. 50 wkts (3): most – 72 (2000). BB 8-95 v Z (Gloucester) 2000. CC BB 7-56 (10-92 match) v Notts (Bristol) 1999. Hat-trick 2000. Awards: BHC 2. LO HS 33* v Somerset (Bristol) 1998 (BHC). LO BB 4-23 v Durham (Bristol) 2001 (BHC).

‡**PEARSON, James** Alexander, b Bristol 11 Sep 1983. LHB. Staff 2002 – awaiting f-c debut. LO HS 7 and BB 1-29 Glos CB v Herefords (Brockhampton) 2001.

POPE, Stephen Patrick (Cheltenham Bournside CS), b Cheltenham 25 Jan 1983. 5'8". RHB, WK. Awaiting f-c debut. LO HS (Glos CB) 15 v Herefords (Brockhampton) 2001 (CGT).

RUSSELL, Robert Charles ('*Jack*') (Archway CS; Bristol Poly – "*briefly*"), b Stroud 15 Aug 1963. 5'8½". LHB, WK, occ OB. Debut 1981 – youngest Glos wicket-keeper (17yr 307d), setting record for most match dismissals on f-c debut – 8 v SL (Bristol); cap 1985; benefit 1994; captain 1995. *Wisden* 1989. MBE 1996. **Tests:** 54 (1988 to 1997-98); HS 128* v A (Manchester) 1989; 11 ct v SA (Jo'burg) 1995-96 (Test record); 27 dis 1995-96 series v SA (Eng record). **LOI:** 40 (1987-88 to 1998-99); HS 50 v I (Nottingham) 1990. Tours: A 1990-91, 1992-93 (Eng A); SA 1995-96; WI 1989-90, 1993-94, 1997-98; NZ 1991-92, 1996-97; P 1987-88; SL 1986-87 (Gs). 1000 runs (1): 1049 (1997). HS 129* Eng XI v Boland (Paarl) 1995-96. Gs HS 124 v Notts (Nottingham) 1996. BB 1-4. Awards: CGT 1; BHC 3. LO HS 119* v Brit U (Bristol) 1998 (BHC).

SILLENCE, Roger John (Highbury SS; Salisbury Art C), b Salisbury, Wilts 29 Jun 1977. 6'3". RHB, RMF. Debut 2001 taking 5-97 v Sussex (Hove). Wiltshire 1996-2001. HS 6 and BB 5-97 (*see above*). LO HS (Wilts) 82 v Northants CB (Northampton) 1999 (NWT). LO BB (Wilts) 3-47 v Middx CB (Southgate) 2000 (NWT).

SMITH, Andrew Michael (Queen Elizabeth GS, Wakefield; Exeter U; West of England U), b Dewsbury, Yorks 1 Oct 1967. 5'9". RHB, LMF. Debut 1991; cap 1995; benefit 2001. **Tests**: 1 (1997); HS 4* v A (Leeds) 1997. Tour: P 1995-96 (Eng A – *part*). HS 61 v Yorks (Gloucester) 1998. 50 wkts (5); most – 83 (1997). BB 8-73 (10-118 match) v Middx (Lord's) 1996. Award: BHC 1. LO HS 26* v Kent (Moreton-in-M) 1996 (SL). LO BB 6-39 v Hants (Southampton) 1995 (BHC).

SNAPE, Jeremy Nicholas (Denstone C; Durham U), b Stoke-on-Trent, Staffs 27 Apr 1973. 5'8½". RHB, OB. Northamptonshire 1992-97. Combined U 1994. Gloucestershire debut/cap 1999. **LOI**: 8 (2001-02); HS 38 v I (Madras) 2001-02; BB 3-43 v Z (Bulawayo) 2001-02. Tour: Z 1994-95 (Nh). HS 131 v Sussex (Cheltenham) 2001. BB 5-65 Nh v Durham (Northampton) 1995. Gs BB 3-27 v Durham (Chester-le-St) 2001. Awards: BHC 3. LO HS 104* v Notts (Nottingham) 2001 (NL). LO BB 5-32 Nh v Leics (Northampton) 1997 (BHC).

‡**SPEARMAN, Craig** Murray, b Auckland, NZ 4 Jul 1972. RHB. Auckland 1993-94 to 1995-96. Central Districts 1996-97 to date. **Tests**: 19 (1995-96 to 2000-01); HS 112 v Z (Auckland) 1995-96. **LOI**: 51 (1995-96 to 2000-01); HS 86 v Z (Harare) 2000-01. Tours (NZ): SA 2000-01; WI 1995-96; I 1999-00; P 1996-97; SL 1997-98; Z 1997-98, 2000-01. HS 147 Auckland v ND (Hamilton) 1994-95. BB 1-37. LO HS 126 CD v Canterbury (Nelson) 1997-98 (SC)

TAYLOR, Christopher Glyn (Colston's Collegiate S), b Southmead, Bristol 27 Sep 1976. 5'7". RHB, OB. Debut 2000, scoring 104 v Middx – first to score a hundred at Lord's in a Championship match on his first-class debut. Cap 2001. HS 196 v Notts (Nottingham) 2001. BB 3-126 v Northants (Cheltenham) 2000. LO HS 63* v Northants (Cheltenham) 2001 (NL).

WILLIAMS, Richard Charles James (**'Reggie'**) (Millfield S), b Southmead, Bristol 8 Aug 1969. 5'9". LHB, WK. Debut 1990; cap 1996. Tour: SL 1992-93 (Gs). HS 90 v OU (Bristol) 1995. CC HS 55* v Derbys (Gloucester) 1991. LO HS 38 v Pak A (Cheltenham) 1997.

WINDOWS, Matthew Guy Newman (Clifton C; Durham U), b Bristol 5 Apr 1973. Son of A.R.Windows (Glos and CU 1960-68). 5'7". RHB, LM. Debut 1992; cap 1998. Combined U 1995. Tours (Eng A): SA 1998-99; Z 1998-99. 1000 runs (2); most – 1173 (1998). HS 184 v Warwks (Cheltenham) 1996. BB (Comb U) 1-6. Gs BB – . Awards: CGT 1; BHC 2. LO HS 117 v Northants (Cheltenham) 2001 (NL).

RELEASED/RETIRED
(Having made a first-class County appearance in 2001)

CAWDRON, M.J. – *see NORTHAMPTONSHIRE*.

CUNLIFFE, R.J. – *see LEICESTERSHIRE*.

HEWSON, D.R. – *see DERBYSHIRE*.

T.P.Cotterell, D.J.Forder and M.D.Sutliff have left the staff having made no f-c appearances in 2001.

GLOUCESTERSHIRE 2001

RESULTS SUMMARY

	Place	Won	Lost	Tied	Drew	No Result
County Championship (2nd Division)	**4th**	5	5		6	
All First-Class Matches		5	5		6	
C & G Trophy	4th Round					
Benson & Hedges Cup	Finalist					
NU National League (1st Division)	**7th**	6	9			1

COUNTY CHAMPIONSHIP AVERAGES

BATTING AND FIELDING

Cap		M	I	NO	HS	Runs	Avge	100	50	Ct/St
1999	J.N.Snape	14	21	3	131	868	48.22	3	5	10
2001	C.G.Taylor	12	20	–	196	930	46.50	3	4	6
1999	K.J.Barnett	14	25	2	114	1029	44.73	1	7	10
1998	J.Lewis	5	8	7	15*	44	44.00	–	–	–
1999	I.J.Harvey	10	15	2	130*	531	40.84	2	1	8
1985	R.C.Russell	10	12	2	91*	373	37.30	–	2	42/2
–	D.R.Hewson	14	25	2	168	816	35.47	2	4	6
1998	M.G.N.Windows	16	27	3	174	840	35.00	3	3	6
1990	M.W.Alleyne	16	26	3	136	718	31.21	2	2	12/1
1996	M.C.J.Ball	12	16	3	68	379	29.15	–	3	21
1998	T.H.C.Hancock	6	11	–	55	230	20.90	–	1	7
–	R.J.Cunliffe	5	8	1	48	141	20.14	–	–	5
1996	R.C.J.Williams	5	9	–	33	123	13.66	–	–	15/1
–	A.N.Bressington	5	5	2	17*	40	13.33	–	–	2
–	M.J.Cawdron	6	9	2	29	82	11.71	–	–	1
–	B.W.Gannon	5	6	4	10*	12	6.00	–	–	–
2001	J.M.M.Averis	15	19	3	7*	35	2.18	–	–	3

Also batted: M.A.Hardinges (4 matches) 22, 20, 14 (2 ct); R.J.Sillence (1) 0, 6; A.M.Smith (1 – cap 1995) 4 (1 ct).

BOWLING

	O	M	R	W	Avge	Best	5wI	10wM
I.J.Harvey	288.4	92	773	41	18.85	5-33	2	–
J.Lewis	175.4	56	454	21	21.61	5-71	1	–
M.C.J.Ball	349.3	94	879	34	25.85	6-23	2	–
M.W.Alleyne	372.4	86	1076	41	26.24	5-50	1	–
A.N.Bressington	120.4	31	397	11	36.09	3-42	–	–
J.M.M.Averis	463.2	100	1621	43	37.69	5-52	1	–
M.J.Cawdron	168	50	498	12	41.50	4-79	–	–

Also bowled:

R.J.Sillence	29.5	5	100	5	20.00	5-97	1	–
B.W.Gannon	97	12	380	8	47.50	3-47	–	–
M.A.Hardinges	79	15	295	6	49.16	2-36	–	–
J.N.Snape	153	34	406	8	50.75	3-27	–	–

K.J.Barnett 16-4-35-0; T.H.C.Hancock 28-5-100-1; D.R.Hewson 3-1-7-0; A.M.Smith 33-11-70-2.

Gloucestershire played no first-class fixtures outside the County Championship in 2001. The First-Class Averages (pp 113-126) give the records of Gloucestershire players in all first-class county matches.

GLOUCESTERSHIRE RECORDS

FIRST-CLASS CRICKET

Highest Total	For 653-6d		v	Glamorgan	Bristol	1928
	V 774-7d		by	Australians	Bristol	1948
Lowest Total	For 17		v	Australians	Cheltenham	1896
	V 12		by	Northants	Gloucester	1907
Highest Innings	For 318 *	W.G.Grace	v	Yorkshire	Cheltenham	1876
	V 296	A.O.Jones	for	Notts	Nottingham	1903

Highest Partnership for each Wicket

1st	395	D.M.Young/R.B.Nicholls	v	Oxford U	Oxford	1962
2nd	256	C.T.M.Pugh/T.W.Graveney	v	Derbyshire	Chesterfield	1960
3rd	336	W.R.Hammond/B.H.Lyon	v	Leics	Leicester	1933
4th	321	W.R.Hammond/W.L.Neale	v	Leics	Gloucester	1937
5th	261	W.G.Grace/W.O.Moberley	v	Yorkshire	Cheltenham	1876
6th	320	G.L.Jessop/J.H.Board	v	Sussex	Hove	1903
7th	248	W.G.Grace/E.L.Thomas	v	Sussex	Hove	1896
8th	239	W.R.Hammond/A.E.Wilson	v	Lancashire	Bristol	1938
9th	193	W.G.Grace/S.A.P.Kitcat	v	Sussex	Bristol	1896
10th	131	W.R.Gouldsworthy/J.G.Bessant	v	Somerset	Bristol	1923

Best Bowling	For	10-40	E.G.Dennett	v	Essex	Bristol	1906
(Innings)	V	10-66	A.A.Mailey	for	Australians	Cheltenham	1921
		10-66	K.Smales	for	Notts	Stroud	1956
Best Bowling	For	17-56	C.W.L.Parker	v	Essex	Gloucester	1925
(Match)	V	15-87	A.J.Conway	for	Worcs	Moreton-in-M	1914

Most Runs – Season	2860	W.R.Hammond	(av 69.75)	1933
Most Runs – Career	33664	W.R.Hammond	(av 57.05)	1920-51
Most 100s – Season	13	W.R.Hammond		1938
Most 100s – Career	113	W.R.Hammond		1920-51
Most Wkts – Season	222	T.W.J.Goddard	(av 16.80)	1937
	222	T.W.J.Goddard	(av 16.37)	1947
Most Wkts – Career	3170	C.W.L.Parker	(av 19.43)	1903-35
Most Career W-K Dismissals	1016†	J.H.Board	(698 ct; 318 st)	1891-1914
Most Career Catches in the Field	718	C.A.Milton		1948-74

† R.C.Russell (1981-2001) has the second-highest aggregate with 975 dismissals (877 ct; 98 st)

LIMITED-OVERS CRICKET

Highest Total	NWT	351-2		v	Scotland	Bristol	1997
	BHC	308-3		v	Ireland	Dublin	1996
	NL	344-6		v	Northants	Cheltenham	2001
Lowest Total	NWT	82		v	Notts	Bristol	1987
	BHC	62		v	Hampshire	Bristol	1975
	NL	49		v	Middlesex	Bristol	1978
Highest Innings	NWT	177	A.J.Wright	v	Scotland	Bristol	1997
	BHC	154*	M.J.Procter	v	Somerset	Taunton	1972
	NL	146*	S.Young	v	Yorkshire	Leeds	1997
Best Bowling	NWT	6-21	C.A.Walsh	v	Kent	Bristol	1990
		6-21	C.A.Walsh	v	Cheshire	Bristol	1992
	BHC	6-13	M.J.Procter	v	Hampshire	Southampton	1977
	NL	6-52	J.N.Shepherd	v	Kent	Bristol	1983

HAMPSHIRE

Formation of Present Club: 12 August 1863
Colours: Blue, Gold and White
Badge: Tudor Rose and Crown
County Champions: (2) 1961, 1973
Gillette/NatWest/C & G Trophy Winners: (1) 1991
Benson and Hedges Cup Winners: (2) 1988, 1992
NU National League (Div 1) Winners: (0); best – 8th 1999
Sunday League Winners: (3) 1975, 1978, 1986
Match Awards: CGT 61; BHC 65

Chief Executive: G.M.Walker, The Hampshire Rose Bowl, Botley Road, West End, Southampton SO30 3XH ▲ Tel: 023 8047 2002 ▲ Fax: 023 8047 2122 ▲ Email: enquiries.hants@ecb.co.uk ▲ Web: www.hampshire.cricket.org

Captain: R.A.Smith. **Vice-Captain:** W.S.Kendall. **Overseas Player:** N.C.Johnson.
2002 Beneficiary: S.D.Udal. **Scorer:** V.H Isaacs. ‡ New registration

ADAMS, James Henry Kenneth (Sherborne S; University C, London), b Winchester 23 Sep 1980. 6'2". LHB, LM. Dorset 1998. Summer Contract – awaiting f-c debut.

AYMES, Adrian Nigel (Bellemoor SM, Southampton), b Southampton 4 Jun 1964. 6'0". RHB, WK. Debut 1987; cap 1991; benefit 2000. HS 133 v Leics (Leicester) 1998. BB 2-101 v Notts (Nottingham) 2001. Awards: CGT 1; BHC 1. LO HS 73* v Middx (Lord's) 1998 (NWT).

‡BENHAM, Christopher Charles (Yately S), b Frimley, Surrey 24 Mar 1983. RHB, OB. Summer Contract – awaiting f-c debut. LO HS (Hants CB) 0 (CGT).

BRUNNSCHWEILER, Iain (King Edward VI S, Southampton), b Southampton 10 Dec 1979. 6'0". RHB, WK. Debut 2000 – awaiting CC debut. HS 19 v NZ A (Portsmouth) 2000 – on debut.

FRANCIS, John Daniel (King Edward VI S, Southampton; Durham U; Loughborough U), b Bromley, Kent 13 Nov 1980. Younger brother of S.R.G.Francis (*see SOMERSET*). 5'11". LHB, SLA. Debut 2001. Summer Contract. HS 72* and BB 1-34 v Notts (Nottingham) 2001. LO HS 78* v Worcs (Worcester) 2001 (NL).

HAMBLIN, James Rupert Christopher (Charterhouse S; W of England U), b Pembury, Kent 16 Aug 1978. Son of C.B.Hamblin (Oxford U 1971-73). 6'0". RHB, RMF. Debut 2001. HS 5 and BB 1-88 v Warwks (Birmingham) 2001 – on debut. LO HS 61 v Sussex (Hove) 2001 (NL). LO BB 4-29 v Middx (Southgate) 2001 (NL).

JOHNSON, Neil Clarkson (Howick HS, Natal; Port Elizabeth U), b Salisbury, Rhodesia 24 Jan 1970. 6'2". LHB, RFM. EP B 1989-90 to 1991-92. Natal 1992-93 to 1997-98. Leicestershire 1997; cap 1997. Matabeleland 1999-00. WP 2000-01 to date. Hampshire debut/cap 2001. **Tests** (Z): 13 (1998-99 to 2000); HS 107 v P (Peshawar) 1998-99; BB 4-77 v WI (Kingston) 1999-00. **LOI** 48 (1998-99 to 2000); HS 132* v A (Lord's) 1999; BB 4-42 v K (Taunton) 1999. **Tours** (Z): E 2000; SA 1999-00; WI 1999-00; P 1998-99; Z 1994-95 (SA A). 1000 (1): 1073 (2001). HS 150 Leics v Lancs (Leicester) 1997. H HS 105* v Notts (Nottingham) 2001. BB 5-79 Natal v Boland (Stellenbosch) 1993-94. H BB 4-20 v Derbys (Southampton) 2001. LO HS 146* Natal v GW (Kimberley) 1996-97 (SBC). LO BB 4-19 Natal v K (Durban) 1996-97 (SBC).

KENDALL, William Salwey (Bradfield C; Keble C, Oxford), b Wimbledon, Surrey 18 Dec 1973. 5'10". RHB, RM. Oxford U 1994-96; blues 1995-96. Hampshire debut 1996; cap 1996. 1000 runs (3); most – 1186 (1999). HS 201 v Sussex (Southampton) 1999. BB 3-37 OU v Derbys (Oxford) 1995. H BB 2-46 v Notts (Southampton) 1996. LO HS 85* v Glam (Southampton) 2000 (NL).

KENWAY, Derek Anthony (St George's S, Southampton; Barton Peveril C, Eastleigh), b Fareham 12 Jun 1978. 5'11". RHB, RM, occ WK. Debut 1997; cap 2001. 1000 runs (1): 1055 (1999). HS 166 v Notts (Southampton) 2001. BB 1-5. LO HS 93* v Derbys (Derby) 2001 (NL).

LANEY, Jason Scott (Pewsey Vale CS; St John's SFC, Marlborough; Leeds Metropolitan U), b Winchester 27 Apr 1973. 5'10". RHB, OB. Debut 1995; cap 1996. Matabeleland 1995-96. 1000 runs (1): 1163 (1996). HS 112 v OU (Oxford) 1996. CC HS 105 v Kent (Canterbury) 1996. BB 1-24. Award: CGT 1. LO HS 153 v Norfolk (Southampton) 1996 (NWT).

MASCARENHAS, Adrian Dimitri (Trinity C, Perth, Australia), b Hammersmith, London 30 Oct 1977. Resident in Australia 1979-96. RHB, RMF. Debut 1996, taking 6-88 v Glamorgan (Southampton); took 16 wickets in first two CC matches; cap 1998. Dorset 1996. HS 104 v Worcs (Southampton) 2001. BB 6-26 v Middx (Southampton) 2001. Awards: CGT 3. LO HS 79 v Worcs (Southampton) 1999 (NL). LO BB 4-25 v Middx (Lord's) 2000 (NWT).

MORRIS, Alexander Corfield (Holgate S; Barnsley C), b Barnsley, Yorks 4 Oct 1976. Elder brother of Z.C.Morris (Hampshire 1998-99). 6'3". LHB, RMF. Yorkshire 1995-97. Yorks 2nd XI debut when 16yr 332d. Hampshire debut 1998; cap 2001. Tour: Z 1995-96 (Y). HS 65 v Sussex (Southampton) 2001. 50 wkts (2): most – 51 (2001). BB 5-39 v Durham (Chester-le-St) 2001. LO HS 48* Y v Durham (Chester-le-St) 1996 (SL). LO BB 5-32 Y v Young A (Leeds) 1995.

MULLALLY, Alan David (Cannington HS, Perth, Australia; Wembley & Carlisle TC), b Southend-on-Sea, Essex 12 Jul 1969. 6'5". RHB, LFM. W Australia 1987-88 to 1989-90. Victoria 1990-91. Hampshire 1988 (1 match), 2000 to date; cap 2000. Leicestershire 1990-99; cap 1993. **Tests:** 19 (1996 to 2001); HS 24 v P (Oval) 1996; BB 5-105 v A (Brisbane) 1998-99. **LOI:** 50 (1996 to 2001); HS 20 v Z (Harare) 1996-97; BB 4-18 v A (Brisbane) 1998-99. Tours: A 1998-99; SA 1999-00; NZ 1996-97; Z 1996-97. HS 75 Le v Middx (Leicester) 1996. H HS 36 v Derbys (Derby) 2001. 50 wkts (5); most – 70 (1996). BB 9-93 (14-188 match) v Derbys (Derby) 2000. Award: CGT 1. LO HS 38 Le v Kent (Leicester) 1994 (SL). LO BB 6-38 Le v NZ (Leicester) 1990.

‡**POTHAS, Nic** (King Edward VII S), b Johannesburg 18 Nov 1973. ECB qualified – EU (Greek) passport. RHB, WK. Transvaal 1993-94 to 2000-01. **LOI** (SA): 3 (2000-01); HS 24 v P (Singapore) 2000 – on debut. Tours (SA): E 1996 (SA A); WI 2000-01 (SA A); SL 1998-99. HS 165 Gauteng v KZ-Natal (Johannesburg) 1998-99. LO HS 101 Transvaal v EP (Jo'burg) 1995-96.

PRITTIPAUL, Lawrence Roland (St John's C, Southsea; Portsmouth C), b Portsmouth 19 Oct 1979. Cousin of S.Chanderpaul (Guyana and West Indies 1991-92 to date). 6'1". RHB, RM. Debut 2000. HS 152 v Derbys (Southampton) 2000. LO HS 61 v Notts (Southampton) 2000 (NL). LO BB 2-53 Hants CB v Suffolk (Bury St Edmunds) 1999 (NWT).

SCHOFIELD, James Edward Knowle (Worcester RGS; Bradford U), b Blackpool, Lancs 1 Nov 1978. RHB, RFM. Debut 2001 taking wicket of M.L.Hayden (Australians) with his first ball. HS 21* v Durham (Chester-le-St) 2001. BB 4-51 v Worcs (Worcester) 2001. LO HS – and BB 1-22 (NL).

SHAH, Irfan Hussain (Loxford HS, Ilford; Haringey Cricket C; City of Westminster C), b Barking, Essex 20 Jun 1979. RHB, OB. MCC YC. Joined staff 2001 – awaiting f-c debut.

SMITH, Robin Arnold (Northlands BHS), b Durban, SA 13 Sep 1963. Younger brother of C.L.Smith (Natal, Glam, Hants and England 1977-78 to 1992) and grandson of Dr V.L.Shearer (Natal). 5'11". RHB, LB. Natal 1980-81 to 1984-85. Hampshire debut 1982; cap 1985; benefit 1996; captain 1998 to date. *Wisden* 1989. **Tests:** 62 (1988 to 1995-96); HS 175 v WI (St John's) 1993-94. **LOI:** 71 (1988 to 1995-96); HS 167* v A (Birmingham) 1993 – Eng record. Tours: A 1990-91; SA 1995-96; WI 1989-90, 1993-94; NZ 1991-92; I/SL 1992-93. 1000 runs (11); most – 1577 (1989). HS 209* v Essex (Southend) 1987. BB 2-11 v Surrey (Southampton) 1985. Awards: CGT 9; BHC 5. LO HS 167* (*see LOI*). LO BB 2-13 v Berks (Southampton) 1985 (NWT).

‡**TOMLINSON, James** Andrew, b Winchester 12 Jun 1982. LHB, LM. Wiltshire 2001. Summer Contract – awaiting f-c debut. LO HS (Hants CB) 4 (NWT). LO BB (Wilts) 1-29 (CGT).

TREMLETT, Christopher Timothy (Thornden S, Chandler's Ford; Taunton's C, Southampton), b Southampton 2 Sep 1981. Son of T.M.Tremlett (Hampshire 1976-91); grandson of M.F.Tremlett (Somerset, CD and England 1947-60). 6'7". RHB, RMF. Debut 2000 – awaiting CC debut. HS 26 v Notts (Southampton) 2001. BB 4-16 v NZ A (Portsmouth) 2000 – on debut. CC BB 4-34 v Durham (Southampton) 2001. LO HS 30* v Glam (Southampton) 2000 (NL). LO BB 3-15 v Derbys (Southampton) 2001 (NL).

UDAL, Shaun David (Cove CS), b Cove, Farnborough 18 Mar 1969. Grandson of G.F.U.Udal (Middx 1932 and Leics 1946); great-great-grandson of J.S.Udal (MCC 1871-75). 6'2". RHB, OB. Debut 1989; cap 1992; benefit 2002. **LOI:** 10 (1994 to 1995); HS 11* v Z (Brisbane) 1994-95; BB 2-37 v A (Sydney) 1994-95. Tours: A 1994-95; P 1995-96 (Eng A). HS 117* v Warwks (Southampton) 1997. 50 wkts (6); most – 74 (1993). BB 8-50 v Sussex (Southampton) 1992. Awards: CGT 1; BHC 1. LO HS 78 v Surrey (Guildford) 1997 (SL). LO BB 5-43 v Surrey (Oval) 1998 (SL).

VAN DER GUCHT, Charles Graham (Radley C; St Hild & St Bede C, Durham U), b Wimbledon, Surrey 14 Jan 1980. Grandson of P.I.Van der Gucht (Gloucestershire 1932-33). 6'0". LHB, LM/SLA. Debut 2000 – awaiting CC debut. Durham UCCE 2001. Summer Contract. HS 38 DU v Lancs (Durham) 2001. H HS 0*. BB 3-75 v Z (Southampton) 2000 – on debut. Award: CGT 1. LO HS 3 and LO BB 3-35 Hants CB v Glam (Southampton) 1999 (NWT).

WHITE, Giles William (Millfield S; Loughborough U), b Barnstaple, Devon 23 Mar 1972. 6'0". RHB, LB. Somerset 1991 (one match). Combined U 1994. Hampshire debut 1994; cap 1998. Devon 1988-94. 1000 runs (1): 1211 (1998). HS 156 v SL (Southampton) 1998. CC HS 145 v Yorks (Portsmouth) 1997. BB 3-23 v Notts (Nottingham) 1999. LO HS 76 v Glam (Southampton) 1998 (SL). LO BB (Devon) 1-45 (NWT).

RELEASED/RETIRED
(Having made a first-class County appearance in 2001)

STEPHENSON, J.P. – *see ESSEX.*

S.R.G.Francis (*see SOMERSET*), Z.C.Morris and A.J.Sexton left the staff having made no f-c appearances in 2001.

HAMPSHIRE 2001

RESULTS SUMMARY

	Place	Won	Lost	Tied	Drew	No Result
County Championship (2nd Division)	**2nd**	7	2		7	
All First-Class Matches		8	2		7	1
C & G Trophy	3rd Round					
Benson & Hedges Cup	6th in South Group					
NU National League (2nd Division)	**4th**	9	6			1

COUNTY CHAMPIONSHIP AVERAGES

BATTING AND FIELDING

Cap		M	I	NO	HS	Runs	Avge	100	50	Ct/St
–	J.D.Francis	2	4	2	72*	131	65.50	–	1	1
2001	N.C.Johnson	16	25	3	105*	948	43.09	2	7	24
1991	A.N.Aymes	16	19	5	112*	572	40.85	1	4	43/2
1996	J.S.Laney	4	5	1	60	137	34.25	–	2	8
2001	D.A.Kenway	15	28	3	166	840	33.60	2	3	14
1998	G.W.White	16	30	4	141	731	28.11	2	1	16/2
1998	A.D.Mascarenhas	14	21	5	104	423	26.43	1	1	8
1995	J.P.Stephenson	3	6	1	51	128	25.60	–	1	1
1999	W.S.Kendall	16	28	3	94	629	25.16	–	3	11
2001	A.C.Morris	16	19	2	65	423	24.88	–	3	10
1992	S.D.Udal	15	18	2	81	397	24.81	–	3	5
–	L.R.Prittipaul	6	7	–	84	155	22.14	–	1	4
1985	R.A.Smith	15	24	2	118	475	21.59	2	1	4
–	C.T.Tremlett	7	9	4	26	83	16.60	–	–	2
2000	A.D.Mullally	12	11	4	36	78	11.14	–	–	4

Also batted: J.R.C.Hamblin (1 match) 5; J.E.K.Schofield (2) 21*, 1, 2 (1 ct).

BOWLING

	O	M	R	W	Avge	Best	5wI	10wM
A.D.Mullally	427.3	135	1047	57	18.36	8-90	5	–
C.T.Tremlett	131.2	37	401	20	20.05	4-34	–	–
A.D.Mascarenhas	389.4	110	990	39	25.38	6-26	2	–
A.C.Morris	472	106	1428	51	28.00	5-39	2	–
S.D.Udal	518	133	1455	49	29.69	7-74	1	–
N.C.Johnson	232.5	38	836	21	39.80	4-20	–	–

Also bowled:

| J.E.K.Schofield | 55 | 12 | 154 | 8 | 19.25 | 4-51 | – | – |

A.N.Aymes 12-0-107-2; J.D.Francis 6-0-34-1; J.R.C.Hamblin 18-1-88-1; W.S.Kendall 16-2-36-0; D.A.Kenway 8-0-66-1; L.R.Prittipaul 25-1-86-0; J.P.Stephenson 17.4-3-60-4; G.W.White 19.1-0-71-1.

The First-Class Averages (pp 113-126) give the records of Hampshire players in all first-class county matches (Hampshire's other opponents being the Australians and Oxford University, the latter fixture being abandoned because of rain), with the exception of C.G.van der Gucht, whose only first-class appearance was in a University match, and:
A.D.Mullally 13-12-5-36-82-11.71-0-0-4ct. 447.1-141-1085-62-17.50-8/90-6-0.

HAMPSHIRE RECORDS

FIRST-CLASS CRICKET

Highest Total	For 672-7d		v	Somerset	Taunton	1899
	V 742		by	Surrey	The Oval	1909
Lowest Total	For 15		v	Warwicks	Birmingham	1922
	V 23		by	Yorkshire	Middlesbrough	1965
Highest Innings	For 316	R.H.Moore	v	Warwicks	Bournemouth	1937
	V 303*	G.A.Hick	for	Worcs	Southampton	1997

Highest Partnership for each Wicket

1st	347	V.P.Terry/C.L.Smith	v	Warwicks	Birmingham	1987
2nd	321	G.Brown/E.I.M.Barrett	v	Glos	Southampton	1920
3rd	344	C.P.Mead/G.Brown	v	Yorkshire	Portsmouth	1927
4th	263	R.E.Marshall/D.A.Livingstone	v	Middlesex	Lord's	1970
5th	235	G.Hill/D.F.Walker	v	Sussex	Portsmouth	1937
6th	411	R.M.Poore/E.G.Wynyard	v	Somerset	Taunton	1899
7th	325	G.Brown/C.H.Abercrombie	v	Essex	Leyton	1913
8th	227	K.D.James/T.M.Tremlett	v	Somerset	Taunton	1985
9th	230	D.A.Livingstone/A.T.Castell	v	Surrey	Southampton	1962
10th	192	H.A.W.Bowell/W.H.Livsey	v	Worcs	Bournemouth	1921

Best Bowling	For	9- 25	R.M.H.Cottam	v	Lancashire	Manchester	1965
(Innings)	V	10- 46	W.Hickton	for	Lancashire	Manchester	1870
Best Bowling	For	16- 88	J.A.Newman	v	Somerset	Weston-s-Mare	1927
(Match)	V	17-119	W.Mead	for	Essex	Southampton	1895

Most Runs – Season	2854	C.P.Mead	(av 79.27)		1928
Most Runs – Career	48892	C.P.Mead	(av 48.84)		1905-36
Most 100s – Season	12	C.P.Mead			1928
Most 100s – Career	138	C.P.Mead			1905-36
Most Wkts – Season	190	A.S.Kennedy	(av 15.61)		1922
Most Wkts – Career	2669	D.Shackleton	(av 18.23)		1948-69
Most Career W-K Dismissals	700	R.J.Parks	(630 ct/70 st)		1980-92
Most Career Catches in the Field	629	C.P.Mead			1905-36

LIMITED-OVERS CRICKET

Highest Total	NWT	371-4		v	Glamorgan	Southampton	1975
	BHC	321-1		v	Minor C (S)	Amersham	1973
	NL	313-2		v	Sussex	Portsmouth	1993
Lowest Total	NWT	98		v	Lancashire	Manchester	1975
	BHC	50		v	Yorkshire	Leeds	1991
	NL	43		v	Essex	Basingstoke	1972
Highest Innings	NWT	177	C.G.Greenidge	v	Glamorgan	Southampton	1975
	BHC	173*	C.G.Greenidge	v	Minor C (S)	Amersham	1973
	NL	172	C.G.Greenidge	v	Surrey	Southampton	1987
Best Bowling	NWT	7-30	P.J.Sainsbury	v	Norfolk	Southampton	1965
	BHC	6-25	S.J.Renshaw	v	Surrey	Southampton	1997
	NL	6-20	T.E.Jesty	v	Glamorgan	Cardiff	1975

KENT

Formation of Present Club: 1 March 1859
Substantial Reorganisation: 6 December 1870
Colours: Maroon and White
Badge: White Horse on a Red Ground
County Champions: (6) 1906, 1909, 1910, 1913, 1970, 1978
Joint Champions: (1) 1977
Gillette/NatWest/C & G Trophy Winners: (2) 1967, 1974
Benson and Hedges Cup Winners: (3) 1973, 1976, 1978
NU National League (Div 1) Winners: (1) 2001
Sunday League Winners: (4) 1972, 1973, 1976, 1995
Match Awards: CGT 53; BHC 94

Chief Executive: P.E.Millman, St Lawrence Ground, Canterbury, CT1 3NZ ▲ Tel: 01227 456886 ▲ Fax: 01227 762168 ▲ Email: kent@ecb.co.uk ▲ Web: www.kentcountycricket.co.uk

Captain: D.P.Fulton. **Limited-Overs Captain:** M.V.Fleming. **Vice-Captain:** No appointment. **Overseas Player:** A.Symonds. **2002 Beneficiaries:** D.W.Headley and M.J.McCague. **Scorer:** J.C.Foley. ‡ New registration

BANES, Matthew John (Tonbridge S; Collingwood C, Durham U), b Pembury 10 Dec 1979. 5'9". RHB, OB. Debut 1999. British U 2000-01. Durham UCCE 2001. HS 53 v NZ (Canterbury) 1999 – on debut. CC HS 5. BB 3-65 DU v Lancs (Durham) 2001. LO HS (Kent CB) 82 v Leics CB (Hinckley) 2001 (CGT).

EALHAM, Mark Alan (Stour Valley SS, Chartham), b Willesborough, Ashford 27 Aug 1969. Son of A.G.E.Ealham (Kent 1966-82). 5'9". RHB, RMF. Debut 1989; cap 1992. **Tests:** 8 (1996 to 1998); HS 53* v A (Birmingham) 1997; BB 4-21 v I (Nottingham) 1996. **LOI:** 64 (1996 to 2001); HS 45 v WI (Bridgetown) 1997-98; BB 5-15 v Z (Kimberley) 1999-00 – Eng record. Tours: A 1996-97 (Eng A); SA 1999-00 (*part*); SL 1997-98; Z 1992-93 (K); K 1997-98. 1000 runs (1): 1055 (1997). HS 153* v Northants (Canterbury) 2001. BB 8-36 (10-74 match) v Warwks (Birmingham) 1996. Awards: CGT 2; BHC 6. LO HS 112 v Derbys (Maidstone) 1995 (off 44 balls – SL record). LO BB 6-53 v Hants (Basingstoke) 1993 (SL).

FERLEY, Robert Steven (King Edward VII HS; Sutton Valence S; Grey C, Durham U), b Norwich, Norfolk 4 Feb 1982. 5'8". RHB, SLA. Durham UCCE 2001. British U 2001. Summer contract – awaiting county debut. Norfolk 2001. HS 17* DU v Worcs (Worcester) 2001. BB 3-52 DU v Lancs (Durham) 2001. LO HS 6 and LO BB 1-13 (Kent CB – CGT).

FLEMING, Matthew Valentine (St Aubyns S, Rottingdean; Eton C), b Macclesfield, Cheshire 12 Dec 1964. 5'11½". RHB, RM. Debut 1989; cap 1990; captain 1999-2001 (l-o captain 2002); benefit 2001. **LOI:** 11 (1997-98 to 1998); HS 33 v WI (Sharjah) 1997-98; BB 4-45 v I (Sharjah) 1997-98 – on debut. Tour: Z 1992-93 (K). HS 138 v Essex (Canterbury) 1997 and 138 v Worcs (Worcester) 1999. BB 5-51 v Notts (Nottingham) 1997. Awards: CGT 2; BHC 7. LO HS 125 v Northants (Canterbury) 2001 (NL). LO BB 5-27 v Hants (Canterbury) 1998 (BHC).

FULTON, David Paul (The Judd S; Kent U), b Lewisham 15 Nov 1971. 6'2". RHB, SLA, occ WK. Debut 1992; cap 1998; captain 2002. 1000 (1): 1892 (2001). HS 208 v Somerset (Canterbury) 2001. Scored 9 hundreds in 2001, including 208*, 104* and 197 in successive innings. BB 1-37. CC BB – . LO HS 82 v Yorks (Leeds) 2001 (NL).

GOLDING, James Matthew (Kent C, Canterbury; University C, Worcester), b Canterbury 19 Jul 1977. 6'4". RHB, RMF. Debut 1999. HS 30 v Glam (Maidstone) 2001. BB 3-23 v Somerset (Taunton) 2001. Award: CGT 1. LO HS 47 Kent CB v Hants (Canterbury) 1999 (NWT). LO BB 3-20 v Middx (Canterbury) 2000 (BHC).

‡**HEWITT, James** Peter (Teddington S; Richmond C; City of Westminster C), b South-wark, London 26 Feb 1976. 6'2½". LHB, RMF. Middlesex 1996-2001; cap 1998. HS 75 M v Essex (Chelmsford) 1997. 50 wkts (1): 60 (1997). BB 6-14 M v Glam (Cardiff) 1997. Took wicket of R.I.Dawson (Glos) with first ball in f-c cricket. LO HS 32* M v Glos (Bristol) 1997 (SL). LO BB 4-24 M v Worcs (Uxbridge) 1998 (SL).

HOCKLEY, James Bernard (Kelsey Park S, Beckenham), b Beckenham 16 Apr 1979. 6'2". RHB, OB. Debut 1998. HS 74 v Z (Canterbury) 2000. CC HS 34 v Glos (Canterbury) 1999. BB 1-21. LO HS 90 v Warwks (Birmingham) 2001 (NL).

JONES, Geraint Owen (Harristown State HS, Toowoomba and MacGregor State HS, Brisbane, Australia), b Kundiawa, Papua New Guinea 14 Jul 1976. Welsh parents. 5'10". RHB, WK. Debut 2001. HS 5. LO HS 39 v Surrey (Oval) 2001 (NL).

KEY, Robert William Trevor (Colfe's S), b East Dulwich, London 12 May 1979. 6'1". RHB, RM/OB. Debut 1998; cap 2001. Tours (Eng A): SA 1998-99; Z 1998-99. 1000 (1): 1281 (2001). HS 132 v Lancs (Manchester) 2001. LO HS 76* v Yorks (Canterbury) 1999 (NL).

KHAN, Amjad (Skolenpa Duevej, Denmark), b Copenhagen, Denmark 14 Oct 1980. 6'0". RHB, RFM. Debut 2001 – awaiting CC debut. Denmark 1998-2000. HS – . BB 1-46. LO HS (Denmark) 2 (NWT). LO BB 2-38 Denmark v Kent CB (Maidstone) 1999 (NWT).

‡**LOUDON, Alexander** Guy Rushworth (Wellesley House; Eton C; Collingwood C, Durham U), b Westminster, London 6 Sep 1980. Younger brother of H.J.H.Loudon (Durham UCCE 2001). 6'3". RHB, OB. Durham UCCE 2001. HS 39 DU v Lancs (Durham) 2001. BB 3-86 DU v Worcs (Worcester) 2001. LO HS 53 Kent CB v Leics CB (Hinckley) 2001 (CGT).

McCAGUE, Martin John (Hedland Sr HS; Carine Tafe C), b Larne, N Ireland 24 May 1969. 6'5". RHB, RFM. W Australia 1990-91 to 1991-92. Kent debut 1991; cap 1992; benefit 2002. **Tests:** 3 (1993 to 1994-95); HS 11 v A (Leeds) 1993; BB 4-121 v A (Nottingham) 1993. Tours: A 1994-95 (*part*); SA 1993-94 (Eng A). HS 72 v Yorks (Canterbury) 2000. 50 wkts (4); most – 76 (1996). BB 9-86 (15-147 match) v Derbys (Derby) 1994. Hat-trick 1996. Award: CGT 1. LO HS 56 v Leics (Canterbury) 2000 (NL). LO BB 5-26 v Middx (Canterbury) 1993 (NWT).

MASTERS, David Daniel (Fort Luton HS; Mid Kent CHE), b Chatham 22 Apr 1978. Son of K.D.Masters (Kent 1981-85, Surrey 1986). 6'4". RHB, RMF. Debut 2000. HS 21 v Hants (Canterbury) 2000. BB 6-27 v Durham (Tunbridge Wells) 2000. LO HS 12* v Middx (Canterbury) 2000 (BHC). LO BB 2-10 v Northants (Canterbury) 2000 (NL).

NIXON, Paul Andrew (Ullswater HS, Penrith), b Carlisle, Cumberland 21 Oct 1970. 6'0". LHB, WK. Leicestershire 1989-99; cap 1994. Kent debut/cap 2000. Cumberland 1987. MCC YC. Tours: SA 1996-97 (Le); I 1994-95 (Eng A); P 2000-01; SL 2000-01 (*no f-c*). 1000 runs (1): 1046 (1994). HS 134* v Hants (Canterbury) 2000. Awards: BHC 2. LO HS 101 Le v SL A (Galle) 1998-99.

PATEL, Minal Mahesh (Dartford GS; Erith TC), b Bombay, India 7 Jul 1970. 5'9". RHB, SLA. Debut 1989; cap 1994. **Tests:** 2 (1996); HS 27 and BB 1-101 v I (Nottingham) 1996. Tour: I 1994-95 (Eng A). HS 67 v Glos (Canterbury) 1999. 50 wkts (3); most – 90 (1994). BB 8-96 v Lancs (Canterbury) 1994. LO HS 27* v Somerset (Canterbury) 2001 (CGT). LO BB 3-22 v Essex (Canterbury) 1999 (NL).

SAGGERS, Martin John (Springwood HS, King's Lynn; Huddersfield U), b King's Lynn, Norfolk 23 May 1972. 6'2". RHB, RMF. Durham 1996-98. Norfolk 1995-96. Kent debut 1999; cap 2001. HS 61* v Lancs (Canterbury) 2001. 50 wkts (2): most 64 (2001). BB 7-79 v Durham (Chester-le-St) 2000. Award: BHC 1. LO HS 34* Minor C v Leics (Jesmond) 1996 (BHC). LO BB 5-22 v Glos (Canterbury) 2001 (NL).

SMITH, Edward Thomas (Tonbridge S; Peterhouse, Cambridge), b Pembury 19 Jul 1977. 6'2". RHB, RM. Cambridge U 1996-98, scoring 101 v Glam (Cambridge) on debut; blue 1996-97 (*injured 1998*). Kent debut 1996; cap 2001. 1000 runs (2): most – 1163 (1997). HS 190 CU v Leics (Cambridge) 1997. K HS 175 v Durham (Chester-le-St) 2000. LO HS 72* v Hants (Portsmouth) 1997 (SL).

SYMONDS, Andrew (All Saints Anglican School, Mudgeeraba, Queensland), b Birmingham 9 Jun 1975. 6'1½". RHB, RMF/OB. Emigrated to Australia when 18 months old. Queensland 1994-95 to date. Australian CA. Gloucestershire 1995-96; cap 1996. Kent 1999, 2001; cap 1999. YC 1995. Surrendered England qualification by appearing for Australia A v WI 1996-97. **LOI** (A): 48 (1998-99 to 2001-02); HS 68* v I (Galle) 1999-00; BB 4-11 v I (Sydney) 1999-00. Tours (Aus A): Sc 1998; NZ 1994-95 (Aus Academy). 1000 runs (2): most – 1438 (1995). HS 254* Gs v Glam (Abergavenny) 1995 (including record 16 sixes); hit record 20 sixes in match. K HS 177 v Leics (Canterbury) 1999. BB 4-39 Q v WA (Perth) 1998-99. K BB 3-28 v Somerset (Canterbury) 2001. Awards: CGT 2; BHC 2. LO HS 95 Gs v Comb Us (Bristol) 1995 (BHC) and 95 v Leics (Canterbury) 1999 (NL). LO BB 6-14 Aus A v Ind A (Los Angeles) 1999.

TREDWELL, James Cullum (Southlands Community CS), b Ashford 27 Feb 1982. LHB, OB. Debut 2001. HS 10 and BB 1-38 v Leics (Leicester) 2001. LO HS 71 and BB 1-39 Kent CB v Bucks (Maidstone) 2001 (CGT).

TROTT, Benjamin James (Court Fields Community S, Wellington; Richard Huish C, Taunton; Plymouth U), b Wellington, Somerset 14 Mar 1975. 6'5". RHB, RMF. Somerset 1997-98. Kent debut 2000. Devon 2000. HS 13 v Glam (Maidstone) and 13 v Leics (Leicester) 2001. K BB 6-13 (11-78 match) v Essex (Tunbridge Wells) 2001. Award: CGT 1. LO HS 2* (NL). LO BB 5-18 v Cumb (Barrow) 2001 (CGT).

WALKER, Matthew Jonathan (King's S, Rochester), b Gravesend 2 Jan 1974. Grandson of Jack Walker (Kent 1949). 5'8". LHB, RM. Debut 1992-93 (Z tour); UK Debut 1994; cap 2000. Tour: Z 1992-93 (K). HS 275* v Somerset (Canterbury) 1996. BB 1-3 (FCC Select XI). K BB 1-4. Awards: BHC 3. LO HS 117 v Warwks (Canterbury) 1997 (BHC). LO BB 4-24 v Yorks (Leeds) 2001 (NL).

RELEASED/RETIRED
(Having made a first-class County appearance in 2001)

CULLINAN, Daryll John (Queens C, Queenstown; Stellenbosch U), b Kimberley, SA 4 Mar 1967. Brother of R.E.Cullinan (Border and OFS 1984-85 to 1992-93). 5'10". RHB, OB. Border 1983-84 to 1984-85 and 1994-95 to 1995-96, making debut whilst at school. WP 1985-86/1990-91. Transvaal/Gauteng 1991-92 to 1993-94 and 1996-97 to date. At 16yr 304d remains youngest player to score f-c hundred in SA. Derbyshire 1995. Kent 2001; cap 2001. **Tests** (SA): 70 (1992-93 to 2000-01); HS 275* (SA record) v NZ (Auckland) 1998-99; BB 1-10. **LOI** (SA): 138 (1992-93 to 2000-01); HS 124 v P (Nairobi) 1996-97; BB 2-30 v E (Manchester) 1998. Tours (SA): E 1994, 1998; A 1993-94, 1997-98; WI 2000-01; NZ 1994-95, 1998-99; I 1996-97, 1999-00; P 1997-98; SL 1993-94, 2000-01; Z 1995-96, 1999-00. 1000 runs (1): 1003 (1995). HS 337* Transvaal v N Transvaal (Jo'burg) 1993-94 (SA f-c record). UK HS 200* SA v Durham (Chester-le-St) 1998. K HS 63 and BB 1-24 v Essex (Tunbridge Wells) 2001. BB 2-27 Border v Natal B (E London) 1983-84. Awards: CGT 1; BHC 1. LO HS 124 (*see LOI*). LO BB 2-30 (*see LOI*).

P.S.Lazenbury, B.J.Phillips (*see NORTHAMPTONSHIRE*) and A.P.Wells left the staff having made no f-c appearances in 2001.

KENT 2001

RESULTS SUMMARY

		Place	Won	Lost	Tied	Drew	No Result
County Championship (1st Division)		3rd	4	3		9	
All First-Class Matches			4	3		11	
C & G Trophy		Quarter-Finalist					
Benson & Hedges Cup		4th in South Group					
NU National League (1st Division)		1st	11	2	1		2

COUNTY CHAMPIONSHIP AVERAGES

BATTING AND FIELDING

Cap		M	I	NO	HS	Runs	Avge	100	50	Ct/St
1998	D.P.Fulton	16	24	2	208*	1729	78.59	8	3	26
1999	A.Symonds	8	12	–	131	563	46.91	2	2	13
2000	M.J.Walker	15	22	3	124	868	45.68	4	3	9
2001	R.W.T.Key	16	24	–	132	1073	44.70	3	6	6
2001	E.T.Smith	16	24	1	116	947	41.17	3	4	5
2000	P.A.Nixon	16	22	5	87*	554	32.58	–	3	42/3
1992	M.A.Ealham	11	13	1	153*	286	23.83	1	–	8
1990	M.V.Fleming	16	21	4	59	381	22.41	–	1	6
1994	M.M.Patel	15	18	2	38	247	15.43	–	–	8
–	J.B.Hockley	5	9	–	29	132	14.66	–	–	6
2001	M.J.Saggers	16	20	5	61*	185	12.33	–	1	1
–	J.M.Golding	4	7	1	30	69	11.50	–	–	1
–	B.J.Trott	13	13	3	13	57	5.70	–	–	3

Also batted: D.J.Cullinan (3 matches – cap 2001) 57, 2, 63; G.O.Jones (1) 5 (1 ct);
M.J.McCague (1 – cap 1992) 4; D.D.Masters (3) 2*, 6, 0* (1 ct); J.C.Tredwell (1) 10.

BOWLING

	O	M	R	W	Avge	Best	5wI	10wM
M.J.Saggers	492.3	112	1520	63	24.12	6- 92	3	–
M.A.Ealham	213	63	555	23	24.13	6- 64	2	–
B.J.Trott	352.5	64	1169	47	24.87	6- 13	4	1
M.M.Patel	476.2	143	1097	36	30.47	8-119	1	1
A.Symonds	106.2	23	333	10	33.30	3- 28	–	–
M.V.Fleming	284	47	888	20	44.40	4- 53	–	–

Also bowled:

	O	M	R	W	Avge	Best	5wI	10wM
J.M.Golding	82.3	15	298	6	49.66	3- 23	–	–
D.D.Masters	73	10	258	5	51.60	3- 52	–	–

D.J.Cullinan 14-6-29-1; D.P.Fulton 1-0-2-0; J.B.Hockley 28-5-109-1; G.O.Jones 1-0-4-0;
R.W.T.Key 1-0-5-0; M.J.McCague 18-3-64-2; J.C.Tredwell 26-5-123-2; M.J.Walker
20-3-69-2.

The First-Class Averages (pp 113-126) give the records of Kent players in all first-class
county matches (Kent's other opponents being the Pakistanis and Cambridge University),
with the exception of M.J.Banes and R.S.Ferley whose only first-class appearances were in
University matches.

KENT RECORDS

FIRST-CLASS CRICKET

Highest Total	For 803-4d		v	Essex	Brentwood	1934
	V 676		by	Australians	Canterbury	1921
Lowest Total	For 18		v	Sussex	Gravesend	1867
	V 16		by	Warwicks	Tonbridge	1913
Highest Innings	For 332	W.H.Ashdown	v	Essex	Brentwood	1934
	V 344	W.G.Grace	for	MCC	Canterbury	1876

Highest Partnership for each Wicket

1st	300	N.R.Taylor/M.R.Benson	v	Derbyshire	Canterbury	1991
2nd	366	S.G.Hinks/N.R.Taylor	v	Middlesex	Canterbury	1990
3rd	321*	A.Hearne/J.R.Mason	v	Notts	Nottingham	1899
4th	368	P.A.de Silva/G.R.Cowdrey	v	Derbyshire	Maidstone	1995
5th	277	F.E.Woolley/L.E.G.Ames	v	New Zealand	Canterbury	1931
6th	315	P.A.de Silva/M.A.Ealham	v	Notts	Nottingham	1995
7th	248	A.P.Day/E.Humphreys	v	Somerset	Taunton	1908
8th	157	A.L.Hilder/A.C.Wright	v	Essex	Gravesend	1924
9th	171	M.A.Ealham/P.A.Strang	v	Notts	Nottingham	1997
10th	235	F.E.Woolley/A.Fielder	v	Worcs	Stourbridge	1909

Best Bowling	For	10- 30	C.Blythe	v	Northants	Northampton	1907
(Innings)	V	10- 48	C.H.G.Bland	for	Sussex	Tonbridge	1899
Best Bowling	For	17- 48	C.Blythe	v	Northants	Northampton	1907
(Match)	V	17-106	T.W.J.Goddard	for	Glos	Bristol	1939

Most Runs – Season	2894	F.E.Woolley	(av 59.06)		1928
Most Runs – Career	47868	F.E.Woolley	(av 41.77)		1906-38
Most 100s – Season	10	F.E.Woolley			1928
	10	F.E.Woolley			1934
Most 100s – Career	122	F.E.Woolley			1906-38
Most Wkts – Season	262	A.P.Freeman	(av 14.74)		1933
Most Wkts – Career	3340	A.P.Freeman	(av 17.64)		1914-36
Most Career W-K Dismissals	1253	F.H.Huish	(901 ct/352 st)		1895-1914
Most Career Catches in the Field	773	F.E.Woolley			1906-38

LIMITED-OVERS CRICKET

Highest Total	NWT	384-6		v	Berkshire	Finchampstead	1994
	BHC	338-6		v	Somerset	Maidstone	1996
	NL	327-6		v	Leics	Canterbury	1993
Lowest Total	NWT	60		v	Somerset	Taunton	1979
	BHC	73		v	Middlesex	Canterbury	1979
	NL	83		v	Middlesex	Lord's	1984
Highest Innings	NWT	136*	C.L.Hooper	v	Berkshire	Finchampstead	1994
	BHC	143	C.J.Tavaré	v	Somerset	Taunton	1985
	NL	145	C.L.Hooper	v	Leics	Leicester	1996
Best Bowling	NWT	8-31	D.L.Underwood	v	Scotland	Edinburgh	1987
	BHC	6-41	T.N.Wren	v	Somerset	Canterbury	1995
	NL	6- 9	R.A.Woolmer	v	Derbyshire	Chesterfield	1979

LANCASHIRE

Formation of Present Club: 12 January 1864
Colours: Red, Green and Blue
Badge: Red Rose
County Champions (since 1890): (7) 1897, 1904, 1926,
1927, 1928, 1930, 1934
Joint Champions: (1) 1950
Gillette/NatWest/C & G Trophy Winners: (7) 1970, 1971,
1972, 1975, 1990, 1996, 1998
Benson and Hedges Cup Winners: (4) 1984, 1990, 1995, 1996
NU National League (Div 1) Winners: (1) 1999.
Sunday League Winners: (4) 1969, 1970, 1989, 1998
Match Awards: CGT 74; BHC 82

Chief Executive: J.Cumbes, Old Trafford, Manchester M16 0PX ▲ Tel: 0161 282 4000 ▲
Fax: 0161 282 4100 ▲ Email: sales.lancs@ecb.co.uk ▲ Web: www.lccc.co.uk

Captain: W.K.Hegg. **Vice-Captain:** No appointment. **Overseas Player:** S.G.Law.
2002 Beneficiary: P.J.Martin. **Scorer:** A.West. ‡ New registration

ANDERSON, James Michael (St Theodore RC HS and SFC, Burnley), b Burnley 30 Jul 1982. 6'2". LHB, RMF. England U-19. Staff 2001 – awaiting f-c debut. LO HS 5* and LO BB 2-64 Lancs CB v Essex CB (Chelmsford) 2000 (NWT).

‡BYAS, David (Scarborough C), b Kilham, Yorks 26 Aug 1963. 6'4". LHB, RM. Yorkshire 1986-2001; cap 1991; captain 1996-2001. Tours (Y): SA 1991-92, 1992-93; Z 1995-96. 1000 runs (5); most – 1913 (1995). HS 213 Y v Worcs (Scarborough) 1995. BB 3-55 Y v Derbys (Chesterfield) 1990. Awards: BHC 3. LO HS 116* Y v Surrey (Oval) 1996 (BHC). LO BB 3-19 Y v Notts (Leeds) 1989 (SL).

CHAPPLE, Glen (West Craven HS; Nelson & Colne C), b Skipton, Yorks 23 Jan 1974. 6'1". RHB, RFM. Debut 1992; cap 1994. Tours (Eng A): A 1996-97; WI 1995-96 (La); I 1994-95. HS 155 v Somerset (Manchester) 2001. Scored 100 off 27 balls in contrived circumstances v Glam (Manchester) 1993. 50 wkts (3); most – 55 (1994). BB 6-42 v Durham (Chester-le-St) 2000. Awards: CGT 1; BHC 1. LO HS 56 v Middx (Manchester) 2001 (NL). LO BB 6-18 v Essex (Lord's) 1996 (NWT).

CHILTON, Mark James (Manchester GS; Durham U), b Sheffield, Yorks 2 Oct 1976. 6'3". RHB, RM. Debut 1997. British U 1998. HS 106* v CU (Cambridge) 1999. CC HS 104 v Northants (Northampton) 2001. BB 1-1. CC BB – . Awards: BHC 2. LO HS 56 Brit U v Kent (Oxford) 1998 (BHC). LO BB 5-26 Brit U v Sussex (Cambridge) 1997 (BHC).

CRAWLEY, John Paul (Manchester GS; Trinity C, Cambridge), b Maldon, Essex 21 Sep 1971. Brother of M.A.Crawley (Oxford U, Lancs and Notts 1987-94) and P.M.Crawley (Cambridge U 1992). 6'1". RHB, RM, occ WK. Debut 1990; cap 1994; captain 1999-2001. Cambridge U 1991-93; blue 1991-92-93; captain 1992-93. YC 1994. **Tests:** 29 (1994 to 1998-99); HS 156* v SL (Oval) 1998. **LOI:** 13 (1994-95 to 1998-99); HS 73 v Z (Harare) 1996-97. Tours: A 1994-95, 1998-99; SA 1993-94 (Eng A), 1995-96; WI 1995-96 (La), 1997-98, 2000-01 (Eng A); NZ 1996-97; Z 1996-97. 1000 runs (7); most – 1851 (1998). HS 286 England A v E Province (Port Elizabeth) 1993-94. La HS 281* v Somerset (Southport) 1994. BB 1-90. Award: BHC 1. LO HS 114 v Notts (Manchester) 1995 (BHC).

DRIVER, Ryan Craig (Redruth Community C; Durham U), b Truro, Cornwall 30 Apr 1979. 6'3½". LHB, RM. Worcestershire 1998-2000. British U 1999. Lancashire debut 2001. Cornwall 1996-97. HS 64 Wo v Sussex (Worcester) 2000. La HS 35 v Leics (Leicester) 2001. BB (Wo) 1-13. Award: CGT 1. LO HS 61* Wo v Glos (Worcester) 2000 (NWT). LO BB (Wo) 1-17 (NL).

47

FAIRBROTHER, Neil Harvey (Lymm GS), b Warrington 9 Sep 1963. 5'8". LHB, LM. Debut 1982; cap 1985; captain 1992-93; benefit 1995. Transvaal 1994-95. **Tests**: 10 (1987 to 1992-93); HS 83 v I (Madras) 1992-93. **LOI**: 75 (1986-87 to 1999); HS 113 v WI (Lord's) 1991. Tours: NZ 1987-88, 1991-92; I/SL 1992-93; P 1987-88, 1990-91 (Eng A); SL 1990-91 (Eng A). 1000 runs (10); most – 1740 (1990). HS 366 v Surrey (Oval) 1990 (ground record), including 311 in a day and 100 or more in each session. BB 2-91 v Notts (Manchester) 1987. Awards: CGT 6; BHC 10. LO HS 145 v Hants (Manchester) 1990 (BHC). LO BB 1-17 (BHC).

FLINTOFF, Andrew (Ribbleton Hall HS), b Preston 6 Dec 1977. 6'4". RHB, RM. Debut 1995; cap 1998. YC 1998. **ECB contract 2000. Tests**: 12 (1998 to 2001-02); HS 42 v SA (Pt Elizabeth) 1999-00; BB 4-50 v I (Bangalore) 2001-02. **LOI**: 39 (1998-99 to 2001-02); HS 84 v P (Karachi) 2000-01; BB 4-17 v NZ (Auckland) 2001-02. Tours (Eng A): SA 1998-99, 1999-00 (Eng); NZ 2001-02; I/SL 1997-98; Z 1998-99; K 1997-98. HS 160 v Yorks (Manchester) 1999. BB 5-24 v Hants (Southampton) 1999. Awards: CGT 3; BHC 1. LO HS 143 (off 66 balls) v Essex (Chelmsford) 1999 (NL). LO BB 4-22 Eng A v Zim A (Harare) 1998-99.

HAYNES, Jamie Jonathan (St Edmunds C, Canberra; Canberra U), b Bristol 5 Jul 1974. 5'11". RHB, WK. Debut 1996. Represented Australian Capital Territory at cricket and Australian Rules football. HS 80 v SL A (Manchester) 1999. CC HS 57 v Surrey (Oval) 2001. LO HS 59* v Warwks CB (Blackpool) 2001 (CGT).

HEGG, Warren Kevin (Unsworth HS, Bury; Stand C, Whitefield), b Whitefield 23 Feb 1968. 5'8". RHB, WK. Debut 1986; cap 1989; benefit 1999; captain 2002. **Tests**: 2 (1998-99); HS 15 v A (Sydney) 1998-99. Tours: A 1996-97 (Eng A), 1998-99; WI 1986-87 (La), 1995-96 (La); NZ 2001-02; SL 1990-91 (Eng A); Z 1988-89 (La). HS 134 v Leics (Manchester) 1996. Held 11 catches (equalling world f-c match record) v Derbys (Chesterfield) 1989. Award: BHC 1. LO HS 81 v Yorks (Manchester) 1996 (BHC).

HOGG, Kyle William (Saddleworth HS), b Birmingham 2 Jul 1983. Son of W.Hogg (Lancashire and Warwickshire 1976-83); grandson of S.Ramadhin (Trinidad, Lancashire and West Indies 1949-50 to 1965). 6'4". LHB, RFM. Debut 2001 – awaiting CC debut. HS 19 and BB 3-17 v Durham UCCE (Durham) 2001. LO HS - . LO BB 1-14 (NL).

KEEDY, Gary (Garforth CS), b Wakefield, Yorks 27 Nov 1974. 6'0". LHB, SLA. Yorkshire 1994 (one match). Lancashire debut 1995; cap 2000. Tour: WI 1995-96 (La). HS 34 v Surrey (Manchester) 2000. BB 6-56 (10-155 match) v Durham (Manchester) 2000. LO HS 2 (NL). LO BB 5-30 v Sussex (Manchester) 2000 (NL).

‡LAW, Stuart Grant (Craigslea State HS), b Herston, Brisbane, Australia 18 Oct 1968. 6'1". RHB, RM/LB. Queensland 1988-89 to date; captain 1994-95 to 1996-97, 1999-00 to date. Essex 1996-2001; cap 1996. Wisden 1997. **Tests**: A: 1 (1995-96); HS 54* v SL (Perth) 1995-96. **LOI** (A): 54 (1994-95 to 1998-99); HS 110 v Z (Hobart) 1994-95; BB 2-22 v P (Sydney) 1996-97. Tours: E 1995 (Young A); Z 1991-92 (Aus B). 1000 runs (5+1); most – 1833 (1999). HS 263 Ex v Somerset (Chelmsford) 1999. BB 5-39 Q v Tasmania (Brisbane) 1995-96. CC BB 3-27 Ex v Worcs (Chelmsford) 1997. Awards: CGT 4; BHC 1. LO HS 163 Young A v Surrey (Oval) 1995. LO BB 5-26 Q v SL (Cairns) 1995-96.

LLOYD, Graham David (Hollins County HS), b Accrington 1 Jul 1969. Son of D.Lloyd (Lancs and England 1965-83). 5'9". RHB, RM. Debut 1988; cap 1992; benefit 2001. **LOI**: 6 (1996 to 1998-99); HS 22 v A (Oval) 1997. Tours: A 1992-93 (Eng A); WI 1995-96 (La). 1000 runs (5); most – 1389 (1992). HS 241 v Essex (Chelmsford) 1996. BB 1-4. Awards: BHC 2. LO HS 134 v Durham (Manchester) 1997 (SL). LO BB 1-23 (NWT).

‡MAIDEN, Gregor Ian, b Glasgow, Scotland 22 Jul 1979. RHB, OB. Scotland 1999-2000. Lancashire staff 2002 – awaiting county debut. HS 23* and BB 2-11 Scot v SA Academy XI (Linlithgow) 1999. LO HS (Scot) 3 (CGT). LO BB 2-27 Scot v Dorset (Glasgow) 1999 (NWT).

MARTIN, Peter James (Danum S, Doncaster), b Accrington 15 Nov 1968. 6'4". RHB, RFM. Debut 1989; cap 1994; benefit 2002. **Tests:** 8 (1995 to 1997); HS 29 v WI (Lord's) 1995; BB 4-60 v SA (Durban) 1995-96. **LOI:** 20 (1995 to 1998-99); HS 6; BB 4-44 v WI (Oval) 1995 – on debut. Tour: SA 1995-96. HS 133 v Durham (Gateshead) 1992. 50 wkts (3); most – 58 (1997). BB 8-32 (13-79 match) v Middx (Uxbridge) 1997. Awards: CGT 2. LO HS 35* v Worcs (Manchester) 1996 (SL). LO BB 5-16 v Warwks CB (Blackpool) 2001 (CGT).

ROBERTS, Timothy William (Bishop's Stopford S, Kettering; Durham U), b Kettering, Northants 4 Mar 1978. Younger brother of A.R.Roberts (Northants 1987-98). 5'7". RHB, OB. British U 1999. Bedfordshire 2000. Lancashire debut 2001. HS 49 Brit U v NZ (Oxford) 1999 – on debut. La HS 17 v DU (Durham) 2001. CC HS 3. LO HS 55 v Derbys (Derby) 2001 (NL).

SCHOFIELD, Christopher Paul (Wardle HS), b Birch Hill, Rochdale 6 Oct 1978. 6'2". LHB, LB. Debut 1998. **ECB contract 2000. Tests:** 2 (2000); HS 57 v Z (Nottingham) 2000. Tours (Eng A): WI 2000-01; NZ 1999-00; B 1999-00. HS 80* v Essex (Colchester) 2001. BB 6-120 Eng A v Bangladesh (Chittagong) 1999-00. La BB 5-48 v CU (Cambridge) 2000. CC BB 5-66 v Durham (Manchester) 1999. LO HS 42 v Leics (Leicester) 2001 (CGT). LO BB 5-31 v Derbys (Manchester) 2001 (NL).

SMETHURST, Michael Paul (Hulme GS, Oldham; Salford U), b Oldham 11 Oct 1976. 6'5". RHB, RM. Debut 1999. HS 66 v Surrey (Manchester) 2000. 50 wkts (1): 56 (2000). BB 7-37 v NZ A (Liverpool) 2000. CC BB 7-50 v Durham (Chester-le-St) 2000. Award: CGT 1. LO HS 10* v Leics (Manchester) 2000 (BHC). LO BB 4-46 v Hants (Southampton) 1999 (NWT).

‡**SWANN, Alec** James (Risade S; Sponne S, Towcester), b Northampton 26 Oct 1976. Son of R.Swann (Northumberland 1969-72; Bedfordshire 1988-95); elder brother of G.P.Swann (*see NORTHAMPTONSHIRE*). 6'1". RHB, RM/OB. Northamptonshire 1996-2001. Bedfordshire 1994. HS 154 Nh v Notts (Northampton) 1999. BB 2-30 Nh v Glos (Northampton) 2000. LO HS 83* Nh v Glos (Bristol) 2001 (BHC).

WOOD, John (Crofton HS; Wakefield District C; Leeds Poly), b Crofton, Yorks 22 Jul 1970. 6'3". RHB, RFM. GW (LO only) 1990-91. Durham 1992-2000; cap 1998. Lancashire debut 2001. HS 63* Du v Notts (Chester-le-St) 1993. La HS 35 v Yorks (Leeds) 2001. 50 wkts (1): 62 (1998). BB 7-58 Du v Yorks (Leeds) 1999. La BB 3-97 v Kent (Canterbury) 2001. LO HS 28* Du v Leics (Leicester) 2000 (BHC) and 28* Du v Notts (Nottingham) 2000 (NL). LO BB 4-17 Du v Kent (Darlington) 1997 (SL).

YATES, Gary (Manchester GS), b Ashton-under-Lyne 20 Sep 1967. 6'0". RHB, OB. Debut 1990; cap 1994. HS 134* v Northants (Manchester) 1993. BB 6-64 v Kent (Manchester) 1999. LO HS 38 v Essex (Chelmsford) 1996 (SL). LO BB 4-34 v Warwks (Birmingham) 1994 (SL).

RELEASED/RETIRED
(Having made a first-class County appearance in 2001)

ATHERTON, Michael Andrew (Manchester GS; Downing C, Cambridge), b Failsworth, Manchester 23 Mar 1968. 5'11". RHB, LB. Cambridge U 1987-89; blue 1987-88-89; captain 1988-89. Lancashire 1987-2001; cap 1989; benefit 1997. YC 1990. *Wisden* 1990. OBE 1997. **ECB contracts 2000, 2001. Tests:** 115 (1989 to 2001, 54 as captain – England record); HS 185* v SA (Johannesburg) 1995-96; BB 1-20. **LOI:** 54 (1990 to 1998, 43 as captain); HS 127 v WI (Lord's) 1995. Tours (C=captain): A 1990-91, 1994-95C, 1998-99; SA 1995-96C, 1999-00; WI 1993-94C, 1995-96 (La), 1997-98C; NZ 1996-97C; I 1992-93; P 2000-01; SL 1992-93, 2000-01; Z 1989-90 (Eng A), 1996-97C. 1000 runs (7); most – 1924 (1990). Scored 1193 in season of f-c debut. HS 268* v Glam (Blackpool) 1999. BB 6-78 v Notts (Nottingham) 1990. Awards: CGT 4; BHC 4. LO HS 127 (*see LOI*). LO BB 4-42 Comb U v Somerset (Taunton) 1989 (BHC). **RELEASED/RETIRED** continued on p 74

LANCASHIRE 2001

RESULTS SUMMARY

	Place	Won	Lost	Tied	Drew	No Result
County Championship (1st Division)	**6th**	4	5		5	2
All First-Class Matches		4	5		6	2
C & G Trophy	Semi-Finalist					
Benson & Hedges Cup	5th in North Group					
NU National League (2nd Division)	**6th**	5	8			3

COUNTY CHAMPIONSHIP AVERAGES

BATTING AND FIELDING

Cap		M	I	NO	HS	Runs	Avge	100	50	Ct/St
1985	N.H.Fairbrother	12	19	4	179*	939	62.60	4	1	16
1989	W.K.Hegg	13	20	4	133	782	48.87	2	5	35/3
1989	M.A.Atherton	4	8	1	160	330	47.14	1	–	4
1994	J.P.Crawley	14	24	2	280	898	40.81	2	5	4
1994	G.Chapple	13	19	3	155	497	31.06	1	2	3
–	M.J.Chilton	13	23	1	104	668	30.36	1	4	10
–	C.P.Schofield	8	13	2	80*	328	29.81	–	3	7
–	J.C.Scuderi	12	17	2	89	444	29.60	–	3	2
1998	A.Flintoff	13	22	1	68	566	26.95	–	2	17
1994	P.J.Martin	9	12	3	51*	169	18.77	–	1	2
–	J.J.Haynes	4	7	–	57	103	14.71	–	1	6
2000	G.Keedy	12	14	8	20*	81	13.50	–	–	6
–	J.Wood	7	9	–	35	112	12.44	–	–	–
–	R.C.Driver	4	7	–	35	77	11.00	–	–	5
1999	M.Muralitharan	7	8	1	21	70	10.00	–	–	4
–	M.P.Smethurst	4	7	1	7	29	4.83	–	–	–
1992	G.D.Lloyd	3	4	–	9	19	4.75	–	–	3

Also batted (1 match each): T.W.Roberts 3, 0; G.Yates (cap 1994) 8* (2 ct).

BOWLING

	O	M	R	W	Avge	Best	5wI	10wM
M.Muralitharan	484.5	159	971	50	19.42	6-53	5	1
G.Chapple	379.2	87	1174	53	22.15	6-46	4	–
P.J.Martin	322.3	86	969	33	29.36	5-52	1	–
A.Flintoff	236.3	44	713	19	37.52	3-36	–	–
G.Keedy	368.3	68	1114	27	41.25	5-73	2	–
C.P.Schofield	234.1	49	704	11	64.00	2-50	–	–

Also bowled:

J.C.Scuderi	115.4	33	318	9	35.33	3-48	–	–
M.P.Smethurst	82	13	315	7	45.00	3-32	–	–
J.Wood	131.3	14	511	9	56.77	3-97	–	–

M.J.Chilton 1-0-5-0; J.P.Crawley 1-0-2-0; R.C.Driver 4-0-33-0; N.H.Fairbrother 6-1-20-1; G.Yates 19.5-4-65-2.

The First-Class Averages (pp 113-126) give the records of Lancashire players in all first-class county matches (Lancashire's other opponents being Durham University), with the exception of M.A.Atherton whose full county figures are as above.

LANCASHIRE RECORDS

FIRST-CLASS CRICKET

Highest Total	For 863		v	Surrey	The Oval	1990
	V 707-9d		by	Surrey	The Oval	1990
Lowest Total	For 25		v	Derbyshire	Manchester	1871
	V 22		by	Glamorgan	Liverpool	1924
Highest Innings	For 424	A.C.MacLaren	v	Somerset	Taunton	1895
	V 315*	T.W.Hayward	for	Surrey	The Oval	1898

Highest Partnership for each Wicket

1st	368	A.C.MacLaren/R.H.Spooner	v	Glos	Liverpool	1903
2nd	371	F.B.Watson/G.E.Tyldesley	v	Surrey	Manchester	1928
3rd	364	M.A.Atherton/N.H.Fairbrother	v	Surrey	The Oval	1990
4th	358	S.P.Titchard/G.D.Lloyd	v	Essex	Chelmsford	1996
5th	249	B.Wood/A.Kennedy	v	Warwicks	Birmingham	1975
6th	278	J.Iddon/H.R.W.Butterworth	v	Sussex	Manchester	1932
7th	248	G.D.Lloyd/I.D.Austin	v	Yorkshire	Leeds	1997
8th	158	J.Lyon/R.M.Ratcliffe	v	Warwicks	Manchester	1979
9th	142	L.O.S.Poidevin/A.Kermode	v	Sussex	Eastbourne	1907
10th	173	J.Briggs/R.Pilling	v	Surrey	Liverpool	1885

Best Bowling	For	10-46	W.Hickton	v	Hampshire	Manchester	1870
(Innings)	V	10-40	G.O.B.Allen	for	Middlesex	Lord's	1929
Best Bowling	For	17-91	H.Dean	v	Yorkshire	Liverpool	1913
(Match)	V	16-65	G.Giffen	for	Australians	Manchester	1886

Most Runs – Season	2633	J.T.Tyldesley	(av 56.02)		1901
Most Runs – Career	34222	G.E.Tyldesley	(av 45.20)		1909-36
Most 100s – Season	11	C.Hallows			1928
Most 100s – Career	90	G.E.Tyldesley			1909-36
Most Wkts – Season	198	E.A.McDonald	(av 18.55)		1925
Most Wkts – Career	1816	J.B.Statham	(av 15.12)		1950-68
Most Career W-K Dismissals	922†	G.Duckworth	(634 ct/288 st)		1923-38
Most Career Catches in the Field	556	K.J.Grieves			1949-64

† *W.K.Hegg (1987-2001) has the second-highest aggregate with 751 dismissals (672 ct; 79 st)*

LIMITED-OVERS CRICKET

Highest Total	NWT	381-3		v	Herts	Radlett	1999
	BHC	353-7		v	Notts	Manchester	1995
	NL	301-6		v	Essex	Chelmsford	1999
Lowest Total	NWT	59		v	Worcs	Worcester	1963
	BHC	82		v	Yorkshire	Bradford	1972
	NL	68		v	Yorkshire	Leeds	2000
Highest Innings	NWT	135*	A.Flintoff	v	Surrey	The Oval	2000
	BHC	136	G.Fowler	v	Sussex	Manchester	1991
	NL	143	A.Flintoff	v	Essex	Chelmsford	1999
Best Bowling	NWT	6-18	G.Chapple	v	Essex	Lord's	1996
	BHC	6-10	C.E.H.Croft	v	Scotland	Manchester	1982
	NL	6-25	G.Chapple	v	Yorkshire	Leeds	1998

LEICESTERSHIRE

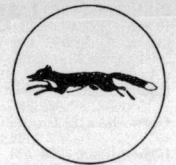

Formation of Present Club: 25 March 1879
Colours: Dark Green and Scarlet
Badge: Gold Running Fox on Green Ground
County Champions: (3) 1975, 1996, 1998
Gillette/NatWest/C & G Trophy Winners: (0); best –
finalist 1992, 2001
Benson and Hedges Cup Winners: (3) 1972, 1975, 1985
NU National League (Div 1) Winners: (0); best – 2nd 2001
Sunday League Champions: (2) 1974, 1977
Match Awards: CGT 47; BHC 75

Secretary/General Manager: J.J.Whitaker, County Ground, Grace Road, Leicester LE2
8AD ▲ Tel: 0116 283 2128 ▲ Fax: 0116 244 0363 ▲ Email: leics@ecb.co.uk ▲ Web:
www.leicestershireccc.co.uk

Captain: V.J.Wells. **Vice-Captain:** I.J.Sutcliffe. **Overseas Player:** M.G.Bevan.
2002 Beneficiary: J.Birkenshaw. **Scorer:** G.A.York. ‡ New registration

ADSHEAD, Stephen John (Bridley Moor HS, Redditch), b Worcester 29 Jan 1980. 5'9".
RHB, WK. Herefordshire 1999. Debut 2000 – awaiting CC debut. HS 0. LO HS 29 Leics
CB v Kent CB (Hinckley) 2001 (CGT).

‡BEVAN, Michael Gwyl (Western Creek HS, Canberra), b Belconnen, ACT, Australia
8 May 1970. 5'11½". LHB, SLC. S Australia 1989-90. NSW 1990-91 to date. Yorkshire
1995-96; cap 1995. Sussex 1998, 2000; cap 1998. **Tests** (A): 18 (1994-95 to 1997-98); HS
91 v P (Lahore) 1994-95; BB 6-82 (10-113 match) v WI (Adelaide) 1996-97. **LOI** (A): 171
(1993-94 to 2001-02); HS 108* v E (Oval) 1997; BB 3-36 v P (Melbourne) 1996-97. Tours
(A): E 1997, 2001; SA 1996-97; I 1996-97; P 1994-95; Z 1991-92 (Aus B). 1000 runs (3);
most – 1598 (1995). HS 203* NSW v WA (Sydney) 1993-94. UK HS 174 Sx v Notts (Hove)
2000. BB 6-82 (*see Tests*). UK BB 3-36 Y v Warwks (Leeds) 1996 and 3-36 Sx v Kent
(Tunbridge W) 1998. Awards: CGT 2; BHC 6. LO HS 157* Sx v Essex (Chelmsford) 2000
(BHC). LO BB 5-29 Y v Sussex (Eastbourne) 1996 (SL).

‡BRANDY, Damien Gareth, b Highgate, London 14 Sep 1981. RHB, RMF. Staff 2002 –
awaiting f-c debut.

‡BRIGNULL, David Stephen (Wyggeston & Queen Elizabeth Inst), b N London 27 Nov
1981. RHB, RMF. Staff 2002 – awaiting f-c debut. LO HS (Leics CB) 9* (NWT). BB 2-35
Leics CB v Warwks CB (Coventry) 2001 (CGT).

BURNS, Neil David (Moulsham HS, Chelmsford), b Chelmsford, Essex 19 Sep 1965. 5'10".
LHB, WK, occ SLA. W Province B 1985-86. Essex 1986. Somerset 1987-93; cap 1987.
Leicestershire debut 2000; cap 2001. Buckinghamshire 1995-99. HS 166 Sm v Glos (Taunton)
1990. Le HS 111 v Glam (Leicester) 2001. LO HS 90* v Northants (Leicester) 2001 (NL).

CROWE, Carl Daniel (Lutterworth GS), b Leicester 25 Nov 1975. 6'0". RHB, OB.
Leicestershire 1995-2001. HS 44* v Northants (Northampton) 1999. BB 4-47 v Surrey
(Oval) 2001. LO HS 19 v SL A (Moratuwa) 1998-99. LO BB 4-30 v Notts (Nottingham)
2001 (NL).

‡CUNLIFFE, Robert John (Banbury S; Banbury TC), b Oxford 8 Nov 1973. 5'10". RHB,
RM. Gloucestershire 1994-2001. Oxfordshire 1991-94. HS 190* v OU (Bristol) 1995. CC
HS 108 v Northants (Northampton) 1999. Awards: BHC 3. LO HS 137* v Surrey (Oval)
1996 (BHC).

‡DAGNALL, Charles Edward (Bridgewater HS, Worsley; UMIST), b Bury, Lancs 10 Jul
1976. 6'3". RHB, RMF. Warwickshire 1999-2001. Cumberland 1997-98. HS (Wa) 6*. BB
6-50 Wa v Derbys (Derby) 2001. Award: BHC 1. LO HS 21* Wa v Worcs (Worcester) 2001
(BHC). LO BB 4-34 Wa v Derbys (Birmingham) 2000 (NL).

DeFREITAS, Phillip Anthony Jason (Willesden HS, London), b Scotts Head, Dominica 18 Feb 1966. 6'0". RHB, RFM. UK resident since 1976. Leicestershire 1985-88; cap 1986. Lancashire 1989-93; cap 1989. Boland 1993-94 and 1995-96. Derbyshire 1994-99; cap 1994; captain 1997 (*part*). *Wisden* 1991. MCC YC. **Tests:** 44 (1986-87 to 1995-96); HS 88 v A (Adelaide) 1994-95; BB 7-70 v SL (Lord's) 1991. **LOI:** 103 (1986-87 to 1997); HS 67 v SL (Faisalabad) 1995-96; BB 4-35 v A (Adelaide) 1986-87. Tours: A 1986-87, 1990-91, 1994-95; WI 1989-90; NZ 1987-88, 1991-92; P 1987-88; I 1992-93; Z 1988-89 (La). HS 123* v Lancs (Leicester) 2000. 50 wkts (12); most – 94 (1986). Took his 1000th f-c wicket 1999. BB 7-21 La v Middx (Lord's) 1989. Le BB 7-44 (13-86 match) v Essex (Southend) 1986. Hat-trick 1994. Awards: CGT 5; BHC 4. LO HS 75* La v Hants (Manchester) 1990 (BHC). LO BB 5-13 La v Cumb (Kendal) 1989 (NWT).

‡**GROVE, Jamie** Oliver (Bury St Edmunds County Upper S), b Bury St Edmunds, Suffolk 3 Jul 1979. 6'1". RHB, RMF. Essex 1998-99. Somerset 2000-01. HS 33 Ex v Surrey (Chelmsford) 1998. Sm HS 19* v Surrey (Taunton) 2001. BB 5-90 v Leics (Leicester) 2000 – on Somerset debut. LO HS 6 (Sm – NL). LO BB 4-36 Sm v Cambs (March) 2001 (CGT).

MADDY, Darren Lee (Wreake Valley C), b Leicester 23 May 1974. 5'9". RHB, RM/OB. Debut 1994; cap 1996. **Tests:** 3 (1999 to 1999-00); HS 24 v SA (Durban) 1999-00. **LOI:** 8 (1998 to 1999-00); HS 53 v Z (Harare) 1999-00. Tours (Eng A): SA 1996-97 (Le), 1998-99, 1999-00 (Eng); SL 1997-98; Z 1998-99; K 1997-98. 1000 runs (2); most – 1060 (1999). HS 202 Eng A v Kenya (Nairobi) 1997-98. Le HS 162 v Durham (Darlington) 1998. BB 5-67 v Northants (Leicester) 2001. Awards: CGT 1; BHC 7 (inc 5 in 1998). LO HS 151 v Minor C (Leicester) 1998 (BHC). LO BB 4-16 v Somerset (Taunton) 2000 (NL).

MALCOLM, Devon Eugene (St Elizabeth THS; Richmond C, Sheffield; Derby CHE), b Kingston, Jamaica 22 Feb 1963. Qualified for England 1987. 6'2". RHB, RF. Derbyshire 1984-97; cap 1989; benefit 1997. Northamptonshire 1998-2000; cap 1999. Leicestershire debut/cap 2001. *Wisden* 1994. **Tests:** 40 (1989 to 1997); HS 29 v A (Sydney) 1994-95; BB 9-57 v SA (Oval) 1994. **LOI:** 10 (1990 to 1993-94); HS 4; BB 3-40 v I (Gwalior) 1992-93. Tours: A 1990-91, 1994-95; SA 1995-96; WI 1989-90, 1991-92 (Eng A), 1993-94; I 1992-93; SL 1992-93. HS 51 De v Surrey (Derby) 1989. Le HS 50 v Somerset (Taunton) 2001. 50 wkts (8); most – 82 (1996). BB 9-57 (*see Tests*). CC BB 8-63 v Surrey (Leicester) 2001. Awards: CGT 1; BHC 2. LO HS 42 De v Surrey (Oval) 1996 (SL). LO BB 7-35 De v Northants (Derby) 1997 (NWT).

NEW, Thomas James, b Sutton in Ashfield, Notts 18 Jan 1985. LHB, WK. Leicestershire summer contract 2001 – awaiting f-c debut. LO HS (Leics CB) 3 (CGT).

STEVENS, Darren Ian (Hinckley C), b Leicester 30 Apr 1976. 5'11". RHB, RM. Debut 1997. HS 130 v Sussex (Arundel) 1999. BB 1-5. Award: CGT 1. LO HS 133 v Northumb (Jesmond) 2000 (NWT). LO BB 2-26 v Wales CB (Swansea) 2001 (CGT).

SUTCLIFFE, Iain John (Leeds GS; Queen's C, Oxford), b Leeds, Yorks 20 Dec 1974. 6'2". LHB, occ OB. Oxford U 1994-96; blue 1995-96; boxing blue 1993-94. Leicestershire debut 1995; cap 1997. Tour (Le): SA 1996-97. 1000 (1): 1004 (2001). HS 203 v Glam (Cardiff) 2001. 167 v Middx (Leicester) 1998. BB 2-21 OU v CU (Lord's) 1996. CC BB 1-7. Awards: CGT 1; BHC 1. LO HS 105* v Notts (Nottingham) 1998 (BHC).

‡**WALKER, George**, b Norwich, Norfolk 12 May 1984. LHB, SLA. Staff 2002 – awaiting f-c debut.

WARD, Trevor Robert (Hextable CS, nr Swanley), b Farningham, Kent 18 Jan 1968. 5'11". RHB, OB. Kent 1986-99; cap 1989; benefit 1999. Leicestershire debut 2000; cap 2001. Tour: Z 1992-93 (K). 1000 runs (6); most – 1648 (1992). HS 235* K v Middx (Canterbury) 1991. Le HS 160* v Northants (Leicester) 2001. BB 2-10 K v Yorks (Canterbury) 1996. Awards: CGT 1; BHC 2. LO HS 131 K v Notts (Nottingham) 1993 (SL). LO BB 3-20 K v Glam (Canterbury) 1989 (SL).

WELLS, Vincent John (Sir William Nottidge S, Whitstable), b Dartford, Kent 6 Aug 1965. 6'0". RHB, RMF. Kent 1988-91. Leicestershire debut 1992; cap 1994; captain 2000 to date; benefit 2001. **LOI:** 9 (1998-99); HS 39 v A (Sydney) 1998-99; BB 3-30 v A (Sydney)

1998-99. Tour (Le): SA 1996-97. 1000 runs (2); most – 1331 (1996). HS 224 v Middx (Lord's) 1997. BB 5-18 v Notts (Worksop) 1998. Hat-trick 1994. Awards: CGT 4; BHC 1. LO HS 201 v Berks (Leicester) 1996 (NWT). LO BB 6-25 v Minor C (Leicester) 1998 (BHC).

WHILEY, Matthew Jeffrey Allen (Harry Carlton CS, East Leake), b Clifton, Nottingham 6 May 1980. 6'5½". RHB, LMF. Nottinghamshire 1998-2000. Leicestershire debut 2001. HS 1*. BB (Nt) 1-44. CC BB 1-54. LO HS – . LO BB 1-68 (v P).

WRIGHT, Ashley Spencer (Belvoir HS; King Edward VII S, Melton Mowbray), b Grantham, Lincs 21 Oct 1980. Elder brother of L.J.Wright. 6'0". RHB, RM. Debut 2001 – awaiting CC debut. Award: CGT 1. HS 30 v P (Leicester) 2001. LO HS 112 Leics CB v Durham CB (Gateshead) 2000 (NWT).

‡WRIGHT, Luke James, b Grantham, Lincs 7 Mar 1985. Younger brother of A.S.Wright. RHB, RM. Staff 2002 – awaiting f-c debut. LO HS 16 Leics CB v Kent CB (Hinckley) 2001 (CGT).

RELEASED/RETIRED
(Having made a first-class County appearance in 2001)

BOSWELL, Scott Antony John (Wolverhampton U), b Fulford, Yorks 11 Sep 1974. 6'5". RHB, RFM. British U 1996. Northamptonshire 1996-98. Leicestershire 1999-2001. HS 35 Nh v Leics (Northampton) 1997. Le HS 20 and Le BB 3-39 v Hants (Southampton) 2000. BB 5-94 Nh v Worcs (Northampton) 1997. LO HS 23* v Yorks (Leicester) 2001 (NL). LO BB 4-44 v Lancs (Leicester) 2001 (CGT).

DAKIN, J. – *see ESSEX.*

DAVIS, Richard Peter (King Ethelbert's S, Birchington; Thanet TC), b Westbrook, Margate, Kent 18 Mar 1966. 6'3". RHB, SLA. Kent 1986-93; cap 1990. Warwickshire 1993-94 to 1995; cap 1994. Gloucestershire 1996-97. Sussex 1998 (L-O matches). Berkshire 2001. Leicestershire debut 2001 taking 6-73 v Northants (Northampton). Tours: SA 1994-95 (Wa); Z 1992-93 (K), 1993-94 (Wa). HS 67 K v Hants (Southampton) 1989. Le HS 51 and BB 6-73 v Northants (Northampton) 2001. 50 wkts (2); most – 74 (1992). BB 7-64 K v Durham (Gateshead) 1992. Award: BHC 1. LO HS 56 Berks v Lincs (Lincoln) 2001 (CGT). LO BB 5-52 K v Somerset (Bath) 1989 (SL).

GRIFFITHS, Paul (Codsall HS, Wolverhampton; Cheltenham & Gloucester CHE, Gloucester), b Wolverhampton, Staffs 14 Sep 1975. 6'7". RHB, RMF. Debut 2000 – awaiting CC debut. HS 4* and BB 2-51 v P (Leicester) 2001.

HABIB, A. – *see ESSEX.*

MARSH, Daniel James (Christ Church GS, Adelaide), b Subiaco, Perth, Australia 14 Jun 1973. Son of R.W.Marsh (WA and Australia 1968-69 to 1983-84). RHB, SLA. S Australia 1993-94 to 1995-96. Tasmania 1996-97 to date. Leicestershire 2001; cap 2001. HS 157 Tas v I (Hobart) 1999-00. Le HS 138* v Somerset (Leicester) 2001. BB 7-57 Tas v NSW (Sydney) 1997-98. Le BB 2-35 v Lancs (Leicester) 2001. LO HS 97* v Surrey (Oval) 2001 (NL). LO BB 4-44 v Notts (Oakham) 2001 (NL).

ORMOND, J. – *see SURREY.*

SHAHID AFRIDI (Ibrahim Alibhai S and Islamia Science C, Karachi), b Kohat 1 Mar 1980. Younger brother of Tariq Afridi (Karachi). 5'11". RHB, LBG. F-c debut (Combined XI v England A) 1995-96. Leicestershire 2001; cap 2001. **Tests** (P): 11 (1998-99 to 2000-01); HS 141 v I (Madras) 1998-99; BB 5-52 v A (Karachi) 1998-99 – on debut. **LOI** (P): 136 (1997-98 to 2001-02); HS 109 v I (Toronto) 1998-99; BB 5-40 v E (Lahore) 2000-01. Scored a 37-ball hundred (*LOI record*) which included 11 sixes (*equalled record*) v SL (Nairobi) 1996-97 in his first LOI innings. HS 164 v Northants (Northampton) 2001. BB 6-101 Habib Bank v KRL (Rawalpindi) 1997-98. Le BB 5-84 v Essex (Chelmsford) 2001. Awards: CGT 2. LO HS 112 Pak A v Ind A (Karachi) 1997-98. LO BB 5-40 (*see LOI*).

SMITH, B.F. – *see WORCESTERSHIRE.*

W.F.Stelling left the staff having made no f-c appearances in 2001.

LEICESTERSHIRE 2001

RESULTS SUMMARY

	Place	Won	Lost	Tied	Drew	No Result
County Championship (1st Division)	5th	5	6		5	
All First-Class Matches		5	7		5	
C & G Trophy	Finalist					
Benson & Hedges Cup	4th in North Group					
NU National League (1st Division)	2nd	11	4			1

COUNTY CHAMPIONSHIP AVERAGES

BATTING AND FIELDING

Cap		M	I	NO	HS	Runs	Avge	100	50	Ct/St
2001	D.J.Marsh	9	16	3	138*	600	46.15	1	5	13
1995	B.F.Smith	16	28	2	180*	1197	46.03	5	2	19
2001	T.R.Ward	12	21	2	160*	872	45.89	4	2	7
2001	Shahid Afridi	5	7	–	164	295	42.14	1	1	6
2001	N.D.Burns	16	26	6	111	834	41.70	1	6	64/3
1998	A.Habib	13	21	2	153	779	41.00	3	3	8
1997	I.J.Sutcliffe	16	29	1	203	911	32.53	2	4	5
1994	V.J.Wells	13	22	1	138	628	29.90	2	2	8
1986	P.A.J.DeFreitas	8	12	1	97	255	23.18	–	2	–
–	D.I.Stevens	7	12	2	63	218	21.80	–	1	2
1996	D.L.Maddy	16	27	1	111	521	20.03	1	2	15
1999	J.Ormond	11	16	5	42	216	19.63	–	–	2
2000	J.M.Dakin	7	11	–	69	211	19.18	–	1	1
–	C.D.Crowe	6	8	1	42	71	10.14	–	–	3
2001	D.E.Malcolm	16	21	7	50	126	9.00	–	1	1
–	M.J.A.Whiley	3	5	1	1*	2	0.50	–	–	–

Also batted (1 match each): S.A.J.Boswell 16*; R.P.Davis 51, 0 (2 ct).

BOWLING

	O	M	R	W	Avge	Best	5wI	10wM
J.M.Dakin	122.3	22	427	16	26.68	4-53	–	–
J.Ormond	452.4	109	1306	48	27.20	5-71	2	–
V.J.Wells	181	47	498	18	27.66	5-36	1	–
P.A.J.DeFreitas	285	62	893	32	27.90	6-65	1	–
D.E.Malcolm	545.1	94	1944	68	28.58	8-63	4	1
D.L.Maddy	224.3	41	777	26	29.88	5-67	1	–
Shahid Afridi	153.1	39	511	11	46.45	5-84	1	–

Also bowled:

	O	M	R	W	Avge	Best	5wI	10wM
R.P.Davis	42	7	161	7	23.00	6-73	1	–
C.D.Crowe	107.1	30	292	8	36.50	4-47	–	–
D.J.Marsh	152.2	43	410	9	45.55	2-35	–	–

S.A.J.Boswell 17-2-74-3; D.I.Stevens 7-1-28-0; I.J.Sutcliffe 17-3-64-3; M.J.A.Whiley 53.1-14-188-2.

The First-Class Averages (pp 113-126) give the records of Leicestershire players in all first-class county matches (their other opponents being the Pakistanis), with the exception of J.Ormond and Shahid Afridi whose full county figures are as above.

LEICESTERSHIRE RECORDS

FIRST-CLASS CRICKET

Highest Total	For 701-4d		v	Worcs	Worcester	1906
	V 761-6d		by	Essex	Chelmsford	1990
Lowest Total	For 25		v	Kent	Leicester	1912
	V 24		by	Glamorgan	Leicester	1971
	24		by	Oxford U	Oxford	1985
Highest Innings	For 261	P.V.Simmons	v	Northants	Leicester	1994
	V 341	G.H.Hirst	for	Yorkshire	Leicester	1905

Highest Partnership for each Wicket

1st	390	B.Dudleston/J.F.Steele	v	Derbyshire	Leicester	1979
2nd	289*	J.C.Balderstone/D.I.Gower	v	Essex	Leicester	1981
3rd	316*	W.Watson/A.Wharton	v	Somerset	Taunton	1961
4th	290*	P.Willey/T.J.Boon	v	Warwicks	Leicester	1984
5th	322	B.F.Smith/P.V.Simmons	v	Notts	Worksop	1998
6th	284	P.V.Simmons/P.A.Nixon	v	Durham	Chester-le-St	1996
7th	219*	J.D.R.Benson/P.Whitticase	v	Hampshire	Bournemouth	1991
8th	172	P.A.Nixon/D.J.Millns	v	Lancashire	Manchester	1996
9th	160	W.W.Odell/R.T.Crawford	v	Worcs	Leicester	1902
10th	228	R.Illingworth/K.Higgs	v	Northants	Leicester	1977

Best Bowling	For 10- 18	G.Geary	v	Glamorgan	Pontypridd	1929
(Innings)	V 10- 32	H.Pickett	for	Essex	Leyton	1895
Best Bowling	For 16- 96	G.Geary	v	Glamorgan	Pontypridd	1929
(Match)	V 16-102	C.Blythe	for	Kent	Leicester	1909

Most Runs – Season		2446	L.G.Berry	(av 52.04)	1937
Most Runs – Career		30143	L.G.Berry	(av 30.32)	1924-51
Most 100s – Season		7	L.G.Berry		1937
		7	W.Watson		1959
		7	B.F.Davison		1982
Most 100s – Career		45	L.G.Berry		1924-51
Most Wkts – Season		170	J.E.Walsh	(av 18.96)	1948
Most Wkts – Career		2130	W.E.Astill	(av 23.19)	1906-39
Most Career W-K Dismissals		903	R.W.Tolchard	(794 ct/109 st)	1965-83
Most Career Catches in the Field		427	M.R.Hallam		1950-70

LIMITED-OVERS CRICKET

Highest Total	NWT	406-5		v	Berkshire	Leicester	1996
	BHC	382-6		v	Minor C	Leicester	1998
	NL	344-4		v	Durham	Chester-le-St	1996
Lowest Total	NWT	56		v	Northants	Leicester	1964
	BHC	56		v	Minor C	Wellington	1982
	NL	36		v	Sussex	Leicester	1973
Highest Innings	NWT	201	V.J.Wells	v	Berkshire	Leicester	1996
	BHC	158*	B.F.Davison	v	Warwicks	Coventry	1972
	NL	152	B.Dudleston	v	Lancashire	Manchester	1975
Best Bowling	NWT	6-20	K.Higgs	v	Staffs	Longton	1975
	BHC	6-25	V.J.Wells	v	Minor C	Leicester	1998
	NL	6-17	K.Higgs	v	Glamorgan	Leicester	1973

MIDDLESEX

Formation of Present Club: 2 February 1864
Colours: Blue
Badge: Three Seaxes
County Champions (since 1890): (10) 1903, 1920, 1921, 1947, 1976, 1980, 1982, 1985, 1990, 1993
Joint Champions: (2) 1949, 1977
Gillette/NatWest/C & G Trophy Winners: (4) 1977, 1980, 1984, 1988
Benson and Hedges Cup Winners: (2) 1983, 1986
NU National League (Div 1) Winners: (0); best – 4th (Div 2) 2000
Sunday League Winners: (1) 1992
Match Awards: CGT 58; BHC 62

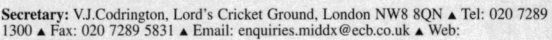

Secretary: V.J.Codrington, Lord's Cricket Ground, London NW8 8QN ▲ Tel: 020 7289 1300 ▲ Fax: 020 7289 5831 ▲ Email: enquiries.middx@ecb.co.uk ▲ Web: www.middlesexccc.com

Captain: A.R.C.Fraser. **Vice-Captain:** A.J.Strauss. **Overseas Player:** Abdul Razzaq.
2002 Beneficiary: P.N.Weekes. **Scorer:** M.J.Smith. ‡ New registration

‡**ABDUL RAZZAQ** (Furqan Model HS, Shahdara, Lahore), b Lahore 2 Dec 1979. 5'11". RHB, RFM. F-c debut (Lahore City) 1996-97. **Tests** (P): 19 (1999-00 to 2001-02); HS 134 v B (Dhaka) 2001-02; BB 4-24 v WI (Sharjah) 2001-02. Hat-trick 1999-00. **LOI** (P): 95 (1996-97 to 2001-02); HS 75* (off 40 balls) v E (Karachi) 2000-01; BB 6-35 v B (Dhaka) 2001-02. Tours: E 2001; A 1999-00; WI 1999-00; SL 1999-00; B 2001-02. HS 117 KRL v Customs (Faisalabad) 1997-98. UK HS 53 P v E (Lord's) 2001. BB 7-51 Lahore City v Karachi Whites (Thatta) 1996-97 – on debut. UK BB 3-61 P v E (Manchester) 2001. LO HS 87* KRL v Islamabad (Rawalpindi) 1997-98. LO BB 5-31 (*see LOI*).

ALLEYNE, David (Enfield GS; Hertford Regional C; City & Islington C), b York 17 Apr 1976. 5'11". RHB, WK. Debut 2001. HS 44 v Glos (Lord's) 2001. LO HS 58 v Notts (Nottingham) 2000 (NL).

BLOOMFIELD, Timothy Francis (Halliford S, Shepperton), b Ashford 31 May 1973. 6'2". RHB, RMF. Debut 1997; cap 2001. Berkshire 1996. HS 28 v Sussex (Hove) 2001. 50 wkts (1): 50 (2001). BB 5-36 v Glam (Cardiff) 1999. Award: CGT 1. LO HS 15 v Warwks (Lord's) 1998 (SL). LO BB 4-17 v Somerset (Southgate) 2000 (NWT).

BROWN, Michael James (Queen Elizabeth GS, Blackburn; Collingwood C, Durham U), b Burnley, Lancs 9 Feb 1980. 6'0". RHB, OB. Debut 1999. Durham UCCE 2001. British U 2001. HS 60* DU v Worcs (Worcester) 2001. M HS 24* v CU (Cambridge) 1999 – on debut. CC HS 10 v Warwks (Lord's) 2001.

‡**COLEMAN, Alan** James (Longford Community S), b Ashford 13 Dec 1983. LO HS 11* v Glam (Cardiff) 2001 (NL). Staff 2002 – awaiting f-c debut.

‡**COMPTON, Nicholas** Richard Denis (Harrow S), b Durban, SA 26 Jun 1983. 6'1". Grandson of D.C.S.Compton (Middlesex, England, Holkar, Europeans, Commonwealth and Cavaliers 1936-64); great-nephew of L.H.Compton (Middlesex 1938-56). RHB, OB. Staff 2002 – awaiting f-c debut. LO HS 6 (NL).

COOK, Simon James (Matthew Arnold S), b Oxford 15 Jan 1977. 6'4". RHB, RM. Debut 1999. HS 93* v Notts (Lord's) 2000. HS 43 v Essex (Lord's) 2000. LO HS 50 v Glam (Cardiff) 2001 (NL). LO BB 3-16 v Glam (Cardiff) 1999 (NL).

CREESE, Matthew Leonard (Goffs S; Durham U), b Enfield 13 Feb 1982. 6'2". LHB, SLA. Debut 1999 – awaiting CC debut. 2nd XI debut when aged 15y 188d. No appearances 2000-01. HS 4 and BB 1-37 v CU (Cambridge) 1999 – on debut.

DALRYMPLE, James William Murray (Radley C; St Peter's C, Oxford), b Nairobi, Kenya 21 Jan 1981. 5'11". RHB, OB. Oxford UCCE 2001. OU 2001; blue 2001. British U 2001. Middlesex debut 2001. HS 70 OU v Warwks (Oxford) 2001. M HS 11 and BB 1-113 v Warwks (Lord's) 2001 – on county debut. BB 4-86 OU v CU (Cambridge) 2001. LO HS 38* v Essex (Colchester) 2001 (NL). LO BB 4-14 v Essex (Southgate) 2001 (NL).

‡**DUNCAN, Ben**, b (in UK) 21 Nov 1983. RHB, RM. Summer contract 2002 – awaiting f-c debut.

FOLLETT, David (Moorland Road HS, Burslem; Stoke-on-Trent TC), b Newcastle-under-Lyme, Staffs 14 Oct 1968. 6'2". RHB, RFM. Middlesex 1995-96. Northamptonshire 1997-99. Staffordshire 1994, 2000-01. HS 19 Nh v Surrey (Northampton) 1999. BB 8-22 (10-87 match) v Durham (Lord's) 1996. Nh BB 3-48 Nh v Glos (Bristol) 1998. LO HS 10* Nh v SL (Northampton) 1998. LO BB 4-17 Staffs v Herts (Welwyn) 2001 (CGT).

FRASER, Angus Robert Charles (Gayton HS, Harrow; Orange Hill HS, Edgware), b Billinge, Lancs 8 Aug 1965. Brother of A.G.J.Fraser (Middx and Essex 1986-92). 6'5". RHB, RMF. Debut 1984; cap 1988; benefit 1997; captain 2001 to date. MBE 1999. *Wisden* 1995. **Tests:** 46 (1989 to 1998-99); HS 32 v SL (Oval) 1998; BB 8-53 (11-110 match) v WI (P-of-S) 1997-98 – record England innings analysis v WI. **LOI:** 42 (1989-90 to 1999); HS 38* v A (Melbourne) 1990-91; BB 4-22 v A (Melbourne) 1994-95. Tours: A 1990-91, 1994-95 (part), 1998-99; SA 1995-96; WI 1989-90, 1993-94, 1997-98. HS 92 v Surrey (Oval) 1990. 50 wkts (7); most – 92 (1989). BB 8-53 (*see Tests*). M BB 7-40 v Leics (Lord's) 1993. LO HS 38* (*see LOI*). LO BB 5-32 v Derbys (Lord's) 1995 (SL).

‡**HOLT, David** Robert (St Benedict's S, Ealing; London U), b Hammersmith, London 29 Dec 1981. RHB, RM. MCC YC 2001. Summer contract 2002 – awaiting f-c debut.

HUNT, Thomas Aaron *'Thos'* (Acton HS; St Clement Danes S), b Melbourne, Australia 19 Jan 1982. 6'2". RHB, RMF. Staff 1999 – awaiting f-c debut. LO HS – . LO BB 1-32 (v A).

HUTTON, Benjamin Leonard (Radley C; Durham U), b Johannesburg, SA 29 Jan 1977. Elder son of R.A.Hutton (Yorkshire, Transvaal & England 1962 to 1975-76); grandson of Sir Leonard (Yorkshire and England 1934-60). 6'2". LHB, RMF. British U 1998-99. Middlesex debut 2001. HS 139 v Derbys (Southgate) 2001. BB 2-9 v Glam (Southgate) 2000. LO HS 77 v Durham (Chester-le-St) 2001 (NL). LO BB 5-45 v Derbys (Southgate) 2001 (NL).

JOYCE, Edmund Christopher (Presentation C, Bray, Co Wicklow; Trinity C, Dublin), b Dublin, Ireland 22 Sep 1978. 5'11". LHB, RM. Ireland 1997 to date. Middlesex debut 1999. HS 108* v Worcs (Worcester) 2001. LO HS 73 Ire v Warwks (Birmingham) 1998 (NWT).

KEEGAN, Chad Blake (Durban HS), b Sandton, near Johannesburg, SA 30 Jul 1979. 6'1". RHB, RF. Debut 2001. MCC YC. HS 30* v Warwks (Birmingham) 2001. BB 4-54 v Hants (Southampton) 2001. LO HS 16 v Essex (Colchester) 2001 (NL). LO BB 5-17 v Hants (Southgate) 2001 (NL).

‡**KOENIG, Sven** Gaetan (Hilton C; Cape Town U), b Durban, SA 9 Dec 1973. ECB qualified – EU (Italian) passport. 5'10". LHB, OB. Western Province 1993-94 to 1996-97. Transvaal/Gauteng 1997-98 to 2000-01. Tour (SA A): E 1996. HS 155 Gauteng v GW (Kimberley) 2000-01. BB 1-0. LO HS 109 Gauteng v Border (Jo'burg) 2000-01 (SBC). LO BB – .

LARAMAN, Aaron William (Enfield GS), b Enfield 10 Jan 1979. 6'5". RHB, RFM. Debut 1998. HS 29 and CC BB 2-20 v Derbys (Southgate) 2001. BB 4-33 v CU (Cambridge) 2000. LO HS 16* v Herefords (Kingsland) 2001 (CGT). LO BB 6-42 v Glam (Cardiff) 2000 (NL).

MAUNDERS, John Kenneth (Ashford HS; Spelthorne C), b Ashford 4 Apr 1981. 5'10". LHB, RM. Debut 1999 (awaiting CC debut). Middx 2nd XI debut aged 16y 19d. No appearances 2000-01. HS 9. LO HS 49 v Glam (Cardiff) 2001 (NL).

NASH, David Charles (Sunbury Manor S; Malvern C), b Chertsey, Surrey 19 Jan 1978. 5'8". RHB, occ LB, WK. Debut 1997; cap 2000. Tour: SL 1997-98 (Eng A). HS 114 v Somerset (Lord's) 1998. BB 1-8. LO HS 58 v Herefords (Kingsland) 2001 (CGT).

‡**RENDELL, Carlo** Stefan (Durham U), b Perth, Australia 9 Dec 1982. RHB, LMF. Summer contract 2002 – awaiting f-c debut.

SHAH, Owais Alam (Isleworth & Syon S), b Karachi, Pakistan 22 Oct 1978. 6'0". RHB, OB. Debut 1996; cap 2000. YC 2001. **LOI**: 9 (2001 to 2001-02); HS 62 v P (Lord's) 2001. Tours (Eng A): A 1996-97; SL 1997-98. 1000 (1): 1040 (2001). HS 203 v Derbys (Southgate) 2001. BB 3-33 v Glos (Bristol) 1999. Award: BHC 1. LO HS 134 v Sussex (Arundel) 1999 (NL). LO BB 2-2 v Glam (Cardiff) 1998 (BHC).

STRAUSS, Andrew John (Radley C; Durham U), b Johannesburg, SA 2 Mar 1977. 5'11". LHB, LM. Debut 1998; cap 2001. Oxfordshire 1996. 1000 (1): 1211 (2001). HS 176 v Durham (Lord's) 2001. LO HS 90 v Durham (Chester-le-St) 2000 (NL).

TUFNELL, Philip Clive Roderick (Highgate S), b Barnet, Herts 29 Apr 1966. 6'0". RHB, SLA. Debut 1986; cap 1990; benefit 1999. MCC YC. **Tests**: 42 (1990-91 to 2001); HS 22* v I (Madras) 1992-93; BB 7-47 (11-147 match) v NZ (Christchurch) 1991-92, took 11-93 v A (Oval) 1997. **LOI**: 20 (1990-91 to 1996-97); HS 5*; BB 4-22 v NZ (Christchurch) 1996-97. Tours: A 1990-91, 1994-95; SA 1999-00; WI 1993-94, 1997-98; NZ 1991-92, 1996-97; I/SL 1992-93, Z 1996-97. HS 67* v Worcs (Lord's) 1996. 50 wkts (9); most – 88 (1991). BB 8-29 v Glam (Cardiff) 1993. Award: CGT 1. LO HS 18 v Warwks (Lord's) 1991 (BHC). LO BB 5-28 v Leics (Lord's) 1993 (SL).

WEEKES, Paul Nicholas (Homerton House SS, Hackney), b Hackney, London 8 Jul 1969. 5'10". LHB, OB. Debut 1990; cap 1993; benefit 2002. Tour: I 1994-95 (Eng A). MCC YC. 1000 runs (1): 1218 (1996). HS 171* v Somerset (Uxbridge) 1996. BB 8-39 v Glam (Lord's) 1996. Awards: CGT 2; BHC 4. LO HS 143* v Cornwall (St Austell) 1995 (NWT). LO BB 4-17 v Kent (Lord's) 2001 (BHC).

WESTON, Robin Michael Swann (Durham S; Loughborough U), b Durham 7 Jun 1975. Brother of W.P.C.Weston (*see WORCESTERSHIRE*). 5'10". RHB, LB. Durham 1995-97. Derbyshire 1998-99 (scored 72, 129*, 22, 124 and 156 in consecutive CC innings 1999). Middlesex debut 2000; cap 2001. Minor C debut 1991 when aged 15yr 355d (Durham record). HS 156 De v Somerset (Derby) 1999. M HS 135* v Hants (Southgate) 2001. BB 1-15 (De). LO HS 80* v Derbys (Southgate) 2001 (NL).

RELEASED/RETIRED
(Having made a first-class County appearance in 2001)

FLEMING, Stephen Paul (Cashmere HS, Canterbury; Christchurch C), b Christchurch, New Zealand 1 Apr 1973. 6'3". LHB. Canterbury 1991-92 to date. Middlesex 2001; cap 2001. **Tests** (NZ): 65 (1993-94 to 2001-02, 43 as captain); HS 174* v SL (Colombo) 1997-98. **LOI** (NZ): 170 (1993-94 to 2001-02, 110 as captain); HS 116* v A (Melbourne) 1997-98; BB 1-8. Tours (NZ) (C=captain): E 1994, 1999C; A 1997-98C, 2001-02C; SA 1993-94 (Cant), 1994-95, 2000-01C; WI 1995-96; I 1995-96, 1999-00C; P 1996-97; SL 1997-98C; Z 1997-98C, 2000-01C. 1000 (1): 1091 (2001). HS 174* (*see Tests*). M HS 151 v Notts (Nottingham) 2001. LO HS 120* Wellington v Otago (Wellington) 2000-01. LO BB (NZ) 1-3.

HEWITT, J.P. – *see KENT*.

ROSEBERRY, Michael Anthony (Durham S), b Sunderland 28 Nov 1966. Elder brother of A.Roseberry (Leics and Glam 1992-94). 6'1". RHB, RM. Middlesex 1986-94 and 1999-2001; cap 1990; benefit 2000. Durham 1995-98; captain 1995-96; cap 1998. Tour: A 1992-93 (Eng A). 1000 runs (4) inc 2000 (1): 2044 (1992). HS 185 v Leics (Lord's) 1993. BB 1-1. Awards: CGT 1; BHC 1. LO HS 121 Du v Herefords (Chester-le-St) 1995 (NWT). LO BB 1-22 (NWT).

R.B.Bryan left the staff having made no f-c appearances in 2001.

MIDDLESEX 2001

RESULTS SUMMARY

	Place	Won	Lost	Tied	Drew	No Result
County Championship (2nd Division)	5th	4	3		9	
All First-Class Matches		4	3		10	
C & G Trophy	3rd Round					
Benson & Hedges Cup	3rd in South Group					
NU National League (2nd Division)	8th	3	9	1		3

COUNTY CHAMPIONSHIP AVERAGES

BATTING AND FIELDING

Cap		M	I	NO	HS	Runs	Avge	100	50	Ct/St
2001	S.P.Fleming	13	21	2	151	1059	55.73	4	6	20
2001	A.J.Strauss	16	26	1	176	1208	48.32	3	6	7
–	E.C.Joyce	3	6	1	108*	234	46.80	2	–	5
2001	R.M.S.Weston	10	17	1	135*	671	41.93	3	1	5
2000	O.A.Shah	14	23	–	203	955	41.52	3	3	13
2000	D.C.Nash	14	18	5	103*	456	35.07	1	4	35/4
–	B.L.Hutton	13	20	1	139	648	34.10	2	2	20
–	S.J.Cook	9	10	3	93*	226	32.28	–	1	3
1993	P.N.Weekes	16	25	4	107	659	31.38	1	4	14
1990	M.A.Roseberry	10	15	2	63	328	25.23	–	1	8
–	D.Alleyne	2	4	–	44	55	13.75	–	–	4
1988	A.R.C.Fraser	12	11	–	41	144	13.09	–	–	3
2001	T.F.Bloomfield	15	15	3	28	85	7.08	–	–	2
–	C.B.Keegan	7	10	2	30*	45	5.62	–	–	1
1998	J.P.Hewitt	4	5	1	10*	22	5.50	–	–	1
1990	P.C.R.Tufnell	15	17	7	11*	44	4.40	–	–	–

Also batted (1 match each): M.J.Brown 0, 10; J.W.M.Dalrymple 11, 0* (2 ct); A.W.Laraman 29 (1 ct).

BOWLING

	O	M	R	W	Avge	Best	5wI	10wM
P.C.R.Tufnell	626.3	155	1510	57	26.49	6-44	3	1
P.N.Weekes	427.5	95	1179	40	29.47	5-90	1	–
C.B.Keegan	170	38	588	18	32.66	4-54	–	–
T.F.Bloomfield	451.4	67	1653	47	35.17	5-58	2	–
A.R.C.Fraser	448.4	129	1176	31	37.93	3-46	–	–
J.P.Hewitt	83	8	386	10	38.60	3-72	–	–
S.J.Cook	196.1	36	663	14	47.35	3-59	–	–

Also bowled: J.W.M.Dalrymple 30-1-113-1; S.P.Fleming 2-0-19-0; B.L.Hutton 9-0-48-0; A.W.Laraman 4.5-1-20-2; O.A.Shah 5-1-38-0; A.J.Strauss 1-0-3-0.

The First-Class Averages (pp 113-126) give the records of Middlesex players in all first-class county matches (Middlesex's other opponents being Oxford University), with the exception of M.J.Brown and J.W.M.Dalrymple, whose full county figures are as above, and: P.C.R.Tufnell 16-18-7-11*-45-4.09-0-0-0ct. 651-164-1547-59-26.22-6/44-3-1.

MIDDLESEX RECORDS

FIRST-CLASS CRICKET

Highest Total	For 642-3d		v	Hampshire	Southampton	1923
	V 665		by	W Indians	Lord's	1939
Lowest Total	For 20		v	MCC	Lord's	1864
	V 31		by	Glos	Bristol	1924
Highest Innings	For 331*	J.D.B.Robertson	v	Worcs	Worcester	1949
	V 316*	J.B.Hobbs	for	Surrey	Lord's	1926

Highest Partnership for each Wicket

1st	372	M.W.Gatting/J.L.Langer	v	Essex	Southgate	1998
2nd	380	F.A.Tarrant/J.W.Hearne	v	Lancashire	Lord's	1914
3rd	424*	W.J.Edrich/D.C.S.Compton	v	Somerset	Lord's	1948
4th	325	J.W.Hearne/E.H.Hendren	v	Hampshire	Lord's	1919
5th	338	R.S.Lucas/T.C.O'Brien	v	Sussex	Hove	1895
6th	270	J.D.Carr/P.N.Weekes	v	Glos	Lord's	1994
7th	271*	E.H.Hendren/F.T.Mann	v	Notts	Nottingham	1925
8th	182*	M.H.C.Doll/H.R.Murrell	v	Notts	Lord's	1913
9th	160*	E.H.Hendren/T.J.Durston	v	Essex	Leyton	1927
10th	230	R.W.Nicholls/W.Roche	v	Kent	Lord's	1899

Best Bowling (Innings)	For 10- 40	G.O.B.Allen	v	Lancashire	Lord's	1929
	V 9- 38	R.C.R-Glasgow†	for	Somerset	Lord's	1924
Best Bowling (Match)	For 16-114	G.Burton	v	Yorkshire	Sheffield	1888
	16-114	J.T.Hearne	v	Lancashire	Manchester	1898
	V 16-109	C.W.L.Parker	for	Glos	Cheltenham	1930

Most Runs – Season	2669	E.H.Hendren	(av 83.41)	1923
Most Runs – Career	40302	E.H.Hendren	(av 48.81)	1907-37
Most 100s – Season	13	D.C.S.Compton		1947
Most 100s – Career	119	E.H.Hendren		1907-37
Most Wkts – Season	158	F.J.Titmus	(av 14.63)	1955
Most Wkts – Career	2361	F.J.Titmus	(av 21.27)	1949-82
Most Career W-K Dismissals	1223	J.T.Murray	(1024 ct/199 st)	1952-75
Most Career Catches in the Field	561	E.H.Hendren		1907-37

LIMITED-OVERS CRICKET

Highest Total	NWT	304-7	v	Surrey	The Oval	1995
		304-8	v	Cornwall	St Austell	1995
	BHC	325-5	v	Leics	Leicester	1992
	NL	290-6	v	Worcs	Lord's	1990
Lowest Total	NWT	41	v	Essex	Westcliff	1972
	BHC	73	v	Essex	Lord's	1985
	NL	23	v	Yorkshire	Leeds	1974
Highest Innings	NWT	158	G.D.Barlow	v	Lancashire	Lord's	1984
	BHC	143*	M.W.Gatting	v	Sussex	Hove	1985
	NL	147*	M.R.Ramprakash	v	Worcs	Lord's	1990
Best Bowling	NWT	6-15	W.W.Daniel	v	Sussex	Hove	1980
	BHC	7-12	W.W.Daniel	v	Minor C (E)	Ipswich	1978
	NL	6- 6	R.W.Hooker	v	Surrey	Lord's	1969

† R.C.Robertson-Glasgow

NORTHAMPTONSHIRE

Formation of Present Club: 31 July 1878
Colours: Maroon
Badge: Tudor Rose
County Champions: (0); best – 2nd 1912, 1957, 1965, 1976
Gillette/NatWest/C & G Trophy Winners: (2) 1976, 1992
Benson and Hedges Cup Winners: (1) 1980
NU National League (Div 1) Winners: (0); best – 3rd 2000
Sunday League Winners: (0); best – 3rd 1991
Match Awards: CGT 55; BHC 58

Chief Executive: S.P.Coverdale, County Ground, Wantage Road, Northampton, NN1 4TJ ▲ Tel: 01604 514455 ▲ Fax: 01604 514488 ▲ Email: post@nccc.co.uk ▲ Web: www.nccc.co.uk

Captain/Overseas Player: M.E.K.Hussey. **Vice-Captain:** A.L.Penberthy.
2002 Beneficiary: A.L.Penberthy. **Scorer:** A.C.Kingston. ‡ New registration

‡**ANDERSON, Ricaldo** Sherman Glenroy (Alperton HS; Barnet C; North West London C; London Cricket C), b Hammersmith, London 22 Sep 1976. 5'10". RHB, RFM. Essex 1999-2001. HS 67* Ex v Sussex (Chelmsford) 2000. 50 wkts (1): 50 (1999). BB 6-34 (11-111 match) Ex v Northants (Ilford) 2000. LO HS 22 Ex v Sussex (Hove) 2001 (NL). LO BB 3-32 Ex v Glos (Bristol) 1999 (NL).

BAILEY, Tobin Michael Barnaby (Bedford S; Loughborough U), b Kettering 28 Aug 1976. 5'10". RHB, WK. Debut 1996. British U 1998. Bedfordshire 1994-96. HS 96* v Worcs (Worcester) 2000. LO HS 52 Brit U v Glos (Bristol) 1997.

‡**BAKER, Thomas** Michael (Whitcliffe Mount S; Huddersfield TC), b Dewsbury, Yorks 6 Jul 1981. 6'4". RHB, RFM. Yorkshire staff 2001 – no f-c appearances. LO HS (Y) 3 (BHC). LO BB 2-13 Y v Derbys (Leeds) 2001 (BHC).

BLAIN, John Angus Rae (Penicuik HS; Jewel & Esk Valley C), b Edinburgh, Scotland 4 Jan 1979. 6'1". RHB, RMF. Scotland 1996-99. Northamptonshire debut 1997. **LOI** (Scot): 5 (1999); HS 9 and BB 4-37 v B (Edinburgh) 1999. HS 34 v Surrey (Northampton) 2001. BB 6-42 v Kent (Canterbury) 2001. LO HS 11 v Worcs (Kidderminster) 2001 (BHC). LO BB 5-24 v Derbys (Derby) 1997 (SL).

‡**BROPHY, Gerard** Louis (Welkom BC; Boksburg BC; Witwatersrand TC), b Welkom, SA 26 Nov 1975. ECB qualified – British/EU passport. RHB, WK. Transvaal 1996-97 to 1998-99. Free State 1999-00 to 2000-01. HS 185 SA Academy v Zim President's XI (Harare) 1998-99. LO HS 50* FS v Gauteng (Jo'burg) 1999-00.

BROWN, Jason Fred (St Margaret Ward HS & SFC), b Newcastle-under-Lyme, Staffs 10 Oct 1974. 6'0". RHB, OB. Debut 1996; cap 2000. Staffordshire 1994-95. Tours: WI 2000-01 (part) (Eng A); SL 2000-01 (no f-c). HS 35* v Leics (Northampton) 2001. 50 wkts (1): 61 (2000). BB 7-78 (11-131 match) v Sussex (Northampton) 2000. LO HS 5* (twice) (BHC). LO BB 4-26 v Leics (Northampton) 1997 (SL).

CASSAR, Matthew Edward (Sir Joseph Banks HS, Sydney; Manchester Metropolitan U), b Sydney, Australia 16 Oct 1972. Husband of Jane Cassar (née Smit; England 1991-92 to date). 6'0". RHB, RFM. Derbyshire 1994-2000. ECB qualified/CC debut 1997. Northamptonshire debut 2001. HS 121 De v Sussex (Horsham) 1998. Nh HS 9. BB 6-76 De v Yorks (Derby) 2000. Award: CGT 1. LO HS 134 De v Northants (Northampton) 1998 (SL). LO BB 4-29 De v Hants (Southampton) 2000 (NL).

‡**CAWDRON, Michael** John (Cheltenham C), b Luton, Beds 7 Oct 1974. 6'2". LHB, RM. Gloucestershire staff 1994-2001; debut 1999 – taking 15 wickets in first four innings. HS 42 and CC BB 5-35 Gs v Hants (Bristol) 1999 – on debut. BB 6-25 (10-74 match) FCC Select XI v NZ A (Milton Keynes) 2000. LO HS 50 Gs v Essex (Cheltenham) 1995 (SL). LO BB 4-17 Gs v Warwks (Cheltenham) 1999 (NL).

COOK, Jeffrey William (James Cook HS, Kogarah, NSW), b Sydney, Australia 2 Feb 1972. 6'4". LHB, RM. Resident in UK since 1993 – ECB qualified 2000. Debut 2000. NSW U-19. HS 137 v Glos (Cheltenham) 2000. BB 1-17. Award: CGT 1. LO HS 130 Northants CB v Wilts (Northampton) 1999 (NWT). LO BB 2-44 v Somerset (Taunton) 2001 (NL).

COUSINS, Darren Mark (Netherhall CS; Impington Village C), b Cambridge 24 Sep 1971. 6'2". RHB, RMF. Essex 1993-98. Surrey (NL only) 1999. Northamptonshire debut/cap 2000. Cambridgeshire 1990, 1999. HS 29* v Glam (Northampton) 2000. 50 wkts (1): 67 (2000). BB 8-102 v Yorks (Leeds) 2001. LO HS 18 v Yorks (Northampton) 2000 (NL). LO BB 4-23 v Worcs (Kidderminster) 2001 (BHC).

‡**GREENIDGE, Carl** Gary (Lodge S and St Michael S, Barbados; Heathcote S, Chingford; W Hatch S; City of Westminster C), b Basingstoke, Hants 20 Apr 1978. Son of C.Gordon Greenidge (Hampshire, Barbados and West Indies 1970-92). RHB, RMF. MCC YC. Surrey 1999-2000. HS 14 Sy v SL A (Oval) 1999. CC HS (Sy) 6. BB 5-60 (8-124 match) Sy v Yorks (Oval) 1999 – on CC debut. LO HS (Sy) 3* (NL). LO BB 2-17 Sy v Somerset (Oval) 2001 (NL).

HUSSEY, Michael Edward Killeen (Prindiville Catholic C; Curtin U), b Morley, Perth, Australia 27 May 1975. 5'11". LHB, RM. W Australia 1994-95 to date. Northamptonshire debut/cap 2001. Captain 2002. Tour (Aus A): Sc/Ire 1998. HS 329* v Essex (Northampton) 2001 – Northants record. 1000 runs (1): 2055 (2001). BB 2-21 WA v Q (Perth) 1998-99. Nh BB 1-14. Awards: BHC 2. LO HS 114* v Glam (Cardiff) 2001 (BHC). LO BB 3-52 WA v Vic (Melbourne) 1999-00 (MM).

INNES, Kevin John (Weston Favell Upper S), b Wellingborough 24 Sep 1975. 5'10". RHB, RM. 2nd XI debut 1990 (aged 14yr 8m – Northamptonshire record). Debut 1994. HS 63 and BB 4-61 v Lancs (Northampton) 1996. LO HS 55 v Worcs (Worcester) 2000 (NL). LO BB 4-36 v Kent (Northampton) 2000 (NL).

LOYE, Malachy Bernhard (Moulton S), b Northampton 27 Sep 1972. 6'2". RHB, OB. Debut 1991; cap 1994. Tours (Eng A): SA 1993-94, 1998-99; Z 1994-95 (Nh), 1998-99. 1000 runs (3); most – 1198 (1998). HS 322* v Glam (Northampton) 1998 – record Northants score until 2001. Awards: CGT 1; BHC 1. LO HS 124* v Northants CB (Northampton) 2001 (CGT).

PANESAR, Mudhsuden Singh *'Monty'* (Stopsley HS; Bedford Modern S; Loughborough U), b Luton, Beds 25 Apr 1982. 6'0". LHB, SLA. Bedfordshire 1998-99. Debut 2001. HS 10 and BB 4-11 (8-131 match) v Leics (Northampton) 2001 – on debut.

PENBERTHY, Anthony Leonard (Camborne CS), b Troon, Cornwall 1 Sep 1969. 6'1". LHB, RM. Debut 1989; cap 1994; benefit 2002. Cornwall 1987-89. Tours (Nh): SA 1991-92; Z 1994-95. RHB, occ WK, occ RM. HS 132* v Glam (Northampton) 2001. BB 5-37 v Glam (Swansea) 1993. Took wicket of M.A.Taylor (A) with his first ball in f-c cricket. Award: CGT 1. LO HS 81* v Surrey (Northampton) 1997 (SL). LO BB 5-29 v Glos (Bristol) 2000 (NL).

‡**PHILLIPS, Ben** James (Langley Park S and SFC, Beckenham), b Lewisham, London 30 Sep 1974. 6'6". RHB, RFM. Kent 1996-99. HS 100* K v Lancs (Manchester) 1997. BB 5-47 K v Sussex (Horsham) 1997. Award: CGT 1. LO HS K 29 v Glam (Cardiff) 1996 (SL). LO BB 4-25 K v Northants (Canterbury) 2000 (NL).

POWELL, Mark John (Campion S, Bugbrooke; Loughborough U), b Northampton 4 Nov 1980. 5'11". RHB, OB. Debut 2000. HS 1 (twice).

ROLLINS, Adrian Stewart (Little Ilford CS), b Barking, Essex 8 Feb 1972. Brother of R.J.Rollins (Essex 1992-99). 6'5". RHB, occ WK, occ RM. Derbyshire 1993-99; cap 1995. Northamptonshire debut 2000. 1000 runs (3); most – 1142 (1997). HS 210 De v Hants (Chesterfield) 1997. Nh HS 100 v Middx (Lord's) 2000. BB (De) 1-19. LO HS 126* De v Surrey (Derby) 1995 (SL).

63

SALES, David John Grimwood (Caterham S; Cumnor House S), b Carshalton, Surrey 3 Dec 1977. 6'0". RHB, RM. Debut 1996 v Worcs (Kidderminster) scoring 0 and 210* – record Championship score on f-c debut; youngest (18yr 237d) to score 200 in a Championship match; cap 1999. Tours (Eng A): NZ 1999-00; SL 1997-98; K 1997-98; B 1999-00. Sustained severe knee injury prior to start of England A tour of WI 2000-01 – no f-c appearances 2001. 1000 runs (1): 1291 (1999). HS 303* v Essex (Northampton) 1999 – youngest Englishman (21yr 240d) to score a f-c 300. BB 4-25 v SL A (Northampton) 1999. CC BB 2-7 v Yorks (Scarborough) 1999. Award: BHC 1. LO HS 91* v SL (Northampton) 1998.

SWANN, Graeme Peter (Sponne SS, Towcester), b Northampton 24 Mar 1979. Son of R.Swann (Northumberland 1969-72; Bedfordshire 1988-95); younger brother of A.J.Swann (see *LANCASHIRE*). 6'0". RHB, OB. Debut 1998; cap 1999. Bedfordshire 1996. **LOI**: 1 (1999-00); dnb v SA (Bloemfontein) 1999-00. Tours (Eng A): SA 1998-99, 1999-00 (Eng); WI 2000-01 (*part*); Z 1998-99. HS 130* v SL A (Northampton) 1999. CC HS 111 v Leics (Leicester) 1998. 50 wkts (1): 57 (1999). BB 6-41 (11-126 match) v Leics (Northampton) 1999. LO HS 83 v Leics (Northampton) 2001 (NL). LO BB 5-35 v Durham (Chester-le-St) 1999 (NL).

WARREN, Russell John (Kingsthorpe Upper S), b Northampton 10 Sep 1971. 6'1". RHB, OB. Debut 1992; cap 1995. 1000 (1): 1303 (2001). HS 201* v Glam (Northampton) 1996. Award: CGT 1. LO HS 100* v Ire (Northampton) 1994 (NWT).

WEEKES, Lesroy Charlesworth (Montserrat HS; Montserrat Sports C), b Montserrat, WI 19 Jul 1971. 6'2". RHB, RFM. Leeward Is 1993-94 to 1996-97. Yorkshire (two matches as an unregistered player) 1994, 2000. Northamptonshire debut 2001. HS 46 Leeward Is v Guyana (Blairmont, Berbice) 1993-94. Nh HS 44* and Nh BB 3-51 v Leics (Leicester) 2001. BB 6-56 Y v WI (Leeds) 2000. LO HS 11 v A (Northampton) 2001. LO BB 4-33 Leeward Is v Guyana (Georgetown) 1994-95 (SST).

WHITE, Robert Allan (Stowe S; Durham U; Loughborough U), b Chelmsford, Essex 15 Oct 1979. 5'11". RHB, LB. Debut 2000. HS 20 v OU (Oxford) 2000 – on debut. CC HS 4.

RELEASED/RETIRED
(Having made a first-class County appearance in 2001)

RIPLEY, David (Royds SS, Leeds), b Leeds, Yorks 13 Sep 1966. 5'9". RHB, WK. Northamptonshire 1984-2001; cap 1987; benefit 1997; captain 2001. Tours (Nh): SA 1991-92; Z 1994-95. HS 209 v Glam (Northampton) 1998. BB 2-89 v Essex (Ilford) 1987. Award: BHC 1. LO HS 52* v Surrey (Northampton) 1993 (SL).

STRONG, Michael Richard (Brighton C; Brunel UC), b Cuckfield, Sussex 28 Jun 1974. 6'1". LHB, RMF. Sussex 1998-99. Northamptonshire 2000-01. HS 35* Sx v Leics (Arundel) 1999. Nh HS 34 v Leics (Northampton) 2001. BB 4-46 v OU (Oxford) 2000 – on Northants debut. CC BB 4-50 v Glam (Cardiff) 2000. Award: CGT 1. LO HS 21 v Glos (Bristol) 2000 (NWT). LO BB 5-39 v Z (Northampton) 2000.

SWANN, A.J. – see *LANCASHIRE*.

TAYLOR, Jonathan Paul (Pingle S, Swadlincote), b Ashby-de-la-Zouch, Leics 8 Aug 1964. 6'2". LHB, LFM. Derbyshire 1984-86. Northamptonshire 1991-2001; cap 1992; benefit 2000. Staffordshire 1989-90. **Tests**: 2 (1992-93 to 1994); HS 17* v I (Calcutta) 1992-93. BB 1-18. **LOI**: 1 (1992-93); HS 1 v SL (Moratuwa) 1992-93. Tours: SA 1993-94 (Eng A – part); I 1992-93; Z 1994-95 (Nh). HS 86 v Glam (Northampton) 1995. 50 wkts (1): most – 69 (1993). BB 7-23 v Hants (Bournemouth) 1992. Award: BHC 1. LO HS 57 v Kent (Canterbury) 2001 (CGT). LO BB 5-45 v Notts (Northampton) 1996 (BHC).

M.C.Dobson left the staff having made no f-c appearances in 2001.

NORTHAMPTONSHIRE 2001

RESULTS SUMMARY

	Place	Won	Lost	Tied	Drew	No Result
County Championship (1st Division)	7th	2	5		9	
All First-Class Matches		2	5		9	
C & G Trophy	4th Round					
Benson & Hedges Cup	5th in Mid/West/Wales Group					
NU National League (1st Division)	9th	3	12			1

COUNTY CHAMPIONSHIP AVERAGES

BATTING AND FIELDING

Cap		M	I	NO	HS	Runs	Avge	100	50	Ct/St
2001	M.E.K.Hussey	16	30	4	329*	2055	79.03	5	9	19
1994	M.B.Loye	12	21	3	197	1003	55.72	3	4	4
1995	R.J.Warren	16	26	2	194	1303	54.29	4	7	8
1994	A.L.Penberthy	15	24	1	132*	942	40.95	3	5	11
–	J.W.Cook	9	16	1	88	391	26.06	–	4	5
1987	D.Ripley	15	25	6	95	481	25.31	–	2	45/3
–	A.S.Rollins	6	10	1	65	214	23.77	–	1	3
–	A.J.Swann	13	22	–	113	479	21.77	1	2	9
1999	G.P.Swann	15	25	–	61	543	21.72	–	3	9
1992	J.P.Taylor	12	17	3	53	273	19.50	–	1	3
–	T.M.B.Bailey	5	7	–	41	113	16.14	–	–	3
–	K.J.Innes	4	7	1	40	86	14.33	–	–	1
–	J.A.R.Blain	5	9	4	34	66	13.20	–	–	–
2000	D.M.Cousins	8	10	3	27	87	12.42	–	–	2
–	M.R.Strong	9	13	4	34	110	12.22	–	–	2
2000	J.F.Brown	11	12	5	35*	56	8.00	–	–	2

Also batted: M.E.Cassar (1 match) 9, 0 (2 ct); M.S.Panesar (2) 10, 2*, 3*; L.C.Weekes (1) 44*, 18; R.A.White (1) 4, 2.

BOWLING

	O	M	R	W	Avge	Best	5wI	10wM
M.S.Panesar	101.3	28	358	11	32.54	4- 11	–	–
D.M.Cousins	333.4	54	1176	36	32.66	8-102	2	–
J.A.R.Blain	153	16	673	17	39.58	6- 42	1	–
A.L.Penberthy	339.2	70	1019	25	40.76	4- 39	–	–
G.P.Swann	422.3	87	1365	30	45.50	5- 34	1	–
J.P.Taylor	379.2	49	1345	29	46.37	4-100	–	–
J.F.Brown	473.5	102	1407	28	50.25	5-107	1	–
M.R.Strong	256.3	46	992	19	52.21	3- 98	–	–

Also bowled:
K.J.Innes   83.5   15   331   9   36.77   4- 76
J.W.Cook 47-16-124-1; M.E.K.Hussey 18-2-78-2; A.J.Swann 16-4-50-1; R.J.Warren 1-1-0-0; L.C.Weekes 26-5-107-3; R.A.White 3-0-7-0.

Northamptonshire played no first-class fixtures outside the County Championship in 2001. The First-Class Averages (pp 113-126) give the records of Northamptonshire players in all first-class county matches.

NORTHAMPTONSHIRE RECORDS

FIRST-CLASS CRICKET

Highest Total	For 781-7d		v	Notts	Northampton	1995
	V 670-9d		by	Sussex	Hove	1921
Lowest Total	For 12		v	Glos	Gloucester	1907
	V 33		by	Lancashire	Northampton	1977
Highest Innings	For 329*	M.E.K.Hussey	v	Essex	Northampton	2001
	V 333	K.S.Duleepsinhji	for	Sussex	Hove	1930

Highest Partnership for each Wicket

1st	372	R.R.Montgomerie/M.B.Loye	v	Yorkshire	Northampton	1996
2nd	344	G.Cook/R.J.Boyd-Moss	v	Lancashire	Northampton	1986
3rd	393	A.Fordham/A.J.Lamb	v	Yorkshire	Leeds	1990
4th	370	R.T.Virgin/P.Willey	v	Somerset	Northampton	1976
5th	401	M.B.Loye/D.Ripley	v	Glamorgan	Northampton	1998
6th	376	R.Subba Row/A.Lightfoot	v	Surrey	The Oval	1958
7th	293	D.J.G.Sales/D.Ripley	v	Essex	Northampton	1999
8th	164	D.Ripley/N.G.B.Cook	v	Lancashire	Manchester	1987
9th	156	R.Subba Row/S.Starkie	v	Lancashire	Northampton	1955
10th	148	B.W.Bellamy/J.V.Murdin	v	Glamorgan	Northampton	1925

Best Bowling	For 10-127	V.W.C.Jupp	v	Kent	Tunbridge W	1932
(Innings)	V 10- 30	C.Blythe	for	Kent	Northampton	1907
Best Bowling	For 15- 31	G.E.Tribe	v	Yorkshire	Northampton	1958
(Match)	V 17- 48	C.Blythe	for	Kent	Northampton	1907

Most Runs – Season	2198	D.Brookes	(av 51.11)		1952
Most Runs – Career	28980	D.Brookes	(av 36.13)		1934-59
Most 100s – Season	8	R.A.Haywood			1921
Most 100s – Career	67	D.Brookes			1934-59
Most Wkts – Season	175	G.E.Tribe	(av 18.70)		1955
Most Wkts – Career	1097	E.W.Clark	(av 21.31)		1922-47
Most Career W-K Dismissals	810	K.V.Andrew	(653 ct/157 st)		1953-66
Most Career Catches in the Field	469	D.S.Steele			1963-84

LIMITED-OVERS CRICKET

Highest Total	NWT	360-2		v	Staffs	Northampton	1990
	BHC	304-6		v	Scotland	Northampton	1995
	NL	306-2		v	Surrey	Guildford	1985
Lowest Total	NWT	62		v	Leics	Leicester	1974
	BHC	85		v	Sussex	Northampton	1978
	NL	41		v	Middlesex	Northampton	1972
Highest Innings	NWT	145	R.J.Bailey	v	Staffs	Stone	1991
	BHC	134	R.J.Bailey	v	Glos	Northampton	1987
	NL	172*	W.Larkins	v	Warwicks	Luton	1983
Best Bowling	NWT	7-37	N.A.Mallender	v	Worcs	Northampton	1984
	BHC	5-14	F.A.Rose	v	Minor C	Luton	1998
	NL	7-39	A.Hodgson	v	Somerset	Northampton	1976

NOTTINGHAMSHIRE

Formation of Present Club: March/April 1841
Substantial Reorganisation: 11 December 1866
Colours: Green and Gold
Badge: Badge of City of Nottingham
County Champions (since 1890): (4) 1907, 1929, 1981, 1987
Gillette/NatWest/C & G Trophy Winners: (1) 1987
Benson and Hedges Cup Winners: (1) 1989
NU National League (Div 1) Winners: (0); best – 5th 2001
Sunday League Winners: (1) 1991
Match Awards: CGT 43; BHC 73

Chief Executive: D.G.Collier, Trent Bridge, Nottingham NG2 6AG ▲ Tel: 0115 982 3000 ▲ Fax: 0115 945 5730 ▲ Email: administration.notts@ecb.co.uk ▲ Web: www.notts.ccc.co.uk

Captain: J.E.R.Gallian. **Vice-Captain:** No appointment. **Overseas Player:** C.L.Cairns.
2002 Beneficiary: C.M.Tolley. **Scorer:** G.Stringfellow. ‡ New registration

AFZAAL, Usman (Manvers Pierrepont CS; S Notts C) b Rawalpindi, Pakistan 9 Jun 1977. 6'0". LHB, SLA. Debut 1995; cap 2000. **Tests:** 3 (2001); HS 54 v A (Oval) 2001; BB 1-49. Tours: SA 1996-97 (Nt); WI 2000-01 (Eng A); NZ 2001-02. 1000 runs (2): most – 1018 (2000). HS 151* v Worcs (Nottingham) 2000. BB 4-101 v Glos (Nottingham) 1998. LO HS 95* v Hants (Southampton) 2000 (NL). LO BB 3-51 v Surrey (Oval) 2001 (BHC).

BICKNELL, Darren John (Robert Haining County SS; Guildford TC) b Guildford, Surrey 24 Jun 1967. Elder brother of M.P.Bicknell (*see SURREY*). 6'4". LHB, SLA. Surrey 1987-99; cap 1990; benefit 1999. Nottinghamshire debut/cap 2000. Tours (Eng A): WI 1991-92; P 1990-91; SL 1990-91; Z 1989-93. 1000 runs (7); most – 1888 (1991). HS 235* Sy v Notts (Nottingham) 1994. Nt HS 180* v Warwks (Birmingham) 2000 – sharing unbroken 1st wkt stand of 406 with G.E.Welton. BB 3-7 Sy v Sussex (Guildford) 1996. Awards: CGT 1; BHC 6. LO HS 135* Sy v Yorks (Oval) 1989 (NWT). LO BB (Sy) 1-11 (SL).

CAIRNS, Christopher Lance (Christchurch BHS) b Picton, NZ 13 Jun 1970. Son of B.L.Cairns (CD, Otago, ND and NZ 1971-86). 6'2". RHB, RFM. Nottinghamshire 1988-89, 1992-93 and 1995-96; cap 1993. N Districts 1988-89. Canterbury 1990-91 to date. **Tests** (NZ): 54 (1989-90 to 2001-02); HS 126 v I (Hamilton) 1998-99; BB 7-27 v WI (Hamilton) 1999-00. **LOI** (NZ): 151 (1990-91 to 2001-02, 1 as captain); HS 115 v I (Christchurch) 1998-99; BB 5-42 v A (Napier) 1997-98. Tours (NZ): E 1999; A 1989-90, 1993-94, 1997-98, 2000-01; WI 1995-96 (part); I 1995-96, 1999-00; P 1996-97; SL 1997-98; Z 1997-98, 2000-01. 1000 runs (1): 1171 (1995). HS 126 (*see Tests*). Nt HS 115 v Middx (Lord's) 1995. 50 wkts (3); most – 56 (1992). BB 8-47 (15-83 match) v Sussex (Arundel) 1995. Awards: CGT 2; BHC 1. LO HS 143 Canterbury v Auckland (Christchurch) 1994-95 (SC). LO BB 6-37 Canterbury v Wellington (Christchurch) 1996-97 (SC).

CLOUGH, Gareth David (Pudsey Grangefield S) b Leeds, Yorks 23 May 1978. 6'0". RHB, RM. Yorkshire 1998. Nottinghamshire debut 2001. HS 33 Y v Glam (Cardiff) 1998 – on debut. Nt HS 8. BB 3-69 v Glos (Nottingham) 2001. LO HS 24 v Northants (Northampton) 2001 (NL). LO BB 2-33 v Surrey (Oval) 2001 (NL).

FRANKS, Paul John (Southwell Minster CS) b Mansfield 3 Feb 1979. 6'2". LHB, RMF. Debut 1996; cap 1999. YC 2000. **LOI:** 1 (2000); HS 4 v WI (Nottingham) 2000. Tours (Eng A): SA 1998-99; WI 2000-01; NZ 1999-00; B 1999-00. Nt HS 85 v Middx (Lord's) 2001. 50 wkts (2); most – 63 (1999). BB 7-56 v Middx (Lord's) 2000. Hat-trick 1997. Award: CGT 1. LO HS 40 v Glam (Nottingham) 1999 (NL). LO BB 6-27 v Durham (Chester-le-St) 2000 (NL).

GALLIAN, Jason Edward Riche (Pittwater House S, Sydney; Keble C, Oxford), b Manly, Sydney, Australia 25 Jun 1971. Qualified for England 1994. 6'0". RHB, RM. Lancashire 1990-97, taking wicket of D.A.Hagan (OU) with his first ball; cap 1994. Oxford U 1992-93; blue 1992-93; captain 1993. Nottinghamshire debut/cap 1998; captain 1998 (part) to date. Captained Australia YC v England YC 1989-90, scoring 158* in 1st 'Test'. **Tests:** 3 (1995 to 1995-96); HS 28 v SA (Pt Elizabeth) 1995-96. Tours: A 1996-97 (Eng A); I 1995-96 (La); SA 1995-96 (part); I 1994-95 (Eng A); P 1995-96 (Eng A). 1000 runs (2); most – 1156 (1996). HS 312 La v Derbys (Manchester) 1996 (record score at Old Trafford). Nt HS 150 v Glam (Nottingham) 2000. BB 6-115 La v Surrey (Southport) 1996. Nt BB 2-28 v Warwks (Nottingham) 1999. Awards: CGT 2; BHC 2. LO HS 134 La v Notts (Manchester) 1995 (BHC). LO BB 5-15 La v Minor C (Leek) 1995 (BHC).

HARRIS, Andrew James (Hadfield CS; Glossopdale Community C), b Ashton-under-Lyne, Lancs 26 Jun 1973. 6'1". RHB, RM. Derbyshire 1994-99; cap 1996. Nottinghamshire debut/cap 2000. Tour: A 1996-97 (Eng A). HS 39 v Worcs (Nottingham) 2000 – on Notts debut. 50 wkts (1): 72 (1996). BB 6-40 (12-83 match) De v Middx (Derby) 1998. Nt BB 6-98 v Sussex (Nottingham) 2001. Award: CGT 1. LO HS 11* De v Kent (Derby) 1996 (NWT). LO BB 5-35 v Hants (Nottingham) 2000 (NL).

JOHNSON, Paul (Grove CS, Balderton), b Newark 24 Apr 1965. 5'7". RHB, RM. Debut 1982; cap 1986; benefit 1995; captain 1996-98. Tours: SA 1996-97 (Nt); WI 1991-92 (Eng A). 1000 runs (9); most – 1518 (1990). HS 187 v Lancs (Manchester) 1993. WI 9-12. CC BB 1-14. Awards: CGT 2; BHC 3. LO HS 167* v Kent (Nottingham) 1993 (SL). LO BB 1-2 (NL).

LOGAN, Richard James (Wolverhampton GS), b Stone, Staffs 28 Jan 1980. 6'1". RHB, RMF. Northamptonshire 1999-2000. Nottinghamshire debut 2001. HS 37* v Hants (Nottingham) 2001. BB 6-93 v Derbys (Nottingham) 2001. Award: CGT 1. LO HS 24 v Northants (Northampton) 2001 (NL). LO BB 5-24 v Suffolk (Mildenhall) 2001 (CGT).

LUCAS, David Scott (Djanogly CTC, Nottingham), b Nottingham 19 Aug 1978. 6'2". RHB, LMF. Debut 1999. HS 46* v Middx (Nottingham) 2000. BB 5-104 v Essex (Nottingham) 1999. LO HS 19* v Sussex (Hove) 1999 (NL). LO BB 4-27 v Derbys (Derby) 2000 (NL).

MALIK, Muhammad Nadeem, (Wilford Meadows CS; Bilborough C), b Nottingham 6 Oct 1982. 6'5". RHB, RFM. Debut 2001. 2nd XI debut 1999 when aged 16y 337d. HS 6*. BB 5-57 v Derbys (Nottingham) 2001. LO HS 3* (NL). LO BB 2-34 v Yorks (Nottingham) 2001 (NL).

NOON, Wayne Michael (Caistor S), b Grimsby, Lincs 5 Feb 1971. 5'9". RHB, WK. Northamptonshire 1989-93. Nottinghamshire debut 1994; cap 1995. Canterbury 1994-95. Worcs 2nd XI debut when aged 15yr 199d. Tours: SA 1991-92 (Nh), 1996-97 (Nt). HS 83 v Northants (Northampton) 1997. LO HS 46 v Warwks (Birmingham) 1998 (BHC).

PIETERSEN, Kevin Peter (Maritzburg C; Natal U), b Pietermaritzburg, SA 27 Jun 1980. ECB qualified – British passport (English mother). 6'4". RHB, OB. Natal/KwaZulu-Natal 1997-98 to 1999-00. Nottinghamshire debut 2001; uncapped. 1000 (1): 1275 (2001). HS 218* v Derbys (Derby) 2001. BB 4-141 KZ-Natal v E (Durban) 1999-00. Nt BB 2-46 v Worcs (Nottingham) 2001. LO HS 78* v Surrey (Oval) 2001 (BHC). LO BB 3-39 v Warwks (Nottingham) 2001 (NL).

RANDALL, Stephen John (W Bridgford S), b Nottingham 9 Jun 1980. 5'10". RHB, OB. Debut 1999. HS 28 v Glos (Bristol) 2001. BB 2-64 v Derbys (Nottingham) 2001. LO HS 15* and BB 3-44 v Glos (Cheltenham) 2001 (NL).

READ, Christopher Mark Wells (Torquay GS; Bath U), b Paignton, Devon 10 Aug 1978. 5'8". RHB, WK. Gloucestershire (L-O) 1997. Nottinghamshire debut 1998; cap 1999. Devon 1995-97. **Tests:** 3 (1999); HS 37 v NZ (Lord's) 1999. **LOI:** 9 (1999-00); HS 26* v SA (Cape Town) 1999-00. Tours (Eng A): SA 1998-99, 1999-00 (Eng); WI 2000-01; SL 1997-98; Z 1998-99; K 1997-98. HS 160 v Warwks (Nottingham) 1999. LO HS 62 v Somerset (Nottingham) 1999 (NL).

SHAFAYAT, Bilal Mustapha (Greenwood Dale; Nottingham Bluecoat SFC), b Nottingham 10 Jul 1984. 5'7". RHB, RMF. Debut 2001, scoring 72 and 24 v Middx (Nottingham). HS 75 v Hants (Nottingham) 2001. LO HS 36 Notts CB v Beds (Luton) 2001 (CGT).

SMITH, Gregory James (Pretoria BHS; Pretoria Technikon), b Pretoria, SA 30 Oct 1971. ECB qualified – British passport. 6'4". RHB, LFM. N Transvaal/Northerns 1993-94 to date. Nottinghamshire debut/cap 2001. Tour (SA A): E 1996. 50 wkts (1): 50 (2001). HS 68 NT v WP (Pretoria) 1995-96. Nt HS 44* v Sussex (Nottingham) 2001. BB 6-35 Northerns v WP (Pretoria) 1997-98. Nt BB 5-37 (10-101 match) v Sussex (Hove) 2001. LO HS 9 (SBC). LO BB 5-11 (SBC) NT v GW (Kimberley) 1995-96.

‡**SMITH, Will** Rew (Bedford S), b Luton, Beds 28 Sep 1982. 5'9". RHB, OB. Awaiting f-c debut. Notts 2nd XI debut 1999 when aged 16y 309d.

TOLLEY, Christopher Mark (King Edward VI C, Stourbridge; Loughborough U), b Kidderminster, Worcs 30 Dec 1967. 5'9". RHB, LMF. Worcestershire 1989-95; cap 1993. Nottinghamshire 1996-2001; cap 1997; benefit 2002; Cricket Development Officer – Elite Squad 2000 to date – available for l-o matches. Tours (Wo): SA 1996-97 (Nt); Z 1990-91, 1993-94. HS 84 Wo v Derbys (Derby) 1994. Nt HS 78 v Glos (Nottingham) 1998. BB 7-45 v Worcs (Kidderminster) 1998. Hat-trick 1997. Awards: CGT 1; BHC 1. LO HS 78 Notts CB v Oxon (Oxford) 2001 (CGT). LO BB 5-16 v Hants (Southampton) 1996 (SL).

WELTON, Guy Edward (Healing CS; Grimsby TC; Nottingham Trent U), b Grimsby, Lincs 4 May 1978. 6'1". RHB, OB. Debut 1997. MCC YC. HS 200* v Warwks (Birmingham) 2000 – sharing unbroken 1st wkt stand of 406 with D.J.Bicknell. Awards: BHC 2. LO HS 104* v Durham (Nottingham) 1999 (NL).

RELEASED/RETIRED
(Having made a first-class County appearance in 2001)

BLEWETT, Gregory Scott (Prince Alfred C), b Adelaide, Australia 28 Oct 1971. Son of R.W.Blewett (South Australia 1975-76 to 1978-79). 6'0". RHB, RM. South Australia 1991-92 to date. Yorkshire 1999; cap 1999. Nottinghamshire 2001; cap 2001. **Tests** (A): 46 (1994-95 to 1999-00); HS 214 v SA (Johannesburg) 1996-97; scored 102* v E (Adelaide) on debut; first to score hundreds in his first 3 Ashes Tests; BB 2-9 v WI (St John's) 1998-99. **LOI** (A): 32 (1994-95 to 1998-99); HS 57* v WI (Melbourne) 1996-97; BB 2-6 v SL (Adelaide) 1998-99. Tours (A): E 1997; SA 1996-97; WI 1994-95, 1998-99; NZ 1999-00; I 1997-98; SL 1999-00; Z 1999-00. 1000 runs (1+4); most – 1292 (2001). HS 268 S Aus v Vic (Melbourne) 1993-94. CC HS 190 Y v Northants (Scarborough) 1999. Nt HS 137* v Durham (Chester-le-St) 2001. BB 5-29 Aus XI v WI (Hobart) 1996-97. CC BB 2-16 Y v Durham (Leeds) 1999. Nt BB 2-20 v Glos (Nottingham) 2001. Award: BHC 1. LO HS 131 Aus A v Z (Brisbane) 2000-01. LO BB 4-18 Y v Lancs (Manchester) 1999 (NWT).

MILLNS, David James (Garibaldi CS; N Notts C; Nottingham Trent U), b Clipstone, Notts 27 Feb 1965. 6'3". LHB, RF. Nottinghamshire 1988-89, 2000-01; cap 2000. Leicestershire 1990-99; cap 1991; benefit 1999. Tasmania 1994-95. Boland 1996-97. Tours: A 1992-93 (Eng A); SA 1996-97 (Le). HS 121 Le v Northants (Northampton) 1997. Nt HS 50* v Northants (Northampton) 2000. 50 wkts (4); most – 76 (1994). BB 9-37 (12-91 match) Le v Derbys (Derby) 1991. Nt BB 5-58 v Northants (Nottingham) 2000. Awards: CGT 1; BHC 1. LO HS 39* Le v Warwks (Birmingham) 1996 (BHC). LO BB 4-26 Le v Durham (Stockton) 1995 (BHC).

MORRIS, John Edward (Shavington CS; Dane Bank CFE), b Crewe, Cheshire 1 Apr 1964. 5'10". RHB, RM. Derbyshire 1982-93; cap 1986. GW 1988-89 and 1993-94. Durham 1994-99; cap 1998; benefit 1999. Nottinghamshire 2000-01; cap 2000. **Tests**: 3 (1990); HS 32 v I (Oval) 1990. **LOI**: 8 (1990-91); HS 63* v NZ (Adelaide) 1990-91. Tour: A 1990-91. 1000 runs (11); most – 1739 (1986). HS 229 De v Glos (Cheltenham) 1993. Nt HS 170 v Derbys (Derby) 2001. BB 1-6 (De). Nt BB 1-26. Awards: CGT 2; BHC 2. LO HS 145 Du v Leics (Leicester) 1996 (BHC). LO BB (GW) 1-44 (NS).

STEMP, Richard David (Britannia HS, Rowley Regis), b Erdington, Birmingham 11 Dec 1967. 6'0". RHB, SLA. Worcestershire 1990-92. Yorkshire 1993-98; cap 2000. Nottinghamshire 1999-2001; cap 2000. Tours (Eng A): SA 1992-93 (Y); I 1994-95; P 1995-96. Nt HS 66 v Hants (Southampton) 2001. Nt HS 18 v Sussex (Hove) 1999. BB 6-37 Y v Durham (Durham) 1994. Nt BB 5-123 v Worcs (Worcester) 2000. Award: BHC 1. LO HS 29* v Somerset (Nottingham) 1999 (NL). LO BB 4-25 Y v Glos (Bristol) 1996 (SL) and Nt v Somerset (Nottingham) 2001 (NL).

C.J.Hewison left the staff having made no f-c appearances in 2001.

NOTTINGHAMSHIRE 2001

RESULTS SUMMARY

	Place	Won	Lost	Tied	Drew	No Result
County Championship (2nd Division)	**7th**	3	7		6	
All First-Class Matches		3	7		6	
C & G Trophy	4th Round					
Benson & Hedges Cup	Semi-Finalist					
NU National League (1st Division)	**5th**	7	8			1

COUNTY CHAMPIONSHIP AVERAGES

BATTING AND FIELDING

Cap		M	I	NO	HS	Runs	Avge	100	50	Ct/St
	K.P.Pietersen	15	26	4	218*	1275	57.95	4	6	14
1999	P.J.Franks	5	8	4	85	217	54.25	–	1	2
2001	G.S.Blewett	16	30	3	137*	1292	47.85	5	5	24
2000	J.E.Morris	8	16	2	170	640	45.71	2	4	3
2000	U.Afzaal	12	22	–	138	928	42.18	1	7	9
–	B.M.Shafayat	3	6	–	75	231	38.50	–	2	–
2000	D.J.Bicknell	16	29	–	167	1050	36.20	3	3	8
1986	P.Johnson	13	24	2	149	684	31.09	2	2	7
1999	C.M.W.Read	16	27	5	78	666	30.27	–	5	43/1
–	D.S.Lucas	5	8	–	41	145	18.12	–	–	–
2001	G.J.Smith	15	20	9	44*	195	17.72	–	–	3
–	G.E.Welton	12	22	–	61	337	15.31	–	2	5
2000	R.D.Stemp	5	7	–	66	105	15.00	–	1	1
–	R.J.Logan	10	15	2	37*	162	12.46	–	–	4
–	S.J.Randall	4	7	1	28	73	12.16	–	–	1
–	M.N.Malik	5	6	5	6*	12	12.00	–	–	–
2000	A.J.Harris	9	15	2	20*	79	6.07	–	–	1
–	G.D.Clough	4	6	–	8	22	3.66	–	–	1

Also played (1 match each): J.E.R.Gallian (cap 1998) 23*; D.J.Millns (cap 2000) 3*, 4 (1 ct); C.M.Tolley (cap 1997) did not bat.

BOWLING

	O	M	R	W	Avge	Best	5wI	10wM
G.J.Smith	446.2	103	1256	50	25.12	5-37	3	1
R.J.Logan	329.1	53	1375	43	31.97	6-93	3	–
P.J.Franks	149.1	33	429	13	33.00	4-65	–	–
A.J.Harris	330.4	84	1097	28	39.17	6-98	1	–
M.N.Malik	104	21	414	10	41.40	5-57	1	–
R.D.Stemp	244.4	51	707	16	44.18	3-39	–	–

Also bowled:

G.D.Clough	100	14	353	6	58.83	3-69	–	–
U.Afzaal	149.2	29	530	9	58.88	3-88	–	–
G.S.Blewett	113	24	374	6	62.33	2-20	–	–
S.J.Randall	132.1	21	465	7	66.42	2-64	–	–
D.S.Lucas	118	8	571	8	71.37	3-80	–	–
K.P.Pietersen	234	52	767	9	85.22	2-46	–	–

P.Johnson 1-1-0-0; D.J.Millns 25.1-4-87-1; J.E.Morris 3.2-0-19-0; C.M.W.Read 3-0-25-0; G.E.Welton 1-0-4-0.

Nottinghamshire played no first-class fixtures outside the County Championship in 2001. The First-Class Averages (pp 113-126) give the records of Nottinghamshire players in all first-class county matches, with the exception of U.Afzaal whose full county figures are as above.

NOTTINGHAMSHIRE RECORDS

FIRST-CLASS CRICKET

Highest Total	For 739-7d		v	Leics	Nottingham	1903
	V 781-7d		by	Northants	Northampton	1995
Lowest Total	For 13		v	Yorkshire	Nottingham	1901
	V 16		by	Derbyshire	Nottingham	1879
	16		by	Surrey	The Oval	1880
Highest Innings	For 312*	W.W.Keeton	v	Middlesex	The Oval	1939
	V 345	C.G.Macartney	for	Australians	Nottingham	1921

Highest Partnership for each Wicket

1st	406*	D.J.Bicknell/G.E.Welton	v	Warwicks	Birmingham	2000
2nd	398	A.Shrewsbury/W.Gunn	v	Sussex	Nottingham	1890
3rd	369	W.Gunn/J.R.Gunn	v	Leics	Nottingham	1903
4th	361	A.O.Jones/J.R.Gunn	v	Essex	Leyton	1905
5th	266	A.Shrewsbury/W.Gunn	v	Sussex	Hove	1884
6th	372*	K.P.Pietersen/J.E.Morris	v	Derbyshire	Derby	2001
7th	301	C.C.Lewis/B.N.French	v	Durham	Chester-le-St	1993
8th	220	G.F.H.Heane/R.Winrow	v	Somerset	Nottingham	1935
9th	170	J.C.Adams/K.P.Evans	v	Somerset	Taunton	1994
10th	152	E.B.Alletson/W.Riley	v	Sussex	Hove	1911
	152	U.Afzaal/A.J.Harris	v	Worcs	Nottingham	2000

Best Bowling	For 10-66	K.Smales	v	Glos	Stroud	1956
(Innings)	V 10-10	H.Verity	for	Yorkshire	Leeds	1932
Best Bowling	For 17-89	F.C.Matthews	v	Northants	Nottingham	1923
(Match)	V 17-89	W.G.Grace	for	Glos	Cheltenham	1877

Most Runs – Season	2620	W.W.Whysall	(av 53.46)	1929
Most Runs – Career	31592	G.Gunn	(av 35.69)	1902-32
Most 100s – Season	9	W.W.Whysall		1928
	9	M.J.Harris		1971
	9	B.C.Broad		1990
Most 100s – Career	65	J.Hardstaff jr		1930-55
Most Wkts – Season	181	B.Dooland	(av 14.96)	1954
Most Wkts – Career	1653	T.G.Wass	(av 20.34)	1896-1920
Most Career W-K Dismissals	957	T.W.Oates	(733 ct/224 st)	1897-1925
Most Career Catches in the Field	466	A.O.Jones		1892-1914

LIMITED-OVERS CRICKET

Highest Total	NWT	344-6		v	Northumb	Jesmond	1994
	BHC	296-6		v	Kent	Nottingham	1989
	NL	329-6		v	Derbyshire	Nottingham	1993
Lowest Total	NWT	123		v	Yorkshire	Scarborough	1969
	BHC	74		v	Leics	Leicester	1987
	NL	66		v	Yorkshire	Bradford	1969
Highest Innings	NWT	149*	D.W.Randall	v	Devon	Torquay	1988
	BHC	130*	C.E.B.Rice	v	Scotland	Glasgow	1982
	NL	167*	P.Johnson	v	Kent	Nottingham	1993
Best Bowling	NWT	6-10	K.P.Evans	v	Northumb	Jesmond	1994
	BHC	6-22	M.K.Bore	v	Leics	Leicester	1980
		6-22	C.E.B.Rice	v	Northants	Northampton	1981
	NL	6-12	R.J.Hadlee	v	Lancashire	Nottingham	1980

SOMERSET

Formation of Present Club: 18 August 1875
Colours: Black, White and Maroon
Badge: Somerset Dragon
County Champions: (0); best – 2nd (Div 1) 2001
Gillette/NatWest/C & G Trophy Winners: (3) 1979, 1983, 2001
Benson and Hedges Cup Winners: (2) 1981, 1982
NU National League (Div 1) Winners: (0); best – 4th 2001
Sunday League Winners: (1) 1979
Match Awards: CGT 59; BHC 70

Chief Executive: P.W.Anderson, County Ground, Taunton TA1 1JT ▲ Tel: 01823 272946 ▲ Fax: 01823 332395 ▲ Email: somerset@ecb.co.uk ▲ Web: None.

Captain: M.E.Trescothick. **Vice-Captain/Overseas Player:** J.Cox.
2002 Beneficiary: R.J.Turner. **Scorer:** G.A.Stickley. ‡ New registration

BLACKWELL, Ian David (Brookfield Community S), b Chesterfield, Derbys 10 Jun 1978. 6'1". LHB, SLA. Derbyshire 1997-99. Somerset debut 2000; cap 2001. HS 122 v Northants (Northampton) 2001. BB 5-115 De v Surrey (Oval) 1998. Sm BB 5-122 v Northants (Taunton) 2001. Award: BHC 1. LO HS 97 De v Glam (Derby) 1999 (NL). LO BB 4-36 v Worcs (Worcester) 2000 (NL).

BOWLER, Peter Duncan (Scots C, Sydney, Aus; Daramalan C, Canberra, Aus; Nottingham Trent U), b Plymouth, Devon 30 Jul 1963. 6'1". RHB, OB, occ WK. Leicestershire 1986 – first to score hundred on f-c debut for Leics (100* and 62 v Hants). Tasmania 1986-87. Derbyshire 1988-94; cap 1989; scored 155* v CU (Cambridge) on debut – first instance of hundreds on debut for two counties. Somerset debut/cap 1995; captain 1997-98; benefit 2000. 1000 runs (9) inc 2000 (1): 2044 (1992). HS 241* De v Hants (Portsmouth) 1992. Sm HS 207 v Surrey (Taunton) 1996. BB 3-25 v Northants (Taunton) 1998. Awards: BHC 4. LO HS 138* De v Somerset (Derby) 1993 (SL). LO BB 3-31 De v Glos (Cheltenham) 1991 (SL).

BULBECK, Matthew Paul Leonard (Taunton S; Richard Huish C), b Taunton 8 Nov 1979. 6'3½". LHB, LMF. Debut 1998. HS 76* v Durham (Chester-le-St) 1999. 50 wkts (1): 51 (1999). BB 5-45 (10-108 match) v Northants (Northampton) 1999. LO HS 5 (NL). LO BB 5-18 v Somerset CB v Norfolk (Hellesdon) 2001 (CGT).

BURNS, Michael (Walney CS), b Barrow-in-Furness, Lancs 6 Feb 1969. 6'0". RHB, RM, WK. Cumberland 1988-90. Warwickshire 1992-96. Somerset debut 1997; cap 1999. Scored earliest hundred in UK f-c matches (160 v OU (Taunton) on 7 Apr 2000). HS 221 v Yorks (Bath) 2001. BB 6-54 v Leics (Taunton) 2001. Awards: CGT 1. BHC 1. LO HS 115* v Middx (Taunton) 1997 (SL). LO BB 4-39 v Glos (Taunton) 1997 (SL).

CADDICK, Andrew Richard (Papanui HS), b Christchurch, NZ 21 Nov 1968. Son of English emigrants – qualified for England 1992. 6'5". RHB, RFM. Debut 1991; cap 1992; benefit 1999. Represented NZ in 1987-88 Youth World Cup. *Wisden* 2000. **ECB contracts 2000, 2001. Tests:** 50 (1993 to 2001); HS 49* v SA (Birmingham) 2001; BB 7-46 v SA (Durban) 1999-00. **LOI:** 38 (1993 to 2001-02); HS 36 v SA (Oval) 2001; BB 4-19 v SA (Jo'burg) 1999-00. Tours: A 1992-93 (Eng A); SA 1999-00; WI 1993-94, 1997-98; NZ 1996-97, 2000-01; SL 2000-01; Z 1996-97. HS 92 v Worcs (Worcester) 1995. 50 wkts (8) inc 100 (1): 105 (1998). BB 9-32 (12-120 match) v Lancs (Taunton) 1993. Awards: CGT 2. LO HS 39 v Hants (Taunton) 1996 (SL). LO BB 6-30 v Glos (Taunton) 1992 (NWT).

COX, Jamie (Wynyard HS; Deakin U), b Burnie, Tasmania, Australia 15 Oct 1969. 6'0". RHB, OB. Tasmania 1987-88 to date; captain 2000-01 to date. Somerset debut/cap 1999; captain 1999-2001. Tours: Z 1991-92 (Aus B), 1995-96 (Tas). 1000 runs (2+2); most – 1617 (1999). HS 245 Tas v NSW (Hobart) 1999-00. Sm HS 216 v Hants (Southampton) 1999. BB 3-46 v Middx (Taunton) 1999. Awards: CGT 2. LO HS 114 v Surrey (Taunton) 1999 (NWT). LO BB 3-28 v Durham (Taunton) 1999 (NL).

DUTCH, Keith Philip (Nower Hill HS; Weald C), b Harrow, Middlesex 21 Mar 1973. 5'10". RHB, OB. Middlesex 1993-2000. Somerset debut/cap 2001. MCC YC. HS 118 v Essex (Taunton) 2001. BB 6-62 M v Essex (Chelmsford) 2000. Sm BB 4-32 v Essex (Chelmsford) 2001. Award: CGT 1. LO HS 61* v Warwks (Taunton) 2001 (CGT). LO BB 6-40 v Northants (Northampton) 2001 (NL).

‡**FRANCIS, Simon** Richard George (Yardley Court, Tonbridge; King Edward VI S, Southampton; Durham U), b Bromley, Kent 15 Aug 1978. Elder brother of J.D.Francis (Hampshire 2001). 6'2". RHB, RMF. Hampshire 1997-2000. British U 1998-99. HS 30* and BB 4-95 H v Surrey (Oval) 2000. LO HS 8* (twice for H – NL). LO BB 2-28 H v Kent (Canterbury) 1999 (NL).

GAZZARD, Carl Matthew (Mounts Bay CS, Penzance; Richard Huish C), b Penzance, Cornwall 15 Apr 1982. 6'0". RHB, WK. Cornwall 1998-2000. Staff 2000 – awaiting f-c debut. LO HS 16 Cornwall v Cumb (Kendal) 1999 (NWT).

HOLLOWAY, Piran Christopher Laity (Millfield S; Taunton S; Loughborough U), b Helston, Cornwall 1 Oct 1970. 5'8". LHB, WK. Warwickshire 1988-93. Somerset debut 1994; cap 1997. Awards: CGT 1; BHC 1. HS 168 v Middx (Uxbridge) 1996. LO HS 117 v Glos (Taunton) 1997 (SL).

HUNKIN, Christopher Andrew (Richard Huish C), b St Austell, Cornwall 14 Dec 1980. RHB, RM. Staff 2001 – awaiting f-c debut. LO HS 10* Somerset CB v Staffs (Walsall) 2000 (NWT). LO BB 2-43 Cornwall v Cheshire (Toft) 2001 (CGT).

JOHNSON, Richard Leonard (Sunbury Manor S; S Pelthorne C), b Chertsey, Surrey 29 Dec 1974. 6'2". RHB, RFM. Middlesex 1992-2000; cap 1995. Somerset debut/cap 2001. Tour: I 1994-95 (Eng A – *part*). HS 69 M v Essex (Chelmsford) 2000. Sm HS 68 v Leics (Taunton) 2001. 50 wkts (3); most – 62 (2001). BB 10-45 M v Derbys (Derby) 1994 (second youngest to take all ten wickets in any f-c match). Sm BB 5-40 v Essex (Chelmsford) 2001. Award: CGT 1. LO HS 45* M v Durham (Southgate) 1998 (NWT). LO BB 5-50 M v Kent (Lord's) 1997 (NWT).

JONES, Philip Steffan (Stradey CS, Llanelli; Neath TC; Loughborough U; Homerton C, Cambridge), b Llanelli, Wales 9 Feb 1974. 6'2". RHB, RMF. Cambridge U 1997; blue 1997. Somerset debut 1997; cap 2001. Wales MC 1992-96. HS 105 v NZ (Taunton) 1999. CC HS 56* v Yorks (Scarborough) 2000. 50 wkts (1): 59 (2001). BB 6-67 CU v OU (Lord's) 1997. Sm BB 5-41 v Surrey (Taunton) 2000. LO HS 27 v Northants (Northampton) 2000 (NL). LO BB 5-23 v Warwks (Taunton) 1998 (SL).

LATHWELL, Mark Nicholas (Braunton S, Devon), b Bletchley, Bucks 26 Dec 1971. 5'8". RHB, OB. Debut 1991; cap 1992. YC 1993. MCC YC. **Tests:** 2 (1993); HS 33 v A (Nottingham) 1993. Tours (Eng A): A 1992-93; SA 1993-94. 1000 runs (5); most – 1230 (1994). HS 206 v Surrey (Bath) 1994. BB 2-21 v Sussex (Hove) 1994. Awards: CGT 1; BHC 2. LO HS 121 v Middx (Lord's) 1996 (BHC). LO BB 1-23 (NWT).

PARSONS, Keith Alan (The Castle S, Taunton; Richard Huish C), b Taunton 2 May 1973. Identical twin brother of K.J.Parsons (Somerset staff 1992-94). 6'1". RHB, RM. Debut 1992; cap 1999. HS 193* v WI (Taunton) 2000. CC HS 139 v Northants (Taunton) 2001. BB 5-13 v Lancs (Taunton) 2000. Award: CGT 1. LO HS 72 v Warwks (Taunton) 2001 (BHC). LO BB 4-43 v Surrey (Taunton) 1999 (NWT).

ROSE, Graham David (Northumberland Park S, Tottenham), b Tottenham, London 12 Apr 1964. 6'4". RHB, RM. Middlesex 1985-86. Somerset debut 1987; cap 1988; benefit 1997. 1000 runs (1): 1000 (1990). HS 191 v Sussex (Taunton) 1997. 50 wkts (5); most – 63 (1997). BB 7-47 (13-88 match) v Notts (Taunton) 1996. Awards: BHC 4. LO HS 148 v Glam (Neath) 1990 (SL). LO BB 4-16 v SL (Taunton) 1990.

SUPPIAH, Arul Vivasvan (Exeter U), b Kuala Lumpur, Malaysia 30 Aug 1983. Son of R.Suppiah (Kuala Lumpur). Brother of R.V.Suppiah (Malaysia – vice-captain). 6'0". RHB, SLA. Summer contract – awaiting f-c debut.

TREGO, Peter David (Wyvern CS, W-s-M), b Weston-super-Mare 12 Jun 1981. 6'0". RHB, RMF. Somerset debut 2000. 2nd XI debut 1997 when aged 16y 20d. Malaysia 1999-2001. HS 62 v Yorks (Taunton) 2000. BB 4-84 v Yorks (Scarborough) 2000. LO HS 21 v Kent (Taunton) 2001 (NL). LO BB 2-21 Somerset CB v Norfolk (Hellesdon) 2001 (CGT).

TRESCOTHICK, Marcus Edward (Sir Bernard Lovell S), b Keynsham 25 Dec 1975. 6'2". LHB, RM. Debut 1993; cap 1999; captain 2002. **ECB contract 2001. Tests:** 19 (2000 to 2001-02); HS 122 v SL (Galle) 2000-01; BB 1-34. **LOI:** 37 (2000 to 2001-02, 1 as captain); HS 137 v P (Lord's) 2001; BB 2-7 v Z (Manchester) 2000. Tours: NZ 1999-00 (Eng A), 2001-02; I 2001-02; P 2000-01; SL 2000-01; B 1999-00 (Eng A). HS 190 v Middx (Taunton) 1999. BB 4-36 (in hat-trick) v Young A (Taunton) 1995. CC BB 4-82 v Yorks (Leeds) 1998. Hat-trick 1995. Awards: CGT 2; BHC 3. LO HS (see LOI). LO BB 4-50 v Northants (Northampton) 2000 (NL).

TUCKER, Joseph Peter (Colston Collegiate S; Richard Huish C), b Bath 14 Sep 1979. 6'3". RHB, RMF. Debut 2000. 2nd XI debut 1995 when aged 15y 257d. HS 14 and BB 1-28 (dismissing B.C.Lara with his 2nd ball) v WI (Taunton) 2000 on debut. CC HS 5*.

TURNER, Robert Julian (Millfield S; Magdalene C, Cambridge), b Malvern, Worcs 25 Nov 1967. 6'1½". RHB, WK. Brother of S.J.Turner (Somerset 1984-85). Cambridge U 1988-91; blue 1988-89-90-91; captain 1991. Somerset debut 1991; cap 1994; benefit 2002. Cambridgeshire 1990. Tours (Eng A): NZ 1999-00; B 1999-00. Held 7 catches in an innings v Northants (Taunton) 2001. 1000 runs (2); most – 1217 (1999). HS 144 v Kent (Taunton) 1997. Award: BHC 1. LO HS 70 v Glam (Cardiff) 1996 (BHC).

WEBLEY, Thomas (King's C, Taunton), b Bristol 2 Mar 1983. RHB, SLA. Staff 2001 – awaiting f-c debut. 2nd XI debut 1999 when aged 16y 49d. LO HS (Somerset CB) 4 (CGT).

WOOD, Matthew James (Exmouth Community C; Exeter U), b Exeter, Devon 30 Sep 1980. 5'11". RHB, OB. Debut 2001. 2nd XI debut 1997 when aged 16y 345d. Devon 1998-2000. HS 122 v Northants (Taunton) 2001. LO HS 43 Devon v Surrey (Exmouth) 2000 (NWT).

RELEASED/RETIRED
(Having made a first-class County appearance in 2001)

GROVE, J.O. – see LEICESTERSHIRE.

KERR, J.I. – see DERBYSHIRE.

I.Jones and J.A.Knott left the staff having made no f-c appearances in 2001.

LANCASHIRE – RELEASED/RETIRED (continued from p 49)
(Having made a first-class County appearance in 2001)

MURALITHARAN, Muthiah (St Anthony's C, Kandy), b Kandy, Sri Lanka 17 Apr 1972. 5'5". RHB, OB. Central Province 1989-90 to date. Tamil Union 1991-92 to date. Lancashire 1999 (taking 7-44 and 7-73 v Warwks at Southport on debut), 2001; cap 1999. Wisden 1998. **Tests** (SL): 72 (1992-93 to 2001-02); HS 67 v I (Kandy) 2001-02; BB 9-51 v Z (Kandy) 2001-02. **LOI** (SL): 183 (1993-94 to 2001-02); HS 18 v E (Lord's) 1998; BB 7-30 v I (Sharjah) 2000-01. Tours (SL): E 1991, 1998; A 1995-96; SA 1992-93 (SL U-24), 1994-95, 1997-98, 2000-01; WI 1996-97; NZ 1994-95, 1996-97; I 1993-94, 1997-98; P 1995-96, 1999-00; Z 1994-95, 1999-00. HS 67 (see Tests). La HS 21 v Kent (Canterbury) 2001. 50 wkts (2+3); most – 66 (1996-97; 1999 – in 7 CC matches). BB 9-51 (see Tests). La BB 7-39 (11-161 match) v Derbys (Derby) 1999. Award: BHC 1. LO HS 18 (see LOI). LO BB 7-30 (see LOI).

SCUDERI, Joseph Charles (Ingham State HS), b Ingham, Queensland, Australia 24 Dec 1968. 5'11". RHB, RM. S Australia 1988-89 to 1997-98. ECB qualified – Italian passport. Italy 1998-1999. Lancashire 2000-01. HS 125* S Aus v WA (Adelaide) 1991-92. La HS 89 v Northants (Manchester) 2001. BB 7-79 S Aus v NSW (Adelaide) 1991-92. La BB 4-58 v Somerset (Taunton) 2000. LO HS 73* v Notts (Nottingham) 2001 (BHC). LO BB 3-28 v Middx (Lord's) 2001 (NL).

I.D.Austin, R.J.Green and M.Watkinson left the playing staff having made no f-c appearances in 2001.

SOMERSET 2001

RESULTS SUMMARY

	Place	Won	Lost	Tied	Drew	No Result
County Championship (1st Division)	2nd	6	2		8	
All First-Class Matches		6	3		8	
C & G Trophy	**Winners**					
Benson & Hedges Cup	Quarter-Finalist					
NU National League (1st Division)	4th	7	7	1		1

COUNTY CHAMPIONSHIP AVERAGES

BATTING AND FIELDING

Cap		M	I	NO	HS	Runs	Avge	100	50	Ct/St
1999	J.Cox	15	25	3	186	1264	57.45	1	9	6
1999	M.E.Trescothick	3	4	–	147	216	54.00	1	–	3
2001	I.D.Blackwell	10	15	–	122	781	52.06	4	3	4
–	M.J.Wood	6	10	–	122	439	43.90	1	3	2
1999	K.A.Parsons	4	6	1	139	213	42.60	1	–	4
1995	P.D.Bowler	13	20	1	164	799	42.05	2	4	14
1999	M.Burns	16	26	1	221	893	35.72	1	6	13
1992	M.N.Lathwell	13	21	1	99	702	35.10	–	8	9
1994	R.J.Turner	16	24	3	115*	710	33.80	1	3	58
2001	R.L.Johnson	13	15	3	68	379	31.58	–	2	3
1997	P.C.L.Holloway	11	19	1	85	560	31.11	–	4	2
2001	J.I.D.Kerr	7	10	5	36	154	30.80	–	–	1
2001	K.P.Dutch	16	22	4	118	530	29.44	1	3	19
–	P.D.Trego	3	5	1	43	117	29.25	–	–	–
2001	P.S.Jones	16	16	5	29*	180	16.36	–	–	3
–	M.P.L.Bulbeck	5	7	2	18	50	10.00	–	–	3
1988	G.D.Rose	3	4	–	15	25	6.25	–	–	–

Also batted: A.R.Caddick (2 matches – cap 1992) 0, 10*, 5*; J.O.Grove (3) 4*, 1, 19* (2 ct); J.P.Tucker (1) 5*, 0*.

BOWLING

	O	M	R	W	Avge	Best	5wI	10wM
A.R.Caddick	88.4	17	319	18	17.72	5- 81	3	1
R.L.Johnson	463.2	89	1474	62	23.77	5- 40	5	–
P.S.Jones	560	100	2015	59	34.15	5-115	1	–
K.P.Dutch	367	64	1268	35	36.22	4- 32	–	–
M.Burns	127.5	21	510	12	42.50	6- 54	1	–
I.D.Blackwell	259.4	69	783	18	43.50	5-122	1	–

Also bowled:

J.I.D.Kerr	150.4	33	504	8	63.00	3- 51	–	–
J.O.Grove	58.2	7	316	5	63.20	2- 46	–	–

P.D.Bowler 2-0-9-0; M.P.L.Bulbeck 110-6-501-4; P.C.L.Holloway 4-0-19-0; M.N.Lathwell 7-0-37-0; K.A.Parsons 24-3-90-1; G.D.Rose 50-15-155-3; P.D.Trego 58-11-243-4; J.P.Tucker 17-2-82-0; R.J.Turner 13-3-29-0; M.J.Wood 7-1-30-0.

The First-Class Averages (pp 113-126) give the records of Somerset players in all first-class county matches (Somerset's other opponents being the Australians), with the exception of A.R.Caddick and M.E.Trescothick, whose full county figures are as above, and:
  Shoaib Akhtar 1-2-1-10-14.00-0-0-0ct. 21-3-90-3-30.00-2/9.

SOMERSET RECORDS

FIRST-CLASS CRICKET

Highest Total	For 675-9d		v	Hampshire	Bath	1924
	V 811		by	Surrey	The Oval	1899
Lowest Total	For 25		v	Glos	Bristol	1947
	V 22		by	Glos	Bristol	1920
Highest Innings	For 322	I.V.A.Richards	v	Warwicks	Taunton	1985
	V 424	A.C.MacLaren	for	Lancashire	Taunton	1895

Highest Partnership for each Wicket

1st	346	H.T.Hewett/L.C.H.Palairet	v	Yorkshire	Taunton	1892
2nd	290	J.C.W.MacBryan/M.D.Lyon	v	Derbyshire	Burton upon T	1924
3rd	319	P.M.Roebuck/M.D.Crowe	v	Leics	Taunton	1984
4th	310	P.W.Denning/I.T.Botham	v	Glos	Taunton	1980
5th	235	J.C.White/C.C.C.Case	v	Glos	Taunton	1927
6th	265	W.E.Alley/K.E.Palmer	v	Northants	Northampton	1961
7th	279	R.J.Harden/G.D.Rose	v	Sussex	Taunton	1997
8th	172	I.V.A.Richards/I.T.Botham	v	Leics	Leicester	1983
	172	A.R.K.Pierson/P.S.Jones	v	N Zealanders	Taunton	1999
9th	183	C.H.M.Greetham/H.W.Stephenson	v	Leics	Weston-s-Mare	1963
	183	C.J.Tavaré/N.A.Mallender	v	Sussex	Hove	1990
10th	143	J.J.Bridges/A.H.D.Gibbs	v	Essex	Weston-s-Mare	1919

Best Bowling	For 10- 49	E.J.Tyler	v	Surrey	Taunton	1895
(Innings)	V 10- 35	A.Drake	for	Yorkshire	Weston-s-Mare	1914
Best Bowling	For 16- 83	J.C.White	v	Worcs	Bath	1919
(Match)	V 17-137	W.Brearley	for	Lancashire	Manchester	1905

Most Runs – Season	2761	W.E.Alley	(av 58.74)	1961
Most Runs – Career	21142	H.Gimblett	(av 36.96)	1935-54
Most 100s – Season	11	S.J.Cook		1991
Most 100s – Career	49	H.Gimblett		1935-54
Most Wkts – Season	169	A.W.Wellard	(av 19.24)	1938
Most Wkts – Career	2166	J.C.White	(av 18.02)	1909-37
Most Career W-K Dismissals	1007	H.W.Stephenson	(698 ct/309 st)	1948-64
Most Career Catches in the Field	381	J.C.White		1909-37

LIMITED-OVERS CRICKET

Highest Total	NWT	413-4		v	Devon	Torquay	1990
	BHC	349-7		v	Ireland	Taunton	1997
	NL	360-3		v	Glamorgan	Neath	1990
Lowest Total	NWT	58		v	Middlesex	Southgate	2000
	BHC	98		v	Middlesex	Lord's	1982
	NL	58		v	Essex	Chelmsford	1977
Highest Innings	NWT	162*	C.J.Tavaré	v	Devon	Torquay	1990
	BHC	177	S.J.Cook	v	Sussex	Hove	1990
	NL	175*	I.T.Botham	v	Northants	Wellingborough	1986
Best Bowling	NWT	7-15	R.P.Lefebvre	v	Devon	Torquay	1990
	BHC	7-24	Mushtaq Ahmed	v	Ireland	Taunton	1997
	NL	6-24	I.V.A.Richards	v	Lancashire	Manchester	1983

SURREY

Formation of Present Club: 22 August 1845
Colours: Chocolate
Badge: Prince of Wales' Feathers
County Champions (since 1890): (17) 1890, 1891, 1892, 1894, 1895, 1899, 1914, 1952, 1953, 1954, 1955, 1956, 1957, 1958, 1971, 1999, 2000
Joint Champions: (1) 1950
Gillette/NatWest/C & G Trophy Winners: (1) 1982
Benson and Hedges Cup Winners: (3) 1974, 1997, 2001
NU National League (Div 1) Winners: (0); best – 8th 2001
Sunday League Winners: (1) 1996
Match Awards: CGT 52; BHC 74

Chief Executive: P.C.J.Sheldon, Kennington Oval, London, SE11 5SS ▲ Tel: (020) 7582 6660 ▲ Fax: (020) 7735 7769 ▲ E-mail: enquiries@surreyccc.co.uk ▲ Web: www.surreyccc.co.uk

Captain: A.J.Hollioake. **Vice-Captain:** No appointment. **Overseas Player:** Saqlain Mushtaq. **2002 Beneficiary:** A.D.Brown. **Scorer:** K.R.Booth. ‡ New registration

BATTY, Jonathan Neil (Wheatley Park S, Oxon; Repton S; Durham U; Keble C, Oxford), b Chesterfield, Derbys 18 Apr 1974. 5'10". RHB, WK. Minor C 1994. Comb U 1995. Oxford U 1996; blue 1996. Surrey debut 1997; cap 2001. Oxfordshire 1993-96. HS 100* v Somerset (Oval) 2000. BB 1-21. LO HS 40 v Derbys (Oval) 1998 (SL).

BICKNELL, Martin Paul (Robert Haining County SS), b Guildford 14 Jan 1969. Younger brother of D.J.Bicknell (*see NOTTINGHAMSHIRE*). 6'3". RHB, RFM. Debut 1986; cap 1989; benefit 1997. *Wisden* 2000. **Tests:** 2 (1993); HS 14 and BB 3-99 v A (Birmingham) 1993. **LOI:** 7 (1990-91); HS 31* v A (Perth) 1990-91; BB 3-55 v NZ (Christchurch) 1990-91. Tours: A 1990-91; SA 1993-94 (Eng A); Z 1989-90 (Eng A). HS 110* v Kent (Canterbury) 2001. 50 wkts (10); most – 72 (2001). BB 9-45 v CU (Oval) 1988. CC BB 9-47 (16-119 match) v Leics (Guildford) 2000. Awards: BHC 3. LO HS 66* v Northants (Oval) 1991 (NWT). LO BB 7-30 v Glam (Oval) 1999 (NL).

BROWN, Alistair Duncan (Caterham S), b Beckenham, Kent 11 Feb 1970. 5'10". RHB, occ LB. Debut 1992; cap 1994; benefit 2002. **LOI:** 16 (1996 to 2001); HS 118 v I (Manchester) 1996. 1000 runs (5); most – 1382 (1993). HS 295* v Leics (Oakham) 2000 – record score (all levels) in Rutland. BB 1-56. Awards: BHC 3. LO HS 203 v Hants (Guildford) 1997 (SL). LO BB 3-39 v Notts (Nottingham) 2000 (NL).

BUTCHER, Mark Alan (Trinity S; Archbishop Tenison's S, Croydon), b Croydon 23 Aug 1972. Son of A.R.Butcher (Surrey, Glamorgan and England 1972-92); brother of G.P.Butcher (Glamorgan 1994-98; Surrey 1999-2001). 5'11". LHB, RM/OB. Debut 1992; cap 1996. **Tests:** 35 (1997 to 2001-02, 1 as captain); HS 173* v A (Leeds) 2001; BB 4-42 v A (Birmingham) 2001. Tours: A 1996-97 (Eng A), 1998-99; SA 1999-00; WI 1997-98; NZ 2001-02; I 2001-02. 1000 runs (6); most – 1604 (1996). HS 259 v Leics (Leicester) 1999. BB 5-86 v Lancs (Manchester) 2000. Awards: CGT 2; BHC 2. LO HS 91 v Somerset (Oval) 1996 (NWT). LO BB 3-23 v Sussex (Oval) 1992 (SL).

CARBERRY, Michael Alexander (St John Rigby Catholic C), b Croydon 29 Sep 1980. 6'0". LHB, OB. Debut 2001. HS 84 v Glam (Cardiff) 2001. LO HS 20 v Glos (Bristol) 2001 (NL).

‡CLARKE, Rikki (Broadwater SS; Godalming C), b Orsett, Essex 29 Sep 1981. 6'4". RHB, RFM. Staff 2002 – awaiting f-c debut. LO HS 7 (NL). LO BB (Surrey CB) 1-14 (CGT).

77

GIDDINS, Edward Simon Hunter (Eastbourne C), b Eastbourne, Sussex 20 Jul 1971. 6'4½". RHB, RFM. Sussex 1991-96; cap 1994. Warwickshire 1998-2000; cap 1998. Surrey debut 2001. MCC YC. **Tests:** 4 (1999 to 2000); HS 7 and BB 5-15 v Z (Lord's) 2000. Tour: P 1995-96 (Eng A). HS 34 Sx v Essex (Hove) 1995. Sy HS 9*. 50 wkts (4); most – 84 (1998). BB 6-47 Sx v Yorks (Eastbourne) 1996. Sy BB 5-48 v Leics (Oval) 2001. Awards: CGT 1; BHC 1. LO HS 13 Sx v Essex (Hove) 1994 (NWT). LO BB 5-21 Wa v Leics (Leicester) 1999 (BHC).

HOLLIOAKE, Adam John (St Joseph's C, Sydney; St Patrick's C, Ballarat; St George's C, Weybridge; Surrey Tutorial C), b Melbourne, Australia 5 Sep 1971. Elder brother of B.C.Hollioake. 5'11". RHB, RMF. Debut 1993, scoring 13 and 123 v Derbys (Ilkeston); cap 1995; captain 1997 to date. Qualified for England 1992. **Tests:** 4 (1997 to 1997-98); HS 45 and BB 2-31 v A (Nottingham) 1997 – on debut. **LOI:** 35 (1996 to 1999, 14 as captain); HS 83* v SA (Dhaka) 1998-99; BB 4-23 v P (Birmingham) 1996 – on debut. Tours: A 1996-97 (Eng A – captain); WI 1997-98. 1000 runs (2); most – 1522 (1996). HS 182 v Middx (Lord's) 1997. BB 5-62 v Glam (Swansea) 1998. Awards: CGT 1; BHC 1. LO HS 111 v Glam (Oval) 2000 (NL). LO BB 5-29 v Durham (Chester-le-St) 2000 (NL).

HOLLIOAKE, Benjamin Caine (Millfield S), b Melbourne, Australia 11 Nov 1977. Younger brother of A.J.Hollioake. 6'2". RHB, RMF. Debut 1996. Surrey 1996. YC 1997. **Tests:** 2 (1997 to 1998); HS 28 v A (Nottingham) 1997 on debut; BB 2-105 v SL (Oval) 1998. **LOI:** 20 (1997 to 2001-02); HS 63 v A (Lord's) 1997 – on debut; BB 2-37 v Z (Harare) 2001-02. Tours: A 1998-99; SL (Eng A) 1997-98. HS 163 Eng A v SL (Moratuwa) 1997-98. Sy HS 118 v Yorks (Oval) 2001. BB 5-51 v Glam (Oval) 1999. Awards: BHC 4. LO HS 98 v Kent (Lord's) 1997 (BHC). LO BB 5-10 v Derbys (Oval) 1996 (SL).

MURTAGH, Timothy James (John Fisher S; St Mary's C), b Lambeth 2 Aug 1981. Nephew of A.J.Murtagh (Hampshire and E Province 1973-7). 6'0". LHB, RFM. British U 2000-01. Surrey debut 2001. HS 22* and BB 6-86 Brit U v P (Nottingham) 2001. Sy HS 2. Sy BB 1-15. LO HS 11 Surrey CB v Hunts (Cheam) 2001 (CGT). LO BB 4-31 v Warwks (Croydon) 2001 (NL).

‡**NEWMAN, Scott** Alexander (Trinity S, Croydon; Coulsdon C; Brighton U), b Epsom 3 Nov 1979. 6'2". LHB, RM. Staff 2002 – awaiting f-c debut. LO HS 49 Surrey CB v Lincs (Bourne) 2001 (CGT).

‡**ORMOND, James** (St Thomas More S, Nuneaton), b Walsgrave, Coventry, Warwks 20 Aug 1977. 6'3". RHB, RFM. Leicestershire 1995-2001; cap 1999. **Tests:** 2 (2001 to 2001-02); HS 18 v A (Oval) 2001; BB 1-70. Tours: NZ 2001-02; I 2001-02; SL 1997-98 (Eng A); K 1997-98 (Eng A). HS 50* Le v Warwks (Leicester) 1999. 50 wkts (1): 52 (1999). BB 6-33 (9-62 match) Le v Somerset (Leicester) 1998. Awards: BHC 2. LO HS 18* Le v Somerset (Lord's) 2001 (CGT). LO BB 4-12 Le v Middx (Leicester) 1998 (SL).

RAMPRAKASH, Mark Ravin (Gayton HS; Harrow Weald SFC), b Bushey, Herts 5 Sep 1969. 5'9". RHB, RM. Middlesex 1987-2000; cap 1990; captain 1997-99. Surrey debut 2001. YC 1991. **ECB contract 2000. Tests:** 49 (1991 to 2001-02); HS 154 v WI (Bridgetown) 1997-98; BB 1-2. **LOI:** 18 (1991 to 2001-02); HS 51 v WI (P-o-S) 1997-98; BB 3-28 v Z (Harare) 2001-02. Tours: A 1994-95 (part), 1998-99; SA 1995-96; WI 1991-92 (Eng A), 1993-94, 1997-98; NZ 1991-92, 2001-02; I 1994-95 (Eng A). P 1990-91 (Eng A); SL 1990-91 (Eng A). 1000 runs (11) inc 2000 (1): 2258 (1995). HS 235 M v Yorks (Leeds) 1995. Sy HS 146 v Kent (Oval) 2001 – on Sy debut. BB 3-32 M v Glam (Lord's) 1998. Sy BB – . Awards: CGT 2; BHC 4. LO HS 147* M v Worcs (Lord's) 1990 (SL). LO BB 5-38 M v Leics (Lord's) 1993 (SL).

RATCLIFFE, Jason David (Sharman's Cross SS; Solihull SFC), b Solihull, Warwks 19 Jun 1969. Son of D.P.Ratcliffe (Warwks 1957-68). 6'4". RHB, RM. Warwickshire 1988-94. Surrey debut 1995; cap 1998. No appearances 2001. Tours (Wa): SA 1991-92, 1992-93; Z 1993-94. HS 135 v Worcs (Worcester) 1997. BB 6-48 v SA (Oval) 1999. BB 3-28 v Kent (Tunbridge W) 1999. Awards: CGT 2. LO HS 105 Wa v Yorks (Leeds) 1993 (NWT). LO BB 3-15 v Sussex (Hove) 2000 (BHC).

SALISBURY, Ian David Kenneth (Moulton CS), b Northampton 21 Jan 1970. 5'11". RHB, LBG. Sussex 1989-96; cap 1991. Surrey debut 1997; cap 1998. MCC YC. YC 1992. *Wisden* 1992. **Tests:** 15 (1992 to 2000-01); HS 50 v P (Manchester) 1992; BB 4-163 v WI (Georgetown) 1993-94. **LOI:** 4 (1992-93 to 1993-94); HS 5; BB 3-41 v WI (P-o-S) 1993-94. Tours: WI 1991-92 (Eng A), 1993-94; I 1992-93; 1994-95 (Eng A); P 1990-91 (Eng A), 1995-96 (Eng A), 2000-01; SL 1990-91 (Eng A). HS 100* v Somerset (Oval) 1999. 50 wkts (6); most – 87 (1992). BB 8-60 (12-91 match) v Somerset (Oval) 2000. Awards: CGT 1; BHC 2. LO HS 48* Sx v Glam (Swansea) 1995 (SL). LO BB 5-30 Sx v Leics (Leicester) 1992 (SL).

‡**SAMPSON, Philip** James (Pretoria BHS, SA), b Manchester 6 Sep 1980. 6'1". RHB, RFM. Staff 2002 – awaiting f-c debut. Buckinghamshire 1999. LO HS (Sy CB) 4* (NWT). LO BB 1-25 (NL).

SAQLAIN MUSHTAQ (Govt Muslim League HS, M.A.O. College, Lahore), b Lahore, Pakistan 29 Dec 1976. Brother of Sibtain Mushtaq (Lahore 1988-89). 5'11". RHB. OB. Islamabad 1994-95. PIA 1994-95 to date. Surrey debut 1997; cap 1998. *Wisden* 1999. **Tests** (P): 39 (1995-96 to 2001-02); HS 101* v NZ (Christchurch) 2000-01; BB 8-164 v E (Lahore) 2000-01. **LOI** (P): 148 (1995-96 to 2001-02); HS 37* v A (Brisbane) 1999-00; BB 5-20 v E (Rawalpindi) 2000-01, 2 hat-tricks. Tours (P): E 1996, 2001; A 1995-96, 1996-97, 1999-00; SA 1997-98; WI 1999-00; NZ 2000-01; I 1998-99, SL 1996-97; Z 1997-98; B 1998-99. HS 101* (*see Tests*). Sy HS 66 v Leics (Oakham) 2000. 50 wkts (4+1); most – 66 (2000). BB 8-65 (11-107 match) v Derbys (Oval) 1988. Took 7-11 v Derbys (Oval) 2000. Hat-tricks 1997 and 1999. Awards: CGT 2. LO HS 38* v Yorks (Leeds) 2001 (NL). LO BB 5-20 (*see LOI*).

SCOTT, Ben James Matthew (Whitton S, Richmond; Richmond C), b Isleworth, Middx 4 Aug 1981. 5'8". RHB, WK. Staff 2001 – awaiting f-c debut. LO HS 11 Middx CB v Cumb (Southgate) 1999 (NWT).

SHAHID, Nadeem (Ipswich S), b Karachi, Pakistan 23 Apr 1969. 6'0". RHB, LB. Essex 1989-94. Surrey debut 1995; cap 1998. Suffolk 1988. 1000 runs (1): 1003 (1990). HS 139 v Yorks (Oval) 1995. BB 3-91 Ex v Surrey (Oval) 1990. Sy BB 3-93 v SA A (Oval) 1996. LO HS 109* v Notts (Nottingham) 2000 (NL). LO BB 3-30 v Bucks (Oval) 1998 (NWT).

STEWART, Alec James (Tiffin S), b Merton 8 Apr 1963. Son of M.J.Stewart (Surrey and England 1954-72). 5'11". RHB, WK. Debut 1981; cap 1985; captain 1992-97; benefit 1994. *Wisden* 1992. MBE 1998. **ECB contracts 2000, 2001. Tests:** 115 (1989-90 to 2001, 15 as captain); HS 190 v P (Birmingham) 1992. **LOI:** 146 – Eng record (1989-90 to 2001, 40 as captain); HS 116 v I (Sharjah) 1997-98. Tours (C=captain): A 1990-91, 1994-95, 1998-99C; SA 1995-96, 1999-00; WI 1989-90, 1993-94, 1997-98; NZ 1991-92, 1996-97; I 1992-93; P 2000-01; SL 1992-93C, 2000-01; Z 1996-97. 1000 runs (8); most – 1665 (1986). HS 271* v Yorks (Oval) 1997. BB 1-7. Held 11 catches (equalling world f-c match record) v Leics (Leicester) 1989. Awards: CGT 5; BHC 6. LO HS 167* v Somerset (Oval) 1994 (BHC).

THORPE, Graham Paul (Weydon CS; Farnham SFC), b Farnham 1 Aug 1969. 5'10". LHB, RM. Debut 1988; cap 1991; benefit 2000. *Wisden* 1997. **ECB contract 2001. Tests:** 70 (1993 to 2001-02); HS 138 v A (Birmingham) 1997 and 138 v P (Manchester) 2001; scored 114* v A (Nottingham) 1993 on debut. **LOI:** 79 (1993 to 2001-02, 3 as captain); HS 89 v I (Brisbane) 1994-95 and 89 v H (Peshawar) 1995-96; BB 2-15 v I (Manchester) 1996. Tours: A 1992-93 (Eng A), 1994-95, 1998-99 (*part*); SA 1995-96; WI 1991-92 (Eng A), 1993-94, 1997-98; NZ 1996-97, 2001-02; I 2001-02 (*part*); P 1990-91 (Eng A), 2000-01; SL 1990-91 (Eng A), 2000-01; Z 1989-90 (Eng A), 1996-97. 1000 runs (8); most – 1895 (1992). HS 223* Eng XI v S Aus (Adelaide) 1998-99. Sy HS 222 v Glam (Oval) 1997. BB 4-40 v A (Oval) 1993. CC BB 2-14 v Derbys (Oval) 1996. Awards: CGT 3; BHC 1. LO HS 145* v Lancs (Oval) 1994 (NWT). LO BB 3-21 v Somerset (Oval) 1991 (SL).

TUDOR, Alex Jeremy (St Mark's S, Hammersmith; City of Westminster C), b West Brompton, London 23 Oct 1977. 6'5". RHB, RF. Debut 1995; cap 1999. YC 1999. **Tests:** 5 (1998-99 to 2001); HS 99* v NZ (Birmingham) 1999 – record score by an England 'night-watchman'. BB 5-44 v A (Nottingham) 2001. Tours: A 1998-99; SA 1999-00; WI 2000-01 (Eng A). HS 116 v Essex (Oval) 2001. BB 7-48 v Lancs (Oval) 2000. LO HS 29* v Essex (Oval) 1995 (SL). LO BB 4-26 v Hants (Oval) 2000 (NL).

WARD, Ian James (Millfield S), b Plymouth, Devon 30 Sep 1972. 5'8½". LHB, RM. Surrey 1992, 1996 to date; cap 2000. **Tests:** 5 (200); HS 39 v P (Lord's) 2001 – on debut. Tours (Eng A): WI 2000-01; NZ 1999-00; B 1999-00. 1000 runs (1): 1018 (1999). HS 158* v Kent (Canterbury) 2000. LO HS 91 v Middx (Guildford) 1998 (SL).

RELEASED/RETIRED
(Having made a first-class County appearance in 2001)

AMIN, Rupesh Mahesh (Riddlesdown HS; John Ruskin C; Croydon C), b Clapham, London 20 Aug 1977. 6'0". RHB, SLA. Surrey 1997-2001. HS 12 v Leics (Oval) 1998. BB 4-87 v Somerset (Oval) 1999. LO HS – (SL). LO BB 2-43 v Lancs (Oval) 1997 (SL).

BATTY, G.J. – *see* WORCESTERSHIRE.

BUTCHER, Gary Paul (Trinity S; Riddlesdown S; Heath Clark C), b Clapham, London 11 Mar 1975. Son of A.R.Butcher (Surrey, Glam and England 1972-92); brother of M.A.Butcher. 5'9". RHB, RM. Glamorgan 1994-98. Surrey 1999-2001. Tours (Gm): SA 1995-96; Z 1994-95. HS 101* Gm v OU (Oxford) 1997. CC HS 89 Gm v Northants (Northampton) 1996. Sy HS 70 v Warwks (Birmingham) 1999. BB 7-77 Gm v Glos (Bristol) 1996. Sy BB 5-18 v Derbys (Oval) 2000 – including 4 wickets in 4 balls. Hat-trick (4 in 4) 2000. LO HS 48 Gm v Beds (Cardiff) 1997 (NWT). LO BB 4-32 Gm v Glos (Bristol) 1996 (SL).

I.E.Bishop, C.G.Greenidge (*see* NORTHAMPTONSHIRE), M.W.Patterson and J.J.Porter have left the staff having made no f-c appearances in 2001.

OVERSEAS REGISTRATIONS 2002

Derbyshire	M.J.Di Venuto
Durham	M.L.Love
Essex	A.Flower
Glamorgan	*tba*
Gloucestershire	I.J.Harvey
Hampshire	N.C.Johnson
Kent	A.Symonds
Lancashire	S.G.Law
Leicestershire	M.G.Bevan
Middlesex	Abdul Razzaq
Northamptonshire	M.E.K.Hussey
Nottinghamshire	C.L.Cairns
Somerset	J.Cox
Surrey	Saqlain Mushtaq
Sussex	M.W.Goodwin
Warwickshire	S.M.Pollock
Worcestershire	A.J.Bichel
Yorkshire	D.S.Lehmann

SURREY 2001

RESULTS SUMMARY

	Place	Won	Lost	Tied	Drew	No Result
County Championship (1st Division)	4th	3	1		11	1
All First-Class Matches		3	1		11	1
C & G Trophy	4th Round					
Benson & Hedges Cup	Winners					
NU National League (1st Division)	8th	6	10			

COUNTY CHAMPIONSHIP AVERAGES

BATTING AND FIELDING

Cap		M	I	NO	HS	Runs	Avge	100	50	Ct/St
1996	M.A.Butcher	10	15	1	230	844	60.28	2	5	11
–	M.R.Ramprakash	9	14	–	146	776	55.42	3	4	4
1989	M.P.Bicknell	15	22	6	110*	748	46.75	1	4	5
1999	A.J.Tudor	7	11	1	116	399	39.90	1	1	2
1995	A.J.Hollioake	13	20	1	97	758	39.89	–	7	15
1985	A.J.Stewart	5	6	1	106	196	39.20	1	–	13/1
1994	A.D.Brown	13	20	–	122	630	31.50	3	2	3
2000	I.J.Ward	11	18	–	79	561	31.16	–	4	5
–	M.A.Carberry	6	10	–	84	311	31.10	–	1	6
1999	B.C.Hollioake	12	19	–	118	586	30.84	1	4	18
1998	I.D.K.Salisbury	15	21	4	54	440	25.88	–	1	9
–	G.P.Butcher	4	8	1	56	175	25.00	–	1	1
1998	N.Shahid	7	12	–	65	208	17.33	–	1	8
2001	J.N.Batty	10	16	1	59	239	15.93	–	1	26/2
1998	Saqlain Mushtaq	9	14	5	38	131	14.55	–	–	1
	E.S.H.Giddins	12	14	8	9*	36	6.00	–	–	2
	R.M.Amin	3	4	1	1	1	0.33	–	–	2

Also batted: G.J.Batty (1 match) 25, 19 (2 ct); T.J.Murtagh (1) 2; G.P.Thorpe (2 – cap 1991) 148, 32 (2 ct).

BOWLING

	O	M	R	W	Avge	Best	5wI	10wM
M.P.Bicknell	541.5	132	1538	72	21.36	7-60	3	1
Saqlain Mushtaq	411.2	109	952	43	22.13	7-58	4	–
E.S.H.Giddins	352.5	83	1102	30	36.73	5-48	1	–
A.J.Tudor	206.2	46	732	19	38.52	5-54	1	–
I.D.K.Salisbury	396.2	72	1151	27	42.62	5-95	1	–

Also bowled:

R.M.Amin	102	28	272	5	54.40	3-80		
B.C.Hollioake	133.2	21	530	9	58.88	2-39		

A.D.Brown 23-1-97-0; G.P.Butcher 34.4-5-138-2; M.A.Butcher 45-5-162-4; A.J.Hollioake 54-11-165-3; T.J.Murtagh 11-5-28-1; M.R.Ramprakash 51-14-84-0; A.J.Stewart 1-1-0-0; G.P.Thorpe 1-0-11-0.

Surrey played no first-class fixtures outside the County Championship in 2001. The First-Class Averages (pp 113-126) give the records of Surrey players in all first-class county matches, with the exception of M.A.Butcher, T.J.Murtagh, M.R.Ramprakash, Saqlain Mushtaq, A.J.Stewart, G.P.Thorpe, A.J.Tudor and I.J.Ward whose full county figures are as above.

SURREY RECORDS

FIRST-CLASS CRICKET

Highest Total	For 811		v	Somerset	The Oval	1899
	V 863		by	Lancashire	The Oval	1990
Lowest Total	For 14		v	Essex	Chelmsford	1983
	V 16		by	MCC	Lord's	1872
Highest Innings	For 357*	R.Abel	v	Somerset	The Oval	1899
	V 366	N.H.Fairbrother	for	Lancashire	The Oval	1990

Highest Partnership for each Wicket

1st	428	J.B.Hobbs/A.Sandham	v	Oxford U	The Oval	1926
2nd	371	J.B.Hobbs/E.G.Hayes	v	Hampshire	The Oval	1909
3rd	413	D.J.Bicknell/D.M.Ward	v	Kent	Canterbury	1990
4th	448	R.Abel/T.W.Hayward	v	Yorkshire	The Oval	1899
5th	308	J.N.Crawford/F.C.Holland	v	Somerset	The Oval	1908
6th	298	A.Sandham/H.S.Harrison	v	Sussex	The Oval	1913
7th	262	C.J.Richards/K.T.Medlycott	v	Kent	The Oval	1987
8th	205	I.A.Greig/M.P.Bicknell	v	Lancashire	The Oval	1990
9th	168	E.R.T.Holmes/E.W.J.Brooks	v	Hampshire	The Oval	1936
10th	173	A.Ducat/A.Sandham	v	Essex	Leyton	1921

Best Bowling	For	10-43	T.Rushby	v	Somerset	Taunton	1921
(Innings)	V	10-28	W.P.Howell	for	Australians	The Oval	1899
Best Bowling	For	16-83	G.A.R.Lock	v	Kent	Blackheath	1956
(Match)	V	15-57	W.P.Howell	for	Australians	The Oval	1899

Most Runs – Season	3246	T.W.Hayward	(av 72.13)	1906
Most Runs – Career	43554	J.B.Hobbs	(av 49.72)	1905-34
Most 100s – Season	13	T.W.Hayward		1906
	13	J.B.Hobbs		1925
Most 100s – Career	144	J.B.Hobbs		1905-34
Most Wkts – Season	252	T.Richardson	(av 13.94)	1895
Most Wkts – Career	1775	T.Richardson	(av 17.87)	1892-1904
Most Career W-K Dismissals	1221	H.Strudwick	(1035 ct/186 st)	1902-27
Most Career Catches in the Field	605	M.J.Stewart		1954-72

LIMITED-OVERS CRICKET

Highest Total	NWT	350	v	Worcs	The Oval	1994
	BHC	361-8	v	Notts	The Oval	2001
	NL	375-4	v	Yorkshire	Scarborough	1994
Lowest Total	NWT	74	v	Kent	The Oval	1967
	BHC	89	v	Notts	Nottingham	1984
	NL	64	v	Worcs	Worcester	1978
Highest Innings	NWT	146	G.S.Clinton	v	Kent	Canterbury	1985
	BHC	167*	A.J.Stewart	v	Somerset	The Oval	1994
	NL	203	A.D.Brown	v	Hampshire	Guildford	1997
Best Bowling	NWT	7-33	R.D.Jackman	v	Yorkshire	Harrogate	1970
	BHC	5-15	S.G.Kenlock	v	Ireland	The Oval	1995
	NL	7-30	M.P.Bicknell	v	Glamorgan	The Oval	1999

SUSSEX

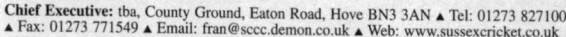

Formation of Present Club: 1 March 1839
Substantial Reorganisation: August 1857
Colours: Dark Blue, Light Blue and Gold
Badge: County Arms of Six Martlets
County Champions: (0); best – 2nd 1902, 1903, 1932,
1933, 1934, 1953, 1981
Gillette/NatWest/C & G Trophy Winners: (4) 1963, 1964,
1978, 1986
Benson and Hedges Cup Winners: (0); best –
semi-finalists 1982, 1999
NU National League (Div 1) Winners: (0); best – 9th 2000
Sunday League Winners: (1) 1982
Match Awards: CGT 57; BHC 60

Chief Executive: tba, County Ground, Eaton Road, Hove BN3 3AN ▲ Tel: 01273 827100
▲ Fax: 01273 771549 ▲ Email: fran@sccc.demon.co.uk ▲ Web: www.sussexcricket.co.uk

Captain: C.J.Adams. **Vice-Captain:** R.J.Kirtley. **Overseas Player:** M.W.Goodwin.
2002 Beneficiary: J.D.Lewry. **Scorer:** L.V.Chandler. ‡ New registration

ADAMS, Christopher John (Repton S), b Whitwell, Derbyshire 6 May 1970. 6'0". RHB,
RM/OB. Derbyshire 1988-97; cap 1992. Sussex debut/cap 1998; captain 1998 to date.
Tests: 5 (1999-00); HS 31 v SA (Cape Town) 1999-00; BB 1-42. **LOI:** 5 (1998 to 1999-00);
HS 42 v SA (Cape Town) 1999-00. Tour: SA 1999-00. 1000 runs (5); most – 1742 (1996).
HS 239 De v Hants (Southampton) 1996. Sx HS 192 v Derbys (Arundel) 2001. BB 4-28 v
Durham (Chester-le-St) 2001. Awards: CGT 3; BHC 5. LO HS 163 v Middx (Arundel) 1999
(NL). LO BB 5-16 v Middx (Hove) 1998 (SL).

AMBROSE, Timothy Raymond (Merewether HS, NSW; TAFE C), b Newcastle, NSW,
Australia 1 Dec 1982. ECB qualified. 5'7". RHB, WK. Debut 2001. HS 52 v Warwks
(Birmingham) 2001 – on debut. LO HS 87 v Lancs (Hove) 2001 (NL).

CARPENTER, James Robert (Birkenhead S), b Birkenhead, Cheshire 20 Oct 1975. 6'1½".
LHB, SLA. MCC YC. Debut 1997. No appearances 2001. HS 65 v Notts (Nottingham)
1998. BB 1-50. LO HS 64* v Notts (Cleethorpes) 1999 (NL).

CLAPP, Dominic Adrian (Lancing C; Worthing SFC), b Southport, Lancs 25 May 1980.
6'0". RHB, RM. Staff 2000 – awaiting f-c debut. 2nd XI debut 1997 when aged 16y 347d.
LO HS 10 Sussex CB v Berks (Hastings) 2000 (NWT). LO BB 3-46 Sussex CB v Herefords
(Colwall) 2000 (NWT).

COTTEY, Phillip Anthony (Bishopston CS, Swansea), b Swansea, Glamorgan 2 Jun 1966.
5'4". RHB, OB. Glamorgan 1986-98; cap 1992. Sussex debut/cap 1999. E Transvaal
1991-92. Tours (Gm): SA 1995-96; Z 1990-91, 1994-95. 1000 runs (7); most – 1543 (1996).
HS 203 and BB 4-49 Gm v Leics (Swansea) 1996. Sx HS 154 v Essex (Chelmsford) 2000.
Sx BB – . LO HS 96 Gm v Sussex (Hove) 1998 (BHC). LO BB 4-56 Gm v Essex
(Chelmsford) 1996 (SL).

DAVIS, Mark Jeffrey Gronow (Grey HS; Pretoria U), b Port Elizabeth, SA 10 Oct 1971.
ECB qualified – British/EU passport. 6'2". RHB, OB. N Transvaal/Northerns 1990-91 to
date. MCC 1999 and 2000. Sussex debut 2001. HS 71 NT v OFS (Bloemfontein) 1995-96.
Sx HS 52 v Derbys (Derby) 2001. BB 8-37 (12-84 match) NT B v W Transvaal
(Potchefstroom) 1994-95. Sx BB 6-116 v Worcs (Horsham) 2001. LO HS 35 NT v EP
(Verwoerdburg) 1994-95 (BHS). LO BB 4-24 v Middx (Richmond) 2001 (NL).

GOODWIN, Murray William (Newton Moore HS, Bunbury, WA), b Salisbury, Rhodesia 11 Dec 1972. Younger brother of D.G.Goodwin (Zimbabwe 1986-97 to 1989-90). 5'9". Emigrated to Australia in Nov 1986. Gained Zimbabwean citizenship in Sep 1997. RHB, LB. Western Australia 1994-95 to 1996-97, 2000-01 to date. Mashonaland 1997-98 to 1998-99. Sussex debut/cap 2001. Holland 1993. **Tests** (Z): 19 (1997-98 to 2000); HS 166* v P (Bulawayo) 1997-98. **LOI** (Z): 71 (1997-98 to 2000); HS 112* v WI (Chester-le-St) 2000; BB 1-12. Tours (Z): E 2000, SA 1999-00; WI 1999-00; NZ 1997-98; P 1998-99; SL 1997-98. 1000 (1): 1654 (2001). HS 203* v Notts (Nottingham) 2001. BB 2-23 Z v Lahore City (Lahore) 1998-99. Sx BB – . Award: BHC 1. LO HS 167 WA v NSW (Perth) 2000-01 (MC) – Australian l-o record. LO BB 1-9 Mashonaland v Eng A (Harare) 1998-99.

HAVELL, Paul Matthew Roger (Mentone GS, Melbourne; Warden Park S; Haywards Heath C), b Melbourne, Australia 4 Jul 1980. 6'3". LHB, RFM. Debut 2001 – awaiting CC debut. HS – . LO HS – (NL).

HOPKINSON, Carl Daniel (Brighton C), b Brighton 14 Sep 1981. 5'11". RHB, RM. Awaiting f-c debut. LO HS 43 Sussex CB v Glos (Horsham) 2001 (CGT). LO BB 1-2 (NL).

HOUSE, William John (Sevenoaks S; Gonville & Caius C, Cambridge), b Sheffield, Yorks 16 Mar 1976. 5'11". LHB, RM. Cambridge U 1996-98, scoring 136 v Derbys on debut; blue 1996-97-98. Kent 1997-99. British U 1998. Sussex debut 2000. HS 136 (see above). CC HS 46 v Notts (Hove) 2001. BB 1-34 (twice – CU, Sx). Awards: BHC 2. LO HS 93 Brit U v Surrey (Oval) 1997 (BHC). LO BB 5-58 Brit U v Glos (Bristol) 1998 (BHC).

‡**HUTCHISON, Paul** Michael (Crawshaw HS, Pudsey), b Leeds, Yorks 9 Jun 1977. 6'3". LHB, LFM. Yorkshire 1995-96 (Y in Zim) to 2001; cap 1998. The Rest 1996. Tours (Eng A): SL 1997-98; Z 1995-96 (Y); K 1997-98. HS 30 Y v Essex (Scarborough) 1998. 50 wkts (1): 59 (1998). BB 7-31 Y v Sussex (Hove) 1998. Award: CGT 1. LO HS (Y) 4* (NWT/BHC). LO BB 4-34 Y v Glos (Gloucester) 1998 (SL).

KIRTLEY, Robert James (Clifton C), b Eastbourne 10 Jan 1975. 6'0". RHB, RFM. Debut 1995; cap 1998. Mashonaland 1996-97. **LOI**: 3 (2001-02); HS 1; BB 2-33 v Z (Harare) 2001-02 – on debut. Tours (Eng A): NZ 1999-00; B 1999-00. HS 59 v Durham (Eastbourne) 1998. 50 wkts (4); most – 75 (1998). BB 7-21 v Hants (Southampton) 1999. Took 5-53 (7-88 match) for Mashonaland v Eng XI (Harare) 1996-97. Award: CGT 1. LO HS 17* v Somerset (Hove) 1999 (NL). LO BB 5-39 v Salop (Hove) 1997 (NWT).

LEWRY, Jason David (Durrington HS, Worthing), b Worthing 2 Apr 1971. 6'2". LHB, LFM. Debut 1994; cap 1996; benefit 2002 Tour: Z 1998-99 (Eng A). HS 47 v Glos (Hove) 2001. 50 wkts (4); most – 62 (1998). BB 7-38 (10-113 match) v Derbys (Derby) 1999. 2 hat-tricks (1998, 2001). LO HS 16 v Lancs (Manchester) 2001 (CGT). LO BB 4-29 v Somerset (Bath) 1995 (SL).

MARTIN-JENKINS, Robin Simon Christopher (Radley C; Durham U), b Guildford, Surrey 28 Oct 1975. Son of C.D.A.Martin-Jenkins (Times Chief Cricket Correspondent/BBC Commentator). 6'5". RHB, RFM. Debut 1995; cap 2000. British U 1996. HS 113 v Glos (Hove) 2001. BB 7-54 v Glam (Hove) 1998. Award: BHC 1. LO HS 45 v Hants (Hove) 2000 (BHC). LO BB (Brit U) 4-57 v Glos (Bristol) 1997 (BHC).

MONTGOMERIE, Richard Robert (Rugby S; Worcester C, Oxford), b Rugby, Warwks 3 Jul 1971. 5'10½". RHB. OB. Oxford U 1991-94; blue 1991-92-93-94; captain 1994; half blues for rackets and real tennis. Northamptonshire 1991-98; cap 1995. Sussex debut/cap 1999. Tour: Z 1994-95 (Nh). 1000 runs (3); most – 1704 (2001). HS 192 Nh v Kent (Canterbury) 1995. Sx HS 160* v Notts (Nottingham) 2001. BB 1-0. LO HS 129* v Z (Hastings) 2000.

PRIOR, Matthew James (Brighton C), b Johannesburg, SA, 24 Feb 82. 6'2". RHB, WK. Debut 2001. HS 66 v Derbys (Arundel) 2001. LO HS 25 v Durham (Chester-le-St) 2001 (NL).

RASHID, Umer Bin Abdul (Ealing Green HS; Ealing Tertiary C; Southbank U), b Southampton, Hants 6 Feb 1976. 6'3". LHB, SLA. Middlesex 1996-98. Sussex debut 1999. HS 110 v Glam (Colwyn Bay) 2000. BB 5-103 v Northants (Northampton) 2000. LO HS 82 Brit U v Hants (Oxford) 1997. LO BB 5-24 v Glam (Swansea) 1999 (NL).

ROBINSON, Mark Andrew (Hull GS), b Hull, Yorkshire 23 Nov 1966. 6'3". RHB, RFM. Northamptonshire 1987-90; cap 1990. Canterbury 1988-89. Yorkshire 1991-95; cap 1992. Sussex 1997-2001; cap 1997. Tours (Y): SA 1991-92, 1992-93. Failed to score in 12 successive f-c innings 1990 – world record. HS 27 v Lancs (Manchester) 1997. 50 wkts (2): most – 56 (2001). BB 9-37 (12-124 match) Y v Northants (Harrogate) 1993. Sx BB 6-78 v Northants (Hove) 1997 on Sussex debut. Awards: BHC 2. LO HS 15* v Lancs (Manchester) 2000 (NL). LO BB 4-23 Y v Northants (Leeds) 1993 (SL) and 4-23 v Leics (Leicester) 2000 (NL). Transferred from playing to coaching staff after 2001 season – available for 1-o matches.

TAYLOR, Billy Victor (Bitterne Park S, Southampton), b Southampton, Hants 11 Jan 1977. Brother of J.L.Taylor (Wiltshire 1998 to date). 6'3". LHB, RMF. Debut 1999. Wiltshire 1996-98. HS 24* v Glos (Cheltenham) 2001. BB 3-27 v Worcs (Worcester) 2000. Award: CGT 1. LO HS 21* v Notts (Cleethorpes) 1999 (NL). LO BB 4-26 v Middx CB (Southgate) 2000 (NWT).

YARDY, Michael Howard (William Parker S, Hastings), b Pembury, Kent 27 Nov 1980. 6'0". LHB, LM. Debut 2000. HS 87* v Hants (Hove) 2001. BB 1-13. LO HS 59 v Middx (Hove) 2001 (BHC). LO BB 2-34 v Derbys (Arundel) 2001 (NL).

ZUIDERENT, Bastiaan ('*Bas*') (Erasmiaans Gymnasium, Rotterdam; Amsterdam U), b Utrecht, Holland 3 Mar 1977. 6'3". RHB, OB. Debut 2001. Holland 1994 to date. **LOI** (H): 5 (1995-96 World Cup); HS 54 v E (Peshawar) 1995-96. HS 122 v Notts (Hove) 2001. Award: BHC 1. LO HS 102* v Hants (Southampton) 2001 (BHC).

RELEASED/RETIRED
(Having made a first-class County appearance in 2001)

WILTON, Nicholas James (Beacon Community C and SFC; City of Westminster C), b Pembury, Kent 23 Sep 1978. 5'11". RHB, WK. Sussex 1998-2001. MCC YC. HS 55 v Leics (Arundel) 1999. LO HS 17 v SL A (Hove) 1999.

COUNTY CAPS AWARDED IN 2001

Derbyshire	S.D.Stubbings, G.Welch
Durham	D.R.Law, M.L.Love, N.Peng, N.C.Phillips, A.Pratt
Essex	J.S.Foster
Glamorgan	J.P.Maher
Gloucestershire	J.M.M.Averis, C.G.Taylor
Hampshire	N.C.Johnson, D.A.Kenway, A.C.Morris
Kent	D.J.Cullinan, R.W.T.Key, M.J.Saggers, E.T.Smith
Lancashire	–
Leicestershire	N.D.Burns, D.E.Malcolm, D.J.Marsh, Shahid Afridi, T.R.Ward
Middlesex	T.F.Bloomfield, S.P.Fleming, A.J.Strauss, R.M.S.Weston
Northamptonshire	M.E.K.Hussey
Nottinghamshire	G.S.Blewett, G.J.Smith
Somerset	I.D.Blackwell, K.P.Dutch, R.L.Johnson, P.S.Jones, J.I.D.Kerr
Surrey	J.N.Batty
Sussex	M.W.Goodwin
Warwickshire	I.R.Bell, M.M.Betts, V.C.Drakes
Worcestershire	A.J.Bichel
Yorkshire	M.J.Wood

SUSSEX 2001

RESULTS SUMMARY

	Place	Won	Lost	Tied	Drew	No Result
County Championship (2nd Division)	**1st**	9	3		4	
All First-Class Matches		9	4		5	
C & G Trophy	4th Round					
Benson & Hedges Cup	Quarter-Finalist					
NU National League (2nd Division)	**5th**	8	7			1

COUNTY CHAMPIONSHIP AVERAGES

BATTING AND FIELDING

Cap		M	I	NO	HS	Runs	Avge	100	50	Ct/St
2001	M.W.Goodwin	16	30	4	203*	1521	58.50	6	5	8
1999	R.R.Montgomerie	16	30	3	160*	1461	54.11	7	4	16
1998	C.J.Adams	14	22	1	192	1020	48.57	3	6	27
2000	R.S.C.Martin-Jenkins	9	15	4	113	524	47.63	1	3	4
–	M.H.Yardy	15	26	4	87*	741	33.68	–	5	9
–	M.J.G.Davis	14	21	4	52	438	25.76	–	1	5
–	B.Zuiderent	15	25	1	122	613	25.54	1	3	17
–	W.J.House	2	4	–	46	80	20.00	–	–	1
–	M.J.Prior	15	24	2	66	433	19.68	–	1	39/2
–	U.B.A.Rashid	12	19	–	106	360	18.94	1	–	–
1996	J.D.Lewry	15	18	4	47	202	14.42	–	–	7
1998	R.J.Kirtley	16	24	6	51*	196	10.88	–	1	8
1997	M.A.Robinson	12	15	7	10	32	4.00	–	–	1

Also batted: T.R.Ambrose (2 matches) 26, 52, 14 (3 ct); P.A.Cottey (1 – cap 1999) 46, 4*
(1 ct); B.V.Taylor (2) 11, 0, 24*.

BOWLING

	O	M	R	W	Avge	Best	5wI	10wM
C.J.Adams	40.2	6	111	10	11.10	4- 28	–	–
M.A.Robinson	392.4	120	978	54	18.11	5- 35	3	–
R.J.Kirtley	566.3	135	1749	75	23.32	6- 34	5	2
J.D.Lewry	489.1	123	1465	57	25.70	7- 42	3	1
R.S.C.Martin-Jenkins	248	63	764	24	31.83	4- 18	–	–
U.B.A.Rashid	120.2	37	333	10	33.30	4- 9	–	–
M.J.G.Davis	337.3	81	900	23	39.13	6-116	1	–

Also bowled:
B.V.Taylor | 38.5 | 17 | 95 | 5 | 19.00 | 2- 5 | – | –
M.W.Goodwin 13-3-40-0; R.R.Montgomerie 5-1-11-1; M.H.Yardy 21-6-53-1.

The First-Class Averages (pp 113-126) give the records of Sussex players in all first-class
county matches (Sussex's other opponents being the Australians and Cambridge University).

SUSSEX RECORDS

FIRST-CLASS CRICKET

Highest Total	For 705-8d			v Surrey	Hastings	1902
	V 726			by Notts	Nottingham	1895
Lowest Total	For 19			v Surrey	Godalming	1830
	19			v Notts	Hove	1873
	V 18			by Kent	Gravesend	1867
Highest Innings	For 333	K.S.Duleepsinhji	v	Northants	Hove	1930
	V 322	E.Paynter	for	Lancashire	Hove	1937

Highest Partnership for each Wicket

1st	490	E.H.Bowley/J.G.Langridge	v	Middlesex	Hove	1933
2nd	385	E.H.Bowley/M.W.Tate	v	Northants	Hove	1921
3rd	298	K.S.Ranjitsinhji/E.H.Killick	v	Lancashire	Hove	1901
4th	326*	J.Langridge/G.Cox	v	Yorkshire	Leeds	1949
5th	297	J.H.Parks/H.W.Parks	v	Hampshire	Portsmouth	1937
6th	255	K.S.Duleepsinhji/M.W.Tate	v	Northants	Hove	1930
7th	344	K.S.Ranjitsinhji/W.Newham	v	Essex	Leyton	1902
8th	229*	C.L.A.Smith/G.Brann	v	Kent	Hove	1902
9th	178	H.W.Parks/A.F.Wensley	v	Derbyshire	Horsham	1930
10th	156	G.R.Cox/H.R.Butt	v	Cambridge U	Cambridge	1908

Best Bowling	For	10- 48	C.H.G.Bland	v	Kent	Tonbridge	1899
(Innings)	V	9- 11	A.P.Freeman	for	Kent	Hove	1922
Best Bowling	For	17-106	G.R.Cox	v	Warwicks	Horsham	1926
(Match)	V	17- 67	A.P.Freeman	for	Kent	Hove	1922

Most Runs – Season	2850	J.G.Langridge	(av 64.77)	1949
Most Runs – Career	34152	J.G.Langridge	(av 37.69)	1928-55
Most 100s – Season	12	J.G.Langridge		1949
Most 100s – Career	76	J.G.Langridge		1928-55
Most Wkts – Season	198	M.W.Tate	(av 13.47)	1925
Most Wkts – Career	2211	M.W.Tate	(av 17.41)	1912-37
Most Career W-K Dismissals	1176	H.R.Butt	(911 ct/265 st)	1890-1912
Most Career Catches in the Field	779	J.G.Langridge		1928-55

LIMITED-OVERS CRICKET

Highest Total	NWT	384-9		v	Ireland	Belfast	1996
	BHC	316-3		v	Essex	Chelmsford	2000
	NL	312-8		v	Hampshire	Portsmouth	1993
Lowest Total	NWT	49		v	Derbyshire	Chesterfield	1969
	BHC	61		v	Middlesex	Hove	1978
	NL	59		v	Glamorgan	Hove	1996
Highest Innings	NWT	158	R.K.Rao	v	Derbyshire	Derby	1997
	BHC	157*	M.G.Bevan	v	Essex	Chelmsford	2000
	NL	163	C.J.Adams	v	Middlesex	Arundel	1999
Best Bowling	NWT	6- 9	A.I.C.Dodemaide	v	Ireland	Downpatrick	1990
	BHC	5- 8	Imran Khan	v	Northants	Northampton	1978
	NL	7-41	A.N.Jones	v	Notts	Nottingham	1986

WARWICKSHIRE

Formation of Present Club: 8 April 1882
Substantial Reorganisation: 19 January 1884
Colours: Dark Blue, Gold and Silver
Badge: Bear and Ragged Staff
County Champions: (5) 1911, 1951, 1972, 1994, 1995
Gillette/NatWest/C & G Trophy Winners: (5) 1966, 1968, 1989, 1993, 1995
Benson and Hedges Cup Winners: (1) 1994
NU National League (Div 1) Winners: (0); best – 3rd 2001
Sunday League Winners: (3) 1980, 1994, 1997
Match Awards: CGT 71; BHC 64

Chief Executive: D.L.Amiss MBE, County Ground, Edgbaston, Birmingham, B5 7QU ▲ Tel: 0121 446 4422 ▲ Fax: 0121 446 4544 ▲ Email: info@warwk.co.org ▲ Web: www.thebears.co.uk
Captain: M.J.Powell. **Vice-Captain:** tba. **Overseas Player:** S.M.Pollock
2002 Beneficiary: N.M.K.Smith. **Scorer:** D.E.Wainwright. ‡ New registration

BELL, Ian Ronald (Princethorpe C), b Walsgrave-on-Sowe 11 Apr 1982. 5'9". RHB, RM. Debut 1999; cap 2001. Tour (Eng A): WI 2000-01 (*part*). HS 135 v Derbys (Derby) 2001. BB 1-24. LO HS 48 v Kent (Birmingham) 2001 (NL).

BETTS, Melvyn Morris (Fyndoune CS, Sacriston), b Sacriston, Co Durham 26 Mar 1975. 5'10". RHB, RFM. Durham 1993-2000; cap 1998. Warwickshire debut/cap 2001. Tour: Z 1998-99. HS 57* Du v Sussex (Hove) 1996. Wa HS 19 v Worcs (Worcester) 2001. BB 9-64 (Durham record; 13-143 match) v Northants (Northampton) 1997. Wa BB 5-22 v Durham (Birmingham) 2001 – on Wa debut. Award: BHC 1. LO HS 21 Du v Hants (Chester-le-St) 1997 (SL). LO BB 4-22 v Somerset (Taunton) 2001 (BHC).

BROWN, Douglas Robert (Alloa Academy; W London IHE), b Stirling, Scotland 29 Oct 1969. 6'2". RHB, RFM. Scotland 1989. Warwickshire debut 1991-92 (SA tour); cap 1995. Wellington 1995-96. **LOI:** 9 (1997-98); HS 21 v WI (Bridgetown) 1997-98; BB 2-28 v WI (Sharjah) 1997-98. Tours (Wa): SA 1991-92, 1994-95; SL 1997-98 (Eng A). HS 203 v Sussex (Hove) 2000. 50 wkts (2); most – 81 (1997). BB 8-89 (11-154 match) F-C Counties XI v Pak A (Chelmsford) 1997. Wa BB 7-66 v Durham (Chester-le-St) 1999. Award: BHC 1. LO HS 78* v Notts (Nottingham) 1995 (SL). LO BB 5-31 v Worcs (Worcester) 1997 (BHC).

CARTER, Neil Miller (Hottentots Holland HS; Cape Technicon), b Cape Town, SA 29 Jan 1975. ECB qualified – British passport. 6'2". LHB, LFM. Boland 1999-00 to 2000-01. Warwickshire debut 2001. HS 37 Boland v EP (Pt Elizabeth) 1999-00. Wa HS 5. BB 6-63 Boland v GW (Kimberley) 2000-01. Wa BB 5-78 v Worcs (Birmingham) 2001. Award: CGT 1. LO HS 40 and BB 4-21 v Essex (Birmingham) 2001 (CGT).

FROST, Tony (James Brinkley HS; Stoke-on-Trent C), b Stoke-on-Trent, Staffs 17 Nov 1975. 5'11". RHB, WK. Debut 1997; cap 1999. HS 111* v OU (Oxford) 1998. CC HS 66 v Sussex (Birmingham) 1999. LO HS 22* v Kent (Birmingham) 1999.

GILES, Ashley Fraser (George Abbot S, Guildford), b Chertsey, Surrey 19 Mar 1973. 6'3". RHB, SLA. Debut 1993; cap 1996. **ECB contract 2001. Tests:** 10 (1998 to 2001-02); HS 37* v P (Lahore) 2000-01; BB 5-67 v I (Ahmedabad) 2001-02. **LOI:** 17 (1997 to 2001-02); HS 21* v NZ (Dunedin) 2001-02; BB 5-57 v I (Delhi) 2001-02. Tours: A 1996-97 (Eng A); NZ 2001-02; I 2001-02; P 2000-01; SL 1997-98 (Eng A), 2000-01; K 1997-98 (Eng A). HS 128* v Sussex (Hove) 2001. 50 wkts (2); most – 64 (1996). BB 8-90 (12-135 match) v Northants (Northampton) 2000. Awards: CGT 2; BHC 1. LO HS 107 v Derbys (Birmingham) 2000 (NWT). LO BB 5-21 v Norfolk (Birmingham) 1997 (NWT).

88

KNIGHT, Nicholas Verity (Felsted S; Loughborough U), b Watford, Herts 28 Nov 1969. 6'0". LHB, occ RM. Essex 1991-94; cap 1994. Warwickshire debut 1994-95 (SA tour); cap 1995. **Tests:** 17 (1995 to 2001); HS 113 v P (Leeds) 1996. **LOI:** 76 (1996 to 2001-02); HS 125* v P (Nottingham) 1996. Tours: SA 1994-95 (Wa), 1999-00 (*part*); NZ 1996-97; I 1994-95 (Eng A); SL 1997-98 (Eng A – captain); P 1995-96 (Eng A); Z 1996-97; K 1997-98 (Eng A – captain). 1000 runs (2); most – 1196 (1996). HS 233 v Glam (Birmingham) 2000. BB 1-61. Awards: CGT 4; BHC 3. LO HS 151 v Somerset (Birmingham) 1995 (NWT). LO BB 1-14 (SL).

‡**MEES, Thomas** (Brookes U, Oxford), b Wolverhampton, Staffs 8 Jun 1981. RHB, RMF. Oxford UCCE 2001. Summer contract – awaiting f-c debut. HS (OU) 4 (twice). BB 6-64 OU v Middx (Oxford) 2001. Award: CGT 1. LO HS (Wa CB) 4* (CGT). LO BB 3-19 Warwks CB v Cambs (March) 2001 (CGT).

OSTLER, Dominic Piers (Princethorpe C; Solihull TC), b Solihull 15 Jul 1970. 6'3". RHB, occ RM. Debut 1990; cap 1991; benefit 1999. Tours: SA 1992-93 (Wa); P 1995-96 (Eng A). 1000 runs (5); most – 1284 (1991). HS 208 v Surrey (Birmingham) 1995. BB 1-46. Awards: CGT 2; BHC 1. LO HS 134* v Glos (Birmingham) 2001 (NL). LO BB 1-4 (NWT).

PENNEY, Trevor Lionel (Prince Edward S, Salisbury), b Salisbury, Rhodesia 12 Jun 1968. 6'0". RHB, RM. Qualified for England 1992. Boland 1991-92. Warwickshire debut 1991-92 (SA tour); UK debut v CU (Cambridge) 1992, scoring 102*; cap 1994. Mashonaland 1993-94; 1997-98 to date. Tours (Wa): SA 1991-92, 1992-93, 1994-95; Z 1993-94. 1000 runs (2); most – 1295 (1996). HS 151 v Middx (Lord's) 1992. BB 3-18 Mashonaland v Mashonaland U-24 (Harare) 1993-94. Wa BB 1-40 (Z tour). CC BB – . Awards: CGT 3. LO HS 90 v Cornwall (St Austell) 1996 (NWT). LO BB 1-8 (NWT).

PIPER, Keith John (Haringey Cricket C), b Leicester 18 Dec 1969. 5'6". RHB, WK. Warwickshire debut 1989; cap 1992; benefit 2001. Tours (Wa): SA 1991-92, 1992-93, 1994-95; I 1994-95 (Eng A); P 1995-96 (Eng A); Z 1993-94. HS 116* v Durham (Birmingham) 1994. BB 1-57. LO HS 38* v Leics (Birmingham) 1999 (NL).

POLLOCK, Shaun Maclean (Northwood HS; Durban U), b Port Elizabeth, SA 16 Jul 1973. Son of P.M.Pollock (EP and SA 1958-59 to 1971-72); nephew of R.G.Pollock (EP, Transvaal and SA 1960-61 to 1986-87). 6'3". RHB, RFM. Natal 1991-92 to date. Warwickshire 1996; cap 1996. **Tests** (SA): 63 (1995-96 to 2001-02, 21 as captain); HS 111 v SL (Pretoria) 2000-01; BB 7-87 v A (Adelaide) 1997-98. **LOI** (SA): 152 (1995-96 to 2001-02, 56 as captain); HS 75 v Z (Jo'burg) 1996-97; BB 6-35 v WI (E London) 1998-99. Tours (SA) (C=captain): E 1998; A 1997-98, 2001-02C; WI 2000-01C; NZ 1998-99; I 1999-00; P 1997-98; SL 2000-01C; Z 1999-00. HS 150* v Glam (Birmingham) 1996. BB 7-33 Natal v Border (E London) 1995-96. Wa BB 6-56 v Middx (Lord's) 1996. Award: BHC 1. LO HS 87 SA v Notts (Nottingham) 1998. LO BB 6-21 v Leics (Birmingham) 1996 (BHC) – inc 4 wkts in 4 balls on Wa debut.

POWELL, Michael James (Lawrence Sheriff S, Rugby), b Bolton, Lancs 5 Apr 1975. 5'11". RHB, RM. Debut 1996; cap 1999; captain 2001 to date. Tour (Eng A): WI 2000-01. 1000 runs (1): 1046 (2000). HS 236 v OU (Oxford) 2001. CC HS 145 v Northants (Northampton) 2000. BB 2-16 v OU (Oxford) 1998. CC BB 1-0. LO HS 78 v Northants (Northampton) 2001 (NL). LO BB 2-13 v Hants (Southampton) 2000 (NL).

RICHARDSON, Alan (Alleyne's HS; Stafford CFE; Durham U), b Newcastle-under-Lyme, Staffs 6 May 1975. 6'2". RHB, RMF. Derbyshire 1995 (one match). Warwickshire debut 1999. Staffordshire 1996-98. HS 17* v Northants (Northampton) 2000. BB 8-51 (10-107 match) v Glos (Birmingham) 1999. LO HS 11* v Leics (Birmingham) 1999 (NL). LO BB 3-17 v Somerset (Birmingham) 2001 (NL).

SHEIKH, Mohammad Avez (Broadway S), b Birmingham 2 Jul 1973. 6'0". LHB, RM. Debut 1997. HS 58* v Northants (Northampton) 2000. BB 4-36 v Hants (Birmingham) 2001. 2-14 v Middx (Birmingham) 1997. LO HS 36 v Hants (Southampton) 2000 (NL). LO BB 4-17 v Yorks (Birmingham) 2001 (NL).

SMITH, Neil Michael Knight (Warwick S), b Birmingham 27 Jul 1967. Son of M.J.K.Smith (Leics, Warwks and England 1951-75). 6'0". RHB, OB. Debut 1987; cap 1993; captain 1999-2000; benefit 2002. MCC YC. **LOI:** 7 (1995-96 to 1996); HS 31 v H (Peshawar) 1995-96; BB 3-29 v UAE (Peshawar) 1995-96. Tours (Wa): SA 1991-92, 1994-95; Z 1993-94. 1000 runs (1): 1002 (1998). HS 161 v Yorks (Leeds) 1989. BB 7-42 v Lancs (Birmingham) 1994. Awards: CGT 1; BHC 2. LO HS 125 v Kent (Canterbury) 1997 (BHC). LO BB 6-33 v Sussex (Birmingham) 1995 (SL).

SPIRES, James Ashley S. (Solihull S), b Solihull 12 Nov 1979. 6'0". RHB, SLA. Debut 2001. HS – and BB 2-73 v Middx (Lord's) 2001 – on debut. LO HS – and BB (Warwks CB) 1-33 (CGT).

TAHIR, Naqaash (Moseley S; Spring Hill C), b Birmingham 14 Nov 1983. 5'10", RHB, RFM. Staff 2001 – awaiting f-c debut.

TROUGHTON, Jamie Oliver (Trinity S; Leamington Spa; Birmingham U), b Camden, London 2 Mar 1979. Great-grandson of H.T.Crichton (Warwicks 1908). 5'11". RHB, SLA. Debut 2001. HS 27 v Worcs (Birmingham) 2001 – on debut. Award: CGT 1. LO HS 115* and BB 4-23 Warwks CB v Cumb (Millom) 2001 (CGT).

WAGG, Graham Grant (Ashlawn S, Rugby), b Rugby, 28 Apr 1983. 6'0". RHB, LM. Staff 2001 – awaiting f-c debut. LO HS (Warwks CB) 0 (NWT).

WAGH, Mark Anant (King Edward's S, Birmingham; Keble C, Oxford), b Birmingham 20 Oct 1976. 6'2". RHB, OB. Oxford U 1996-98; blue 1996-97-98; captain 1997. Warwickshire debut 1997; cap 2000. British U 1998. Mashonaland A 1998-99. 1000 runs (2): 1277 (2001). HS 315 v Middx (Lord's) 2001. BB 4-11 v Middx (Lord's) 1998. LO HS 70* v Somerset (Birmingham) 2001 (NL). LO BB 1-39 (Brit U – BHC).

WARREN, Nick Alexander (Wheelers Lane S; Solihull SFC), b Moseley, Birmingham 26 Jun 1982. 5'11". RHB, RMF. Staff 2000 – awaiting f-c debut. 2nd XI debut 1998 when aged 16y 76d. LO HS (Warwks CB) 0 (CGT).

WILSON, Elliot James (The Deanes S, Thundersley; SE Essex C; Stamford C), b Hertford, Herts 10 Nov 1979. 5'9". RHB, RM. Staff 2001 – awaiting f-c debut. Lincolnshire 2000.

RELEASED/RETIRED
(Having made a first-class County appearance in 2001)

DAGNALL, C.E. – see *LEICESTERSHIRE*.

DRAKES, Vasbert Conneil (St Lucy SS), b St James, Barbados 5 Aug 1969. 6'2". RHB, RFM. Barbados 1991-92 to 1997-98. Sussex 1996-97; cap 1996. Border 1996-97 to date. Nottinghamshire 1999; cap 1999. Warwickshire 2001; cap 2001. **LOI** (WI): 5 (1994-95); HS 16 v A (P-o-S) 1994-95; BB 1-36. Tour (WI): E 1995. HS 180* Barbados v Leeward Is (Anguilla) 1994-95. UK HS 145* Sx v Essex (Chelmsford) 1996. Wa HS 50 v Sussex (Birmingham) 2001. 50 wkts (2+2); most – 80 (1999). BB 8-59 Border v Natal (Durban) 1996-97. UK BB 6-39 (12-110 match) Nt v Warwks (Nottingham) 1999. Wa BB 5-37 v Glos (Birmingham) 2001. LO HS 104 Border v Boland (Paarl) 1996-97 (SBC). LO BB 5-19 v Ire (Hove) 1996 (BHC). Took 4 wkts in 4 balls v Derbys (Nottingham) 1999 (NL).

HEMP, D.L. – see *GLAMORGAN*.

G.D.Franklin and R.E.Sierra have left the staff having made no f-c appearances in 2001.

WARWICKSHIRE 2001

RESULTS SUMMARY

	Place	Won	Lost	Tied	Drew	No Result
County Championship (2nd Division)	3rd	5	1		10	
All First-Class Matches		5	1		11	
C & G Trophy	Semi-Finalist					
Benson & Hedges Cup	Quarter-Finalist					
NU National League (1st Division)	3rd	8	5			3

COUNTY CHAMPIONSHIP AVERAGES

BATTING AND FIELDING

Cap		M	I	NO	HS	Runs	Avge	100	50	Ct/St
2001	I.R.Bell	10	15	3	135	706	58.83	2	4	10
2000	M.A.Wagh	15	22	2	315	1170	58.50	3	5	4
1995	N.V.Knight	12	17	2	140	744	49.60	2	3	16
1991	D.P.Ostler	10	12	1	121	520	47.27	2	2	22
1997	D.L.Hemp	16	23	4	186*	852	44.84	3	2	12
1995	D.R.Brown	15	18	3	104	629	41.93	1	6	15
1992	K.J.Piper	15	17	5	92*	426	35.50	–	2	39/1
1999	M.J.Powell	16	23	–	133	519	22.56	1	2	13
1993	N.M.K.Smith	14	14	2	54	254	21.16	–	1	2
2001	V.C.Drakes	14	13	3	50	209	20.90	–	1	1
2001	M.M.Betts	12	11	3	19	92	11.50	–	–	9
–	A.Richardson	12	9	4	6*	20	4.00	–	–	6
–	N.M.Carter	5	4	1	5	10	3.33	–	–	2

Also played: C.E.Dagnall (2 matches) 1; A.F.Giles (2 – cap 1996) 0, 40*, 24 (4 ct);
T.L.Penney (1 – cap 1994) 1 (3 ct); M.A.Sheikh (3) 19, 0, 14; J.A.S.Spires (1) did not bat;
J.O.Troughton (1) 27, 5*.

BOWLING

	O	M	R	W	Avge	Best	5wI	10wM
C.E.Dagnall	69	15	214	11	19.45	6-50	1	–
M.M.Betts	308.2	72	979	37	26.45	5-22	2	–
A.Richardson	369.5	102	918	32	28.68	5-89	1	–
D.R.Brown	461.5	123	1264	42	30.09	6-60	1	1
N.M.K.Smith	314	75	813	25	32.52	4-76	–	–
N.M.Carter	95	8	362	11	32.90	5-78	1	–
M.A.Wagh	179	36	466	13	35.84	3- 3	–	–
V.C.Drakes	505.2	107	1537	42	36.59	5-37	1	–

Also bowled:

M.A.Sheikh	99.1	36	238	7	34.00	4-36	–	–
A.F.Giles	89	22	241	5	48.20	2-54	–	–

I.R.Bell 17-4-40-1; D.L.Hemp 12-1-28-0; K.J.Piper 1-0-3-0; M.J.Powell 34-2-100-2;
J.A.S.Spires 50-8-155-2; J.O.Troughton 2-0-17-0.

The First-Class Averages (pp 113-126) give the records of Warwickshire's players in all
first-class county matches (Warwickshire's other opponents being Oxford University), with
the exception of N.V.Knight, whose full county figures are as above, and:
  A.F.Giles 3-5-2-40*-65-21.66-0-0-4ct. 129.5-41-321-11-29.18-5/46-1-0.

WARWICKSHIRE RECORDS

FIRST-CLASS CRICKET

Highest Total	For 810-4d		v	Durham	Birmingham	1994
	V 887		by	Yorkshire	Birmingham	1896
Lowest Total	For 16		v	Kent	Tonbridge	1913
	V 15		by	Hampshire	Birmingham	1922
Highest Innings	For 501*	B.C.Lara	v	Durham	Birmingham	1994
	V 322	I.V.A.Richards	for	Somerset	Taunton	1985

Highest Partnership for each Wicket

1st	377*	N.F.Horner/K.Ibadulla	v	Surrey	The Oval	1960
2nd	465*	J.A.Jameson/R.B.Kanhai	v	Glos	Birmingham	1974
3rd	327	S.P.Kinneir/W.G.Quaife	v	Lancashire	Birmingham	1901
4th	470	A.I.Kallicharran/G.W.Humpage	v	Lancashire	Southport	1982
5th	322*	B.C.Lara/K.J.Piper	v	Durham	Birmingham	1994
6th	220	H.E.Dollery/J.Buckingham	v	Derbyshire	Derby	1938
7th	289	D.Brown/A.F.Giles	v	Sussex	Hove	2000
8th	228	A.J.W.Croom/R.E.S.Wyatt	v	Worcs	Dudley	1925
9th	154	G.W.Stephens/A.J.W.Croom	v	Derbyshire	Birmingham	1925
10th	141	A.F.Giles/T.A.Munton	v	Worcs	Worcester	1996

Best Bowling	For	10-41	J.D.Bannister	v	Comb Servs	Birmingham	1959
(Innings)	V	10-36	H.Verity	for	Yorkshire	Leeds	1931
Best Bowling	For	15-76	S.Hargreave	v	Surrey	The Oval	1903
(Match)	V	17-92	A.P.Freeman	for	Kent	Folkestone	1932

Most Runs – Season	2417	M.J.K.Smith	(av 60.42)	1959
Most Runs – Career	35146	D.L.Amiss	(av 41.64)	1960-87
Most 100s – Season	9	A.I.Kallicharran		1984
	9	B.C.Lara		1994
Most 100s – Career	78	D.L.Amiss		1960-87
Most Wkts – Season	180	W.E.Hollies	(av 15.13)	1946
Most Wkts – Career	2201	W.E.Hollies	(av 20.45)	1932-57
Most Career W-K Dismissals	800	E.J.Smith	(662 ct/138 st)	1904-30
Most Career Catches in the Field	422	M.J.K.Smith		1956-75

LIMITED-OVERS CRICKET

Highest Total	NWT	392-5		v	Oxfordshire	Birmingham	1984
	BHC	369-8		v	Minor C	Jesmond	1996
	NL	301-6		v	Essex	Colchester	1982
Lowest Total	NWT	98		v	Leics	Leicester	1998
	BHC	94		v	Glos	Bristol	2000
	NL	59		v	Yorks	Leeds	2001
Highest Innings	NWT	206	A.I.Kallicharran	v	Oxfordshire	Birmingham	1984
	BHC	137*	T.A.Lloyd	v	Lancashire	Birmingham	1985
	NL	134*	D.P.Ostler	v	Glos	Birmingham	2001
Best Bowling	NWT	6-32	K.Ibadulla	v	Hampshire	Birmingham	1965
		6-32	A.I.Kallicharran	v	Oxfordshire	Birmingham	1984
	BHC	7-32	R.G.D.Willis	v	Yorkshire	Birmingham	1981
	NL	6-15	A.A.Donald	v	Yorkshire	Birmingham	1995

WORCESTERSHIRE

Formation of Present Club: 11 March 1865
Colours: Dark Green and Black
Badge: Shield Argent a Fess between three Pears Sable
County Championships: (5) 1964, 1965, 1974, 1988, 1989
Gillette/NatWest/C & G Trophy Winners: (1) 1994
Benson and Hedges Cup Winners: (1) 1991
NU National League (Div 1) Winners: (0); best – 2nd 1999
Sunday League Winners: (3) 1971, 1987, 1988
Match Awards: CGT 45; BHC 68

Chief Executive: M.Newton, County Ground, New Road, Worcester, WR2 4QQ ▲ Tel: 01905 748474 ▲ Fax: 01905 748005 ▲ Email: admin@wccc.co.uk ▲ Web: www.wccc.co.uk

Captain: G.A.Hick. **Vice-Captain:** S.J.Rhodes. **Overseas Player:** A.J.Bichel.
2002 Beneficiary: R.McLaren (Head Groundsman). **Scorer:** W.Clarke.
‡ New registration

ALI, Kabir (Moseley CS and SFC), b Moseley, Birmingham 24 Nov 1980. 6'0". RHB, RMF. Debut 1999. HS 50* v Notts (Worcester) 2000. BB 5-22 v Glos (Worcester) 2001. Award: BHC 1. LO HS 11 v NZ A (Worcester) 2000. LO BB 4-22 v Derbys (Derby) 2001 (NL).

ALI, Kadeer (Handsworth GS), b Moseley, Birmingham 7 Mar 1983. 6'1". RHB, LB. Debut 2000. HS 38 v Middx (Worcester) 2001. LO HS 24 Worcs CB v Kent CB (Maidstone) 1999 (NWT).

‡BATTY, Gareth Jon (Bingley GS), b Bradford, Yorks 13 Oct 1977. Younger brother of J.D.Batty (Yorkshire and Somerset 1989-96). 5'11". RHB, OB. Yorkshire 1997. Surrey 1999-2001. HS 25* and BB 2-45 Sy v SL A (Oval) 1999. CC HS 25 Sy v Somerset (Taunton) 2001. LO HS 83* Sy v Yorks (Oval) 2001 (NL). LO BB 4-36 Sy v Kent (Canterbury) 2001 (NL).

BICHEL, Andrew John (Laidley HS; Ipswich C, Queensland), b Laidley, Queensland 27 Aug 1970. RHB, RFM. 5'11". Queensland 1992-93 to date. Worcestershire debut/cap 2001. **Tests:** 6 (1996-97 to 2001-02); HS 18 v WI (Perth) 1996-97; BB 5-60 v WI (Melbourne) 2000-01. **LOI:** 23 (1996-97 to 2001-02); HS 27* v SA (Perth) 1997-98; BB 5-19 v SA (Sydney) 2001-02. Tours (A): E 1997; Scot 1998 (Aus A); SA 1996-97, 2001-02; WI 1998-99. HS 110 (off 110 balls) Q v Vic (Brisbane) 1997-98. Wo HS 78 v Hants (Worcester) 2001. 50 wkts (1+1): most – 66 (2001). BB 6-44 v Glos (Bristol) 2001. Award: BHC 1. LO HS 100 v Glam (Cardiff) 2001 (BHC). LO BB 5-21 v Essex (Chelmsford) 2001 (NL).

CATTERALL, Duncan Neil (Queen Elizabeth's GS, Blackburn; Loughborough U), b Preston, Lancs 19 Sep 1978. 5'11". RHB, RMF. Debut 1998. No appearances 2001. HS 60 v Essex (Chelmsford) 1999 and 60 v Middx (Worcester) 1999 – in successive innings. BB 4-50 v WI (Worcester) 2000. CC BB 2-16 v Essex (Chelmsford) 1999. LO HS 21* v NZ A (Worcester) 2000. LO BB 2-35 v Yorks (Worcester) 1999 (NL).

HICK, Graeme Ashley (Prince Edward HS, Salisbury), b Salisbury, Rhodesia 23 May 1966. 6'3". RHB, OB. Zimbabwe 1983-84 to 1985-86. Worcestershire debut 1984; cap 1986; benefit 1999; captain 2000 to date. N Districts 1987-88 to 1988-89. Queensland 1990-91. *Wisden* 1986. **ECB contract 2000.** Tests: 65 (1991 to 2000-01); HS 178 v I (Bombay) 1992-93; BB 4-126 v NZ (Wellington) 1991-92. Took wicket with third ball in Test cricket. **LOI:** 120 (1991 to 2000-01); HS 126* v SL (Adelaide) 1998-99; BB 5-33 v Z (Harare) 1999-00. Tours: E 1985 (Z); A 1994-95, 1998-99 (*part*); SA 1995-96, 1999-00 (*part*); WI 1993-94; NZ 1991-92; I 1992-93; P 2000-01; SL 1983-84 (Z), 1992-93, 2000-01; Z 1990-91 (Wo), 1996-97 (Wo). 1000 runs (16+1) inc 2000 (3); most – 2713 (1988); youngest to score 2000 (1986). Scored 1019 runs before June 1988, including a record 410 runs in April. Fewest innings for 10,000 runs in county cricket (179). Youngest (24) to score 50 f-c hundreds. Second-youngest (32) to score 100 f-c hundreds. Scored 645 runs without being dismissed (UK record) in 1990. HS 405* (Worcs record and then second highest in UK f-c matches) v Somerset (Taunton) 1988. BB 5-18 v Leics (Worcester) 1995. Awards: CGT 5; BHC 11. LO HS 172* v Devon (Worcester) 1987 (NWT). LO BB 5-19 E v Pak A (Lahore) 1998-99.

‡**KANDOLA, Gurdeep** Singh (Barking Abbey S), b Forest Gate, Essex 6 Mar 1980. RHB, LB. Staff 2002 – awaiting f-c debut. LO HS (Worcs CB) 8 (CGT).

LAMPITT, Stuart Richard (Kingswinford S; Dudley TC), b Wolverhampton, Staffs 29 Jul 1966. 5'11". RHB, RMF. Debut 1985; cap 1989; benefit 2000. Tours (Wo): Z 1990-91, 1993-94, 1996-97. HS 122 v Middx (Lord's) 1994. 50 wkts (7); most – 64 (1994). BB 7-45 v Warwks (Worcester) 2000. Awards: CGT 1; BHC 4. LO HS 54 v Scot (Edinburgh) 1998 (NWT). LO BB 6-26 v Derbys (Derby) 1994 (BHC).

LEATHERDALE, David Anthony (Pudsey Grangefield S), b Bradford, Yorks 26 Nov 1967. 5'10½". RHB, RM. Debut 1988; cap 1994. Tours (Wo): Z 1993-94, 1996-97. 1000 runs (1): 1001 (1998). HS 157 v Somerset (Worcester) 1991. BB 5-20 v Glos (Worcester) 1998. LO HS 70* v Yorks (Worcester) 1999 (NL). LO BB 5-10 v A (Worcester) 1997.

LIPTROT, Christopher George (The Deanery HS), b Wigan, Lancs 13 Feb 1980. 6'2". LHB, RFM. Debut 1999. HS 61 v Warwks (Birmingham) 1999. BB 6-44 v Warwks (Worcester) 2000. LO HS 15* and LO BB 3-44 v Kent (Canterbury) 2000 (NL).

‡**MASON, Matthew** Sean (Mazenod C, Lesmurdie, WA), b Claremont, Perth, Australia 20 Mar 1974. ECB qualified – British passport. 6'5". RHB, RFM. W Australia 1996-97 to 1997-98. HS (WA) 3 and BB 2-60 WA v Q (Perth) 1997-98. LO HS (WA) 2 (MC). LO BB 2-61 WA v S Australia (Perth) 1997-98 (MC).

PATEL, Depesh Balvant (Moseley Park GS; Bilston Community C), b Wolverhampton, Staffs 23 Sep 1981. 6'3". RHB, RMF. Awaiting f-c debut. LO HS 19* and LO BB 1-36 Worcs CB v Kent CB (Maidstone) 1999 (NWT).

‡**PETERS, Stephen** David (Coopers Coborn & Co S), b Harold Wood, Essex 10 Dec 1978. 5'11". RHB, occ LB. Essex 1996-2001, scoring 110 and 12* v CU (Cambridge) on debut. HS 110 (as above). CC HS 81 Ex v Glam (Cardiff) 1999. BB (Ex) 1-19 (not CC). Award: CGT 1. LO HS 73* Ex v Glam (Southend) 2000 (NL).

PIPE, David James (Queensbury S, Bradford), b Bradford, Yorks 16 Dec 1977. 5'11". RHB, WK. Debut 1998. HS 54 v Warwks (Worcester) 2000 – on CC debut. LO HS 56 Worcs CB v Kent CB (Kidderminster) 2000 (NWT). Held 8 catches v Herts (Hertford) 2001 (CGT) to equal l-o record.

POLLARD, Paul Raymond (Gedling CS), b Carlton, Nottingham 24 Sep 1968. 5'11". LHB, RM. Nottinghamshire 1987-98; cap 1992. Worcestershire debut 1999. Tour (Nt): SA 1996-97. 1000 runs (3); most – 1463 (1993). HS 180 Nt v Derbys (Nottingham) 1993. Wo HS 131* v DU (Worcester) 2000. BB 2-79 Nt v Glos (Bristol) 1993. Award: BHC 1. LO HS 132* Nt v Somerset (Nottingham) 1995 (SL).

RAWNSLEY, Matthew James (Shenley Court CS, Birmingham), b Birmingham 8 Jun 1976. 6'2". RHB, SLA. Debut 1996. HS 39 v Hants (Worcester) 2001. BB 6-44 (11-116 match) v OU (Oxford) 1998. CC BB 5-125 v Middx (Southgate) 2000. LO HS 12 v Leics (Worcester) 2001 (CGT). LO BB 5-26 v Kent (Tunbridge W) 1999 (NL).

RHODES, Steven John (Lapage Middle S; Carlton-Bolling S, Bradford), b Bradford, Yorks 17 Jun 1964. Son of W.E.Rhodes (Notts 1961-64). 5'7". RHB, WK. Yorkshire 1981-84. Worcestershire debut 1985; cap 1986; benefit 1996. *Wisden* 1994. **Tests:** 11 (1994 to 1994-95); HS 65* v SA (Leeds) 1994. **LOI:** 9 (1989 to 1994-95); HS 56 v SA (Manchester) 1994. Tours: A 1994-95; SA 1993-94 (Eng A); WI 1991-92 (Eng A); SL 1985-86 (Eng B), 1990-91 (Eng A); Z 1989-90 (Eng A), 1990-91 (Wo), 1993-94 (Wo), 1996-97 (Wo – captain). 1000 runs (2); most – 1018 (1995). HS 122* v Young A (Worcester) 1995. CC HS 116* v Warwks (Worcester) 1992. Awards: CGT 1; BHC 2. LO HS 105 v Lancs (Manchester) 1991 (RAC).

‡**ROUND, Nathan** William (Cradley HS; Halesowen C), b Stourbridge 21 Aug 1980. RHB, RM. Herefordshire 1999-2001. Staff 2002 – awaiting f-c debut. LO HS 66 Herefords v Middx (Kingsland) 2001 (CGT). LO BB 2-28 Herefords v Sussex CB (Colwall) 2000 (NWT).

SHERIYAR, Alamgir (George Dixon S; Joseph Chamberlain SFC; Oxford Poly), b Birmingham 15 Nov 1973. 6'1". RHB, LFM. Leicestershire 1994-95. Worcestershire debut 1996; cap 1997. Tours (Eng A): NZ 1999-00; B 1999-00. HS 21 v Notts (Nottingham) 1997 and 21 v Pak A (Worcester) 1997. 50 wkts (3); most – 92 (1999). BB 7-130 (10-172 match) v Hants (Southampton) 1999. Hat-tricks (2): 1994 (Le), 1999. LO HS 19 v Derbys (Chesterfield) 1996 (SL). LO BB 4-18 v Yorks (Leeds) 1997 (SL).

SINGH, Anurag (King Edward's, Birmingham; Gonville & Caius C, Cambridge), b Kanpur, India 9 Sep 1975. 5'11½". RHB, OB. Warwickshire 1995-2000. Cambridge U 1996-98; blue 1996-97-98; captain 1997-98. British U 1998 (captain). Worcestershire debut 2001. 1000 (1): 1054 (2001). HS 168 v Middx (Worcester) 2001. Award: BHC 1. LO HS 123 Brit U v Somerset (Taunton) 1996 (BHC).

‡**SMITH, Benjamin** Francis (Kibworth HS), b Corby, Northants 3 Apr 1972. 5'9". RHB, RM. Leicestershire 1990-2001; cap 1995. Central Districts 2001-02. Tour (Le): SA 1996-97. 1000 runs (3); most – 1243 (1996). HS 204 Le v Surrey (Oval) 1998. BB (Le) 1-5. Award: CGT 1. LO HS 115 Le v Somerset (Weston-s-M) 1995 (SL). LO BB (Le) 1-26.

SOLANKI, Vikram Singh (Regis S, Wolverhampton), b Udaipur, India 1 Apr 1976. 6'0". RHB, OB. Debut 1995; cap 1998. Tours (Eng A): SA 1999-00 (Eng – *part*); WI 2000-01; NZ 1999-00; Z 1996-97 (Wo), 1998-99; B 1999-00. **LOI:** 8 (1999-00); HS 24 v Z (Bulawayo) 1999-00. 1000 runs (2); most – 1339 (1999). HS 185 Eng A v Bangladesh (Chittagong) 1999-00. Wo HS 171 v Glos (Cheltenham) 1999. BB 5-69 v Middx (Lord's) 1996. LO HS 120* v Derbys (Derby) 1998 (SL). LO BB 2-40 Eng A v Zim Academy (Harare) 1998-99.

SPIRING, Karl Reuben (Monmouth S; Durham U), b Southport, Lancs 13 Nov 1974. 5'11". RHB, OB. Worcestershire debut 1994; cap 1997. No appearances 2001. 1000 runs (1): 1084 (1996). HS 150 v Essex (Chelmsford) 1997. LO HS 71 v Sussex (Hove) 2000 (NL).

WESTON, William Philip Christopher (Durham S), b Durham 16 Jun 1973. Son of M.P.Weston (Durham; England RFU); brother of R.M.S.Weston (*see MIDDLESEX*). 6'3". LHB, LM. Debut 1991; cap 1995. Tours (Wo): Z 1993-94, 1996-97. 1000 runs (4); most – 1389 (1996). HS 205 v Northants (Northampton) 1997. BB 2-39 v P (Worcester) 1992. CC BB – . LO HS 134 v Derbys (Derby) 2001 (NL). LO BB 1-2 (SL).

RELEASED/RETIRED
(Having made a first-class County appearance in 2001)

BOULTON, Nicholas Ross (King's C, Taunton), b Johannesburg, SA 22 Mar 1979. 6'1½". LHB, RM. Somerset 1997 (1 match). Worcestershire 2001. HS 47 v DU (Worcester) 2001. CC HS 21 v Notts (Worcester) 2001. LO HS 39 v Herts (Hertford) 2001 (CGT).

E.J.Wilson left the staff having made no f-c appearances in 2001.

WORCESTERSHIRE 2001

RESULTS SUMMARY

	Place	Won	Lost	Tied	Drew	No Result
County Championship (2nd Division)	6th	4	5		7	
All First-Class Matches		4	6		8	
C & G Trophy	Quarter-Finalist					
Benson & Hedges Cup	4th in Mid/West/Wales Group					
NU National League (2nd Division)	3rd	9	5			2

COUNTY CHAMPIONSHIP AVERAGES

BATTING AND FIELDING

Cap		M	I	NO	HS	Runs	Avge	100	50	Ct/St
1986	G.A.Hick	16	26	3	201	1390	60.43	6	3	19
1995	W.P.C.Weston	16	28	4	192	1044	43.50	2	6	11
1986	S.J.Rhodes	15	20	7	52	442	34.00	–	1	51/1
–	A.Singh	16	28	2	168	853	32.80	1	3	4
2001	A.J.Bichel	16	24	–	78	627	26.12	–	3	5
1998	V.S.Solanki	16	26	–	112	678	26.07	2	2	16
1989	S.R.Lampitt	10	13	5	42*	205	25.62	–	–	4
1994	D.A.Leatherdale	16	25	3	93	476	21.63	–	1	5
–	P.R.Pollard	9	11	–	45	178	16.18	–	–	5
–	M.J.Rawnsley	13	18	4	39	186	13.28	–	–	6
–	C.G.Liptrot	10	12	2	22	111	11.10	–	–	3
–	Kadeer Ali	3	5	–	38	44	8.80	–	–	–
1997	A.Sheriyar	14	17	8	20	63	7.00	–	–	2
–	N.R.Boulton	3	4	–	21	28	7.00	–	–	–

Also batted: Kabir Ali (2 matches) 13, 25; D.J.Pipe (1) 22, 0 (3 ct).

BOWLING

	O	M	R	W	Avge	Best	5wI	10wM
Kabir Ali	56	16	143	10	14.30	5-22	1	–
A.Sheriyar	472.3	115	1534	65	23.60	6-88	3	–
C.G.Liptrot	242.4	67	749	28	26.75	3-12	–	–
A.J.Bichel	555.5	137	1804	66	27.33	6-44	4	1
S.R.Lampitt	203.2	49	669	24	27.87	5-22	1	–
D.A.Leatherdale	153	39	534	16	33.37	4-70	–	–
M.J.Rawnsley	337.2	88	922	18	51.22	3-72	–	–

Also bowled:

G.A.Hick	105.4	30	287	7	41.00	3-33	–	–

N.R.Boulton 4-1-15-0; Kadeer Ali 8-2-27-0; V.S.Solanki 46.4-6-161-0; W.P.C.Weston 2.4-0-19-0.

The First-Class Averages (pp 113-126) give the records of Worcestershire's players in all first-class county matches (Worcestershire's other opponents being the Australians and Durham University).

WORCESTERSHIRE RECORDS

FIRST-CLASS CRICKET

Highest Total	For 670-7d		v	Somerset	Worcester	1995
	V 701-4d		by	Leics	Worcester	1906
Lowest Total	For 24		v	Yorkshire	Huddersfield	1903
	V 30		by	Hampshire	Worcester	1903
Highest Innings	For 405*	G.A.Hick	v	Somerset	Taunton	1988
	V 331*	J.D.B.Robertson	for	Middlesex	Worcester	1949

Highest Partnership for each Wicket

1st	309	F.L.Bowley/H.K.Foster	v	Derbyshire	Derby	1901
2nd	300	W.P.C.Weston/G.A.Hick	v	Indians	Worcester	1996
3rd	438*	G.A.Hick/T.M.Moody	v	Hampshire	Southampton	1997
4th	281	J.A.Ormrod/Younis Ahmed	v	Notts	Nottingham	1979
5th	393	E.G.Arnold/W.B.Burns	v	Warwicks	Birmingham	1909
6th	265	G.A.Hick/S.J.Rhodes	v	Somerset	Taunton	1988
7th	205	G.A.Hick/P.J.Newport	v	Yorkshire	Worcester	1988
8th	184	S.J.Rhodes/S.R.Lampitt	v	Derbyshire	Kidderminster	1991
9th	181	J.A.Cuffe/R.D.Burrows	v	Glos	Worcester	1907
10th	119	W.B.Burns/G.A.Wilson	v	Somerset	Worcester	1906

Best Bowling (Innings)	For 9- 23	C.F.Root	v	Lancashire	Worcester	1931
	V 10- 51	J.Mercer	for	Glamorgan	Worcester	1936
Best Bowling (Match)	For 15- 87	A.J.Conway	v	Glos	Moreton-in-M	1914
	V 17-212	J.C.Clay	for	Glamorgan	Swansea	1937

Most Runs – Season	2654	H.H.I.Gibbons	(av 52.03)	1934
Most Runs – Career	34490	D.Kenyon	(av 34.18)	1946-67
Most 100s – Season	10	G.M.Turner		1970
	10	G.A.Hick		1988
Most 100s – Career	87	G.A.Hick		1984-2001
Most Wkts – Season	207	C.F.Root	(av 17.52)	1925
Most Wkts – Career	2143	R.T.D.Perks	(av 23.73)	1930-55
Most Career W-K Dismissals	1015†	R.Booth	(868 ct/147 st)	1946-67
Most Career Catches in the Field	412	D.W.Richardson		1952-67

† S.J.Rhodes (1985-2001) has made 945 dismissals (856 ct; 89 st)

LIMITED-OVERS CRICKET

Highest Total	NWT	404-3		v	Devon	Worcester	1987
	BHC	314-5		v	Lancashire	Manchester	1980
	NL	307-4		v	Derbyshire	Worcester	1975
Lowest Total	NWT	98		v	Durham	Chester-le-St	1968
	BHC	81		v	Leics	Worcester	1983
	NL	86		v	Yorkshire	Leeds	1969
Highest Innings	NWT	180*	T.M.Moody	v	Surrey	The Oval	1994
	BHC	143*	G.M.Turner	v	Warwicks	Birmingham	1976
	NL	160	T.M.Moody	v	Kent	Worcester	1991
Best Bowling	NWT	7-19	N.V.Radford	v	Beds	Bedford	1991
	BHC	6- 8	N.Gifford	v	Minor C (S)	High Wycombe	1979
	NL	6-26	A.P.Pridgeon	v	Surrey	Worcester	1978

YORKSHIRE

Formation of Present Club: 8 January 1863
Substantial Reorganisation: 10 December 1891
Colours: Dark Blue, Light Blue and Gold
Badge: White Rose
County Championships (since 1890): (30) 1893, 1896, 1898, 1900, 1901, 1902, 1905, 1908, 1912, 1919, 1922, 1923, 1924, 1925, 1931, 1932, 1933, 1935, 1937, 1938, 1939, 1946, 1959, 1960, 1962, 1963, 1966, 1967, 1968, 2001
Joint Champions: (1) 1949
Gillette/NatWest/C & G Trophy Winners: (2) 1965, 1969
Benson and Hedges Cup Winners: (1) 1987
NU National League (Div 1) Winners: (0); best – 2nd 2000
Sunday League Winners: (1) 1983
Match Awards: CGT 40; BHC 78

Chief Executive: C.D.Hassell, Headingley Cricket Ground, Leeds, LS6 3BU ▲ Tel: 0113 278 7394 ▲ Fax: 0113 278 4099 ▲ Email: cricket@yorkshireccc.org.uk ▲ Web: www.yorkshireccc.org.uk

Captain/Overseas Player: D.S.Lehmann. **Vice-Captain:** tba.
2002 Beneficiary: C.White. **Scorer:** J.T.Potter. ‡ New registration

BLAKEY, Richard John (Rastrick GS), b Huddersfield 15 Jan 1967. 5'9". RHB, WK. Debut 1985; cap 1987; benefit 1998. YC 1987. **Tests:** 2 (1992-93); HS 6. **LOI:** 3 (1992 to 1992-93); HS 25 v P (Lord's) 1992 – on debut. Tours: SA 1991-92 (Y); WI 1986-87 (Y); I 1992-93; P 1990-91 (Eng A); SL 1990-91 (Eng A); Z 1989-90 (Eng A), 1995-96 (Y). 1000 runs (5); most – 1361 (1987). HS 221 Eng A v Z (Bulawayo) 1989-90. Y HS 204* v Glos (Leeds) 1987. BB 1-68. Awards: BHC 2. LO HS 130* v Kent (Scarborough) 1991 (SL).

BRESNAN, Timothy Thomas (Castleford HS and TC; Pontefract New C), b Pontefract 28 Feb 1985. 6'0". RHB, RMF. Awaiting f-c debut. LO HS 7 and BB 2-27 v Leics (Leicester) 2001 (NL).

CRAVEN, Victor John (Harrogate GS), b Harrogate 31 Jul 1980. 6'0". LHB, RM. Debut 2000. HS 58 v Derbys (Derby) 2000. LO HS 55 v Kent (Leeds) 2001 (NL).

DAWSON, Richard Kevin James (Batley GS; Exeter U), b Doncaster 4 Aug 1980. 6'3". RHB, OB. British U 2000. Yorkshire debut 2001. Devon 1999-2000. **Tests:** 3 (2000-02); HS 11 and BB 4-134 v I (Chandigarh) 2001-02 – on debut. Tours: NZ 2001-02; I 2001-02. HS 37 v Leics (Leeds) 2001 – on debut. BB 6-82 v Glam (Scarborough) 2001. LO HS 10* v Surrey (Leeds) 2001 (NL). LO BB 3-28 v Northants (Northampton) 2001 (NL).

ELSTUB, Christopher John (Whitcliffe Mount S and SFC; Leeds Metropolitan U), b Dewsbury 3 Feb 1981. 5'11". RHB, RMF. Debut 2000. British U 2001. No county f-c appearances 2001. HS (Brit U) 6*. BB 3-37 v WI (Leeds) 2000. CC HS 4* and CC BB 2-40 v Lancs (Leeds) 2000. LO HS 0* (NL). LO BB 4-25 v Surrey (Leeds) 2001 (NL).

FELLOWS, Gary Matthew (N Halifax GS), b Halifax 30 Jul 1978. 5'9". RHB, RM. Matabeleland 1996-97. Yorkshire debut 1998. HS 63 v Somerset (twice) (Leeds and Bath) 2001. BB 3-23 v Essex (Chelmsford) 2001. Award: CGT 1. LO HS 80 * v Surrey (Leeds) 2001 (CGT). LO BB 3-34 v Glos (Bristol) 2001 (NL).

GOUGH, Darren (Priory CS, Lundwood), b Barnsley 18 Sep 1970. 5'11". RHB, RF. Debut 1989; cap 1993; benefit 2001. *Wisden* 1998. **ECB contracts 2000, 2001. Tests:** 56 (1994 to 2001); HS 65 v NZ (Manchester) 1994 – on debut; BB 6-42 v SA (Leeds) 1998; hat-trick v A (Sydney) 1998-99 – first for E v A since 1899. **LOI:** 106 (1994 to 2001-02); HS 45 v A (Melbourne) 1994-95; BB 5-44 v Z (Sydney) 1994-95 and 5-44 v A (Lord's) 1997. Took wickets with his sixth balls in both Tests and LOIs. Tours: A 1994-95, 1998-99; SA 1991-92 (Y), 1992-93 (Y), 1993-94 (Eng A), 1995-96, 1999-00; NZ 1996-97; P 2000-01; SL 2000-01; Z 1996-97. HS 121 v Warwks (Leeds) 1996. 50 wkts (5); most – 67 (1996). BB 7-28 (10-80 match) v Lancs (Leeds) 1995 (not CC). CC BB 7-42 (10-96 match) v Somerset (Taunton) 1993. 2 hat-tricks (1995, 1998-99); took 4 wkts in 5 balls v Kent (Leeds) 1995. Awards: CGT 2; BHC 1. LO HS 72* v Leics (Leicester) 1991 (SL). LO BB 7-27 v Ire (Leeds) 1997 (NWT).

GRAY, Andrew Kenneth Donovan, b Western Australia 19 May 1974. RHB, OB. Debut 2001. HS 3 and BB 4-128 v Surrey (Oval) 2001. LO HS 19* and BB 1-45 v Notts (Nottingham) 2001 (NL).

GUY, Simon Mark (Wickersley CS), b Rotherham 17 Nov 1978. 5'7". RHB, WK. Debut 2000. HS 42 v Somerset (Taunton) 2000.

HAMILTON, Gavin Mark (Hurstmere SS, Kent), b Broxburn, Scotland 16 Sep 1974. 6'1". LHB, RFM. Scotland 1993-94. Yorkshire debut 1994; cap 1998. **Tests:** 1 (1999-00); HS 0 v SA (Jo'burg) 1999-00. **LOI** (Scot): 5 (1999); HS 76 and BB 2-36 v P (Chester-le-St) 1999. Tours: SA 1999-00; Z 1995-96 (Y). HS 125 v Hants (Leeds) 2000. 50 wkts (1): 59 (1998). BB 7-50 (11-72 match) v Surrey (Leeds) 1998. Match double (79, 70; 5-69, 5-43) v Glam (Cardiff) 1998 – first instance for Yorks since 1964 (R.Illingworth). Award: BHC 1. LO HS 76 *(see LOI)*. LO BB 5-16 v Hants (Leeds) 1998 (SL).

HOGGARD, Matthew James (Grangefield S, Pudsey), b Leeds 31 Dec 1976. 6'2". RHB, RFM. Debut 1996; cap 2000. Free State 1998-99 to 1999-00. **ECB contract 2001. Tests:** 5 (2000 to 2001-02); HS 12* v WI (Lord's) 2000 – on debut; BB 4-80 v I (Bangalore) 2001-02. **LOI:** 12 (2001-02); HS 4*; BB 5-49 v Z (Harare) 2001-02. Tours: NZ 2001-02; I 2001-02; P 2000-01; SL 2000-01. HS 21* FS v Gauteng (Jo'burg) 1999-00. Y HS 21 v Somerset (Taunton) 1999. 50 wkts (1): 50 (2000). BB 6-51 v Essex (Scarborough) 2001. LO HS 5* (NL). LO BB 5-28 v Leics (Leicester) 2000 (NL).

KIRBY, Steven Paul (Elton HS; Bury C), b Ainsworth, nr Bolton, Lancs 4 Oct 1977. 6'3½". RHB, RF. Leicestershire staff 1998 – no f-c appearances. Debut 2001, sub for M.J.Hoggard (England duty) taking 7-50 v Kent (Leeds). HS 15* v Lancs (Leeds) 2001. BB 7-50 *(see above)*. LO HS 4* (NL). LO BB 3-35 v Warwks (Leeds) 2001 (NL).

LEHMANN, Darren Scott (Gawler HS), b Gawler, South Australia 5 Feb 1970. 5'10. LHB, SLA. South Australia 1987-88 to 1989-90, 1993-94 to date; captain 1998-99 to date. Victoria 1990-91 to 1992-93. Yorkshire 1997-98, 2000; cap 1997; captain 2002. *Wisden* 2000. **Tests** (A): 5 (1997-98 to 1998-99); HS 98 v P (Rawalpindi) 1998-99; BB 1-6. **LOI** (A): 70 (1996-97 to 2001-02); HS 110* v WI (St George's, Grenada) 1998-99; BB 2-4 v I (Colombo) 1999-00. Tours: E 1991 (Vic); SA 2001-02; I 1997-98; P 1998-99. 1000 runs (3+5); most – 1575 (1997). HS 255 S Aus v Queensland (Adelaide) 1996-97. Y HS 252 v Lancs (Leeds) 2001. BB 4-42 v Kent (Maidstone) 1998. Awards: CGT 1; BHC 5. LO HS 191 v Notts (Scarborough) 2001 (NL). LO BB 3-14 A v SA (Kuala Lumpur) 1998-99.

LUMB, Michael John (St Stithians C, Jo'burg), b Johannesburg, SA 12 Feb 1980. Son of R.G.Lumb (Yorkshire 1970-84); nephew of A.J.S.Smith (SAU and Natal 1971-72 to 1983-84). 6'0". LHB, RM. Debut 2000. ECB qualified and CC debut 2001. HS 122 v Leics (Leeds) 2001. BB 2-10 v Kent (Canterbury) 2001. LO HS 66 v Kent (Leeds) 2001 (NL).

McGRATH, Anthony (Yorkshire Martyrs Collegiate S), b Bradford 6 Oct 1975. 6'2". RHB, RM. Debut 1995; cap 1999. Tours (Eng A): A 1996-97; P 1995-96; Z 1995-96 (Y). HS 142* v Middx (Leeds) 1999. BB 3-18 v Surrey (Oval) 1999. Awards: CGT 1; BHC 1. LO HS 109* v Minor C (Leeds) 1997 (BHC). LO BB 2-10 v Scot (Leeds) 1996 (BHC).

RICHARDSON, Scott Andrew (Hulme GS, Oldham; Manchester GS), b Oldham, Lancs 5 Sep 1977. 6'2". RHB, RM. Debut 2000. HS 69 v Kent (Leeds) 2001.

SIDEBOTTOM, Ryan Jay (King James's GS, Almondbury), b Huddersfield 15 Jan 1978. Son of A.Sidebottom (Yorks, OFS and England 1973-91). 6'3". LHB, LFM. Debut 1997; cap 2000. **Tests**: 1 (2001); HS 4 v P (Lord's) 2001; **LOI**: 2 (2001-02); HS 2*; BB 1-42 (twice). Tour (Eng A): WI 2000-01. HS 54 v Glam (Cardiff) 1998. BB 6-16 (11-43 match) v Kent (Leeds) 2000. LO HS 24* v Hants (Basingstoke) 1999 (NL). LO BB 6-40 v Glam (Cardiff) 1998 (SL).

SILVERWOOD, Christopher Eric Wilfred (Garforth CS), b Pontefract 5 Mar 1975. 6'1". RHB, RFM. Debut 1993; cap 1996. YC 1996. **Tests**: 5 (1996-97 to 1999-00); HS 7*; BB 5-91 v SA (Cape Town) 1999-00. **LOI**: 7 (1996-97 to 2001-02); HS 12 v NZ (Auckland) 1996-97; BB 3-43 v Z (Bulawayo) 2001-02. Tours: SA 1999-00 (*part*); WI 1997-98, 2000-01 (Eng A); NZ 1996-97; Z 1995-96 (Y), 1996-97.HS 70 v Essex (Chelmsford) 2001. 50 wkts (2); most – 59 (1999). BB 7-93 (12-148 match) v Kent (Leeds) 1997. Awards: BHC 2. LO HS 38* Eng A v NZ Academy (Lincoln) 1999-00. LO BB 5-28 v Scot (Leeds) 1996 (BHC).

STEAD, Roger Alexander (Hipperholme & Lightcliffe HS; St Chads C, Durham U), b Dewsbury 18 Apr 1980. RHB, RM. 6'0". Durham UCCE 2001. Awaiting county debut. HS 28 DU v Worcs (Worcester) 2001.

TAYLOR, Christopher Robert (Benton Park HS, Rawdon), b Leeds 21 Feb 1981. 6'4". RHB, RMF. Debut 2001. HS 18 v Surrey (Oval) 2001.

VAUGHAN, Michael Paul (Silverdale CS, Sheffield), b Manchester, Lancs 29 Oct 1974. 6'2". RHB, OB. Debut 1993; cap 1995. **ECB contracts 2000, 2001. Tests**: 13 (1999-00 to 2001-02); HS 120 v P (Manchester) 2001. **LOI**: 13 (2000-01 to 2001-02); HS 63 v I (Cuttack) 2001-02; BB 2-37 v I (Bombay) 2001-02. Tours (C=captain): A 1996-97 (Eng A); SA 1998-99C (Eng A), 1999-00; NZ 2001-02; I 1994-95 (Eng A), 2001-02; P 2000-01; SL 2000-01; Z 1995-96 (Y), 1998-99C (Eng A). 1000 runs (4); most – 1244 (1995). HS 183 v Glam (Cardiff) 1996. BB 4-39 v OU (Oxford) 1994. CC BB 4-47 v Somerset (Leeds) 2001. Awards: CGT 2; BHC 2. LO HS 125* v Somerset (Taunton) 2001 (BHC). LO BB 4-27 v Glos (Bristol) 2000 (NL).

WHITE, Craig (Flora Hill HS, Bendigo, Australia; Bendigo HS), b Morley 16 Dec 1969. 6'0". RHB, RFM. Debut 1990; cap 1993; benefit 2002. Victoria 1990-91 (2 matches). **ECB contracts 2000, 2001. Tests**: 24 (1994 to 2001-02); HS 121 v I (Ahmedabad) 2001-02; BB 5-32 v WI (Oval) 2000. **LOI**: 42 (1994-95 to 2000-01); HS 38 v NZ (Napier) 1996-97; BB 5-21 v Z (Bulawayo) 1999-00. Tours: A 1994-95, 1996-97 (Eng A); SA 1991-92 (Y), 1992-93 (Y); NZ 1996-97, 2001-02; I 2001-02; P 1995-96 (Eng A), 2000-01; SL 2000-01; Z 1996-97 (*part*). HS 186 v Lancs (Manchester) 2001. BB 8-55 v Glos (Gloucester) 1998 – inc hat-trick. Hat-trick 1998. Awards: CGT 2; BHC 3. LO HS 148 v Leics (Leicester) 1997 (SL). LO BB 5-21 (*see LOI*).

WOOD, Matthew James (Shelley HS & SFC), b Huddersfield 6 Apr 1977. 5'9". RHB, OB. Debut 1997; cap 2001. 1000 runs (2): most – 1080 (1998). HS 200* v Warwks (Leeds) 1998. LO HS 68 v Warwks (Leeds) 2001 (NL).

RELEASED/RETIRED
(Having made a first-class County appearance in 2001)

BYAS, D. – *see LANCASHIRE*.

FISHER, I.D. – *see GLOUCESTERSHIRE*.

HUTCHISON, P.M. – *see SUSSEX*.

MIDDLEBROOK, J.D. – *see ESSEX*.

WIDDUP, Simon (Ridgewood CS; Danum SFC), b Doncaster 10 Nov 1977. 6'0". RHB, OB. Yorkshire 2000-01. HS 44 and BB 1-22 v Somerset (Scarborough) 2000. LO HS 38 v Somerset (Taunton) 2000 (NL).

T.M.Baker (*see NORTHAMPTONSHIRE*), G.A.Lambert and G.Ramsden left the staff having made no f-c appearances in 2001.

YORKSHIRE 2001

	Place	Won	Lost	Tied	Drew	No Result
County Championship (1st Division)	**1st**	9	3		4	
All First-Class Matches		9	3		4	
C & G Trophy	Quarter-Finalist					
Benson & Hedges Cup	Semi-Finalist					
NU National League (1st Division)	**6th**	7	9			

COUNTY CHAMPIONSHIP AVERAGES
BATTING AND FIELDING

Cap		M	I	NO	HS	Runs	Avge	100	50	Ct/St
1997	D.S.Lehmann	13	19	2	252	1416	83.29	5	5	6
1995	M.P.Vaughan	7	13	–	133	673	51.76	2	4	6
–	J.D.Middlebrook	4	4	1	84	145	48.33	–	1	2
2001	M.J.Wood	14	23	1	124	1060	48.18	4	6	10
1991	D.Byas	16	24	5	110*	853	44.89	4	2	38
1993	C.White	9	15	1	186	567	40.50	2	–	5
–	M.J.Lumb	4	7	1	122	218	36.33	1	1	–
1999	A.McGrath	9	15	2	116*	417	32.07	1	2	6
–	G.M.Fellows	12	17	1	63	455	28.43	–	3	4
1987	R.J.Blakey	15	21	6	78*	405	27.00	–	3	49/5
–	S.A.Richardson	7	11	2	69	215	23.88	–	2	6
1996	C.E.W.Silverwood	8	9	1	70	167	20.87	–	1	2
2000	R.J.Sidebottom	8	8	4	40*	78	19.50	–	–	3
1998	G.M.Hamilton	8	9	–	34	114	12.66	–	–	1
–	V.J.Craven	2	4	1	23*	33	11.00	–	–	2
–	S.Widdup	2	4	–	27	44	11.00	–	–	5
–	C.R.Taylor	3	6	–	18	60	10.00	–	–	1
–	R.K.J.Dawson	9	11	1	37	95	9.50	–	–	6
–	S.P.Kirby	10	10	2	15*	49	6.12	–	–	4
2000	M.J.Hoggard	7	6	1	4	11	2.20	–	–	–
–	A.K.D.Gray	3	4	–	3	4	1.00	–	–	2

Also batted: I.D.Fisher (1 match) 28*; D.Gough (2 – cap 1993) 11*, 2, 96; S.M.Guy (1) 0, 12*; P.M.Hutchison (3 – cap 1998) 9*, 11*, 2*.

BOWLING

	O	M	R	W	Avge	Best	5wI	10wM
C.E.W.Silverwood	209.1	42	644	33	19.51	5- 20	3	–
S.P.Kirby	280.3	60	980	47	20.85	7- 50	3	1
M.J.Hoggard	192	50	561	26	21.57	6- 51	2	–
R.J.Sidebottom	258.2	73	646	27	23.92	4- 49	–	–
C.White	167.3	45	410	16	25.62	4- 57	–	–
G.M.Hamilton	211.2	43	672	26	25.84	5- 27	1	–
A.K.D.Gray	92	23	281	10	28.10	4-128	–	–
D.S.Lehmann	139.1	33	368	12	30.66	3- 13	–	–
G.M.Fellows	156	43	398	12	33.16	3- 23	–	–
R.K.J.Dawson	315.5	69	1014	30	33.80	6- 82	2	–

Also bowled:

	O	M	R	W	Avge	Best	5wI	10wM
M.P.Vaughan	63.5	14	165	7	23.57	4- 47		
P.M.Hutchison	60	11	224	7	32.00	2- 33		
D.Gough	88	18	275	8	34.37	4- 65		
J.D.Middlebrook	82	15	265	5	53.00	3- 49		

V.J.Craven 13-1-69-0; I.D.Fisher 13-3-32-1; M.J.Lumb 4-1-10-2; A.McGrath 17-4-53-3.
Yorkshire played no first-class fixtures outside the County Championship in 2001. The First-Class Averages (pp 113-126) give the records of Yorkshire players in all first-class county matches, with the exception of D.Gough, M.J.Hoggard, R.J.Sidebottom, M.P.Vaughan and C.White whose full county figures are as above, and C.J.Elstub and R.A.Stead whose only first-class appearances were in University matches.

YORKSHIRE RECORDS

FIRST-CLASS CRICKET

Highest Total	For 887		v	Warwicks	Birmingham	1896
	V 681-7d		by	Leics	Bradford	1996
Lowest Total	For 23		v	Hampshire	Middlesbrough	1965
	V 13		by	Notts	Nottingham	1901
Highest Innings	For 341	G.H.Hirst	v	Leics	Leicester	1905
	V 318*	W.G.Grace	for	Glos	Cheltenham	1876

Highest Partnership for each Wicket

1st	555	P.Holmes/H.Sutcliffe	v	Essex	Leyton	1932
2nd	346	W.Barber/M.Leyland	v	Middlesex	Sheffield	1932
3rd	323*	H.Sutcliffe/M.Leyland	v	Glamorgan	Huddersfield	1928
4th	312	D.Denton/G.H.Hirst	v	Hampshire	Southampton	1914
5th	340	E.Wainwright/G.H.Hirst	v	Surrey	The Oval	1899
6th	276	M.Leyland/E.Robinson	v	Glamorgan	Swansea	1926
7th	254	W.Rhodes/D.C.F.Burton	v	Hampshire	Dewsbury	1919
8th	292	R.Peel/Lord Hawke	v	Warwicks	Birmingham	1896
9th	192	G.H.Hirst/S.Haigh	v	Surrey	Bradford	1898
10th	149	G.Boycott/G.B.Stevenson	v	Warwicks	Birmingham	1982

Best Bowling	For 10-10	H.Verity	v	Notts	Leeds	1932
(Innings)	V 10-37	C.V.Grimmett	for	Australians	Sheffield	1930
Best Bowling	For 17-91	H.Verity	v	Essex	Leyton	1933
(Match)	V 17-91	H.Dean	for	Lancashire	Liverpool	1913

Most Runs – Season	2883	H.Sutcliffe	(av 80.08)		1932
Most Runs – Career	38561	H.Sutcliffe	(av 50.20)		1919-45
Most 100s – Season	12	H.Sutcliffe			1932
Most 100s – Career	112	H.Sutcliffe			1919-45
Most Wkts – Season	240	W.Rhodes	(av 12.72)		1900
Most Wkts – Career	3608	W.Rhodes	(av 16.00)		1898-1930
Most Career W-K Dismissals	1186	D.Hunter	(863 ct/323 st)		1888-1909
Most Career Catches in the Field	665	J.Tunnicliffe			1891-1907

LIMITED-OVERS CRICKET

Highest Total	NWT	345-5		v	Notts	Leeds	1996
	BHC	317-5		v	Scotland	Leeds	1986
	NL	352-6		v	Notts	Scarborough	2001
Lowest Total	NWT	76		v	Surrey	Harrogate	1970
	BHC	88		v	Worcs	Leeds	1995
	NL	56		v	Warwicks	Birmingham	1995
Highest Innings	NWT	146	G.Boycott	v	Surrey	Lord's	1965
	BHC	142	G.Boycott	v	Worcs	Worcester	1980
	NL	191	D.S.Lehmann	v	Notts	Scarborough	2001
Best Bowling	NWT	7-27	D.Gough	v	Ireland	Leeds	1997
	BHC	6-27	A.G.Nicholson	v	Minor C (N)	Middlesbrough	1972
	NL	7-15	R.A.Hutton	v	Worcs	Leeds	1969

FIRST-CLASS UMPIRES 2002

† New Appointment

BENSON, Mark Richard (Sutton Valence S), b Shoreham, Sussex 6 Jul 1958. LHB, OB. Kent 1980-95; cap 1981; captain 1991-96 (did not play in 1996); benefit 1991. **Tests**: 1 (1986); HS 30 v I (Birmingham) 1986. **LOI**: 1 (1986; HS 24). 1000 runs (11); most – 1725 (1987). HS 257 K v Hants (Southampton) 1991. BB 2-55 K v Surrey (Dartford) 1986. F-c career: 292 matches; 18387 runs @ 40.23, 48 hundreds; 5 wickets @ 98.60; 140 ct. Appointed 2000.

BURGESS, Graham Iefvion (Millfield S), b Glastonbury, Somerset 5 May 1943. RHB, RM. Somerset 1966-79; cap 1968; testimonial 1977. HS 129 Sm v Glos (Taunton) 1973. BB 7-43 (13-75 match) Sm v OU (Oxford) 1975. F-c career: 252 matches; 7129 runs @ 18.90, 2 hundreds; 474 wickets @ 28.57. Appointed 1991.

CLARKSON, Anthony (Harrogate GS), b Killinghall, Harrogate, Yorks 5 Sep 1939. RHB, OB. Yorkshire 1963. Somerset 1966-71; cap 1968. Devon. 1000 runs (2); most – 1246 (1970). HS 131 Sm v Northants (Northampton) 1969. BB 3-51 Sm v Essex (Yeovil) 1967. F-c career: 110 matches; 4458 runs @ 25.18, 2 hundreds; 13 wickets @ 28.23. Appointed 1996.

CONSTANT, David John, b Bradford-on-Avon, Wilts 9 Nov 1941. LHB, SLA. Kent 1961-63. Leicestershire 1965-68. HS 80 Le v Glos (Bristol) 1966. BB 1-28. F-c career: 61 matches; 1517 runs @ 19.20; 1 wicket @ 36.00. Appointed 1969. Umpired 36 Tests (1971 to 1988) and 33 LOI (1972 to 2001). Represented Gloucestershire at bowls 1984-86.

COWLEY, Nigel Geoffrey (Dutchy Manor SS, Mere), b Shaftesbury, Dorset 1 Mar 1953. RHB, OB. Dorset 1972. Hampshire 1974-89; cap 1978; benefit 1988. Glamorgan 1990. 1000 runs (1): 1042 (1984). HS 109* H v Somerset (Taunton) 1977. BB 6-48 H v Leics (Southampton) 1982. F-c career: 271 matches; 7309 runs @ 23.35, 2 hundreds; 437 wickets @ 34.04. Appointed 2000.

DUDLESTON, Barry (Stockport S), b Bebington, Cheshire 16 Jul 1945. RHB, SLA. Leicestershire 1966-80; cap 1969; benefit 1980. Gloucestershire 1981-83. Rhodesia 1976-77 to 1979-80. 1000 runs (8); most – 1374 (1970). HS 202 Le v Derbys (Leicester) 1979. BB 4-6 Le v Surrey (Leicester) 1972. F-c career: 295 matches; 14747 runs @ 32.48, 32 hundreds; 47 wickets @ 29.04. Appointed 1984. Umpired 2 Tests (1991 to 1992) and 4 LOI (1992 to 2001).

EVANS, Jeffery Howard, b Llanelli, Carms 7 Aug 1954. No f-c appearances. Appointed 2001.

†GOULD, Ian James (Westgate SS, Chippenham), b Taplow, Bucks 19 Aug 1957. LHB, WK. Middlesex 1975 to 1980-81, 1996; cap 1977. Auckland 1979-80. Sussex 1981-90; cap 1981; captain 1987; benefit 1990. MCC YC. **LOI**: 18 (1982-83 to 1983; HS 42). Tours: A 1982-83; P 1980-81 (Int); Z 1980-81 (M). HS 128 M v Worcs (Worcester) 1978. BB 3-10 Sx v Surrey (Oval) 1989. Middlesex coach 1991-2000. Reappeared in one match (v OU) 1996. F-c career: 298 matches; 8756 runs @ 26.05, 4 hundreds; 7 wickets @ 52.14; 603 dismissals (536 ct, 67 st). Appointed 2002.

HAMPSHIRE, John Harry (Oakwood THS, Rotherham), b Thurnscoe, Yorks 10 Feb 1941. RHB, LB. Son of J. (Yorks 1937); brother of A.W. (Yorks 1975). Yorkshire 1961-81; cap 1963; benefit 1976; captain 1979-80. Leicestershire 1980-81 (tour). Derbyshire 1982-84; cap 1982. Tasmania 1967-68 to 1978-79. **Tests**: 8 (1969 to 1975); 403 runs @ 26.86, HS 107 v WI (Lord's) 1969 on debut (only England player to score hundred at Lord's on Test debut). Tours: A 1970-71; SA 1972-73 (DHR), 1974-75 (DHR); WI 1964-65 (Cav); NZ 1970-71; P 1967-68 (Cwlth XI); SL 1969-70; Z 1980-81 (Le XI). 1000 runs (15); most – 1596 (1978). HS 183* Y v Sussex (Hove) 1971. BB 7-52 Y v Glam (Cardiff) 1963. F-c career: 577 matches; 28059 runs @ 34.55, 43 hundreds; 30 wickets @ 54.56; 445 ct. Appointed 1985. Umpired 21 Tests (1989 to 2001-02) and 20 LOI (1989 to 2001), including one Sharjah tournament. **International Panel 1999 to date.**

HARRIS, Michael John ('*Pasty*') (Gerrans S, nr Truro), b St Just-in-Roseland, Cornwall 25 May 1944. RHB, LB, WK. Middlesex 1964-68; cap 1967. Nottinghamshire 1969-82; cap

103

1970; benefit 1977. E Province 1971-72. Wellington 1975-76. 1000 runs (11); most – 2238 (1971). Equalled Notts record with 9 hundreds in 1971. HS 201* Nt v Glam (Nottingham) 1973. BB 4-16 Nt v Warwks (Nottingham) 1969. F-c career: 344 matches; 19,196 runs @ 36.70, 41 hundreds; 79 wickets @ 43.78; 302 dismissals (288 ct, 14 st). Appointed 1998.

HOLDER, John Wakefield (Combermere S), b St George, Barbados 19 Mar 1945. RHB, RFM. Hampshire 1968-72. HS 33 H v Sussex (Hove) 1971. BB 7-79 H v Glos (Gloucester) 1972. Hat-trick 1972. F-c career: 47 matches; 374 runs @ 10.68; 139 wickets @ 24.56. Appointed 1983. Umpired 11 Tests (1988 to 2001) and 19 LOI (1988 to 2001) including 1989-90 Nehru Cup and one Sharjah tournament.

HOLDER, Vanburn Alonza (Richmond SM), b Deans Village, St Michael, Barbados 8 Oct 1945. RHB, RFM. Barbados 1966-67 to 1977-78. Worcestershire 1968-80; cap 1970; benefit 1979. Shropshire 1981. **Tests** (WI): 40 (1969 to 1978-79); 682 runs @ 14.20, HS 42 v NZ (P-o-S) 1971-72; 109 wkts @ 33.27, BB 6-28 v A (P-o-S) 1977-78. **LOI** (WI): 12. Tours (WI): E 1969, 1973, 1976; A 1975-76; I 1974-75, 1978-79; P 1973-74 (RW), 1974-75; SL 1974-75, 1978-79. HS 122 Barbados v Trinidad (Bridgetown) 1973-74. BB 7-40 Wo v Glam (Cardiff) 1974. F-c career: 311 matches; 3559 runs @ 13.03, 1 hundred; 947 wickets @ 24.48. Appointed 1992.

JESTY, Trevor Edward (Privet County SS, Gosport), b Gosport, Hants 2 Jun 1948. RHB, RM. Hampshire 1966-84; cap 1971; benefit 1982. Surrey 1985-87; cap 1985; captain 1985. Lancashire 1987-88 to 1991; cap 1989. Border 1973-74. GW 1974-75 to 1980-81. Canterbury 1979-80. **Wisden** 1982. **LOI**: 10. Tours: WI 1987-88 (La), 1982-83 (Int); Z 1988-89 (La). 1000 runs (10); most – 1645 (1982). HS 248 H v CU (Cambridge) 1984. Scored 102* La v OU (Oxford) 1991 in his final f-c innings. 90 wkts (2); most – 52 (1981). BB 7-75 H v Worcs (Southampton) 1976. F-c career: 490 matches; 21916 runs @ 32.71, 35 hundreds; 585 wickets @ 27.47. Appointed 1994.

JONES, Allan Arthur (St John's C, Horsham), b Horley, Surrey 9 Dec 1947. RHB, RFM. Sussex 1966-69. Somerset 1970-75; cap 1972. Middlesex 1976-79; cap 1976. Glamorgan 1980-81. Northern Transvaal 1972-73. Orange Free State 1976-77. HS 33 M v Kent (Canterbury) 1978. BB 9-51 Sm v Sussex (Hove) 1972. F-c career: 214 matches; 799 runs @ 5.39; 549 wickets @ 28.07. Appointed 1985. Umpired 1 LOI (1996).

KITCHEN, Mervyn John (Backwell SM, Nailsea), b Nailsea, Somerset 1 Aug 1940. LHB, RM. Somerset 1960-79; cap 1966; testimonial 1973. Tour: Rhodesia 1972-73 (Int W). 1000 runs (7); most – 1730 (1968). HS 189 Sm v Pakistanis (Taunton) 1967. BB 1-4. F-c career: 354 matches; 15230 runs @ 26.25, 17 hundreds; 2 wickets @ 54.50. Appointed 1982. Umpired 20 Tests (1990 to 2000) and 28 LOI (1983 to 2001), including tournaments in Sharjah (1) and Nairobi (1). International Panel 1995-99.

LEADBEATER, Barrie (Harehills SS), b Harehills, Leeds, Yorks 14 Aug 1943. RHB, RM. Yorkshire 1966-79; cap 1969; joint benefit with G.A.Cope 1980. Tour: WI 1969-70 (DN). HS 140* Y v Hants (Portsmouth) 1976. BB 1-1. F-c career: 147 matches; 5373 runs @ 25.34, 1 hundred; 1 wicket @ 5.00. Appointed 1981. Umpired 5 LOI (1983 to 2000).

†**LLONG, Nigel** James (Ashford North S), b Ashford, Kent 11 Feb 1969. LHB, OB. Kent 1990-98; cap 1993. Tour: Z 1992-93 (K). HS 130 K v Hants (Canterbury) 1996. BB 5-21 K v Middx (Canterbury) 1996. F-c career: 68 matches; 3024 runs @ 31.17, 6 hundreds; 35 wickets @ 35.97. Appointed 2002.

LLOYDS, Jeremy William (Blundells S), b Penang, Malaya 17 Nov 1954. LHB, OB. Somerset 1979-84; cap 1982. Gloucestershire 1985-91; cap 1985. Orange Free State 1983-84 to 1987-88, Tour (Glos): SL 1986-87. 1000 runs (3); most – 1295 (1985). HS 132* Sm v Northants (Northampton) 1982. BB 7-88 Sm v Essex (Chelmsford) 1982. F-c career: 267 matches; 10,679 runs @ 31.04, 10 hundreds; 333 wickets @ 38.86; 229 ct. Appointed 1998. Umpired 2 LOI (2000 to 2001).

MALLENDER, Neil Alan (Beverley GS), b Kirk Sandall, Yorks 13 Aug 1961. RHB, RFM. Northamptonshire 1980-86 and 1995-96; cap 1984. Somerset 1987-94; cap 1987; benefit 1994. Otago 1983-84 to 1992-93; captain 1990-91 to 1992-93. **Tests**: 2 (1992); 8 runs @ 2.66, HS 4; 10 wkts @ 21.50, BB 5-50 v P (Leeds) 1992 – on debut. Tour: Z 1994-95 (Nh).

HS 100* Otago v CD (Palmerston N) 1991-92. UK HS 87* Sm v Sussex (Hove) 1990. 50 wkts (6); most – 56 (1983). BB 7-27 Otago v Auckland (Auckland) 1984-85. UK BB 7-41 Nh v Derbys (Northampton) 1982. F-c career: 345 matches; 4,709 runs @ 17.18, 1 hundred; 937 wickets @ 26.31; 111 ct. Appointed 1999. Umpired 2 LOI (2001).

PALMER, Kenneth Ernest (Southbroom SM, Devizes), b Winchester, Hants 22 Apr 1937. RHB, RFM. Brother of R. (*below*) and father of G.V. (Somerset 1982-88). Somerset 1955-69; cap 1958; testimonial 1968. Tours: WI 1963-64 (Cav); P 1963-64 (Cwlth XI). **Tests:** 1 (1964-65; while coaching in South Africa); 10 runs; 1 wicket. 1000 runs (1): 1036 (1961). 100 wickets (4); most – 139 (1963). HS 125* Sm v Northants (Northampton) 1961. BB 9-57 Sm v Notts (Nottingham) 1963. F-c career: 314 matches; 7761 runs @ 20.64, 2 hundreds; 866 wickets @ 21.34. Appointed 1972. Umpired 22 Tests (1978 to 1994) and 23 LOI (1977 to 2001). International Panel 1994.

PALMER, Roy (Southbroom SM, Devizes), b Devizes, Wilts 12 Jul 1942. RHB, RFM. Brother of K.E. (*see above*). Somerset 1965-70. HS 84 Sm v Leics (Taunton) 1967. BB 6-45 Sm v Middx (Lord's) 1967. F-c career: 74 matches; 1037 runs @ 13.29; 172 wickets @ 31.62. Appointed 1980. Umpired 2 Tests (1992 to 1993) and 8 LOI (1983 to 1995).

SHARP, George (Elwick Road SS, Hartlepool), b West Hartlepool, Co Durham 12 Mar 1950. RHB, WK, occ LM. Northamptonshire 1968-85; cap 1973; benefit 1982. HS 98 Nh v Yorks (Northampton) 1983. BB 1-47. F-c career: 306 matches; 6254 runs @ 19.85; 1 wicket @ 70.00; 655 dismissals (565 ct, 90 st). Appointed 1992. Umpired 14 Tests (1996 to 2001) and 31 LOI (1995-96 to 2001-02), including tournaments in Nairobi (1), Sharjah (3) and Singapore (1). **International Panel 1996 to date.**

SHEPHERD, David Robert (Barnstaple GS; St Luke's C, Exeter), b Bideford, Devon 27 Dec 1940. RHB, RM. Gloucestershire 1965-79; cap 1969; joint benefit with J.Davey 1978. Scored 108 on debut (v OU). Devon 1959-64. 1000 runs (2); most – 1079 (1970). HS 153 Gs v Middx (Bristol) 1968. BB 1-1. F-c career: 282 matches; 10672 runs @ 24.47, 12 hundreds; 2 wickets @ 53.00. Appointed 1981. Umpired 59 Tests (1985 to 2001-02) and 97 LOI (1983 to 2001), including 1987-88, 1991-92, 1995-96 and 1999 World Cups (2 finals), and tournaments in Sri Lanka (3), Dhaka (2), Sharjah (6), Toronto (1) and Nairobi (1). **International Panel 1994 to date.**

STEELE, John Frederick (Endon SS), b Brown Edge, Staffs 23 Jul 1946. RHB, SLA. Brother of D.S. (Northants, Derbys and England 1963-84). Leicestershire 1970-83; cap 1971; benefit 1983. Glamorgan 1984-86; cap 1984. Natal 1973-74 to 1977-78. Staffordshire 1965-69. Tour: SA 1974-75 (DHR). 1000 runs (6); most – 1347 (1972). HS 195 Le v Derbys (Leicester) 1971. BB 7-29 Natal B v GW (Umzinto) 1973-74 and 7-29 Le v Glos (Leicester) 1980. F-c career: 379 matches; 15054 runs @ 28.95, 21 hundreds; 584 wickets @ 27.04; 413 ct. Appointed 1997.

WHITEHEAD, Alan Geoffrey Thomas, b Butleigh, Somerset 28 Oct 1940. LHB, SLA. Somerset 1957-61. HS 15 Sm v Hants (Bournemouth) 1959 and 15 Sm v Leics (Leicester) 1960. BB 6-74 Sm v Sussex (Eastbourne) 1959. F-c career: 38 matches; 137 runs @ 5.70; 67 wickets @ 34.41. Appointed 1970. Umpired 5 Tests (1982 to 1987) and 14 LOI (1979 to 2001).

WILLEY, Peter (Seaham SS), b Sedgefield, Co Durham 6 Dec 1949. RHB, OB. Northamptonshire 1966-83; cap 1971; benefit 1981. Leicestershire 1984-91; cap 1984; captain 1987. E Province 1982-83 to 1984-85. Northumberland 1992. **Tests:** 26 (1976 to 1986); 1184 runs @ 26.90, HS 102* v WI (St John's) 1980-81; 7 wkts @ 65.14, BB 2-73 v WI (Lord's) 1980. **LOI:** 26. Tours: A 1979-80; SA 1972-73 (DHR), 1981-82 (SAB); WI 1980-81, 1985-86; I 1979-80; SL 1977-78 (DHR). 1000 runs (10); most – 1783 (1982). HS 227 Nh v Somerset (Northampton) 1976. 50 wkts (3); most – 52 (1979). BB 7-37 Nh v OU (Oxford) 1975. F-c career: 559 matches; 24361 runs @ 30.56, 44 hundreds; 756 wickets @ 30.95. Appointed 1993. Umpired 24 Tests (1995-96 to 2001) and 23 LOI (1996 to 2001), including 1999 World Cup and tournaments in Dhaka and Nairobi. **International Panel 1996 to date.**

RESERVE FIRST-CLASS LIST: P.Adams, N.L.Bainton, M.Dixon, †P.J.Hartley, †A.Hill, C.S.Kelly, †R.A.Kettleborough, K.J.Lyons, †R.T.Robinson, K.Shuttleworth.

Test Match and LOI statistics to 30 January 2002. See page 11 for key to abbreviations.

TOURING TEAM FIRST-CLASS REGISTER 2001

AUSTRALIA

Full Names	Birthdate	Birthplace	Team	Type	F-C Debut
BEVAN, Michael Gwyl	8. 5.70	Belconnen	NSW	LHB/SLC	1989-90
BRACKEN, Nathan Wade	12. 9.77	Penrith	NSW	RHB/LFM	1998-99
FLEMING, Damien William	24. 4.70	Perth, WA	Victoria	RHB/RFM	1989-90
GILCHRIST, Adam Craig	14.11.71	Bellingen, NSW	W Australia	LHB/WK	1992-93
GILLESPIE, Jason Neil	19. 4.75	Darlinghurst, NSW	S Australia	RHB/RF	1994-95
HAYDEN, Matthew Lawrence	29.10.71	Kingaroy	Queensland	LHB/RM	1991-92
KATICH, Simon Mathew	21. 8.75	Middle Swan	W Australia	LHB/SLC	1996-97
LANGER, Justin Lee	21.11.70	Perth	W Australia	LHB/RM/WK	1991-92
LEE, Brett	8.11.76	Wollongong	NSW	RHB/RF	1994-95
McGRATH, Glenn Donald	9. 2.70	Dubbo	NSW	RHB/RFM	1992-93
MARTYN, Damien Richard	21.10.71	Darwin, NT	W Australia	RHB/RM	1990-91
MILLER, Colin Reid	6. 2.64	Footscray, Vic	Tasmania	RHB/RMF/OB	1985-86
NOFFKE, Ashley Allan	30. 4.77	Nambour	Queensland	RHB/RFM	1998-99
PONTING, Ricky Thomas	19.12.74	Launceston	Tasmania	RHB/RM/OB	1992-93
SECCOMBE, Wade Anthony	30.10.71	Murgon	Queensland	RHB/WK	1992-93
SLATER, Michael Jonathon	21. 2.70	Wagga	NSW	RHB/RM	1991-92
WARNE, Shane Keith	13. 9.69	Ferntree Gully, Mel	Victoria	RHB/LBG	1990-91
WAUGH, Mark Edward	2. 6.65	Canterbury, Sydney	NSW	RHB/RM/OB	1985-86
WAUGH, Stephen Rodger	2. 6.65	Canterbury, Sydney	NSW	RHB/RM	1984-85

PAKISTAN

Full Names	Birthdate	Birthplace	Team	Type	F-C Debut
AZHAR MAHMOOD	28. 2.75	Multan	PIA	RHB/RMF	1993-94
FAISAL IQBAL	30.12.81	Karachi	PNSC	RHB/RM	1998-99
IMRAN FARHAT	20. 5.82	Lahore	Habib Bank	LHB/LB	1998-99
INZAMAM-UL-HAQ	3. 3.70	Multan	Multan	RHB/SLA	1985-86
MOHAMMAD SAMI	24. 2.81	Karachi	Karachi	RHB/RF	1999-00
MOHAMMAD WASIM	8. 8.77	Rawalpindi	KRL	RHB/LB	1994-95
MUSHTAQ AHMED	28. 6.70	Sahiwal	National Bank	RHB/LBG	1986-87
RASHID LATIF	14.10.68	Karachi	Allied Bank	RHB/WK	1986-87
SAEED ANWAR	6. 9.68	Karachi	Karachi	LHB/SLA	1986-87
SALIM ELAHI	20.11.76	Sahiwal	Habib Bank	RHB/OB/WK	1995-96
WAQAR YOUNIS	16.11.69	Vehari	REDCO	RHB/RF	1987-88
WASIM AKRAM	3. 6.66	Lahore	PIA	LHB/LF	1984-85
YOUNIS KHAN	29.11.77	Mardan	Habib Bank	RHB/LB	1998-99
YOUSUF YOUHANA	27. 8.74	Lahore	PIA	RHB	1996-97

See MIDDLESEX, SURREY and SOMERSET for details of ABDUL RAZZAQ, SAQLAIN MUSHTAQ and SHOAIB AKHTAR respectively.

MCC FIRST-CLASS REGISTER 2001

Full Names	Birthdate	Birthplace	Team	Type	F-C Debut
ADAMS, James Clive	9. 1.68	Port Maria, Jamaica	Jamaica	LHB/SLA/WK	1984-85
AMINUL ISLAM	2. 2.68	Dhaka, Bangladesh	Bangladesh	RHB/OB	1997-98
ASIF MUJTABA, Mohammad	4.11.67	Karachi, Pakistan	Karachi/PIA	LHB/SLA	1984-85
DAWES, Joseph Henry	29. 8.70	Preston	Queensland	RHB/RFM	1997-98
KRUIS, Gideon Jacobus	9. 5.74	Pretoria, SA	Griqualand W	RHB/RFM	1993-94
METSON, Colin Peter	7. 7.63	Goffs Oak, Herts	Ex Middx/Glam	RHB/WK	1981
RICHARDSON, Mark Hunter	11. 6.71	Hastings, NZ	Otago	LHB/LM	1989-90
WARD, David Mark	10. 2.61	Croydon	Ex Surrey	RHB/OB	1985
WILLOUGHBY, Charl Miles	3.12.74	Cape Town, SA	Boland	LHB/LFM	1994-95

See PAKISTAN (*above*) and LEICESTERSHIRE for details of AZHAR MAHMOOD and SHAHID AFRIDI respectively.

UNIVERSITY FIRST-CLASS REGISTER 2001

CAMBRIDGE (‡ Blue 2001)

Full Names	Birthdate	Birthplace	College	Type	F-C Debut
‡BLOCK, Stuart Anthony Allen	6. 1.79	Hereford	Downing	LHB/SLC	2000
‡CLARKE, Adam Charles Spencer	10.11.81	Nottingham	Downing	RHB/RMF	2001
CLIFFE, Joel Alexander	2. 4.80	Oxford	Gonville & Caius	LHB/LMF	2001
‡COLLINS, Benjamin James	4.11.77	London	Girton	RHB	1998
‡DILL, Graham John	14. 9.70	Luton	Homerton	RHB/RMF	2001
‡HUGHES, Toby Roger	15. 2.79	Stourport-on-Severn	Homerton	RHB/RMF	2000
‡JOHNSON, Adam Hugh Vyvyan	28.11.78	Sheffield	Jesus	RHB/WK	2001
‡KUMAR, Vikram Harsh	21. 1.81	Beckenham	St John's	RHB/WK	2001
‡PARKER, James William Ralph	6.11.80	Durban, SA	St Catharine's	LHB/LM	2001
‡PYEMONT, James Patrick	10. 4.78	Eastbourne	Trinity Hall	RHB/OB	1997
‡SAYERS, Christopher Allan	19.12.78	Harrow	Trinity Hall	RHB/RMF	1999
‡SCOTT, James Beattie	27.11.78	West London	Downing	LHB/LMF	2001
SYMCOX, Alexander David	13.12.79	Eastbourne	Robinson	RHB	2001

DURHAM

Full Names	Birthdate	Birthplace	College	Type	F-C Debut
BANES, Matthew John	10.12.79	Pembury, Kent	Collingwood	RHB/OB	1999
BROWN, Michael James	9. 2.80	Burnley	Collingwood	RHB/OB	1999
BRUCE, James Thomas Anthony	17.12.79	London	St Hild & St Bede	RHB/RMF	2001
FERLEY, Robert Steven	4. 2.82	Norwich	Grey	RHB/SLA	2001
FOSTER, James Savin	15. 6.80	Whipps Cross	Collingwood	RHB/WK	2000
GILBERT, Richard George	29. 6.80	Scarborough	Van Mildert	RHB/RFM	2000
JEFFERSON, William Ingleby	25.10.79	Derby	St Hild & St Bede	RHB/RMF	2000
LOUDON, Alexander Guy Rushworth	6. 9.80	Westminster	Collingwood	RHB/OB	2001
LOUDON, Hugo John Hope	11.12.78	Westminster	St Hild & St Bede	RHB/SLA	2001
PHILLIPS, Timothy James	13. 3.81	Cambridge	St Hild & St Bede	LHB/SLA	1999
ROWE, James George Castell	4. 7.79	Farnborough, Kent	Hatfield	LHB/SLA	2001
STEAD, Roger Alexander	18. 4.80	Dewsbury	St Chads	RHB/RM	2001
THORBURN, Mark	11. 8.78	Bath	Collingwood	RHB/RMF	2001
VAN DER GUCHT, Charles Graham	14. 1.80	Wimbledon	St Hild & St Bede	LHB/LM/SLA	2001

OXFORD (‡ Blue 2001)

Full Names	Birthdate	Birthplace	College	Type	F-C Debut
BONES, Andrew Stephen	18. 2.78	Crewe	(Brookes U)	RHB/WK/OB	2000
‡BUTCHER, Graham Robert	25. 9.81	Epsom	Oriel	RHB	2001
‡DALRYMPLE, James William Murray	21. 1.81	Nairobi, Kenya	St Peter's	RHB/OB	2001
DANIELS, Timothy John	24.10.80	Brighton	(Brookes U)	RHB	2001
‡FLOYD, Matthew Kabir	30.11.80	Hampstead	Keble	RHB/OB	2001
‡GOFTON, Alan Frederick	4.10.79	Chesterfield	Wadham	RHB/OB	1999
‡HAWINKELS, Stephen John	12. 3.82	Cape Town, SA	University	RHB	2001
‡HICKS, Thomas Charles	28. 8.79	Farnborough, Kent	St Catherine's	RHB/OB	1999
JONES, Huw Rhys	23.11.80	Oxford	(Brookes U)	RHB/LB	2001
‡KHAN, Salman Haider	4. 6.71	Rawalpindi, Pak	Wadham	RHB	1998
MEES, Thomas	8. 6.81	Wolverhampton	(Brookes U)	RHB/RMF	2001
‡MILLAR, Neil	3. 2.81	London	Christ Church	RHB/RM	2000
PORTER, Joseph James	5. 5.80	London	(Brookes U)	LHB/SLA	2001
SANKLECHA, Pranay	3.11.83	Cochin, India	Lincoln	RHB/RM/SLA	2001
SHARPE, Toby John	5. 7.81	London	(Brookes U)	RHB/RMF	2001
‡SMALLEY, Richard George	20. 3.79	Newcastle-u-Tyne	Keble	LHB/WK	1999
‡WARREN, Charles Christopher Morel	11. 3.79	Portadown	Worcester	RHB	2001
‡WORTLEY, Thomas Henry	22. 2.81	Sutton	Jesus	RHB/LB	2001

BRITISH UNIVERSITIES
(Excluding players listed either above or in the County Register)

Full Names	Birthdate	Birthplace	University	Type	F-C Debut
TOURNIER, Mark Andrew	3.5.71	Melbourne, Aust	Loughborough	RHB/RFM	2000

THE 2001 FIRST-CLASS SEASON
STATISTICAL HIGHLIGHTS

HIGHEST INNINGS TOTALS († *Second innings*)

701-9d	Surrey v Glamorgan	Cardiff
650	Somerset v Northamptonshire	Taunton
641-4d	Australia v England (5)	The Oval
633-6d	Northamptonshire v Essex	Northampton
631-6d	Worcestershire v Durham UCCE	Worcester
631-9d	Warwickshire v Middlesex	Lord's
612-8d	Leicestershire v Kent	Canterbury
608-8d	Gloucestershire v Nottinghamshire	Bristol
607	Surrey v Northamptonshire	Northampton
600-6d	Lancashire v Northamptonshire	Manchester
600-8d	Somerset v Glamorgan	Taunton
589-5	Yorkshire v Somerset	Bath
588	Leicestershire v Glamorgan	Cardiff
580-9d	Yorkshire v Glamorgan	Scarborough
576-8d†	Kent v Northamptonshire	Canterbury
576	Australia v England (1)	Birmingham
572	Derbyshire v Nottinghamshire	Derby
569-9d†	Australians v Essex	Chelmsford
567	Northamptonshire v Somerset	Northampton
560-8d	Gloucestershire v Derbyshire	Derby
559	Leicestershire v Essex	Chelmsford
557-5†	Nottinghamshire v Derbyshire	Derby
556-7d	Glamorgan v Northamptonshire	Cardiff
553-5d	Somerset v Yorkshire	Bath
548-6d	Glamorgan v Northamptonshire	Northampton
546-8d	Glamorgan v Essex	Cardiff
543	Middlesex v Derbyshire	Southgate
540-7d†	Essex v Glamorgan	Chelmsford
533-5d	Essex v Cambridge UCCE	Cambridge
531	Yorkshire v Lancashire	Leeds
527	Middlesex v Nottinghamshire	Nottingham
526	Nottinghamshire v Derbyshire	Derby
524	Worcestershire v Warwickshire	Birmingham
520	Gloucestershire v Sussex	Cheltenham
518-5d	Kent v Essex	Tunbridge Wells
516-9d	Surrey v Yorkshire	The Oval
508	Gloucestershire v Derbyshire	Bristol
502-7d	Middlesex v Warwickshire	Lord's
500-7d	Sussex v Hampshire	Southampton
500	Yorkshire v Leicestershire	Leeds

HIGHEST FOURTH INNINGS TOTALS

478-9 (set 536)	Surrey v Leicestershire	Leicester
461-3 (set 458)	Nottinghamshire v Worcestershire	Worcester
403-7 (set 401)	Kent v Leicestershire	Leicester

LOWEST INNINGS TOTALS

67	Durham UCCE v Durham	Chester-le-Street
68	Essex v Kent	Tunbridge Wells
74	British U v Pakistanis	Nottingham
81	Hampshire v Sussex	Hove
85	Leicestershire v Northamptonshire	Northampton

87	Gloucestershire v Worcestershire	Worcester
95	Derbyshire v Durham	Chester-le-Street
96	Leicestershire v Pakistanis	Leicester
97	Australians v Hampshire	Southampton
99	Leicestershire v Yorkshire	Leeds

MATCH AGGREGATES OF 1500 RUNS

1795-34	Somerset (650, 250-6) v Northamptonshire (463-9d, 432-9d)	Taunton
1655-25	Derbyshire (572) v Nottinghamshire (526, 557-5)	Derby
1583-34	Leicestershire (425, 365-7d) v Kent (390, 403-7)	Leicester

FOUR HUNDREDS IN AN INNINGS

Essex (533-5d) v Cambridge UCCE   Cambridge
   P.J.Prichard 111, A.P.Grayson 127, D.D.J.Robinson 109, G.R.Napier 104
Middlesex (502-7d) v Warwickshire   Lord's
   S.P.Fleming 102, E.C.Joyce 104, P.N.Weekes 107, D.C.Nash 103*

FIRST TO INDIVIDUAL TARGETS

1000 RUNS	D.P.Fulton	Kent	4 July
2000 RUNS	M.E.K.Hussey	Northamptonshire	13 September
100 WICKETS	–	*(most 75 – R.J.Kirtley for Sussex)*	

TRIPLE HUNDREDS

M.E.K.Hussey	329*	Northamptonshire v Essex	Northampton
M.A.Wagh	315	Warwickshire v Middlesex	Lord's

DOUBLE HUNDREDS

M.Burns		221	Somerset v Yorkshire	Bath
M.A.Butcher		230	Surrey v Glamorgan	Cardiff
J.P.Crawley		280	Lancashire v Northamptonshire	Manchester
A.Dale		204	Glamorgan v Northamptonshire	Northampton
D.P.Fulton		208*	Kent v Somerset	Canterbury
M.W.Goodwin		203*	Sussex v Nottinghamshire	Nottingham
G.A.Hick	(2)	201	Worcestershire v Warwickshire	Birmingham
		200*	Worcestershire v Durham	Chester-le-Street
M.E.K.Hussey	(3)	329*	Northamptonshire v Essex	Northampton
			Record Northamptonshire score	
		232	Northamptonshire v Leicestershire	Northampton
		208	Northamptonshire v Somerset	Taunton
D.S.Lehmann		252	Yorkshire v Lancashire	Leeds
			Record score in Roses matches	
J.P.Maher		217	Glamorgan v Essex	Cardiff
K.P.Pietersen		218*	Nottinghamshire v Derbyshire	Derby
M.J.Powell		236	Warwickshire v Oxford UCCE	Oxford
Saeed Anwar		201	Pakistanis v Kent	Canterbury
O.A.Shah		203	Middlesex v Derbyshire	Southgate
I.J.Sutcliffe		203	Leicestershire v Glamorgan	Cardiff
M.A.Wagh		315	Warwickshire v Middlesex	Lord's

HUNDREDS IN THREE CONSECUTIVE INNINGS

D.P.Fulton (Kent) 208* and 104* v Somerset (Canterbury), 197 v Northamptonshire (Northampton).
B.F.Smith (Leicestershire) 179 v Surrey (Leicester), 117 v Glamorgan (Cardiff), 111 v Kent (Leicester).

HUNDRED IN EACH INNINGS OF A MATCH

C.W.G.Bassano	186*	106	Derbyshire v Gloucestershire	Derby
			On Championship debut – first instance	
I.D.Blackwell	103	122	Somerset v Northamptonshire	Northampton

D.P.Fulton	208*	104*	Kent v Somerset	Canterbury
M.W.Goodwin	115	203*	Sussex v Nottinghamshire	Nottingham
A.P.Grayson	173	149	Essex v Northamptonshire	Northampton
S.G.Law	116*	123*	Essex v Lancashire	Manchester
J.E.Morris	170	136*	Nottinghamshire v Derbyshire	Derby
D.D.J.Robinson	102	118*	Essex v Leicestershire	Chelmsford

FASTEST HUNDRED (WALTER LAWRENCE TROPHY)
I.J.Harvey   61 balls   Gloucestershire v Derbyshire   Bristol

HUNDRED BEFORE LUNCH
A.P.Grayson   0*-114* 1st day   Essex v Cambridge UCCE   Cambridge

CARRIED BAT THROUGH COMPLETED INNINGS († One man absent)
S.A.A.Block	56*	Cambridge UCCE (129) v Kent	Cambridge
M.A.Butcher	145*	Surrey (281) v Glamorgan	The Oval
M.K.Floyd	128*	Oxford U (325) v Cambridge U	Cambridge
S.P.James	61*	Glamorgan (146) v Leicestershire	Leicester
M.H.Richardson	64*	MCC (124) v Australians	Arundel
A.J.Strauss	112*	Middlesex (253) v Hampshire	Southampton
L.D.Sutton	140*	Derbyshire (263) v Sussex	Derby
		(Last out for 54 out of 117 in 2nd innings)	

AN HOUR WITHOUT ADDING TO SCORE
60 min   A.L.Penberthy (20)   Northamptonshire v Essex   Chelmsford

FIRST-WICKET PARTNERSHIP OF 100 IN EACH INNINGS
163 147   J.Cox/M.J.Wood Somerset v Northamptonshire   Taunton

OTHER NOTABLE PARTNERSHIPS († County record)
First Wicket
372*	M.W.Goodwin/R.R.Montgomerie	Sussex v Nottinghamshire	Nottingham
343	M.J.Powell/I.R.Bell	Warwickshire v Oxford UCCE	Oxford
309	C.White/M.J.Wood	Yorkshire v Lancashire	Manchester
307	Saeed Anwar/Salim Elahi	Pakistanis v Kent	Canterbury

Second Wicket
258†   J.J.B.Lewis/M.L.Love   Durham v Nottinghamshire   Chester-le-Street

Third Wicket
306	M.G.N.Windows/C.G.Taylor	Gloucestershire v Nottinghamshire	Bristol
300	B.F.Smith/A.Habib	Leicestershire v Somerset	Taunton
287	M.E.K.Hussey/R.J.Warren	Northamptonshire v Somerset	Taunton
284	J.P.Maher/M.J.Powell	Glamorgan v Essex	Cardiff
267	M.P.Vaughan/G.P.Thorpe	England v Pakistan (2)	Manchester

Fourth Wicket
316	U.Afzaal/J.E.Morris	Nottinghamshire v Derbyshire	Derby
292	O.A.Shah/B.L.Hutton	Middlesex v Derbyshire	Southgate

Fifth Wicket
248   A.Dale/K.Newell   Glamorgan v Northamptonshire   Northampton

Sixth Wicket
372*†	K.P.Pietersen/J.E.Morris	Nottinghamshire v Derbyshire	Derby
251*	D.R.Martyn/A.C.Gilchrist	Australians v Essex	Chelmsford
250	R.J.Warren/A.L.Penberthy	Northamptonshire v Glamorgan	Northampton

Seventh Wicket
222	R.J.Turner/K.P.Dutch	Somerset v Essex	Taunton
206	A.J.Stewart/A.J.Tudor	Surrey v Essex	The Oval

Tenth Wicket

135	C.M.W.Read/R.D.Stemp	Nottinghamshire v Hampshire	Southampton
129	G.Chapple/G.Keedy	Lancashire v Somerset	Manchester
109*	M.P.Bicknell/I.D.K.Salisbury	Surrey v Leicestershire	Leicester
107	I.D.Blackwell/J.O.Grove	Somerset v Surrey	Taunton
103	A.J.Stewart/A.R.Caddick	England v Australia (1)	Birmingham

EIGHT OR MORE WICKETS IN AN INNINGS

D.M.Cousins	8-102	Northamptonshire v Yorkshire	Leeds
D.E.Malcolm	8- 63	Leicestershire v Surrey	Leicester
A.D.Mullally	8- 90	Hampshire v Warwickshire	Southampton
Mushtaq Ahmed	8- 49	Pakistanis v British U	Nottingham
M.M.Patel	8-119	Kent v Somerset	Canterbury

TEN OR MORE WICKETS IN A MATCH

A.J.Bichel		10- 86	Worcestershire v Gloucestershire	Worcester
M.P.Bicknell		11-117	Surrey v Glamorgan	The Oval
D.R.Brown		10- 80	Warwickshire v Derbyshire	Derby
A.R.Caddick		10-173	Somerset v Yorkshire	Leeds
R.D.B.Croft		10-191	Glamorgan v Northamptonshire	Cardiff
K.J.Dean		10-105	Derbyshire v Durham	Chester-le-Street
S.P.Kirby		12- 72	Yorkshire v Leicestershire	Leeds
R.J.Kirtley	(2)	10- 95	Sussex v Durham	Hove
		10- 93	Sussex v Gloucestershire	Hove
J.D.Lewry		13- 79	Sussex v Hampshire	Hove
D.E.Malcolm		10-187	Leicestershire v Surrey	Leicester
M.Muralitharan		10-123	Lancashire v Essex	Manchester
Mushtaq Ahmed		10- 51	Pakistanis v British U	Nottingham
M.M.Patel		12-144	Kent v Somerset	Canterbury
G.J.Smith		10-101	Nottinghamshire v Sussex	Hove
B.J.Trott		11- 78	Kent v Essex	Tunbridge Wells
P.C.R.Tufnell		11-133	Middlesex v Derbyshire	Southgate
S.K.Warne		11-229	Australia v England (5)	The Oval

HAT-TRICKS

J.D.Lewry	Sussex v Hampshire	Hove
Waqar Younis	Pakistanis v Leicestershire	Leicester

WICKET WITH FIRST BALL IN FIRST-CLASS CRICKET

J.E.K.Schofield	Hampshire v Australians	Southampton

SIX OR MORE WICKET-KEEPING DISMISSALS IN AN INNINGS

N.D.Burns	(3)	7ct	Leicestershire v Somerset	Leicester
		6ct	Leicestershire v Yorkshire	Leicester
		6ct	Leicestershire v Glamorgan	Leicester
C.M.W.Read		6ct	Nottinghamshire v Middlesex	Nottingham
R.J.Turner	(2)	7ct	Somerset v Northamptonshire	Taunton
		6ct	Somerset v Surrey	Taunton

NINE OR MORE WICKET-KEEPING DISMISSALS IN A MATCH

N.D.Burns (2)	9 ct		Leicestershire v Somerset	Leicester
	8 ct	1st	Leicestershire v Yorkshire	Leicester
R.J.Turner	9 ct		Somerset v Surrey	Taunton

NO BYES CONCEDED IN TOTAL OF 500 OR MORE

607	T.M.B.Bailey	Northamptonshire v Surrey	Northampton
576-8d	D.Ripley	Northamptonshire v Kent	Canterbury
567	R.J.Turner	Somerset v Northamptonshire	Northampton

FIVE OR MORE CATCHES IN AN INNINGS IN THE FIELD

M.J.Di Venuto   5 ct   Derbyshire v Durham   Chester-le-Street

SEVEN OR MORE CATCHES IN A MATCH IN THE FIELD

D.P.Fulton   7 ct   Kent v Somerset   Canterbury

SIXTY EXTRAS IN AN INNINGS

B	LB	W	NB			
68	23	31	10	4	Surrey (478-9) v Leicestershire	Leicester
66	8	24	20	14	Sussex (404) v Nottinghamshire	Hove
61	16	13	6	26	Gloucestershire (520) v Sussex	Cheltenham

150 EXTRAS IN A MATCH

B	LB	W	NB			
185	17	55	41	72	Sussex (404, 298-8d) v Nottinghamshire (332, 208)	Hove
159	8	45	30	76	Derbyshire (572) v Nottinghamshire (526, 557-5)	Derby

Under ECB regulations (Test matches excluded), two extras were scored for each no-ball, in addition to any runs scored off that ball, and two extras were also scored for each wide (one in tourist matches). Penalty points awarded as five runs when the ball struck a helmet parked behind the wicket-keeper were also included. There were a further 13 instances of 50-59 extras in an innings.

YOUNG CRICKETER OF THE YEAR

This annual award, made by The Cricket Writers' Club (founded 1946), is currently restricted to players qualified for England, meeting that requirement at the time of his award, and under the age of 23 on 1 May. In 1986 their ballot resulted in a dead heat. To 12 March 2002 their selections have gained a tally of 1,742 England caps (shown in brackets).

1950	R.Tattersall (16)		1977	I.T.Botham (102)
1951	P.B.H.May (66)		1978	D.I.Gower (117)
1952	F.S.Trueman (67)		1979	P.W.G.Parker (1)
1953	M.C.Cowdrey (114)		1980	G.R.Dilley (41)
1954	P.J.Loader (13)		1981	M.W.Gatting (79)
1955	K.F.Barrington (82)		1982	N.G.Cowans (19)
1956	B.Taylor		1983	N.A.Foster (29)
1957	M.J.Stewart (8)		1984	R.J.Bailey (4)
1958	A.C.D.Ingleby-Mackenzie		1985	D.V.Lawrence (5)
1959	G.Pullar (28)		1986	A.A.Metcalfe
1960	D.A.Allen (39)			J.J.Whitaker (1)
1961	P.H.Parfitt (37)		1987	R.J.Blakey (2)
1962	P.J.Sharpe (12)		1988	M.P.Maynard (4)
1963	G.Boycott (108)		1989	N.Hussain (66)
1964	J.M.Brearley (39)		1990	M.A.Atherton (115)
1965	A.P.E.Knott (95)		1991	M.R.Ramprakash (49)
1966	D.L.Underwood (86)		1992	I.D.K.Salisbury (15)
1967	A.W.Greig (58)		1993	M.N.Lathwell (2)
1968	R.M.H.Cottam (4)		1994	J.P.Crawley (29)
1969	A.Ward (5)		1995	A.Symonds
1970	C.M.Old (46)		1996	C.E.W.Silverwood (5)
1971	J.Whitehouse		1997	B.C.Hollioake (2)
1972	D.R.Owen-Thomas		1998	A.Flintoff (12)
1973	M.Hendrick (30)		1999	A.J.Tudor (5)
1974	P.H.Edmonds (51)		2000	P.J.Franks
1975	A.Kennedy		2001	O.A.Shah
1976	G.Miller (34)			

2001 FIRST-CLASS AVERAGES

These averages involve the 450 cricketers who appeared in the 168 first-class matches played by 28 teams in the British Isles during the 2001 season.

'Cap' denotes the season in which the player was awarded a 1st XI cap by the county he represented in 2001.

Team abbreviations: A – Australia(ns); BU – British Universities; CU – Cambridge University/Cambridge UCCE; De – Derbyshire; Du – Durham; DU – Durham UCCE; E – England; Ex – Essex; Gm – Glamorgan; Gs – Gloucestershire; H – Hampshire; K – Kent; La – Lancashire; Le – Leicestershire; M – Middlesex; MCC – Marylebone Cricket Club; Nh – Northamptonshire; Nt – Nottinghamshire; OU – Oxford University/Oxford UCCE; P – Pakistan(is); Sm – Somerset; Sy – Surrey; Sx – Sussex; Wa – Warwickshire; Wo – Worcestershire; Y – Yorkshire.

† Left-handed batsman.

BATTING AND FIELDING

	Cap	M	I	NO	HS	Runs	Avge	100	50	Ct/St
†Aamir Sohail (Sm)	–	1	2	–	50	86	43.00	–	1	–
Abdul Razzaq (P)	–	5	7	1	53	133	22.16	–	1	2
Adams, C.J.(Sx)	1998	15	23	2	192	1086	51.71	3	7	28
†Adams, J.C.(MCC)	–	1	2	1	81*	81	81.00	–	1	2
†Afzaal, U.(Nt/E)	2000	15	28	1	138	1011	37.44	1	8	9
Aldred, P.(De)	1999	8	13	1	35	120	10.00	–	–	5
Ali, Kabir (Wo)	–	4	5	1	50*	138	34.50	–	1	–
Ali, Kadeer (Wo)	–	5	8	–	38	65	8.12	–	–	2
Alleyne, D.(M)	–	2	4	–	44	55	13.75	–	–	4
Alleyne, M.W.(Gs)	1990	16	26	3	136	718	31.21	2	2	12/1
Ambrose, T.R.(Sx)	–	2	3	–	52	92	30.66	–	1	3
Amin, R.M.(Sy)	–	3	4	1	1	1	0.33	–	–	2
Aminul Islam (MCC)	–	1	2	–	20	21	10.50	–	–	2
Anderson, R.S.G.(Ex)	–	8	11	–	45	154	14.00	–	–	2
†Asif Mujtaba (MCC)	–	1	2	–	22	22	11.00	–	–	1
Atherton, M.A.(La/E)	1989	11	21	1	160	649	32.45	1	3	17
Averis, J.M.M.(Gs)	2001	15	19	3	7*	35	2.18	–	–	3
Aymes, A.N.(H)	1991	16	19	5	112*	572	40.85	1	4	43/2
Azhar Mahmood (P/MCC)	–	4	7	1	80*	209	34.83	–	1	1
Bailey, R.J.(De)	2000	14	25	1	136*	515	21.45	1	2	8
Bailey, T.M.B.(Nh)	–	5	7	–	41	113	16.14	–	–	3
Ball, M.C.J.(Gs)	1996	12	16	3	68	379	29.15	–	3	21
Banes, M.J.(DU/BU)	–	4	6	1	25*	60	12.00	–	–	1
Banks, O.A.C.(Le)	–	1	2	–	4	4	2.00	–	–	–
Barnett, K.J.(Gs)	1999	14	25	2	114	1029	44.73	1	7	10
Bassano, C.W.G.(De)	–	8	14	2	186*	523	43.58	2	2	5
Batty, G.J.(Sy)	–	1	2	–	25	44	22.00	–	–	2
Batty, J.N.(Sy)	2001	10	16	1	59	239	15.93	–	1	26/2
Bell, I.R.(Wa)	2001	11	16	3	135	836	64.30	3	4	11
Betts, M.M.(Wa)	2001	12	11	3	19	92	11.50	–	–	9
†Bevan, M.G.(A)	–	1	2	–	34	67	33.50	–	–	–
Bichel, A.J.(Wo)	2001	16	24	–	78	627	26.12	–	3	5
†Bicknell, D.J.(Nt)	2000	16	29	–	167	1050	36.20	3	3	8
Bicknell, M.P.(Sy)	1989	15	22	6	110*	748	46.75	1	4	5
Bishop, J.E.(Ex)	–	8	12	2	18	74	7.40	–	–	–
†Blackwell, I.D.(Sm)	2001	11	17	–	122	839	49.35	4	3	5
Blain, J.A.R.(Nh)	–	5	9	4	34	66	13.20	–	–	–
Blakey, R.J.(Y)	1987	15	21	6	78*	405	27.00	–	3	49/5
Blewett, G.S.(Nt)	2001	16	30	3	137*	1292	47.85	5	5	24
†Block, S.A.A.(CU)	–	4	7	1	56*	139	23.16	–	1	1

113

	Cap	M	I	NO	HS	Runs	Avge	100	50	Ct/St
Bloomfield, T.F.(M)	2001	16	16	4	28	85	7.08	–	–	2
Bones, A.S.(OU)	–	1	1	–	3	3	3.00	–	–	2
Boswell, S.A.J.(Le)	–	2	3	1	16*	20	10.00	–	–	2
†Boulton, N.R.(Wo)	–	4	5	–	47	75	15.00	–	–	1
Bowler, P.D.(Sm)	1995	14	22	2	164	827	41.35	2	4	14
Bracken, N.W.(A)	–	1	2	2	9*	10	–	–	–	1
†Bressington, A.N.(Gs)	–	5	5	2	17*	40	13.33	–	–	2
Bridge, G.D.(Du)	–	7	13	2	39*	125	11.36	–	–	5
Brinkley, J.E.(Du)	–	10	13	2	65	111	10.09	–	1	4
Brown, A.D.(Sy)	1994	13	20	–	122	630	31.50	3	2	3
Brown, D.R.(Wa)	1995	16	20	3	104	666	39.17	1	6	16
Brown, J.F.(Nh)	2000	11	12	5	35*	56	8.00	–	–	2
Brown, M.J.(DU/BU/Mx)	–	5	10	2	60*	203	25.37	–	2	2
Brown, S.J.E.(Du)	1998	4	5	2	29	64	21.33	–	–	1
Bruce, J.T.A.(DU)	–	3	3	1	14*	19	9.50	–	–	
Brunnschweiler, I.(H)	–	1	2	1	10*	11	11.00	–	–	5
†Bulbeck, M.P.L.(Sm)	–	5	7	2	18	50	10.00	–	–	3
Burns, M.(Sm)	1999	17	28	1	221	961	35.59	1	7	13
†Burns, N.D.(Le)	2001	17	28	7	111	862	41.04	1	6	65/3
Butcher, G.P.(Sy)	–	4	8	1	56	175	25.00	–	1	1
Butcher, G.R.(OU)	–	1	2	–	10	16	8.00	–	–	
†Butcher, M.A.(Sy/E)	1996	15	25	2	230	1300	56.52	3	6	15
†Byas, D.(Y)	1991	16	24	5	110*	853	44.89	4	2	38
Caddick, A.R.(Sm/E)	1992	9	15	4	49*	122	11.09	–	–	1
†Carberry, M.A.(Sy)	–	6	10	–	84	311	31.10	–	1	6
†Carter, N.M.(Wa)	–	6	4	1	5	10	3.33	–	–	2
Cassar, M.E.(Nh)	–	1	2	–	9	9	4.50	–	–	2
†Cawdron, M.J.(Gs)	–	6	9	2	29	82	11.71	–	–	1
Chapple, G.(La)	1994	13	19	3	155	497	31.06	1	2	3
Chilton, M.J.(La)	–	14	24	1	104	684	29.73	1	4	10
Clarke, A.C.S.(CU)	–	2	2	–	44	44	22.00	–	–	
†Cliffe, J.A.(CU)	–	3	3	–	2	2	0.66	–	–	
†Clinton, R.S.(Ex)	–	8	15	1	58*	283	20.21	–	1	2
Clough, G.D.(Nt)	–	4	6	–	8	22	3.66	–	–	1
Collingwood, P.D.(Du)	1998	13	24	3	153	1108	52.76	3	6	10
Collins, B.J.(CU)	–	4	6	1	28*	79	15.80	–	–	
†Cook, J.W.(Nh)	–	9	16	1	88	391	26.06	–	4	5
Cook, S.J.(M)	–	10	11	3	93*	236	29.50	–	1	3
Cork, D.G.(De/E)	1993	7	11	–	128	262	23.81	1	–	6
Cosker, D.A.(Gm)	2000	11	15	4	35	175	15.90	–	–	10
Cottey, P.A.(Sx)	1999	2	3	1	46	70	35.00	–	–	1
Cousins, D.M.(Nh)	2000	8	10	3	27	87	12.42	–	–	
Cowan, A.P.(Ex)	1997	15	24	3	68	360	17.14	–	2	8
Cox, J.(Sm)	1999	15	25	3	186	1264	57.45	1	9	6
†Craven, V.J.(Y)	–	2	4	1	23*	33	11.00	–	–	2
Crawley, J.P.(La)	1994	14	24	2	280	898	40.81	2	5	4
Croft, R.D.B.(Gm/E)	1992	10	15	2	93	353	27.15	–	3	6
Crowe, C.D.(Le)	–	7	10	1	42	73	8.11	–	–	4
Cullinan, D.J.(K)	2001	3	–	63	122	40.66	–	2	–	1
Cunliffe, R.J.(Gs)	–	5	8	1	48	141	20.14	–	–	5
Dagnall, C.E.(Wa)	–	3	1	–	1	1	1.00	–	–	
†Dakin, J.M.(Le)	2000	7	11	–	69	211	19.18	–	1	1
Dale, A.(Gm)	1992	15	23	3	204	1026	51.30	3	4	9
Daley, J.A.(Du)	1999	9	16	1	128*	428	28.53	1	1	4
Dalrymple, J.W.M.(OU/BU/M)	–	5	10	1	70	203	22.55	–	1	8
Daniels, T.J.(OU)	–	1	1	–	0	0	0.00	–	–	1/2
†Davies, A.P.(Gm)	–	4	7	1	40	85	14.16	–	–	2
Davies, M.K.(Ex)	–	2	4	1	10*	22	7.33	–	–	–

114

	Cap	M	I	NO	HS	Runs	Avge	100	50	Ct/St
Davis, M.J.G.(Sx)	–	15	22	4	52	439	24.38	–	1	5
Davis, R.P.(Le)	–	1	2	–	51	51	25.50	–	1	2
Dawes, J.H.(MCC)	–	1	2	–	10	11	5.50	–	–	–
Dawson, R.K.J.(Y)	–	9	11	1	37	95	9.50	–	–	6
†Dean, K.J.(De)	1998	8	12	2	23	117	11.70	–	–	2
DeFreitas, P.A.J.(Le)	1986	9	14	1	97	256	19.69	–	2	–
Dill, G.J.(CU)	–	4	6	1	8	27	5.40	–	–	3
†Di Venuto, M.J.(De)	2000	14	25	1	165	1082	45.08	4	5	15
†Dowman, M.P.(De)	2000	14	26	1	145*	567	22.68	1	1	4
Drakes, V.C.(Wa)	2001	14	13	3	50	209	20.90	–	1	1
†Driver, R.C.(La)	–	5	8	–	35	93	11.62	–	–	5
Dumelow, N.R.C.(De)	–	9	15	1	61	304	21.71	–	2	2
Dutch, K.P.(Sm)	2001	16	22	4	118	530	29.44	1	3	19
Ealham, M.A.(K)	1992	12	15	2	153*	299	23.00	1	–	8
Edwards, A.D.(De)	–	1	2	1	23	27	27.00	–	–	–
Elstub, C.J.(DU)	–	1	2	1	6*	6	6.00	–	–	–
Evans, A.W.(Gm)	–	2	3	–	41	54	18.00	–	–	1
†Fairbrother, N.H.(La)	1985	12	19	4	179*	939	62.60	4	1	16
Faisal Iqbal (P)	–	4	4	–	83	178	44.50	–	2	–
Fellows, G.M.(Y)	–	12	17	1	63	455	28.43	–	3	4
Ferley, R.S.(DU/BU)	–	4	5	1	17*	41	10.25	–	–	1
†Fisher, I.D.(Y)	–	1	1	1	28*	28	–	–	–	–
Fleming, D.W.(A)	–	5	6	–	20	49	8.16	–	–	–
Fleming, M.V.(K)	1990	17	23	5	59	393	21.83	–	1	6
†Fleming, S.P.(M)	2001	14	23	2	151	1091	51.95	4	6	22
Flintoff, A.(La)	1998	14	23	1	120	686	31.18	1	2	17
Floyd, M.K.(OU)	–	3	6	1	128*	174	34.80	1	–	–
Foster, J.S.(DU/BU/Ex)	2001	16	25	–	103	664	26.56	1	4	31/8
†Francis, J.D.(H)	–	2	4	2	72*	131	65.50	–	1	1
†Franks, P.J.(Nt)	1999	5	8	4	85	217	54.25	–	1	2
Fraser, A.R.C.(M)	1988	13	12	–	41	149	12.41	–	–	4
†Frost, T.(Wa)	1999	1	2	1	17	17	17.00	–	–	5/2
Fulton, D.P.(K)	1998	18	27	2	208*	1892	75.68	9	3	27
Gallian, J.E.R.(Nt)	1998	1	1	1	23*	23	–	–	–	–
Gannon, B.W.(Gs)	–	5	6	4	10*	12	6.00	–	–	–
Giddins, E.S.H.(Sy)	–	12	14	8	9*	36	6.00	–	–	2
Gilbert, R.G.(DU)	–	1	1	–	0	0	0.00	–	–	–
†Gilchrist, A.C.(A)	–	8	10	2	152	663	82.87	3	2	28/4
Giles, A.F.(Wa/E)	1996	4	7	2	40*	72	14.40	–	–	3
Gillespie, J.N.(A)	–	8	9	3	27*	94	15.66	–	–	3
Gofton, A.F.(OU)	–	1	2	1	4*	8	8.00	–	–	–
Golding, J.M.(K)	–	5	8	2	30	90	15.00	–	–	2
Goodwin, M.W.(Sx)	2001	17	32	5	203*	1654	61.25	7	5	8
Gough, D.(Y/E)	1993	9	15	5	96	219	21.90	–	1	–
Gough, M.A.(Du)	–	13	23	–	79	450	19.56	–	1	8
Grant, J.B.(Ex)	–	1	1	1	1*	1	–	–	–	–
Gray, A.K.D.(Y)	–	3	4	–	3	4	1.00	–	–	–
Grayson, A.P.(Ex)	1996	16	29	3	189	1275	49.03	6	1	7
Griffiths, P.(Le)	–	2	1	–	4*	5	5.00	–	–	–
Grove, J.O.(Sm)	–	4	5	2	19*	30	10.00	–	–	2
Guy, S.M.(Y)	–	1	2	1	12*	12	12.00	–	–	1
Habib, A.(Le)	1998	13	21	2	153	779	41.00	3	3	8
Hamblin, J.R.C.(H)	–	1	1	–	5	5	5.00	–	–	–
†Hamilton, G.M.(Y)	1998	8	9	–	34	114	12.66	–	–	1
Hancock, T.H.C.(Gs)	1998	6	11	–	55	230	20.90	–	1	7
Hardinges, M.A.(Gs)	–	4	3	–	22	56	18.66	–	–	2
Harmison, S.J.(Du)	1999	12	14	4	27	97	9.70	–	–	–
Harris, A.J.(Nt)	2000	9	15	2	20*	79	6.07	–	–	–

	Cap	M	I	NO	HS	Runs	Avge	100	50	Ct/St
Harvey, I.J.(Gs)	1999	10	15	2	130*	531	40.84	2	1	8
Hatch, N.G.(Du)	–	9	16	8	24	129	16.12	–	–	1
†Havell, P.M.R.(Sx)	–	1	–	–	–	–	–	–	–	–
Hawinkels, S.J.(OU)	–	1	2	–	26	28	14.00	–	–	–
†Hayden, M.L.(A)	–	10	17	1	142	636	39.75	1	3	6
Haynes, J.J.(La)	–	5	8	–	57	133	16.62	–	1	7
Hegg, W.K.(La)	1989	13	20	4	133	782	48.87	2	5	35/3
†Hemp, D.L.(Wa)	1997	17	25	5	186*	987	49.35	4	2	12
†Hewitt, J.P.(M)	1998	4	5	1	10*	22	5.50	–	–	1
Hewson, D.R.(Gs)	–	14	25	2	168	816	35.47	2	4	6
Hick, G.A.(Wo)	1986	17	28	3	201	1409	56.36	6	3	19
Hicks, T.C.(OU)	–	3	4	–	58	103	25.75	–	1	7
Hockley, J.B.(K)	–	7	13	1	29	166	13.83	–	–	6
†Hogg, K.W.(La)	–	1	1	–	19	19	19.00	–	–	–
Hoggard, M.J.(Y/E)	2000	8	8	2	4	11	1.83	–	–	–
Hollioake, A.J.(Sy)	1995	13	20	1	97	758	39.89	–	7	15
Hollioake, B.C.(Sy)	1999	12	19	–	118	586	30.84	1	4	18
†Holloway, P.C.L.(Sm)	1997	12	21	1	85	567	28.35	–	4	3
†House, W.J.(Sx)	–	3	4	–	46	80	20.00	–	–	1
Hughes, J.(Gm)	–	1	2	–	49	87	43.50	–	–	–
Hughes, T.R.(CU)	–	3	5	–	7	12	2.40	–	–	–
Hunter, I.D.(Du)	–	8	14	3	37	199	18.09	–	–	4
Hussain, N.(Ex/E)	1989	6	10	1	64	306	34.00	–	3	5
†Hussey, M.E.K.(Nh)	2001	16	30	4	329*	2055	79.03	5	9	19
†Hutchison, P.M.(Y)	1998	3	3	1	11*	22	–	–	–	–
†Hutton, B.L.(M)	–	14	22	2	139	786	39.30	3	2	20
Hyam, B.J.(Ex)	1999	6	9	2	63	150	21.42	–	1	20/1
Illingworth, R.K.(De)	–	5	8	1	61*	125	17.85	–	1	–
†Ilott, M.C.(Ex)	1993	10	12	1	34	186	16.90	–	–	6
†Imran Farhat (P)	–	1	2	1	46	69	69.00	–	–	2
Innes, K.J.(Nh)	–	4	7	1	40	86	14.33	–	–	1
Inzamam-ul-Haq (P)	–	6	7	–	114	299	42.71	1	1	4
Irani, R.C.(Ex)	1994	17	29	2	119	779	28.85	1	6	4
James, S.P.(Gm)	1992	9	15	3	156	568	47.33	1	4	5
Jefferson, W.I.(Du/BU/Ex)	–	3	5	–	69	160	32.00	–	1	2
Johnson, A.H.V.(CU)	–	4	5	1	55*	72	18.00	–	1	5
†Johnson, N.C.(H)	2001	17	27	3	105*	1073	44.70	2	8	28
Johnson, P.(Nt)	1986	13	24	2	149	684	31.09	2	2	7
Johnson, R.L.(Sm)	2001	13	15	3	68	379	31.58	–	2	3
Jones, G.O.(K)	–	1	1	–	5	5	5.00	–	–	1
Jones, H.R.(OU)	–	2	4	1	57	90	30.00	–	1	2
Jones, P.S.(Sm)	2001	16	16	5	29*	180	16.36	–	–	3
†Jones, S.P.(Gm)	–	8	11	1	46	83	8.30	–	–	–
†Joyce, E.C.(M)	–	3	6	1	108*	234	46.80	2	–	5
†Katich, S.M.(A)	–	5	7	3	168*	288	72.00	1	1	7
†Keedy, G.(La)	2000	13	15	8	20*	81	11.57	–	–	6
Keegan, C.B.(M)	–	7	10	2	30*	45	5.62	–	–	1
Kendall, W.S.(H)	1999	17	30	3	94	638	23.62	–	3	11
Kenway, D.A.(H)	2001	16	30	3	166	932	34.51	2	4	16
Kerr, J.I.D.(Sm)	2001	8	12	5	36	167	23.85	–	–	1
Key, R.W.T.(K)	2001	18	28	–	132	1281	45.75	4	7	7
Khan, A.(K)	–	1	–	–	–	–	–	–	–	–
Khan, R.M.(De)	–	1	2	–	13	18	9.00	–	–	–
Khan, S.H.(OU)	–	2	2	–	6	7	3.50	–	–	1
†Khan, W.G.(De)	–	1	1	–	1	1	1.00	–	–	–
†Killeen, N.(Du)	1999	4	3	–	5	6	2.00	–	–	–
Kirby, S.P.(Y)	–	10	10	2	15*	49	6.12	–	–	4
Kirtley, R.J.(Sx)	1998	16	24	6	51*	196	10.88	–	1	8

116

	Cap	M	I	NO	HS	Runs	Avge	100	50	Ct/St
†Knight, N.V.(Wa/E)	1995	13	19	2	140	759	44.64	2	3	18
Krikken, K.M.(De)	1992	14	25	5	93*	435	21.75	–	3	33/1
Kruis, G.J.(MCC)	–	1	2	–	2	2	1.00	–	–	2
Kumar, V.H.(CU)	–	4	7	1	86*	199	33.16	–	1	2
Lampitt, S.R.(Wo)	1989	10	13	5	42*	205	25.62	–	–	4
Laney, J.S.(H)	1996	4	5	1	60	137	34.25	–	2	8
†Langer, J.L.(A)	–	6	11	2	104*	285	31.66	2	–	5
Laraman, A.W.(M)	–	1	1	–	29	29	29.00	–	–	1
Lathwell, M.N.(Sm)	1992	13	21	1	99	702	35.10	–	8	9
Law, D.R.(Du)	2001	16	26	1	103	586	23.44	1	1	10
Law, S.G.(Ex)	1996	13	23	3	153	1311	65.55	4	8	18
Leatherdale, D.A.(Wo)	1994	17	27	3	93	570	23.75	–	2	7
Lee, B.(A)	–	8	7	–	79	127	18.14	–	1	–
†Lehmann, D.S.(Y)	1997	13	19	2	252	1416	83.29	5	5	6
Lewis, J.(Gs)	1998	5	8	7	15*	44	44.00	–	–	–
Lewis, J.J.B.(Du)	1998	17	32	–	129	1000	31.25	3	3	6
†Lewry, J.D.(Sx)	1996	17	18	4	47	202	14.42	–	–	7
†Liptrot, C.G.(Wo)	–	12	14	4	22	128	12.80	–	–	4
Lloyd, G.D.(La)	1992	3	4	–	9	19	4.75	–	–	3
Logan, R.J.(Nt)	–	10	15	2	37*	162	12.46	–	–	4
Loudon, A.G.R.(DU)	–	2	2	–	39	42	21.00	–	–	1
Loudon, H.J.H.(DU)	–	3	4	1	16	26	8.66	–	–	1
Love, M.L.(Du)	2001	15	29	2	149*	1364	50.51	4	13	21
Loye, M.B.(Nh)	1994	12	21	3	197	1003	55.72	3	4	4
Lucas, D.S.(Nt)	–	5	8	–	41	145	18.12	–	–	1
†Lumb, M.J.(Y)	–	4	7	1	122	218	36.33	1	1	–
†Lungley, T.(De)	–	6	11	4	47	108	15.42	–	–	4
McCague, M.J.(K)	1992	2	1	–	4	4	4.00	–	–	1
McGarry, A.C.(Ex)	–	6	8	6	4*	5	2.50	–	–	2
McGrath, A.(Y)	1999	9	15	2	116*	417	32.07	1	2	6
McGrath, G.D.(A)	–	7	6	3	38	53	17.66	–	–	1
Maddy, D.L.(Le)	1996	17	29	1	111	521	18.60	1	2	15
†Maher, J.P.(Gm)	2001	14	23	2	217	1133	53.95	4	3	13
Malcolm, D.E.(Le)	2001	16	21	7	50	126	9.00	–	1	1
Malik, M.N.(Nt)	–	5	6	5	6*	12	12.00	–	–	–
Marsh, D.J.(Le)	2001	9	16	3	138*	600	46.15	1	5	13
Martin, P.J.(La)	1994	9	12	3	51*	169	18.77	–	1	2
Martin-Jenkins, R.S.C.(Sx)	2000	9	15	4	113	524	47.63	1	3	4
Martyn, D.R.(A)	–	9	14	5	176*	942	104.66	5	3	3
Mascarenhas, A.D.(H)	1998	15	23	5	104	447	24.83	1	1	8
Mason, T.J.(Ex)	–	3	5	2	41*	85	28.33	–	–	1
Masters, D.D.(K)	–	4	3	2	6	8	8.00	–	–	2
Maynard, M.P.(Gm)	1987	13	20	–	145	621	31.05	1	3	6
Mees, T.(OU)	–	2	2	–	4	8	4.00	–	–	1
Metson, C.P.(MCC)	–	1	2	–	3	3	1.50	–	–	1
Middlebrook, J.D.(Y)	–	4	4	1	84	145	48.33	–	1	2
Millar, N.(OU)	–	3	5	1	36	87	21.75	–	–	1
Miller, C.R.(A)	–	5	4	1	62	68	22.66	–	1	2
†Millns, D.J.(Nt)	2000	1	2	1	4	7	7.00	–	–	1
Mohammad Sami (P)	–	2	1	–	15	15	15.00	–	–	–
Mohammad Wasim (P)	–	3	3	–	36	78	26.00	–	–	2
Montgomerie, R.R.(Sx)	1999	18	33	4	160*	1704	58.75	8	5	17
Morris, A.C.(H)	2001	16	19	2	65	423	24.88	–	3	10
Morris, J.E.(Nt)	2000	8	16	2	170	640	45.71	2	4	3
Mullally, A.D.(H/E)	2000	14	13	5	36	82	10.25	–	–	4
Munton, T.A.(De)	2000	9	13	1	50	145	12.08	–	1	2
Muralitharan, M.(La)	1999	7	8	1	21	70	10.00	–	–	4
†Murtagh, T.J.(BU/Sy)	–	2	3	1	22*	24	12.00	–	–	–

117

	Cap	M	I	NO	HS	Runs	Avge	100	50	Ct/St
Mushtaq Ahmed (P)	–	3	2	–	0	0	0.00	–	–	–
Napier, G.R.(Ex)	–	10	16	–	104	506	31.62	1	2	4
Nash, D.C.(M)	2000	15	19	5	103*	458	32.71	1	4	39/4
Newell, K.(Gm)	–	7	11	2	103	296	32.88	1	1	5
†Nixon, P.A.(K)	2000	18	24	7	87*	651	38.29	–	4	44/4
Noffke, A.A.(A)	–	3	3	–	28	69	23.00	–	–	1
Ormond, J.(Le/E)	1999	12	18	5	42	251	19.30	–	–	2
Ostler, D.P.(Wa)	1991	10	12	1	121	520	47.27	2	2	22
†Panesar, M.S.(Nh)	–	2	3	2	10	15	15.00	–	–	–
†Parker, J.W.R.(CU)	–	1	2	–	83	127	63.50	–	1	–
Parkin, O.T.(Gm)	–	1	1	–	0	0	0.00	–	–	1
Parsons, K.A.(Sm)	1999	5	8	1	139	254	36.28	1	–	5
Patel, M.M.(K)	1994	17	19	3	38	247	15.43	–	–	9
†Penberthy, A.L.(Nh)	1994	15	24	1	132*	942	40.95	3	5	11
Peng, N.(Du)	2001	13	23	2	101	551	26.23	1	3	8
Penney, T.L.(Wa)	1994	1	1	–	1	1	1.00	–	–	3
Peters, S.D.(Ex)	–	15	26	3	56*	508	22.08	–	1	6
Pettini, M.L.(Ex)	–	1	2	–	41	42	21.00	–	–	1
Phillips, N.C.(Du)	2001	7	11	4	30	87	12.42	–	–	6
†Phillips, T.J.(DU/Ex)	–	6	8	–	27	80	10.00	–	–	–
Pierson, A.R.K.(De)	–	1	2	1	9	10	10.00	–	–	1
Pietersen, K.P.(Nt)	–	15	26	4	218*	1275	57.95	4	6	14
Pipe, D.J.(Wo)	–	3	5	–	24	59	11.80	–	–	4/1
Piper, K.J.(Wa)	1992	15	17	5	92*	426	35.50	–	2	39/1
†Pollard, P.R.(Wo)	–	10	12	1	131*	309	28.09	1	–	5
Ponting, R.T.(A)	–	9	15	1	147*	844	60.28	3	5	11
†Porter, J.J.(OU/BU)	–	3	6	1	46	102	20.40	–	–	3
Powell, M.J.(Gm)	2000	15	25	2	108	681	29.60	2	4	12
Powell, M.J.(Wa)	1999	17	24	–	236	755	31.45	2	2	14
†Pratt, A.(Du)	2001	16	28	4	68*	476	19.83	–	3	49/7
†Pratt, G.J.(Du)	–	2	4	–	37	53	13.25	–	–	–
Prichard, P.J.(Ex)	1986	7	11	–	111	201	18.27	1	1	–
Prior, M.J.(Sx)	–	16	24	2	66	433	19.68	–	1	39/2
Prittipaul, L.R.(H)	–	7	9	–	84	165	18.33	–	1	6
Pyemont, J.P.(CU/BU)	–	5	9	1	70	167	20.87	–	1	4
Ramprakash, M.R.(Sy/E)	–	13	22	–	146	1094	49.72	4	4	7
Randall, S.J.(Nt)	–	4	7	1	28	73	12.16	–	–	1
†Rashid, U.B.A.(Sx)	–	14	21	1	106	367	18.35	1	1	6
Rashid Latif (P)	–	5	6	–	71	137	22.83	–	1	15/1
Rawnsley, M.J.(Wo)	–	15	21	5	39	210	13.12	–	–	6
Read, C.M.W.(Nt)	1999	16	27	5	78	666	30.27	–	5	43/1
Rhodes, S.J.(Wo)	1986	15	20	7	52	442	34.00	–	1	51/1
Richardson, A.(Wa)	–	13	9	4	6*	20	4.00	–	–	6
†Richardson, M.H.(MCC)	–	1	2	1	64*	81	81.00	–	1	–
Richardson, S.A.(Y)	–	7	11	2	69	215	23.88	–	2	6
Ripley, D.(Nh)	1987	15	25	6	95	481	25.31	–	2	45/3
Roberts, T.W.(La)	–	2	3	–	17	20	6.66	–	–	1
Robinson, D.D.J.(Ex)	1997	18	31	2	118*	955	32.93	3	4	11
Robinson, M.A.(Sx)	1997	14	15	7	10	32	4.00	–	–	1
Rollins, A.S.(Nh)	–	6	10	1	65	214	23.77	–	1	3
Rose, G.D.(Sm)	1988	3	4	–	15	25	6.25	–	–	–
Roseberry, M.A.(M)	1990	11	17	2	87	420	28.00	–	2	9
†Rowe, J.G.C.(DU)	–	3	5	2	74*	128	42.66	–	1	1
†Russell, R.C.(Gs)	1985	10	12	2	91*	373	37.30	–	2	42/2
†Saeed Anwar (P)	–	4	6	–	201	351	58.50	1	1	1
Saggers, M.J.(K)	2001	17	20	5	61*	185	12.33	–	1	1
Salim Elahi (P)	–	3	4	1	94*	172	57.33	–	2	1
Salisbury, I.D.K.(Sy)	1998	15	21	4	54	440	25.88	–	1	9

	Cap	M	I	NO	HS	Runs	Avge	100	50	Ct/St
Sanklecha, P.(OU)	–	1	2	1	15*	23	23.00	–	–	1
Saqlain Mushtaq (P/Sy)	1998	13	18	6	38	164	13.66	–	–	2
Sayers, C.A.(CU)	–	4	6	1	23	42	8.40	–	–	3
†Schofield, C.P.(La)	–	9	14	2	80*	390	32.50	–	4	8
Schofield, J.E.K.(H)	–	3	5	2	21*	25	8.33	–	–	1
Scott, G.M.(Du)	–	1	2	–	25	33	16.50	–	–	1
†Scott, J.B.(CU)	–	4	5	1	14	27	6.75	–	–	
Scuderi, J.C.(La)	–	12	17	2	89	444	29.60	–	3	2
Seccombe, W.A.(A)	–	4	5	–	76	157	31.40	–	1	8/2
†Selwood, S.A.(De)	–	2	4	–	18	43	10.75	–	–	1
Shafayat, B.M.(Nt)	–	3	6	–	75	231	38.50	–	2	–
Shah, O.A.(M)	2000	15	25	–	203	1040	41.60	3	4	14
Shahid, N.(Sy)	1998	7	12	–	65	208	17.33	–	1	8
Shahid Afridi (MCC/Le)	2001	6	9	–	164	325	36.11	1	1	8
†Sharif, Z.K.(Ex)	–	1	2	–	15	17	8.50	–	–	1
Sharpe, T.J.(OU)	–	2	2	–	0*	0		–	–	
Shaw, A.D.(Gm)	1999	5	6	1	62	143	28.60	–	1	11
†Sheikh, M.A.(Wa)	–	4	4	–	33	66	16.50	–	–	–
Sheriyar, A.(Wo)	1997	16	19	8	20	71	6.45	–	–	3
Shoaib Akhtar (P/Sm)	–	4	6	3	16	33	11.00	–	–	1
†Sidebottom, R.J.(Y/E)	2000	9	9	4	40*	82	16.40	–	–	3
Sillence, R.J.(Gs)	–	1	2	–	6	6	3.00	–	–	
Silverwood, C.E.W.(Y)	1996	8	9	1	70	167	20.87	–	1	2
Simcox, A.D.(CU)	–	3	5	1	19	56	14.00	–	–	3
Singh, A.(Wo)	–	18	31	2	168	1054	36.34	2	4	5
Slater, M.J.(A)	–	8	13	1	77	341	28.41	–	2	1
†Smalley, R.G.(OU)	–	1	2	–	67	69	34.50	–	1	3/1
Smethurst, M.P.(La)	–	5	8	1	7	29	4.14	–	–	–
Smith, A.M.(Gs)	1995	1	1	–	4	4	4.00	–	–	1
Smith, B.F.(Le)	1995	17	30	2	180*	1222	43.64	5	2	19
Smith, E.T.(K)	2001	18	28	1	116	1054	39.03	3	4	5
Smith, G.J.(Nt)	2001	15	20	9	44*	195	17.72	–	–	3
Smith, N.M.K.(Wa)	1993	14	14	2	54	254	21.16	–	1	2
Smith, R.A.(H)	1985	16	26	2	118	598	24.91	3	1	4
†Smith, T.M.(De)	–	6	10	2	19	79	9.87	–	–	4
Snape, J.N.(Gs)	1999	14	21	3	131	868	48.22	3	5	10
Solanki, V.S.(Wo)	1998	18	29	–	112	802	27.65	3	2	17
Speak, N.J.(Du)	1998	3	4	1	45*	95	31.66	–	–	1
Speight, M.P.(Du)	1998	8	15	3	67*	304	25.33	–	1	3
Spires, J.A.S.(Wa)	–	1	–	–				–	–	
Stead, R.A.(DU)	–	2	2	–	28	28	14.00	–	–	1
Stemp, R.D.(Nt)	2000	5	7	–	66	105	15.00	–	1	1
Stephenson, J.P.(H)	1995	3	6	1	51	128	25.60	–	1	1
Stevens, D.I.(Le)	–	8	14	2	63	259	21.58	–	1	2
Stewart, A.J.(Sy/E)	1985	12	18	3	106	581	38.73	1	2	36/1
†Strauss, A.J.(M)	2001	17	28	1	176	1211	44.85	3	6	7
†Strong, M.R.(Nh)	–	9	13	4	34	110	12.22	–	–	2
†Stubbings, S.D.(De)	2001	17	31	–	127	1047	33.77	3	6	6
Such, P.M.(Ex)	1991	15	20	9	25	117	10.63	–	–	7
†Sutcliffe, I.J.(Le)	1997	17	31	1	203	1004	33.46	2	5	5
Sutton, L.D.(De)	–	15	27	3	140*	688	28.66	2	1	9
Swann, A.J.(Nh)	–	13	22	–	113	479	21.77	1	2	9
Swann, G.P.(Nh)	1999	15	25	–	61	543	21.72	–	3	9
Symonds, A.(K)	1999	8	12	–	131	563	46.91	2	2	13
†Taylor, B.V.(Sx)	–	4	3	1	24*	35	17.50	–	–	
Taylor, C.G.(Gs)	2001	12	20	–	196	930	46.50	3	4	6
Taylor, C.R.(Y)	–	3	6	–	18	60	10.00	–	–	1
†Taylor, J.P.(Nh)	1992	12	17	3	53	273	19.50	–	1	3

	Cap	M	I	NO	HS	Runs	Avge	100	50	Ct/St
†Thomas, I.J.(Gm)	–	6	11	1	59	194	19.40	–	1	2
†Thomas, S.D.(Gm)	1997	15	21	2	138	562	29.57	1	4	5
Thorburn, M.(DU)	–	2	2	1	11	19	19.00	–	–	–
†Thorpe, G.P.(Sy/E)	1991	5	7	–	148	430	61.42	2	1	8
Titchard, S.P.(De)	–	3	5	–	39	92	18.40	–	–	–
Tolley, C.M.(Nt)	1997	1	2	–	–	–	–	–	–	–
Tournier, M.A.(BU)	–	1	2	–	13	13	6.50	–	–	–
†Tredwell, J.C.(K)	–	1	1	–	10	10	10.00	–	–	–
Trego, P.D.(Sm)	–	3	5	1	43	117	29.25	–	–	–
Tremlett, C.T.(H)	–	7	9	4	26	83	16.60	–	–	2
†Trescothick, M.E.(Sm/E)	1999	10	17	–	147	700	41.17	2	3	9
Trott, B.J.(K)	–	14	13	3	13	57	5.70	–	–	3
†Troughton, J.O.(Wa)	–	1	2	1	27	32	32.00	–	–	–
Tucker, J.P.(Sm)	–	1	2	2	5*	5	–	–	–	–
Tudor, A.J.(Sy/E)	1999	9	14	1	116	413	31.76	1	1	2
Tufnell, P.C.R.(M/E)	1990	17	20	8	11*	52	4.33	–	–	4
Turner, R.J.(Sm)	1994	17	26	3	115*	761	33.08	1	3	59
Udal, S.D.(H)	1992	16	20	2	81	414	23.00	–	3	5
†Van der Gucht, C.G.(DU)	–	1	1	–	38	38	38.00	–	–	–
Vaughan, M.P.(Y/E)	1995	9	16	–	133	839	52.43	3	4	8
Wagh, M.A.(Wa)	2000	16	24	2	315	1277	58.04	3	6	4
†Walker, M.J.(K)	2000	17	25	3	124	985	44.77	4	3	9
†Wallace, M.A.(Gm)	–	10	16	3	80*	290	22.30	–	2	27/1
Waqar Younis (P)	–	5	7	2	50*	105	21.00	–	1	1
Ward, D.M.(MCC)	–	1	2	–	57	61	30.50	–	1	2
†Ward, I.J.(Sy/E)	2000	16	27	1	79	690	26.53	–	4	6
Ward, T.R.(Le)	2001	12	21	2	160*	872	45.89	4	2	7
Warne, S.K.(A)	–	8	10	2	69	237	29.62	–	2	13
Warren, C.C.M.(OU)	–	3	6	1	40*	96	19.20	–	–	4
Warren, R.J.(Nh)	1995	16	26	2	194	1303	54.29	4	7	8
†Wasim Akram (P)	–	5	6	1	36	93	18.60	–	–	2
Watkin, S.L.(Gm)	1989	15	17	7	38	188	18.80	–	–	5
Waugh, M.E.(A)	–	9	15	6	120	644	71.55	2	2	12
Waugh, S.R.(A)	–	7	11	2	157*	583	64.77	3	–	5
Weekes, L.C.(Nh)	–	1	2	1	44*	62	62.00	–	–	–
†Weekes, P.N.(M)	1993	17	27	5	107	719	32.68	1	5	15
Welch, G.(De)	2001	16	29	2	64	511	18.92	–	1	3
Wells, V.J.(Le)	1994	13	22	1	138	628	29.90	2	2	8
Welton, G.E.(Nt)	–	12	22	–	61	337	15.31	–	2	5
Weston, R.M.S.(M)	2001	10	17	1	135*	671	41.93	3	1	5
†Weston, W.P.C.(Wo)	1995	18	31	4	192	1132	41.92	2	7	12
Wharf, A.G.(Gm)	2000	3	4	1	31	59	19.66	–	–	1
†Wharton, L.J.(De)	–	11	18	9	13*	29	3.22	–	–	1
Whiley, M.J.A.(Le)	–	3	5	1	1*	2	0.50	–	–	–
White, C.(Y/E)	1993	12	21	2	186	605	31.84	2	–	6
White, G.W.(H)	1998	17	32	4	141	739	26.39	2	1	17/2
White, R.A.(Nh)	–	1	2	–	4	6	3.00	–	–	–
Widdup, S.(Y)	–	2	4	–	27	44	11.00	–	–	5
†Williams, R.C.J.(Gs)	1996	5	9	–	33	123	13.66	–	–	15/1
†Willoughby, C.M.(MCC)	–	1	2	–	8	8	4.00	–	–	–
Wilton, N.J.(Sx)	–	1	1	–	1	1	1.00	–	–	–/1
Windows, M.G.N.(Gs)	1998	16	27	3	174	840	35.00	3	3	6
Wood, J.(La)	–	8	10	1	35	127	14.11	–	–	–
Wood, M.J.(Sm)	–	7	12	–	122	529	44.08	1	4	2
Wood, M.J.(Y)	2001	14	23	1	124	1060	48.18	4	6	10
Wortley, T.H.(OU)	–	1	1	–	0	0	0.00	–	–	1
Wright, A.S.(Le)	–	1	2	–	30	30	15.00	–	–	–
†Yardy, M.H.(Sx)	–	17	29	6	87*	796	34.60	–	5	9

	Cap	M	I	NO	HS	Runs	Avge	100	50	Ct/St
Yates, G.(La)	1994	2	2	1	57	65	65.00	–	1	2
Younis Khan (P)	–	4	6	–	65	185	30.83	–	1	2
Yousuf Youhana (P)	–	6	8	–	80	174	21.75	–	1	1
Zuiderent, B.(Sx)	–	17	27	1	122	619	23.80	1	3	18

BOWLING

See BATTING and FIELDING section for details of matches, caps and teams

	Cat	O	M	R	W	Avge	Best	5wI	10wM
Aamir Sohail	SLA	3	0	16	0			–	–
Abdul Razzaq	RFM	105.3	19	359	10	35.90	3- 61	–	–
Adams, C.J.	RM/OB	40.2	6	111	10	11.10	4- 28	–	–
Adams, J.C.	SLA	6	0	45	1	45.00	1- 45	–	–
Afzaal, U.	SLA	158.2	29	579	10	57.90	3- 88	–	–
Aldred, P.	RM	189.3	30	742	13	57.07	3-102	–	–
Ali, Kabir	RMF	84.2	18	253	14	18.07	5- 22	1	–
Ali, Kadeer	LB	17	5	57	0			–	–
Alleyne, M.W.	RM	372.4	86	1076	41	26.24	5- 50	1	–
Amin, R.M.	SLA	102	28	272	5	54.40	3- 80	–	–
Aminul Islam	OB	5.5	0	22	3	7.33	3- 14	–	–
Anderson, R.S.G.	RMF	231.1	54	699	35	19.97	5- 21	3	–
Asif Mujtaba	SLA	16	1	77	0			–	–
Averis, J.M.M.	RMF	463.2	100	1621	43	37.69	5- 52	1	–
Aymes, A.N.	(WK)	12	0	107	2	53.50	2-101	–	–
Azhar Mahmood	RMF	77	19	259	5	51.80	4- 50	–	–
Bailey, R.J.	OB	76.3	17	245	7	35.00	2- 17	–	–
Ball, M.C.J.	OB	349.3	94	879	34	25.85	6- 23	2	–
Banes, M.J.	OB	46	8	162	3	54.00	3- 65	–	–
Banks, O.A.C.	OB	9	0	38	0			–	–
Barnett, K.J.	RM/LB	16	4	35	0			–	–
Bassano, C.W.G.	LB	2	0	11	0			–	–
Bell, I.R.	RM	17	4	40	1	40.00	1- 24	–	–
Betts, M.M.	RFM	308.2	72	979	37	26.45	5- 22	2	–
Bevan, M.G.	SLC	5	0	28	0			–	–
Bichel, A.J.	RFM	555.5	137	1804	66	27.33	6- 44	4	1
Bicknell, M.P.	RFM	541.5	132	1538	72	21.36	7- 60	3	1
Bishop, J.E.	LMF	224	39	915	24	38.12	5-148	1	–
Blackwell, I.D.	SLA	291.4	72	896	20	44.80	5-122	1	–
Blain, J.A.R.	RMF	153	16	673	17	39.58	6- 42	1	–
Blewett, G.S.	RM	113	24	374	6	62.33	2- 20	–	–
Bloomfield, T.F.	RMF	479.4	79	1709	50	34.18	5- 58	2	–
Boswell, S.A.J.	RFM	45.3	7	161	6	26.83	3- 74	–	–
Boulton, N.R.	RM	17	4	48	0			–	–
Bowler, P.D.	OB	2	0	9	0			–	–
Bracken, N.W.	LFM	24	5	61	5	12.20	3- 29	–	–
Bressington, A.N.	RFM	120.4	31	397	11	36.09	3- 42	–	–
Bridge, G.D.	SLA	172	48	413	18	22.94	6- 84	1	–
Brinkley, J.E.	RFM	222.1	57	663	31	21.38	6- 14	2	–
Brown, A.D.	LB	23	1	97	0			–	–
Brown, D.R.	RFM	472.1	123	1284	42	30.57	6- 60	1	1
Brown, J.F.	OB	473.5	102	1407	28	50.25	5-107	1	–
Brown, S.J.E.	LFM	115	29	333	14	23.78	6- 70	1	–
Bruce, J.T.A.	RMF	48	6	211	0			–	–
Bulbeck, M.P.L.	LMF	110	6	501	4	125.25	2- 46	–	–
Burns, M.	RM	138.5	23	539	12	44.91	6- 54	1	–
Butcher, G.P.	RM	34.4	5	138	2	69.00	1- 8	–	–
Butcher, M.A.	RM	59	9	225	8	28.12	4- 42	–	–
Caddick, A.R.	RFM	351.2	53	1376	47	29.27	5- 81	4	1

	Cat	O	M	R	W	Avge	Best	5wI	10wM
Carter, N.M.	LFM	120	12	456	14	32.57	5- 78	1	–
Cawdron, M.J.	RMF	168	50	498	12	41.50	4- 79	–	–
Chapple, G.	RFM	379.2	87	1174	53	22.15	6- 46	4	–
Chilton, M.J.	RM	5	0	18	0			–	–
Clarke, A.C.S.	RMF	37.2	7	102	6	17.00	3- 44	–	–
Cliffe, J.A.	LMF	52.4	7	190	2	95.00	2- 71	–	–
Clinton, R.S.	RM	9	1	30	2	15.00	2- 30	–	–
Clough, G.D.	RM	100	14	353	6	58.83	3- 69	–	–
Collingwood, P.D.	RMF	165	50	465	9	51.66	2- 2	–	–
Cook, J.W.	RM	47	16	124	1	124.00	1- 17	–	–
Cook, S.J.	RM	218.1	47	696	20	34.80	3- 10	–	–
Cork, D.G.	RFM	206.5	44	618	12	51.50	4-122	–	–
Cosker, D.A.	SLA	423.5	84	1390	33	42.12	4- 48	–	–
Cousins, D.M.	RMF	333.4	54	1176	36	32.66	8-102	2	–
Cowan, A.P.	RFM	461.5	103	1518	33	46.00	3- 64	–	–
Craven, V.J.	RM	13	1	69	0			–	–
Crawley, J.P.	RM	1	0	2	0			–	–
Croft, R.D.B.	OB	328.3	86	927	24	38.62	5- 95	2	1
Crowe, C.D.	OB	117.1	30	326	9	36.22	4- 47	–	–
Cullinan, D.J.	OB	14	6	29	1	29.00	1- 24	–	–
Dagnall, C.E.	RM	83	16	279	12	23.25	6- 50	1	–
Dakin, J.M.	RM	122.3	22	427	16	26.68	4- 53	–	–
Dale, A.	RMF	117	25	410	7	58.57	3- 34	–	–
Dalrymple, J.W.M.	OB	203.3	47	578	10	57.80	4- 86	–	–
Davies, A.P.	RMF	86	16	341	9	37.88	3- 76	–	–
Davies, M.K.	SLA	38	4	141	3	47.00	3-121	–	–
Davis, M.J.G.	OB	349.3	82	956	24	39.83	6-116	1	–
Davis, R.P.	SLA	42	7	161	7	23.00	6- 73	1	–
Dawes, J.H.	RFM	31	6	125	5	25.00	4- 74	–	–
Dawson, R.K.J.	OB	315.5	69	1014	30	33.80	6- 82	2	–
Dean, K.J.	LMF	250.5	58	888	34	26.11	6- 73	2	1
DeFreitas, P.A.J.	RFM	303	66	934	34	27.47	6- 65	1	–
Dill, G.J.	RMF	81	17	301	5	60.20	2- 54	–	–
Di Venuto, M.J.	RM/LB	30	2	124	1	124.00	1- 16	–	–
Dowman, M.P.	RMF	10	3	53	0			–	–
Drakes, V.C.	RFM	505.2	107	1537	42	36.59	5- 37	1	–
Driver, R.C.	RM	4	0	33	0			–	–
Dumelow, N.R.C.	OB	185.5	34	723	14	51.64	4- 81	–	–
Dutch, K.P.	OB	367	64	1268	35	36.22	4- 32	–	–
Ealham, M.A.	RMF	226.5	68	574	25	22.96	6- 64	2	–
Edwards, A.D.	RFM	13	3	40	0			–	–
Elstub, C.J.	RMF	17	4	65	2	32.50	2- 65	–	–
Evans, A.W.	RM	1	0	2	0			–	–
Fairbrother, N.H.	LM	6	1	20	1	20.00	1- 18	–	–
Faisal Iqbal	RM	3	0	19	0			–	–
Fellows, G.M.	RM	156	43	398	12	33.16	3- 23	–	–
Ferley, R.S.	SLA	100	26	337	7	48.14	3- 52	–	–
Fisher, I.D.	SLA	13	3	32	1	32.00	1- 32	–	–
Fleming, D.W.	RFM	138	32	390	19	20.52	6- 59	1	–
Fleming, M.V.	RM	302.4	59	910	22	41.36	4- 53	–	–
Fleming, S.P.	RSM	2	0	19	0			–	–
Flintoff, A.	RFM	245.3	48	736	19	38.73	3- 36	–	–
Foster, J.S.	(WK)	2	0	6	0			–	–
Francis, J.D.	SLA	6	0	34	1	34.00	1- 34	–	–
Franks, P.J.	RMF	149.1	33	429	13	33.00	4- 65	–	–
Fraser, A.R.C.	RMF	469.4	140	1204	32	37.62	3- 46	–	–
Fulton, D.P.	SLA	1	0	2	0			–	–
Gannon, B.W.	RMF	97	12	380	8	47.50	3- 47	–	–

	Cat	O	M	R	W	Avge	Best	5wI	10wM
Giddins, E.S.H.	RFM	352.5	83	1102	30	36.73	5- 48	1	–
Gilbert, R.G.	RFM	18	5	54	0				
Giles, A.F.	SLA	154.5	41	429	12	35.75	5- 46	1	–
Gillespie, J.N.	RF	228	54	801	29	27.62	5- 37	2	–
Gofton, A.F.	RM	8	1	36	0				
Golding, J.M.	RMF	94.3	17	330	6	55.00	3- 23	–	–
Goodwin, M.W.	RM/LB	13	3	40	0				
Gough, D.	RF	321.4	55	1212	39	31.07	5- 61	2	–
Gough, M.A.	OB	157.3	34	449	14	32.07	5- 66	1	–
Grant, J.B.	RFM	19	0	101	3	33.66	3- 81	–	–
Gray, A.K.D.	OB	92	23	281	10	28.10	4-128	–	–
Grayson, A.P.	SLA	162	24	602	9	66.88	5- 20	1	–
Griffiths, P.	RMF	20	7	51	2	25.50	2- 51	–	–
Grove, J.O.	RMF	88.2	8	489	6	81.50	2- 46	–	–
Hamblin, J.R.C.	RMF	18	1	88	1	88.00	1- 88	–	–
Hamilton, G.M.	RFM	211.2	43	672	26	25.84	5- 27	1	–
Hancock, T.H.C.	RM	28	5	100	1	100.00	1- 67	–	–
Hardinges, M.A.	RMF	79	15	295	6	49.16	2- 36	–	–
Harmison, S.J.	RF	419.5	86	1262	35	36.05	6-111	2	–
Harris, A.J.	RM	330.4	84	1097	28	39.17	6- 98	1	–
Harvey, I.J.	RM	288.4	92	773	41	18.85	5- 33	2	–
Hatch, N.G.	RM	248.4	43	867	26	33.34	3- 42	–	–
Havell, P.M.R.	RFM	7	3	16	0				
Hawinkels, S.J.	RM	4	3	3	0				
Hayden, M.L.	RM	11	2	44	0				
Hemp, D.L.	RM	14	1	37	0				
Hewitt, J.P.	RM	83	8	386	10	38.60	3- 72	–	–
Hewson, D.R.	RM	3	1	7	0				
Hick, G.A.	OB	105.4	30	287	7	41.00	3- 33	–	–
Hicks, T.C.	OB	143	30	394	13	30.30	5- 77	1	–
Hockley, J.B.	OB	46	7	176	2	88.00	1- 21	–	–
Hogg, K.W.	RFM	12	3	30	3	10.00	3- 17	–	–
Hoggard, M.J.	RFM	240	58	733	32	22.90	6- 51	2	–
Hollioake, A.J.	RMF	54	11	165	3	55.00	1- 19	–	–
Hollioake, B.C.	RFM	133.2	21	530	9	58.88	2- 39	–	–
Holloway, P.C.L.	RM	4	0	19	0				
Hughes, T.R.	RMF	89	18	277	7	39.57	2- 38	–	–
Hunter, I.D.	RMF	181.3	27	700	16	43.75	4- 55	–	–
Hussain, N.	LB	1	0	1	0				
Hussey, M.E.K.	RM	18	2	78	2	39.00	1- 14	–	–
Hutchison, P.M.	LFM	60	11	224	7	32.00	2- 33	–	–
Hutton, B.L.	RMF	24	4	91	1	91.00	1- 24	–	–
Illingworth, R.K.	SLA	126.4	39	316	10	31.60	4- 37	–	–
Ilott, M.C.	LFM	287	65	921	27	34.11	5- 85	1	–
Imran Farhat	LB	7	0	48	1	48.00	1- 44	–	–
Innes, K.J.	RM	83.5	15	331	9	36.77	4- 76	–	–
Irani, R.C.	RMF	354.5	97	1040	32	32.50	6- 79	3	–
Johnson, N.C.	RFM	252.5	42	911	23	39.60	4- 20	–	–
Johnson, P.	RM	1	1	0	0				
Johnson, R.L.	RFM	463.2	89	1474	62	23.77	5- 40	5	–
Jones, G.O.	(WK)	1	0	4	0				
Jones, P.S.	RMF	560	100	2015	59	34.15	5-115	1	–
Jones, S.P.	RF	198.2	29	887	17	52.17	3- 36	–	–
Katich, S.M.	SLC	24	2	106	4	26.50	3- 21	–	–
Keedy, G.	SLA	387.1	76	1150	28	41.07	5- 73	2	–
Keegan, C.B.	RFM	170	38	588	18	32.66	4- 54	–	–
Kendall, W.S.	RM	16	2	36	0				
Kenway, D.A.	RM	8	0	66	1	66.00	1- 66	–	–

	Cat	O	M	R	W	Avge	Best	5wI	10wM
Kerr, J.I.D.	RMF	186.4	36	645	9	71.66	3- 51	–	–
Key, R.W.T.	RM/OB	1	0	5	0			–	–
Khan, A.	RFM	8.2	2	46	1	46.00	1- 46	–	–
Khan, S.H.	RM	72	20	162	4	40.50	2- 53	–	–
Killeen, N.	RFM	89	29	222	11	20.18	3- 14	–	–
Kirby, S.P.	RFM	280.3	60	980	47	20.85	7- 50	3	1
Kirtley, R.J.	RFM	566.3	135	1749	75	23.32	6- 34	5	2
Krikken, K.M.	(WK)	7	0	27	0				
Kruis, G.J.	RFM	23	3	108	1	108.00	1- 52	–	–
Lampitt, S.R.	RMF	203.2	49	669	24	27.87	5- 22	1	–
Langer, J.L.	RM	2	0	5	0				
Laraman, A.W.	RFM	4.5	1	20	2	10.00	2- 20	–	–
Lathwell, M.N.	OB	7	0	37	0				
Law, D.R.	RFM	351	70	1103	42	26.26	6- 53	3	–
Leatherdale, D.A.	RM	158	39	580	16	36.25	4- 70	–	–
Lee, B.	RF	186.5	29	752	17	44.23	3- 17	–	–
Lehmann, D.S.	SLA	139.1	33	368	12	30.66	3- 13	–	–
Lewis, J.	RMF	175.4	56	454	21	21.61	5- 71	1	–
Lewry, J.D.	LFM	512.1	126	1548	59	26.23	7- 42	3	1
Liptrot, C.G.	RFM	308.4	80	966	35	27.60	3- 12	–	–
Logan, R.J.	RMF	329.1	53	1375	43	31.97	6- 93	3	–
Loudon, A.G.R.	OB	20	5	86	3	28.66	3- 86	–	–
Lucas, D.S.	LFM	118	8	571	8	71.37	3- 80	–	–
Lumb, M.J.	RM	4	1	10	2	5.00	2- 10	–	–
Lungley, T.	RMF	115.4	14	527	12	43.91	3- 58	–	–
McCague, M.J.	RFM	27	5	99	2	49.50	1- 28	–	–
McGarry, A.C.	RFM	148	19	637	10	63.70	3- 77	–	–
McGrath, A.	RM	17	4	53	3	17.66	2- 22	–	–
McGrath, G.D.	RFM	234.5	74	624	40	15.60	7- 76	4	–
Maddy, D.L.	RM/OB	237.3	45	804	28	28.71	5- 67	1	–
Maher, J.P.	RM	21	3	88	0				
Malcolm, D.E.	RF	545.1	94	1944	68	28.58	8- 63	4	1
Malik, M.N.	RM	104	21	414	10	41.40	5- 57	1	–
Marsh, D.J.	SLA	152.2	43	410	9	45.55	2- 35	–	–
Martin, P.J.	RFM	322.3	86	969	33	29.36	5- 52	1	–
Martin-Jenkins, R.S.C.	RFM	248	63	764	24	31.83	4- 18	–	–
Martyn, D.R.	RM	9	1	53	2	26.50	2- 38	–	–
Mascarenhas, A.D.	RMF	399.3	112	1015	40	25.37	6- 26	2	–
Mason, T.J.	OB	39	13	98	6	16.33	5- 40	1	–
Masters, D.D.	RMF	88	16	279	7	39.85	3-'52	–	–
Maynard, M.P.	RM	1	1	0	0				
Mees, T.	RMF	67.3	9	222	7	31.71	6- 64	1	–
Middlebrook, J.D.	OB	82	15	265	5	53.00	3- 49	–	–
Millar, N.	RM	35	4	122	2	61.00	2- 50	–	–
Miller, C.R.	RMF/OB	157.2	37	586	18	32.55	4- 41	–	–
Millns, D.J.	RF	25.1	4	87	1	87.00	1- 69	–	–
Mohammad Sami	RF	45	8	148	6	24.66	2- 27	–	–
Mohammad Wasim	LB	2	0	5	0				
Montgomery, R.R.	OB	6	1	17	1	17.00	1- 0	–	–
Morris, A.C.	RMF	472	106	1428	51	28.00	5- 39	2	–
Morris, J.E.	RM	3.2	0	19	0				
Mullally, A.D.	LFM	477.4	151	1184	64	18.50	8- 90	6	–
Munton, T.A.	RMF	242.1	61	659	19	34.68	5- 85	1	–
Muralitharan, M.	OB	484.5	159	971	50	19.42	6- 53	5	1
Murtagh, T.J.	RFM	33.5	8	114	7	16.28	6- 86	1	–
Mushtaq Ahmed	LBG	69.2	18	176	14	12.57	8- 49	1	1
Napier, G.R.	RM	104.1	15	453	12	37.75	3- 55	–	–
Newell, K.	RM	13	0	48	0				

	Cat	O	M	R	W	Avge	Best	5wI	10wM
Noffke, A.A.	RFM	67.4	16	258	6	43.00	3- 66	–	–
Ormond, J.	RFM	486.4	113	1421	49	29.00	5- 71	2	–
Panesar, M.S.	SLA	101.3	28	358	11	32.54	4- 11	–	–
Parker, J.W.R.	LM	1	0	8	0			–	–
Parkin, O.T.	RFM	44	4	176	4	44.00	2- 45	–	–
Parsons, K.A.	RM	46	5	193	1	193.00	1- 22	–	–
Patel, M.M.	SLA	524.2	158	1228	40	30.70	8-119	1	1
Penberthy, A.L.	RM	339.2	70	1019	25	40.76	4- 39	–	–
Phillips, N.C.	OB	285.5	60	939	23	40.82	5- 64	1	–
Phillips, T.J.	SLA	144	24	582	6	97.00	2- 80	–	–
Pierson, A.R.K.	OB	10	0	28	0			–	–
Pietersen, K.P.	OB	234	52	767	9	85.22	2- 46	–	–
Piper, K.J.	(WK)	1	0	3	0			–	–
Ponting, R.T.	RM/OB	7.3	1	15	0			–	–
Porter, J.J.	SLA	22.2	1	84	4	21.00	3- 50	–	–
Powell, M.J.(Wa)	RM	34	2	100	2	50.00	1- 25	–	–
Prittipaul, L.R.	RM/OB	25	1	86	0			–	–
Pyemont, J.P.	OB	146	31	512	10	51.20	4-101	–	–
Ramprakash, M.R.	RM	59	14	115	0			–	–
Randall, S.J.	OB	132.1	21	465	7	66.42	2- 64	–	–
Rashid, U.B.A.	SLA	134.2	38	398	11	36.18	4- 9	–	–
Rawnsley, M.J.	SLA	446.2	122	1211	27	44.85	3- 55	–	–
Read, C.M.W.	(WK)	3	0	25	0			–	–
Richardson, A.	RMF	395.5	111	983	36	27.30	5- 89	1	–
Robinson, D.D.J.	RMF	10	0	54	0			–	–
Robinson, M.A.	RFM	415.4	125	1083	56	19.33	5- 35	3	–
Rose, G.D.	RM	50	15	155	3	51.66	1- 36	–	–
Saggers, M.J.	RMF	512.3	118	1551	64	24.23	6- 92	3	–
Salisbury, I.D.K.	LBG	396.2	72	1151	27	42.62	5- 95	1	–
Saqlain Mushtaq	OB	567.2	157	1286	62	20.74	7- 58	5	–
Schofield, C.P.	LB	252.1	52	757	14	54.07	3- 53	–	–
Schofield, J.E.K.	RFM	89.1	17	285	13	21.92	4- 51	–	–
Scott, G.M.	OB	3	1	11	0			–	–
Scott, J.B.	LMF	86.2	16	320	4	80.00	1- 33	–	–
Scuderi, J.C.	RMF	115.4	33	318	9	35.33	3- 48	–	–
Shah, O.A.	OB	5	1	38	0			–	–
Shahid Afridi	LB	166.1	41	569	13	43.76	5- 84	1	–
Sharif, Z.K.	LB	2	0	23	0			–	–
Sharpe, T.J.	RMF	41	10	150	1	150.00	1- 49	–	–
Sheikh, M.A.	RM	109.1	40	255	8	31.87	4- 36	–	–
Sheriyar, A.	LFM	536.1	125	1795	71	25.28	6- 88	3	–
Shoaib Akhtar	RF	76	12	264	6	44.00	2- 9	–	–
Sidebottom, R.J.	LFM	278.2	75	710	27	26.29	4- 49	–	–
Sillence, R.J.	RMF	29.5	5	100	5	20.00	5- 97	1	–
Silverwood, C.E.W.	RFM	209.1	42	644	33	19.51	5- 20	3	–
Slater, M.J.	RM	3.2	0	23	1	23.00	1- 23	–	–
Smethurst, M.P.	RM	103	17	371	7	53.00	3- 32	–	–
Smith, A.M.	LMF	33	11	70	2	35.00	2- 24	–	–
Smith, G.J.	LFM	446.2	103	1256	50	25.12	5- 37	3	1
Smith, N.M.K.	OB	314	75	813	25	32.52	4- 76	–	–
Smith, T.M.	RFM	91.3	15	383	11	34.81	4- 61	–	–
Snape, J.N.	OB	153	34	406	8	50.75	3- 27	–	–
Solanki, V.S.	OB	83.4	17	265	2	132.50	2- 41	–	–
Spires, J.A.S.	SLA	50	8	155	2	77.50	2- 73	–	–
Stead, R.A.	RM	35	5	107	0			–	–
Stemp, R.D.	SLA	244.4	51	707	16	44.18	3- 39	–	–
Stephenson, J.P.	RM	17.4	3	60	4	15.00	3- 48	–	–
Stevens, D.I.	RM	7	1	28	0				

125

	Cat	O	M	R	W	Avge	Best	5wI	10wM
Stewart, A.J.	(WK)	1	1	0	0			–	–
Strauss, A.J.	LM	1	0	3	0				
Strong, M.R.	RMF	256.3	46	992	19	52.21	3- 98	–	–
Stubbings, S.D.	OB	4	0	36	0				
Such, P.M.	OB	433	98	1362	24	56.75	5-131	1	–
Sutcliffe, I.J.	OB	18	3	67	3	22.33	1- 7	–	–
Swann, A.J.	RM/OB	16	4	50	1	50.00	1- 31	–	–
Swann, G.P.	OB	422.3	87	1365	30	45.50	5- 34	1	–
Symonds, A.	RMF/OB	106.2	23	333	10	33.30	3- 28	–	–
Taylor, B.V.	RMF	72.4	20	258	8	32.25	2- 5	–	–
Taylor, J.P.	LFM	379.2	49	1345	29	46.37	4-100	–	–
Thomas, I.J.	OB	3	1	2	0				
Thomas, S.D.	RFM	420.1	56	1668	33	50.54	4- 54	–	–
Thorburn, M.	RMF	34	5	159	2	79.50	1- 76	–	–
Thorpe, G.P.	RM	1	0	11	0				
Tournier, M.A.	RFM	19	6	67	0				
Tredwell, J.C.	OB	26	5	123	2	61.50	1- 38	–	–
Trego, P.D.	RM	58	11	243	4	60.75	3- 85	–	–
Tremlett, C.T.	RMF	131.2	37	401	20	20.05	4- 34	–	–
Trescothick, M.E.	RM	5	1	16	0				
Trott, B.J.	RFM	372.5	68	1235	47	26.27	6- 13	4	1
Troughton, J.O.	SLA	2	0	17	0				
Tucker, J.P.	RMF	17	2	82	0				
Tudor, A.J.	RF	251.1	53	927	26	35.65	5- 44	2	–
Tufnell, P.C.R.	SLA	690	166	1721	60	28.68	6- 44	3	1
Turner, R.J.	(WK)	10	3	29	0				
Udal, S.D.	OB	566.1	143	1610	54	29.81	7- 74	1	–
Van der Gucht, C.G.	SLA	12	1	63	1	63.00	1- 63	–	–
Vaughan, M.P.	OB	66.5	14	198	7	28.28	4- 47	–	–
Wagh, M.A.	OB	184	37	473	13	36.38	3- 3	–	–
Walker, M.J.	RM	20	3	69	2	34.50	1- 9	–	–
Waqar Younis	RF	119.1	23	399	18	22.16	5- 23	1	–
Warne, S.K.	LBG	263	56	784	42	18.66	7-165	3	1
Warren, R.J.	OB	1	1	0	0				
Wasim Akram	LFM	153	44	385	15	25.66	4- 18	–	–
Watkin, S.L.	RMF	472.4	113	1400	43	32.55	6- 67	1	–
Waugh, M.E.	OB	24	2	121	2	60.50	1- 33	–	–
Weekes, L.C.	RFM	26	5	107	3	35.66	3- 51	–	–
Weekes, P.N.	OB	439.5	100	1198	40	29.95	5- 90	1	–
Welch, G.	RM	502.3	108	1631	44	37.06	6- 30	3	–
Wells, V.J.	RMF	181	47	498	18	27.66	5- 36	1	–
Welton, G.E.	OB	1	0	4	0				
Weston, W.P.C.	LM	7.4	0	41	0				
Wharf, A.G.	RMF	127.4	19	448	14	32.00	5- 63	1	–
Wharton, L.J.	SLA	217.3	58	644	8	80.50	2- 74	–	–
Whiley, M.J.A.	LMF	53.1	14	188	2	94.00	1- 54	–	–
White, C.	RFM	214.1	52	599	17	35.23	4- 57	–	–
White, G.W.	LB	27.1	0	109	2	54.50	1- 29	–	–
White, R.A.	LB	3	0	7	0				
Willoughby, C.M.	LFM	35	8	109	5	21.80	3- 66	–	–
Wood, J.	RFM	139.5	16	540	9	60.00	3- 97	–	–
Wood, M.J.(Sm)	OB	7	1	30	0				
Wortley, T.H.	LBG	20	6	50	3	16.66	2- 17	–	–
Yardy, M.H.	LM	23	6	61	1	61.00	1- 13	–	–
Yates, G.	OB	38.5	10	88	4	22.00	2- 23	–	–
Younis Khan	LB	8	1	42	0				

COUNTY CHAMPIONSHIP 2001
CRICINFO FINAL TABLES

DIVISION 1

		P	W	L	D	A	Bonus Points Bat	Bonus Points Bowl	Deduct Points	Total Points
1	YORKSHIRE (3)	16	9	3	4	–	50	45	0.00	219.00
2	Somerset (5)	16	6	2	8	–	55	44	0.00	203.00
3	Kent (6)	16	4	3	9	–	48	44	1.00	175.00
4	Surrey (1)	15	3	1	11	1	43	43	0.50	169.50
5	Leicestershire (4)	16	5	5	5	–	38	47	0.00	165.00
6	Lancashire (2)	14	4	5	5	2	38	39	0.00	153.00
7	Northamptonshire	16	2	5	9	–	52	36	0.00	148.00
8	Glamorgan	15	2	5	8	1	36	37	0.00	133.00
9	Essex	16	2	7	7	–	28	36	0.00	116.00

Lancashire's fixtures at Old Trafford v Surrey (April 26-28) and Glamorgan (May 16-19) were abandoned without a ball being bowled – see note (g) below.

DIVISION 2

		P	W	L	D	A	Bonus Points Bat	Bonus Points Bowl	Deduct Points	Total Points
1	SUSSEX (9)	16	9	3	4	–	42	44	0.00	208.00
2	Hampshire	16	7	2	7	–	34	44	0.00	192.00
3	Warwickshire (6)	16	5	1	10	–	46	40	0.25	185.75
4	Gloucestershire (4)	16	5	5	6	–	46	43	0.00	173.00
5	Middlesex (8)	16	4	3	9	–	46	42	0.00	172.00
6	Worcestershire (5)	16	4	5	7	–	35	41	0.25	151.75
7	Nottinghamshire (7)	16	3	7	6	–	44	38	0.75	141.25
8	Durham	16	3	6	7	–	32	44	0.00	140.00
9	Derbyshire	16	1	9	6	–	20	37	0.75	92.25

2000 final positions for that division are shown in brackets.

SCORING OF POINTS 2001

(a) For a win, 12 points, plus any points scored in the first innings.

(b) In a tie, each side to score six points, plus any points scored in the first innings.

(c) In a drawn match, each side to score four points, plus any points scored in the first innings (see also paragraph (f) below).

(d) If the scores are equal in a drawn match, the side batting in the fourth innings to score six points plus any points scored in the first innings, and the opposing side to score four points plus any points scored in the first innings.

(e) **First Innings Points** (awarded only for performances **in the first 130 overs** of each first innings and retained whatever the result of the match).
  • A maximum of five batting points to be available as under:-
  200 to 249 runs – 1 point; 250 to 299 runs – 2 points; 300 to 349 runs – 3 points;
  350 to 399 runs – 4 points; 400 runs or over – 5 points.
  • A maximum of three bowling points to be available as under:-
  3 to 5 wickets taken – 1 point; 6 to 8 wickets taken – 2 points; 9 to 10 wickets taken – 3 points.

(f) If play starts when less than eight hours playing time remains (in which event a one innings match shall be played as provided for in First Class Playing Condition 18), no first innings points shall be scored. The side winning on the one innings to score 12 points. In a tie, each side to score six points. In a drawn match, each side to score four points. If the scores are equal in a drawn match, the side batting in the second innings to score six points and the opposing side to score four points.

(g) If a match is abandoned without a ball being bowled, each side to score four points.

(h) The side which has the highest aggregate of points gained at the end of the season shall be the Champion County of their respective Division. Should any sides in the Championship table be equal on points, the following tie-breakers will be applied in the order stated: most wins, least losses, team achieving most points in contests between teams level on points, most wickets taken, most runs scored. At the end of the season, the top three teams from the Second Division will be promoted and the bottom three teams from the First Division will be relegated.

COUNTY CHAMPIONS

The English County Championship was not officially constituted until December 1889. Prior to that date there was no generally accepted method of awarding the title; although the 'least matches lost' method existed, it was not consistently applied. Rules governing playing qualifications were agreed in 1873 and the first unofficial points system 15 years later.

Research has produced a list of champions dating back to 1826, but at least seven different versions exist for the period from 1864 to 1889 (see *The Wisden Book of Cricket Records*). Only from 1890 can any authorised list of county champions commence.

That first official Championship was contested between eight counties: Gloucestershire, Kent, Lancashire, Middlesex, Nottinghamshire, Surrey, Sussex and Yorkshire. The remaining counties were admitted in the following seasons: 1891 – Somerset, 1895 – Derbyshire, Essex, Hampshire, Leicestershire and Warwickshire, 1899 – Worcestershire, 1905 – Northamptonshire, 1921 – Glamorgan, and 1992 – Durham.

The Championship pennant was introduced by the 1951 champions, Warwickshire, and the Lord's Taverners' Trophy was first presented in 1973. The first sponsors, Schweppes (1977 to 1983), were succeeded by Britannic Assurance (1984 to 1998), by PPP Healthcare (1999-2000). Based on their previous season's positions, the 18 counties were separated into two divisions in 2001, the first sponsor of this format being CricInfo.

1890	Surrey	1929	Nottinghamshire	1968	Yorkshire
1891	Surrey	1930	Lancashire	1969	Glamorgan
1892	Surrey	1931	Yorkshire	1970	Kent
1893	Yorkshire	1932	Yorkshire	1971	Surrey
1894	Surrey	1933	Yorkshire	1972	Warwickshire
1895	Surrey	1934	Lancashire	1973	Hampshire
1896	Yorkshire	1935	Yorkshire	1974	Worcestershire
1897	Lancashire	1936	Derbyshire	1975	Leicestershire
1898	Yorkshire	1937	Yorkshire	1976	Middlesex
1899	Surrey	1938	Yorkshire	1977	Kent / Middlesex
1900	Yorkshire	1939	Yorkshire		
1901	Yorkshire	1946	Yorkshire	1978	Kent
1902	Yorkshire	1947	Middlesex	1979	Essex
1903	Middlesex	1948	Glamorgan	1980	Middlesex
1904	Lancashire	1949	Middlesex / Yorkshire	1981	Nottinghamshire
1905	Yorkshire			1982	Middlesex
1906	Kent	1950	Lancashire / Surrey	1983	Essex
1907	Nottinghamshire			1984	Essex
1908	Yorkshire	1951	Warwickshire	1985	Middlesex
1909	Kent	1952	Surrey	1986	Essex
1910	Kent	1953	Surrey	1987	Nottinghamshire
1911	Warwickshire	1954	Surrey	1988	Worcestershire
1912	Yorkshire	1955	Surrey	1989	Worcestershire
1913	Kent	1956	Surrey	1990	Middlesex
1914	Surrey	1957	Surrey	1991	Essex
1919	Yorkshire	1958	Surrey	1992	Essex
1920	Middlesex	1959	Yorkshire	1993	Middlesex
1921	Middlesex	1960	Yorkshire	1994	Warwickshire
1922	Yorkshire	1961	Hampshire	1995	Warwickshire
1923	Yorkshire	1962	Yorkshire	1996	Leicestershire
1924	Yorkshire	1963	Yorkshire	1997	Glamorgan
1925	Yorkshire	1964	Worcestershire	1998	Leicestershire
1926	Lancashire	1965	Worcestershire	1999	Surrey
1927	Lancashire	1966	Yorkshire	2000	Surrey
1928	Lancashire	1967	Yorkshire	2001	Yorkshire

COUNTY CHAMPIONSHIP RESULTS 2001

DIVISION 1

	ESSEX	GLAM	KENT	LANCS	LEICS	N'HANTS	SOM'T	SURREY	YORKS
ESSEX	–	Chelms Gm 6w	S'end K I/132	Col Drawn	Chelms Drawn	Chelms Drawn	Chelms Sm 9w	Ilford Drawn	Chelms Drawn
GLAM	Cardiff Drawn	–	Swansea Drawn	Col Bay Drawn	Cardiff Le I/90	Cardiff Drawn	Cardiff Drawn	Cardiff Drawn	Swansea Y 328
KENT	Tun W K I/152	Maid Drawn	–	Cant K 268	Cant Le I/149	Cant Drawn	Cant Drawn	Cant Drawn	Cant Y 4w
LANCS	Man La 9w	Man Aban'd	Man Drawn	–	Man La 6w	Man Drawn	Man Sm 10w	Man Aban'd	Man Y I/37
LEICS	Leics E I/9	Leics Le 10w	Leics K 3w	Leics Le 6	–	Leics Le 9w	Leics Drawn	Leics Drawn	Leics Y 168
N'HANTS	No'ton Nh 10w	No'ton Drawn	No'ton Drawn	No'ton La 3w	No'ton Nh 202	–	No'ton Drawn	No'ton Drawn	No'ton Drawn
SOM'T	Taunton Sm I/60	Taunton Sm I/67	Taunton Drawn	Taunton La I/4	Taunton Drawn	Taunton Sm 4w	–	Taunton Drawn	Bath Drawn
SURREY	Oval Drawn	Oval Gm 3w	Oval Drawn	Oval Drawn	Oval Drawn	Guild Sy I/55	Oval Sy 6w	–	Oval Sy I/46
YORKS	Scar E 51	Scar Y I/112	Leeds Y 9w	Leeds Y 7w	Leeds Y 227	Leeds Y 4w	Leeds Sm 161	Leeds Drawn	–

DIVISION 2

	DERBYS	DURHAM	GLOS	HANTS	MIDDX	NOTTS	SUSSEX	WARWKS	WORCS
DERBYS	–	Derby Drawn	Derby Drawn	Derby H 9w	Derby Drawn	Derby Drawn	Derby Sx 130	Derby Wa I/100	Derby Wo I/3
DURHAM	C-le-St De 4w	–	C-le-St Drawn	C-le-St H 7w	C-le-St Drawn	C-le-St Du 8w	C-le-St Sx 133	C-le-St Drawn	C-le-St Drawn
GLOS	Bristol Gs I/20	Glos Drawn	–	Chelt Drawn	Bristol M 5w	Bristol Gs I/120	Chelt Gs 10w	Bristol Drawn	Bristol Wo 252
HANTS	So'ton H 10w	So'ton H 47	So'ton Drawn	–	So'ton Drawn	So'ton H 5w	So'ton Drawn	So'ton Drawn	So'ton H 124
MIDDX	S'gate M I/185	Lord's M I/74	Lord's Gs I/59	S'gate Drawn	–	Lord's Drawn	Lord's Drawn	Lord's Drawn	Lord's Drawn
NOTTS	N'ham Nt 7w	N'ham Drawn	N'ham Gs 187	N'ham Drawn	N'ham Drawn	–	N'ham Sx 161	N'ham Drawn	N'ham Nt 61
SUSSEX	Arundel Sx I/34	Hove Du 71	Hove Drawn	Hove Sx I/113	Hove Sx 192	Hove Sx 162	–	Hove Wa 8w	Horsham Sx 33
WARWKS	B'ham Drawn	B'ham Wa 7w	B'ham Wa 10w	B'ham Drawn	B'ham M 129	B'ham Wa 139	B'ham Drawn	–	B'ham Drawn
WORCS	Worcs Drawn	Kidd Du 7w	Worcs Wo 7w	Worcs Wo 112	Worcs Drawn	Worcs Nt 7w	Worcs Drawn	Worcs Drawn	–

COUNTY CHAMPIONSHIP RESULTS 2002

KEEP YOUR OWN RECORD (see page 129)

DIVISION 1

	HANTS	KENT	LANCS	LEICS	SOM'T	SURREY	SUSSEX	WARWKS	YORKS
HANTS	–	So'ton	So'ton	So'ton	So'ton	So'ton	So'ton	So'ton	So'ton
KENT	Cant	–	Cant	Cant	Cant	Cant	Tun W	Maid	Cant
LANCS	Man	L'pool	–	Man	B'pool	Man	Man	Man	Man
LEICS	Leics	Leics	Leics	–	Leics	Leics	Leics	Leics	Leics
SOM'T	Bath	Taunton	Taunton	Taunton	–	Taunton	Taunton	Taunton	Taunton
SURREY	Oval	Oval	Oval	Oval	Oval	–	Oval	Oval	Guild
SUSSEX	Hove	Hove	Hove	Horsham	Hove	Hove	–	Hove	Arundel
WARWKS	B'ham	B'ham	B'ham	B'ham	B'ham	B'ham	B'ham	–	B'ham
YORKS	Leeds	Leeds	Leeds	Scar	Scar	Leeds	Leeds	Leeds	–

DIVISION 2

	DERBYS	DURHAM	ESSEX	GLAM	GLOS	MIDDX	N'HANTS	NOTTS	WORCS
DERBYS	–	Derby	Derby	Derby	Derby	Derby	Derby	Derby	Derby
DURHAM	Dar'ton	–	C-le-St	C-le-St	C-le-St	C-le-St	C-le-St	C-le-St	C-le-St
ESSEX	Chelms	Colch'r	–	Chelms	Chelms	Chelms	Ilford	Chelms	S'end
GLAM	Cardiff	Cardiff	Swansea	–	Cardiff	Cardiff	Cardiff	Col Bay	Cardiff
GLOS	Bristol	Bristol	Glos	Chelt	–	Chelt	Bristol	Bristol	Bristol
MIDDX	Lord's	Lord's	S'gate	Lord's	S'gate	–	Lord's	Lord's	Lord's
N'HANTS	No'ton	No'ton	No'ton	No'ton	No'ton	No'ton	–	No'ton	No'ton
NOTTS	N'ham	N'ham	N'ham	N'ham	N'ham	N'ham	N'ham	–	N'ham
WORCS	Worcs	Worcs	Worcs	Worcs	Worcs	Worcs	Worcs	Kidd	–

NATWEST TRIANGULAR SERIES 2001

Birmingham 7 June (floodlit)

Toss: Pakistan. PAKISTAN beat **England** by 108 runs. Pakistan 273-6 (50 overs) (Inzamam-ul-Haq 79, Saeed Anwar 77). England 165 (47.2 overs) (N.V.Knight 59*; Shahid Afridi 3-15). Award: Saeed Anwar.

Cardiff 9 June

Toss: Pakistan. AUSTRALIA beat **Pakistan** by seven wickets. Pakistan 257 (49.5 overs) (Yousuf Youhana 91*, Rashid Latif 66; S.K.Warne 3-52). Australia 258-3 (45.4 overs) (R.T.Ponting 70, M.G.Bevan 56*, S.R.Waugh 54*). Award: R.T.Ponting.

Bristol 10 June

Toss: England. AUSTRALIA beat **England** by five wickets. England 268-4 (50 overs) (N.V.Knight 84, M.E.Trescothick 69). Australia 272-5 (49.3 overs) (R.T.Ponting 102). Award: R.T.Ponting.

Lord's 12 June

Toss: England. PAKISTAN beat **England** by two runs. Pakistan 242-8 (50 overs) (Yousuf Youhana 81). England 240 (50 overs) (M.E.Trescothick 137, O.A.Shah 62). Award: M.E.Trescothick.

Manchester 14 June (floodlit)

Toss: England. AUSTRALIA beat **England** by 125 runs (D/L Method). Australia 208-7 (48 overs) (S.R.Waugh 64, D.R.Martyn 51*; A.D.Mullally 3-50). England (set 212 from 44 overs) 86 (32.4 overs) (J.N.Gillespie 3-20). Award: J.N.Gillespie.

Chester-le-Street 16 June

Toss: –. Australia v Pakistan – match abandoned without a ball bowled – rain.

Leeds 17 June

Toss: Pakistan. PAKISTAN beat **England** who conceded the match after a second crowd invasion and serious injury to a steward. England 156 (45.2 overs) (B.C.Hollioake 53; Waqar Younis 7-36). Pakistan 153-4 (Abdul Razzaq 75). Award: Waqar Younis.

Nottingham 19 June (floodlit)

Toss: Pakistan. PAKISTAN beat **Australia** by 36 runs. Pakistan 290-9 (50 overs) (Salim Elahi 79). Australia 254 (46.3) (A.C.Gilchrist 70, S.R.Waugh 56; Waqar Younis 6-59). Award: Waqar Younis.

The Oval 21 June

Toss: England. AUSTRALIA beat **England** by eight wickets. England 176 (43.2 overs) (B.Lee 3-63). Australia 177-2 (30.1 overs) (A.C.Gilchrist 80, R.T.Ponting 70*). Award: R.T.Ponting.

	Played	Won	Lost	Abandoned	Points	NRR
Australia	5	4	1	1	9	0.93
Pakistan	5	4	1	1	9	0.70
England	6	–	6	–	0	–1.33

Final – Lord's 23 June

Toss: Pakistan. AUSTRALIA beat **Pakistan** by nine wickets. Pakistan 152 (42.3 overs) (S.K.Warne 3-56). Australia 156-1 (A.C.Gilchrist 76*). Award: A.C.Gilchrist. Series Award: Waqar Younis.

CHELTENHAM & GLOUCESTER TROPHY 2001 RESULTS CHART

THIRD ROUND 27 June	FOURTH ROUND 11, 12 July	QUARTER-FINALS 24, 25 July	SEMI-FINALS 11, 12, 13 August	FINAL 1 September
Wales†				
LEICESTERSHIRE	LEICESTERSHIRE			
Suffolk†		LEICESTERSHIRE		
NOTTINGHAMSHIRE	Nottinghamshire†			
Hertfordshire†			LEICESTERSHIRE†	
WORCESTERSHIRE	WORCESTERSHIRE†			
Middlesex		Worcestershire† (£11,500)		
HEREFORDSHIRE†	Herefordshire			
Warwickshire Board†				Leicestershire (£27,000)
LANCASHIRE	LANCASHIRE†			
Cornwall†		LANCASHIRE†		
SUSSEX	Sussex			
Hampshire			Lancashire (£16,500)	
DURHAM†	DURHAM			
Sussex Board†		Durham (£11,500)		
GLOUCESTERSHIRE	Gloucestershire†			
Bedfordshire†				
YORKSHIRE	YORKSHIRE†			
Surrey Board†		Yorkshire† (£11,500)		
SURREY	Surrey			
Kent Board†			Warwickshire (£16,500)	
WARWICKSHIRE	WARWICKSHIRE†			
Berkshire†		WARWICKSHIRE		
ESSEX	Essex			
Northamptonshire Board†				SOMERSET (£53,000)
NORTHAMPTONSHIRE	Northamptonshire			
Cumberland†		Kent† (£11,500)		
KENT	KENT†			
Derbyshire†			SOMERSET†	
GLAMORGAN	Glamorgan			
Cambridgeshire†		SOMERSET		
SOMERSET	SOMERSET†			

† Home team. Winning teams are in capitals. Prize-money shown in brackets.

2001 C & G TROPHY FINAL

LEICESTERSHIRE v SOMERSET

At Lord's, London on 1 September.
Result: **SOMERSET won by 41 runs.**
Toss: Somerset. Award: K.A.Parsons.

SOMERSET		Runs	Balls	4/6	Fall
M.E.Trescothick	c Afridi b Ormond	18	18	3	1- 40
P.D.Bowler	b Afridi	42	85	6	2-107
* J.Cox	b Afridi	44	64	4	4-149
I.D.Blackwell	b Afridi	15	16	1/1	3-132
M.Burns	c Maddy b Wells	21	23	1	5-176
K.A.Parsons	not out	60	52	3/3	
† R.J.Turner	not out	37	42	2	
K.P.Dutch					
R.L.Johnson					
A.R.Caddick					
P.S.Jones					
Extras	(LB 19, W 15)	34			
Total	(50 overs; 5 wickets; 202 minutes)	**271**			

LEICESTERSHIRE		Runs	Balls	4/6	Fall
T.R.Ward	b Parsons	54	65	10	2-105
Shahid Afridi	c Turner b Johnson	20	10	3	1- 20
D.L.Maddy	c and b Dutch	49	71	3	5-156
* V.J.Wells	c Turner b Parsons	3	8	–	3-111
B.F.Smith	c Trescothick b Dutch	15	18	1	4-142
D.I.Stevens	lbw b Jones	23	32	1	7-182
† N.D.Burns	c Turner b Jones	6	9	1	6-171
A.Habib	c Dutch b Blackwell	15	19	1	8-194
P.A.J.DeFreitas	b Johnson	14	23	1	9-225
J.Ormond	not out	18	18	1/1	
S.A.J.Boswell	b Jones	2	4	–	10-230
Extras	(LB 3, W 2, NB 6)	11			
Total	(45.4 overs; 185 minutes)	**230**			

LEICS	O	M	R	W	SOMERSET	O	M	R	W
Ormond	10	2	38	1	Caddick	10	2	33	0
Boswell	2	0	23	0	Johnson	8	0	39	2
DeFreitas	10	1	57	0	Jones	7.4	0	40	3
Wells	10	1	40	1	Parsons	6	0	40	2
Maddy	8	0	47	0	Dutch	10	0	50	2
Shahid Afridi	10	0	47	3	Blackwell	4	0	25	1

Scores after 15 overs: Somerset 60-1; Leicestershire 66-1.

Umpires: B.Dudleston and G.Sharp.

CHELTENHAM & GLOUCESTER TROPHY
PRINCIPAL RECORDS 1963-2001
(Including Gillette Cup and NatWest Trophy Matches)

Highest Total		413-4	Somerset v Devon	Torquay	1990
Highest Total in a Final		322-5	Warwicks v Sussex	Lord's	1993
Highest Total Batting Second		350	Surrey v Worcs	The Oval	1994
Highest Total to Win Batting Second		329-5	Sussex v Derbyshire	Derby	1997
Lowest Total		39	Ireland v Sussex	Hove	1985
Lowest Total in a Final		57	Essex v Lancashire	Lord's	1996
Lowest Total to Win Batting First		98	Worcs v Durham	Chester-le-St	1968

Highest Score	206	A.I.Kallicharran	Warwicks v Oxon	Birmingham	1984
Fastest Hundred	36 balls	G.D.Rose	Somerset v Devon	Torquay	1990
Most Hundreds	8	R.A.Smith	Hampshire		1985-99
Most Runs	2,547	(av 48.98)	G.A.Gooch	Essex	1973-96

Highest Partnership for each Wicket

1st	311	A.J.Wright/N.J.Trainor	Glos v Scotland	Bristol	1997
2nd	286	I.S.Anderson/A.Hill	Derbys v Cornwall	Derby	1986
3rd	309*	T.S.Curtis/T.M.Moody	Worcs v Surrey	The Oval	1994
4th	234*	D.Lloyd/C.H.Lloyd	Lancashire v Glos	Manchester	1978
5th	166	M.A.Lynch/G.R.J.Roope	Surrey v Durham	The Oval	1982
6th	226	N.J.Llong/M.V.Fleming	Kent v Cheshire	Bowdon	1999
7th	160*	C.J.Richards/I.R.Payne	Surrey v Lincs	Sleaford	1983
8th	112	A.L.Penberthy/J.E.Emburey	Northants v Lancs	Manchester	1996
9th	87	M.A.Nash/A.E.Cordle	Glamorgan v Lincs	Swansea	1974
10th	81	S.Turner/R.E.East	Essex v Yorkshire	Leeds	1982

Best Bowling	8-21	M.A.Holding	Derbys v Sussex	Hove	1988
	8-31	D.L.Underwood	Kent v Scotland	Edinburgh	1987
Most Wickets	87	(av 14.24)	A.A.Donald	Warwicks	1987-2000

Most Wicket-Keeping Dismissals in an Innings

8	(8ct)	D.J.Pipe	Worcs v Herts	Hertford	2001

Most Match Wins 82 – Lancashire   **Most Cup/Trophy Wins** 7 – Lancashire

GILLETTE CUP WINNERS

1963	Sussex	1969	Yorkshire	1975	Lancashire
1964	Sussex	1970	Lancashire	1976	Northamptonshire
1965	Yorkshire	1971	Lancashire	1977	Middlesex
1966	Warwickshire	1972	Lancashire	1978	Sussex
1967	Kent	1973	Gloucestershire	1979	Somerset
1968	Warwickshire	1974	Kent	1980	Middlesex

NATWEST TROPHY WINNERS

1981	Derbyshire	1988	Middlesex	1995	Warwickshire
1982	Surrey	1989	Warwickshire	1996	Lancashire
1983	Somerset	1990	Lancashire	1997	Essex
1984	Middlesex	1991	Hampshire	1998	Lancashire
1985	Essex	1992	Northamptonshire	1999	Gloucestershire
1986	Sussex	1993	Warwickshire	2000	Gloucestershire
1987	Nottinghamshire	1994	Worcestershire		

NORWICH UNION NATIONAL LEAGUE 2001

FIRST DIVISION

		P	W	L	T	NR	Pts	NRR
1	Kent (5)	16	11	2	1	2	50	+4.264
2	Leicestershire (4)	16	11	4	–	1	46	+7.805
3	Warwickshire	16	8	5	–	3	38	+1.580
4	Somerset (6)	16	7	7	1	1	32	+4.604
5	Nottinghamshire	16	7	8	–	1	30	–8.015
6	Yorkshire (2)	16	7	9	–	–	28	+9.656
7	Gloucestershire (1)	16	6	9	–	1	26	+1.481
8	Surrey	16	6	10	–	–	24	–5.051
9	Northamptonshire (3)	16	3	12	–	1	14	–9.021

SECOND DIVISION

		P	W	L	T	NR	Pts	NRR
1	Glamorgan (6)	16	11	3	–	2	48	+15.20
2	Durham (7)	16	9	4	–	3	42	+1.740
3	Worcestershire	16	9	5	–	2	40	+9.617
4	Hampshire (8)	16	9	6	–	1	38	+5.289
5	Sussex	16	8	7	–	1	34	–1.103
6	Lancashire	16	5	8	–	3	26	–3.709
7	Essex (5)	16	5	9	1	1	24	–9.923
8	Middlesex (4)	16	3	9	1	3	20	–8.311
9	Derbyshire (9)	16	4	12	–	–	16	–7.207

Win = 4 points. Tie (T)/No Result (NR) = 2 points. Positions of counties finishing equal on points are decided by most wins or, if equal, by higher net run-rate (NRR – overall run-rate in all matches, i.e. total runs scored x 100 divided by balls received, minus the run-rate of its opponents in those same matches). Horizontal rules segregate the counties relegated and promoted for the 2001 competition. 2000 final positions for that division are shown in brackets.

SUNDAY LEAGUE CHAMPIONS

1969	Lancashire	1979	Somerset	1989	Lancashire
1970	Lancashire	1980	Warwickshire	1990	Derbyshire
1971	Worcestershire	1981	Essex	1991	Nottinghamshire
1972	Kent	1982	Sussex	1992	Middlesex
1973	Kent	1983	Yorkshire	1993	Glamorgan
1974	Leicestershire	1984	Essex	1994	Warwickshire
1975	Hampshire	1985	Essex	1995	Kent
1976	Kent	1986	Hampshire	1996	Surrey
1977	Leicestershire	1987	Worcestershire	1997	Warwickshire
1978	Hampshire	1988	Worcestershire	1998	Lancashire

NATIONAL LEAGUE CHAMPIONS

1999	Lancashire	2000	Gloucestershire	2001	Kent

NATIONAL (SUNDAY) LEAGUE 1969-2001
PRINCIPAL RECORDS

Highest Total		375-4		Surrey v Yorkshire	Scarborough	1994
Highest Total Batting Second		317-6		Surrey v Notts	The Oval	1993
Lowest Total		23		Middlesex v Yorks	Leeds	1974
Highest Score	203	A.D.Brown		Surrey v Hampshire	Guildford	1997
Fastest Hundred	44 balls	M.A.Ealham		Kent v Derbyshire	Maidstone	1995

Highest Partnership for each Wicket

1st	239	G.A.Gooch/B.R.Hardie	Essex v Notts	Nottingham	1985
2nd	273	G.A.Gooch/K.S.McEwan	Essex v Notts	Nottingham	1983
3rd	223	S.J.Cook/G.D.Rose	Somerset v Glam	Neath	1990
4th	219	C.G.Greenidge/C.L.Smith	Hampshire v Surrey	Southampton	1987
5th	220*	C.C.Lewis/P.A.Nixon	Leics v Kent	Canterbury	1999
6th	137	M.P.Speight/I.D.K.Salisbury	Sussex v Surrey	Guildford	1996
7th	132	K.R.Brown/N.F.Williams	Middx v Somerset	Lord's	1988
8th	110*	C.L.Cairns/B.N.French	Notts v Surrey	The Oval	1993
9th	105	D.G.Moir/R.W.Taylor	Derbyshire v Kent	Derby	1984
10th	82	G.Chapple/P.J.Martin	Lancashire v Worcs	Manchester	1996
Best Bowling	8-26	K.D.Boyce	Essex v Lancashire	Manchester	1971
	7-15	R.A.Hutton	Yorkshire v Worcs	Leeds	1969
	7-16	S.D.Thomas	Glamorgan v Surrey	Swansea	1998
	7-30	M.P.Bicknell	Surrey v Glamorgan	The Oval	1999
	7-39	A.Hodgson	Northants v Somerset	Northampton	1976
	7-41	A.N.Jones	Sussex v Notts	Nottingham	1986
Four Wkts in Four Balls		A.Ward	Derbyshire v Sussex	Derby	1970
		V.C.Drakes	Notts v Derbys	Nottingham	1999

Most Wicket-Keeping Dismissals in an Innings

7	(6ct, 1st)	R.W.Taylor	Derbyshire v Lancs	Manchester	1975

Most Catches in an Innings

5		J.M.Rice	Hampshire v Warwicks	Southampton	1978

BENSON & HEDGES CUP 2001
FINAL GROUP TABLES

NORTH	P	W	L	NR	Points	Run-Rate
Nottinghamshire	5	4	1	–	8	0.77
Durham	5	3	2	–	6	0.33
Yorkshire	5	3	2	–	6	0.04
Leicestershire	5	3	2	–	6	−0.32
Lancashire	5	1	4	–	2	−0.27
Derbyshire	5	1	4	–	2	−0.61

MID/WEST/WALES	P	W	L	NR	Points	Run-Rate
Somerset	5	4	1	–	8	0.75
Gloucestershire	5	4	1	–	8	−0.27
Warwickshire	5	3	2	–	6	0.31
Worcestershire	5	2	3	–	4	0.17
Northamptonshire	5	2	3	–	4	−0.54
Glamorgan	5	–	5	–	0	−0.44

SOUTH	P	W	L	NR	Points	Run-Rate
Sussex	5	3	–	2	8	0.89
Surrey	5	2	1	2	6	0.25
Middlesex	5	2	2	1	5	−0.59
Kent	5	2	2	1	5	−0.03
Essex	5	1	2	2	4	0.34
Hampshire	5	–	3	2	2	−0.72

2001 B & H CUP FINAL

SURREY v GLOUCESTERSHIRE

At Lord's, London on 14 July.
Result: **SURREY won by 47 runs.**
Toss: Surrey. Award: B.C.Hollioake.

SURREY		Runs	Balls	4/6	Fall
M.A.Butcher	lbw b Harvey	0	7	–	1- 7
I.J.Ward	c Russell b Hardinges	54	59	5	5-118
M.R.Ramprakash	c Taylor b Alleyne	39	33	7	2- 71
† A.J.Stewart	c Snape b Alleyne	8	18	–	3- 89
A.D.Brown	c Harvey b Alleyne	3	10	–	4- 97
* A.J.Hollioake	lbw b Ball	39	65	–	6-202
B.C.Hollioake	c Alleyne b Averis	73	76	4/2	8-242
A.J.Tudor	lbw b Ball	1	7	–	7-204
M.P.Bicknell	b Harvey	19	21	–/1	9-244
Saqlain Mushtaq	not out	1	2	–	
E.S.H.Giddins	b Harvey	0	1	–	10-244
Extras	(LB 4, W 3)	7			
Total	(49.5 overs; 199 minutes)	**244**			

GLOUCESTERSHIRE		Runs	Balls	4/6	Fall
† R.C.Russell	c Stewart b Tudor	62	96	7	5-131
K.J.Barnett	b Giddins	7	30	–	1- 35
D.R.Hewson	c Bicknell b Saqlain	11	12	1	2- 68
I.J.Harvey	lbw b Giddins	1	5	–	3- 71
M.G.N.Windows	b Giddins	10	15	2	4- 89
* M.W.Alleyne	c and b Saqlain	26	32	1/1	6-133
J.N.Snape	c Stewart b Tudor	22	35	–	8-190
C.G.Taylor	b Saqlain	12	16	2	7-161
M.A.Hardinges	c Stewart b Bicknell	12	21	–	9-194
M.C.J.Ball	not out	3	7	–	
J.M.M.Averis	b Tudor	1	6	–	10-197
Extras	(LB 16, W 14)	30			
Total	(45.5 overs; 200 minutes)	**197**			

GLOS	O	M	R	W	SURREY	O	M	R	W
Harvey	9.5	2	43	3	Bicknell	10	1	38	1
Averis	10	1	65	1	Tudor	9.5	3	28	3
Alleyne	10	1	51	3	Giddins	8	1	31	3
Ball	10	0	39	2	Saqlain Mushtaq	8	0	37	3
Hardinges	7	0	31	1	B.C.Hollioake	10	0	47	0
Barnett	3	0	11	0					

Scores after 15 overs: Surrey 88-2; Gloucestershire: 48-1.

Umpires: J.H.Hampshire and K.E.Palmer.

BENSON AND HEDGES CUP

RESULTS CHART 2001

QUARTER-FINALS	SEMI-FINALS	FINAL
22, 23 May	*25 June*	*14 July*

QUARTER-FINALS	SEMI-FINALS	FINAL
NOTTINGHAMSHIRE†	Nottinghamshire (£15,500)	
Warwickshire (£10,500)		SURREY
Sussex† (£10,500)		(£52,000)
SURREY	SURREY†	
Somerset† (£10,500)		
YORKSHIRE	Yorkshire† (£15,500)	
GLOUCESTERSHIRE†		Gloucestershire
Durham (£10,500)	GLOUCESTERSHIRE	(£26,000)

† Home team. Winning teams are in capitals. Prize-money in brackets.

PRINCIPAL RECORDS 1972-2001

Highest Total		388-7	Essex v Scotland	Chelmsford	1992
Highest Total Batting Second		318-5	Lancashire v Leics	Manchester	1995
Lowest Total		50	Hampshire v Yorks	Leeds	1991
Highest Score	198*	G.A.Gooch	Essex v Sussex	Hove	1982
Fastest Hundred	62 min	M.A.Nash	Glamorgan v Hants	Swansea	1976
Highest Partnership for each Wicket					
1st	252	V.P.Terry/C.L.Smith	Hants v Combined U	Southampton	1990
2nd	285*	C.G.Greenidge/D.R.Turner	Hants v Minor C (S)	Amersham	1973
3rd	271	C.J.Adams/M.G.Bevan	Sussex v Essex	Chelmsford	2000
4th	207	R.C.Russell/A.J/Wright	Glos v British U	Bristol	1998
5th	160	A.J.Lamb/D.J.Capel	Northants v Leics	Northampton	1986
6th	167*	M.G.Bevan/R.J.Blakey	Yorkshire v Lancs	Manchester	1996
7th	149*	J.D.Love/C.M.Old	Yorks v Scotland	Bradford	1981
8th	109	R.E.East/N.Smith	Essex v Northants	Chelmsford	1977
9th	83	P.G.Newman/M.A.Holding	Derbyshire v Notts	Nottingham	1985
10th	80*	D.L.Bairstow/M.Johnson	Yorkshire v Derbys	Derby	1981
Best Bowling	7-12	W.W.Daniel	Middx v Minor C (E)	Ipswich	1978
	7-22	J.R.Thomson	Middx v Hampshire	Lord's	1981
	7-24	Mushtaq Ahmed	Somerset v Ireland	Taunton	1997
	7-32	R.G.D.Willis	Warwicks v Yorks	Birmingham	1981
Four Wickets in Four Balls		S.M.Pollock	Warwicks v Leics	Birmingham	1996
Most Wicket-Keeping Dismissals in an Innings					
8 (8ct)		D.J.S.Taylor	Somerset v Combined U	Taunton	1982
Most Catches in an Innings					
5		V.J.Marks	Combined U v Kent	Oxford	1976

BENSON AND HEDGES CUP WINNERS

1972	Leicestershire	1982	Somerset
1973	Kent	1983	Middlesex
1974	Surrey	1984	Lancashire
1975	Leicestershire	1985	Leicestershire
1976	Kent	1986	Middlesex
1977	Gloucestershire	1987	Yorkshire
1978	Kent	1988	Hampshire
1979	Essex	1989	Nottinghamshire
1980	Northamptonshire	1990	Lancashire
1981	Somerset	1991	Worcestershire

1992	Hampshire
1993	Derbyshire
1994	Warwickshire
1995	Lancashire
1996	Lancashire
1997	Surrey
1998	Essex
1999	Gloucestershire
2000	Gloucestershire
2001	Surrey

MINOR COUNTIES CHAMPIONSHIP

FINAL TABLE 2001

	P	W	L	D	Bonus Points Bat	Bonus Points Bowl	Total Points
EASTERN DIVISION							
LINCOLNSHIRE	6	3	1	2	13	23	92
Staffordshire	6	2	–	4	14	24	86
Northumberland	6	2	–	4	12	22	82
Hertfordshire	6	2	1	3	13	20	77
Cumberland	6	2	2	2	10	23	73
Norfolk	6	1	1	4	10	16	58
Cambridgeshire	6	4	–	2	9	24	52†
Buckinghamshire	6	–	2	4	7	16	39
Suffolk	6	–	4	2	6	17	31
Bedfordshire	6	–	5	1	6	19	29
WESTERN DIVISION							
CHESHIRE	6	4	–	2	15	21	108
Shropshire	6	3	–	3	10	23	93
Devon	6	3	1	2	14	22	92
Herefordshire	6	3	2	1	12	23	87
Berkshire	6	3	3	–	8	22	78
Wales MC	9	1	2	3	14	20	62
Cornwall	6	1	2	3	4	23	53‡
Oxfordshire	6	1	3	2	5	17	46
Wiltshire	6	1	3	2	2	19	45
Dorset	6	–	4	2	11	20	39

† 53 points deducted for fielding inelible player.
‡ 2 points deducted for slow over rate.

CHAMPIONSHIP FINAL

At Grantham CC on 9, 10, 11 September: **LINCOLNSHIRE drew with CHESHIRE.**
Lincolnshire 254-5 closed (70 overs; J.C.Harrison 110, R.W.J.Howitt 74, R.W.Fisher 4-84)
and 391-5 dec (J.Trower 149, S.Plumb 103*, J.Clarke 53). Cheshire 295-6 closed (70 overs;
A.J.Hall 120, M.R.Currie 70) and 99-2 (P.R.J.Bryson 50).

ECB 38-COUNTY CUP

At Lord's on 4 September: **NORFOLK beat DEVON by 114 runs.** Norfolk 202-9 closed
(50 overs; C.J.Rogers 54, J.Rhodes 3-43). Devon 88 (28.1 overs; C.Brown 4-15,
P.J.Bradshaw 3-10).

MINOR COUNTIES RECORDS

Highest Total	621		Surrey II v Devon	The Oval	1928
Lowest Total	14		Cheshire v Staffs	Stoke	1909
Highest Score	282	E.Garnett	Berkshire v Wiltshire	Reading	1908
Most Runs – Season	1212	A.F.Brazier	Surrey II		1949
Record Partnership:					
2nd	388*	T.H.Clark and A.F.Brazier	Surrey II v Sussex II	The Oval	1949
Best Bowling – Innings	10- 11	S.Turner	Cambs v Cumberland	Penrith	1987
– Match	18-100	N.W.Harding	Kent II v Wiltshire	Swindon	1937
Most Wickets – Season	119	S.F.Barnes	Staffordshire		1906

MINOR COUNTIES CHAMPIONS

1895	{ Norfolk	1930	Durham	1970	Bedfordshire
	Durham	1931	Leicestershire II	1971	Yorkshire II
	Worcestershire	1932	Buckinghamshire	1972	Bedfordshire
1896	Worcestershire	1933	*Undecided*	1973	Shropshire
1897	Worcestershire	1934	Lancashire II	1974	Oxfordshire
1898	Worcestershire	1935	Middlesex II	1975	Hertfordshire
1899	{ Northamptonshire	1936	Hertfordshire	1976	Durham
	Buckinghamshire	1937	Lancashire II	1977	Suffolk
	{ Glamorgan	1938	Buckinghamshire	1978	Devon
1900	Durham	1939	Surrey II	1979	Suffolk
	Northamptonshire	1946	Suffolk	1980	Durham
1901	Durham	1947	Yorkshire II	1981	Durham
1902	Wiltshire	1948	Lancashire II	1982	Oxfordshire
1903	Northamptonshire	1949	Lancashire II	1983	Hertfordshire
1904	Northamptonshire	1950	Surrey II	1984	Durham
1905	Norfolk	1951	Kent II	1985	Cheshire
1906	Staffordshire	1952	Buckinghamshire	1986	Cumberland
1907	Lancashire II	1953	Berkshire	1987	Buckinghamshire
1908	Staffordshire	1954	Surrey II	1988	Cheshire
1909	Wiltshire	1955	Surrey II	1989	Oxfordshire
1910	Norfolk	1956	Kent II	1990	Hertfordshire
1911	Staffordshire	1957	Yorkshire II	1991	Staffordshire
1912	*In abeyance*	1958	Yorkshire II	1992	Staffordshire
1913	Norfolk	1959	Warwickshire II	1993	Staffordshire
1920	Staffordshire	1960	Lancashire II	1994	Devon
1921	Staffordshire	1961	Somerset II	1995	Devon
1922	Buckinghamshire	1962	Warwickshire II	1996	Devon
1923	Buckinghamshire	1963	Cambridgeshire	1997	Devon
1924	Berkshire	1964	Lancashire II	1998	Staffordshire
1925	Buckinghamshire	1965	Somerset II	1999	Cumberland
1926	Durham	1966	Lincolnshire	2000	Dorset
1927	Staffordshire	1967	Cheshire	2001	{ Cheshire
1928	Berkshire	1968	Yorkshire II		Lincolnshire
1929	Oxfordshire	1969	Buckinghamshire		

LEADING BATTING AVERAGES
(Qualifications: 8 innings; average 30.00)

		M	I	NO	HS	Runs	Avge	100	50
D.M.Ward	Herts	5	10	2	172	636	79.50	2	3
J.Trower	Lincs	5	8	2	149	393	65.50	1	3
R.I.Dawson	Devon	6	10	1	221	559	62.11	1	4
J.A.Knott	Beds	4	8	2	75*	360	60.00	–	2
M.A.Fell	Lincs	7	11	4	69	416	59.42	–	2
A.J.Hall	Cheshire	5	8	2	120	338	56.33	1	2
J.C.Harrison	Lincs	6	12	2	117	549	54.90	2	3
R.J.Rollins	Cambs	6	12	1	204*	597	54.27	1	4
J.B.Windows	Northumb	4	8	3	93	270	54.00	–	3
P.J.Caley	Suffolk	6	10	2	95	393	49.12	–	4
D.G.Wilson	Cambs	6	12	4	82	393	49.12	–	4
D.R.Drepaul	Bucks	5	8	2	135	288	48.00	1	–
P.F.Shaw	Staffs	6	10	–	131	480	48.00	1	1
M.R.Currie	Cheshire	5	10	2	121	383	47.87	1	1
G.J.Byram	Salop	4	8	3	74*	238	47.60	–	2
D.Lowe	Herts	4	8	1	142*	323	46.14	2	–
P.R.J.Bryson	Cheshire	4	8	1	113	318	45.42	1	1
A.R.Roberts	Beds	6	11	–	113	484	44.00	1	4
R.W.Sylvester	Wales MC	5	9	2	124*	308	44.00	1	1
M.J.Marvell	Salop	6	12	2	141*	437	43.70	1	2

		M	I	NO	HS	Runs	Avge	100	50
T.R.Bristow	Beds	4	8	1	114*	304	43.42	1	–
R.J.Rowe	Wilts	6	12	1	89*	471	42.81	–	5
C.W.Boroughs	Herefords	6	10	–	124	420	42.00	2	1
G.D.T.Paskins	Bucks	5	10	–	122	417	41.70	1	2
S.J.Lowe	Herts	6	12	–	116	500	41.66	2	2
C.Amos	Norfolk	6	10	–	138	405	40.50	1	3
O.A.Dawkins	Wales MC	5	9	2	75	283	40.42	–	3
M.I.Humphries	Staffs	6	8	3	62	201	40.20	–	1
S.C.Goldsmith	Norfolk	6	9	1	109	320	40.00	1	2
M.Swarbrick	Dorset	5	9	–	149	437	39.72	1	2
D.W.Cowley	Dorset	5	9	–	114	355	39.44	1	2
A.P.Cook	Oxon	6	11	3	70*	311	38.87	–	3
B.J.Thompson	Oxon	4	8	1	121*	271	38.71	1	1
P.D.Atkins	Bucks	6	10	2	95*	302	37.75	–	3
G.F.Archer	Staffs	6	10	–	108	363	36.30	1	2
S.A.Kellett	Cambs	5	10	1	100*	312	34.66	1	2
B.Parker	Northumb	6	11	2	81	307	34.11	–	2
J.R.Wood	Berks	6	10	–	65	341	34.10	–	3
S.J.Dean	Staffs	6	10	–	127	338	33.80	1	1
S.G.Plumb	Lincs	6	12	2	103*	333	33.30	1	–
I.Cockbain	Cheshire	7	12	2	110	331	33.10	1	1
C.S.Carey	Norfolk	5	8	4	72*	132	33.00	–	1
G.R.Treagus	Dorset	6	11	–	115	352	32.00	1	1
I.Dawood	Herefords	5	9	–	68	286	31.77	–	2
M.D.Coxon	Wilts	5	10	1	144	284	31.55	1	1
R.G.Hignett	Cheshire	7	12	1	110	340	30.90	1	1
S.Chapman	Northumb	5	8	1	92	216	30.85	–	2
J.A.Graham	Northumb	5	8	–	85	241	30.12	–	2

LEADING BOWLING AVERAGES
(Qualification: 20 wickets)

		O	M	R	W	Avge	BB	5w	10w
K.E.Cooper	Herefords	141.1	46	285	30	9.50	5- 35	6	3
I.E.Bishop	Devon	169.3	56	377	31	12.16	6- 20	3	1
J.B.Grant	Cambs	104.3	25	260	21	12.38	6- 34	2	–
N.D.Cross	Cheshire	116.4	40	293	21	13.95	7- 40	2	–
S.Chapman	Northumb	154.3	47	337	24	14.04	5- 63	1	–
J.C.J.Stephens	Cornwall	194.1	59	462	32	14.43	6- 32	3	1
G.M.Kirk	Suffolk	130.4	43	314	21	14.95	5- 46	2	–
R.P.Davis	Berks	219.2	63	576	36	16.00	7- 95	4	–
M.A.Sharp	Cumb	185.2	77	354	21	16.85	4- 31	–	–
D.B.Pennett	Cumb	142.4	37	441	24	18.37	7- 65	2	1
D.Follett	Staffs	163.2	35	436	23	18.95	7- 27	2	1
D.R.Womble	Staffs	140.3	24	494	26	19.00	5- 41	1	–
Ajaz Akhtar	Cambs	235.3	79	551	27	20.40	4- 38	–	–
G.Angus	Northumb	158.1	41	439	21	20.90	3- 31	–	–
S.J.Renshaw	Cheshire	164.2	34	534	25	21.36	5- 57	3	–
R.W.Fisher	Cheshire	172.3	44	459	21	21.85	7- 73	1	1
C.S.Lamb	Cheshire	187.4	56	483	22	21.95	7- 49	1	–
D.J.P.Boden	Salop	157.5	52	441	20	22.05	6- 32	2	–
I.D.Graham	Suffolk	140.1	32	477	21	22.71	5- 79	1	–
P.J.Humphries	Herefords	171.2	44	507	22	23.04	5- 55	1	–
R.D.Bedbrook	Wilts	231.4	46	861	37	23.27	7- 97	4	2
A.R.Roberts	Beds	182.5	42	541	23	23.52	5- 70	2	–
S.G.Plumb	Lincs	198.2	55	551	22	25.04	4- 42	–	–
D.J.Pipes	Lincs	184.3	38	585	23	25.43	6- 51	1	–
R.A.Cooper	Staffs	174.5	43	516	20	25.80	4- 36	–	–
R.J.Chapman	Lincs	152.1	27	542	21	25.80	5- 55	1	–
V.J.Pike	Dorset	251.2	57	739	28	26.39	5-104	1	–
C.Brown	Norfolk	189	46	577	21	27.47	5-111	1	–
C.E.Shreck	Cornwall	238.2	59	809	27	29.96	4- 47	–	–

SECOND XI CHAMPIONSHIP 2001
FINAL TABLE

	P	W	L	D	Bonus Points Bat	Bowl	Total Points	Avge
1 HAMPSHIRE (11)	11	8	–	3	28	33	†171	15.55
2 Yorkshire (5)	13	8	2	3	35	34	177	13.62
3 Nottinghamshire (4)	15	9	3	3	35	37	192	12.80
4 Gloucestershire (9)	13	7	3	3	45	25	166	12.77
5 Northamptonshire (14)	14	5	4	5	40	42	162	11.57
6 Kent (2)	11	5	4	2	20	31	119	10.82
7 Surrey (8)	12	4	4	4	28	36	128	10.67
8 Warwickshire (3)	12	3	3	6	22	32	†116	9.67
9 Lancashire (7)	11	3	4	4	19	29	100	9.09
10 Durham (12)	11	1	3	7	22	36	98	8.91
11 Middlesex (1)	13	2	5	6	28	38	114	8.77
12 Leicestershire (15)	12	2	4	6	30	27	105	8.75
13 Worcestershire (17)	11	1	4	6	31	29	96	8.73
14 Essex (10)	10	2	4	4	16	31	87	8.70
15 Somerset (16)	10	2	4	4	25	22	87	8.70
16 Glamorgan (13)	11	3	5	3	16	30	94	8.55
17 Sussex (6)	10	2	6	2	20	23	75	7.50
18 Derbyshire (18)	12	1	6	5	11	31	77	6.42

Win = 12 points, plus any first-innings points. † Includes 2 extra draw points in match where scores were level. Essex (13.3) gained precedence over Somerset (13.2) by virtue of higher average number of wickets taken per match. 2000 final positions are shown in brackets.

ECB SECOND XI AWARDS 2001

Players of the Month:
G.J.Batty (Surrey); T.M.B.Bailey (Northamptonshire);
J.W.M.Dalrymple (Middlesex); J.R.C.Hamblin (Hampshire)

Player of the Season:
G.J.Batty (Surrey)

SECOND XI CHAMPIONS

1959 Gloucestershire	1974 Middlesex	1989 Middlesex
1960 Northamptonshire	1975 Surrey	1990 Sussex
1961 Kent	1976 Kent	1991 Yorkshire
1962 Worcestershire	1977 Yorkshire	1992 Surrey
1963 Worcestershire	1978 Sussex	1993 Middlesex
1964 Lancashire	1979 Warwickshire	1994 Somerset
1965 Glamorgan	1980 Glamorgan	1995 Hampshire
1966 Surrey	1981 Hampshire	1996 Warwickshire
1967 Hampshire	1982 Worcestershire	1997 Lancashire
1968 Surrey	1983 Leicestershire	1998 Northamptonshire
1969 Kent	1984 Yorkshire	1999 Middlesex
1970 Kent	1985 Nottinghamshire	2000 Middlesex
1971 Hampshire	1986 Lancashire	2001 Hampshire
1972 Nottinghamshire	1987 Kent/Yorkshire	
1973 Essex	1988 Surrey	

FIRST-CLASS CAREER RECORDS

Compiled by **PHILIP BAILEY**

The following career records are for all players who appeared in first-class or limited-overs cricket during the 2001 season and are complete to the end of that season. Some players who did not appear in 2001 but may do so in 2002 are also included.

BATTING AND FIELDING

'1000' denotes instances of scoring 1000 runs in a season. Where these have been achieved outside the British Isles they are shown after a plus sign.

	M	I	NO	HS	Runs	Avge	100	50	1000	Ct/St
Aamer Sohail	195	331	17	205	12213	38.89	29	50	1+2	153
Abdul Razzaq	46	67	8	117	1700	28.81	4	11	–	14
Adams, C.J.	231	376	29	239	12936	37.27	30	65	5	279
Adams, J.C.	189	319	54	208*	10550	39.81	23	52	–	166
Adshead, S.J.	1	1	0	0	0	0.00	–	–	–	–/1
Afzaal, U.	101	176	15	151*	4891	30.37	7	29	2	47
Aldred, P.	58	78	11	83	766	11.43	–	1	–	32
Ali, Kabir	15	21	4	50*	362	21.29	–	2	–	5
Ali, Kadeer	9	15	0	38	78	5.20	–	–	–	3
Alleyne, D.	2	4	0	44	55	13.75	–	–	–	4
Alleyne, M.W.	300	491	45	256	13957	31.29	21	67	6	246/3
Ambrose, T.R.	2	3	0	52	92	30.66	–	1	–	3
Amin, R.M.	14	18	8	12	35	3.50	–	–	–	6
Aminul Islam	23	40	5	153	1252	35.77	4	4	–	11
Anderson, R.S.G.	32	39	5	67*	471	13.85	–	1	–	7
Asif Mujtaba	255	395	77	240	15956	50.17	42	85	1+3	231
Atherton, M.A.	336	584	47	268*	21929	40.83	54	107	7	268
Austin, I.D.	124	172	37	115*	3778	27.98	2	20	–	35
Averis, J.M.M.	34	48	11	42	417	11.27	–	–	–	6
Aymes, A.N.	210	307	77	133	7286	31.67	8	38	–	500/43
Azhar Mahmood	74	118	16	136	2791	27.36	4	13	–	50
Bailey, R.J.	374	628	89	224*	21844	40.52	47	111	13	272
Bailey, T.M.B.	18	22	3	96*	394	20.73	–	1	–	22/2
Ball, M.C.J.	154	237	42	71	3779	19.37	–	12	–	189
Banes, M.J.	7	11	1	53	171	17.10	–	2	–	2
Banks, O.A.C.	7	12	1	43	160	14.54	–	–	–	3
Barnett, K.J.	471	769	73	239*	27952	40.16	58	152	16	283
Bassano, C.W.G.	8	14	2	186*	523	43.58	2	2	–	5
Batty, G.J.	3	6	1	25*	98	19.60	–	–	–	2
Batty, J.N.	69	90	15	100*	1641	21.88	1	6	–	161/23
Bell, I.R.	13	19	3	135	886	55.37	3	4	–	13
Betts, M.M.	80	116	26	57*	1049	11.65	–	2	–	30
Bevan, M.G.	189	316	56	203*	14420	55.46	49	64	3	105
Bichel, A.J.	83	111	8	110	2089	20.28	1	8	–	40
Bicknell, D.J.	243	426	38	235*	15108	38.93	37	65	7	89
Bicknell, M.P.	243	293	71	110*	5092	22.93	1	22	–	83
Bishop, J.E.	10	13	2	18	91	8.27	–	–	–	3
Blackwell, I.D.	54	79	4	122	2073	27.64	5	9	–	23
Blain, J.A.R.	9	11	5	34	97	16.16	–	–	–	3
Blakey, R.J.	319	506	78	221	13165	30.75	11	78	5	717/55
Blewett, G.S.	179	319	22	268	13608	45.81	35	67	1+4	152
Block, S.A.A.	6	11	1	56*	170	17.00	–	1	–	1
Bloomfield, T.F.	49	54	22	28	222	6.93	–	–	–	6

143

	M	I	NO	HS	Runs	Avge	100	50	1000	Ct/St
Bones, A.S.	5	8	0	7	27	3.37	–	–	–	2
Boswell, S.A.J.	22	30	10	35	249	12.45	–	–	–	6
Boulton, N.R.	5	7	0	47	90	12.85	–	–	–	1
Bowler, P.D.	279	475	50	241*	17290	40.68	42	86	9	188/1
Bracken, N.W.	14	19	10	30	102	11.33	–	–	–	7
Bressington, A.N.	6	6	3	17*	42	14.00	–	–	–	3
Bridge, G.D.	8	15	2	39*	136	10.46	–	–	–	6
Brinkley, J.E.	29	35	7	65	300	10.71	–	1	–	12
Brophy, G.L.	23	38	3	185	1030	29.42	1	5	–	73/5
Brown, A.D.	154	241	24	295*	9356	43.11	27	37	5	162/1
Brown, D.R.	130	194	25	203	4811	28.46	3	28	–	84
Brown, J.F.	40	50	22	35*	139	4.96	–	–	–	9
Brown, M.J.	7	13	4	60*	251	27.88	–	2	–	4
Brown, S.J.E.	158	221	72	69	1796	12.05	–	2	–	42
Bruce, J.T.A.	3	3	1	14*	19	9.50	–	–	–	–
Brunnschweiler, I.	2	4	1	19	33	11.00	–	–	–	9
Bulbeck, M.P.L.	31	35	17	76*	462	25.66	–	1	–	6
Burns, M.	95	147	6	221	4251	30.14	5	28	–	92/7
Burns, N.D.	189	283	63	166	6656	30.25	6	35	–	417/36
Butcher, G.P.	53	78	12	101*	1841	27.89	1	12	–	19
Butcher, G.R.	1	2	0	10	16	8.00	–	–	–	–
Butcher, M.A.	167	288	23	259	10292	38.83	19	58	6	160
Byas, D.	268	449	42	213	14398	35.37	28	79	5	351
Caddick, A.R.	181	242	46	92	2937	14.98	–	5	–	61
Cairns, C.L.	183	286	33	126	8903	35.18	11	60	1	70
Carberry, M.A.	6	10	0	84	311	31.10	–	1	–	6
Carpenter, J.R.	13	24	0	65	383	15.95	–	2	–	5
Carter, N.M.	15	19	3	37	144	9.00	–	–	–	4
Cassar, M.E.	56	89	11	121	1812	23.23	1	9	–	16
Catterall, D.N.	4	5	0	60	157	31.40	–	2	–	1
Cawdron, M.J.	18	26	4	42	333	15.13	–	–	–	3
Chapple, G.	130	176	47	155	2785	21.58	2	8	–	40
Cherry, D.D.	1	1	0	11	11	11.00	–	–	–	–
Chilton, M.J.	46	75	5	106*	1964	28.05	3	8	–	41
Clarke, A.C.S.	2	2	0	44	44	22.00	–	–	–	–
Cliffe, J.A.	3	3	0	2	2	0.66	–	–	–	–
Clinton, R.S.	8	15	1	58*	283	20.21	–	1	–	2
Clough, G.D.	5	8	0	33	56	7.00	–	–	–	2
Collingwood, P.D.	84	145	10	153	4094	30.32	7	22	1	87
Collins, B.J.	18	26	3	46	310	13.47	–	–	–	9
Cook, J.W.	20	33	2	137	893	28.80	2	5	–	9
Cook, S.J.	27	37	6	93*	618	19.93	–	2	–	8
Cork, D.G.	195	289	41	200*	6225	25.10	5	34	–	133
Cosker, D.A.	83	96	27	49	752	10.89	–	–	–	55
Cottey, P.A.	238	384	51	203	12209	36.66	24	65	7	162
Cousins, D.M.	39	58	15	29*	456	10.60	–	–	–	8
Cowan, A.P.	90	134	26	94	1873	17.34	–	7	–	42
Cox, J.	185	326	23	245	13910	45.90	41	60	2+2	81
Craven, V.J.	10	15	2	58	284	21.84	–	2	–	8
Crawley, J.P.	237	387	36	286	16530	47.09	40	90	7	162
Croft, R.D.B.	249	362	72	143	7180	24.75	2	32	–	126
Crowe, C.D.	26	33	6	44*	409	15.14	–	–	–	14
Cullinan, D.J.	219	373	53	337*	14110	44.09	38	67	1	209
Cunliffe, R.J.	62	103	6	190*	2421	24.95	3	10	–	52
Dagnall, C.E.	6	4	2	6*	12	6.00	–	–	–	–
Dakin, J.M.	49	71	6	190	1957	30.10	5	10	–	16

144

	M	I	NO	HS	Runs	Avge	100	50	1000	Ct/St
Dale, A.	213	349	30	214*	10829	33.94	20	53	4	85
Daley, J.A.	91	158	12	159*	4142	28.36	4	19	–	43
Dalrymple, J.W.M.	5	10	1	70	203	22.55	–	1	–	8
Daniels, T.J.	1	1	0	0	0	0.00	–	–	–	1/2
Davies, A.P.	13	16	3	40	164	12.61	–	–	–	3
Davies, M.K.	33	48	14	32*	338	9.94	–	–	–	8
Davis, M.J.G.	85	133	21	71	1953	17.43	–	5	–	51
Davis, R.P.	170	210	46	67	2503	15.26	–	5	–	157
Dawes, J.H.	26	33	10	23*	206	8.95	–	–	–	6
Dawson, R.K.J.	10	12	1	37	96	8.72	–	–	–	6
Dean, K.J.	56	70	25	27*	447	9.93	–	–	–	7
DeFreitas, P.A.J.	323	458	43	123*	9433	22.73	8	48	–	110
Dill, G.J.	4	6	1	8	27	5.40	–	–	–	3
Di Venuto, M.J.	134	231	11	189	8755	39.79	17	57	2	117
Dowman, M.P.	93	164	11	149	4350	28.43	9	17	1	50
Drakes, V.C.	131	205	24	180*	4026	22.24	4	16	–	40
Driver, R.C.	20	35	4	64	573	18.48	–	1	–	8
Dumelow, N.R.C.	9	15	1	61	304	21.71	–	2	–	2
Dutch, K.P.	43	57	6	118	1027	20.13	1	6	–	41
Ealham, M.A.	161	255	40	153*	6635	30.86	6	42	1	64
Edwards, A.D.	16	25	3	23	183	8.31	–	–	–	11
Elstub, C.J.	5	6	4	6*	12	6.00	–	–	–	1
Evans, A.W.	38	63	7	125	1503	26.83	1	6	–	24
Fairbrother, N.H.	354	561	79	366	20206	41.92	46	104	10	280
Faisal Iqbal	32	45	4	200	1532	37.36	1	9	–	18
Fellows, G.M.	32	48	6	63	957	22.78	–	4	–	13
Ferley, R.S.	4	5	1	17*	41	10.25	–	–	–	1
Fisher, I.D.	24	32	9	68*	545	23.69	–	2	–	1
Fleming, D.W.	107	128	36	71*	1345	14.61	–	4	–	53
Fleming, M.V.	214	340	42	138	8995	30.18	10	42	–	83
Fleming, S.P.	137	226	21	174*	8517	41.54	16	53	1	179
Flintoff, A.	80	124	10	160	3941	34.57	7	20	–	100
Flower, A.	116	191	38	232*	8047	52.59	23	42	–	236/18
Floyd, M.K.	3	6	1	128*	174	34.80	1	–	–	–
Follett, D.	18	22	8	19	87	6.21	–	–	–	5
Foster, J.S.	23	34	3	103	911	29.38	1	6	–	46/9
Francis, J.D.	2	4	2	72*	131	65.50	–	1	–	1
Francis, S.R.G.	16	22	10	30*	91	7.58	–	–	–	1
Franks, P.J.	71	105	19	85	1862	21.65	–	8	–	30
Fraser, A.R.C.	288	342	82	92	2898	11.14	–	2	–	54
Frost, T.	31	45	6	111*	912	23.38	1	3	–	77/5
Fulton, D.P.	125	217	14	208*	7185	35.39	16	30	1	185
Gait, A.I.	19	35	0	112	937	26.77	2	5	–	19
Gallian, J.E.R.	141	245	23	312	8124	36.59	18	36	2	112
Gannon, B.W.	24	28	12	28	156	9.75	–	–	–	7
Giddins, E.S.H.	137	164	69	34	501	5.27	–	–	–	21
Gilbert, R.G.	1	1	0	0	0	0.00	–	–	–	–
Gilchrist, A.C.	105	158	28	203*	5618	43.21	16	22	–	432/25
Giles, A.F.	108	146	33	128*	3166	28.01	3	13	–	47
Gillespie, J.N.	66	86	17	58	951	13.78	–	3	–	26
Gofton, A.F.	12	17	3	47*	240	17.14	–	–	–	–
Golding, J.M.	7	11	4	30	111	15.85	–	–	–	2
Goodwin, M.W.	72	128	13	203*	5283	45.93	15	25	1	50
Gough, D.	192	260	50	121	3379	16.09	1	12	–	41
Gough, M.A.	46	80	1	123	1752	22.17	1	8	–	43
Grant, J.B.	15	19	9	36*	90	9.00	–	–	–	6

145

	M	I	NO	HS	Runs	Avge	100	50	1000	Ct/St
Gray, A.K.D.	3	4	0	3	4	1.00	–	–	–	2
Grayson, A.P.	158	261	23	189	7593	31.90	14	37	4	109
Greenidge, C.G.	5	5	0	14	29	5.80	–	–	–	3
Griffiths, P.	2	2	1	4*	5	5.00	–	–	–	–
Grove, J.O.	22	27	9	33	191	10.61	–	–	–	2
Guy, S.M.	7	11	3	42	148	18.50	–	–	–	21/2
Habib, A.	103	150	23	215	5686	44.77	15	26	2	47
Hamblin, J.R.C.	1	1	0	5	5	5.00	–	–	–	–
Hamilton, G.M.	78	103	20	125	2230	26.86	1	14	–	27
Hancock, T.H.C.	150	262	16	220*	6737	27.38	6	40	1	95
Hardinges, M.A.	7	7	0	22	60	8.57	–	–	–	2
Harmison, S.J.	58	81	22	36	540	9.15	–	–	–	9
Harris, A.J.	66	94	24	39	624	8.91	–	–	–	20
Harrison, D.S.	3	4	0	27	56	14.00	–	–	–	–
Harvey, I.J.	92	154	11	136	4371	30.56	7	24	–	69
Hatch, N.G.	9	16	8	24	129	16.12	–	–	–	1
Havell, P.M.R.	1									–
Hawinkels, S.J.	1	2	0	26	28	14.00	–	–	–	–
Hayden, M.L.	195	338	34	235*	15752	51.81	48	68	3+3	170
Haynes, J.J.	11	17	3	80	348	24.85	–	2	–	28/2
Hegg, W.K.	288	421	81	134	9524	28.01	7	49	–	698/79
Hemp, D.L.	161	268	24	186*	8465	34.69	17	44	3	107
Hewison, C.J.	1	2	0	24	30	15.00	–	–	–	5
Hewitt, J.P.	60	81	12	75	1216	17.62	–	3	–	23
Hewson, D.R.	51	94	7	168	2172	24.96	2	13	–	23
Hick, G.A.	422	695	65	405*	33793	53.63	117	127	16+1	522
Hicks, T.C.	16	20	2	58	301	16.72	–	2	–	16
Hockley, J.B.	14	21	1	74	341	17.05	–	1	–	8
Hogg, K.W.	1	1	0	19	19	19.00	–	–	–	–
Hoggard, M.J.	53	63	19	21*	269	6.11	–	–	–	11
Hollioake, A.J.	139	212	17	182	7538	38.65	13	45	2	130
Hollioake, B.C.	75	114	6	163	2794	25.87	3	14	–	68
Holloway, P.C.L.	119	200	28	168	5358	31.15	9	28	–	82/1
House, W.J.	37	57	8	136	1443	29.44	2	8	–	21
Hughes, J.	1	2	0	49	87	43.50	–	–	–	–
Hughes, T.R.	9	8	2	13*	26	4.33	–	–	–	1
Hunter, I.D.	11	18	3	63	282	18.80	–	1	–	4
Hussain, N.	286	463	47	207	17349	41.70	44	86	5	314
Hussey, M.E.K.	88	161	12	329*	7437	49.91	18	32	1	70
Hutchison, P.M.	44	45	25	30	200	10.00	–	–	–	9
Hutton, B.L.	33	53	4	139	1315	26.83	3	5	–	33
Hyam, B.J.	60	95	11	63	1381	16.44	–	3	–	168/11
Illingworth, R.K.	376	435	122	120*	7027	22.45	4	21	–	161
Ilott, M.C.	186	240	49	60	2785	14.58	–	4	–	50
Imran Farhat	37	65	5	216	2780	46.33	6	13	–	48
Innes, K.J.	21	32	6	63	522	20.07	–	1	–	10
Inzamam-ul-Haq	186	295	45	201*	12539	50.15	34	65	0+2	140
Irani, R.C.	161	266	32	168*	8461	36.15	15	49	5	64
James, S.P.	230	400	32	309*	14764	40.11	43	55	8	165
Jefferson, W.I.	5	8	0	69	206	25.75	–	1	–	3
Johnson, A.H.V.	4	5	1	55*	72	18.00	–	1	–	5
Johnson, N.C.	125	193	23	150	5744	33.78	8	40	1	157
Johnson, P.	357	599	57	187	19872	36.66	40	114	9	229/1
Johnson, R.L.	105	145	17	69	2127	16.61	–	5	–	45
Jones, G.O.	1	1	0	5	5	5.00	–	–	–	1
Jones, H.R.	2	4	1	57	90	30.00	–	1	–	2

146

	M	I	NO	HS	Runs	Avge	100	50	1000	Ct/St
Jones, I.	3	4	1	35	78	26.00	–	–	–	–
Jones, P.S.	54	64	18	105	756	16.43	1	1	–	14
Jones, S.P.	26	30	7	46	175	7.60	–	–	–	3
Joyce, E.C.	12	19	2	108*	520	30.58	2	1	–	14
Katich, S.M.	62	111	21	228*	4695	52.16	15	20	1+2	67
Keedy, G.	78	89	49	34	444	11.10	–	–	–	21
Keegan, C.B.	7	10	2	30*	45	5.62	–	–	–	1
Kendall, W.S.	106	172	22	201	5488	36.58	9	27	3	93
Kenway, D.A.	54	95	11	166	2812	33.47	4	15	1	44/1
Kerr, J.I.D.	58	83	16	80	1394	20.80	–	5	–	16
Key, R.W.T.	70	118	3	132	3365	29.26	7	18	1	44
Khan, A.	1	–	–	–	–	–	–	–	–	–
Khan, R.M.	1	2	0	13	18	9.00	–	–	–	–
Khan, S.H.	17	15	1	87	266	19.00	–	1	–	5
Khan, W.G.	58	102	8	181	2835	30.15	5	17	–	36
Killeen, N.	45	64	12	48	629	12.09	–	–	–	12
Kirby, S.P.	10	10	2	15*	49	6.12	–	–	–	4
Kirtley, R.J.	93	131	38	59	969	10.41	–	2	–	29
Knight, N.V.	166	274	27	233	10024	40.58	24	48	2	231
Koenig, S.G.	75	131	5	155	4642	36.84	7	25	–	45
Krikken, K.M.	204	305	59	104	5541	22.52	1	25	–	499/31
Kruis, G.J.	50	76	15	59	802	13.14	–	2	–	22
Kumar, V.H.	4	7	1	86*	199	33.16	–	1	–	2
Lampitt, S.R.	236	311	74	122	5649	23.83	1	20	–	148
Laney, J.S.	80	140	5	112	4125	30.55	5	25	1	65
Langer, J.L.	197	346	37	274*	15612	50.52	49	59	3+3	171
Laraman, A.W.	3	1	0	29	29	29.00	–	–	–	2
Lathwell, M.N.	156	272	14	206	8727	33.43	12	57	5	105
Law, D.R.	96	150	6	115	2918	20.26	2	12	–	52
Law, S.G.	234	390	41	263	17590	50.40	54	84	5+1	263
Leatherdale, D.A.	196	316	37	157	9016	32.31	12	48	1	145
Lee, B.	35	38	9	79	515	17.75	–	2	–	7
Lehmann, D.S.	190	323	22	255	16890	56.11	54	77	3+5	104
Lewis, J.	86	127	25	62	1206	11.82	–	2	–	19
Lewis, J.J.B.	140	249	21	210*	7624	33.43	13	44	3	90
Lewry, J.D.	91	126	27	47	965	9.74	–	–	–	17
Liptrot, C.G.	27	33	11	61	271	12.31	–	1	–	9
Lloyd, G.D.	196	310	27	241	10830	38.26	24	59	5	136
Logan, R.J.	18	25	3	37*	214	9.72	–	–	–	6
Loudon, A.G.R.	2	2	0	39	42	21.00	–	–	–	1
Loudon, H.J.H.	3	4	1	16	26	8.66	–	–	–	1
Love, M.L.	105	182	13	228	7647	45.24	18	38	1+1	130
Loye, M.B.	138	221	21	322*	7581	37.90	17	34	3	68
Lucas, D.S.	21	27	8	46*	387	20.36	–	–	–	3
Lumb, M.J.	5	9	2	122	286	40.85	1	2	–	–
Lungley, T.	7	11	4	47	108	15.42	–	–	–	–
McCague, M.J.	135	186	45	72	2324	16.48	–	6	–	75
McGarry, A.C.	10	12	9	4*	6	2.00	–	–	–	2
McGrath, A.	102	173	12	142*	4717	29.29	8	21	–	63
McGrath, G.D.	131	137	45	55	665	7.22	–	1	–	35
Maddy, D.L.	138	218	11	202	6278	30.32	14	27	2	134
Maher, J.P.	106	185	24	217	6622	41.13	14	30	1+1	106
Maiden, G.I.	3	3	1	23*	32	16.00	–	–	–	1
Malcolm, D.E.	284	340	105	51	1820	7.74	–	2	–	41
Malik, M.N.	5	6	5	6*	12	12.00	–	–	–	–
Marsh, D.J.	66	109	20	157	3464	38.92	7	18	–	67

147

	M	I	NO	HS	Runs	Avge	100	50	1000	Ct/St
Martin, P.J.	180	211	54	133	2993	19.06	1	6	–	43
Martin–Jenkins, R.S.C.	53	84	10	113	1936	26.16	1	10	–	15
Martyn, D.R.	141	242	35	203*	10172	49.14	30	53	–	114/2
Mascarenhas, A.D.	70	102	11	104	2104	23.12	2	11	–	26
Mason, M.S.	3	5	1	3	10	2.50	–	–	–	1
Mason, T.J.	20	25	5	52*	311	15.55	–	1	–	8
Masters, D.D.	20	23	9	21	79	5.64	–	–	–	6
Maunders, J.K.	1	2	0	9	13	6.50	–	–	–	1
Maynard, M.P.	350	569	56	243	21518	41.94	48	117	11	332/7
Mees, T.	2	2	0	4	8	4.00	–	–	–	1
Metson, C.P.	232	304	71	96	4062	17.43	–	7	–	561/51
Middlebrook, J.D.	23	31	3	84	485	17.32	–	1	–	14
Millar, N.	5	6	1	36	87	17.40	–	–	–	1
Miller, C.R.	122	145	30	62	1498	13.02	–	3	–	39
Millns, D.J.	171	203	63	121	3082	22.01	3	8	–	76
Mohammad Sami	15	16	10	15	55	9.16	–	–	–	5
Mohammad Wasim	88	139	6	192	4140	31.12	11	15	–	92/5
Montgomerie, R.R.	148	260	26	192	8508	36.35	21	42	3	137
Morris, A.C.	58	76	12	65	1289	20.14	–	7	–	32
Morris, J.E.	362	612	35	229	21539	37.32	52	104	11	156
Mullally, A.D.	199	222	57	75	1456	8.82	–	2	–	40
Munton, T.A.	252	272	98	54*	1827	10.50	–	4	–	82
Muralitharan, M.	135	164	52	67	1258	11.23	–	1	–	71
Murtagh, T.J.	3	4	2	22*	36	18.00	–	–	–	–
Mushtaq Ahmed	193	243	31	90	2884	13.60	–	9	–	89
Napier, G.R.	16	24	2	104	613	27.86	1	2	–	10
Nash, D.C.	71	100	17	114	2356	28.38	3	11	–	135/13
Newell, K.	72	123	14	135	2930	26.88	5	11	–	25
Nixon, P.A.	220	309	70	134*	7617	31.87	12	30	1	570/46
Noffke, A.A.	9	8	2	43	132	22.00	–	–	–	3
Noon, W.M.	89	140	22	83	2474	20.96	–	12	–	187/20
Ormond, J.	62	71	17	50*	737	13.64	–	1	–	12
Ostler, D.P.	186	303	24	208	9698	34.75	14	61	5	232
Panesar, M.S.	2	3	2	10	15	15.00	–	–	–	–
Parker, J.W.R.	1	2	0	83	127	63.50	–	1	–	–
Parkin, O.T.	37	44	20	24*	203	8.45	–	–	–	10
Parsons, K.A.	92	148	15	193*	3704	27.84	5	19	–	82
Patel, M.M.	144	194	38	67	2364	15.15	–	6	–	79
Penberthy, A.L.	163	242	26	132*	6210	28.75	8	35	–	99
Peng, N.	21	37	2	101	782	22.34	1	4	–	9
Penney, T.L.	157	246	45	151	7954	39.57	15	36	2	93/2
Peters, S.D.	62	102	15	110	2245	25.80	2	10	–	46
Pettini, M.L.	1	2	0	41	42	21.00	–	–	–	1
Phillips, B.J.	27	39	4	100*	584	16.68	1	2	–	8
Phillips, N.C.	54	80	16	53	945	14.76	–	3	–	31
Phillips, T.J.	9	12	0	27	107	8.91	–	–	–	1
Pierson, A.R.K.	180	224	70	108*	2651	17.21	1	5	–	87
Pietersen, K.P.	25	39	6	218*	1528	46.30	4	8	1	24
Pipe, D.J.	8	12	0	54	187	15.58	–	1	–	6/2
Piper, K.J.	187	256	42	116*	4318	20.17	2	13	–	476/32
Pollard, P.R.	192	332	24	180	9685	31.44	15	48	3	158
Pollock, S.M.	112	160	29	150*	4314	32.93	5	20	–	73
Ponting, R.T.	130	219	31	233	10016	53.27	34	45	–	125
Porter, J.J.	9	16	1	93	399	26.60	–	4	–	3
Pothas, N.	86	133	25	165	3889	36.00	7	17	–	237/22
Powell, M.J. (Gm)	70	114	12	200*	3710	36.37	8	18	1	39

	M	I	NO	HS	Runs	Avge	100	50	1000	Ct/St
Powell, M.J. (Nh)	1	2	0	1	2	1.00	–	–	–	–
Powell, M.J. (Wa)	67	105	3	236	3348	32.82	7	17	1	53
Pratt, A.	26	41	5	68*	707	19.63	–	3	–	60/7
Pratt, G.J.	4	7	0	37	92	13.14	–	–	–	2
Prichard, P.J.	330	540	49	245	16834	34.28	32	97	8	202
Prior, M.J.	16	24	2	66	433	19.68	–	1	–	39/2
Prittipaul, L.R.	11	15	0	152	463	30.86	1	2	–	7
Pyemont, J.P.	34	51	4	124	1005	21.38	1	5	–	20
Ramprakash, M.R.	300	495	62	235	20142	46.51	55	101	11	177
Randall, S.J.	8	12	2	28	103	10.30	–	–	–	4
Rashid Latif	126	177	31	131*	3935	26.95	2	23	–	331/47
Rashid, U.B.A.	41	63	7	110	1421	25.37	2	7	–	12
Ratcliffe, J.D.	135	242	13	135	6545	28.58	5	38	–	68
Rawnsley, M.J.	42	53	8	39	502	11.15	–	–	–	21
Read, C.M.W.	81	122	19	160	2533	24.59	1	11	–	218/7
Rhodes, S.J.	397	561	149	122*	13461	32.67	11	66	2	1020/114
Richardson, A.	33	27	14	17*	76	5.84	–	–	–	10
Richardson, M.H.	97	166	25	306	6252	44.34	13	28	0+1	48
Richardson, S.A.	8	13	2	69	229	20.81	–	2	–	6
Ripley, D.	307	410	104	209	8693	28.40	9	34	–	678/85
Roberts, T.W.	3	5	0	49	108	21.60	–	–	–	1
Robinson, D.D.J.	107	186	9	200	5083	28.71	10	23	–	87
Robinson, M.A.	228	257	111	27	580	3.97	–	–	–	41
Rollins, A.S.	123	221	19	210	6871	34.01	12	38	3	103/1
Rose, G.D.	248	343	63	191	8653	30.90	11	41	1	116
Roseberry, M.A.	236	401	43	185	11950	33.37	21	58	4	165
Rowe, J.G.C.	3	5	2	74*	128	42.66	–	1	–	1
Russell, R.C.	435	644	134	129*	15404	30.20	8	81	1	1119/122
Saeed Anwar	141	224	7	221	9913	45.68	29	50	1+1	63
Saggers, M.J.	43	55	15	61*	404	10.10	–	1	–	7
Saleem Elahi	67	110	7	229	3566	34.62	5	18	–	52/1
Sales, D.J.G.	74	115	10	303*	3711	35.34	8	15	1	53
Salisbury, I.D.K.	247	316	66	100*	4861	19.44	1	17	–	160
Sanklecha, P.	1	2	1	15*	23	23.00	–	–	–	1
Saqlain Mushtaq	120	171	47	101*	1922	15.50	1	6	–	49
Sayers, C.A.	14	18	6	46	122	10.16	–	–	–	8
Schofield, C.P.	49	68	11	80*	1572	27.57	–	13	–	27
Schofield, J.E.K.	3	5	2	21*	25	8.33	–	–	–	1
Scott, G.M.	1	2	0	25	33	16.50	–	–	–	1
Scott, J.B.	4	5	1	14	27	6.75	–	–	–	–
Scuderi, J.C.	82	130	18	125*	3372	30.10	3	17	–	26
Seccombe, W.A.	73	105	17	151	2246	25.52	2	6	–	333/16
Selwood, S.A.	2	4	0	18	43	10.75	–	–	–	1
Shafayat, B.M.	3	6	0	75	231	38.50	–	2	–	–
Shah, O.A.	78	130	8	203	3991	32.71	9	18	1	56
Shahid Afridi	56	93	3	164	2912	32.35	6	13	–	44
Shahid, N.	128	203	25	139	5556	31.21	7	30	1	125
Sharif, Z.K.	1	2	0	15	17	8.50	–	–	–	1
Sharpe, T.J.	2	2	2	0*	0	–	–	–	–	–
Shaw, A.D.	76	102	16	140	1873	21.77	1	9	–	180/14
Sheikh, M.A.	9	11	2	58*	223	24.77	–	1	–	–
Sheriyar, A.	109	114	41	21	576	7.89	–	–	–	18
Shoaib Akhtar	72	95	38	26	468	8.21	–	–	–	25
Sidebottom, R.J.	38	47	15	54	367	11.46	–	1	–	15
Sillence, R.J.	1	2	0	6	6	3.00	–	–	–	–
Silverwood, C.E.W.	110	142	30	70	1730	15.44	–	5	–	23

149

	M	I	NO	HS	Runs	Avge	100	50	1000	Ct/St
Simcox, A.D.	3	5	1	19	56	14.00	–	–	–	3
Singh, A.	61	98	5	168	2883	31.00	6	11	1	20
Slater, M.J.	196	347	18	221	13722	41.70	33	66	1+1	107
Smalley, R.G.	8	12	1	83	341	31.00	–	2	–	9/5
Smethurst, M.P.	26	31	11	66	195	9.75	–	1	–	4
Smith, A.M.	134	177	48	61	1594	12.35	–	4	–	26
Smith, B.F.	187	284	35	204	9714	39.01	23	41	3	97
Smith, E.T.	79	131	7	190	4561	36.78	9	21	2	23
Smith, G.J.	82	103	39	68	820	12.81	–	2	–	15
Smith, N.M.K.	191	266	34	161	6308	27.18	4	32	1	64
Smith, R.A.	401	677	85	209*	24801	41.89	59	123	11	218
Smith, T.M.	32	42	11	53*	377	12.16	–	1	–	11
Snape, J.N.	85	126	23	131	3123	30.32	3	19	–	60
Solanki, V.S.	126	209	14	185	6882	35.29	12	37	2	158
Speak, N.J.	177	307	34	232	9692	35.50	15	56	3	108
Spearman, C.M.	85	151	8	147	4889	34.18	9	24	–	83
Speight, M.P.	193	323	31	184	9225	31.59	13	48	3	292/5
Spires, J.A.S.	1	–	–	–	–	–	–	–	–	–
Stead, R.A.	2	2	0	28	28	14.00	–	–	–	1
Stelling, W.F.	18	28	2	53	475	18.26	–	1	–	8
Stemp, R.D.	165	196	63	66	1649	12.39	–	3	–	68
Stephenson, J.P.	281	474	45	202*	13847	32.27	24	72	5	174
Stevens, D.I.	37	60	2	130	1316	22.68	1	6	–	21
Stewart, A.J.	417	689	75	271*	24334	39.63	47	133	8	635/27
Strauss, A.J.	46	79	4	176	2707	36.09	4	14	1	19
Strong, M.R.	15	23	8	35*	235	15.66	–	–	–	4
Stubbings, S.D.	41	75	4	135*	2176	30.64	4	10	1	13
Such, P.M.	306	327	125	54	1645	8.14	–	2	–	119
Sutcliffe, I.J.	105	163	13	203	4647	30.98	7	24	1	54
Sutton, L.D.	28	49	7	140*	1136	27.04	2	3	–	39/1
Swann, A.J.	44	70	2	154	1765	25.95	5	7	–	28
Swann, G.P.	74	110	7	130*	2699	26.20	2	12	–	48
Symington, M.J.	3	3	2	36	52	52.00	–	–	–	1
Symonds, A.	123	204	17	254*	7878	42.12	24	31	2	78
Taylor, B.V.	10	11	5	24*	58	9.66	–	–	–	1
Taylor, C.G.	24	42	3	196	1422	36.46	4	4	–	14
Taylor, C.R.	3	6	0	18	60	10.00	–	–	–	1
Taylor, J.P.	183	213	65	86	2253	15.22	–	9	–	61
Thomas, I.J.	10	17	3	82	380	27.14	–	2	–	7
Thomas, S.D.	127	171	36	138	2785	20.62	1	13	–	43
Thorburn, M.	2	2	1	11	19	19.00	–	–	–	–
Thorpe, G.P.	276	459	64	223*	17703	44.81	40	98	8	244
Titchard, S.P.	107	186	14	163	5319	30.92	6	30	–	54
Tolley, C.M.	107	148	31	84	2666	22.78	–	13	–	42
Tournier, M.A.	2	2	0	13	13	6.50	–	–	–	–
Tredwell, J.C.	1	1	0	10	10	10.00	–	–	–	–
Trego, P.D.	10	13	2	62	251	22.81	–	1	–	3
Tremlett, C.T.	8	11	4	26	116	16.57	–	–	–	2
Trescothick, M.E.	124	207	8	190	6444	32.38	10	36	–	131
Trott, B.J.	19	17	6	13	58	5.27	–	–	–	5
Troughton, J.O.	1	2	1	27	32	32.00	–	–	–	–
Tucker, J.P.	2	3	2	14	19	19.00	–	–	–	–
Tudor, A.J.	72	94	24	116	1609	22.98	1	4	–	20
Tufnell, P.C.R.	302	334	128	67*	1977	9.59	–	1	–	103
Turner, R.J.	193	296	51	144	7564	30.87	9	38	2	505/39
Udal, S.D.	183	260	46	117*	4777	22.32	1	21	–	83

	M	I	NO	HS	Runs	Avge	100	50	1000	Ct/St
Van der Gucht, C.G.	2	2	1	38	38	38.00	–	–	–	–
Vaughan, M.P.	159	280	14	183	9360	35.18	21	43	4	77
Wagh, M.A.	82	130	13	315	4571	39.06	12	18	2	35
Walker, M.J.	87	142	15	275*	3830	30.15	7	14	–	56
Wallace, M.A.	16	25	5	80*	504	25.20	–	4	–	49/1
Waqar Younis	198	238	54	55	2278	12.38	–	3	–	47
Ward, D.M.	156	246	34	294*	8139	38.39	16	33	2	122/3
Ward, I.J.	80	134	12	158*	4308	35.31	7	29	1	46
Ward, T.R.	225	386	22	235*	12879	35.38	28	72	6	212
Warne, S.K.	180	240	32	86	3505	16.85	–	11	–	140
Warren, C.C.M.	6	11	2	40*	137	15.22	–	–	–	5
Warren, R.J.	104	169	20	201*	5398	36.22	9	30	1	105/3
Wasim Akram	248	345	39	257*	7036	22.99	7	24	–	96
Watkin, S.L.	266	297	109	51	2037	10.83	–	1	–	71
Waugh, M.E.	331	532	70	229*	24632	53.31	78	120	5+1	399
Waugh, S.R.	304	471	79	216*	20707	52.82	66	86	2	243
Weekes, L.C.	24	36	6	46	535	17.83	–	–	–	17
Weekes, P.N.	160	251	30	171*	7119	32.21	11	34	1	146
Welch, G.	94	138	20	84*	2406	20.38	–	9	–	33
Wells, V.J.	173	268	19	224	8336	33.47	16	41	2	114
Welton, G.E.	45	82	3	200*	1773	22.44	1	8	–	21
Weston, R.M.S.	51	89	4	156	2397	28.20	6	7	–	33
Weston, W.P.C.	162	284	29	205	8817	34.57	17	44	4	82
Wharf, A.G.	43	60	8	101*	908	17.46	2	3	–	22
Wharton, L.J.	18	27	13	13*	44	3.14	–	–	–	3
Whiley, M.J.A.	6	9	2	1*	2	0.28	–	–	–	1
White, C.	191	295	41	186	7886	31.04	11	36	–	133
White, G.W.	120	209	19	156	5961	31.37	9	30	1	101/2
White, R.A.	2	4	0	20	37	9.25	–	–	–	2
Widdup, S.	11	18	1	44	245	14.41	–	–	–	11
Williams, R.C.J.	44	59	9	90	911	18.22	–	5	–	123/17
Willoughby, C.M.	54	75	30	17*	190	4.22	–	–	–	10
Wilton, N.J.	17	26	4	55	353	16.04	–	1	–	37/3
Windows, M.G.N.	112	198	15	184	6296	34.40	13	32	2	67
Wood, J.	96	142	21	63*	1462	12.08	–	2	–	23
Wood, M.J. (Sm)	7	12	0	122	529	44.08	1	4	–	2
Wood, M.J. (Y)	63	106	10	200*	3027	31.53	9	13	2	43
Wortley, T.H.	1	1	0	0	0	0.00	–	–	–	1
Wright, A.S.	1	2	0	30	30	15.00	–	–	–	–
Yardy, M.H.	21	37	7	87*	860	28.66	–	5	–	9
Yates, G.	81	105	36	134*	1772	25.68	3	5	–	38
Younis Khan	47	71	10	221	3235	53.03	12	12	0+1	51
Yousuf Youhana	57	94	6	203	3640	41.81	9	22	–	44
Zuiderent, B.	17	27	1	122	619	23.80	1	3	–	18

BOWLING

'50wS' denotes instances of taking 50 or more wickets in a season. Where these have been achieved outside the British Isles they are shown after a plus sign.

	Runs	Wkts	Avge	Best	5wI	10wM	50wS
Aamer Sohail	5983	157	38.10	7- 53	2	1	–
Abdul Razzaq	4543	144	31.54	7- 51	6	2	–
Adams, C.J.	1830	41	44.63	4- 28	–	–	–
Adams, J.C.	3943	99	39.82	5- 17	1	–	–
Afzaal, U.	3153	62	50.85	4-101	–	–	–
Aldred, P.	4351	127	34.25	7-101	5	1	1

151

	Runs	Wkts	Avge	Best	5wI	10wM	50wS
Ali, Kabir	1122	37	30.32	5- 22	1	–	–
Ali, Kadeer	57	0					
Alleyne, M.W.	12009	377	31.85	6- 49	8	–	1
Amin, R.M.	1053	25	42.12	4- 87	–	–	–
Aminul Islam	258	5	51.60	3- 14	–	–	–
Anderson, R.S.G.	2701	109	24.77	6- 34	8	1	1
Asif Mujtaba	7422	328	22.62	6- 17	18	4	0+2
Atherton, M.A.	4733	108	43.82	6- 78	3	–	–
Austin, I.D.	7954	262	30.35	6- 43	6	1	–
Averis, J.M.M.	3579	76	47.09	5- 52	2	–	–
Aymes, A.N.	438	6	73.00	2-101	–	–	–
Azhar Mahmood	6020	245	24.57	7- 65	9	2	0+1
Bailey, R.J.	5144	121	42.51	5- 54	2	–	–
Ball, M.C.J.	10770	291	37.01	8- 46	10	1	–
Banes, M.J.	162	3	54.00	3- 65	–	–	–
Banks, O.A.C.	481	21	22.90	7- 70	1	1	–
Barnett, K.J.	7034	186	37.81	6- 28	3	–	–
Bassano, C.W.G.	11	0					
Batty, G.J.	128	4	32.00	2- 45	–	–	–
Batty, J.N.	61	1	61.00	1- 21	–	–	–
Bell, I.R.	40	1	40.00	1- 24	–	–	–
Betts, M.M.	7227	262	27.58	9- 64	12	2	–
Bevan, M.G.	4952	112	44.21	6- 82	1	1	–
Bichel, A.J.	8560	354	24.18	6- 44	20	3	1+1
Bicknell, D.J.	789	23	34.30	3- 7	–	–	–
Bicknell, M.P.	21681	898	24.14	9- 45	35	4	10
Bishop, J.E.	1095	27	40.55	5-148	1	–	–
Blackwell, I.D.	3252	71	45.80	5-115	2	–	–
Blain, J.A.R.	955	20	47.75	6- 42	1	–	–
Blakey, R.J.	68	1	68.00	1- 68	–	–	–
Blewett, G.S.	4802	111	43.26	5- 29	1	–	–
Bloomfield, T.F.	4468	141	31.68	5- 36	6	–	1
Boswell, S.A.J.	1665	42	39.64	5- 94	1	–	–
Boulton, N.R.	48	0					
Bowler, P.D.	2018	33	61.15	3- 25	–	–	–
Bracken, N.W.	1148	45	25.51	5- 22	2	–	–
Bressington, A.N.	446	16	27.87	4- 36	–	–	–
Bridge, G.D.	523	19	27.52	6- 84	1	–	–
Brinkley, J.E.	2116	82	25.80	6- 14	4	–	–
Brown, A.D.	425	1	425.00	1- 56	–	–	–
Brown, D.R.	9336	349	26.75	8- 89	13	4	2
Brown, J.F.	4433	154	28.78	7- 78	9	3	1
Brown, S.J.E.	15735	548	28.71	7- 51	36	2	7
Bruce, J.T.A.	211	0					
Bulbeck, M.P.L.	2675	94	28.45	5- 45	3	1	1
Burns, M.	1630	38	42.89	6- 54	1	–	–
Burns, N.D.	8	0					
Butcher, G.P.	2390	63	37.93	7- 77	2	–	–
Butcher, M.A.	3705	112	33.08	5- 86	1	–	–
Byas, D.	727	12	60.58	3- 55	–	–	–
Caddick, A.R.	19468	784	24.83	9- 32	53	14	8
Cairns, C.L.	15625	566	27.60	8- 47	26	6	3
Carpenter, J.R.	81	1	81.00	1- 50	–	–	–
Carter, N.M.	1406	49	28.69	6- 63	3	–	–
Cassar, M.E.	2287	75	30.49	6- 76	2	–	–
Catterall, D.N.	308	11	28.00	4- 50	–	–	–

	Runs	Wkts	Avge	Best	5wI	10wM	50wS
Cawdron, M.J.	1298	53	24.49	6- 25	5	1	–
Chapple, G.	10725	384	27.92	6- 42	15	–	3
Chilton, M.J.	171	2	85.50	1- 1	–	–	–
Clarke, A.C.S.	102	6	17.00	3- 44	–	–	–
Cliffe, J.A.	190	2	95.00	2- 71	–	–	–
Clinton, R.S.	30	2	15.00	2- 30	–	–	–
Clough, G.D.	364	6	60.66	3- 69	–	–	–
Collingwood, P.D.	2143	51	42.01	3- 7	–	–	–
Cook, J.W.	131	1	131.00	1- 17	–	–	–
Cook, S.J.	1985	58	34.22	4- 13	–	–	–
Cork, D.G.	16360	608	26.90	9- 43	20	2	5
Cosker, D.A.	7191	203	35.42	6-140	2	–	–
Cottey, P.A.	862	16	53.87	4- 49	–	–	–
Cousins, D.M.	3632	130	27.93	8-102	4	–	1
Cowan, A.P.	7930	239	33.17	6- 47	7	–	1
Cox, J.	323	4	80.75	3- 46	–	–	–
Craven, V.J.	84	0					
Crawley, J.P.	201	1	201.00	1- 90	–	–	–
Croft, R.D.B.	24402	676	36.09	8- 66	30	5	5
Crowe, C.D.	1332	41	32.48	4- 47	–	–	–
Cullinan, D.J.	329	7	47.00	2- 27	–	–	–
Dagnall, C.E.	548	23	23.82	6- 50	1	–	–
Dakin, J.M.	2750	74	37.16	4- 27	–	–	–
Dale, A.	7614	208	36.60	6- 18	4	–	–
Daley, J.A.	81	1	81.00	1- 12	–	–	–
Dalrymple, J.W.M.	578	10	57.80	4- 86	–	–	–
Davies, A.P.	944	25	37.76	3- 76	–	–	–
Davies, M.K.	2566	96	26.72	6- 49	5	–	–
Davis, M.J.G.	5687	165	34.46	8- 37	4	1	–
Davis, R.P.	14704	421	34.92	7- 64	17	2	2
Dawes, J.H.	2474	113	21.89	7- 98	4	1	–
Dawson, R.K.J.	1129	31	36.41	6- 82	2	–	–
Dean, K.J.	4725	208	22.71	8- 52	11	2	1
DeFreitas, P.A.J.	30302	1094	27.69	7- 21	55	5	12
Dill, G.J.	301	5	60.20	2- 54	–	–	–
Di Venuto, M.J.	401	5	80.20	1- 0	–	–	–
Dowman, M.P.	1171	25	46.84	3- 10	–	–	–
Drakes, V.C.	12848	508	25.29	8- 59	23	3	2+2
Driver, R.C.	77	2	38.50	1- 13	–	–	–
Dumelow, N.R.C.	723	14	51.64	4- 81	–	–	–
Dutch, K.P.	2459	73	33.68	6- 62	1	–	–
Ealham, M.A.	10166	359	28.31	8- 36	16	1	–
Edwards, A.D.	1109	26	42.65	5- 34	1	–	–
Elstub, C.J.	240	10	24.00	3- 37	–	–	–
Evans, A.W.	5	0					
Fairbrother, N.H.	473	7	67.57	2- 91	–	–	–
Faisal Iqbal	56	0					
Fellows, G.M.	865	22	39.31	3- 23	–	–	–
Ferley, R.S.	337	7	48.14	3- 52	–	–	–
Fisher, I.D.	1384	43	32.18	5- 35	2	–	–
Fleming, D.W.	10117	363	27.87	7- 90	13	1	–
Fleming, M.V.	10123	284	35.64	5- 51	2	–	–
Fleming, S.P.	129	0					
Flintoff, A.	2412	71	33.97	5- 24	1	–	–
Flower, A.	189	4	47.25	1- 1	–	–	–
Follett, D.	1509	44	34.29	8- 22	3	1	–

153

	Runs	Wkts	Avge	Best	5wI	10wM	50wS
Foster, J.S.	6	0					
Francis, J.D.	34	1	34.00	1- 34	–	–	–
Francis, S.R.G.	1232	25	49.28	4- 95	–	–	–
Franks, P.J.	6434	233	27.61	7- 56	8	–	2
Fraser, A.R.C.	24087	879	27.40	8- 53	35	5	7
Frost, T.	6	0					
Fulton, D.P.	112	1	112.00	1- 37	–	–	–
Gallian, J.E.R.	3825	94	40.69	6-115	1	–	–
Gannon, B.W.	2104	70	30.05	6- 80	3	–	–
Giddins, E.S.H.	12490	443	28.19	6- 47	22	2	4
Gilbert, R.G.	54	0					
Giles, A.F.	8658	329	26.31	8- 90	15	2	2
Gillespie, J.N.	5868	241	24.34	7- 34	11	–	0+1
Gofton, A.F.	724	10	72.40	3- 41	–	–	–
Golding, J.M.	442	8	55.25	3- 23	–	–	–
Goodwin, M.W.	337	7	48.14	2- 23	–	–	–
Gough, D.	18627	705	26.42	7- 28	27	3	5
Gough, M.A.	1109	25	44.36	5- 66	1	–	–
Grant, J.B.	980	23	42.60	3- 43	–	–	–
Gray, A.K.D.	281	10	28.10	4-128	–	–	–
Grayson, A.P.	5242	119	44.05	5- 20	1	–	–
Greenidge, C.G.	337	12	28.08	5- 60	1	–	–
Griffiths, P.	116	3	38.66	2- 51	–	–	–
Grove, J.O.	1873	41	45.68	5- 90	1	–	–
Guy, S.M.	8	0					
Habib, A.	52	0					
Hamblin, J.R.C.	88	1	88.00	1- 88	–	–	–
Hamilton, G.M.	6002	238	25.21	7- 50	9	2	1
Hancock, T.H.C.	1658	44	37.68	3- 5	–	–	–
Hardinges, M.A.	454	10	45.40	2- 16	–	–	–
Harmison, S.J.	5753	183	31.43	6-111	4	–	2
Harris, A.J.	6990	209	33.44	6- 40	9	1	1
Harrison, D.S.	109	1	109.00	1- 15	–	–	–
Harvey, I.J.	6806	250	27.22	7- 44	10	1	–
Hatch, N.G.	867	26	33.34	3- 42	–	–	–
Havell, P.M.R.	16	0					
Hawinkels, S.J.	3	0					
Hayden, M.L.	671	17	39.47	3- 10	–	–	–
Hegg, W.K.	7	0					
Hemp, D.L.	778	17	45.76	3- 23	–	–	–
Hewitt, J.P.	4856	170	28.56	6- 14	5	–	–
Hewson, D.R.	44	1	44.00	1- 7	–	–	–
Hick, G.A.	10126	231	43.83	5- 18	5	1	–
Hicks, T.C.	1636	37	44.21	5- 54	2	–	–
Hockley, J.B.	233	3	77.66	1- 21	–	–	–
Hogg, K.W.	30	3	10.00	3- 17	–	–	–
Hoggard, M.J.	4460	197	22.63	6- 51	8	–	1
Hollioake, A.J.	4159	103	40.37	5- 62	1	–	–
Hollioake, B.C.	4215	126	33.45	5- 51	1	–	–
Holloway, P.C.L.	69	0					
House, W.J.	964	4	241.00	1- 34	–	–	–
Hughes, T.R.	685	16	42.81	3- 55	–	–	–
Hunter, I.D.	928	22	42.18	4- 55	–	–	–
Hussain, N.	323	2	161.50	1- 38	–	–	–
Hussey, M.E.K.	248	5	49.60	2- 21	–	–	–
Hutchison, P.M.	3562	155	22.98	7- 31	7	1	1

154

	Runs	Wkts	Avge	Best	5wI	10wM	50wS
Hutton, B.L.	576	9	64.00	2- 9	–	–	–
Hyam, B.J.	8	0					
Illingworth, R.K.	26213	831	31.54	7- 50	27	6	5
Ilott, M.C.	16898	617	27.38	9- 19	27	3	6
Imran Farhat	1002	32	31.31	7- 31	2	–	–
Innes, K.J.	1117	38	29.39	4- 61	–	–	–
Inzamam-ul-Haq	1294	37	34.97	5- 80	2	–	–
Irani, R.C.	9171	301	30.46	6- 79	8	–	1
James, S.P.	3	0					
Johnson, N.C.	6299	197	31.97	5- 79	2	–	–
Johnson, P.	605	6	100.83	1- 9	–	–	–
Johnson, R.L.	9186	337	27.25	10- 45	12	2	4
Jones, G.O.	4	0					
Jones, I.	341	6	56.83	3- 81	–	–	–
Jones, P.S.	5138	147	34.95	6- 67	3	–	1
Jones, S.P.	2382	53	44.94	5- 31	1	–	–
Joyce, E.C.	102	0					
Katich, S.M.	861	15	57.40	3- 21	–	–	–
Keedy, G.	7132	198	36.02	6- 56	6	2	–
Keegan, C.B.	588	18	32.66	4- 54	–	–	–
Kendall, W.S.	453	10	45.30	3- 37	–	–	–
Kenway, D.A.	142	3	47.33	1- 5	–	–	–
Kerr, J.I.D.	4558	113	40.33	7- 23	2	–	–
Key, R.W.T.	40	0					
Khan, A.	46	1	46.00	1- 46	–	–	–
Khan, S.H.	1485	21	70.71	3- 70	–	–	–
Khan, W.G.	62	0					
Killeen, N.	3838	139	27.61	7- 85	6	–	1
Kirby, S.P.	980	47	20.85	7- 50	3	1	–
Kirtley, R.J.	8837	350	25.24	7- 21	20	3	4
Knight, N.V.	191	1	191.00	1- 61	–	–	–
Koenig, S.G.	67	1	67.00	1- 0	–	–	–
Krikken, K.M.	121	1	121.00	1- 54	–	–	–
Kruis, G.J.	4750	161	29.50	7- 58	6	–	–
Lampitt, S.R.	17224	601	28.65	7- 45	20	–	7
Laney, J.S.	224	2	112.00	1- 24	–	–	–
Langer, J.L.	199	5	39.80	2- 17	–	–	–
Laraman, A.W.	75	6	12.50	4- 33	–	–	–
Lathwell, M.N.	721	13	55.46	2- 21	–	–	–
Law, D.R.	6317	194	32.56	6- 53	8	–	–
Law, S.G.	3883	80	48.53	5- 39	1	–	–
Leatherdale, D.A.	3434	111	30.93	5- 20	2	–	–
Lee, B.	3400	145	23.44	6- 25	7	–	–
Lehmann, D.S.	2041	48	42.52	4- 42	–	–	–
Lewis, J.	7625	294	25.93	8- 95	13	1	3
Lewis, J.J.B.	121	1	121.00	1- 73	–	–	–
Lewry, J.D.	8489	330	25.72	7- 38	20	3	4
Liptrot, C.G.	1955	62	31.53	6- 44	2	–	–
Lloyd, G.D.	440	2	220.00	1- 4	–	–	–
Logan, R.J.	2006	62	32.35	6- 93	4	–	–
Loudon, A.G.R.	86	3	28.66	3- 86	–	–	–
Love, M.L.	5	1	5.00	1- 5	–	–	–
Loye, M.B.	43	0					
Lucas, D.S.	1853	50	37.06	5-104	1	–	–
Lumb, M.J.	10	2	5.00	2- 10	–	–	–
Lungley, T.	568	18	31.55	3- 10	–	–	–

	Runs	Wkts	Avge	Best	5wI	10wM	50wS
McCague, M.J.	12392	456	27.17	9- 86	25	2	4
McGarry, A.C.	1013	20	50.65	3- 29	–	–	–
McGrath, A.	581	18	32.27	3- 18	–	–	–
McGrath, G.D.	12184	598	20.37	8- 38	34	7	1+1
Maddy, D.L.	1889	55	34.34	5- 67	1	–	–
Maher, J.P.	500	10	50.00	3- 11	–	–	–
Maiden, G.I.	139	6	23.16	2- 11	–	–	–
Malcolm, D.E.	29789	980	30.39	9- 57	41	8	8
Malik, M.N.	414	10	41.40	5- 57	1	–	–
Marsh, D.J.	4974	120	41.45	7- 57	1	–	–
Martin, P.J.	13937	502	27.76	8- 32	15	1	3
Martin-Jenkins, R.S.C.	3830	127	30.15	7- 54	2	–	–
Martyn, D.R.	1372	34	40.35	4- 30	–	–	–
Mascarenhas, A.D.	4393	139	31.60	6- 26	4	–	–
Mason, M.S.	249	4	62.25	2- 60	–	–	–
Mason, T.J.	1252	30	41.73	5- 40	1	–	–
Masters, D.D.	1440	55	26.18	6- 27	3	–	–
Maynard, M.P.	861	6	143.50	3- 21	–	–	–
Mees, T.	222	7	31.71	6- 64	1	–	–
Metson, C.P.	0	0					
Middlebrook, J.D.	1458	49	29.75	6- 82	1	1	–
Millar, N.	139	2	69.50	2- 50	–	–	–
Miller, C.R.	13380	440	30.40	7- 49	16	3	0+1
Millns, D.J.	15129	553	27.35	9- 37	23	4	4
Mohammad Sami	1476	66	22.36	6- 72	5	–	–
Mohammad Wasim	144	3	48.00	2- 12	–	–	–
Montgomerie, R.R.	89	1	89.00	1- 0	–	–	–
Morris, A.C.	4007	156	25.68	5- 39	5	1	2
Morris, J.E.	958	8	119.75	1- 6	–	–	–
Mullally, A.D.	17422	627	27.78	9- 93	29	4	5
Munton, T.A.	19065	737	25.86	8- 89	35	6	6
Muralitharan, M.	14562	722	20.16	9- 65	60	16	2+3
Murtagh, T.J.	120	8	15.00	6- 86	1	–	–
Mushtaq Ahmed	21310	802	26.57	9- 93	53	16	4+1
Napier, G.R.	638	17	37.52	3- 55	–	–	–
Nash, D.C.	19	1	19.00	1- 8	–	–	–
Newell, K.	1023	24	42.62	4- 61	–	–	–
Nixon, P.A.	14	0					
Noffke, A.A.	905	30	30.16	5- 41	1	–	–
Noon, W.M.	34	0					
Ormond, J.	5731	225	25.47	6- 33	13	–	1
Ostler, D.P.	249	1	249.00	1- 46	–	–	–
Panesar, M.S.	358	11	32.54	4- 11	–	–	–
Parker, J.W.R.	8	0					
Parkin, O.T.	2745	100	27.45	5- 24	2	–	–
Parsons, K.A.	2722	63	43.20	5- 13	2	–	–
Patel, M.M.	13278	434	30.59	8- 96	22	9	3
Penberthy, A.L.	8164	214	38.14	5- 37	4	–	–
Penney, T.L.	184	6	30.66	3- 18	–	–	–
Peters, S.D.	19	1	19.00	1- 19	–	–	–
Phillips, B.J.	1914	65	29.44	5- 47	2	–	–
Phillips, N.C.	4890	103	47.47	6- 97	4	1	–
Phillips, T.J.	860	14	61.42	4- 42	–	–	–
Pierson, A.R.K.	13787	363	37.98	8- 42	14	–	1
Pietersen, K.P.	1529	32	47.78	4-141	–	–	–
Piper, K.J.	60	1	60.00	1- 57	–	–	–

	Runs	Wkts	Avge	Best	5wI	10wM	50wS
Pollard, P.R.	272	4	68.00	2- 79	–	–	–
Pollock, S.M.	9054	420	21.55	7- 33	18	1	–
Ponting, R.T.	632	12	52.66	2- 10	–	–	–
Porter, J.J.	134	4	33.50	3- 50	–	–	–
Pothas, N.	5	0					
Powell, M.J. (Gm)	111	2	55.50	2- 39	–	–	–
Powell, M.J. (Wa)	309	7	44.14	2- 16	–	–	–
Prichard, P.J.	497	2	248.50	1- 28	–	–	–
Prittipaul, L.R.	86	0					
Pyemont, J.P.	673	11	61.18	4-101	–	–	–
Ramprakash, M.R.	2041	32	63.78	3- 32	–	–	–
Randall, S.J.	811	8	101.37	2- 64	–	–	–
Rashid Latif	158	5	31.60	2- 17	–	–	–
Rashid, U.B.A.	2073	49	42.30	5-103	1	–	–
Ratcliffe, J.D.	897	26	34.50	6- 48	1	–	–
Rawnsley, M.J.	3009	72	41.79	6- 44	3	1	–
Read, C.M.W.	25	0					
Rhodes, S.J.	30	0					
Richardson, A.	2622	89	29.46	8- 51	2	1	–
Richardson, M.H.	1861	41	45.39	5- 77	1	–	–
Ripley, D.	103	2	51.50	2- 89	–	–	–
Robinson, D.D.J.	99	0					
Robinson, M.A.	17669	579	30.51	9- 37	13	2	2
Rollins, A.S.	122	1	122.00	1- 19	–	–	–
Rose, G.D.	17868	604	29.58	7- 47	15	1	5
Roseberry, M.A.	406	4	101.50	1- 1	–	–	–
Russell, R.C.	68	1	68.00	1- 4	–	–	–
Saeed Anwar	412	9	45.77	3- 83	–	–	–
Saggers, M.J.	3660	160	22.87	7- 79	7	–	2
Saleem Elahi	47	0					
Sales, D.J.G.	163	9	18.11	4- 25	–	–	–
Salisbury, I.D.K.	22088	690	32.01	8- 60	34	6	6
Saqlain Mushtaq	11832	566	20.90	8- 65	46	12	4+1
Sayers, C.A.	357	2	178.50	2- 21	–	–	–
Schofield, C.P.	4295	137	31.35	6-120	4	–	–
Schofield, J.E.K.	285	13	21.92	4- 51	–	–	–
Scott, G.M.	11	0					
Scott, J.B.	320	4	80.00	1- 33	–	–	–
Scuderi, J.C.	6073	179	33.92	7- 79	8	1	–
Seccombe, W.A.	3	0					
Shah, O.A.	612	17	36.00	3- 33	–	–	–
Shahid Afridi	3557	125	28.45	6-101	5	–	–
Shahid, N.	1999	43	46.48	3- 91	–	–	–
Sharif, Z.K.	23	0					
Sharpe, T.J.	150	1	150.00	1- 49	–	–	–
Shaw, A.D.	7	0					
Sheikh, M.A.	442	15	29.46	4- 36	–	–	–
Sheriyar, A.	10970	376	29.17	7-130	16	3	3
Shoaib Akhtar	7000	234	29.91	6- 69	16	–	0+1
Sidebottom, R.J.	2529	103	24.55	6- 16	5	1	–
Sillence, R.J.	100	5	20.00	5- 97	1	–	–
Silverwood, C.E.W.	9528	361	26.39	7- 93	18	1	2
Singh, A.	111	0					
Slater, M.J.	97	3	32.33	1- 4	–	–	–
Smethurst, M.P.	1909	76	25.11	7- 37	3	–	1
Smith, A.M.	11217	456	24.59	8- 73	20	5	5

	Runs	Wkts	Avge	Best	5wI	10wM	50wS
Smith, B.F.	261	2	130.50	1- 5	–	–	–
Smith, E.T.	45	0					
Smith, G.J.	6952	251	27.69	6- 35	9	1	1
Smith, N.M.K.	13149	358	36.72	7- 42	17	–	–
Smith, R.A.	993	14	70.92	2- 11	–	–	–
Smith, T.M.	2135	73	29.24	6- 32	5	1	–
Snape, J.N.	4380	95	46.10	5- 65	1	–	–
Solanki, V.S.	3172	72	44.05	5- 69	3	1	–
Speak, N.J.	191	2	95.50	1- 0	–	–	–
Spearman, C.M.	55	1	55.00	1- 37	–	–	–
Speight, M.P.	32	2	16.00	1- 2	–	–	–
Spires, J.A.S.	155	2	77.50	2- 73	–	–	–
Stead, R.A.	107	0					
Stelling, W.F.	1029	33	31.18	5- 49	1	–	–
Stemp, R.D.	13495	384	35.14	6- 37	14	1	–
Stephenson, J.P.	11253	332	33.89	7- 51	10	–	–
Stevens, D.I.	53	1	53.00	1- 5	–	–	–
Stewart, A.J.	423	3	141.00	1- 7	–	–	–
Strauss, A.J.	16	0					
Strong, M.R.	1426	31	46.00	4- 46	–	–	–
Stubbings, S.D.	77	0					
Such, P.M.	25936	849	30.54	8- 93	48	9	6
Sutcliffe, I.J.	279	8	34.87	2- 21	–	–	–
Swann, A.J.	246	5	49.20	2- 30	–	–	–
Swann, G.P.	6148	190	32.35	6- 41	8	1	1
Symington, M.J.	215	7	30.71	3- 55	–	–	–
Symonds, A.	3606	91	39.62	4- 39	–	–	–
Taylor, B.V.	771	16	48.18	3- 27	–	–	–
Taylor, C.G.	136	3	45.33	3-126	–	–	–
Taylor, J.P.	16618	559	29.72	7- 23	18	4	6
Thomas, I.J.	2	0					
Thomas, S.D.	12230	396	30.88	8- 50	15	–	4
Thorburn, M.	159	2	79.50	1- 76	–	–	–
Thorpe, G.P.	1305	25	52.20	4- 40	–	–	–
Titchard, S.P.	195	4	48.75	1- 11	–	–	–
Tolley, C.M.	6623	189	35.04	7- 45	5	–	–
Tournier, M.A.	184	3	61.33	3-117	–	–	–
Tredwell, J.C.	123	2	61.50	1- 38	–	–	–
Trego, P.D.	846	22	38.45	4- 84	–	–	–
Tremlett, C.T.	492	26	18.92	4- 16	–	–	–
Trescothick, M.E.	1434	36	39.83	4- 36	–	–	–
Trott, B.J.	1552	58	26.75	6- 13	4	1	–
Troughton, J.O.	17	0					
Tucker, J.P.	129	1	129.00	1- 28	–	–	–
Tudor, A.J.	5872	219	26.81	7- 48	12	–	–
Tufnell, P.C.R.	29636	1012	29.28	8- 29	49	6	9
Turner, R.J.	58	0					
Udal, S.D.	17247	506	34.08	8- 50	25	4	6
Van der Gucht, C.G.	138	4	34.50	3- 75	–	–	–
Vaughan, M.P.	4703	108	43.54	4- 39	–	–	–
Wagh, M.A.	2199	43	51.13	4- 11	–	–	–
Walker, M.J.	390	8	48.75	1- 3	–	–	–
Waqar Younis	18610	848	21.94	8- 17	59	14	4+1
Ward, D.M.	113	2	56.50	2- 66	–	–	–
Ward, I.J.	102	0					
Ward, T.R.	647	8	80.87	2- 10	–	–	–

	Runs	Wkts	Avge	Best	5wI	10wM	50wS
Warne, S.K.	19693	752	26.18	8- 71	36	5	3+1
Warren, R.J.	0	0					
Wasim Akram	21886	1011	21.64	8- 30	70	16	5
Watkin, S.L.	25191	902	27.92	8- 59	31	4	9
Waugh, M.E.	8002	204	39.22	6- 68	3	–	–
Waugh, S.R.	7783	243	32.02	6- 51	5	–	–
Weekes, L.C.	1871	69	27.11	6- 56	2	–	–
Weekes, P.N.	7937	203	39.09	8- 39	4	–	–
Welch, G.	7867	228	34.50	6- 30	7	1	1
Wells, V.J.	6984	261	26.75	5- 18	4	–	–
Welton, G.E.	5	0					
Weston, R.M.S.	104	2	52.00	1- 15	–	–	–
Weston, W.P.C.	640	4	160.00	2- 39	–	–	–
Wharf, A.G.	3391	102	33.24	5- 63	2	–	–
Wharton, L.J.	1108	20	55.40	5- 96	1	–	–
Whiley, M.J.A.	432	4	108.00	1- 44	–	–	–
White, C.	9129	334	27.33	8- 55	9	–	–
White, G.W.	565	11	51.36	3- 23	–	–	–
White, R.A.	7	0					
Widdup, S.	22	1	22.00	1- 22	–	–	–
Willoughby, C.M.	4459	178	25.05	5- 26	3	–	0+1
Windows, M.G.N.	111	2	55.50	1- 6	–	–	–
Wood, J.	9059	269	33.67	7- 58	11	–	1
Wood, M.J. (Sm)	30	0					
Wood, M.J. (Y)	16	0					
Wortley, T.H.	50	3	16.66	2- 17	–	–	–
Yardy, M.H.	145	1	145.00	1- 13	–	–	–
Yates, G.	6949	184	37.76	6- 64	5	–	–
Younis Khan	398	7	56.85	3- 24	–	–	–
Yousuf Youhana	11	0					

STOP PRESS

ICC ELITE UMPIRES PANEL

As we go to press the ICC has revealed the names of the eight umpires appointed to the elite panel which will supervise all Test matches from 11 April 2002. Appointed for a two-year period, this panel will also provide one umpire for every limited-overs international from 10 April. Peter Willey was originally selected for this octet but declined to accept for family reasons. The elite eight are: S.A.Bucknor (West Indies), E.A.R.de Silva (Sri Lanka), D.J.Harper (Australia), R.E.Koertzen and D.L.Orchard (South Africa), D.R.Shepherd (England), R.B.Tiffin (Zimbabwe) and S.Venkataraghavan (India).

LEADING CURRENT PLAYERS

The leading career batting/bowling averages and wicket-keeping/fielding aggregates among players currently registered for first-class county cricket. All figures are to the end of the 2001 English season.

BATTING

(Qualification: 100 innings)

	Runs	Avge
D.S.Lehmann	16890	56.11
M.G.Bevan	14420	55.46
G.A.Hick	33793	53.63
A.Flower	8047	52.59
S.G.Law	17590	50.40
M.E.K.Hussey	7437	49.91
J.P.Crawley	16530	47.09
M.R.Ramprakash	20142	46.51
M.W.Goodwin	5283	45.93
J.Cox	13910	45.90
M.L.Love	7647	45.24
G.P.Thorpe	17703	44.81
A.Habib	5686	44.77
A.D.Brown	9356	43.11
A.Symonds	7878	42.12
M.P.Maynard	21518	41.94
N.H.Fairbrother	20206	41.92
R.A.Smith	24801	41.89
N.Hussain	17349	41.70
J.P.Maher	6622	41.13
P.D.Bowler	17290	40.68
N.V.Knight	10024	40.58
R.J.Bailey	21844	40.52
K.J.Barnett	27952	40.16
S.P.James	14764	40.11
M.J.Di Venuto	8755	39.79
A.J.Stewart	24334	39.63
T.L.Penney	7954	39.57
M.A.Wagh	4571	39.06
B.F.Smith	9714	39.01
D.J.Bicknell	15108	38.93
M.A.Butcher	10292	38.83
A.J.Hollioake	7538	38.65
G.D.Lloyd	10830	38.26
M.B.Loye	7581	37.90
C.J.Adams	12936	37.27

BOWLING

(Qualification: 100 wickets)

	Wkts	Avge
Saqlain Mushtaq	566	20.90
S.M.Pollock	420	21.55
M.J.Hoggard	197	22.63
K.J.Dean	208	22.71
M.J.Saggers	160	22.87
P.M.Hutchison	155	22.98
M.P.Bicknell	898	24.14
A.J.Bichel	354	24.18
R.J.Sidebottom	103	24.55
A.M.Smith	456	24.59
R.S.G.Anderson	109	24.77
A.R.Caddick	784	24.83
G.M.Hamilton	238	25.21
R.J.Kirtley	350	25.24
J.Ormond	225	25.47
A.C.Morris	156	25.68
J.D.Lewry	330	25.72
T.A.Munton	737	25.86
J.Lewis	294	25.93
A.F.Giles	329	26.31
C.E.W.Silverwood	361	26.39
D.Gough	705	26.42
D.R.Brown	349	26.750
V.J.Wells	261	26.758
A.J.Tudor	219	26.81
D.G.Cork	608	26.90
M.J.McCague	456	27.17
I.J.Harvey	250	27.22
R.L.Johnson	337	27.25
C.White	334	27.33
M.C.Ilott	617	27.38
A.R.C.Fraser	879	27.40
O.T.Parkin	100	27.45
M.M.Betts	262	27.58
C.L.Cairns	566	27.60
N.Killeen	139	27.611
P.J.Franks	233	27.613
G.J.Smith	251	27.697
P.A.J.DeFreitas	1094	27.698

WICKET-KEEPING

	Total	Ct	St
R.C.Russell	1241	1119	122
S.J.Rhodes	1134	1020	114
W.K.Hegg	777	698	79
R.J.Blakey	772	717	55
A.J.Stewart	662	635	27
P.A.Nixon	616	570	46
R.J.Turner	544	505	39
A.N.Aymes	543	500	43
K.M.Krikken	530	499	31
K.J.Piper	508	476	32

FIELDING

	Ct
G.A.Hick	522
M.P.Maynard	332
N.Hussain	314
K.J.Barnett	283
N.H.Fairbrother	280
C.J.Adams	279
R.J.Bailey	272
S.G.Law	263

LIMITED-OVERS CAREER RECORDS

Compiled by **PHILIP BAILEY**

The following career records, to the end of the 2001 season, include all players currently registered with first-class counties. These records are restricted to performances in limited-overs matches of 'List A' status as defined by the Association of Cricket Statisticians and Historians. The following matches qualify for List A status and are included in the figures that follow:

> Limited-Overs Internationals
> Other international matches (e.g. Commonwealth Games, 'A' team internationals)
> Premier domestic limited-overs tournaments in Test status countries
> Official tourist matches against the main first-class teams

The following matches do NOT qualify for inclusion:

> World Cup warm-up games
> Tourist matches against first-class teams outside the major domestic competitions (e.g. Universities, Minor Counties, etc.)
> Festival and pre-season friendly games

	M	Runs	Avge	HS	100	50	Wkts	Avge	Best	Ct/St
Abdul Razzaq	103	1745	24.92	87*	–	10	142	25.49	5-31	14
Adams, C.J.	258	8095	39.48	163	16	51	32	37.09	5-16	124
Adshead, S.J.	5	72	24.00	29	–	–				5/3
Afzaal, U.	61	1566	38.19	95*	–	13	20	31.15	3-51	17
Aldred, P.	82	360	12.00	39*	–	–	93	29.23	4-30	14
Ali, Kabir	28	49	5.44	11	–	–	42	19.92	4-22	6
Ali, Kadeer	3	58	19.33	24	–	–				
Alleyne, D.	15	208	13.86	58	–	1				16/6
Alleyne, M.W.	366	7246	27.65	134*	5	29	337	30.13	5-27	154/1
Ambrose, T.R.	4	164	41.00	87	–	1				3/3
Amin, R.M.	3	–	–	–	–	–	2	32.00	2-43	1
Anderson, J.M.	3	5	–	5*	–	–	4	32.75	2-64	
Anderson, R.S.G.	20	64	5.33	22	–	–	11	65.09	3-32	1
Atherton, M.A.	287	9343	36.49	127	14	59	24	29.62	4-42	111
Austin, I.D.	314	2285	18.13	97	–	4	359	28.04	5-56	53
Averis, J.M.M.	69	177	8.85	23*	–	–	111	21.91	5-20	9
Aymes, A.N.	221	2210	23.26	73*	–	6	–	–	–	215/53
Bailey, R.J.	395	12057	38.89	153*	10	79	69	36.92	5-45	111
Bailey, T.M.B.	26	169	12.07	52	–	1				19/11
Baker, T.M.	4	3	3.00	3	–	–	4	22.25	2-13	3
Ball, M.C.J.	201	1332	13.59	51	–	1	183	33.76	5-42	89
Banes, M.J.	1	82	82.00	82	–	1				
Barnett, K.J.	506	15085	35.24	136	16	88	111	25.78	6-24	168
Bassano, C.W.G.	9	189	23.62	45	–	–				3
Batty, G.J.	23	457	26.88	83*	–	3	17	37.23	4-36	8
Batty, J.N.	65	424	12.11	40	–	–				57/10
Bell, I.R.	2	58	29.00	48	–	–				
Benham, C.C.	1	0	0.00	0	–	–				
Betts, M.M.	75	303	10.10	21	–	–	89	30.48	4-22	12
Bevan, M.G.	311	11584	60.64	157*	10	92	90	33.08	5-29	98
Bichel, A.J.	90	875	19.88	100	1	–	117	27.76	5-21	32
Bicknell, D.J.	211	6992	39.06	135*	10	48	3	27.33	1-11	53
Bicknell, M.P.	293	1358	16.16	66*	–	2	380	24.81	7-30	70
Bishop, J.E.	17	49	5.44	16*	–	–	19	28.52	3-33	3
Blackwell, I.D.	78	1516	24.45	97	–	10	53	31.98	4-36	25
Blain, J.A.R.	21	44	7.33	11	–	–	31	29.58	5-24	5
Blakey, R.J.	334	7047	32.47	130*	3	36	–	–	–	324/48
Blewett, G.S.	140	4009	32.59	131	3	23	88	34.45	4-18	50
Bloomfield, T.F.	43	51	7.28	15	–	–	35	38.05	4-17	7

161

L-O	M	Runs	Avge	HS	100	50	Wkts	Avge	Best	Ct/St
Bopara, R.S.	1	1	1.00	1	–	–	–	–	–	–
Boswell, S.A.J.	47	63	5.72	23*	–	–	41	36.48	4-44	5
Boulton, N.R.	7	93	18.60	39	–	–	–	–	–	–
Bowler, P.D.	299	8722	32.30	138*	6	68	13	40.84	3-31	113/2
Bresnan, T.T.	4	12	12.00	7	–	–	4	21.50	2-27	2
Bressington, A.N.	6	118	29.50	54	–	1	6	30.33	3-21	4
Bridge, G.D.	13	50	10.00	15	–	–	12	38.08	3-44	5
Brignull, D.S.	2	15	15.00	9*	–	–	4	21.25	2-35	1
Brinkley, J.E.	42	136	8.50	30*	–	–	40	31.35	3-55	6
Brophy, G.J.	22	276	21.23	50*	–	1	–	–	–	22/4
Brown, A.D.	263	7503	31.39	203	15	28	9	34.00	3-39	81
Brown, D.R.	196	3052	21.95	78*	–	18	218	26.48	5-31	50
Brown, J.F.	40	35	4.37	5*	–	–	38	36.15	4-26	8
Brown, S.J.E.	113	217	6.57	18	–	–	132	30.77	6-30	23
Bulbeck, M.P.L.	11	8	2.66	5	–	–	10	28.50	5-18	2
Burns, M.	154	3207	25.45	115*	2	19	40	28.80	4-39	63/12
Burns, N.D.	207	2388	19.90	90*	–	8	–	–	–	219/39
Butcher, G.P.	67	684	16.68	48	–	–	26	48.92	4-52	6
Butcher, M.A.	145	2834	27.51	91	–	15	49	44.55	3-23	46
Byas, D.	313	7782	29.14	116*	5	44	25	26.36	3-19	131
Caddick, A.R.	192	586	10.28	39	–	–	255	24.92	6-30	32
Cairns, C.L.	296	7301	31.88	143	8	36	334	27.18	6-37	84
Carberry, M.A.	7	56	8.00	20	–	–	–	–	–	1
Carpenter, J.R.	53	768	23.27	64*	–	5	0	–	–	26
Carter, N.M.	24	107	10.70	40	–	–	37	21.83	4-21	2
Cassar, M.E.	58	1508	29.56	134	4	7	33	30.75	4-29	16
Catterall, D.N.	13	49	9.80	21*	–	–	5	70.60	2-35	3
Cawdron, M.J.	55	303	15.15	50	–	1	55	31.47	4-17	5
Chapple, G.	159	591	11.58	56	–	2	179	29.42	6-18	33
Chilton, M.J.	46	834	20.85	56	–	3	23	23.56	5-26	11
Clapp, D.A.	2	14	7.00	10	–	–	3	15.33	3-46	–
Clarke, A.J.	12	19	3.16	9	–	–	8	40.25	2-39	1
Clarke, R.	3	9	3.00	7	–	–	1	14.00	1-14	1
Clinton, R.S.	10	138	27.60	56	–	1	0	–	–	–
Clough, G.D.	20	73	10.42	24	–	–	20	36.85	2-33	3
Coleman, A.J.	3	15	–	11*	–	–	0	–	–	1
Collingwood, P.D.	119	2840	27.84	95*	–	18	62	33.88	4-31	55
Compton, N.R.D.	1	6	6.00	6	–	–	–	–	–	–
Cook, J.W.	33	722	22.56	130	1	2	3	58.00	2-44	14
Cook, S.J.	50	370	11.56	50	–	1	56	29.37	3-16	8
Cork, D.G.	188	2632	20.88	93	–	15	242	27.66	6-21	74
Cosker, D.A.	77	221	8.50	27*	–	–	87	29.82	3-18	22
Cottey, P.A.	239	4297	25.12	96	–	25	19	35.36	4-56	80
Cousins, D.M.	79	134	5.82	18	–	–	102	26.53	4-23	13
Cowan, A.P.	114	834	13.67	45	–	–	135	29.21	5-14	38
Cox, J.	120	3759	32.97	114	3	28	3	37.00	3-28	39
Craven, V.J.	10	170	17.00	55	–	1	–	–	–	6
Crawley, J.P.	206	5473	29.90	114	3	34	0	–	–	60/4
Croft, R.D.B.	284	3855	22.54	114*	1	18	284	32.55	6-20	69
Crowe, C.D.	10	68	22.66	19	–	–	6	29.66	4-30	2
Cullinan, D.J.	297	7989	32.21	124	7	47	6	43.16	2-30	142
Cunliffe, R.J.	80	1874	27.97	137*	3	11	–	–	–	22
Dagnall, C.E.	21	31	10.33	21*	–	–	30	20.16	4-34	2
Dakin, J.M.	140	2090	19.90	179	2	2	114	28.83	5-30	28
Dale, A.	259	5708	28.68	110	2	28	218	31.41	6-22	57
Daley, J.A.	68	1639	30.92	105	1	10	0	–	–	11
Dalrymple, J.W.M.	10	114	22.80	38*	–	–	8	24.25	4-14	2

162

L-O	M	Runs	Avge	HS	100	50	Wkts	Avge	Best	Ct/St
Davies, A.M.	13	20	2.85	10	–	–	17	21.05	4-13	1
Davies, A.P.	24	65	13.00	24	–	–	35	22.02	5-39	4
Davies, M.K.	10	8	4.00	4	–	–	8	42.87	3-11	–
Davis, M.J.G.	86	368	13.14	35	–	–	75	39.29	4-24	19
Davis, R.P.	145	457	10.15	56	–	1	141	32.04	5-52	56
Dawson, R.K.J.	15	39	4.33	10*	–	–	14	30.35	3-28	5
Dean, K.J.	73	140	12.72	16*	–	–	85	29.20	5-32	13
DeFreitas, P.A.J.	429	4437	18.33	75*	–	11	489	28.08	5-13	91
Di Venuto, M.J.	135	4055	34.07	173*	4	22	5	31.20	1-10	49
Dobson, M.C.	1	1	1.00	1	–	–	1	58.00	1-58	–
Dowman, M.P.	124	2373	21.57	92	–	10	41	34.75	3-21	30
Drakes, V.C.	159	1440	15.82	104	1	1	204	25.88	5-19	29
Driver, R.C.	15	205	14.64	61*	–	2	1	65.00	1-17	1
Dumelow, N.R.C.	14	219	19.90	33	–	–	14	34.35	3-32	1
Dutch, K.P.	105	1239	18.49	61*	–	4	112	25.11	6-40	37
Ealham, M.A.	306	4706	24.38	112	1	19	336	28.10	6-53	73
Edwards, A.D.	37	186	9.30	43	–	–	26	48.00	3-34	10
Elstub, C.J.	8	0	–	0*	–	–	1	22.80	4-25	–
Evans, A.W.	42	662	20.68	108	1	3	–	–	–	13
Fairbrother, N.H.	493	14711	42.88	145	9	107	3	58.66	1-17	183
Fellows, G.M.	65	970	20.20	80*	–	4	11	43.81	3-34	14
Ferley, R.S.	1	6	6.00	6	–	–	1	13.00	1-13	–
Fisher, I.D.	28	68	7.55	20	–	–	29	24.41	3-20	6
Fleming, M.V.	292	5572	24.43	125	4	22	350	25.66	5-27	75
Fleming, S.P.	253	7029	33.00	120*	7	46	2	15.50	1- 3	118
Flintoff, A.	130	2940	27.22	143	3	17	84	21.89	4-22	45
Flower, A.	233	7048	34.38	120*	3	57	0	–	–	174/40
Follett, D.	32	34	8.50	10*	–	–	49	23.91	4-17	8
Forder, D.J.	3	6	–	3*	–	–	1	117.00	1-25	1
Foster, J.S.	21	321	26.75	56*	–	1	–	–	–	25/2
Francis, J.D.	6	189	63.00	78*	–	2	–	–	–	1
Francis, S.R.G.	12	25	8.33	8*	–	–	6	49.00	2-28	2
Franks, P.J.	80	575	17.96	40	–	–	112	24.78	6-27	11
Fraser, A.R.C.	332	864	11.67	38*	–	–	389	26.40	5-32	56
Frost, T.	28	104	11.55	22*	–	–	–	–	–	22/4
Fulton, D.P.	48	799	16.64	82	–	3	0	–	–	30
Gait, A.I.	11	415	41.50	138*	1	1	–	–	–	1
Gallian, J.E.R.	145	4194	32.26	134	7	23	52	32.75	5-15	50
Gannon, B.W.	2	3	3.00	2	–	–	3	23.66	2-29	–
Gazzard, C.M.	1	16	16.00	16	–	–	–	–	–	2
Giddins, E.S.H.	165	76	2.11	13	–	–	189	29.12	5-21	30
Gidman, A.P.R.	4	57	14.25	23	–	–	1	106.00	1-43	1
Giles, A.F.	144	1487	20.09	107	1	3	189	22.60	5-21	44
Golding, J.M.	19	177	17.70	47	–	–	16	34.06	3-20	4
Goodwin, M.W.	132	3993	33.55	167	5	27	7	39.71	1- 9	37
Gough, D.	277	1515	12.83	72*	–	1	397	23.85	7-27	49
Gough, M.A.	32	532	21.28	58	–	1	13	41.38	3-36	8
Grant, J.B.	12	36	18.00	14	–	–	9	42.55	3-10	1
Gray, A.K.D.	2	21	21.00	19*	–	–	1	49.00	1-45	1
Grayson, A.P.	204	2794	19.40	82*	–	9	186	31.84	4-25	55
Greenidge, C.G.	17	6	3.00	3*	–	–	10	54.40	2-17	7
Grove, J.O.	14	9	3.00	6	–	–	13	39.53	4-36	3
Gunter, N.E.L.	1	5	5.00	5	–	–	0	–	–	–
Habib, A.	122	2250	26.16	111	1	9	2	7.50	2- 5	43
Hamblin, J.R.C.	14	129	21.50	61	–	1	17	25.35	4-29	5
Hamilton, G.M.	108	1281	22.87	76	–	4	128	24.42	5-16	16
Hancock, T.H.C.	184	3565	21.60	110	1	16	47	24.72	6-58	58

L-O	M	Runs	Avge	HS	100	50	Wkts	Avge	Best	Ct/St
Hardinges, M.A.	11	127	14.11	65	–	1	7	37.28	2-50	2
Harmison, S.J.	36	45	5.00	11*	–	–	34	38.05	4-43	4
Harris, A.J.	87	113	5.94	11*	–	–	114	28.67	5-35	21
Harrison, D.S.	3	11	5.50	5*	–	–	0	–	–	1
Harvey, I.J.	153	2803	23.95	92	–	13	237	21.22	5-19	41
Hatch, N.G.	6	13	13.00	8*	–	–	9	21.66	3-26	–
Havell, P.M.R.	1	–	–	–	–	–	0	–	–	–
Haynes, J.J.	9	111	27.75	59*	–	1	–	–	–	8/2
Hegg, W.K.	337	2682	20.95	81	–	4	–	–	–	374/51
Hemp, D.L.	160	3166	24.73	121	4	15	8	20.87	4-32	56
Hewison, C.J.	3	39	13.00	20	–	–	–	–	–	2
Hewitt, J.P.	76	326	11.64	32*	–	–	68	33.27	4-24	24
Hewson, D.R.	33	531	19.66	64	–	2	–	–	–	10
Hick, G.A.	527	18535	42.80	172*	34	122	223	29.14	5-19	242
Hockley, J.B.	35	847	29.20	90	–	5	–	–	–	11
Hogg, K.W.	2	–	–	–	–	–	1	36.00	1-14	1
Hoggard, M.J.	59	26	2.36	5*	–	–	87	20.73	5-28	5
Hollioake, A.J.	236	4806	27.78	111	1	25	285	24.00	5-29	71
Hollioake, B.C.	128	2351	23.98	98	–	14	135	27.86	5-10	41
Holloway, P.C.L.	124	2579	28.03	117	2	17	–	–	–	52/8
Hopkinson, C.D.	4	68	34.00	43	–	–	1	90.00	1- 2	6
House, W.J.	74	1271	22.29	93	–	3	23	29.86	5-58	15
Hunkin, C.A.	3	10	5.00	10*	–	–	3	37.33	2-43	1
Hunt, T.A.	1	–	–	–	–	–	1	32.00	1-32	–
Hunter, I.D.	31	100	7.69	21	–	–	36	27.11	4-29	5
Hussain, N.	302	8441	35.31	118	6	61	–	–	–	143
Hussey, M.E.K.	64	2178	41.09	114*	2	18	9	22.44	3-52	29
Hutchison, P.M.	35	18	4.50	4*	–	–	45	20.28	4-34	5
Hutton, B.L.	35	531	21.24	77	–	3	21	28.52	5-45	18
Hyam, B.J.	45	356	13.69	37	–	–	–	–	–	33/6
Illingworth, R.K.	379	1393	14.21	36*	–	–	410	27.05	5-24	93
Ilott, M.C.	185	797	12.07	56*	–	2	232	26.39	5-21	31
Innes, K.J.	58	503	20.95	55	–	1	55	32.50	4-36	14
Irani, R.C.	203	4529	28.66	124	3	25	238	25.63	5-33	50
James, S.P.	221	6672	34.93	135	7	46	–	–	–	58
Jefferson, W.I.	4	119	29.75	65	–	2	–	–	–	1
Johnson, N.C.	180	5606	37.37	146*	12	31	136	33.27	4-19	87
Johnson, P.	370	9925	32.43	167*	13	57	1	23.00	1- 2	112
Johnson, R.L.	131	845	12.07	45*	–	–	147	32.12	5-50	15
Jones, G.O.	5	59	14.75	39	–	–	–	–	–	1
Jones, H.R.	1	10	10.00	10	–	–	–	–	–	–
Jones, I.	3	11	11.00	6	–	–	6	16.66	3-14	1
Jones, P.S.	85	212	11.77	27	–	–	123	25.66	5-23	15
Jones, S.P.	3	12	–	12*	–	–	1	116.00	1-39	–
Joyce, E.C.	20	465	31.00	73	–	1	–	–	–	6
Kandola, G.S.	2	8	8.00	8	–	–	–	–	–	–
Keedy, G.	13	3	1.50	3	–	–	12	33.41	5-30	1
Keegan, C.B.	20	76	7.60	16	–	–	33	21.78	5-17	3
Kendall, W.S.	91	1463	20.60	85*	–	4	0	–	–	38
Kenway, D.A.	58	1377	27.00	93*	–	9	–	–	–	32/6
Kerr, J.I.D.	96	542	12.04	56	–	1	109	29.71	4-28	13
Key, R.W.T.	53	1271	29.55	76*	–	11	–	–	–	7
Khan, A.	4	2	1.00	2	–	–	4	32.00	2-38	–
Khan, R.M.	1	29	29.00	29	–	–	–	–	–	–
Khan, W.G.	29	276	11.50	33	–	–	1	53.00	1- 7	7
Killeen, N.	105	368	8.76	32	–	–	136	26.77	6-31	20
Kirby, S.P.	5	4	4.00	4*	–	–	7	30.14	3-35	1

L-O	M	Runs	Avge	HS	100	50	Wkts	Avge	Best	Ct/St
Kirtley, R.J.	100	222	11.10	17*	–	–	151	22.52	5-39	26
Knight, N.V.	275	8313	36.78	151	16	42	2	44.50	1-14	109
Koenig, S.G.	32	609	19.03	109	1	1	–	–	–	4
Krikken, K.M.	195	1652	18.77	55	–	1	–	–	–	191/43
Lampitt, S.R.	277	2024	18.40	54	–	1	348	24.04	6-26	83
Laney, J.S.	116	2706	24.37	153	2	10	0	–	–	29
Laraman, A.W.	14	51	10.20	16*	–	–	25	14.60	6-42	6
Lathwell, M.N.	167	4409	28.26	121	5	26	1	193.00	1-23	47
Law, D.R.	134	2167	22.11	82	–	6	74	31.54	3-26	27
Law, S.G.	265	7901	33.76	163	18	33	86	36.09	5-26	105
Leatherdale, D.A.	242	3534	20.66	70*	–	14	109	22.48	5-10	104
Lehmann, D.S.	239	8256	42.77	191	13	55	66	28.40	3-14	73
Lewis, J.	85	358	11.93	33*	–	–	96	30.47	4-23	17
Lewis, J.J.B.	161	3318	29.10	102	1	19	0	–	–	25
Lewry, J.D.	56	149	7.84	16	–	–	74	27.27	4-29	7
Liptrot, C.G.	8	23	23.00	15*	–	–	8	24.87	3-44	2
Lloyd, G.D.	273	5727	29.36	134	3	29	1	103.00	1-23	60
Logan, R.J.	21	84	9.33	24	–	–	26	31.38	5-24	6
Loudon, A.G.R.	1	53	53.00	53	–	1	0	–	–	–
Love, M.L.	77	2312	35.03	124	1	13	0	–	–	37
Loye, M.B.	169	4679	32.49	124*	4	29	–	–	–	37
Lucas, D.S.	20	45	9.00	19*	–	–	21	35.95	4-27	2
Lumb, M.J.	16	217	19.72	66	–	1	–	–	–	5
Lungley, T.	13	103	14.71	45	–	–	24	18.66	4-28	1
McCague, M.J.	163	771	11.68	56	–	1	207	26.97	5-26	30
McGarry, A.C.	12	1	1.00	1	–	–	8	29.00	2-20	1
McGrath, A.	129	3375	32.45	109*	3	18	10	25.90	2-10	43
Maddy, D.L.	196	4921	30.94	151	6	28	104	25.92	4-16	66
Maher, J.P.	81	2921	41.72	142*	5	16	3	46.33	2-43	31
Maiden, G.I.	5	3	1.50	3	–	–	4	32.50	2-27	2
Malcolm, D.E.	181	313	5.30	42	–	–	242	27.74	7-35	19
Malik, M.N.	8	5	5.00	3*	–	–	6	47.83	2-34	1
Mann, C.	1	7	7.00	7	–	–	–	–	–	1
Marsh, A.J.	4	73	18.25	53	–	1	–	–	–	2
Marsh, D.J.	56	1201	33.36	97*	–	6	32	47.68	4-44	26
Martin, P.J.	207	392	13.06	35*	–	–	286	23.03	5-16	36
Martin–Jenkins, R.S.C.	78	531	10.41	45	–	–	81	29.76	4-57	20
Mascarenhas, A.D.	97	1499	20.53	79	–	11	110	24.95	4-25	24
Mason, M.S.	2	2	2.00	2	–	–	3	34.33	2-61	1
Mason, T.J.	88	454	12.61	36	–	–	56	44.73	4-12	22
Masters, D.D.	22	52	5.77	12*	–	–	12	52.33	2-10	3
Maunders, J.K.	3	66	22.00	49	–	–	0	–	–	1
Maynard, M.P.	381	11690	35.42	151*	14	70	3	94.66	1-13	157/5
Mees, T.	4	4	4.00	4*	–	–	3	48.00	3-19	–
Metson, C.P.	230	943	11.78	30*	–	–	–	–	–	222/60
Middlebrook, J.D.	18	61	7.62	15*	–	–	13	40.76	3-16	5
Millns, D.J.	91	338	14.69	39*	–	–	83	37.87	4-26	18
Montgomerie, R.R.	121	3926	36.69	129*	3	29	0	–	–	25
Morris, A.C.	42	285	17.81	48*	–	–	39	26.23	5-32	8
Morris, J.E.	349	8362	27.06	145	10	40	1	66.00	1-44	83
Morris, Z.C.	4	7	2.33	7*	–	–	3	43.00	3-31	1
Muchall, G.J.	1	19	19.00	19	–	–	0	–	–	–
Mullally, A.D.	257	447	6.98	38	–	–	310	27.15	6-38	37
Munton, T.A.	271	342	8.55	18	–	–	280	28.71	5-23	49
Muralitharan, M.	227	360	6.10	18	–	–	329	23.64	7-30	94
Murtagh, T.J.	11	25	6.25	11	–	–	13	34.61	4-31	2
Mustard, P.	5	14	4.66	8	–	–	–	–	–	7/3

L-O	M	Runs	Avge	HS	100	50	Wkts	Avge	Best	Ct/St
Napier, G.R.	45	631	18.02	79	–	4	16	31.50	6-29	7
Nash, D.C.	71	784	19.12	58	–	2	–	–	–	60/15
New, T.J.	1	3	3.00	3	–	–	–	–	–	–
Newell, K.	119	2470	25.20	129	1	10	39	38.05	5-33	20
Newman, S.A.	5	110	22.00	49	–	–	–	–	–	1
Nixon, P.A.	240	3721	23.11	101	1	16	–	–	–	249/49
Noon, W.M.	118	751	13.90	46	–	–	–	–	–	89/27
Ormond, J.	76	252	10.08	18*	–	–	101	22.57	4-12	15
Ostler, D.P.	248	6663	32.98	134*	2	48	1	14.00	1- 4	87
Parkin, O.T.	87	62	3.10	8	–	–	115	25.60	5-28	20
Parsons, K.A.	143	2437	26.20	72	–	11	84	36.36	4-43	56
Patel, D.B.	1	19	–	19*	–	–	1	36.00	1-36	–
Patel, M.M.	73	216	9.00	27*	–	–	74	31.31	3-22	22
Pattison, I.	4	57	28.50	48*	–	–	3	29.33	1-25	2
Pearson, J.A.	2	7	3.50	7	–	–	–	29.00	1-29	–
Penberthy, A.L.	225	3587	24.73	81*	–	20	225	30.56	5-29	57
Peng, N.	28	765	29.42	121	3	2	–	–	–	5
Penney, T.L.	233	4109	28.73	90	–	16	1	21.00	1- 8	91/1
Peters, S.D.	75	1162	18.74	73*	–	6	–	–	–	21
Pettini, M.L.	2	14	14.00	14	–	–	–	–	–	1
Phillips, B.J.	26	59	7.37	29	–	–	33	20.18	4-25	9
Phillips, N.C.	91	500	10.41	38*	–	–	99	29.42	4-13	27
Phillips, T.J.	2	1	1.00	1	–	–	2	34.00	2-56	1
Pierson, A.R.K.	119	385	10.13	31*	–	–	100	35.70	5-36	45
Pietersen, K.P.	31	602	35.41	78*	–	4	18	53.16	3-39	17
Pipe, D.J.	11	248	27.55	56	–	2	–	–	–	13/1
Piper, K.J.	204	861	15.37	38*	–	–	–	–	–	218/46
Pollard, P.R.	185	5177	33.61	132*	5	33	0	–	–	62
Pollock, S.M.	228	2391	22.77	87	–	10	319	22.06	6-21	76
Pope, S.P.	5	22	5.50	15	–	–	–	–	–	10/1
Porter, J.J.	1	23	23.00	23	–	–	–	–	–	–
Pothas, N.	100	1574	34.21	101	1	6	–	–	–	91/21
Powell, M.J. (Gm)	81	1607	24.72	86	–	6	–	–	–	24
Powell, M.J. (Wa)	49	873	24.25	78	–	3	8	38.75	2-13	18
Pratt, A.	32	393	24.56	86	–	2	–	–	–	27/13
Pratt, G.J.	1	32	32.00	32	–	–	–	–	–	–
Prichard, P.J.	300	7220	28.65	114	6	38	–	–	–	84
Prior, M.J.	18	85	6.53	25	–	–	–	–	–	12/3
Prittipaul, L.R.	25	363	20.16	61	–	1	4	39.25	2-53	11
Pyemont, J.P.	23	301	13.68	50	–	1	–	–	–	10
Ramprakash, M.R.	280	8619	37.80	147*	7	56	36	28.50	5-38	99
Randall, S.J.	3	29	29.00	15*	–	–	3	43.00	3-44	–
Rashid, U.B.A.	71	564	13.75	82	–	1	73	33.34	5-24	23
Ratcliffe, J.D.	107	1803	22.82	105	1	9	33	34.09	3-15	28
Rawnsley, M.J.	50	75	4.41	12	–	–	47	31.61	5-26	11
Read, C.M.W.	99	1136	18.93	62	–	1	–	–	–	116/20
Rhodes, S.J.	416	3853	19.07	105	1	5	0	–	–	470/114
Richardson, A.	18	24	4.80	11*	–	–	16	32.81	3-17	1
Ripley, D.	281	1885	18.48	52*	–	1	–	–	–	227/36
Roberts, T.W.	3	68	22.66	55	–	1	0	–	–	–
Robinson, D.D.J.	127	2804	25.72	137*	3	12	1	26.00	1- 7	32
Robinson, M.A.	236	143	2.97	15*	–	–	248	30.36	4-23	25
Rollins, A.S.	101	1911	22.22	126*	2	8	0	–	–	40
Rose, G.D.	291	5001	23.92	148	2	24	300	29.53	4-16	67
Roseberry, M.A.	218	5674	30.83	121	6	38	1	51.00	1-22	71
Round, N.W.	6	192	38.40	66	–	1	2	36.00	2-28	1
Russell, R.C.	434	6171	24.58	119*	2	24	–	–	–	413/84

L-O	M	Runs	Avge	HS	100	50	Wkts	Avge	Best	Ct/St
Saggers, M.J.	43	158	14.36	34*	–	–	68	21.58	5-22	8
Sales, D.J.G.	94	2055	27.77	91*	–	12	0	–	–	35
Salisbury, I.D.K.	212	1207	12.70	48*	–	–	216	32.26	5-30	70
Sampson, P.J.	4	8	8.00	4*	–	–	1	118.00	1-25	1
Saqlain Mushtaq	238	1008	11.32	38*	–	–	396	20.84	5-20	61
Schofield, C.P.	44	376	16.34	42	–	–	63	20.95	5-31	12
Schofield, J.E.K.	1	–	–	–	–	–	1	22.00	1-22	–
Scott, B.J.M.	1	11	11.00	11	–	–	–	–	–	–
Scott, G.M.	2	30	15.00	20	–	–	3	18.00	2-32	–
Scuderi, J.C.	64	893	23.50	73*	–	5	50	38.96	3-28	9
Selwood, S.A.	3	75	25.00	37	–	–	0	–	–	–
Shafayat, B.M.	8	120	15.00	36	–	–	–	–	–	3
Shah, O.A.	109	2467	27.41	134	3	11	8	31.12	2-	30
Shahid Afridi	181	4447	26.00	112	3	25	145	38.59	5-40	67
Shahid, N.	145	2490	24.65	109*	2	9	5	50.80	3-30	45
Sharpe, T.J.	1	0	0.00	0	–	–	1	56.00	1-56	–
Shaw, A.D.	85	759	15.48	48	–	–	–	–	–	59/17
Sheikh, M.A.	50	154	11.00	36	–	–	59	23.54	4-17	13
Sheriyar, A.	98	116	7.73	19	–	–	112	26.62	4-18	7
Sidebottom, R.J.	71	149	9.31	24*	–	–	75	29.05	6-40	13
Sillence, R.J.	4	89	29.66	82	–	1	4	18.75	3-47	–
Silverwood, C.E.W.	139	387	9.92	38*	–	–	192	22.85	5-28	21
Singh, A.	67	1635	25.15	123	1	13	–	–	–	18
Smethurst, M.P.	24	25	5.00	10*	–	–	21	33.57	4-46	4
Smith, A.M.	212	465	10.56	26*	–	–	241	27.41	6-39	39
Smith, B.F.	238	5849	28.67	115	2	34	1	68.00	1-26	78
Smith, E.T.	31	439	16.88	72*	–	2	–	–	–	5
Smith, G.J.	63	45	4.09	9	–	–	98	22.81	5-11	10
Smith, N.M.K.	296	4683	21.88	125	2	25	280	26.47	6-33	94
Smith, R.A.	426	14472	41.46	167*	27	78	3	5.33	2-13	155
Smith, T.M.	21	93	11.62	27	–	–	24	31.29	4-38	4
Snape, J.N.	160	2072	22.04	104*	1	7	132	28.57	5-32	59
Solanki, V.S.	155	2845	23.70	120*	1	14	9	45.77	2-40	52
Speak, N.J.	159	3713	28.56	102*	1	20	0	–	–	28
Spearman, C.M.	130	2926	23.22	126	1	17	0	–	–	36
Speight, M.P.	251	5688	25.73	126	3	29	–	–	–	143/17
Spires, J.A.S.	1	–	–	–	–	–	1	33.00	1-33	–
Stelling, W.F.	40	606	37.87	76*	–	3	41	31.39	3-18	13
Stemp, R.D.	152	226	7.79	29*	–	–	160	31.38	4-25	30
Stephenson, J.P.	290	7009	30.60	142	8	38	248	26.31	6-33	107
Stevens, D.I.	62	1238	23.35	133	1	7	3	23.00	2-26	19
Stewart, A.J.	467	14061	35.77	167*	19	88	0	–	–	402/42
Strauss, A.J.	50	963	21.88	90	–	6	–	–	–	11
Strong, M.R.	19	63	7.00	21	–	–	41	25.58	5-39	4
Stubbings, S.D.	47	753	18.82	96*	–	3	–	–	–	4
Such, P.M.	210	275	7.85	19*	–	–	209	31.52	5-29	51
Sutcliffe, I.J.	59	1470	27.22	105*	2	7	–	–	–	14
Sutliff, M.D.R.	3	30	10.00	24	–	–	–	–	–	–
Sutton, L.D.	33	487	17.39	60	–	2	–	–	–	17/3
Swann, A.J.	29	770	38.50	83*	–	5	0	–	–	4
Swann, G.P.	79	1194	21.70	83	–	7	68	31.98	5-35	21
Symington, M.J.	10	43	5.37	16	–	–	4	70.50	1-15	4
Symonds, A.	172	3764	27.47	95	–	19	105	26.66	6-14	71
Taylor, B.V.	35	68	8.50	21*	–	–	46	23.95	4-26	8
Taylor, C.G.	45	437	15.06	63*	–	1	–	–	–	16
Taylor, J.P.	209	468	9.55	57	–	1	244	29.52	5-45	46
Thomas, I.J.	12	305	25.41	53	–	1	–	–	–	4

167

L-O	M	Runs	Avge	HS	100	50	Wkts	Avge	Best	Ct/St
Thomas, S.D.	112	911	14.46	40	–	–	147	25.57	7-16	19
Thorpe, G.P.	311	9496	39.56	145*	7	71	16	40.56	3-21	140
Titchard, S.P.	63	1292	24.37	96	–	5	1	99.00	1-19	8
Tolley, C.M.	139	1526	20.34	78	–	5	127	30.98	5-16	34
Tomlinson, J.A.	2	4	2.00	4	–	–	1	46.00	1-29	–
Tredwell, J.C.	6	166	33.20	71	–	2	3	56.33	1-31	1
Trego, P.D.	12	70	8.75	21	–	–	10	30.50	2-21	1
Tremlett, C.T.	19	99	12.37	30*	–	–	28	22.10	3-15	4
Trescothick, M.E.	149	4321	35.13	137	9	19	54	26.74	4-50	48
Trott, B.J.	17	5	1.66	2*	–	–	24	24.04	5-18	3
Troughton, J.O.	4	222	74.00	115*	1	1	7	11.85	4-23	2
Tudor, A.J.	47	239	9.95	29*	–	–	72	20.91	4-26	11
Tufnell, P.C.R.	93	125	8.92	18	–	–	103	32.30	5-28	17
Turner, R.J.	184	2676	25.24	70	–	8	–	–	–	189/21
Udal, S.D.	262	1743	15.02	78	–	6	290	30.86	5-43	87
Van der Gucht, C.G.	3	4	2.00	4	–	–	5	19.00	3-35	–
Vaughan, M.P.	163	3862	26.45	125*	1	21	57	28.15	4-27	50
Wagg, G.G.	1	0	0.00	0	–	–	–	–	–	–
Wagh, M.A.	31	527	19.51	70*	–	3	3	53.33	1-39	1
Walker, M.J.	139	2833	24.63	117	2	15	18	20.38	4-24	36
Wallace, M.A.	7	18	4.50	8*	–	–	–	–	–	7/3
Ward, D.M.	234	5336	30.49	112	5	32	0	–	–	100/3
Ward, I.J.	94	2117	27.85	91	–	14	0	–	–	19
Ward, T.R.	285	8093	30.19	131	7	55	10	35.10	3-20	63
Warren, N.A.	1	0	0.00	–	–	–	–	–	–	2
Warren, R.J.	135	2438	24.13	100*	1	11	–	–	–	118/10
Watkin, S.L.	252	427	6.37	31*	–	–	309	26.82	5-23	39
Webley, T.	1	4	4.00	4	–	–	–	–	–	–
Weekes, L.C.	28	57	6.33	11	–	–	27	40.14	4-33	3
Weekes, P.N.	231	4478	26.18	143*	3	20	251	27.81	4-17	95
Welch, G.	136	1426	18.76	71	–	4	110	37.62	5-22	17
Wells, V.J.	238	5179	25.89	201	4	24	219	27.22	6-25	66
Welton, G.E.	41	873	22.97	104*	1	4	–	–	–	11
Weston, R.M.S.	47	843	20.56	80*	–	4	–	–	–	10
Weston, W.P.C.	128	2157	20.94	134	2	7	1	2.00	1- 2	29
Wharf, A.G.	52	334	14.52	38*	–	–	50	36.12	4-29	8
Wharton, L.J.	18	26	–	9*	–	–	17	34.94	3-23	2
Whiley, M.J.A.	1	–	–	–	–	–	1	68.00	1-68	–
White, C.	252	4620	24.83	148	2	17	266	25.56	5-21	72
White, G.W.	113	2193	21.71	76	–	14	1	86.00	1-45	37
Widdup, S.	4	49	12.25	38	–	–	–	–	–	2
Williams, R.C.J.	37	266	16.62	38	–	–	–	–	–	40/8
Wilton, N.J.	17	45	4.50	17	–	–	–	–	–	12/3
Windows, M.G.N.	144	2905	24.41	117	2	10	0	–	–	49
Wood, J.	116	538	11.20	28*	–	–	114	34.84	4-17	16
Wood, M.J. (Y)	47	707	20.79	68	–	4	–	–	–	15
Wood, M.J. (Sm)	7	129	21.50	43	–	–	–	–	–	1
Wright, A.S.	5	188	37.60	112	1	1	0	–	–	1
Wright, L.J.	1	16	16.00	16	–	–	–	–	–	–
Yardy, M.H.	16	153	10.92	59	–	1	6	52.66	2-34	5
Yates, G.	164	600	14.28	38	–	–	155	31.71	4-34	38
Zuiderent, B.	36	763	23.84	102*	1	5	0	–	–	16

LIMITED-OVERS INTERNATIONALS CAREER RECORDS

These records, complete to 10 January 2002, include all players registered for county cricket in 2002 at the time of going to press, plus those who have appeared in LOI matches since 15 August 2000.

ENGLAND – BATTING AND FIELDING

	M	I	NO	HS	Runs	Avge	100	50	Ct/St
C.J.Adams	5	4	–	42	71	17.75	–	–	3
M.W.Alleyne	10	8	1	53	151	21.57	–	1	3
R.J.Bailey	4	4	2	43*	137	68.50	–	–	1
K.J.Barnett	1	1	–	84	84	84.00	–	1	–
M.P.Bicknell	7	6	2	31*	96	24.00	–	–	2
R.J.Blakey	3	2	–	25	25	12.50	–	–	2/1
A.D.Brown	16	16	–	118	354	22.12	1	1	6
D.R.Brown	9	8	4	21	99	24.75	–	–	1
A.R.Caddick	35	22	9	36	145	11.15	–	–	8
P.D.Collingwood	7	7	1	77	189	31.50	–	2	1
D.G.Cork	30	19	2	31*	174	10.23	–	–	6
J.P.Crawley	13	12	1	73	235	21.36	–	2	1/1
R.D.B.Croft	50	36	12	32	345	14.37	–	–	11
P.A.J.DeFreitas	103	66	23	67	690	16.04	–	1	26
M.A.Ealham	64	45	4	45	716	17.46	–	–	9
N.H.Fairbrother	75	71	18	113	2092	39.47	1	16	33
M.V.Fleming	11	10	1	33	139	15.44	–	–	1
A.Flintoff	28	21	2	84	450	23.68	–	2	6
J.S.Foster	5	1	1	11*	11	–	–	–	4/4
P.J.Franks	1	1	–	4	4	4.00	–	–	1
A.R.C.Fraser	42	20	9	38*	141	12.81	–	–	5
A.F.Giles	9	6	2	11	38	9.50	–	–	1
D.Gough	95	62	24	45	415	10.92	–	–	14
A.P.Grayson	2	2	–	6	6	3.00	–	–	1
G.A.Hick	120	118	15	126*	3846	37.33	5	27	64
M.J.Hoggard	4	–	–	–	–	–	–	–	–
A.J.Hollioake	35	30	6	83*	606	25.25	–	3	13
B.C.Hollioake	17	14	2	63	259	21.58	–	2	6
N.Hussain	54	54	9	95	1404	31.20	–	11	30
R.C.Irani	10	10	2	45*	78	9.75	–	–	4
R.J.Kirtley	3	1	–	1	1	1.00	–	–	2
N.V.Knight	65	65	8	125*	2446	42.91	3	17	26
G.D.Lloyd	6	5	1	22	39	9.75	–	–	2
D.L.Maddy	8	6	–	53	113	18.83	–	1	1
D.E.Malcolm	10	5	2	4	9	3.00	–	–	1
P.J.Martin	20	13	7	6	38	6.33	–	–	4
M.P.Maynard	14	12	1	41	156	14.18	–	–	4
A.D.Mullally	50	25	10	20	86	5.73	–	–	8
M.R.Ramprakash	18	18	4	51	376	26.85	–	1	8
C.M.W.Read	9	6	2	26*	70	17.50	–	–	11/2
S.J.Rhodes	9	8	2	56	107	17.83	–	1	9/2
R.C.Russell	40	31	7	50	423	17.62	–	1	41/6
I.D.K.Salisbury	4	2	1	5	7	7.00	–	–	1
O.A.Shah	6	6	1	62	104	20.80	–	1	2
R.J.Sidebottom	2	1	1	2*	2	–	–	–	–
C.E.W.Silverwood	7	4	1	12	17	4.25	–	–	1
N.M.K.Smith	7	6	1	31	100	20.00	–	–	1
R.A.Smith	71	70	8	167*	2419	39.01	4	15	26
J.S.Snape	4	1	1	24*	24	–	–	–	3
V.S.Solanki	8	7	1	24	96	16.00	–	–	2
A.J.Stewart	146	141	11	116	4100	31.53	4	23	136/11
G.P.Swann	1	–	–	–	–	–	–	–	–

ENGLAND – BATTING AND FIELDING (continued)

	M	I	NO	HS	Runs	Avge	100	50	Ct/St
G.P.Thorpe	71	66	11	89	2120	38.54	–	19	38
M.E.Trescothick	26	26	1	137	883	35.32	1	5	7
P.C.R.Tufnell	20	10	9	5*	15	15.00	–	–	4
S.D.Udal	10	6	4	11*	35	17.50	–	–	1
M.P.Vaughan	6	6	–	26	42	7.00	–	–	1
V.J.Wells	9	7	–	39	141	20.14	–	–	7
C.White	37	29	2	38	337	12.48	–	–	8

ENGLAND – BOWLING

	O	R	W	Avge	Best	4wI	R/Over
M.W.Alleyne	61	280	10	28.00	3-27	–	4.59
R.J.Bailey	6	25	0	–	–	–	4.17
M.P.Bicknell	68.5	347	13	26.69	3-55	–	5.04
A.D.Brown	1	5	0	–	–	–	5.00
D.R.Brown	54	305	7	43.57	2-28	–	5.65
A.R.Caddick	322	1216	45	27.02	4-19	1	3.78
P.D.Collingwood	28.1	161	2	80.50	1-31	–	5.72
D.G.Cork	281.5	1286	41	31.36	3-27	–	4.56
R.D.B.Croft	411	1743	45	38.73	3-51	–	4.24
P.A.J.DeFreitas	952	3775	115	32.82	4-35	1	3.97
M.A.Ealham	537.5	2197	67	32.79	5-15	3	4.08
N.H.Fairbrother	1	9	0	–	–	–	9.00
M.V.Fleming	87.1	434	17	25.52	4-45	1	4.98
A.Flintoff	74.5	391	13	30.07	2- 3	–	5.22
P.J.Franks	9	48	0	–	–	–	5.33
A.R.C.Fraser	398.4	1412	47	30.04	4-22	1	3.54
A.F.Giles	71	336	8	42.00	2-37	–	4.73
D.Gough	874	3661	147	24.90	5-44	8	4.19
A.P.Grayson	15	60	3	20.00	3-40	–	4.00
G.A.Hick	206	1026	30	34.20	5-33	1	4.98
M.J.Hoggard	38	139	10	13.90	5-49	1	3.66
A.J.Hollioake	201.2	1019	32	31.84	4-23	2	5.06
B.C.Hollioake	92	448	7	64.00	2-37	–	4.87
R.C.Irani	54.5	246	4	61.50	1-23	–	4.49
R.J.Kirtley	24.2	94	3	31.33	2-33	–	3.86
D.E.Malcolm	87.4	404	16	25.25	3-40	–	4.61
P.J.Martin	174.4	806	27	29.85	4-44	1	4.61
A.D.Mullally	449.5	1728	63	27.42	4-18	2	3.84
M.R.Ramprakash	22	108	4	27.00	3-28	–	4.91
I.D.K.Salisbury	31	177	5	35.40	3-41	–	5.71
R.J.Sidebottom	14	84	2	42.00	1-42	–	6.00
C.E.W.Silverwood	51	244	6	40.66	3-43	–	4.78
N.M.K.Smith	43.3	190	6	31.66	3-29	–	4.37
J.S.Snape	38.3	167	7	23.85	3-43	–	4.34
G.P.Swann	5	24	0	–	–	–	4.80
G.P.Thorpe	20	97	2	48.50	2-15	–	4.85
M.E.Trescothick	7.4	45	2	22.50	2- 7	–	5.87
P.C.R.Tufnell	170	699	19	36.78	4-22	1	4.11
S.D.Udal	95	371	8	46.37	2-37	–	3.91
M.P.Vaughan	3	20	0	–	–	–	6.67
V.J.Wells	36.4	189	8	23.62	3-30	–	5.15
C.White	278	1206	47	25.65	5-21	2	4.34

AUSTRALIA – BATTING AND FIELDING

	M	I	NO	HS	Runs	Avge	100	50	Ct/St
M.G.Bevan	164	145	51	108*	5384	57.27	5	36	54
A.J.Bichel	17	11	4	27*	99	14.14	–	–	2
N.W.Bracken	9	–	–	–	–	–	–	–	2
M.J.Di Venuto	9	9	–	89	241	26.77	–	2	1
D.W.Fleming	88	31	18	29	152	11.69	–	–	14
A.C.Gilchrist	119	115	5	154	3848	34.98	6	22	153/29

AUSTRALIA – BATTING AND FIELDING (continued)

	M	I	NO	HS	Runs	Avge	100	50	Ct/St
J.N.Gillespie	24	15	3	26	114	9.50	–	–	1
B.J.Haddin	1	1	–	13	13	13.00	–	–	–/1
I.J.Harvey	35	25	8	47*	363	21.35	–	–	10
M.L.Hayden	27	25	2	111	788	34.26	1	7	10
S.M.Katich	1	–	–	–	–	–	–	–	–
S.G.Law	54	51	5	110	1237	26.89	1	7	12
B.Lee	29	9	2	31	80	11.42	–	–	1
S.Lee	45	35	8	47	477	17.66	–	–	23
D.S.Lehmann	69	62	11	110*	1727	33.86	2	10	14
G.D.McGrath	140	41	24	11	70	4.11	–	–	17
J.P.Maher	2	2	–	13	21	10.50	–	–	–
D.R.Martyn	79	65	23	144*	1679	39.97	2	9	29
R.T.Ponting	123	123	15	145	4546	42.09	8	26	39
A.Symonds	44	31	6	68*	693	27.72	–	2	16
S.K.Warne	167	91	26	55	835	12.84	–	1	70
M.E.Waugh	237	229	19	173	8374	39.87	18	49	105
S.R.Waugh	317	281	57	120*	7382	32.95	3	44	108

AUSTRALIA – BOWLING

	O	R	W	Avge	Best	4wI	R/Over
M.G.Bevan	323.4	1628	36	45.22	3-36	–.	5.03
A.J.Bichel	148.2	701	21	33.38	3-17	–	4.73
N.W.Bracken	71	303	10	30.30	2-21	–	4.27
D.W.Fleming	769.5	3402	134	25.38	5-36	5	4.42
J.N.Gillespie	212.1	947	32	29.59	4-26	1	4.46
I.J.Harvey	276.4	1260	38	33.15	4-28	1	4.55
M.L.Hayden	1	18	0	–	–	–	18.00
S.G.Law	134.3	635	12	52.91	2-22	–	4.72
B.Lee	255.1	1236	50	24.72	5-27	2	4.84
S.Lee	284.2	1245	48	25.93	5-33	2	4.38
D.S.Lehmann	90.4	489	12	40.75	2- 4	–	5.39
G.D.McGrath	1252	5002	212	23.59	5-14	10	4.00
D.R.Martyn	103.4	548	10	54.80	2-21	–	5.29
R.T.Ponting	25	104	3	34.66	1-12	–	4.16
A.Symonds	236.2	1173	40	29.32	4-11	2	4.96
S.K.Warne	1539.3	6541	262	24.96	5-33	13	4.25
M.E.Waugh	603.3	2892	83	34.84	5-24	2	4.79
S.R.Waugh	1470.3	6705	195	34.38	4-33	3	4.56

SOUTH AFRICA – BATTING AND FIELDING

	M	I	NO	HS	Runs	Avge	100	50	Ct/St
S.Abrahams	1	1	1	16*	16	–	–	–	1
P.R.Adams	16	8	4	15*	33	8.25	–	–	4
N.Boje	60	36	8	129·	807	28.82	2	2	19
M.V.Boucher	101	67	19	68	1077	22.43	–	8	145/6
D.J.Cullinan	138	133	16	124	3860	32.99	3	23	62
A.C.Dawson	4	1	–	6	6	6.00	–	–	–
H.H.Dippenaar	24	19	4	81	712	47.46	–	7	6
A.A.Donald	136	33	14	12	88	4.63	–	–	18
H.H.Gibbs	80	80	4	125	2519	33.14	6	11	33
A.J.Hall	18	17	1	81	391	24.43	–	1	8
M.Hayward	19	5	1	4	12	3.00	–	–	4
C.W.Henderson	4	–	–	–	–	–	–	–	–
J.H.Kallis	135	130	23	113*	4698	43.90	7	32	55
J.M.Kemp	11	4	1	46	59	19.66	–	–	5
G.Kirsten	161	161	15	188*	6124	42.11	12	40	53/1
L.Klusener	122	100	36	103*	2780	43.43	2	15	24
C.K.Langeveldt	2	–	–	–	–	–	–	–	–
N.D.McKenzie	36	30	6	131*	957	39.87	2	3	8
A.Nel	7	2	2	3*	3	–	–	–	2
M.Ntini	31	5	2	3*	6	2.00	–	–	13

	M	I	NO	HS	Runs	Avge	100	50	Ct/St
J.L.Ontong	7	3	–	32	45	15.00	–	–	2
S.M.Pollock	142	91	31	75	1460	24.33	–	5	53
N.Pothas	3	1	–	24	24	24.00	–	–	4/1
J.N.Rhodes	210	189	43	121	4867	33.33	1	24	93
R.Telemachus	25	7	2	13	27	5.40	–	–	1
D.J.Terbrugge	4	2	1	5	5	5.00	–	–	–

SOUTH AFRICA – BOWLING

	O	R	W	Avge	Best	4wI	R/Over
S.Abrahams	10	40	0	–	–	–	4.00
P.R.Adams	124.5	554	23	24.08	3-26	–	4.44
N.Boje	379.5	1682	46	36.56	4-25	1	4.43
D.J.Cullinan	31.4	130	5	26.00	2-30	–	4.11
A.C.Dawson	37	188	5	37.60	3-36	–	5.08
A.A.Donald	1187.3	4835	226	21.39	6-23	12	4.07
A.J.Hall	35.4	167	5	33.40	2- 8	–	4.68
M.Hayward	149.3	748	20	37.40	4-31	1	5.00
C.W.Henderson	36.1	132	7	18.85	4-17	1	3.40
J.H.Kallis	796	3687	122	30.22	5-30	2	4.63
J.M.Kemp	72	319	15	21.26	3-20	–	4.43
G.Kirsten	5	23	0	–	–	–	4.60
L.Klusener	886.2	4147	146	28.40	6-49	6	4.68
C.K.Langeveldt	19.3	66	6	11.00	4-21	1	3.38
N.D.McKenzie	7.4	27	0	–	–	–	3.52
A.Nel	59.5	241	10	24.10	3-20	–	4.03
M.Ntini	244.1	1017	39	26.07	5-37	2	4.17
J.L.Ontong	47	192	3	64.00	2-12	–	4.09
S.M.Pollock	1243.5	4675	206	22.69	6-35	10	3.76
J.N.Rhodes	2.2	4	0	–	–	–	1.71
R.Telemachus	220.4	976	37	26.37	4-43	1	4.42
D.J.Terbrugge	21	105	4	26.25	4-20	1	5.00

WEST INDIES – BATTING AND FIELDING

	M	I	NO	HS	Runs	Avge	100	50	Ct/St
J.C.Adams	127	105	28	82	2204	28.62	–	14	68/5
M.I.Black	5	2	–	4	4	2.00	–	–	–
D.Brown	2	1	1	1*	1	–	–	–	–
C.O.Browne	28	19	4	26	187	12.46	–	–	40/6
S.L.Campbell	90	87	–	105	2283	26.24	2	14	23
S.Chanderpaul	106	100	13	150	3093	35.55	2	19	27
P.T.Collins	7	4	2	10*	14	7.00	–	–	2
C.D.Collymore	17	6	3	13*	26	8.66	–	–	2
C.E.Cuffy	29	17	8	17*	53	5.88	–	–	4
M.Dillon	58	30	13	21*	151	8.88	–	–	8
D.Ganga	22	22	–	71	611	27.77	–	8	7
L.V.Garrick	3	3	–	76	99	33.00	–	1	–
C.H.Gayle	39	38	1	152	1053	28.45	1	7	14
R.O.Hinds	2	2	2	16*	31	–	–	–	1
W.W.Hinds	41	40	2	116*	1051	27.65	1	7	17
C.L.Hooper	202	184	37	113*	5146	35.00	6	28	98
R.D.Jacobs	89	77	18	80*	1425	24.15	–	7	114/21
K.C.B.Jeremy	6	4	2	8*	17	8.50	–	–	–
S.C.Joseph	4	4	–	28	57	14.25	–	–	1
R.D.King	48	22	13	12*	62	6.88	–	–	4
B.C.Lara	193	189	18	169	7257	42.43	14	47	82
J.J.C.Lawson	2	1	–	3	3	3.00	–	–	–
N.C.McGarrell	17	10	2	19	60	7.50	–	–	9
N.A.M.McLean	44	33	8	50*	309	12.36	–	1	8
M.V.Nagamootoo	15	13	2	33	136	12.36	–	–	5
R.L.Powell	51	47	3	124	1006	22.86	1	4	23
D.Ramnarine	4	3	–	2	5	1.66	–	–	–

WEST INDIES – BATTING AND FIELDING (continued)

	M	I	NO	HS	Runs	Avge	100	50	Ct/St
M.N.Samuels	29	28	4	68	683	28.45	–	5	6
R.R.Sarwan	9	9	3	38	194	32.33	–	–	1
C.E.L.Stuart	5	1	1	3*	3	–	–	–	1
L.R.Williams	15	13	2	41	124	11.27	–	–	8

WEST INDIES – BOWLING

	O	R	W	Avge	Best	4wI	R/Over
J.C.Adams	309.2	1499	43	34.86	5-37	1	4.85
M.I.Black	38	196	0	–	–	–	5.16
D.Brown	20	93	4	23.25	3-21	–	4.65
S.L.Campbell	32.4	170	8	21.25	4-30	1	5.20
S.Chanderpaul	116	600	14	42.85	3-18	–	5.17
P.T.Collins	62.4	269	6	44.83	2-24	–	4.29
C.D.Collymore	160.1	634	25	25.36	5-51	2	3.96
C.E.Cuffy	259.5	978	31	31.54	4-24	1	3.76
M.Dillon	493.3	2178	69	31.56	5-51	3	4.41
D.Ganga	0.1	4	0	–	–	–	24.00
C.H.Gayle	197.5	887	22	40.31	2-18	–	4.48
R.O.Hinds	5	27	0	–	–	–	5.40
W.W.Hinds	18	100	3	33.33	1- 6	–	5.56
C.L.Hooper	1418.3	6150	176	34.94	4-34	3	4.34
K.C.B.Jeremy	32	163	4	40.75	2-42	–	5.09
R.D.King	413.5	1696	73	23.23	4-25	2	4.10
B.C.Lara	7.1	46	4	11.50	2- 5	–	6.42
J.J.C.Lawson	14	76	2	38.00	2-47	–	5.43
N.C.McGarrell	143.1	681	15	45.40	3-32	–	4.76
N.A.M.McLean	347.2	1691	46	36.76	3-21	–	4.87
M.V.Nagamootoo	127.1	617	11	56.09	4-32	1	4.85
R.L.Powell	28.3	198	4	49.50	2- 5	–	6.95
D.Ramnarine	33.2	164	3	54.66	2-52	–	4.92
M.N.Samuels	152.5	772	25	30.88	3-25	–	5.05
R.R.Sarwan	3	23	0	–	–	–	7.67
C.E.L.Stuart	43	205	8	25.62	5-44	1	4.77
L.R.Williams	109.5	556	18	30.88	3-16	–	5.06

NEW ZEALAND – BATTING AND FIELDING

	M	I	NO	HS	Runs	Avge	100	50	Ct/St
A.R.Adams	3	3	2	13*	18	18.00	–	–	–
G.I.Allott	31	11	6	7*	17	3.40	–	–	5
N.J.Astle	139	136	5	120	4661	35.58	11	27	56
M.D.Bell	7	7	–	66	133	19.00	–	1	1
G.E.Bradburn	11	10	3	30	60	8.57	–	–	2
C.L.Cairns	137	124	12	115	3216	28.71	3	16	44
S.P.Fleming	156	150	14	116*	4165	30.62	3	26	70
J.E.C.Franklin	14	8	1	25*	53	7.57	–	–	3
C.Z.Harris	188	159	51	130	3349	31.00	1	12	70
C.D.McMillan	94	88	6	104*	2091	25.50	1	11	22
C.S.Martin	7	5	1	3	6	1.50	–	–	2
K.D.Mills	8	6	2	18*	27	6.75	–	–	1
D.J.Nash	77	50	13	42	579	15.64	–	–	24
C.J.Nevin	13	12	–	74	291	24.25	–	3	6/2
S.B.O'Connor	38	13	6	8	24	3.42	–	–	11
J.D.P.Oram	17	16	1	59	229	15.26	–	1	5
A.C.Parore	169	152	29	108	3206	26.06	1	14	100/25
A.J.Penn	5	3	1	15	23	11.50	–	–	1
M.S.Sinclair	19	19	1	118*	528	29.33	2	2	4
C.M.Spearman	51	50	–	86	936	18.72	–	5	15
S.B.Styris	30	20	2	48	262	14.55	–	–	8
G.P.Sulzberger	3	2	1	6*	9	9.00	–	–	–
D.R.Tuffey	19	10	6	20*	46	11.50	–	–	5
R.G.Twose	87	81	11	103	2718	38.82	1	20	37

	M	I	NO	HS	Runs	Avge	100	50	Ct/St
D.L.Vettori	72	47	14	25*	342	10.36	–	–	18
L.Vincent	17	17	2	45	328	21.86	–	–	5
B.G.K.Walker	7	4	3	5*	13	13.00	–	–	3
P.J.Wiseman	14	6	5	16	43	43.00	–	–	2

NEW ZEALAND – BOWLING

	O	R	W	Avge	Best	4wI	R/Over
A.R.Adams	18	89	2	44.50	1-38	–	4.94
G.I.Allott	254.4	1207	52	23.21	4-35	4	4.74
N.J.Astle	683.1	3146	86	36.58	4-43	1	4.61
G.E.Bradburn	64.1	318	6	53.00	2-18	–	4.96
C.L.Cairns	935.2	4419	131	33.73	5-42	3	4.72
S.P.Fleming	4.5	28	1	28.00	1- 8	–	5.79
J.E.C.Franklin	107	525	14	37.50	3-44	–	4.91
C.Z.Harris	1422.1	6098	173	35.24	5-42	3	4.29
C.D.McMillan	206.3	1076	36	29.88	3-20	–	5.21
C.S.Martin	54	270	5	54.00	2-56	–	5.00
K.D.Mills	53.2	228	10	22.80	3-30	–	4.28
D.J.Nash	541.2	2498	58	43.06	4-38	1	4.61
S.B.O'Connor	247.5	1396	46	30.34	5-39	3	5.63
J.D.P.Oram	89	431	11	39.18	3-40	–	4.84
A.J.Penn	26.3	201	1	201.00	1-50	–	7.59
C.M.Spearman	0.3	6	0	–	–	–	12.00
S.B.Styris	235.2	1178	27	43.62	4-57	1	5.01
G.P.Sulzberger	22	102	3	34.00	1-28	–	4.64
D.R.Tuffey	133	623	25	24.92	4-24	1	4.68
R.G.Twose	45.2	237	4	59.25	2-31	–	5.23
D.L.Vettori	542.4	2447	65	37.64	4-24	2	4.51
B.G.K.Walker	43	249	3	83.00	2-43	–	5.79
P.J.Wiseman	69	341	11	31.00	4-45	1	4.94

INDIA – BATTING AND FIELDING

	M	I	NO	HS	Runs	Avge	100	50	Ct/St
A.B.Agarkar	81	47	15	67*	514	16.06	–	1	30
H.K.Badani	23	22	5	100	566	33.29	1	3	9
V.Dahiya	19	15	2	51	216	16.61	–	1	19/5
S.S.Das	3	3	1	5*	9	4.50	–	–	–
D.Dasgupta	5	4	1	24*	51	17.00	–	–	2/1
S.S.Dighe	23	17	6	94*	256	23.27	–	1	19/5
R.Dravid	163	151	14	153	5689	37.87	7	35	81/4
S.C.Ganguly	181	175	14	183	7097	44.08	18	41	64
Harbhajan Singh	35	19	4	46	165	11.00	–	–	8
Harvinder Singh	16	5	1	3*	6	1.50	–	–	6
S.B.Joshi	69	45	11	61*	584	17.17	–	1	19
V.G.Kambli	104	97	21	106	2477	32.59	2	14	15
A.R.Kapoor	17	6	–	19	43	7.16	–	–	1
S.S.Karim	34	27	4	55	362	15.73	–	1	27/3
Z.Khan	29	16	9	32*	141	20.14	–	–	7
A.R.Khurasiya	12	11	–	57	149	13.54	–	1	3
A.Kumble	215	106	35	26	724	10.19	–	–	73
V.V.S.Laxman	29	27	2	101	627	25.08	1	4	14
J.J.Martin	10	8	1	39	158	22.57	–	–	6
D.S.Mohanty	45	11	6	18*	28	5.60	–	–	10
D.Mongia	4	4	–	37	51	12.75	–	–	–
A.Nehra	10	3	2	2*	6	6.00	–	–	1
B.K.V.Prasad	161	63	32	19	221	7.12	–	–	37
V.Sehwag	22	20	3	100	459	27.00	1	3	6
R.R.Singh	136	113	23	100	2338	25.97	1	9	33
R.S.Sodhi	17	13	3	67	279	27.90	–	2	9
J.Srinath	198	105	31	53	837	11.31	–	1	31
S.Sriram	6	5	1	12	21	5.25	–	–	1

	M	I	NO	HS	Runs	Avge	100	50	Ct/St
S.R.Tendulkar	280	272	25	186*	10803	43.73	31	53	89
Yuvraj Singh	28	24	2	98*	498	22.63	–	2	14

INDIA – BOWLING

	O	R	W	Avge	Best	4wI	R/Over
A.B.Agarkar	716.2	3662	124	29.53	4-25	5	5.11
H.K.Badani	10	53	2	26.50	1- 7	–	5.30
R.Dravid	31	170	4	42.50	2-43	–	5.48
S.C.Ganguly	455.4	2262	67	33.76	5-16	3	4.96
Harbhajan Singh	320	1283	44	29.15	3-27	–	4.01
Harvinder Singh	114.2	609	24	25.37	3-44	–	5.33
S.B.Joshi	564.2	2509	69	36.36	5- 6	2	4.45
V.G.Kambli	0.4	7	1	7.00	1- 7	–	10.50
A.R.Kapoor	150	612	8	76.50	2-33	–	4.08
Z.Khan	249.5	1199	42	28.54	4-42	2	4.80
A.Kumble	1929.1	8073	281	28.72	6-12	9	4.18
V.V.S.Laxman	6	32	0	–	–	–	5.33
D.S.Mohanty	332.4	1662	57	29.15	4-56	1	5.00
A.Nehra	87.4	389	13	29.92	3-30	–	4.44
B.K.V.Prasad	1354.5	6332	196	32.30	5-27	4	4.67
V.Sehwag	106.4	567	13	43.61	3-59	–	5.32
R.R.Singh	622.2	2985	69	43.26	5-22	2	4.80
R.S.Sodhi	77	365	5	73.00	2-31	–	4.74
J.Srinath	1722.4	7697	268	28.72	5-23	7	4.47
S.Sriram	35	194	5	38.80	3-47	–	5.54
S.R.Tendulkar	969	4792	103	46.52	5-32	4	4.95
Yuvraj Singh	107	453	12	37.75	2-24	–	4.23

PAKISTAN – BATTING AND FIELDING

	M	I	NO	HS	Runs	Avge	100	50	Ct/St
Abdul Razzaq	89	75	15	75*	1514	25.23	–	9	10
Arshad Khan	48	27	16	20	106	9.63	–	–	9
Atiq-uz-Zaman	3	3	1	18	34	17.00	–	–	3/1
Azhar Mahmood	111	84	19	67	1206	18.55	–	3	34
Danish Kaneria	1	1	1	3*	3	–	–	–	–
Faisal Iqbal	3	3	1	17*	33	16.50	–	–	–
Fazal-e-Akber	2	1	–	7	7	7.00	–	–	–
Humayun Farhat	5	3	–	39	60	20.00	–	–	4/3
Ijaz Ahmed	250	232	29	139*	6564	32.33	10	37	90
Imran Abbas	2	2	–	28	29	14.50	–	–	1
Imran Farhat	4	4	–	33	48	12.00	–	–	2
Imran Nazir	35	35	1	105*	788	23.17	1	4	11
Inzamam-ul-Haq	251	237	35	137*	8195	40.56	8	60	76
Kabir Khan	10	5	4	5	10	10.00	–	–	1
Kashif Raza	1	1	1	2*	2	–	–	–	–
Mohammad Sami	4	2	2	4*	5	–	–	–	2
Moin Khan	190	159	35	69*	2853	23.00	–	9	191/66
Mushtaq Ahmed	143	76	34	34*	399	9.50	–	–	30
Naved Latif	3	3	–	113	143	47.66	1	–	1
Rashid Latif	112	74	20	66	917	16.98	–	2	111/29
Saeed Anwar	230	227	17	194	8348	39.75	19	41	41
Salim Elahi	28	28	2	102*	805	30.96	1	5	8
Saqlain Mushtaq	144	85	31	37*	648	12.00	–	–	35
Shahid Afridi	136	132	5	109	3128	24.62	2	18	53
Shoaib Akhtar	49	23	16	36	86	12.28	–	–	8
Shoaib Malik	19	11	3	44	145	18.12	–	–	8
Taufiq Umar	2	2	–	18	28	14.00	–	–	2
Waqar Younis	220	118	41	37	855	11.10	–	–	24
Wasim Akram	323	254	46	86	3359	16.14	–	6	85
Yasir Arafat	2	2	–	6	10	5.00	–	–	–

PAKISTAN – BATTING AND FIELDING (continued)

	M	I	NO	HS	Runs	Avge	100	50	Ct/St
Younis Khan	34	33	1	59	653	21.76	–	2	14
Yousuf Youhana	89	85	13	104*	2798	38.86	3	17	25

PAKISTAN – BOWLING

	O	R	W	Avge	Best	4wI	R/Over
Abdul Razzaq	691	3052	120	25.43	5-31	5	4.42
Arshad Khan	395.3	1627	44	36.97	3-22	–	4.11
Azhar Mahmood	842.5	3820	108	35.37	6-18	5	4.53
Danish Kaneria	7	43	0	–	–	–	6.14
Faisal Iqbal	2	16	0	–	–	–	8.00
Fazal-e-Akber	12	48	0	–	–	–	4.00
Ijaz Ahmed	106.1	476	5	95.20	2-31	–	4.48
Imran Farhat	1.3	12	0	–	–	–	8.00
Imran Nazir	4.1	19	1	19.00	1- 3	–	4.56
Inzamam-ul-Haq	6.4	52	2	26.00	1- 4	–	7.80
Kabir Khan	61.5	303	12	25.25	2-23	–	4.90
Kashif Raza	5	36	1	36.00	1-36	–	7.20
Mohammad Sami	29	137	3	45.66	2-41	–	4.72
Mushtaq Ahmed	1247.1	5296	161	32.89	5-36	4	4.25
Saeed Anwar	36.2	176	5	35.20	2- 9	–	4.84
Saqlain Mushtaq	1256.1	5370	257	20.89	5-20	16	4.28
Shahid Afridi	832.4	3913	95	41.18	5-40	1	4.70
Shoaib Akhtar	369.1	1707	83	20.56	5-19	2	4.62
Shoaib Malik	146.1	665	19	35.00	3-42	–	4.55
Waqar Younis	1803	8318	357	23.29	7-36	25	4.61
Wasim Akram	2757.1	10643	446	23.86	5-15	21	3.86
Yasir Arafat	12	65	2	32.50	1-28	–	5.42
Younis Khan	6	29	0	–	–	–	4.83

SRI LANKA – BATTING AND FIELDING

	M	I	NO	HS	Runs	Avge	100	50	Ct/St
R.P.Arnold	72	63	17	103	1900	41.30	1	14	24
M.S.Atapattu	143	141	18	132*	4563	37.09	5	35	41
U.D.U.Chandana	81	61	8	50	826	15.58	–	1	50
S.I.de Saram	15	13	2	38	183	16.63	–	–	9
P.A.de Silva	275	266	26	145	8430	35.12	11	57	95
H.D.P.K.Dharmasena	123	74	29	69*	1032	22.93	–	4	34
T.M.Dilshan	14	12	3	53	230	25.55	–	1	6
C.R.D.Fernando	19	6	5	12*	21	21.00	–	–	4
T.C.B.Fernando	5	3	2	3	4	4.00	–	–	1
I.S.Gallage	3	2	1	14	17	17.00	–	–	–
W.C.A.Ganegama	2	1	–	0	0	0.00	–	–	–
D.A.Gunawardena	37	37	–	132	1108	29.94	1	7	8
S.T.Jayasuriya	252	244	9	189	7235	30.78	11	47	86
D.P.M.deS.Jayawardena	94	88	8	128	2656	33.20	6	13	41
R.S.Kalpage	86	69	28	51	844	20.58	–	1	33
R.S.Kaluwitharana	170	162	13	102*	3349	22.47	2	21	123/70
D.K.Liyanage	16	11	2	43	144	16.00	–	–	6
M.Muralitharan	183	84	36	18	270	5.62	–	–	82
R.A.P.Nissanka	4	1	–	2	2	2.00	–	–	2
A.S.A.Perera	20	13	2	56*	195	17.72	–	1	4
T.T.Samaraweera	8	5	–	27	66	13.20	–	–	2
K.Sangakkara	40	34	5	85	646	22.27	–	2	25/9
L.P.C.Silva	8	6	–	55	95	15.83	–	1	1
K.E.A.Upashantha	12	8	1	15	49	7.00	–	–	2
W.P.U.C.J.Vaas	175	115	39	50*	1079	14.19	–	1	31
K.Weeraratne	10	4	1	14*	40	13.33	–	–	1
G.P.Wickremasinghe	132	62	23	32	339	8.69	–	–	26
D.N.T.Zoysa	57	26	13	32	180	13.84	–	–	8

LOI   **SRI LANKA – BOWLING**

	O	R	W	Avge	Best	4wI	R/Over
R.P.Arnold	248.5	1127	26	43.34	2-12	–	4.53
M.S.Atapattu	8.3	41	0	–	–	–	4.82
U.D.U.Chandana	530.5	2485	80	31.06	4-31	3	4.68
P.A.de Silva	727.5	3561	91	39.13	4-45	1	4.89
H.D.P.K.Dharmasena	1028	4446	127	35.00	4-37	1	4.32
C.R.D.Fernando	133.2	716	27	26.51	3-43	–	5.37
T.C.B.Fernando	39.4	191	8	23.87	5-67	1	4.82
I.S.Gallage	24	115	3	38.33	2-42	–	4.79
W.C.A.Ganegama	4	27	2	13.50	2-27	–	6.75
S.T.Jayasuriya	1565	7477	214	34.93	6-29	8	4.78
D.P.M.deS.Jayawardena	82.4	459	7	65.57	2-56	–	5.55
R.S.Kalpage	660	2975	73	40.75	4-36	2	4.51
D.K.Liyanage	107	510	10	51.00	3-49	–	4.77
M.Muralitharan	1672.4	6559	267	24.56	7-30	11	3.92
R.A.P.Nissanka	26	171	3	57.00	2-24	–	6.58
A.S.A.Perera	96.3	522	13	40.15	2-25	–	5.41
T.T.Samaraweera	71	328	7	46.85	3-34	–	4.62
K.E.A.Upashantha	94	480	12	40.00	4-37	1	5.12
W.P.U.C.J.Vaas	1416.5	5968	218	27.37	8-19	5	4.21
K.Weeraratne	64	288	6	48.00	3-46	–	4.50
G.P.Wickremasinghe	943.2	4265	108	39.49	4-48	1	4.52
D.N.T.Zoysa	436.2	1936	60	32.26	4-28	2	4.44

ZIMBABWE – BATTING AND FIELDING

	M	I	NO	HS	Runs	Avge	100	50	Ct/St
A.M.Blignaut	14	12	2	27	127	12.70	–	–	3
G.B.Brent	34	26	10	24	158	9.87	–	–	8
A.D.R.Campbell	172	168	14	131*	4794	31.12	7	26	68
S.V.Carlisle	91	88	7	121*	2221	27.41	2	8	33
D.D.Ebrahim	26	25	2	121	547	23.78	1	1	4
S.M.Ervine	8	6	1	47	75	15.00	–	–	–
A.Flower	191	188	14	142*	5797	33.31	3	46	135/32
G.W.Flower	177	175	14	142*	5415	33.63	5	33	67
T.J.Friend	30	20	5	22	134	8.93	–	–	7
T.R.Gripper	5	5	–	26	41	8.20	–	–	3
D.T.Hondo	2	2	1	5	5	5.00	–	–	–
A.J.Mackay	3	–	–	–	–	–	–	–	1
T.N.Madondo	13	13	1	71	191	15.91	–	1	2
D.A.Marillier	25	24	3	52*	340	16.19	–	1	5
H.Masakadza	3	3	–	11	16	5.33	–	–	–
M.Mbangwa	26	12	5	11	33	4.71	–	–	3
B.A.Murphy	21	13	8	20*	58	11.60	–	–	8
D.T.Mutendera	9	4	2	10	20	10.00	–	–	1
M.L.Nkala	33	20	2	36	148	8.22	–	–	4
H.K.Olonga	43	24	13	11	48	4.36	–	–	12
G.J.Rennie	36	33	6	76	567	21.00	–	2	13
B.C.Strang	49	26	8	19	92	5.11	–	–	15
P.A.Strang	95	73	24	47	1090	22.24	–	–	30
H.H.Streak	142	118	41	79*	1848	24.00	–	5	31
T.Taibu	7	6	3	19*	22	7.33	–	–	3/1
M.A.Vermeulen	1	1	–	22	22	22.00	–	–	–
D.P.Viljoen	53	43	7	63*	512	14.22	–	2	18
G.J.Whittall	139	136	22	83	2613	22.92	–	11	34
C.B.Wishart	66	61	4	102	1229	21.56	1	4	18

ZIMBABWE – BOWLING

	O	R	W	Avge	Best	4wI	R/Over
A.M.Blignaut	103.4	485	12	40.41	2-24	–	4.68
G.B.Brent	275	1334	42	31.76	4-53	1	4.85
A.D.R.Campbell	80.5	411	12	34.25	2-20	–	5.08
D.D.Ebrahim	0.3	6	0	–	–	–	12.00

LOI **ZIMBABWE – BOWLING (continued)**

	O	R	W	Avge	Best	4wI	R/Over
S.M.Ervine	60	301	8	37.62	3-29	–	5.02
A.Flower	5	23	0	–	–	–	4.60
G.W.Flower	658.2	3054	81	37.70	4-32	2	4.64
T.J.Friend	232	1261	28	45.03	4-55	1	5.44
T.R.Gripper	10	22	0	–	–	–	2.20
D.T.Hondo	9	66	0	–	–	–	7.33
A.J.Mackay	22	137	0	–	–	–	6.23
D.A.Marillier	129.2	596	16	37.25	4-38	1	4.61
M.Mbangwa	200.1	1030	10	103.00	2-24	–	5.15
B.A.Murphy	160	786	20	39.30	3-43	–	4.91
D.T.Mutendera	65	334	9	37.11	3-23	–	5.14
M.L.Nkala	193.3	1089	18	60.50	3-12	–	5.63
H.K.Olonga	305.1	1771	49	36.14	6-19	3	5.80
G.J.Rennie	1	11	0	–	–	–	11.00
B.C.Strang	415.4	1718	46	37.34	6-20	2	4.13
P.A.Strang	725.1	3174	96	33.06	5-21	4	4.38
H.H.Streak	1186.3	5358	177	30.27	5-32	6	4.52
D.P.Viljoen	345.5	1639	44	37.25	3-20	–	4.74
G.J.Whittall	639.1	3276	84	39.00	4-35	1	5.13
C.B.Wishart	2	12	0	–	–	–	6.00

BANGLADESH – BATTING AND FIELDING

	M	I	NO	HS	Runs	Avge	100	50	Ct/St
Akram Khan	38	38	2	65	857	23.80	–	5	7
Al Sahariar	10	10	1	62*	206	22.88	–	2	2
Aminul Islam	38	38	5	70	763	23.12	–	3	13
Enamul Haque	26	23	5	19	190	10.55	–	–	5
Fahim Muntasir	2	2	1	1*	1	1.00	–	–	1
Habibul Bashar	20	20	–	74	431	21.55	–	4	6
Hasibul Hussain	28	22	3	21*	161	8.47	–	–	6
Javed Omar	16	16	3	85*	437	33.61	–	4	2
Khaled Mahmud	23	21	–	50	308	14.66	–	1	3
Khaled Masud	37	34	7	53*	340	12.59	–	1	25/7
Manjurul Islam	13	7	6	6*	16	16.00	–	–	3
Mashrafe Bin Mortaza	3	3	–	18	20	6.66	–	–	–
Mehrab Hossain	12	12	–	101	351	29.25	1	2	4
Mohammed Ashraful	4	4	–	16	46	11.50	–	–	–
Mohammed Rafique	26	26	2	77	318	13.25	–	1	5
Mohammed Sharif	5	5	3	13*	36	18.00	–	–	1
Mushfiqur Rahman	6	4	1	31	60	20.00	–	–	–
Naimur Rahman	24	23	2	47	441	21.00	–	–	6
Sanwar Hossain	6	6	–	52	85	14.16	–	1	2
Tushar Imran	1	1	–	6	6	6.00	–	–	–

BANGLADESH – BOWLING

	O	R	W	Avge	Best	4wI	R/Over
Akram Khan	19.3	138	0	–	–	–	7.08
Aminul Islam	68.4	411	7	58.71	3-57	–	5.99
Enamul Haque	183.2	930	16	58.12	2-40	–	5.07
Fahim Muntasir	18.1	71	0	–	–	–	3.91
Habibul Bashar	27.1	122	1	122.00	1-31	–	4.49
Hasibul Hussain	206.1	1187	28	42.39	4-56	1	5.76
Khaled Mahmud	182.1	871	20	43.55	3-31	–	4.78
Manjurul Islam	97.1	484	12	40.33	3-37	–	4.98
Mashrafe Bin Mortaza	27.2	116	4	29.00	2-26	–	4.24
Mehrab Hossain	2	18	0	–	–	–	9.00
Mohammed Ashraful	9	54	1	54.00	1-24	–	6.00
Mohammed Rafique	218.1	1084	21	51.61	3-56	–	4.97
Mohammed Sharif	47	232	4	58.00	3-48	–	4.94
Mushfiqur Rahman	52.5	255	3	85.00	1-20	–	4.83

LOI

BANGLADESH – BOWLING (continued)

	O	R	W	Avge	Best	4wI	R/Over
Naimur Rahman	151.4	761	8	95.12	2-51	–	5.02
Sanwar Hossain	1	17	0	–	–	–	17.00

KENYA – BATTING AND FIELDING

	M	I	NO	HS	Runs	Avge	100	50	Ct/St
J.Ababu	3	2	–	17	28	14.00	–	–	1
J.O.Angara	8	3	1	6	12	6.00	–	–	–
S.K.Gupta	10	10	1	41	121	13.44	–	–	–
J.K.Kamande	10	6	3	32*	85	28.33	–	–	–
H.S.Modi	37	32	5	78*	687	25.44	–	4	7
C.O.Obuya	9	7	2	27	84	16.80	–	–	2
D.O.Obuya	8	8	–	34	109	13.62	–	–	4/1
K.O.Obuya	40	39	1	144	993	26.13	2	4	13/9
T.M.Odoyo	42	39	5	53	765	22.50	–	2	13
M.O.Odumbe	41	39	2	83	946	25.56	–	8	7
P.O.Ongando	6	5	2	36	41	13.66	–	–	1
L.N.Onyango	4	4	1	23	29	9.66	–	–	1
B.J.Patel	6	1	–	6	6	6.00	–	–	1
R.D.Shah	26	26	–	71	786	30.23	–	8	8
M.Sheikh	21	15	5	15*	68	6.80	–	–	7
A.O.Suji	28	24	4	67	267	13.35	–	1	7
M.A.Suji	40	32	16	15	127	7.93	–	–	8
S.O.Tikolo	43	41	2	106*	1190	30.51	1	10	17

KENYA – BOWLING

	O	R	W	Avge	Best	4wI	R/Over
J.Ababu	16	75	1	75.00	1-26	–	4.69
J.O.Angara	57	317	8	39.62	3-30	–	5.56
J.K.Kamande	28.5	165	2	82.50	1-16	–	5.72
H.S.Modi	2.1	18	0	–	–	–	8.31
C.O.Obuya	69.4	334	3	111.33	1-32	–	4.79
T.M.Odoyo	309	1557	40	38.92	3-25	–	5.04
M.O.Odumbe	258.5	1242	27	46.00	3-14	–	4.80
P.O.Ongando	27	137	1	137.00	1-10	–	5.07
L.N.Onyango	13.3	130	1	130.00	1-45	–	9.63
B.J.Patel	15.1	91	2	45.50	1-15	–	6.00
R.D.Shah	10	72	0	–	–	–	7.20
M.Sheikh	129.4	625	19	32.89	4-36	1	4.82
A.O.Suji	125.5	654	10	65.40	2-24	–	5.20
M.A.Suji	302	1419	27	52.55	4-24	1	4.70
S.O.Tikolo	192.2	1010	24	42.08	3-22	–	5.25

SCOTLAND – BATTING AND FIELDING

	M	I	NO	HS	Runs	Avge	100	50	Ct/St
J.A.R.Blain	5	5	1	9	15	3.75	–	–	1
J.E.Brinkley	5	5	–	23	52	10.40	–	–	1
G.M.Hamilton	5	5	1	76	217	54.25	–	2	1

SCOTLAND – BOWLING

	O	R	W	Avge	Best	4wI	R/Over
J.A.R.Blain	37.1	210	10	21.00	4-37	1	5.65
J.E.Brinkley	28	117	2	58.50	1-29	–	4.18
G.M.Hamilton	35.4	149	3	49.66	2-36	–	4.18

TEST CAREER RECORDS

These records are complete to 30 January 2002 and include all players registered for county cricket in 2002 at the time of going to press, plus those who have played Test cricket since 4 September 2000.

ENGLAND – BATTING AND FIELDING

	M	I	NO	HS	Runs	Avge	100	50	Ct/St
C.J.Adams	5	8	–	31	104	13.00	–	–	6
U.Afzaal	3	6	1	54	83	16.60	–	1	–
M.A.Atherton	115	212	7	185*	7728	37.69	16	46	83
R.J.Bailey	4	8	–	43	119	14.87	–	–	–
K.J.Barnett	4	7	–	80	207	29.57	–	2	1
M.P.Bicknell	2	4	–	14	26	6.50	–	–	–
R.J.Blakey	2	4	–	6	7	1.75	–	–	2
S.J.E.Brown	1	2	1	10*	11	11.00	–	–	1
M.A.Butcher	35	67	3	173*	1924	30.06	3	7	30
A.R.Caddick	50	77	9	49*	739	10.86	–	–	17
D.G.Cork	34	53	8	59	781	17.35	–	2	17
J.P.Crawley	29	47	5	156*	1329	31.64	3	7	26
R.D.B.Croft	21	34	8	37*	421	16.19	–	–	10
R.K.J.Dawson	3	5	1	11	27	6.75	–	–	1
P.A.J.DeFreitas	44	68	5	88	934	14.82	–	4	14
M.A.Ealham	8	13	3	53*	210	21.00	–	2	4
N.H.Fairbrother	10	15	1	83	219	15.64	–	1	4
A.Flintoff	12	19	–	42	259	13.63	–	–	5
J.S.Foster	3	5	–	48	96	19.20	–	–	5/1
A.R.C.Fraser	46	67	15	32	388	7.46	–	–	9
J.E.R.Gallian	3	6	–	28	74	12.33	–	–	1
E.S.H.Giddins	4	7	3	7	10	2.50	–	–	–
A.F.Giles	10	16	4	37*	138	11.50	–	–	5
D.Gough	56	83	18	65	806	12.40	–	2	12
A.Habib	2	3	–	19	26	8.66	–	–	–
G.M.Hamilton	1	2	–	0	0	0.00	–	–	–
W.K.Hegg	2	4	–	15	30	7.50	–	–	8
G.A.Hick	65	114	6	178	3383	31.32	6	18	90
M.J.Hoggard	5	8	4	12*	18	4.50	–	–	1
A.J.Hollioake	4	6	–	45	65	10.83	–	–	4
B.C.Hollioake	2	4	–	28	44	11.00	–	–	2
N.Hussain	66	118	12	207	3726	35.15	9	19	46
M.C.Ilott	5	6	2	15	28	7.00	–	–	–
R.C.Irani	3	5	–	41	86	17.20	–	–	2
S.P.James	2	4	–	36	71	17.75	–	–	–
N.V.Knight	17	30	–	113	719	23.96	1	4	26
M.N.Lathwell	2	4	–	33	78	19.50	–	–	–
M.J.McCague	3	5	–	11	21	4.20	–	–	1
D.L.Maddy	3	4	–	24	46	11.50	–	–	4
D.E.Malcolm	40	58	19	29	236	6.05	–	–	7
P.J.Martin	8	13	–	29	115	8.84	–	–	6
M.P.Maynard	4	8	–	35	87	10.87	–	–	3
A.D.Mullally	19	27	4	24	127	5.52	–	–	6
T.A.Munton	2	2	1	25*	25	25.00	–	–	1
J.Ormond	2	4	1	18	38	12.66	–	–	–
M.M.Patel	2	2	–	27	45	22.50	–	–	2
M.R.Ramprakash	49	87	6	154	2273	28.06	2	12	37
C.M.W.Read	3	4	–	37	38	9.50	–	–	10/1
S.J.Rhodes	11	17	5	65*	294	24.50	–	1	46/3
R.C.Russell	54	86	16	128*	1897	27.10	2	6	153/12
I.D.K.Salisbury	15	25	3	50	368	16.72	–	1	5

ENGLAND – BATTING AND FIELDING (continued)

	M	I	NO	HS	Runs	Avge	100	50	Ct/St
C.P.Schofield	2	3	–	57	67	22.33	–	1	–
R.J.Sidebottom	1	1	–	4	4	4.00	–	–	–
C.E.W.Silverwood	5	6	3	7*	19	6.33	–	–	2
A.M.Smith	1	2	1	4*	4	4.00	–	–	–
R.A.Smith	62	112	15	175	4236	43.67	9	28	39
A.J.Stewart	115	207	17	190	7469	39.31	14	38	220/11
P.M.Such	11	16	5	14*	67	6.09	–	–	4
G.P.Thorpe	70	128	16	138	4583	40.91	9	29	74
M.E.Trescothick	19	36	2	122	1311	38.55	2	9	15
A.J.Tudor	5	9	3	99*	180	30.00	–	1	–
P.C.R.Tufnell	42	59	29	22*	153	5.10	–	–	12
M.P.Vaughan	13	21	1	120	679	33.95	1	3	11
I.J.Ward	5	9	1	39	129	16.12	–	–	1
C.White	24	39	4	121	745	21.28	1	2	13

ENGLAND – BOWLING

	O	R	W	Avge	Best	5wI	10wM
C.J.Adams	20	59	1	59.00	1- 42	–	–
U.Afzaal	9	49	1	49.00	1- 49	–	–
M.A.Atherton	68	302	2	151.00	1- 20	–	–
K.J.Barnett	6	32	0				
M.P.Bicknell	87	263	4	65.75	3- 99	–	–
S.J.E.Brown	33	138	2	69.00	1- 60	–	–
M.A.Butcher	76.2	251	8	31.37	4- 42	–	–
A.R.Caddick	1788	5392	181	29.79	7- 46	10	–
D.G.Cork	1199.1	3647	124	29.41	7- 43	5	–
R.D.B.Croft	769.5	1825	49	37.24	5- 95	1	–
R.K.J.Dawson	90	279	6	46.50	4-134	–	–
P.A.J.DeFreitas	1639.4	4700	140	33.57	7- 70	4	–
M.A.Ealham	176.4	488	17	28.70	4- 21	–	–
N.H.Fairbrother	2	9	0				
A.Flintoff	229.5	574	13	44.15	4- 50	–	–
A.R.C.Fraser	1812.4	4836	177	27.32	8- 53	13	2
J.E.R.Gallian	14	62	0				
E.S.H.Giddins	74	240	12	20.00	5- 15	1	–
A.F.Giles	472.4	1131	32	35.34	5- 67	2	–
D.Gough	1917.1	6288	228	27.57	6- 42	9	–
G.M.Hamilton	15	63	0				
G.A.Hick	509.3	1306	23	56.78	4-126	–	–
M.J.Hoggard	162.5	502	15	33.46	4- 80	–	–
A.J.Hollioake	24	67	2	33.50	2- 31	–	–
B.C.Hollioake	42	199	4	49.75	2-105	–	–
N.Hussain	5	15	0				
M.C.Ilott	173.4	542	12	45.16	3- 48	–	–
R.C.Irani	32	112	3	37.33	1- 22	–	–
M.J.McCague	98.5	390	6	65.00	4-121	–	–
D.L.Maddy	14	40	0				
D.E.Malcolm	1413.2	4748	128	37.09	9- 57	5	2
P.J.Martin	242	580	17	34.11	4- 60	–	–
A.D.Mullally	754.1	1812	58	31.24	5-105	1	–
T.A.Munton	67.3	200	4	50.00	2- 22	–	–
J.Ormond	62	185	2	92.50	1- 70	–	–
M.M.Patel	46	180	1	180.00	1-101	–	–
M.R.Ramprakash	149.1	477	4	119.25	1- 2	–	–
I.D.K.Salisbury	415.2	1539	20	76.95	4-163	–	–
C.P.Schofield	18	73	0				
R.J.Sidebottom	20	64	0				

ENGLAND – BOWLING (continued)

	O	R	W	Avge	Best	5wI	10wM
C.E.W.Silverwood	134	415	11	37.72	5-91	1	–
A.M.Smith	23	89	0				
R.A.Smith	4	6	0				
A.J.Stewart	3.2	13	0				
P.M.Such	520.4	1242	37	33.56	6-67	2	–
G.P.Thorpe	23	37	0				
M.E.Trescothick	20	52	1	52.00	1-34	–	–
A.J.Tudor	103.1	434	15	28.93	5-44	1	–
P.C.R.Tufnell	1881.2	4560	121	37.68	7-47	5	2
M.P.Vaughan	29	131	0				
C.White	489	1510	40	37.75	5-32	2	–

AUSTRALIA – BATTING AND FIELDING

	M	I	NO	HS	Runs	Avge	100	50	Ct/St
M.G.Bevan	18	30	3	91	785	29.07	–	6	8
A.J.Bichel	6	8	–	18	63	7.87	–	–	4
D.W.Fleming	20	19	3	71*	305	19.06	–	2	9
A.C.Gilchrist	28	39	6	152	1687	51.12	4	10	109/9
J.N.Gillespie	30	39	12	46	400	14.81	–	–	9
M.L.Hayden	27	47	4	203	2045	47.55	7	7	25
M.S.Kasprowicz	17	23	5	25	234	13.00	–	–	6
S.M.Katich	1	2	1	15	15	15.00	–	–	1
J.L.Langer	48	80	5	223	3364	44.85	12	14	32
S.G.Law	1	1	1	54*	54	–	–	1	1
B.Lee	18	17	3	62*	357	25.50	–	2	2
D.S.Lehmann	5	8	–	98	228	28.50	–	2	3
S.C.G.MacGill	17	23	2	43	228	10.85	–	–	12
G.D.McGrath	81	93	32	39	405	6.63	–	–	24
D.R.Martyn	22	35	9	124*	1413	54.34	4	9	7
C.R.Miller	18	24	3	43	174	8.28	–	–	6
R.T.Ponting	53	84	11	197	3196	43.78	9	15	68
M.J.Slater	74	131	7	219	5312	42.83	14	21	33
S.K.Warne	98	134	12	99	1962	16.08	–	6	78
M.E.Waugh	122	200	17	153*	7780	42.51	20	45	167
S.R.Waugh	145	228	41	200	9505	50.82	27	44	101

AUSTRALIA – BOWLING

	O	R	W	Avge	Best	5wI	10wM
M.G.Bevan	214.1	703	29	24.24	6-82	1	1
A.J.Bichel	161.5	517	13	39.76	5-60	1	–
D.W.Fleming	688.1	1942	75	25.89	5-30	3	–
J.N.Gillespie	958.1	2918	115	25.37	7-37	6	–
M.L.Hayden	9	40	0				
M.S.Kasprowicz	556.2	1739	47	37.00	7-36	2	–
J.L.Langer	1	3	0				
S.G.Law	3	9	0				
B.Lee	555.3	1837	74	24.82	5-47	4	–
D.S.Lehmann	17	45	2	22.50	1- 6	–	–
S.C.G.MacGill	689.5	2051	82	25.01	7-50	4	1
G.D.McGrath	3247.4	8297	377	22.00	8-38	22	3
D.R.Martyn	23	60	1	60.00	1- 3	–	–
C.R.Miller	681.5	1805	69	26.15	5-32	3	1
R.T.Ponting	63.5	160	4	40.00	1- 0	–	–
G.R.Robertson	149.4	515	13	39.61	4-72	–	–
M.J.Slater	4.1	10	1	10.00	1- 4	–	–
S.K.Warne	4562.1	11493	430	26.72	8-71	20	5

AUSTRALIA – BOWLING (continued)

	O	R	W	Avge	Best	5wI	10wM
M.E.Waugh	768	2280	57	40.00	5-40	1	–
S.R.Waugh	1195.5	3181	89	35.74	5-28	3	–

SOUTH AFRICA – BATTING AND FIELDING

	M	I	NO	HS	Runs	Avge	100	50	Ct/St
P.R.Adams	34	41	11	29	197	6.56	–	–	21
N.Boje	18	26	3	85	537	23.34	–	2	8
M.V.Boucher	49	66	7	125	1737	29.44	3	10	182/5
D.J.Cullinan	70	115	12	275*	4554	44.21	14	20	67
H.H.Dippenaar	14	21	–	100	486	23.14	1	1	7
A.A.Donald	71	92	32	37	649	10.81	–	–	18
H.H.Gibbs	35	59	2	211*	2264	39.71	5	9	23
M.Hayward	10	13	7	14	52	8.66	–	–	1
C.W.Henderson	5	7	–	30	65	9.28	–	–	2
J.H.Kallis	57	94	15	189*	3787	47.93	9	20	51
J.M.Kemp	3	4	–	16	18	4.50	–	–	3
G.Kirsten	80	142	12	275	5479	42.14	14	25	68
L.Klusener	48	68	11	174	1904	33.40	4	8	33
N.D.McKenzie	21	34	2	120	1168	36.50	2	8	23
A.Nel	2	–	–	–	–	–	–	–	–
M.Ngam	3	1	1	0*	0	–	–	–	1
M.Ntini	20	19	6	23	104	8.00	–	–	6
J.L.Ontong	1	2	–	32	41	20.50	–	–	–
S.M.Pollock	63	91	20	111	2242	31.57	2	10	41

SOUTH AFRICA – BOWLING

	O	R	W	Avge	Best	5wI	10wM
P.R.Adams	1101	3063	96	31.90	6- 55	1	–
N.Boje	543.3	1299	48	27.06	5- 62	2	–
D.J.Cullinan	20	71	2	35.50	1- 10	–	–
A.A.Donald	2571.1	7272	329	22.10	8- 71	20	3
M.Hayward	324.5	1003	32	31.34	4- 75	–	–
C.W.Henderson	284.1	833	19	43.84	4-116	–	–
J.H.Kallis	1242.5	3145	106	29.66	6- 67	2	–
J.M.Kemp	65.5	151	8	18.87	3- 33	–	–
G.Kirsten	56.1	141	2	70.50	1- 0	–	–
L.Klusener	1114.5	2924	78	37.48	8- 64	1	–
N.D.McKenzie	1	4	0				
A.Nel	54.5	168	6	28.00	4- 53	–	–
M.Ngam	65.2	189	11	17.18	3- 26	–	–
M.Ntini	559.1	1617	45	35.93	6- 66	1	–
J.L.Ontong	2	10	0				
S.M.Pollock	2357.3	5409	261	20.72	7- 87	14	1

WEST INDIES – BATTING AND FIELDING

	M	I	NO	HS	Runs	Avge	100	50	Ct/St
J.C.Adams	54	90	17	208*	3012	41.26	6	14	48
M.I.Black	5	9	3	6	12	2.00	–	–	–
C.O.Browne	14	21	6	39*	263	17.53	–	–	63/1
S.L.Campbell	51	91	8	208	2856	32.82	4	18	46
S.Chanderpaul	49	81	9	137*	2833	39.34	2	22	21
P.T.Collins	6	9	–	13	18	2.00	–	–	4
C.E.Cuffy	5	8	3	13*	26	5.20	–	–	2
M.Dillon	19	36	2	36	275	8.08	–	–	9
D.Ganga	13	23	–	89	423	18.39	–	1	6
L.V.Garrick	1	2	–	27	27	13.50	–	–	2
C.H.Gayle	14	24	1	175	672	29.21	1	2	21

	M	I	NO	HS	Runs	Avge	100	50	Ct/St
W.W.Hinds	18	33	1	165	936	29.25	1	6	17
C.L.Hooper	90	154	14	178*	4866	34.75	10	24	103
R.D.Jacobs	35	64	13	113*	1404	27.52	1	7	123/5
R.D.King	14	19	5	12*	50	3.57	–	–	2
B.C.Lara	83	147	4	375	7221	50.49	18	34	107
N.C.McGarrell	4	6	2	33	61	15.25	–	–	2
N.A.M.McLean	19	32	2	46	368	12.26	–	–	5
M.V.Nagamootoo	2	4	–	68	111	27.75	–	1	–
D.Ramnarine	11	19	4	35*	106	7.06	–	–	8
M.N.Samuels	12	22	1	60*	535	25.47	–	4	5
R.R.Sarwan	17	33	5	91	1059	37.82	–	9	9
C.E.L.Stuart	6	9	2	12*	24	3.42	–	–	2
C.A.Walsh	132	185	61	30*	936	7.54	–	–	29

WEST INDIES – BOWLING

	O	R	W	Avge	Best	5wI	10wM
J.C.Adams	475.3	1336	27	49.48	5- 17	1	–
M.I.Black	127.1	508	9	56.44	4- 83	–	–
S.Chanderpaul	231	697	6	116.16	1- 2	–	–
P.T.Collins	227	739	17	43.47	4- 78	–	–
C.E.Cuffy	152.2	476	11	43.27	3- 80	–	–
M.Dillon	670.4	2112	66	32.00	5-111	1	–
C.H.Gayle	54.3	135	4	33.75	3- 25	–	–
W.W.Hinds	18.3	50	3	16.66	2- 23	–	–
C.L.Hooper	2042.1	5015	101	49.65	5- 26	4	–
R.D.King	414.1	1222	44	27.77	5- 51	1	–
B.C.Lara	10	28	0	–	–	–	–
N.C.McGarrell	202	453	17	26.64	4- 23	–	–
N.A.M.McLean	549.5	1873	44	42.56	3- 53	–	–
M.V.Nagamootoo	87	239	6	39.83	3-119	–	–
D.Ramnarine	534.3	1207	42	28.73	5- 78	1	–
M.N.Samuels	75.5	239	3	79.66	2- 49	–	–
R.R.Sarwan	5	27	0	–	–	–	–
C.E.L.Stuart	186	628	20	31.40	3- 33	–	–
C.A.Walsh	5003.1	12688	519	24.44	7- 37	22	3

NEW ZEALAND – BATTING AND FIELDING

	M	I	NO	HS	Runs	Avge	100	50	Ct/St
N.J.Astle	50	85	7	156*	2903	37.21	7	13	43
M.D.Bell	13	23	1	105	484	22.00	1	2	10
S.E.Bond	4	3	1	8	12	6.00	–	–	3
G.E.Bradburn	7	10	2	30*	105	13.12	–	–	6
C.L.Cairns	54	90	4	126	2830	32.90	4	20	14
C.J.Drum	2	1	–	4	4	4.00	–	–	1
S.P.Fleming	65	111	9	174*	3898	37.48	3	32	95
J.E.C.Franklin	2	2	–	0	0	0.00	–	–	1
M.J.Horne	30	55	2	157	1646	31.05	4	5	17
C.D.McMillan	36	59	5	142	2337	43.27	5	15	14
H.J.H.Marshall	1	1	1	40*	40	–	–	–	–
C.S.Martin	9	8	3	7	12	2.40	–	–	3
D.J.Nash	32	45	14	89*	729	23.51	–	4	13
S.B.O'Connor	19	27	9	20	105	5.83	–	–	6
A.C.Parore	75	123	19	110	2783	26.75	2	14	187/7
M.H.Richardson	14	21	1	143	1088	54.40	2	8	11
M.S.Sinclair	18	30	5	214	1079	43.16	3	1	16
C.M.Spearman	19	37	2	112	922	26.34	1	3	21
D.R.Tuffey	7	8	1	13	33	4.71	–	–	3

	M	I	NO	HS	Runs	Avge	100	50	Ct/St
D.L.Vettori	36	52	10	90	720	17.14	–	4	17
L.Vincent	3	4	–	104	181	45.25	1	1	6
B.G.K.Walker	4	6	1	27*	103	20.60	–	–	–
K.P.Walmsley	3	5	–	5	13	2.60	–	–	–
P.J.Wiseman	14	21	5	23	107	6.68	–	–	7

NEW ZEALAND – BOWLING

	O	R	W	Avge	Best	5wI	10wM
N.J.Astle	699.1	1550	31	50.00	2- 22	–	–
S.E.Bond	123.1	439	14	31.35	4- 47	–	–
G.E.Bradburn	144.3	460	6	76.66	3-134	–	–
C.L.Cairns	1721.5	5609	194	28.91	7- 27	12	1
C.J.Drum	22	56	4	14.00	2- 26	–	–
J.E.C.Franklin	54.5	150	7	21.42	4- 26	–	–
M.J.Horne	11	26	0				
C.D.McMillan	346.5	1024	24	42.66	3- 57	–	–
H.J.H.Marshall	1	4	0				
C.S.Martin	271	970	31	31.29	5- 71	1	–
D.J.Nash	1032.4	2649	93	28.48	6- 27	3	1
S.B.O'Connor	611.1	1724	53	32.52	5- 51	1	–
M.H.Richardson	10	17	1	17.00	1- 16	–	–
M.S.Sinclair	4	13	0				
D.R.Tuffey	217.5	763	19	40.15	4- 39	–	–
D.L.Vettori	1579.5	4035	125	32.28	7- 87	7	1
B.G.K.Walker	96.4	302	3	100.66	2- 92	–	–
K.P.Walmsley	129	391	9	43.44	3- 70	–	–
P.J.Wiseman	509.4	1490	34	43.82	5- 82	2	–

INDIA – BATTING AND FIELDING

	M	I	NO	HS	Runs	Avge	100	50	Ct/St
A.B.Agarkar	11	17	1	41*	125	7.81	–	–	3
H.K.Badani	4	7	1	38	94	15.66	–	–	6
S.V.Bahutule	2	4	1	21*	39	13.00	–	–	1
S.B.Bangar	1	1	–	36	36	36.00	–	–	–
V.Dahiya	2	1	1	2*	2	–	–	–	6
S.S.Das	16	29	2	110	1053	39.00	1	9	23
D.Dasgupta	5	9	1	100	291	36.37	1	2	10
S.S.Dighe	6	10	1	47	141	15.66	–	–	12/2
R.Dravid	53	92	10	200*	4257	51.91	9	23	61
S.C.Ganguly	51	87	9	173	3155	40.44	7	15	36
Harbhajan Singh	20	29	9	66	255	12.75	–	1	3
Harvinder Singh	3	4	1	6	6	2.00	–	–	–
S.B.Joshi	15	19	2	92	352	20.70	–	1	7
M.Kaif	4	8	1	37	141	20.14	–	–	1
S.S.Karim	1	1	–	15	15	15.00	–	–	1
M.Kartik	4	5	–	43	61	12.20	–	–	1
Z.Khan	9	13	3	45	85	8.50	–	–	3
N.M.Kulkarni	3	2	1	4	5	5.00	–	–	1
A.Kumble	66	87	15	88	1286	17.86	–	3	32
V.V.S.Laxman	29	49	3	281	1703	37.02	2	10	40
N.R.Mongia	44	68	8	152	1442	24.03	1	6	99/8
A.Nehra	4	5	3	17*	26	13.00	–	–	–
B.K.V.Prasad	33	47	20	30*	203	7.51	–	–	6
S.L.V.Raju	28	34	10	31	240	10.00	–	–	6
S.Ramesh	19	37	1	143	1367	37.97	2	8	18
R.L.Sanghvi	1	2	–	2	2	1.00	–	–	–
Sarandeep Singh	2	1	–	4	4	4.00	–	–	–

INDIA – BATTING AND FIELDING (continued)

	M	I	NO	HS	Runs	Avge	100	50	Ct/St
V.Sehwag	4	5	–	105	235	47.00	1	1	5
I.R.Siddiqui	1	2	1	24	29	29.00	–	–	1
J.Srinath	57	80	21	76	831	14.08	–	4	22
S.R.Tendulkar	89	143	15	217	7419	57.96	27	30	60
T.Yohannan	2	2	2	3*	5	–	–	–	1

INDIA – BOWLING

	O	R	W	Avge	Best	5wI	10wM
A.B.Agarkar	373	1088	26	41.84	3- 43	–	–
H.K.Badani	8	17	0				
S.V.Bahutule	61	203	3	67.66	1- 32	–	–
S.B.Bangar	5	17	0				
S.S.Das	3	7	0				
R.Dravid	11	21	0				
S.C.Ganguly	300.2	1012	23	44.00	3- 28	–	–
Harbhajan Singh	856.2	2367	81	29.22	8- 84	6	2
Harvinder Singh	45.3	185	4	46.25	2- 62	–	–
S.B.Joshi	575.1	1470	41	35.85	5-142	1	–
M.Kaif	3	4	0				
M.Kartik	147.3	309	9	34.33	3-123	–	–
Z.Khan	280.1	956	22	43.45	4- 76	–	–
N.M.Kulkarni	123	332	2	166.00	1- 70	–	–
A.Kumble	3444	8412	300	28.04	10- 74	18	4
V.V.S.Laxman	25	68	0				
A.Nehra	128.4	441	14	31.50	4- 72	–	–
B.K.V.Prasad	1173.3	3360	96	35.00	6- 33	7	1
S.L.V.Raju	1267	2857	93	30.72	6- 12	5	1
S.Ramesh	9	43	0				
R.L.Sanghvi	12.2	78	2	39.00	2- 67	–	–
Sarandeep Singh	92	260	9	28.88	4-136	–	–
V.Sehwag	10	32	0				
I.R.Siddiqui	19	48	1	48.00	1- 32	–	–
J.Srinath	2202.2	6377	216	29.52	8- 86	10	1
S.R.Tendulkar	316	996	25	39.84	3- 10	–	–
T.Yohannan	56	213	4	53.25	2- 56	–	–

PAKISTAN – BATTING AND FIELDING

	M	I	NO	HS	Runs	Avge	100	50	Ct/St
Abdul Razzaq	17	25	2	134	741	32.21	3	3	7
Arshad Khan	8	7	1	9*	30	5.00	–	–	–
Azhar Mahmood	21	34	4	136	900	30.00	3	1	14
Danish Kaneria	5	5	4	8*	15	15.00	–	–	2
Faisal Iqbal	5	8	1	63	201	28.71	–	2	3
Fazal-e-Akber	4	6	4	15*	15	7.50	–	–	1
Humayun Farhat	1	2	–	28	54	27.00	–	–	–
Ijaz Ahmed	60	92	4	211	3315	37.67	12	12	45
Imran Farhat	3	5	–	63	115	23.00	–	1	4
Imran Nazir	5	8	–	131	244	30.50	1	1	1
Inzamam-ul-Haq	77	126	13	200*	5372	47.53	15	30	62
Misbah-ul-Haq	1	2	–	28	38	19.00	–	–	–
Mohammad Akram	9	15	6	10*	24	2.66	–	–	4
Mohammad Sami	2	1	1	0*	0	–	–	–	–
Moin Khan	63	95	7	117*	2493	28.32	3	15	114/20
Mushtaq Ahmed	50	70	15	59	636	11.56	–	2	22
Qaiser Abbas	1	1	–	2	2	2.00	–	–	–
Rashid Latif	27	40	5	94	902	25.77	–	5	88/9
Saeed Anwar	55	91	2	188*	4052	45.52	11	25	18

PAKISTAN – BATTING AND FIELDING (continued)

	M	I	NO	HS	Runs	Avge	100	50	Ct/St
Salim Elahi	9	16	–	72	310	19.37	–	1	9/1
Saqlain Mushtaq	37	58	13	101*	726	16.13	1	2	14
Shadab Kabir	5	7	–	55	148	21.14	–	1	11
Shahid Afridi	11	20	1	141	594	31.26	1	3	7
Shoaib Akhtar	17	25	8	26	109	6.41	–	–	5
Shoaib Malik	1	–	–	–	–	–	–	–	1
Taufiq Umar	3	3	–	104	204	68.00	1	1	2
Waqar Younis	76	102	20	45	824	10.04	–	–	17
Wasim Akram	104	147	19	257*	2898	22.64	3	7	43
Younis Khan	16	25	2	149*	943	41.00	4	4	16
Yousuf Youhana	35	57	4	204*	2511	47.37	8	13	39

PAKISTAN – BOWLING

	O	R	W	Avge	Best	5wI	10wM
Abdul Razzaq	427.1	1173	30	39.10	4- 56	–	–
Arshad Khan	381	852	30	28.40	5- 38	1	–
Azhar Mahmood	502.3	1402	39	35.94	4- 50	–	–
Danish Kaneria	185.4	495	29	17.06	7- 77	3	1
Faisal Iqbal	1	7	0				
Fazal-e-Akber	106.2	349	10	34.90	3- 85	–	–
Ijaz Ahmed	30	77	2	38.50	1- 9	–	–
Inzamam-ul-Haq	1.3	8	0				
Mohammad Akram	246.1	859	17	50.52	5-138	1	–
Mohammad Sami	93.4	245	8	30.62	5- 36	1	–
Mushtaq Ahmed	2037.4	5901	183	32.24	7- 56	10	3
Qaiser Abbas	16	35	0				
Rashid Latif	2	10	0				
Saeed Anwar	8	23	0				
Saqlain Mushtaq	1822.4	4544	158	28.75	8-164	12	2
Shadab Kabir	1	9	0				
Shahid Afridi	197.5	584	20	29.20	5- 52	1	–
Shoaib Akhtar	508.4	1740	50	34.80	5- 43	2	–
Shoaib Malik	6.1	26	2	13.00	2- 18	–	–
Waqar Younis	2434.4	7780	344	22.61	7- 76	22	5
Wasim Akram	3771.1	9779	414	23.62	7-119	25	5
Younis Khan	33	115	1	115.00	1- 47	–	–
Yousuf Youhana	1	3	0				

SRI LANKA – BATTING AND FIELDING

	M	I	NO	HS	Runs	Avge	100	50	Ct/St
R.P.Arnold	36	56	4	123	1503	28.90	2	8	45
M.S.Atapattu	54	94	11	223	3197	38.51	9	10	37
M.R.C.N.Bandaratilake	7	9	1	25	93	11.62	–	–	–
U.D.U.Chandana	6	8	1	92	204	29.14	–	1	3
P.A.de Silva	89	153	11	267	5952	41.91	19	21	43
H.D.P.K.Dharmasena	25	41	6	62*	735	21.00	–	3	12
T.M.Dilshan	10	16	2	163*	372	26.57	1	–	18
C.R.D.Fernando	9	12	3	5*	34	3.77	–	–	5
T.C.B.Fernando	4	2	–	45	46	23.00	–	–	1
D.A.Gunawardena	3	6	–	43	121	20.16	–	–	1
D.Hettiarachchi	1	2	1	0*	0	0.00	–	–	–
S.T.Jayasuriya	69	117	12	340	4339	41.32	9	20	53
A.V.P.Jayawardena	1	–	–	–	–	–	–	–	–
D.P.M.deS.Jayawardena	40	62	3	242	2875	48.72	8	14	55
R.S.Kaluwitharana	40	64	4	132*	1629	27.15	3	7	74/20
D.K.Liyanage	9	9	–	23	69	7.66	–	–	–
M.Muralitharan	72	90	36	67	703	13.01	–	1	34

187

SRI LANKA – BATTING AND FIELDING (continued)

	M	I	NO	HS	Runs	Avge	100	50	Ct/St
A.S.A.Perera	3	4	1	43*	77	25.66	–	–	1
P.D.R.L.Perera	6	7	5	10	18	9.00	–	–	1
K.R.Pushpakumara	23	31	12	44	166	8.73	–	–	10
T.T.Samaraweera	8	8	3	123*	515	103.00	2	3	3
K.Sangakkara	19	29	1	140	1293	46.17	3	7	50/5
H.P.Tillekeratne	66	103	19	204*	3694	43.97	9	18	101/2
W.P.U.C.J.Vaas	58	80	14	74*	1288	19.51	–	6	16
M.G.Vandort	1	1	–	36	36	36.00	–	–	1
G.P.Wickremasinghe	40	64	5	51	555	9.40	–	1	18
D.N.T.Zoysa	21	27	2	26	207	8.28	–	–	2

SRI LANKA – BOWLING

	O	R	W	Avge	Best	5wI	10wM
R.P.Arnold	212.2	577	11	52.45	3- 76	–	–
M.S.Atapattu	8	24	1	24.00	1- 9	–	–
M.R.C.N.Bandaratilake	287	698	23	30.34	5- 36	1	–
U.D.U.Chandana	152.2	513	16	32.06	6-179	1	–
P.A.de Silva	394	1103	27	40.85	3- 30	–	–
H.D.P.K.Dharmasena	935.3	2276	58	39.24	6- 72	3	–
C.R.D.Fernando	217.5	782	20	39.10	5- 42	2	–
T.C.B.Fernando	74.5	249	7	35.57	4- 27	–	–
D.Hettiarachchi	27	41	2	20.50	2- 36	–	–
S.T.Jayasuriya	835.1	2091	65	32.16	5- 43	1	–
D.P.M.deS.Jayawardena	68.2	212	4	53.00	2- 32	–	–
D.K.Liyanage	225.5	666	17	39.17	4- 56	–	–
M.Muralitharan	4026.2	9508	404	23.53	9- 51	33	10
A.S.A.Perera	68	180	1	180.00	1-104	–	–
P.D.R.L.Perera	137	483	12	40.25	3- 40	–	–
K.R.Pushpakumara	632	2242	58	38.65	7-116	4	–
T.T.Samaraweera	88	244	5	48.80	1- 7	–	–
H.P.Tillekeratne	10.4	24	0				
W.P.U.C.J.Vaas	2114.5	5475	190	28.81	7- 71	7	2
G.P.Wickremasinghe	1210	3559	85	41.87	6- 60	3	–
D.N.T.Zoysa	449.4	1245	36	34.58	4- 76	–	–

ZIMBABWE – BATTING AND FIELDING

	M	I	NO	HS	Runs	Avge	100	50	Ct/St
A.M.Blignaut	6	10	1	92	220	24.44	–	1	8
G.B.Brent	4	6	–	25	35	5.83	–	–	1
A.D.R.Campbell	56	101	4	103	2613	26.93	2	16	54
S.V.Carlisle	25	43	4	64	987	25.30	–	6	24
D.D.Ebrahim	11	20	1	71	430	22.63	–	3	7
A.Flower	59	104	19	232*	4552	53.55	12	25	147/9
G.W.Flower	59	108	5	201*	3068	29.78	6	13	37
T.J.Friend	8	11	1	81	230	23.00	–	1	1
T.R.Gripper	12	23	1	112	465	21.13	1	2	9
D.T.Hondo	1	2	1	6	7	7.00	–	–	1
T.N.Madondo	3	4	1	74*	90	30.00	–	1	1
D.A.Marillier	5	7	1	73	185	30.83	–	2	2
H.Masakadza	5	10	1	119	322	35.77	1	1	–
M.Mbangwa	15	25	8	8	34	2.00	–	–	2
B.A.Murphy	11	15	3	30	123	10.25	–	–	11
D.T.Mutendera	1	2	–	10	10	5.00	–	–	1
M.L.Nkala	6	7	1	47	90	15.00	–	–	3
H.K.Olonga	28	41	10	24	165	5.32	–	–	10
R.W.Price	6	9	3	4	14	2.33	–	–	2
G.J.Rennie	22	44	1	93	989	23.00	–	7	12

TEST   ZIMBABWE – BATTING AND FIELDING (continued)

	M	I	NO	HS	Runs	Avge	100	50	Ct/St
J.A.Rennie	4	6	1	22	62	12.40	–	–	1
B.C.Strang	26	45	9	53	465	12.91	–	1	11
P.A.Strang	24	41	10	106*	839	27.06	1	2	15
H.H.Streak	49	78	14	87	1388	21.68	–	8	14
T.Taibu	2	4	–	10	29	7.25	–	–	4
D.P.Viljoen	2	4	–	38	57	14.25	–	–	1
B.T.Watambwa	4	4	3	4*	6	6.00	–	–	–
G.J.Whittall	45	80	7	203*	2198	30.10	4	10	19
C.B.Wishart	21	38	1	114	760	20.54	1	4	9

ZIMBABWE – BOWLING

	O	R	W	Avge	Best	5wI	10wM
A.M.Blignaut	212.5	687	19	36.15	5- 73	2	–
G.B.Brent	136.2	314	7	44.85	3- 21	–	–
A.D.R.Campbell	11	28	0				
A.Flower	0.1	0	0				
G.W.Flower	508	1368	23	59.47	4- 41	–	–
T.J.Friend	263.2	842	22	38.27	5- 31	1	–
T.R.Gripper	70.4	272	3	90.66	2- 91	–	–
D.T.Hondo	19	87	1	87.00	1- 87	–	–
D.A.Marillier	102.4	322	11	29.27	4- 57	–	–
H.Masakadza	4	12	1	12.00	1- 9	–	–
M.Mbangwa	432.4	1006	32	31.43	3- 23	–	–
B.A.Murphy	358.5	1113	18	61.83	3- 32	–	–
D.T.Mutendera	14	29	0				
M.L.Nkala	152	432	7	61.71	3- 82	–	–
H.K.Olonga	692	2377	59	40.28	5- 70	1	–
R.W.Price	279.4	826	16	51.62	5-181	1	–
G.J.Rennie	21	84	1	84.00	1- 40	–	–
J.A.Rennie	120.4	293	3	97.66	2- 22	–	–
B.C.Strang	905.2	2203	56	39.33	5-101	1	–
P.A.Strang	952.2	2522	70	36.02	8-109	4	1
H.H.Streak	1784.3	4605	174	26.46	6- 87	6	–
D.P.Viljoen	17.3	65	1	65.00	1- 14	–	–
B.T.Watambwa	111.2	356	13	27.38	4- 64	–	–
G.J.Whittall	745	1982	50	39.64	4- 18	–	–

BANGLADESH – BATTING AND FIELDING

	M	I	NO	HS	Runs	Avge	100	50	Ct/St
Akram Khan	5	10	–	44	169	16.90	–	–	2
Al Sahariar	9	18	–	68	344	19.11	–	2	7
Aminul Islam	11	22	1	145	513	24.42	1	2	5
Enamul Haque	6	11	3	24*	120	15.00	–	–	–
Fahim Muntasir	2	4	–	33	44	11.00	–	–	–
Habibul Bashar	11	22	1	108	812	38.66	1	9	6
Hasibul Hussain	5	10	1	31	97	10.77	–	–	1
Javed Omar	9	18	1	85*	433	25.47	–	3	1
Khaled Mahmud	3	5	–	45	65	13.00	–	–	–
Khaled Masud	10	18	4	32	205	14.64	–	–	12
Manjural Islam	9	17	8	9	29	3.22	–	–	3
Mashrafe Bin Mortaza	4	7	–	29	51	7.28	–	–	2
Mehrab Hossain	7	14	–	71	208	14.85	–	1	5
Mohammed Ashraful	6	12	1	114	260	23.63	1	–	–
Mohammed Rafique	1	2	–	22	26	13.00	–	–	1
Mohammed Sharif	8	16	2	24*	86	6.14	–	–	5
Mushfiqur Rahman	2	4	1	4	10	3.33	–	–	2
Naimur Rahman	7	13	–	48	204	15.69	–	1	2

TEST   BANGLADESH – BATTING AND FIELDING (continued)

	M	I	NO	HS	Runs	Avge	100	50	Ct/St
Ranjan Das	1	2	–	2	2	1.00	–	–	1
Sanwar Hossain	4	8	–	45	119	14.87	–	–	1
Shahriar Hossain	1	2	–	12	19	9.50	–	–	–/1

BANGLADESH – BOWLING

	O	R	W	Avge	Best	5wI	10wM
Aminul Islam	33	149	1	149.00	1- 66	–	–
Enamul Haque	235.4	639	12	53.25	4-136	–	–
Fahim Muntasir	59	240	3	80.00	3-131	–	–
Habibul Bashar	13	73	0				
Hasibul Hussain	130	571	6	95.16	2-125	–	–
Javed Omar	1	12	0				
Khaled Mahmud	36	141	1	141.00	1- 40	–	–
Manjural Islam	256	870	17	51.17	6- 81	1	–
Mashrafe Bin Mortaza	104.4	374	12	31.16	4-106	–	–
Mohammed Ashraful	49	223	1	223.00	1- 62	–	–
Mohammed Rafique	53	120	3	40.00	3-117	–	–
Mohammed Sharif	225.3	911	14	65.07	4- 98	–	–
Mushfiqur Rahman	37	112	0				
Naimur Rahman	184.1	600	11	54.54	6-132	1	–
Ranjan Das	22	72	1	72.00	1- 64	–	–

LEADING TEST AGGREGATES 2001

1000 RUNS

	M	I	NO	HS	Runs	Avge	100	50
M.L.Hayden (A)	14	25	3	203	1391	63.22	5	5
B.C.Lara (WI)	9	18	–	221	1151	63.94	3	4
H.H.Gibbs (SA)	13	22	1	196	1124	53.52	3	6
J.H.Kallis (SA)	13	23	7	189*	1120	70.00	2	7
D.P.M.deS.Jayawardena (SL)	13	19	–	150	1053	55.42	4	4
S.R.Tendulkar (I)	10	18	2	155	1003	62.68	3	6

50 WICKETS

	M	O	R	W	Avge	Best	5wI	10wM
M.Muralitharan (SL)	12	781.2	1699	80	21.23	8- 87	7	4
G.D.McGrath (A)	14	584.4	1473	68	21.66	7- 76	4	–
Harbhajan Singh (I)	12	570.4	1557	60	25.95	8- 84	6	2
W.P.U.C.J.Vaas (SL)	12	489.1	1323	58	22.81	7- 71	3	1
S.K.Warne (A)	13	583.3	1809	58	31.18	7-165	4	1
S.M.Pollock (SA)	13	521	1176	55	21.38	6- 30	4	1

FIRST-CLASS CRICKET RECORDS

To 15 September 2001 inclusive

TEAM RECORDS

HIGHEST INNINGS TOTALS

1107	Victoria v New South Wales	Melbourne	1926-27
1059	Victoria v Tasmania	Melbourne	1922-23
952-6d	Sri Lanka v India	Colombo	1997-98
951-7d	Sind v Baluchistan	Karachi	1973-74
944-6d	Hyderabad v Andhra	Secunderabad	1993-94
918	New South Wales v South Australia	Sydney	1900-01
912-8d	Holkar v Mysore	Indore	1945-46
910-6d	Railways v Dera Ismail Khan	Lahore	1964-65
903-7d	England v Australia	The Oval	1938
887	Yorkshire v Warwickshire	Birmingham	1896
863	Lancashire v Surrey	The Oval	1990
860-6d	Tamil Nadu v Goa	Panjim	1988-89

Excluding penalty runs in India, there have been 30 innings totals of 800 runs or more in first-class cricket. Tamil Nadu's total of 860-6d was boosted to 912 by 52 penalty runs.

HIGHEST SECOND INNINGS TOTAL

770	New South Wales v South Australia	Adelaide	1920-21

HIGHEST FOURTH INNINGS TOTAL

654-5	England v South Africa	Durban	1938-39

HIGHEST MATCH AGGREGATE

2376	Maharashtra v Bombay	Poona	1948-49

RECORD MARGIN OF VICTORY

Innings and 851 runs: Railways v Dera Ismail Khan	Lahore	1964-65

MOST RUNS IN A DAY

721	Australians v Essex	Southend	1948

MOST HUNDREDS IN AN INNINGS

6	Holkar v Mysore	Indore	1945-46

LOWEST INNINGS TOTALS

12	†Oxford University v MCC and Ground	Oxford	1877
12	Northamptonshire v Gloucestershire	Gloucester	1907
13	Auckland v Canterbury	Auckland	1877-78
13	Nottinghamshire v Yorkshire	Nottingham	1901
14	Surrey v Essex	Chelmsford	1983
15	MCC v Surrey	Lord's	1839
15	†Victoria v MCC	Melbourne	1903-04
15	†Northamptonshire v Yorkshire	Northampton	1908
15	Hampshire v Warwickshire	Birmingham	1922

† Batted one man short

There have been 27 instances of a team being dismissed for under 20.

LOWEST MATCH AGGREGATE BY ONE TEAM

34 (16 and 18)	Border v Natal	East London	1959-60

LOWEST COMPLETED MATCH AGGREGATE BY BOTH TEAMS

105	MCC v Australians	Lord's	1878

FEWEST RUNS IN AN UNINTERRUPTED DAY'S PLAY

95	Australia (80) v Pakistan (15-2)	Karachi	1956-57

TIED MATCHES

Before 1949 a match was considered to be tied if the scores were level after the fourth innings, even if the side batting last had wickets in hand when play ended. Law 22 was amended in 1948 and since then a match has been tied only when the scores are level after the fourth innings has been completed. There have been 53 tied first-class matches, five of which would not have qualified under the current law. The most recent is:

Worcestershire (203/325-8d) v Nottinghamshire (233/295)	Nottingham	1993

BATTING RECORDS
HIGHEST INDIVIDUAL INNINGS

501*	B.C.Lara	Warwickshire v Durham	Birmingham	1994
499	Hanif Mohammed	Karachi v Bahawalpur	Karachi	1958-59
452*	D.G.Bradman	New South Wales v Queensland	Sydney	1929-30
443*	B.B.Nimbalkar	Maharashtra v Kathiawar	Poona	1948-49
437	W.H.Ponsford	Victoria v Queensland	Melbourne	1927-28
429	W.H.Ponsford	Victoria v Tasmania	Melbourne	1922-23
428	Aftab Baloch	Sind v Baluchistan	Karachi	1973-74
424	A.C.MacLaren	Lancashire v Somerset	Taunton	1895
405*	G.A.Hick	Worcestershire v Somerset	Taunton	1988
394	Naved Latif	Sargodha v Gujranwala	Gujranwala	2000-01
385	B.Sutcliffe	Otago v Canterbury	Christchurch	1952-53
383	C.W.Gregory	New South Wales v Queensland	Brisbane	1906-07
377	S.V.Manjrekar	Bombay v Hyderabad	Bombay	1990-91
375	B.C.Lara	West Indies v England	St John's	1993-94
369	D.G.Bradman	South Australia v Tasmania	Adelaide	1935-36
366	N.H.Fairbrother	Lancashire v Surrey	The Oval	1990
366	M.V.Sridhar	Hyderabad v Andhra	Secunderabad	1993-94
365*	C.Hill	South Australia v NSW	Adelaide	1900-01
365*	G.St A.Sobers	West Indies v Pakistan	Kingston	1957-58
364	L.Hutton	England v Australia	The Oval	1938
359*	V.M.Merchant	Bombay v Maharashtra	Bombay	1943-44
359	R.B.Simpson	New South Wales v Queensland	Brisbane	1963-64
357*	R.Abel	Surrey v Somerset	The Oval	1899
357	D.G.Bradman	South Australia v Victoria	Melbourne	1935-36
356	B.A.Richards	South Australia v W Australia	Perth	1970-71
355*	G.R.Marsh	W Australia v S Australia	Perth	1989-90
355	B.Sutcliffe	Otago v Auckland	Dunedin	1949-50
353	W.V.S.Laxman	Hyderabad v Karnataka	Bangalore	1999-00
352	W.H.Ponsford	Victoria v New South Wales	Melbourne	1926-27
350	Rashid Israr	Habib Bank v National Bank	Lahore	1976-77

There have been 133 triple hundreds in first-class cricket, W.V.Raman (313) and Arjan Kripal Singh (302*) for Tamil Nadu v Goa at Panjim in 1988-89 providing the only instance of two batsmen scoring 300 in the same innings.

MOST HUNDREDS IN SUCCESSIVE INNINGS

6	C.B.Fry	Sussex and Rest of England	1901
6	D.G.Bradman	South Australia and D.G.Bradman's XI	1938-39
6	M.J.Procter	Rhodesia	1970-71

TWO DOUBLE HUNDREDS IN A MATCH

| 244 | 202* | A.E.Fagg | Kent v Essex | Colchester | 1938 |

TRIPLE HUNDRED AND HUNDRED IN A MATCH

| 333 | 123 | G.A.Gooch | England v India | Lord's | 1990 |

DOUBLE HUNDRED AND HUNDRED IN A MATCH MOST TIMES

| 4 | Zaheer Abbas | Gloucestershire | 1976-81 |

TWO HUNDREDS IN A MATCH MOST TIMES

| 8 | Zaheer Abbas | Gloucestershire and PIA | 1976-82 |
| 7 | W.R.Hammond | Gloucestershire, England and MCC | 1927-45 |

MOST HUNDREDS IN A SEASON

| 18 | D.C.S.Compton | 1947 | 16 | J.B.Hobbs | 1925 |

100 HUNDREDS IN A CAREER

| | Total | | 100th Hundred | |
	Hundreds	Inns	Season	Inns
J.B.Hobbs	197	1315	1923	821
E.H.Hendren	170	1300	1928-29	740
W.R.Hammond	167	1005	1935	679
C.P.Mead	153	1340	1927	892
G.Boycott	151	1014	1977	645
H.Sutcliffe	149	1088	1932	700
F.E.Woolley	145	1532	1929	1031
L.Hutton	129	814	1951	619
G.A.Gooch	128	990	1992-93	820
W.G.Grace	126	1493	1895	1113
D.C.S.Compton	123	839	1952	552
T.W.Graveney	122	1223	1964	940
D.G.Bradman	117	338	1947-48	295
G.A.Hick	117	695	1998	574
I.V.A.Richards	114	796	1988-89	658
Zaheer Abbas	108	768	1982-83	658
A.Sandham	107	1000	1935	871
M.C.Cowdrey	107	1130	1973	1035
T.W.Hayward	104	1138	1913	1076
G.M.Turner	103	792	1982	779
J.H.Edrich	103	979	1977	945
L.E.G.Ames	102	951	1950	915
G.E.Tyldesley	102	961	1934	919
D.L.Amiss	102	1139	1986	1081

MOST 400s: 2 – W.H.Ponsford
MOST 300s or more: 6 – D.G.Bradman; 4 – W.R.Hammond
MOST 200s or more: 37 – D.G.Bradman; 36 – W.R.Hammond; 22 – E.H.Hendren

MOST RUNS IN A MONTH

| 1294 (avge 92.42) | L.Hutton | Yorkshire | June 1949 |

MOST RUNS IN A SEASON

Runs			I	NO	HS	Avge	100	Season
3816	D.C.S.Compton	Middlesex	50	8	246	90.85	18	1947
3539	W.J.Edrich	Middlesex	52	8	267*	80.43	12	1947
3518	T.W.Hayward	Surrey	61	8	219	66.37	13	1906

The feat of scoring 3000 runs in a season has been achieved 28 times, the most recent instance being by W.E.Alley (3019) in 1961. The highest aggregate in a season since 1969 is 2755 by S.J.Cook in 1991.

1000 RUNS IN A SEASON MOST TIMES

28   W.G.Grace (Gloucestershire), F.E.Woolley (Kent)

HIGHEST BATTING AVERAGE IN A SEASON

(Qualification: 12 innings)

Avge			I	NO	HS	Runs	100	Season
115.66	D.G.Bradman	Australians	26	5	278	2429	13	1938
104.66	D.R.Martyn	Australians	14	5	176*	942	5	2001
102.53	G.Boycott	Yorkshire	20	5	175*	1538	6	1979
102.00	W.A.Johnston	Australians	17	16	28*	102	–	1953
101.70	G.A.Gooch	Essex	30	3	333	2746	12	1990
100.12	G.Boycott	Yorkshire	30	5	233	2503	13	1971

FASTEST HUNDRED AGAINST AUTHENTIC BOWLING

35 min	P.G.H.Fender	Surrey v Northamptonshire	Northampton	1920

FASTEST DOUBLE HUNDRED

113 min	R.J.Shastri	Bombay v Baroda	Bombay	1984-85

FASTEST TRIPLE HUNDRED

181 min	D.C.S.Compton	MCC v NE Transvaal	Benoni	1948-49

MOST SIXES IN AN INNINGS

16	A.Symonds	Gloucestershire v Glamorgan	Abergavenny	1995

MOST SIXES IN A MATCH

20	A.Symonds	Gloucestershire v Glamorgan	Abergavenny	1995

MOST SIXES IN A SEASON

80	I.T.Botham	Somerset and England		1985

MOST FOURS IN AN INNINGS

72	B.C.Lara	Warwickshire v Durham	Birmingham	1994

MOST RUNS OFF ONE OVER

36	G.St A.Sobers	Nottinghamshire v Glamorgan	Swansea	1968
36	R.J.Shastri	Bombay v Baroda	Bombay	1984-85

Both batsmen hit for six all six balls of overs bowled by M.A.Nash and Tilak Raj respectively.

MOST RUNS IN A DAY

390*	B.C.Lara	Warwickshire v Durham	Birmingham	1994

There have been 19 instances of a batsman scoring 300 or more runs in a day.

1015 min R.Nayyar (271)   Himachal Pradesh v Jammu & Kashmir Chamba   1999-00

HIGHEST PARTNERSHIPS FOR EACH WICKET

First Wicket
561	Waheed Mirza/Mansoor Akhtar	Karachi W v Quetta	Karachi	1976-77
555	P.Holmes/H.Sutcliffe	Yorkshire v Essex	Leyton	1932
554	J.T.Brown/J.Tunnicliffe	Yorkshire v Derbys	Chesterfield	1898

Second Wicket
576	S.T.Jayasuriya/R.S.Mahanama	Sri Lanka v India	Colombo (RPS)	1997-98
475	Zahir Alam/L.S.Rajput	Assam v Tripura	Gauhati	1991-92
465*	J.A.Jameson/R.B.Kanhai	Warwickshire v Glos	Birmingham	1974

Third Wicket
467	A.H.Jones/M.D.Crowe	N Zealand v Sri Lanka	Wellington	1990-91
456	Khalid Irtiza/Aslam Ali	United Bank v Multan	Karachi	1975-76
451	Mudassar Nazar/Javed Miandad	Pakistan v India	Hyderabad	1982-83
445	P.E.Whitelaw/W.N.Carson	Auckland v Otago	Dunedin	1936-37
438*	G.A.Hick/T.M.Moody	Worcestershire v Hants	Southampton	1997

Fourth Wicket
577	V.S.Hazare/Gul Mahomed	Baroda v Holkar	Baroda	1946-47
574*	C.L.Walcott/F.M.M.Worrell	Barbados v Trinidad	Port-of-Spain	1945-46
502*	F.M.M.Worrell/J.D.C.Goddard	Barbados v Trinidad	Bridgetown	1943-44
470	A.I.Kallicharran/G.W.Humpage	Warwickshire v Lancs	Southport	1982

Fifth Wicket
464*	M.E.Waugh/S.R.Waugh	NSW v W Australia	Perth	1990-91
405	S.G.Barnes/D.G.Bradman	Australia v England	Sydney	1946-47
401	M.B.Loye/D.Ripley	Northants v Glamorgan	Northampton	1998

Sixth Wicket
487*	G.A.Headley/C.C.Passailaigue	Jamaica v Tennyson's	Kingston	1931-32
428	W.W.Armstrong/M.A.Noble	Australians v Sussex	Hove	1902
411	R.M.Poore/E.G.Wynyard	Hampshire v Somerset	Taunton	1899

Seventh Wicket
460	Bhupinder Singh jr/P.Dharmani	Punjab v Delhi	Delhi	1994-95
347	D.St E.Atkinson/C.C.Depeiza	W Indies v Australia	Bridgetown	1954-55
344	K.S.Ranjitsinhji/W.Newham	Sussex v Essex	Leyton	1902

Eighth Wicket
433	V.T.Trumper/A.Sims	Australians v C'bury	Christchurch	1913-14
313	Wasim Akram/Saqlain Mushtaq	Pakistan v Zimbabwe	Sheikhupura	1996-97
292	R.Peel/Lord Hawke	Yorkshire v Warwicks	Birmingham	1896

Ninth Wicket
283	J.Chapman/A.Warren	Derbys v Warwicks	Blackwell	1910
268	J.B.Commins/N.Boje	SA 'A' v Mashonaland	Harare	1994-95
251	J.W.H.T.Douglas/S.N.Hare	Essex v Derbyshire	Leyton	1921

Tenth Wicket
307	A.F.Kippax/J.E.H.Hooker	NSW v Victoria	Melbourne	1928-29
249	C.T.Sarwate/S.N.Banerjee	Indians v Surrey	The Oval	1946
235	F.E.Woolley/A.Fielder	Kent v Worcs	Stourbridge	1909

35000 RUNS IN A CAREER

	Career	I	NO	HS	Runs	Avge	100
J.B.Hobbs	1905-34	1315	106	316*	61237	50.65	197
F.E.Woolley	1906-38	1532	85	305*	58969	40.75	145
E.H.Hendren	1907-38	1300	166	301*	57611	50.80	170
C.P.Mead	1905-36	1340	185	280*	55061	47.67	153
W.G.Grace	1865-1908	1493	105	344	54896	39.55	126
W.R.Hammond	1920-51	1005	104	336*	50551	56.10	167
H.Sutcliffe	1919-45	1088	123	313	50138	51.95	149
G.Boycott	1962-86	1014	162	261*	48426	56.83	151
T.W.Graveney	1948-71/72	1223	159	258	47793	44.91	122
G.A.Gooch	1973-2000	990	75	333	44846	49.01	128
T.W.Hayward	1893-1914	1138	96	315*	43551	41.79	104
D.L.Amiss	1960-87	1139	126	262*	43423	42.86	102
M.C.Cowdrey	1950-76	1130	134	307	42719	42.89	107
A.Sandham	1911-37/38	1000	79	325	41284	44.82	107
L.Hutton	1934-60	814	91	364	40140	55.51	129
M.J.K.Smith	1951-75	1091	139	204	39832	41.84	69
W.Rhodes	1898-1930	1528	237	267*	39802	30.83	58
J.H.Edrich	1956-78	979	104	310*	39790	45.47	103
R.E.S.Wyatt	1923-57	1141	157	232	39405	40.04	85
D.C.S.Compton	1936-64	839	88	300	38942	51.85	123
G.E.Tyldesley	1909-36	961	106	256*	38874	45.46	102
J.T.Tyldesley	1895-1923	994	62	295*	37897	40.60	86
K.W.R.Fletcher	1962-88	1167	170	228*	37665	37.77	63
C.G.Greenidge	1970-92	889	75	273*	37354	45.88	92
J.W.Hearne	1909-36	1025	116	285*	37252	40.98	96
L.E.G.Ames	1926-51	951	95	295	37248	43.51	102
D.Kenyon	1946-67	1159	59	259	37002	33.63	74
W.J.Edrich	1934-58	964	92	267*	36965	42.39	86
J.M.Parks	1949-76	1227	172	205*	36673	34.76	51
M.W.Gatting	1975-98	861	123	258	36549	49.52	94
D.Denton	1894-1920	1163	70	221	36479	33.37	69
G.H.Hirst	1891-1929	1215	151	341	36323	34.13	60
I.V.A.Richards	1971/72-93	796	63	322	36212	49.40	114
A.Jones	1957-83	1168	72	204*	36049	32.89	56
W.G.Quaife	1894-1928	1203	185	255*	36012	35.37	72
R.E.Marshall	1945/46-72	1053	59	228*	35725	35.94	68
G.Gunn	1902-32	1061	82	220	35208	35.96	62

BOWLING RECORDS

ALL TEN WICKETS IN AN INNINGS

This feat has been achieved 78 times in first-class matches (excluding 12-a-side fixtures).

Three Times: A.P.Freeman (1929, 1930, 1931)
Twice: V.E.Walker (1859, 1865); H.Verity (1931, 1932); J.C.Laker (1956)

Instances since 1945:

W.E.Hollies	Warwickshire v Notts	Birmingham	1946
J.M.Sims	East v West	Kingston on Thames	1948
J.K.R.Graveney	Gloucestershire v Derbyshire	Chesterfield	1949
T.E.Bailey	Essex v Lancashire	Clacton	1949
R.Berry	Lancashire v Worcestershire	Blackpool	1953
S.P.Gupte	President's XI v Combined XI	Bombay	1954-55
J.C.Laker	Surrey v Australians	The Oval	1956
K.Smales	Nottinghamshire v Glos	Stroud	1956

G.A.R.Lock	Surrey v Kent	Blackheath	1956
J.C.Laker	England v Australia	Manchester	1956
P.M.Chatterjee	Bengal v Assam	Jorhat	1956-57
J.D.Bannister	Warwicks v Combined Services	Birmingham (M & B)	1959
A.J.G.Pearson	Cambridge U v Leicestershire	Loughborough	1961
N.I.Thomson	Sussex v Warwickshire	Worthing	1964
P.J.Allan	Queensland v Victoria	Melbourne	1965-66
I.J.Brayshaw	Western Australia v Victoria	Perth	1967-68
Shahid Mahmood	Karachi Whites v Khairpur	Karachi	1969-70
E.E.Hemmings	International XI v W Indians	Kingston	1982-83
P.Sunderam	Rajasthan v Vidarbha	Jodhpur	1985-86
S.T.Jefferies	Western Province v OFS	Cape Town	1987-88
Imran Adil	Bahawalpur v Faisalabad	Faisalabad	1989-90
G.P.Wickremasinghe	Sinhalese v Kalutara	Colombo	1991-92
R.L.Johnson	Middlesex v Derbyshire	Derby	1994
Naeem Akhtar	Rawalpindi B v Peshawar	Peshawar	1995-96
A.Kumble	India v Pakistan	Delhi	1998-99
D.S.Mohanty	East Zone v South Zone	Agartala	2000-01

MOST WICKETS IN A MATCH

| 19 | J.C.Laker | England v Australia | Manchester | 1956 |

MOST WICKETS IN A SEASON

Wkts		Season	Matches	Overs	Mdns	Runs	Avge
304	A.P.Freeman	1928	37	1976.1	423	5489	18.05
298	A.P.Freeman	1933	33	2039	651	4549	15.26

The feat of taking 250 wickets in a season has been achieved on 12 occasions, the last instance being by A.P.Freeman in 1933. 200 or more wickets in a season have been taken on 59 occasions, the last being by G.A.R.Lock (212 wickets, average 12.02) in 1957.

The highest aggregates of wickets taken in a season since the reduction of County Championship matches in 1969 are as follows:

Wkts		Season	Matches	Overs	Mdns	Runs	Avge
134	M.D.Marshall	1982	22	822	225	2108	15.73
131	L.R.Gibbs	1971	23	1024.1	295	2475	18.89
125	F.D.Stephenson	1988	22	819.1	196	2289	18.31
121	R.D.Jackman	1980	23	746.2	220	1864	15.40

Since 1969 there have been 49 instances of bowlers taking 100 wickets in a season.

MOST HAT-TRICKS IN A CAREER

7	D.V.P.Wright
6	T.W.J.Goddard, C.W.L.Parker
5	S.Haigh, V.W.C.Jupp, A.E.G.Rhodes, F.A.Tarrant

2000 WICKETS IN A CAREER

	Career	Runs	Wkts	Avge	100w
W.Rhodes	1898-1930	69993	4187	16.71	23
A.P.Freeman	1914-36	69577	3776	18.42	17
C.W.L.Parker	1903-35	63817	3278	19.46	16
J.T.Hearne	1888-1923	54352	3061	17.75	15
T.W.J.Goddard	1922-52	59116	2979	19.84	16
W.G.Grace	1865-1908	51545	2876	17.92	10
A.S.Kennedy	1907-36	61034	2874	21.23	15
D.Shackleton	1948-69	53303	2857	18.65	20
G.A.R.Lock	1946-70/71	54709	2844	19.23	14

	Career	Runs	Wkts	Avge	100w
F.J.Titmus	1949-82	63313	**2830**	22.37	16
M.W.Tate	1912-37	50571	**2784**	18.16	13+1
G.H.Hirst	1891-1929	51282	**2739**	18.72	15
C.Blythe	1899-1914	42136	**2506**	16.81	14
D.L.Underwood	1963-87	49993	**2465**	20.28	10
W.E.Astill	1906-39	57783	**2431**	23.76	9
J.C.White	1909-37	43759	**2356**	18.57	14
W.E.Hollies	1932-57	48656	**2323**	20.94	14
F.S.Trueman	1949-69	42154	**2304**	18.29	12
J.B.Statham	1950-68	36999	**2260**	16.37	13
R.T.D.Perks	1930-55	53771	**2233**	24.07	16
J.Briggs	1879-1900	35431	**2221**	15.95	12
D.J.Shepherd	1950-72	47302	**2218**	21.32	12
E.G.Dennett	1903-26	42571	**2147**	19.82	12
T.Richardson	1892-1905	38794	**2104**	18.43	10
T.E.Bailey	1945-67	48170	**2082**	23.13	9
R.Illingworth	1951-83	42023	**2072**	20.28	10
F.E.Woolley	1906-38	41066	**2068**	19.85	8
N.Gifford	1960-88	48731	**2068**	23.56	4
G.Geary	1912-38	41339	**2063**	20.03	11
D.V.P.Wright	1932-57	49307	**2056**	23.98	10
J.A.Newman	1906-30	51111	**2032**	25.15	9
A.Shaw	1864-97	24580	**2026+1**	12.12	9
S.Haigh	1895-1913	32091	**2012**	15.94	11

ALL-ROUND RECORDS

THE 'DOUBLE'

3000 runs and 100 wickets: J.H.Parks (1937)
2000 runs and 200 wickets: G.H.Hirst (1906)
2000 runs and 100 wickets: F.E.Woolley (4), J.W.Hearne (3), W.G.Grace (2), G.H.Hirst (2), W.Rhodes (2), T.E.Bailey, D.E.Davies, G.L.Jessop, V.W.C.Jupp, J.Langridge, F.A.Tarrant, C.L.Townsend, L.F.Townsend
1000 runs and 200 wickets: M.W.Tate (3), A.E.Trott (2), A.S.Kennedy

Most Doubles: 16 – W.Rhodes; 14 – G.H.Hirst; 10 – V.W.C.Jupp

Double in Debut Season: D.B.Close (1949) – aged 18, the youngest to achieve this feat.
 The feat of scoring 1000 runs and taking 100 wickets in a season has been achieved on 305 occasions, R.J.Hadlee (1984) and F.D.Stephenson (1988) being the only players to complete the 'double' since the reduction of County Championship matches in 1969.

WICKET-KEEPING RECORDS

EIGHT DISMISSALS IN AN INNINGS

9	(8ct, 1st)	Tahir Rashid	Habib Bank v PACO	Gujranwala	1992-93
9	(7ct, 2st)	W.R.James	Matabeleland v Mashonaland CD	Bulawayo	1995-96
8	(8ct)	A.T.W.Grout	Queensland v W Australia	Brisbane	1959-60
8	(8ct)	D.E.East	Essex v Somerset	Taunton	1985
8	(8ct)	S.A.Marsh	Kent v Middlesex	Lord's	1991
8	(6ct, 2st)	T.J.Zoehrer	Australians v Surrey	The Oval	1993
8	(7ct, 1st)	D.S.Berry	Victoria v South Australia	Melbourne	1996-97
8	(7ct,1st)	Y.S.S.Mendis	Bloomfield v Kurunegala Youth	Colombo	2000-01

TWELVE DISMISSALS IN A MATCH

13	(11ct, 2st)	W.R.James	Matabeleland v Mashonaland CD	Bulawayo	1995-96
12	(8ct, 4st)	E.Pooley	Surrey v Sussex	The Oval	1868
12	(9ct, 3st)	D.Tallon	Queensland v NSW	Sydney	1938-39
12	(9ct, 3st)	H.B.Taber	NSW v South Australia	Adelaide	1968-69

MOST DISMISSALS IN A SEASON

128	(79ct, 49st)	L.E.G.Ames	1929

1000 DISMISSALS IN A CAREER

	Career	Dismissals	Ct	St
R.W.Taylor	1960-88	**1649**	1473	176
J.T.Murray	1952-75	**1527**	1270	257
H.Strudwick	1902-27	**1497**	1242	255
A.P.E.Knott	1964-85	**1344**	1211	133
F.H.Huish	1895-1914	**1310**	933	377
B.Taylor	1949-73	**1294**	1083	211
D.Hunter	1889-1909	**1253**	906	347
R.C.Russell	1981-2001	**1241**	1119	122
H.R.Butt	1890-1912	**1228**	953	275
J.H.Board	1891-1914/15	**1207**	852	355
H.Elliott	1920-47	**1206**	904	302
J.M.Parks	1949-76	**1181**	1088	93
S.J.Rhodes	1981-2001	**1134**	1020	114
R.Booth	1951-70	**1126**	948	178
L.E.G.Ames	1926-51	**1121**	703	418
D.L.Bairstow	1970-90	**1099**	961	138
G.Duckworth	1923-47	**1096**	753	343
H.W.Stephenson	1948-64	**1082**	748	334
J.G.Binks	1955-75	**1071**	895	176
T.G.Evans	1939-69	**1066**	816	250
A.Long	1960-80	**1046**	922	124
G.O.Dawkes	1937-61	**1043**	895	148
R.W.Tolchard	1965-83	**1037**	912	125
W.L.Cornford	1921-47	**1017**	675	342

FIELDING RECORDS

MOST CATCHES IN AN INNINGS

7	M.J.Stewart	Surrey v Northamptonshire	Northampton	1957
7	A.S.Brown	Gloucestershire v Nottinghamshire	Nottingham	1966

MOST CATCHES IN A MATCH

10	W.R.Hammond	Gloucestershire v Surrey	Cheltenham	1928

MOST CATCHES IN A SEASON

78	W.R.Hammond	1928	77	M.J.Stewart	1957

750 CATCHES IN A CAREER

1018	F.E.Woolley	1906-38	784	J.G.Langridge	1928-55
887	W.G.Grace	1865-1908	764	W.Rhodes	1898-1930
830	G.A.R.Lock	1946-70/71	758	C.A.Milton	1948-74
819	W.R.Hammond	1920-51	754	E.H.Hendren	1907-38
813	D.B.Close	1949-86			

UNIVERSITY MATCH RESULTS

Played: 156. Wins: Cambridge 56; Oxford 49. Drawn: 51. Abandoned: 1

In 2001, for the very first time, Cambridge hosted the University Match, cricket's oldest surviving first-class fixture, after the ECB's re-organisation of university cricket around six centres of excellence had removed it from Lord's. Dating from 1827 it has, wartime interruptions apart, been played annually since 1838. With the exception of five matches played in the area of Oxford (1829, 1843, 1846, 1848 and 1850), all the previous fixtures had been staged at Lord's. Last season's contest was the first to be played over four days.

As in 2001, Oxford (with Brookes), Cambridge (with Anglia) and Durham will again each play three first-class matches against counties. The other three centres – Cardiff (with UWIC and Glamorgan), Leeds (with Bradford and Leeds Metropolitan), and Loughborough – will also play three counties apiece but without first-class status, an honour they are expected to be granted for 2003.

1827	Drawn	1875	Oxford	1919	Oxford	1965	Drawn
1829	Oxford	1876	Cambridge	1920	Drawn	1966	Oxford
1836	Oxford	1877	Oxford	1921	Cambridge	1967	Drawn
1838	Oxford	1878	Cambridge	1922	Cambridge	1968	Drawn
1839	Cambridge	1879	Cambridge	1923	Oxford	1969	Drawn
1840	Cambridge	1880	Cambridge	1924	Cambridge	1970	Drawn
1841	Cambridge	1881	Oxford	1925	Drawn	1971	Drawn
1842	Cambridge	1882	Cambridge	1926	Cambridge	1972	Cambridge
1843	Cambridge	1883	Cambridge	1927	Cambridge	1973	Drawn
1844	Drawn	1884	Oxford	1928	Drawn	1974	Drawn
1845	Cambridge	1885	Cambridge	1929	Drawn	1975	Drawn
1846	Oxford	1886	Oxford	1930	Cambridge	1976	Oxford
1847	Cambridge	1887	Oxford	1931	Oxford	1977	Drawn
1848	Oxford	1888	Drawn	1932	Drawn	1978	Drawn
1849	Cambridge	1889	Cambridge	1933	Drawn	1979	Cambridge
1850	Oxford	1890	Cambridge	1934	Drawn	1980	Drawn
1851	Cambridge	1891	Cambridge	1935	Cambridge	1981	Drawn
1852	Oxford	1892	Oxford	1936	Cambridge	1982	Cambridge
1853	Oxford	1893	Cambridge	1937	Oxford	1983	Drawn
1854	Oxford	1894	Oxford	1938	Drawn	1984	Oxford
1855	Oxford	1895	Cambridge	1939	Oxford	1985	Drawn
1856	Cambridge	1896	Oxford	1946	Oxford	1986	Cambridge
1857	Oxford	1897	Cambridge	1947	Drawn	1987	Drawn
1858	Oxford	1898	Oxford	1948	Oxford	1988	Abandoned
1859	Cambridge	1899	Drawn	1949	Cambridge	1989	Drawn
1860	Cambridge	1900	Drawn	1950	Drawn	1990	Drawn
1861	Cambridge	1901	Drawn	1951	Oxford	1991	Drawn
1862	Cambridge	1902	Cambridge	1952	Drawn	1992	Cambridge
1863	Oxford	1903	Oxford	1953	Cambridge	1993	Oxford
1864	Oxford	1904	Drawn	1954	Drawn	1994	Drawn
1865	Oxford	1905	Cambridge	1955	Drawn	1995	Oxford
1866	Oxford	1906	Cambridge	1956	Drawn	1996	Drawn
1867	Cambridge	1907	Cambridge	1957	Drawn	1997	Drawn
1868	Cambridge	1908	Oxford	1958	Cambridge	1998	Cambridge
1869	Cambridge	1909	Drawn	1959	Oxford	1999	Drawn
1870	Cambridge	1910	Oxford	1960	Drawn	2000	Drawn
1871	Oxford	1911	Oxford	1961	Drawn	2001	Oxford
1872	Cambridge	1912	Cambridge	1962	Drawn		
1873	Oxford	1913	Cambridge	1963	Drawn		
1874	Oxford	1914	Oxford	1964	Drawn		

CAMBRIDGE UNIVERSITY RECORDS
ALL FIRST-CLASS MATCHES

Highest Total	For 703-9d		v	Sussex	Hove	1890
	V 730-3		by	W Indians	Cambridge	1950
Lowest Total	For 30		v	Yorkshire	Cambridge	1928
	V 32		by	Oxford U	Lord's	1878
Highest Innings	For 254*	K.S.Duleepsinhji	v	Middlesex	Cambridge	1927
	V 304*	E.de C.Weekes	for	W Indians	Cambridge	1950
Highest Partnership						
(2nd wicket)	429*	J.G.Dewes/G.H.G.Doggart	v	Essex	Cambridge	1949
Best Innings Bowling	10-69	S.M.J.Woods	v	Thornton's XI	Cambridge	1890
Best Match Bowling	15-88	S.M.J.Woods	v	Thornton's XI	Cambridge	1890
Most Runs – Season	1581	D.S.Sheppard	(av 79.05)			1952
Most Runs – Career	4310	J.M.Brearley	(av 38.48)			1961-68
Most 100s – Season	7	D.S.Sheppard				1952
Most 100s – Career	14	D.S.Sheppard				1950-52
Most Wkts – Season	80	O.S.Wheatley	(av 17.63)			1958
Most Wkts – Career	208	G.Goonesena	(av 21.82)			1954-57

UNIVERSITY MATCH RECORDS

Highest Total	432-9d		1936
Lowest Total	39		1858
Highest Innings	211	G.Goonesena	1957
Best Innings Bowling	8-44	G.E.Jeffery	1873
Best Match Bowling	13-73	A.G.Steel	1878

Hat-Tricks: F.C.Cobden (1870), A.G.Steel (1879), P.H.Morton (1880), J.F.Ireland (1911), R.G.H.Lowe (1926).

OXFORD UNIVERSITY RECORDS
ALL FIRST-CLASS MATCHES

Highest Total	For 651		v	Sussex	Hove	1895
	V 679-7d		by	Australians	Oxford	1938
Lowest Total	For 12		v	MCC	Oxford	1877
	V 24		by	MCC	Oxford	1846
Highest Innings	For 281	K.J.Key	v	Middlesex	Chiswick Park	1887
	V 338	W.W.Read	for	Surrey	The Oval	1888
Highest Partnership						
(7th wicket)	340	K.J.Key/H.Philipson	v	Middlesex	Chiswick Park	1887
Best Innings Bowling	10-38	S.E.Butler	v	Cambridge U	Lord's	1871
Best Match Bowling	15-65	B.J.T.Bosanquet	v	Sussex	Oxford	1900
Most Runs – Season	1307	Nawab of Pataudi sr	(av 93.35)			1931
Most Runs – Career	3319	N.S.Mitchell-Innes	(av 47.41)			1934-37
Most 100s – Season	6	Nawab of Pataudi sr				1931
Most 100s – Career	9	A.M.Crawley				1927-30
	9	Nawab of Pataudi sr				1928-31
	9	N.S.Mitchell-Innes				1934-37
	9	M.P.Donnelly				1946-47
Most Wkts – Season	70	I.A.R.Peebles	(av 18.15)			1930
Most Wkts – Career	182	R.H.B.Bettington	(av 19.38)			1920-23

UNIVERSITY MATCH RECORDS

Highest Total	513-6d		1996
Lowest Total	32		1878
Highest Innings	238*	Nawab of Pataudi sr	1931
Best Innings Bowling	10-38	S.E.Butler	1871
Best Match Bowling	15-95	S.E.Butler	1871

Match Doubles: P.R.le Couteur (160 and 11-66 in 1910); G.J.Toogood (149 and 10-93 in 1985)

LIMITED-OVERS INTERNATIONALS RESULTS

1970-71 to 10 January 2002

Columns E–UAE indicate matches **Won** by each country.

Team	Opponents	Matches	E	A	SA	WI	NZ	I	P	SL	Z	B	C	EA	H	K	SC	UAE	Tied	NR
England	Australia	70	31	37															1	1
	South Africa	23	7		16															3
	West Indies	61	26			32													1	3
	New Zealand	47	23				20													1
	India	36	19					16												1
	Pakistan	49	28						20											
	Sri Lanka	23	13							10										
	Zimbabwe	21	14								7									
	Bangladesh	1	1									0								
	Canada	1	1										0							
	East Africa	1	1											0						
	Holland	1	1												0					
	Kenya	1	1													0				
	U A Emirates	1	1															0		
Australia	South Africa	45		21	22															2
	West Indies	98		43		52													2	1
	New Zealand	80		55			22													3
	India	67		39				25												3
	Pakistan	60		33					24										1	2
	Sri Lanka	43		28						13										2
	Zimbabwe	19		18							1									
	Bangladesh	2		2								0								
	Canada	1		1									0							
	Kenya	1		1												0				
	Scotland	1		1													0			
S Africa	West Indies	25			17	8														
	N Zealand	27			17		7													3
	India	42			27			14												1
	Pakistan	29			19				10											
	Sri Lanka	25			14					10										1
	Zimbabwe	15			12						2									1
	Holland	1			1										0					
	Kenya	6			6											0				
	U A Emirates	1			1													0		
W Indies	New Zealand	30				19	9													2
	India	66				41		23											1	1
	Pakistan	95				59			34										2	
	Sri Lanka	35				22				12										1
	Zimbabwe	19				14					5									
	Bangladesh	3				3						0								
	Kenya	4				3										1				
	Scotland	1				1											0			
N Zealand	India	61					27	31											1	3
	Pakistan	59					22		35										1	1
	Sri Lanka	50					16			21										1
	Zimbabwe	25					16				7									2
	Bangladesh	2					2					0								
	East Africa	1					1							0						
	Holland	1					1								0					
	Scotland	1					1										0			
	U A Emirates	1					1											0		
India	Pakistan	85						29	52											4
	Sri Lanka	70						36		29										5
	Zimbabwe	36						28			6									2
	Bangladesh	8						8				0								
	East Africa	1						1						0						
	Kenya	10						8								2				
	U A Emirates	1						1										0		
Pakistan	Sri Lanka	90							56	31									1	2
	Zimbabwe	24							21		2								1	
	Bangladesh	8							7			1								
	Canada	1							1				0							

Opponents	Matches	E	A	SA	WI	NZ	I	P	SL	Z	B	C	EA	H	K	SC	UAE	Tied	NR
Holland	1						1							0					
Kenya	1						1								0				
Scotland	1						1									0			
U A Emirates	2						2										0		
Sri Lanka Zimbabwe	27								21	5									1
Bangladesh	6								6		0								
Kenya	3								3						0				
Zimbabwe Bangladesh	10									10	0								
Kenya	11									10					0				1
Bangladesh Kenya	6										1				5				
Scotland	1										1					0			
Holland U A Emirates	1													0			1		
	1782	167	279	152	254	155	220	265	156	55	3	0	0	0	8	0	1	17	50

MERIT TABLE OF ALL L-O INTERNATIONALS
1970-71 to 10 January 2002

	Matches	Won	Lost	Tied	No Result	% Won (exc NR)
South Africa	239	152	79	–	6	65.23
West Indies	437	254	170	5	8	59.20
Australia	487	279	190	6	12	58.73
Pakistan	505	265	224	6	10	53.53
England	336	167	158	2	9	51.07
India	483	220	242	3	18	47.31
New Zealand	385	155	208	4	18	42.23
Sri Lanka	372	156	200	2	14	43.57
Zimbabwe	207	55	144	4	4	27.09
Kenya	43	8	34	–	1	19.04
Bangladesh	47	3	44	–	–	6.38
Associate Members	23	1	22	–	–	4.34

TEAM RECORDS
HIGHEST TOTALS

398-5	(50 overs)	Sri Lanka v Kenya	Kandy	1995-96
376-2	(50 overs)	India v New Zealand	Hyderabad, India	1999-00
373-6	(50 overs)	India v Sri Lanka	Taunton	1999
371-9	(50 overs)	Pakistan v Sri Lanka	Nairobi	1996-97
363-3	(50 overs)	South Africa v Zimbabwe	Bulawayo	2001-02
363-7	(55 overs)	England v Pakistan	Nottingham	1992
360-4	(50 overs)	West Indies v Sri Lanka	Karachi	1987-88
354-3	(50 overs)	South Africa v Kenya	Cape Town	2001-02
351-3	(50 overs)	India v Kenya	Paarl	2001-02
349-6	(50 overs)	Australia v New Zealand	Christchurch	1999-00
349-9	(50 overs)	Sri Lanka v India	Singapore	1995-96
349-9	(50 overs)	New Zealand v India	Rajkot	1999-00

The highest for Zimbabwe is 325-6 (v K, Dhaka, 1998-99); for Bangladesh 267-9 (v Z, Dhaka, 2001-02); and for Kenya 347-3 (v B, Nairobi, 1997-98).

HIGHEST TOTALS BATTING SECOND

WINNING:	316-4	(48.5 overs)	Australia v Pakistan	Lahore	1998-99
	316-7	(47.5 overs)	India v Pakistan	Dhaka	1997-98
LOSING:	329	(49.3 overs)	Sri Lanka v West Indies	Sharjah	1995-96

HIGHEST MATCH AGGREGATE

664-19	(99.4 overs)	Sri Lanka (349-9) v Pakistan (315)	Singapore	1995-96

LARGEST RUNS MARGINS OF VICTORY

245 runs	Sri Lanka beat India	Sharjah	2000-01
233 runs	Pakistan v Bangladesh	Dhaka	1999-00
232 runs	Australia beat Sri Lanka	Adelaide	1984-85
208 runs	South Africa v Kenya	Cape Town	2001-02

206 runs		New Zealand beat Australia	Adelaide	1985-86
202 runs		England beat India	Lord's	1975
202 runs		South Africa beat Kenya	Nairobi	1996-97
202 runs		Zimbabwe beat Kenya	Dhaka	1998-99

LOWEST TOTALS (Excluding reduced innings)

38	(15.4 overs)	Zimbabwe v Sri Lanka	Colombo (SSC)	2001-02
43	(19.5 overs)	Pakistan v West Indies	Cape Town	1992-93
45	(40.3 overs)	Canada v England	Manchester	1979
54	(26.3 overs)	India v Sri Lanka	Sharjah	2000-01
55	(28.3 overs)	Sri Lanka v West Indies	Sharjah	1986-87
63	(25.5 overs)	India v Australia	Sydney	1980-81
64	(35.5 overs)	New Zealand v Pakistan	Sharjah	1985-86
68	(31.3 overs)	Scotland v West Indies	Leicester	1999
69	(28 overs)	South Africa v Australia	Sydney	1993-94
70	(25.2 overs)	Australia v England	Birmingham	1977
70	(26.3 overs)	Australia v New Zealand	Adelaide	1985-86

The lowest for England is 86 (v A, Manchester, 2001); for West Indies 87 (v A, Sydney, 1992-93); for Bangladesh 87 (v P, Dhaka, 1999-00), and for Kenya 90 (v I, Bloemfontein, 2001-02).

LOWEST MATCH AGGREGATE

78-11	(20 overs)	Sri Lanka (40-1) v Zimbabwe (38)	Colombo (SSC)	2001-02

BATTING RECORDS
HIGHEST INDIVIDUAL INNINGS

194	Saeed Anwar	Pakistan v India	Madras	1996-97
189*	I.V.A.Richards	West Indies v England	Manchester	1984
189	S.T.Jayasuriya	Sri Lanka v India	Sharjah	2000-01
188*	G.Kirsten	South Africa v UAE	Rawalpindi	1995-96
186*	S.R.Tendulkar	India v New Zealand	Hyderabad	1999-00
183	S.C.Ganguly	India v Sri Lanka	Taunton	1999
181	I.V.A.Richards	West Indies v Sri Lanka	Karachi	1987-88
175*	Kapil Dev	India v Zimbabwe	Tunbridge Wells	1983
173	M.E.Waugh	Australia v West Indies	Melbourne	2000-01
171*	G.M.Turner	New Zealand v East Africa	Birmingham	1975
169*	D.J.Callaghan	South Africa v New Zealand	Pretoria	1994-95
169	B.C.Lara	West Indies v Sri Lanka	Sharjah	1995-96
167*	R.A.Smith	England v Australia	Birmingham	1993
161	A.C.Hudson	South Africa v Holland	Rawalpindi	1995-96
158	D.I.Gower	England v New Zealand	Brisbane	1982-83
154	A.C.Gilchrist	Australia v Sri Lanka	Melbourne	1998-99
153*	I.V.A.Richards	West Indies v Australia	Melbourne	1979-80
153*	M.Azharuddin	India v Zimbabwe	Cuttack	1997-98
153*	S.C.Ganguly	India v New Zealand	Gwalior	1999-00
153	B.C.Lara	West Indies v Pakistan	Sharjah	1993-94
153	R.Dravid	India v New Zealand	Hyderabad	1999-00
152*	D.L.Haynes	West Indies v India	Georgetown	1988-89
152	C.H.Gayle	West Indies v Kenya	Nairobi	2001-02
151*	S.T.Jayasuriya	Sri Lanka v India	Bombay	1996-97
150	S.Chanderpaul	West Indies v South Africa	East London	1998-99

The highest for Zimbabwe is 142* by G.W.Flower (v B, Bulawayo, 2000-01) and by A.Flower (v E, Harare, 2001-02); for Bangladesh 101 by Mehrab Hossain (v Z, Dhaka, 1998-99); and for Kenya 144 by K.O.Obuya (v B, Nairobi, 1997-98).

HUNDRED ON DEBUT

D.L.Amiss	103	England v Australia	Manchester	1972
D.L.Haynes	148	West Indies v Australia	St John's	1977-78
A.Flower	115*	Zimbabwe v Sri Lanka	New Plymouth	1991-92
Salim Elahi	102*	Pakistan v Sri Lanka	Gujranwala	1995-96

Shahid Afridi scored 102 for P v SL, Nairobi, 1996-97, in his second match having not batted in his first.

Fastest 100	37 balls	Shahid Afridi (102)	P v SL	Nairobi	1996-97
Fastest 50	17 balls	S.T.Jayasuriya (76)	SL v P	Singapore	1995-96

CARRYING BAT THROUGH COMPLETED INNINGS (ALL OUT)

G.W.Flower	84*	Zimbabwe (205) v England	Sydney	1994-95
Saeed Anwar	103*	Pakistan (219) v Zimbabwe	Harare	1994-95
N.V.Knight	125*	England (246) v Pakistan	Nottingham	1996
R.D.Jacobs	49*	West Indies (110) v Australia	Manchester	1999
D.R.Martyn	116*	Australia (191) v New Zealand	Auckland	1999-00
H.H.Gibbs	59*	South Africa (101) v Pakistan	Sharjah	1999-00
A.J.Stewart	100*	England (192) v West Indies	Nottingham	2000
Javed Omar	33*	Bangladesh (103) v Zimbabwe	Harare	2000-01

5000 RUNS IN A CAREER

		LOI	I	NO	HS	Runs	Avge	100	50
S.R.Tendulkar	I	280	272	25	186*	10803	43.73	31	53
M.Azharuddin	I	334	308	54	153*	9378	36.92	7	58
D.L.Haynes	WI	238	237	28	152*	8648	41.37	17	57
P.A.de Silva	SL	275	266	26	145	8430	35.12	11	57
M.E.Waugh	A	237	229	19	173	8374	39.87	18	49
Saeed Anwar	P	230	227	17	194	8348	39.75	19	41
Inzamam-ul-Haq	P	251	237	35	137*	8195	40.56	8	60
A.Ranatunga	SL	269	255	47	131*	7454	35.83	4	49
S.R.Waugh	A	317	281	57	120*	7382	32.95	3	44
Javed Miandad	P	233	218	41	119*	7381	41.70	8	50
B.C.Lara	WI	193	189	18	169	7257	42.43	14	47
S.T.Jayasuriya	SL	252	244	9	189	7235	30.78	11	47
Salim Malik	P	283	256	38	102	7171	32.89	5	47
S.C.Ganguly	I	181	175	14	183	7097	44.08	18	41
I.V.A.Richards	WI	187	167	24	189*	6721	47.00	11	45
Ijaz Ahmed	P	250	232	29	139*	6564	32.33	10	37
A.R.Border	A	273	252	39	127*	6524	30.62	3	39
R.B.Richardson	WI	224	217	30	122	6248	33.41	5	44
G.Kirsten	SA	161	161	15	188*	6149	42.11	12	40
D.M.Jones	A	164	161	25	145	6068	44.61	7	46
D.C.Boon	A	181	177	16	122	5964	37.04	5	37
Ramiz Raja	P	198	197	15	119*	5841	32.09	9	31
A.Flower	Z	191	188	14	142*	5797	33.31	3	46
W.J.Cronje	SA	188	175	31	112	5565	38.64	2	39
G.W.Flower	Z	177	175	14	142*	5415	33.63	5	33
M.G.Bevan	A	164	145	51	108*	5384	57.27	5	36
A.Jadeja	I	196	179	36	119	5359	37.47	6	30
R.Dravid	I	163	151	14	153	5189	37.87	7	35
R.S.Mahanama	SL	213	198	23	119*	5162	29.49	4	35
C.L.Hooper	WI	202	184	37	113*	5146	35.00	6	28
C.G.Greenidge	WI	128	127	13	133*	5134	45.03	11	31

The most for England is 4290 in 122 innings by G.A.Gooch; for New Zealand 4704 (140) by M.D.Crowe; for Bangladesh 857 (38) by Akram Khan; and for Kenya 1190 (41) by S.O.Tikolo.

17 HUNDREDS

		Inns	100	E	A	SA	WI	NZ	I	P	SL	Z	B	K
S.R.Tendulkar	I	272	31	–	6	3	2	3	–	2	6	5	–	4
Saeed Anwar	P	227	19	–	1	–	2	4	3 ·	–	7	2	–	–
S.C.Ganguly	I	175	18	1	–	3	3	–	3	2	4	3	1	1
M.E.Waugh	A	229	18	1	–	2	3	3	4	1	1	3	–	–
D.L.Haynes	WI	237	17	2	6	–	2	2	4	1	–	–	–	–

The most for England is 8 by G.A.Gooch; for South Africa 12 by G.Kirsten; for New Zealand 11 by N.J.Astle; for Sri Lanka 11 by P.A.de Silva and S.T.Jayasuriya; for Zimbabwe 7 by A.D.R.Campbell; for Bangladesh 1 by Mehrab Hossein; and for Kenya 2 by K.O.Obuya.

HIGHEST PARTNERSHIP FOR EACH WICKET

1st	258	S.C.Ganguly/S.R.Tendulkar	India v Kenya	Paarl	2001-02
2nd	331	S.R.Tendulkar/R.Dravid	India v New Zealand	Hyderabad (Ind)	1999-00
3rd	237*	R.Dravid/S.R.Tendulkar	India v Kenya	Bristol	1999
4th	275*	M.Azharuddin/A.Jadeja	India v Zimbabwe	Cuttack	1997-98
5th	223	M.Azharuddin/A.Jadeja	India v Sri Lanka	Colombo (RPS)	1997-98

6th	161	M.O.Odumbe/A.V.Vadher	Kenya v Sri Lanka	Southampton	1999
7th	130	A.Flower/H.H.Streak	Zimbabwe v England	Harare	2001-02
8th	119	P.R.Reiffel/S.K.Warne	Australia v South Africa	Port Elizabeth	1993-94
9th	126*	Kapil Dev/S.M.H.Kirmani	India v Zimbabwe	Tunbridge Wells	1983
10th	106*	I.V.A.Richards/M.A.Holding	West Indies v England	Manchester	1984

BOWLING RECORDS
SIX WICKETS IN AN INNINGS

8-19	W.P.U.C.J Vaas	Sri Lanka v Zimbabwe	Colombo (SSC)	2001-02
7-30	M.Muralitharan	Sri Lanka v India	Sharjah	2000-01
7-36	Waqar Younis	Pakistan v England	Leeds	2001
7-37	Aqib Javed	Pakistan v India	Sharjah	1991-92
7-51	W.W.Davis	West Indies v Australia	Leeds	1983
6-12	A.Kumble	India v West Indies	Calcutta	1993-94
6-14	G.J.Gilmour	Australia v England	Leeds	1975
6-14	Imran Khan	Pakistan v India	Sharjah	1984-85
6-15	C.E.H.Croft	West Indies v England	Kingstown	1980-81
6-18	Azhar Mahmood	Pakistan v West Indies	Sharjah	1999-00
6-19	H.K.Olonga	Zimbabwe v England	Cape Town	1999-00
6-20	B.C.Strang	Zimbabwe v Bangladesh	Nairobi	1997-98
6-23	A.A.Donald	South Africa v Kenya	Nairobi	1996-97
6-26	Waqar Younis	Pakistan v Sri Lanka	Sharjah	1989-90
6-29	B.P.Patterson	West Indies v India	Nagpur	1987-88
6-29	S.T.Jayasuriya	Sri Lanka v England	Moratuwa	1992-93
6-30	Waqar Younis	Pakistan v New Zealand	Auckland	1993-94
6-35	S.M.Pollock	South Africa v West Indies	East London	1998-99
6-39	H.M.MacLeay	Australia v India	Nottingham	1983
6-41	I.V.A.Richards	West Indies v India	Delhi	1989-90
6-44	Waqar Younis	Pakistan v New Zealand	Sharjah	1996-97
6-49	L.Klusener	South Africa v Sri Lanka	Lahore	1997-98
6-50	A.H.Gray	West Indies v Australia	Port-of-Spain	1990-91
6-59	Waqar Younis	Pakistan v Australia	Nottingham	2001

The best for England is 5-15 by M.A.Ealham (v Z, Kimberley, 1999-00); for New Zealand 5-22 by M.N.Hart (v WI, Margao, 1994-95); for Bangladesh 4-36 by Saiful Islam (v SL, Sharjah, 1994-95); and for Kenya 5-33 by A.Y.Karim (v B, Nairobi, 1997-98).

150 WICKETS IN A CAREER

		LOI	O	R	W	Avge	Best	4w	R/Over
Wasim Akram	P	323	2757.1	10643	446	23.86	5-15	21	3.86
Waqar Younis	P	220	1803	8318	357	23.29	7-36	25	4.61
A.Kumble	I	215	1929.1	8073	281	28.72	6-12	9	4.18
J.Srinath	I	198	1722.4	7697	268	28.72	5-23	7	4.47
M.Muralitharan	SL	183	1672.4	6558	267	24.56	7-30	11	3.92
S.K.Warne	A	167	1539.3	6541	262	24.96	5-33	13	4.25
Saqlain Mushtaq	P	144	1256.1	5370	257	20.89	5-20	16	4.28
Kapil Dev	I	225	1867	6945	253	27.45	5-43	4	3.72
C.A.Walsh	WI	205	1803.4	6915	227	30.46	5- 1	7	3.83
A.A.Donald	SA	136	1187.3	4835	226	21.39	6-23	12	4.07
C.E.L.Ambrose	WI	176	1558.5	5430	225	24.13	5-17	10	3.48
W.P.U.C.J.Vaas	SL	175	1416.5	5969	218	27.38	8-19	5	4.21
S.T.Jayasuriya	SL	252	1565	7477	214	34.93	6-29	8	4.78
G.D.McGrath	A	140	1252	5002	212	23.59	5-14	10	4.00
S.M.Pollock	SA	142	1243.5	4675	206	22.69	6-35	10	3.76
C.J.McDermott	A	138	1243.5	5018	203	24.71	5-44	5	4.04
B.K.V.Prasad	I	161	1354.5	6332	196	32.30	5-27	4	4.67
S.R.Waugh	A	317	1470.3	6705	195	34.38	4-33	3	4.56
Aqib Javed	P	163	1335.3	5721	182	31.43	7-37	6	4.28
Imran Khan	P	175	1243.3	4845	182	26.62	6-14	3	3.90
H.H.Streak	Z	142	1186.3	5358	177	30.27	5-32	6	4.52
C.L.Hooper	WI	202	1418.3	6150	176	34.94	4-34	3	4.34
C.Z.Harris	NZ	188	1422.1	6098	173	35.24	5-42	3	4.29
Mushtaq Ahmed	P	143	1247.1	5296	161	32.89	5-36	4	4.25
R.J.Hadlee	NZ	115	1030.2	3407	158	21.56	5-25	6	3.31
M.Prabhakar	I	129	1060	4534	157	28.87	5-33	6	4.28
M.D.Marshall	WI	136	1195.5	4233	157	26.96	4-18	6	3.54

The most for England is 147 in 95 matches by D.Gough; for Bangladesh 28 (28) by Hasibul Hussain; and for Kenya 40 (42) by T.M.Odoyo.

HAT-TRICKS

Jalaluddin	Pakistan v Australia	Hyderabad	1982-83
B.A.Reid	Australia v New Zealand	Sydney	1985-86
C.Sharma	India v New Zealand	Nagpur	1987-88
Wasim Akram	Pakistan v West Indies	Sharjah	1989-90
Wasim Akram	Pakistan v Australia	Sharjah	1989-90
Kapil Dev	India v Sri Lanka	Calcutta	1990-91
Aqib Javed	Pakistan v India	Sharjah	1991-92
D.K.Morrison	New Zealand v India	Napier	1993-94
Waqar Younis	Pakistan v New Zealand	East London	1994-95
Saqlain Mushtaq	Pakistan v Zimbabwe	Peshawar	1996-97
E.A.Brandes	Zimbabwe v England	Harare	1996-97
A.M.Stuart	Australia v Pakistan	Melbourne	1996-97
Saqlain Mushtaq	Pakistan v Zimbabwe	The Oval	1999
W.P.U.C.J.Vaas	Sri Lanka v Zimbabwe	Colombo (SSC)	2001-02

WICKET-KEEPING RECORDS
SIX DISMISSALS IN AN INNINGS

6	(6ct)	A.C.Gilchrist	Australia v South Africa	Cape Town	1999-00
6	(6ct)	A.J.Stewart	England v Zimbabwe	Manchester	2000
6	(5ct/1st)	R.D.Jacobs	West Indies v Sri Lanka	Colombo (RPS)	2001-02

100 DISMISSALS IN A CAREER
(Including catches taken in the field)

		LOI	Ct	St	Dis
Moin Khan	Pakistan	190	191	66	257
I.A.Healy	Australia	168	195	39	234
P.J.L.Dujon	West Indies	169	183	21	204
R.S.Kaluwitharana	Sri Lanka	170	123	70	193
A.C.Gilchrist	Australia	119	153	29	182
A.Flower	Zimbabwe	191	135	32	167
D.J.Richardson	South Africa	122	149	16	165
N.R.Mongia	India	140	112	44	156
M.V.Boucher	South Africa	101	145	6	151
A.J.Stewart	England	146	136	11	147
Rashid Latif	Pakistan	112	111	29	140
R.D.Jacobs	West Indies	89	114	21	135
A.C.Parore	New Zealand	169	100	25	125
R.W.Marsh	Australia	92	120	4	124
Salim Yousuf	Pakistan	86	80	22	102

FIELDING RECORDS
FIVE CATCHES IN AN INNINGS

5	J.N.Rhodes	South Africa v West Indies	Bombay	1993-94

100 CATCHES IN A CAREER
(Excluding catches taken while keeping wicket)

		LOI	Ct
M.Azharuddin	India	334	156
A.R.Border	Australia	273	127
R.S.Mahanama	Sri Lanka	213	109
S.R.Waugh	Australia	317	108
M.E.Waugh	Australia	237	105
I.V.A.Richards	West Indies	187	101

The most for England is 64 in 120 matches by G.A.Hick; for South Africa 93 (210) by J.N.Rhodes; for New Zealand 70 (156) by S.P.Fleming and (188) C.Z.Harris; for Pakistan 90 (250) by Ijaz Ahmed; and for Zimbabwe 67 (177) by G.W.Flower.

ALL-ROUND RECORDS
50 RUNS AND 5 WICKETS IN A MATCH

I.V.A.Richards	119	5-41	West Indies v New Zealand	Dunedin	1986-87
K.Srikkanth	70	5-27	India v New Zealand	Vishakhapatnam	1988-89
M.E.Waugh	57	5-24	Australia v West Indies	Melbourne	1992-93
L.Klusener	54	6-49	South Africa v Sri Lanka	Lahore	1997-98
Abdul Razzaq	70*	5-48	Pakistan v India	Hobart	1999-00
G.A.Hick	80	5-33	England v Zimbabwe	Harare	1999-00
Shahid Afridi	61	5-40	Pakistan v England	Lahore	2000-01
S.C.Ganguly	71*	5-34	India v Zimbabwe	Kanpur	2000-01

1000 RUNS AND 100 WICKETS

		LOI	Runs	Wkts
Abdul Razzaq	Pakistan	89	1514	120
Azhar Mahmood	Pakistan	111	1206	108
I.T.Botham	England	116	2113	145
C.L.Cairns	New Zealand	137	3216	131
W.J.Cronje	South Africa	188	5565	114
H.D.P.K.Dharmasena	Sri Lanka	123	1032	127
R.J.Hadlee	New Zealand	115	1751	158
C.Z.Harris	New Zealand	188	3349	173
C.L.Hooper	West Indies	202	5146	176
Imran Khan	Pakistan	175	3709	182
S.T.Jayasuriya	Sri Lanka	252	7235	214
J.H.Kallis	South Africa	135	4698	122
Kapil Dev	India	225	3783	253
L.Klusener	South Africa	122	2780	146
Mudassar Nazar	Pakistan	122	2653	111
S.P.O'Donnell	Australia	87	1242	108
S.M.Pollock	South Africa	142	1460	206
M.Prabhakar	India	130	1858	157
I.V.A.Richards	West Indies	187	6721	118
R.J.Shastri	India	150	3108	129
H.H.Streak	Zimbabwe	142	1848	177
S.R.Tendulkar	India	280	10803	103
W.P.U.C.J.Vaas	Sri Lanka	175	1079	218
Wasim Akram	Pakistan	323	3359	446
S.R.Waugh	Australia	317	7382	195

APPEARANCE RECORDS
250 MATCHES

334	M.Azharuddin	India	273	A.R.Border	Australia
323	Wasim Akram	Pakistan	269	A.Ranatunga	Sri Lanka
317	S.R.Waugh	Australia	252	S.T.Jayasuriya	Sri Lanka
283	Salim Malik	Pakistan	251	Inzamam-ul-Haq	Pakistan
280	S.R.Tendulkar	India	250	Ijaz Ahmed	Pakistan
275	P.A.de Silva	Sri Lanka			

The most for England is 146 by A.J.Stewart; for South Africa 210 by J.N.Rhodes; for West Indies 238 by D.L.Haynes; for New Zealand 188 by C.Z.Harris; and for Zimbabwe 191 by A.Flower.

100 MATCHES AS CAPTAIN

193	A.Ranatunga	Sri Lanka	138	W.J.Cronje	South Africa
178	A.R.Border	Australia	109	Wasim Akram	Pakistan
174	M.Azharuddin	India	108	I.V.A.Richards	West Indies
139	Imran Khan	Pakistan			

The most for England is 50 by G.A.Gooch; for New Zealand 96 by S.P.Fleming; and for Zimbabwe 78 by A.D.R.Campbell.

WOMEN'S TEST CRICKET RECORDS

1934-35 to 30 January 2002

Compiled by Marion Collin

RESULTS SUMMARY

	Opponents	Tests	E	A	NZ	SA	WI	I	P	SL	Ire	Drawn
England	Australia	38	6	9	–	–	–	–	–	–	–	23
	New Zealand	22	6	–	0	–	–	–	–	–	–	16
	South Africa	4	1	–	–	0	–	–	–	–	–	3
	West Indies	3	2	–	–	–	0	–	–	–	–	1
	India	8	1	–	–	–	–	0	–	–	–	7
Australia	New Zealand	13	–	4	1	–	–	–	–	–	–	8
	West Indies	2	–	0	–	–	0	–	–	–	–	2
	India	8	–	3	–	–	–	0	–	–	–	5
New Zealand	South Africa	3	–	–	1	0	–	–	–	–	–	2
	India	5	–	–	0	–	–	0	–	–	–	5
West Indies	India	6	–	–	–	–	1	1	–	–	–	4
Pakistan	Sri Lanka	1	–	–	–	–	–	–	0	1	–	–
	Ireland	1	–	–	–	–	–	–	0	–	1	–
		114	16	16	2	0	1	1	0	1	1	76

	Tests	Won	Lost	Drawn	Toss Won
England	75	16	9	50	47
Australia	61	16	7	38	19
New Zealand	43	2	10	31	21
South Africa	7	–	2	5	4
West Indies	11	1	3	7	5†
India	27	1	5	21	11†
Pakistan	2	–	2	–	1
Sri Lanka	1	1	–	–	1
Ireland	1	1	–	–	1

† *Results of tosses in five of the six India v West Indies Tests in 1976-77 are not known*

TEAM RECORDS

HIGHEST INNINGS TOTALS

569-6d	Australia v England	Guildford	1998
525	Australia v India	Ahmedabad	1983-84
517-8	New Zealand v England	Scarborough	1996
503-5d	England v New Zealand	Christchurch	1934-35
427-4d	Australia v England	Worcester	1998
426-9d	India v England	Blackpool	1986
414	England v New Zealand	Scarborough	1996
414	England v Australia	Guildford	1998
403-8d	New Zealand v India	Nelson	1994-95

The highest totals for countries not included above are:

282	West Indies v Australia	Montego Bay	1975-76
266-8d	South Africa v England	Cape Town	1960-61
193-3d	Ireland v Pakistan	Dublin	2000
171	Pakistan v Sri Lanka	Colombo	1997-98

LOWEST INNINGS TOTALS

35	England v Australia	Melbourne	1957-58
38	Australia v England	Melbourne	1957-58
44	New Zealand v England	Christchurch	1934-35
47	Australia v England	Brisbane	1934-35
53	Pakistan v Ireland	Dublin	2000

The lowest innings totals for countries not included above are:

67	West Indies v England	Canterbury	1979
89	South Africa v New Zealand	Durban	1971-72
65	India v West Indies	Jammu	1976-77

BATTING RECORDS
1000 RUNS IN TESTS

			M	I	NO	HS	Avge	100
1935	J.A.Brittin	England	27	44	5	167	49.61	5
1594	R.Heyhoe-Flint	England	22	38	3	179	45.54	3
1301	D.A.Hockley	New Zealand	19	29	4	126*	52.04	4
1164	C.A.Hodges	England	18	31	2	158*	40.13	2
1110	S.Agarwal	India	13	23	1	190	50.45	4
1078	E.Bakewell	England	12	22	4	124	59.88	4
1007	M.E.Maclagan	England	14	25	1	119	41.95	2

HIGHEST INDIVIDUAL INNINGS

209*	K.L.Rolton	A v E	Leeds	2001
204	K.E.Flavell	NZ v E	Scarborough	1996
204‡	M.A.J.Goszko	A v E	Shenley	2001
200	J.Broadbent	A v E	Guildford	1998
193	D.A.Annetts	A v E	Collingham	1987
190	S.Agarwal	I v E	Worcester	1986
189	E.A.Snowball	E v NZ	Christchurch	1934-35
179	R.Heyhoe-Flint	E v A	The Oval	1976
176*	K.L.Rolton	A v E	Worcester	1998
167	J.A.Brittin	E v A	Harrogate	1998
161*	E.C.Drumm	E v A	Christchurch	1994-95
160	B.A.Daniels	E v NZ	Scarborough	1996
158*	C.A.Hodges	E v NZ	Canterbury	1984
155*	P.F.McKelvey	NZ v E	Wellington	1968-69

‡ *On debut*

5 HUNDREDS

						Opponents					
		M	I	E	A	NZ	SA	WI	IND	P	SL	IRE
5	J.A.Brittin (E)	27	44	–	3	1	–	1	–	–	–

HIGHEST PARTNERSHIP FOR EACH WICKET

1st	200	C.Atkins/A.Thompson	E v I	Lucknow	2001-02
2nd	235	E.A.Snowball/M.E.Hide	E v NZ	Christchurch	1934-35
3rd	309	L.A.Reeler/D.A.Annetts	A v E	Collingham	1987
4th	253	K.L.Rolton/L.C.Broadfoot	A v E	Leeds	2001
5th	135	E.R.Wilson/V.Batty	A v E	Adelaide	1957-58
6th	132	B.A.Daniels/K.M.Leng	E v NZ	Scarborough	1996
7th	110	K.Smithies/J.M.Chamberlain	E v A	Hove	1987
8th	181	S.J.Griffiths/D.L.Wilson	A v NZ	Auckland	1989-90
9th	107	B.Botha/M.Payne	SA v NZ	Cape Town	1971-72
10th	78	E.Barker/H.Hegarty	E v A	Adelaide	1957-58
	78	S.Gupta/S.Chakraborty	I v A	Lucknow	1983-84

BOWLING RECORDS
50 WICKETS IN TESTS

Wkts			M	Balls	Runs	Avge	Best
77	M.B.Duggan	E	17	3734	1039	13.49	7- 6
68	E.R.Wilson	A	11	2885	803	11.80	7- 7
63	D.F.Edulji	I	20	5098†	1624	25.77	6- 64
60	M.E.Maclagan	E	14	3432	935	15.58	7- 10
57	R.H.Thompson	A	16	4304	1040	18.24	5- 33
55	J.Lord	NZ	15	3108	1049	19.07	6-119
50	E.Bakewell	E	12	2697	831	16.62	7- 61

† Excludes balls bowled in Sixth Test v West Indies 1976-77

TEN WICKETS IN A TEST

11-16	E.R.Wilson	A v E	Melbourne	1957-58
11-63	J.Greenwood	E v WI	Canterbury	1979
10-65	E.R.Wilson	A v NZ	Wellington	1947-48
10-75	E.Bakewell	E v WI	Birmingham	1979
10-107	K.Price	A v I	Lucknow	1983-84
10-118	D.A.Gordon	A v E	Melbourne	1968-69
10-137	J.Lord	NZ v A	Melbourne	1978-79

SEVEN WICKETS IN AN INNINGS

8-53	N.David	I v E	Jamshedpur	1995-96
7-6	M.B.Duggan	E v A	Melbourne	1957-58
7-7	E.R.Wilson	A v E	Melbourne	1957-58
7-10	M.E.Maclagan	E v A	Brisbane	1934-35
7-18	A.Palmer	A v E	Brisbane	1934-35
7-24	L.Johnston	A v NZ	Melbourne	1971-72
7-34	G.E.McConway	E v I	Worcester	1986
7-41	J.Burley	NZ v E	The Oval	1966
7-61	E.Bakewell	E v WI	Birmingham	1979

HAT-TRICK

E.R.Wilson	Australia v England	Melbourne	1957-58

WICKET-KEEPING AND FIELDING RECORDS
25 DISMISSALS IN TESTS

Total			Tests	Ct	St
58	C.Matthews	Australia	20	46	12
36	S.A.Hodges	England	11	19	17
28	B.Brentnall	New Zealand	10	16	12

EIGHT DISMISSALS IN A TEST

9 (8ct, 1 st)	C.Matthews	A v I	Adelaide	1990-91
8 (6ct, 2st)	L.Nye	E v NZ	New Plymouth	1991-92

SIX DISMISSALS IN AN INNINGS

8 (6ct, 2st)	L.Nye	E v NZ	New Plymouth	1991-92
6 (2ct, 4st)	B.Brentnall	NZ v SA	Johannesburg	1971-72

20 CATCHES IN THE FIELD IN TESTS

Total			Tests
25	C.A.Hodges	England	18
20	L.A.Fullston	Australia	12

APPEARANCE RECORDS
25 TEST MATCH APPEARANCES

27	J.A.Brittin	England	1979-98

TEST MATCHES RESULTS SUMMARY
Matches completed before 30 January 2002

	Opponents	Tests	Won by										Tied	Drawn
			E	A	SA	WI	NZ	I	P	SL	Z	B		
England	Australia	301	94	121	–	–	–	–	–	–	–	–	–	86
	South Africa	120	50	–	23	–	–	–	–	–	–	–	–	47
	West Indies	126	31	–	–	52	–	–	–	–	–	–	–	43
	New Zealand	82	37	–	–	–	6	–	–	–	–	–	–	39
	India	87	32	–	–	–	–	15	–	–	–	–	–	40
	Pakistan	60	16	–	–	–	–	–	10	–	–	–	–	34
	Sri Lanka	9	5	–	–	–	–	–	–	3	–	–	–	1
	Zimbabwe	4	1	–	–	–	–	–	–	–	0	–	–	3
Australia	South Africa	68	–	37	14	–	–	–	–	–	–	–	–	17
	West Indies	95	–	42	–	31	–	–	–	–	–	–	1	21
	New Zealand	41	–	18	–	–	7	–	–	–	–	–	–	16
	India	60	–	29	–	–	–	13	–	–	–	–	1	17
	Pakistan	46	–	18	–	–	–	–	11	–	–	–	–	17
	Sri Lanka	13	–	7	–	–	–	–	–	1	–	–	–	5
	Zimbabwe	1	–	1	–	–	–	–	–	–	0	–	–	–
South Africa	West Indies	11	–	–	7	2	–	–	–	–	–	–	–	2
	New Zealand	27	–	–	15	–	3	–	–	–	–	–	–	9
	India	14	–	–	7	–	–	2	–	–	–	–	–	5
	Pakistan	7	–	–	3	–	–	–	1	–	–	–	–	3
	Sri Lanka	11	–	–	6	–	–	–	–	1	–	–	–	4
	Zimbabwe	5	–	–	4	–	–	–	–	–	0	–	–	1
West Indies	New Zealand	30	–	–	–	10	6	–	–	–	–	–	–	14
	India	70	–	–	–	28	–	7	–	–	–	–	–	35
	Pakistan	37	–	–	–	13	–	–	10	–	–	–	–	14
	Sri Lanka	6	–	–	–	1	–	–	–	3	–	–	–	2
	Zimbabwe	4	–	–	–	3	–	–	–	–	–	–	–	1
New Zealand	India	40	–	–	–	–	7	14	–	–	–	–	–	19
	Pakistan	42	–	–	–	–	6	–	19	–	–	–	–	17
	Sri Lanka	18	–	–	–	–	7	–	–	4	–	–	–	7
	Zimbabwe	11	–	–	–	–	5	–	–	–	0	–	–	6
	Bangladesh	2	–	–	–	–	2	–	–	–	–	0	–	–
India	Pakistan	47	–	–	–	–	–	5	9	–	–	–	–	33
	Sri Lanka	23	–	–	–	–	–	8	–	3	–	–	–	12
	Zimbabwe	7	–	–	–	–	–	3	–	–	2	–	–	2
	Bangladesh	1	–	–	–	–	–	1	–	–	–	0	–	–
Pakistan	Sri Lanka	27	–	–	–	–	–	–	13	5	–	–	–	9
	Zimbabwe	12	–	–	–	–	–	–	6	–	2	–	–	4
	Bangladesh	3	–	–	–	–	–	–	3	–	–	0	–	–
Sri Lanka	Zimbabwe	13	–	–	–	–	–	–	–	8	0	–	–	5
	Bangladesh	1	–	–	–	–	–	–	–	1	–	0	–	–
Zimbabwe	Bangladesh	4	–	–	–	–	–	–	–	–	3	0	–	1
		1586	266	273	79	140	49	68	82	29	7	0	2	591

	Tests	Won	Lost	Drawn	Tied	Toss Won
England	789	266	230	293	–	381
Australia	625	273	171	179	2	319
South Africa	263	79	96	88	–	120
West Indies	379	140	106	132	1	200
New Zealand	293	49	117	127	–	148
India	349	68	117	163	1	179
Pakistan	281	82	68	131	–	134
Sri Lanka	121	29	47	45	–	66
Zimbabwe	61	7	31	23	–	34
Bangladesh	11	–	10	1	–	5

TEST CRICKET RECORDS

To 30 January 2002

TEAM RECORDS

HIGHEST INNINGS TOTALS

952-6d	Sri Lanka v India	Colombo (RPS)	1997-98
903-7d	England v Australia	The Oval	1938
849	England v West Indies	Kingston	1929-30
790-3d	West Indies v Pakistan	Kingston	1957-58
758-8d	Australia v West Indies	Kingston	1954-55
729-6d	Australia v England	Lord's	1930
708	Pakistan v England	The Oval	1987
701	Australia v England	The Oval	1934
699-5	Pakistan v India	Lahore	1989-90
695	Australia v England	The Oval	1930
692-8d	West Indies v England	The Oval	1995
687-8d	West Indies v England	The Oval	1976
681-8d	West Indies v England	Port-of-Spain	1953-54
676-7	India v Sri Lanka	Kanpur	1986-87
674-6	Pakistan v India	Faisalabad	1984-85
674	Australia v India	Adelaide	1947-48
671-4	New Zealand v Sri Lanka	Wellington	1990-91
668	Australia v West Indies	Bridgetown	1954-55
660-5d	West Indies v New Zealand	Wellington	1994-95
659-8d	Australia v England	Sydney	1946-47
658-8d	England v Australia	Nottingham	1938
657-7d	India v Australia	Calcutta	2000-01
657-8d	Pakistan v West Indies	Bridgetown	1957-58
656-8d	Australia v England	Manchester	1964
654-5	England v South Africa	Durban	1938-39
653-4d	England v India	Lord's	1990
653-4d	Australia v England	Leeds	1993
652-7d	England v India	Madras	1984-85
652-8d	West Indies v England	Lord's	1973
652	Pakistan v India	Faisalabad	1982-83
650-6d	Australia v West Indies	Bridgetown	1964-65

The highest for South Africa is 622-9d (v A, Durban, 1969-70), for Zimbabwe 563-9d (v WI, Harare, 2001), and for Bangladesh 400 (v I, Dhaka, 2000-01).

LOWEST INNINGS TOTALS

26	New Zealand v England	Auckland	1954-55
30	South Africa v England	Port Elizabeth	1895-96
30	South Africa v England	Birmingham	1924
35	South Africa v England	Cape Town	1898-99
36	Australia v England	Birmingham	1902
36	South Africa v Australia	Melbourne	1931-32
42	Australia v England	Sydney	1887-88
42	New Zealand v Australia	Wellington	1945-46
42	India v England	Lord's	1974
43	South Africa v England	Cape Town	1888-89
44	Australia v England	The Oval	1896
45	England v Australia	Sydney	1886-87
45	South Africa v Australia	Melbourne	1931-32
46	England v West Indies	Port-of-Spain	1993-94
47	South Africa v England	Cape Town	1888-89
47	New Zealand v England	Lord's	1958

The lowest for West Indies is 51 (v A, Port-of-Spain, 1998-99), for Pakistan 62 (v A, Perth, 1981-82), for Sri Lanka 71 (v P, Kandy, 1994-95), and for Zimbabwe 63 (v WI, Port-of-Spain, 1999-00), and for Bangladesh 90 (v SL, Colombo, 2001-02).

BATTING RECORDS
4000 RUNS IN A TEST CAREER

Runs			M	I	NO	HS	Avge	100	50
11174	A.R.Border	A	156	265	44	205	50.56	27	63
10122	S.M.Gavaskar	I	125	214	16	236*	51.12	34	45
9505	S.R.Waugh	A	145	228	41	200	50.82	27	44
8900	G.A.Gooch	E	118	215	6	333	42.58	20	46
8832	Javed Miandad	P	124	189	21	280*	52.57	23	43
8540	I.V.A.Richards	WI	121	182	12	291	50.23	24	45
8231	D.I.Gower	E	117	204	18	215	44.25	18	39
8114	G.Boycott	E	108	193	23	246*	47.72	22	42
8032	G.St A.Sobers	WI	93	160	21	365*	57.78	26	30
7780	M.E.Waugh	A	122	200	17	153*	42.51	20	45
7728	M.A.Atherton	E	115	212	7	185*	37.70	16	46
7624	M.C.Cowdrey	E	114	188	15	182	44.06	22	38
7558	C.G.Greenidge	WI	108	185	16	226	44.72	19	34
7525	M.A.Taylor	A	104	186	13	334*	43.49	19	40
7515	C.H.Lloyd	WI	110	175	14	242*	46.67	19	39
7487	D.L.Haynes	WI	116	202	25	184	42.29	18	39
7469	A.J.Stewart	E	115	207	17	190	39.31	14	38
7422	D.C.Boon	A	107	190	20	200	43.65	21	32
7419	S.R.Tendulkar	I	89	143	15	217	57.96	27	30
7249	W.R.Hammond	E	85	140	16	336*	58.45	22	24
7221	B.C.Lara	WI	83	147	4	375	50.49	18	34
7110	G.S.Chappell	A	87	151	19	247*	53.86	24	31
6996	D.G.Bradman	A	52	80	10	334	99.94	29	13
6971	L.Hutton	E	79	138	15	364	56.67	19	33
6868	D.B.Vengsarkar	I	116	185	22	166	42.13	17	35
6806	K.F.Barrington	E	82	131	15	256	58.67	20	35
6227	R.B.Kanhai	WI	79	137	6	256	47.53	15	28
6215	M.Azharuddin	I	99	147	9	199	45.03	22	21
6149	R.N.Harvey	A	79	137	10	205	48.41	21	24
6080	G.R.Viswanath	I	91	155	10	222	41.93	14	35
5952	P.A.de Silva	SL	89	153	11	267	41.92	19	21
5949	R.B.Richardson	WI	86	146	12	194	44.39	16	27
5807	D.C.S.Compton	E	78	131	15	278	50.06	17	28
5768	Salim Malik	P	103	154	22	237	43.69	15	29
5479	G.Kirsten	SA	80	142	12	275	42.14	14	25
5444	M.D.Crowe	NZ	77	131	11	299	45.36	17	18
5410	J.B.Hobbs	E	61	102	7	211	56.94	15	28
5372	Inzamam-ul-Haq	P	77	126	13	200*	47.53	15	30
5357	K.D.Walters	A	74	125	14	250	48.26	15	33
5345	I.M.Chappell	A	75	136	10	196	42.42	14	26
5334	J.G.Wright	NZ	82	148	7	185	37.82	12	23
5312	M.J.Slater	A	74	131	7	219	42.84	14	21
5248	Kapil Dev	I	131	184	15	163	31.05	8	27
5234	W.M.Lawry	A	67	123	12	210	47.15	13	27
5200	I.T.Botham	E	102	161	6	208	33.54	14	22
5138	J.H.Edrich	E	77	127	9	310*	43.54	12	24
5105	A.Ranatunga	SL	93	155	12	135*	35.69	4	38
5062	Zaheer Abbas	P	78	124	11	274	44.79	12	20
4882	T.W.Graveney	E	79	123	13	258	44.38	11	20

Runs			M	I	NO	HS	Avge	100	50
4869	R.B.Simpson	A	62	111	7	311	46.81	10	27
4866	C.L.Hooper	WI	90	154	14	178*	34.75	10	24
4737	I.R.Redpath	A	66	120	11	171	43.45	8	31
4656	A.J.Lamb	E	79	139	10	142	36.09	14	18
4583	G.P.Thorpe	E	70	128	16	138	40.91	9	29
4555	H.Sutcliffe	E	54	84	9	194	60.73	16	23
4554	D.J.Cullinan	SA	70	115	12	275*	44.21	14	20
4552	A.Flower	Z	59	104	19	232*	53.55	12	25
4537	P.B.H.May	E	66	106	9	285*	46.77	13	22
4502	E.R.Dexter	E	62	102	8	205	47.89	9	27
4455	E.de C.Weekes	WI	48	81	5	207	58.61	15	19
4415	K.J.Hughes	A	70	124	6	213	37.41	9	22
4409	M.W.Gatting	E	79	138	14	207	35.55	10	21
4399	A.I.Kallicharran	WI	66	109	10	187	44.43	12	21
4389	A.P.E.Knott	E	95	149	15	135	32.75	5	30
4378	M.Amarnath	I	69	113	10	138	42.50	11	24
4356	I.A.Healy	A	119	182	23	161*	27.39	4	22
4339	S.T.Jayasuriya	SL	69	117	12	340	41.32	9	20
4334	R.C.Fredericks	WI	59	109	7	169	42.49	8	26
4257	R.Dravid	I	53	92	10	200*	51.91	9	23
4236	R.A.Smith	E	62	112	15	175	43.67	9	28
4114	Mudassar Nazar	P	76	116	8	231	38.09	10	17
4052	Saeed Anwar	P	55	91	2	188*	45.52	11	25

The most for Bangladesh is 812 by Habibul Bashar (22 innings).

750 RUNS IN A SERIES

Runs		Series		M	I	NO	HS	Avge	100	50
974	D.G.Bradman	A v E	1930	5	7	–	334	139.14	4	–
905	W.R.Hammond	E v A	1928-29	5	9	1	251	113.12	4	–
839	M.A.Taylor	A v E	1989	6	11	1	219	83.90	2	5
834	R.N.Harvey	A v SA	1952-53	5	9	–	205	92.66	4	3
829	I.V.A.Richards	WI v E	1976	4	7	–	291	118.42	3	2
827	C.L.Walcott	WI v A	1954-55	5	10	–	155	82.70	5	2
824	G.St A.Sobers	WI v P	1957-58	5	8	2	365*	137.33	3	3
810	D.G.Bradman	A v E	1936-37	5	9	–	270	90.00	3	1
806	D.G.Bradman	A v SA	1931-32	5	5	1	299*	201.50	4	–
798	B.C.Lara	WI v E	1993-94	5	8	–	375	99.75	2	2
779	E.de C.Weekes	WI v I	1948-49	5	7	–	194	111.28	4	2
774	S.M.Gavaskar	I v WI	1970-71	4	8	3	220	154.80	4	3
765	B.C.Lara	WI v E	1995	6	10	1	179	85.00	3	3
761	Mudassar Nazar	P v I	1982-83	6	8	2	231	126.83	4	1
758	D.G.Bradman	A v E	1934	5	8	–	304	94.75	2	1
753	D.C.S.Compton	E v SA	1947	5	6	–	208	94.12	4	2
752	G.A.Gooch	E v I	1990	3	6	–	333	125.33	3	2

HIGHEST INDIVIDUAL INNINGS

375	B.C.Lara	WI v E	St John's	1993-94
365*	G.St A.Sobers	WI v P	Kingston	1957-58
364	L.Hutton	E v A	The Oval	1938
340	S.T.Jayasuriya	SL v I	Colombo (RPS)	1997-98
337	Hanif Mohammed	P v WI	Bridgetown	1957-58
336*	W.R.Hammond	E v NZ	Auckland	1932-33
334*	M.A.Taylor	A v P	Peshawar	1998-99
334	D.G.Bradman	A v E	Leeds	1930
333	G.A.Gooch	E v I	Lord's	1990

325	A.Sandham	E v WI	Kingston	1929-30
311	R.B.Simpson	A v E	Manchester	1964
310*	J.H.Edrich	E v NZ	Leeds	1965
307	R.M.Cowper	A v E	Melbourne	1965-66
304	D.G.Bradman	A v E	Leeds	1934
302	L.G.Rowe	WI v E	Bridgetown	1973-74
299*	D.G.Bradman	A v SA	Adelaide	1931-32
299	M.D.Crowe	NZ v SL	Wellington	1990-91
291	I.V.A.Richards	WI v E	The Oval	1976
287	R.E.Foster	E v A	Sydney	1903-04
285*	P.B.H.May	E v WI	Birmingham	1957
281	V.V.S.Laxman	I v A	Calcutta	2000-01
280*	Javed Miandad	P v I	Hyderabad	1982-83
278	D.C.S.Compton	E v P	Nottingham	1954
277	B.C.Lara	WI v A	Sydney	1992-93
275*	D.J.Cullinan	SA v NZ	Auckland	1998-99
275	G.Kirsten	SA v E	Durban	1999-00
274	R.G.Pollock	SA v A	Durban	1969-70
274	Zaheer Abbas	P v E	Birmingham	1971
271	Javed Miandad	P v NZ	Auckland	1988-89
270*	G.A.Headley	WI v E	Kingston	1934-35
270	D.G.Bradman	A v E	Melbourne	1936-37
268	G.N.Yallop	A v P	Melbourne	1983-84
267*	B.A.Young	NZ v SL	Dunedin	1996-97
267	P.A.de Silva	SL v NZ	Wellington	1990-91
266	W.H.Ponsford	A v E	The Oval	1934
266	D.L.Houghton	Z v SL	Bulawayo	1994-95
262*	D.L.Amiss	E v WI	Kingston	1973-74
261	F.M.M.Worrell	WI v E	Nottingham	1950
260	C.C.Hunte	WI v P	Kingston	1957-58
260	Javed Miandad	P v E	The Oval	1987
259	G.M.Turner	NZ v WI	Georgetown	1971-72
258	T.W.Graveney	E v WI	Nottingham	1957
258	S.M.Nurse	WI v NZ	Christchurch	1968-69
257*	Wasim Akram	P v Z	Sheikhupura	1996-97
256	R.B.Kanhai	WI v I	Calcutta	1958-59
256	K.F.Barrington	E v A	Manchester	1964
255*	D.J.McGlew	SA v NZ	Wellington	1952-53
254	D.G.Bradman	A v E	Lord's	1930
251	W.R.Hammond	E v A	Sydney	1928-29
250	K.D.Walters	A v NZ	Christchurch	1976-77
250	S.F.A.F.Bacchus	WI v I	Kanpur	1978-79

The highest for Bangladesh is 145 by Aminul Islam (v I, Dhaka, 2000-01).

18 HUNDREDS

			200	I	E	A	SA	Opponents WI	NZ	I	P	SL	Z	B
34	S.M.Gavaskar	I	4	214	4	8	–	13	2	–	5	2	–	–
29	D.G.Bradman	A	12	80	19	–	4	2	–	4	–	–	–	–
27	S.R.Tendulkar	I	2	143	5	6	3	1	3	–	1	6	2	–
27	S.R.Waugh	A	1	228	9	–	2	6	2	2	2	3	1	–
27	A.R.Border	A	2	265	8	–	–	3	5	4	6	1	–	–
26	G.St A.Sobers	WI	2	160	10	4	–	–	1	8	3	–	–	–
24	G.S.Chappell	A	4	151	9	–	–	5	3	1	6	–	–	–
24	I.V.A.Richards	WI	3	182	8	5	–	–	1	8	2	–	–	–
23	Javed Miandad	P	6	189	2	6	–	2	7	5	–	1	–	–

216

Opponents

		200	I	E	A	SA	WI	NZ	I	P	SL	Z	B
22	W.R.Hammond	E	7	140	–	9	6	1	4	2	–	–	–	–
22	M.Azharuddin	I	–	147	6	2	4	–	2	–	–	3	5	–
22	M.C.Cowdrey	E	–	188	–	5	3	6	2	3	3	–	–	–
22	G.Boycott	E	1	193	–	7	1	5	2	4	3	–	–	–
21	R.N.Harvey	A	2	137	6	–	8	3	–	4	–	–	–	–
21	D.C.Boon	A	1	190	7	–	3	–	3	6	1	1	–	–
20	K.F.Barrington	E	1	131	–	5	2	3	3	3	4	–	–	–
20	M.E.Waugh	A	–	200	6	–	4	1	1	3	1	1	–	–
20	G.A.Gooch	E	2	215	–	4	–	5	4	5	1	1	–	–
19	L.Hutton	E	4	138	–	5	3	5	3	2	–	–	–	–
19	P.A.de Silva	SL	1	153	2	1	–	2	5	8	–	–	1	–
19	C.H.Lloyd	WI	1	175	5	6	–	–	–	7	1	–	–	–
19	C.G.Greenidge	WI	4	185	7	4	–	–	2	5	1	–	–	–
19	M.A.Taylor	A	2	186	6	–	2	1	2	2	4	2	–	–
18	B.C.Lara	WI	4	147	6	6	–	–	1	1	–	4	–	–
18	D.L.Haynes	WI	1	202	5	5	–	–	3	2	3	–	–	–
18	D.I.Gower	E	2	204	–	9	–	4	4	2	2	–	–	–

The most for South Africa is 14 by D.J.Cullinan (115 innings) and G.Kirsten (142), for New Zealand 17 by M.D.Crowe (131), and for Zimbabwe 12 by A.Flower (104). The most double hundreds by batsmen not included above is 4 by Zaheer Abbas (12 hundreds for Pakistan) and 3 by R.B.Simpson (10 for Australia).

HIGHEST PARTNERSHIP FOR EACH WICKET

1st	413	V.Mankad/Pankaj Roy	I v NZ	Madras	1955-56
2nd	576	S.T.Jayasuriya/R.S.Mahanama	SL v I	Colombo (RPS)	1997-98
3rd	467	A.H.Jones/M.D.Crowe	NZ v SL	Wellington	1990-91
4th	411	P.B.H.May/M.C.Cowdrey	E v WI	Birmingham	1957
5th	405	S.G.Barnes/D.G.Bradman	A v E	Sydney	1946-47
6th	346	J.H.W.Fingleton/D.G.Bradman	A v E	Melbourne	1936-37
7th	347	D.St E.Atkinson/C.C.Depeiza	WI v A	Bridgetown	1954-55
8th	313	Wasim Akram/Saqlain Mushtaq	P v Z	Sheikhupura	1996-97
9th	195	M.V.Boucher/P.L.Symcox	SA v P	Johannesburg	1997-98
10th	151	B.F.Hastings/R.O.Collinge	NZ v P	Auckland	1972-73
	151	Azhar Mahmood/Mushtaq Ahmed	P v SA	Rawalpindi	1997-98

BOWLING RECORDS
200 WICKETS IN TESTS

Wkts			M	Balls	Runs	Avge	5 wI	10 wM
519	C.A.Walsh	WI	132	30019	12688	24.45	22	3
434	Kapil Dev	I	131	27740	12867	29.64	23	2
431	R.J.Hadlee	NZ	86	21918	9612	22.29	36	9
430	S.K.Warne	A	98	27373	11493	26.72	20	5
414	Wasim Akram	P	104	22627	9779	23.62	25	5
405	C.E.L.Ambrose	WI	98	22104	8500	20.98	22	3
404	M.Muralitharan	SL	72	24158	9508	23.53	33	10
383	I.T.Botham	E	102	21815	10878	28.40	27	4
377	G.D.McGrath	A	81	19486	8297	22.00	22	3
376	M.D.Marshall	WI	81	17584	7876	20.94	22	4
362	Imran Khan	P	88	19458	8258	22.81	23	6
355	D.K.Lillee	A	70	18467	8493	23.92	23	7
344	Waqar Younis	P	76	14608	7780	22.61	22	5
329	A.A.Donald	SA	71	15427	7272	22.10	20	3
325	R.G.D.Willis	E	90	17357	8190	25.20	16	–

Wkts			M	Balls	Runs	Avge	5 wI	10 wM
309	L.R.Gibbs	WI	79	27115	8989	29.09	18	2
307	F.S.Trueman	E	67	15178	6625	21.57	17	3
300	A.Kumble	I	66	20664	8412	28.04	18	4
297	D.L.Underwood	E	86	21862	7674	25.83	17	6
291	C.J.McDermott	A	71	16586	8332	28.63	14	2
266	B.S.Bedi	I	67	21364	7637	28.71	14	1
261	S.M.Pollock	SA	63	14145	5409	20.72	14	1
259	J.Garner	WI	58	13169	5433	20.97	7	–
252	J.B.Statham	E	70	16056	6261	24.84	9	1
249	M.A.Holding	WI	60	12680	5898	23.68	13	2
248	R.Benaud	A	63	19108	6704	27.03	16	1
246	G.D.McKenzie	A	60	17681	7328	29.78	16	3
242	B.S.Chandrasekhar	I	58	15963	7199	29.74	16	2
236	A.V.Bedser	E	51	15918	5876	24.89	15	5
236	Abdul Qadir	P	67	17126	7742	32.80	15	5
235	G.St A.Sobers	WI	93	21599	7999	34.03	6	–
228	D.Gough	E	56	11503	6288	27.57	9	–
228	R.R.Lindwall	A	61	13650	5251	23.03	12	–
216	C.V.Grimmett	A	37	14513	5231	24.21	21	7
216	J.Srinath	I	57	13214	6377	29.52	10	1
212	M.G.Hughes	A	53	12285	6017	28.38	7	1
202	A.M.E.Roberts	WI	47	11136	5174	25.61	11	2
202	J.A.Snow	E	49	12021	5387	26.66	8	1
200	J.R.Thomson	A	51	10535	5601	28.00	8	–

The most for Zimbabwe is 174 in 49 Tests by H.H.Streak and for Bangladesh 17 in 9 Tests by Manjural Islam.

35 WICKETS IN A SERIES

Wkts			Series	M	Balls	Runs	Avge	5 wI	10 wM
49	S.F.Barnes	E v SA	1913-14	4	1356	536	10.93	7	3
46	J.C.Laker	E v A	1956	5	1703	442	9.60	4	2
44	C.V.Grimmett	A v SA	1935-36	5	2077	642	14.59	5	3
42	T.M.Alderman	A v E	1981	6	1950	893	21.26	4	–
41	R.M.Hogg	A v E	1978-79	6	1740	527	12.85	5	2
41	T.M.Alderman	A v E	1989	6	1616	712	17.36	6	1
40	Imran Khan	P v I	1982-83	6	1339	558	13.95	4	2
39	A.V.Bedser	E v A	1953	5	1591	682	17.48	5	1
39	D.K.Lillee	A v E	1981	6	1870	870	22.30	2	1
38	M.W.Tate	E v A	1924-25	5	2528	881	23.18	5	1
37	W.J.Whitty	A v SA	1910-11	5	1395	632	17.08	2	–
37	H.J.Tayfield	SA v E	1956-57	5	2280	636	17.18	4	1
36	A.E.E.Vogler	SA v E	1909-10	5	1349	783	21.75	4	1
36	A.A.Mailey	A v E	1920-21	5	1465	946	26.27	4	2
36	G.D.McGrath	A v E	1997	6	1499	701	19.47	2	–
35	G.A.Lohmann	E v SA	1895-96	3	520	203	5.80	4	2
35	B.S.Chandrasekhar	I v E	1972-73	5	1747	662	18.91	4	–
35	M.D.Marshall	WI v E	1988	5	1219	443	12.65	3	1

The most for New Zealand is 33 by R.J.Hadlee (v A, 1985-86), for Sri Lanka 30 by M.Muralitharan (v Z, 2001-02), and for Zimbabwe 22 by H.H.Streak (v P, 1994-95).

15 WICKETS IN A TEST († On debut)

19- 90	J.C.Laker	E v A	Manchester	1956
17-159	S.F.Barnes	E v SA	Johannesburg	1913-14
16-136†	N.D.Hirwani	I v WI	Madras	1987-88

16-137†	R.A.L.Massie	A v E	Lord's	1972
16-220	M.Muralitharan	SL v E	The Oval	1998
15- 28	J.Briggs	E v SA	Cape Town	1888-89
15- 45	G.A.Lohmann	E v SA	Port Elizabeth	1895-96
15- 99	C.Blythe	E v SA	Leeds	1907
15-104	H.Verity	E v A	Lord's	1934
15-123	R.J.Hadlee	NZ v A	Brisbane	1985-86
15-124	W.Rhodes	E v A	Melbourne	1903-04
15-217	Harbhajan Singh	I v A	Madras	2000-01

The best analysis for South Africa is 13-165 by H.J.Tayfield (v A, Melbourne, 1952-53), for West Indies 14-149 by M.A.Holding (v E, The Oval, 1976), for Pakistan 14-116 by Imran Khan (v SL, Lahore, 1981-82), and for Zimbabwe 11-257 by A.G.Huckle (v NZ, Bulawayo, 1997-98).

NINE WICKETS IN AN INNINGS

10- 53	J.C.Laker	E v A	Manchester	1956
10- 74	A.Kumble	I v P	Delhi	1998-99
9- 28	G.A.Lohmann	E v SA	Johannesburg	1895-96
9- 37	J.C.Laker	E v A	Manchester	1956
9- 51	M.Muralitharan	SL v Z	Kandy	2001-02
9- 52	R.J.Hadlee	NZ v A	Brisbane	1985-86
9- 56	Abdul Qadir	P v E	Lahore	1987-88
9- 57	D.E.Malcolm	E v SA	The Oval	1994
9- 65	M.Muralitharan	SL v E	The Oval	1998
9- 69	J.M.Patel	I v A	Kanpur	1959-60
9- 83	Kapil Dev	I v WI	Ahmedabad	1983-84
9- 86	Sarfraz Nawaz	P v A	Melbourne	1978-79
9- 95	J.M.Noreiga	WI v I	Port-of-Spain	1970-71
9-102	S.P.Gupte	I v WI	Kanpur	1958-59
9-103	S.F.Barnes	E v SA	Johannesburg	1913-14
9-113	H.J.Tayfield	SA v E	Johannesburg	1956-57
9-121	A.A.Mailey	A v E	Melbourne	1920-21

The best analysis for Zimbabwe is 8-109 by P.A.Strang (v NZ, Bulawayo, 2000-01), and for Bangladesh 6-81 by Manjural Islam (v Z, Bulawayo, 2000-01 – on debut).

HAT-TRICKS

F.R.Spofforth	Australia v England	Melbourne	1878-79
W.Bates	England v Australia	Melbourne	1882-83
J.Briggs	England v Australia	Sydney	1891-92
G.A.Lohmann	England v South Africa	Port Elizabeth	1895-96
J.T.Hearne	England v Australia	Leeds	1899
H.Trumble	Australia v England	Melbourne	1901-02
H.Trumble	Australia v England	Melbourne	1903-04
T.J.Matthews (2)[2]	Australia v South Africa	Manchester	1912
M.J.C.Allom[1]	England v New Zealand	Christchurch	1929-30
T.W.J.Goddard	England v South Africa	Johannesburg	1938-39
P.J.Loader	England v West Indies	Leeds	1957
L.F.Kline	Australia v South Africa	Cape Town	1957-58
W.W.Hall	West Indies v Pakistan	Lahore	1958-59
G.M.Griffin	South Africa v England	Lord's	1960
L.R.Gibbs	West Indies v Australia	Adelaide	1960-61
P.J.Petherick[1]	New Zealand v Pakistan	Lahore	1976-77
C.A.Walsh[3]	West Indies v Australia	Brisbane	1988-89
M.G.Hughes[3]	Australia v West Indies	Perth	1988-89
D.W.Fleming[1]	Australia v Pakistan	Rawalpindi	1994-95
S.K.Warne	Australia v England	Melbourne	1994-95

219

D.G.Cork	England v West Indies	Manchester	1995
D.Gough	England v Australia	Sydney	1998-99
Wasim Akram[4]	Pakistan v Sri Lanka	Lahore	1998-99
Wasim Akram[4]	Pakistan v Sri Lanka	Dhaka	1998-99
D.N.T.Zoysa[3]	Sri Lanka v Zimbabwe	Harare	1999-00
Abdul Razzaq	Pakistan v Sri Lanka	Galle	2000-01
G.D.McGrath	Australia v West Indies	Perth	2000-01
Harbhajan Singh	India v Australia	Calcutta	2000-01

[1] On debut. [2] Hat-trick in each innings. [3] Involving both innings. [4] In successive Tests.
[5] His first 3 balls (second over of the match).

WICKET-KEEPING RECORDS
100 DISMISSALS IN TESTS

Total			Tests	Ct	St
395	I.A.Healy	Australia	119	366	29
355	R.W.Marsh	Australia	96	343	12
272†	P.J.L.Dujon	West Indies	81	267	5
269	A.P.E.Knott	England	95	250	19
231†	A.J.Stewart	England	115	220	11
228	Wasim Bari	Pakistan	81	201	27
219	T.G.Evans	England	91	173	46
198	S.M.H.Kirmani	India	88	160	38
194†	A.C.Parore	New Zealand	75	187	7
189	D.L.Murray	West Indies	62	181	8
187	M.V.Boucher	South Africa	49	182	5
187	A.T.W.Grout	Australia	51	163	24
176	I.D.S.Smith	New Zealand	63	168	8
174	R.W.Taylor	England	57	167	7
165	R.C.Russell	England	54	153	12
156†	A.Flower	Zimbabwe	59	147	9
152	D.J.Richardson	South Africa	42	150	2
141	J.H.B.Waite	South Africa	50	124	17
134†	Moin Khan	Pakistan	63	114	20
130	K.S.More	India	49	110	20
130	W.A.S.Oldfield	Australia	54	78	52
128	R.D.Jacobs	West Indies	35	123	5
118	A.C.Gilchrist	Australia	28	109	9
114†	J.M.Parks	England	46	103	11
107	N.R.Mongia	India	44	99	8
104	Salim Yousuf	Pakistan	32	91	13
103†	H.P.Tillekeratne	Sri Lanka	66	101	2

† Including catches taken in the field

25 DISMISSALS IN A SERIES

28	R.W.Marsh	Australia v England	1982-83
27 (inc 2st)	R.C.Russell	England v South Africa	1995-96
27 (inc 2st)	I.A.Healy	Australia v England (6 Tests)	1997
26 (inc 3st)	J.H.B.Waite	South Africa v New Zealand	1961-62
26	R.W.Marsh	Australia v West Indies (6 Tests)	1975-76
26 (inc 5st)	I.A.Healy	Australia v England (6 Tests)	1993
26 (inc 1st)	M.V.Boucher	South Africa v England	1998
26 (inc 2st)	A.C.Gilchrist	Australia v England	2001
25 (inc 2st)	I.A.Healy	Australia v England	1994-95

TEN DISMISSALS IN A TEST

11	R.C.Russell	England v South Africa	Johannesburg	1995-96
10	R.W.Taylor	England v India	Bombay	1979-80
10	A.C.Gilchrist	Australia v New Zealand	Hamilton	1999-00

SEVEN DISMISSALS IN AN INNINGS

7	Wasim Bari	Pakistan v New Zealand	Auckland	1978-79
7	R.W.Taylor	England v India	Bombay	1979-80
7	I.D.S.Smith	New Zealand v Sri Lanka	Hamilton	1990-91
7	R.D.Jacobs	West Indies v Australia	Melbourne	2000-01

FIVE STUMPINGS IN AN INNINGS

5	K.S.More	India v West Indies	Madras	1987-88

FIELDING RECORDS
100 CATCHES IN TESTS

Total			Tests	Total			Tests
167	M.E.Waugh	Australia	122	109	G.St A.Sobers	West Indies	93
157	M.A.Taylor	Australia	104	108	S.M.Gavaskar	India	125
156	A.R.Border	Australia	156	107	B.C.Lara	West Indies	83
122	G.S.Chappell	Australia	87	105	I.M.Chappell	Australia	75
122	I.V.A.Richards	West Indies	121	105	M.Azharuddin	India	99
120	I.T.Botham	England	102	103	C.L.Hooper	West Indies	90
120	M.C.Cowdrey	England	114	103	G.A.Gooch	England	118
110	R.B.Simpson	Australia	62	101	S.R.Waugh	Australia	145
110	W.R.Hammond	England	85				

The most for South Africa is 68 by G.Kirsten (80 Tests), for New Zealand 95 by S.P.Fleming (65), for Pakistan 93 by Javed Miandad (124), for Sri Lanka 68 by H.P.Tillekeratne (54), and for Zimbabwe 54 by A.D.R.Campbell (56).

15 CATCHES IN A SERIES

15	J.M.Gregory	Australia v England	1920-21

SEVEN CATCHES IN A TEST

7	G.S.Chappell	Australia v England	Perth	1974-75
7	Yajurvindra Singh	India v England	Bangalore	1976-77
7	H.P.Tillekeratne	Sri Lanka v New Zealand	Colombo (SSC)	1992-93
7	S.P.Fleming	New Zealand v Zimbabwe	Harare	1997-98

FIVE CATCHES IN AN INNINGS

5	V.Y.Richardson	Australia v South Africa	Durban	1935-36
5	Yajurvindra Singh	India v England	Bangalore	1976-77
5	M.Azharuddin	India v Pakistan	Karachi	1989-90
5	K.Srikkanth	India v Australia	Perth	1991-92
5	S.P.Fleming	New Zealand v Zimbabwe	Harare	1997-98

APPEARANCE RECORDS
100 TEST MATCH APPEARANCES

156	A.R.Border	Australia		116	D.B.Vengsarkar	India
145	S.R.Waugh	Australia		115	M.A.Atherton	England
132	C.A.Walsh	West Indies		115	A.J.Stewart	England
131	Kapil Dev	India		114	M.C.Cowdrey	England
125	S.M.Gavaskar	India		110	C.H.Lloyd	West Indies
124	Javed Miandad	Pakistan		108	G.Boycott	England
122	M.E.Waugh	Australia		108	C.G.Greenidge	West Indies
121	I.V.A.Richards	West Indies		107	D.C.Boon	Australia
119	I.A.Healy	Australia		104	M.A.Taylor	Australia
118	G.A.Gooch	England		104	Wasim Akram	Pakistan
117	D.I.Gower	England		103	Salim Malik	Pakistan
116	D.L.Haynes	West Indies		102	I.T.Botham	England

The most for South Africa is 80 by G.Kirsten, for New Zealand 86 by R.J.Hadlee, for Sri Lanka 93 by A.Ranatunga, and for Zimbabwe 59 by A.Flower and G.W.Flower.

100 CONSECUTIVE TEST APPEARANCES

153	A.R.Border	Australia	March 1979 to March 1994
106	S.M.Gavaskar	India	January 1975 to February 1987
101	M.E.Waugh	Australia	June 1993 to January 2002

75 TESTS AS CAPTAIN

93	A.R.Border	Australia	December 1984 to March 1994

50 TEST UMPIRING APPEARANCES

66	H.D.Bird	(England)	July 1973 to June 1996
63	S.A.Bucknor	(West Indies)	April 1989 to December 2001
59	D.R.Shepherd	(England)	August 1985 to January 2002
50	S.Venkataraghavan	(India)	January 1992 to January 2002

INDIA v AUSTRALIA (1st Test)

At Wankhede Stadium, Bombay, on 27, 28 February, 1 March 2001.
Toss: Australia. Result: **AUSTRALIA** won by ten wickets.
Debuts: India – R.L.Sanghvi.

INDIA

S.S.Das	c Hayden b Gillespie	14		c S.R.Waugh b Gillespie	7
S.Ramesh	c Gilchrist b McGrath	2		c Ponting b McGrath	44
R.Dravid	c Gilchrist b Fleming	9		b Warne	39
S.R.Tendulkar	c Gilchrist b McGrath	76	(5)	c Ponting b M.E.Waugh	65
*S.C.Ganguly	c Hayden b Warne	8	(6)	run out	1
V.V.S.Laxman	c Ponting b McGrath	20	(7)	c Gilchrist b M.E.Waugh	12
†N.R.Mongia	not out	26	(4)	c Gilchrist b Gillespie	28
A.B.Agarkar	c and b Warne	0		b M.E.Waugh	0
J.Srinath	c M.E.Waugh b Warne	12	(11)	b McGrath	0
Harbhajan Singh	c S.R.Waugh b Warne	0	(9)	not out	17
R.L.Sanghvi	c Gilchrist b Gillespie	2	(10)	b Gillespie	0
Extras	(B 2, LB 3, W 1, NB 1)	7		(B 4, LB 1, NB 1)	6
Total		**176**			**219**

AUSTRALIA

M.J.Slater	b Agarkar	10	(2)	not out	19
M.L.Hayden	c Mongia b Srinath	119	(1)	not out	28
J.L.Langer	c Dravid b Harbhajan	19			
M.E.Waugh	c Ganguly b Harbhajan	0			
*S.R.Waugh	c Dravid b Sanghvi	15			
R.T.Ponting	c Das b Harbhajan	0			
†A.C.Gilchrist	st Mongia b Harbhajan	122			
S.K.Warne	c Tendulkar b Sanghvi	39			
J.N.Gillespie	c Mongia b Srinath	0			
D.W.Fleming	c Srinath b Agarkar	6			
G.D.McGrath	not out	0			
Extras	(B 9, LB 7, NB 3)	19			
Total		**349**		(0 wickets)	**47**

AUSTRALIA	O	M	R	W	O	M	R	W		FALL OF WICKETS			
McGrath	19	13	19	3	17.1	9	25	2			I	A	I	A
Fleming	15	3	55	1	15	1	44	0		Wkt	1st	1st	2nd	2nd
Gillespie	15.3	4	50	2	(4) 19	8	45	3		1st	7	21	33	–
Warne	22	7	47	4	(3) 28	11	60	1		2nd	25	71	57	–
M.E.Waugh					15	5	40	3		3rd	31	71	154	–
										4th	55	98	156	–
INDIA										5th	130	99	174	–
Srinath	16	3	60	2	2	0	17	0		6th	139	296	174	–
Agarkar	12	1	50	2	1	0	8	0		7th	140	326	193	–
Harbhajan Singh	28	3	121	4	2	0	11	0		8th	165	327	210	–
Sanghvi	10.2	2	67	2	2	1	11	0		9th	166	349	216	–
Tendulkar	7	1	35	0						10th	176	349	219	–

Umpires: D.R.Shepherd (*England*) (55) and S.Venkataraghavan (43).
Referee: C.W.Smith (*West Indies*) (31). **Test No. 1533/58 (I337/A612)**

INDIA v AUSTRALIA (2nd Test)

At Eden Gardens, Calcutta, on 11, 12, 13, 14, 15 March 2001.
Toss: Australia. Result: **INDIA** won by 171 runs.
Debuts: None.

AUSTRALIA

Batsman	1st innings	Runs	2nd innings	Runs
M.J.Slater	c Mongia b Khan	42	(2) c Ganguly b Harbhajan	43
M.L.Hayden	c sub (H.K.Badani) b Harbhajan	97	(1) lbw b Tendulkar	67
J.L.Langer	c Mongia b Khan	58	c Ramesh b Harbhajan	28
M.E.Waugh	c Mongia b Harbhajan	22	lbw b Raju	0
*S.R.Waugh	lbw b Harbhajan	110	c sub (H.K.Badani) b Harbhajan	24
R.T.Ponting	lbw b Harbhajan	6	c Das b Harbhajan	0
†A.C.Gilchrist	lbw b Harbhajan	0	lbw b Tendulkar	0
S.K.Warne	c Ramesh b Harbhajan	0	(9) lbw b Tendulkar	0
M.S.Kasprowicz	lbw b Ganguly	7	(10) not out	13
J.N.Gillespie	c Ramesh b Harbhajan	46	(8) c Das b Harbhajan	6
G.D.McGrath	not out	21	lbw b Harbhajan	12
Extras	(B 19, LB 10, NB 7)	36	(B 6, NB 8, P 5)	19
Total		**445**		**212**

INDIA

Batsman	1st innings	Runs	2nd innings	Runs
S.S.Das	c Gilchrist b McGrath	20	hit wicket b Gillespie	39
S.Ramesh	c Ponting b Gillespie	0	c M.E.Waugh b Warne	30
R.Dravid	b Warne	25	(6) run out	180
S.R.Tendulkar	lbw b McGrath	10	c Gilchrist b Gillespie	10
*S.C.Ganguly	c S.R.Waugh b Kasprowicz	23	(5) c Gilchrist b McGrath	48
V.V.S.Laxman	c Hayden b Warne	59	(3) c Gilchrist b McGrath	281
†N.R.Mongia	c Gilchrist b Kasprowicz	2	b McGrath	4
Harbhajan Singh	c Ponting b Gillespie	4	(9) not out	8
Z.Khan	b McGrath	3	(8) not out	23
S.L.V.Raju	lbw b McGrath	4		
B.K.V.Prasad	not out	7		
Extras	(LB 2, NB 12)	14	(B 4, LB 14, W 2, NB 14)	34
Total		**171**	(7 wickets declared)	**657**

INDIA	O	M	R	W	O	M	R	W
Khan	28.4	6	89	2	8	4	30	0
Prasad	30	5	95	0	3	1	7	0
Ganguly	13.2	3	44	1	(6) 1	0	2	0
Raju	20	2	58	0	(4) 15	3	58	1
Harbhajan Singh	37.5	7	123	7	(3) 30.3	8	73	6
Tendulkar	2	0	7	0	(5) 11	3	31	3

AUSTRALIA	O	M	R	W	O	M	R	W
McGrath	14	8	18	4	39	12	103	3
Gillespie	11	0	47	2	31	6	115	2
Kasprowicz	13	2	39	2	(5) 35	6	139	0
Warne	20.1	3	65	2	(3) 34	2	152	1
M.E.Waugh					(4) 18	1	58	0
Ponting					12	1	41	0
Hayden					6	0	24	0
Slater					2	1	4	0
Langer					3	0	3	0

FALL OF WICKETS

	A	I	A	I
Wkt	1st	1st	2nd	2nd
1st	103	0	52	74
2nd	193	34	97	106
3rd	214	48	115	116
4th	236	88	232	166
5th	252	88	608	166
6th	252	92	624	167
7th	252	97	629	173
8th	269	113	–	174
9th	402	129	–	191
10th	445	171	–	212

Umpires: S.K.Bansal (6) and P.Willey (*England*) (22).
Referee: C.W.Smith (*West Indies*) (32).

Test No. 1534/59 (I338/A613)

INDIA v AUSTRALIA (3rd Test)

At M.A.Chidambaram Stadium, Chepauk, Madras, on 18, 19, 20, 21, 22 March 2001.
Toss: Australia. Result: **INDIA** won by two wickets.
Debuts: India – S.V.Bahutule, S.S.Dighe.

AUSTRALIA

M.J.Slater	c Laxman b Khan	4	(2) c Laxman b Harbhajan	48
M.L.Hayden	c Ganguly b Harbhajan	203	(1) c Khan b Kulkarni	35
J.L.Langer	c Dravid b Harbhajan	35	(4) c Laxman b Bahutule	21
M.E.Waugh	c sub (H.K.Badani) b Bahutule	70	(5) c Dravid b Harbhajan	57
*S.R.Waugh	handled the ball	47	(6) c Das b Harbhajan	47
R.T.Ponting	st Dighe b Harbhajan	0	(7) c Dravid b Harbhajan	11
†A.C.Gilchrist	lbw b Harbhajan	1	(3) lbw b Harbhajan	1
S.K.Warne	c Das b Harbhajan	0	lbw b Harbhajan	11
J.N.Gillespie	c Ganguly b Harbhajan	0	c Dravid b Harbhajan	2
C.R.Miller	c Bahutule b Harbhajan	0	lbw b Harbhajan	2
G.D.McGrath	not out	3	not out	11
Extras	(B 8, LB 10, NB 10)	28	(B 8, LB 6, NB 4)	18
Total		**391**		**264**

INDIA

S.S.Das	lbw b McGrath	84	c and b McGrath	9
S.Ramesh	c Ponting b Warne	61	run out	25
V.V.S.Laxman	c M.E.Waugh b McGrath	65	c M.E.Waugh b Miller	66
S.R.Tendulkar	c Gilchrist b Gillespie	126	c M.E.Waugh b Gillespie	17
*S.C.Ganguly	c Gilchrist b McGrath	22	c M.E.Waugh b Gillespie	4
R.Dravid	c Gilchrist b Gillespie	81	c S.R.Waugh b Miller	4
†S.S.Dighe	lbw b Warne	4	not out	22
S.V.Bahutule	not out	21	c Warne b Miller	0
Z.Khan	c and b Miller	4	c M.E.Waugh b McGrath	0
Harbhajan Singh	c M.E.Waugh b Miller	2	not out	3
N.M.Kulkarni	lbw b Miller	4		
Extras	(B 19, LB 2, W 1, NB 5)	27	(LB 3, NB 2)	5
Total		**501**	(8 wickets)	**155**

INDIA	O	M	R	W	O	M	R	W		FALL OF WICKETS			
Khan	15	5	57	1	4	0	13	0			A	I	A	I
Ganguly	2	1	11	0	1	0	8	0		*Wkt*	*1st*	*1st*	*2nd*	*2nd*
Harbhajan Singh	38.2	6	133	7	41.5	20	84	8		1st	4	123	82	18
Kulkarni	23	5	67	0	30	11	70	1		2nd	67	211	84	76
Bahutule	21	3	70	1	(6) 9	0	32	1		3rd	217	237	93	101
Tendulkar	16	1	35	0	(5) 12	0	43	0		4th	340	284	141	117
										5th	340	453	193	122
AUSTRALIA										6th	344	468	211	135
McGrath	36	15	75	3	11.1	3	21	2		7th	374	470	241	135
Gillespie	35	11	88	2	15	2	49	2		8th	376	475	246	151
Miller	46	6	160	3	9	1	41	3		9th	385	477	251	
Warne	42	7	140	2	6	0	41	0		10th	391	501	264	
Ponting	2	1	2	0										
M.E.Waugh	3	0	8	0										
Hayden	1	0	7	0										

Umpires: A.V.Jayaprakash (9) and R.E.Koertzen (*South Africa*) (24).
Referee: C.W.Smith (*West Indies*) (33).   Test No. 1535/60 (I339/A614)

INDIA v AUSTRALIA 2000-01

INDIA – BATTING AND FIELDING

	M	I	NO	HS	Runs	Avge	100	50	Ct/St
V.V.S.Laxman	3	6	–	281	503	83.83	1	3	3
R.Dravid	3	6	–	180	338	56.33	1	1	6
S.R.Tendulkar	3	6	–	126	304	50.66	1	2	1
S.S.Das	3	6	–	84	173	28.83	–	1	5
S.Ramesh	3	6	–	61	162	27.00	–	1	3
N.R.Mongia	2	4	1	28	60	20.00	–	–	5/1
S.C.Ganguly	3	6	–	48	106	17.66	–	–	4
Harbhajan Singh	3	6	3	17*	34	11.33	–	–	–
Z.Khan	2	4	1	23*	30	10.00	–	–	1

Played in one Test: A.B.Agarkar 0, 0; S.V.Bahutule 21*, 0 (1 ct); S.S.Dighe 4, 22* (1 st);
N.M.Kulkarni 4; B.K.V.Prasad 7*; S.L.V.Raju 4; R.L.Sanghvi 2, 0; J.Srinath 12, 0 (1 ct).

INDIA – BOWLING

	O	M	R	W	Avge	Best	5wI	10wM
Harbhajan Singh	178.3	44	545	32	17.03	8-84	4	2
A.B.Agarkar	13	1	58	2	29.00	2-50	–	–
J.Srinath	18	3	77	2	38.50	2-60	–	–
R.L.Sanghvi	12.2	3	78	2	39.00	2-67	–	–
S.R.Tendulkar	48	5	151	3	50.33	3-31	–	–
S.V.Bahutule	30	3	102	2	51.00	1-32	–	–
Z.Khan	55.4	15	189	3	63.00	2-89	–	–

Also bowled: S.C.Ganguly 17.2-4-65-1; N.M.Kulkarni 53-16-137-1; B.K.V.Prasad
33-6-102-0; S.L.V.Raju 35-5-116-1.

AUSTRALIA – BATTING AND FIELDING

	M	I	NO	HS	Runs	Avge	100	50	Ct/St
M.L.Hayden	3	6	1	203	549	109.80	2	2	3
S.R.Waugh	3	5	–	110	243	48.60	1	–	4
G.D.McGrath	3	5	4	21*	47	47.00	–	–	1
M.J.Slater	3	6	1	48	166	33.20	–	–	–
J.L.Langer	3	5	–	58	161	32.20	–	1	–
M.E.Waugh	3	5	–	70	149	29.80	–	2	8
A.C.Gilchrist	3	5	–	122	124	24.80	1	–	13
J.N.Gillespie	3	5	–	46	54	10.80	–	–	–
S.K.Warne	3	5	–	39	50	10.00	–	–	2
R.T.Ponting	3	5	–	11	17	3.40	–	–	7

Played in one Test: D.W.Fleming 6; M.S.Kasprowicz 7, 13*; C.R.Miller 0, 2 (1 ct).

AUSTRALIA – BOWLING

	O	M	R	W	Avge	Best	5wI	10wM
G.D.McGrath	136.2	60	261	17	15.35	4-18	–	–
J.N.Gillespie	126.3	31	394	13	30.30	3-45	–	–
C.R.Miller	55	7	201	6	33.50	3-41	–	–
M.E.Waugh	36	6	106	3	35.33	3-40	–	–
S.K.Warne	152.1	31	505	10	50.50	4-47	–	–
M.S.Kasprowicz	48	8	178	2	89.00	2-39	–	–

Also bowled: D.W.Fleming 30-4-99-1; M.L.Hayden 7-0-31-0; J.L.Langer 1-0-3-0;
R.T.Ponting 14-2-43-0; M.J.Slater 2-1-4-0.

NEW ZEALAND v PAKISTAN (1st Test)

At Eden Park, Auckland, on 8, 9, 10, 11, 12 March 2001.
Toss: New Zealand. Result: **PAKISTAN** won by 299 runs.
Debuts: New Zealand – J.E.C.Franklin; Pakistan – Faisal Iqbal, Imran Farhat,
Misbah-ul-Haq, Mohammad Sami.

PAKISTAN

Imran Farhat	c Parore b Martin	23		c and b Wiseman	63
Salim Elahi	c Parore b Tuffey	24		c Wiseman b Tuffey	7
Misbah-ul-Haq	c Sinclair b McMillan	28		c Parore b Tuffey	10
Yousuf Youhana	c Parore b Martin	51		c Astle b Franklin	42
Younis Khan	c McMillan b Tuffey	91	(6)	not out	149
Faisal Iqbal	c Fleming b Tuffey	42	(7)	not out	52
*†Moin Khan	c Parore b Tuffey	47			
Saqlain Mushtaq	c Fleming b Martin	2	(5)	c Parore b Tuffey	2
Waqar Younis	lbw b Martin	4			
Mushtaq Ahmed	c Parore b Franklin	19			
Mohammad Sami	not out	0			
Extras	(B 2, LB 7, NB 6)	15		(B 4, LB 6, NB 1)	11
Total		**346**		**(5 wickets declared)**	**336**

NEW ZEALAND

M.H.Richardson	b Sami	1		c Imran b Saqlain	59
M.D.Bell	c Moin b Waqar	0		run out	28
M.S.Sinclair	c Imran b Sami	34	(4)	c Youhana b Sami	10
*S.P.Fleming	b Saqlain	86	(5)	lbw b Saqlain	5
N.J.Astle	b Mushtaq Ahmed	0	(6)	b Saqlain	1
C.D.McMillan	c Younis Khan b Waqar	54	(7)	c Saqlain b Sami	0
†A.C.Parore	not out	32	(8)	not out	0
J.E.C.Franklin	lbw b Saqlain	0	(9)	b Sami	0
P.J.Wiseman	lbw b Saqlain	9	(3)	b Sami	8
D.R.Tuffey	b Saqlain	2		b Sami	0
C.S.Martin	b Sami	0		b Saqlain	0
Extras	(B 8, LB 20, NB 6)	34		(B 12, LB 7, NB 1)	20
Total		**252**			**131**

NEW ZEALAND	O	M	R	W	O	M	R	W
Tuffey	34	13	96	4	17	3	43	3
Martin	22	1	106	4	12	2	65	0
Franklin	21	6	55	1	18	2	59	1
Wiseman	7	0	35	0	36	6	107	1
McMillan	14	5	34	1	7	0	27	0
Astle	8	3	11	0	13	6	25	0

PAKISTAN	O	M	R	W	O	M	R	W
Waqar Younis	22	8	44	2	11	2	31	0
Mohammad Sami	31.4	11	70	3	15	4	36	5
Saqlain Mushtaq	20	3	48	4	25.4	12	24	4
Mushtaq Ahmed	23	8	62	1	8	2	21	0

FALL OF WICKETS

	P	NZ	P	NZ
Wkt	1st	1st	2nd	2nd
1st	46	1	21	91
2nd	52	1	59	105
3rd	130	82	97	121
4th	138	83	110	126
5th	270	194	189	127
6th	271	217	–	130
7th	286	217	–	130
8th	294	237	–	130
9th	346	251	–	130
10th	346	252	–	131

Umpires: D.B.Cowie (20) and R.B.Tiffin (*Zimbabwe*) (18).
Referee: R.S.Madugalle (*Sri Lanka*) (33).   Test No. 1536/40 (NZ286/P274)

NEW ZEALAND v PAKISTAN (2nd Test)

At Lancaster Park, Christchurch, on 15, 16, 17, 18, 19 March 2001.
Toss: Pakistan. Result: **MATCH DRAWN**.
Debuts: New Zealand – C.J.Drum.

NEW ZEALAND

M.H.Richardson	b Saqlain	46	not out		73
M.D.Bell	c Faisal b Saqlain	75	lbw b Younis Khan		40
M.S.Sinclair	not out	204	not out		50
*S.P.Fleming	run out	32			
N.J.Astle	c Moin b Waqar	6			
G.E.Bradburn	c Imran b Fazal	0			
C.D.McMillan	c Younis Khan b Fazal	20			
†A.C.Parore	lbw b Saqlain	46			
D.R.Tuffey	lbw b Fazal	13			
C.J.Drum	c Moin b Waqar	4			
C.S.Martin	b Waqar				
Extras	(B 2, LB 17, W 1, NB 10)	30	(B 15, LB 4, NB 14)		33
Total		**476**	(1 wicket declared)		**196**

PAKISTAN

Imran Farhat	c Drum b Martin	4
Ijaz Ahmed	hit wicket b Drum	11
Faisal Iqbal	c Fleming b McMillan	63
Inzamam-ul-Haq	c Fleming b Martin	130
Yousuf Youhana	c and b Richardson	203
Younis Khan	c Parore b Tuffey	0
*†Moin Khan	c Martin b Bradburn	28
Saqlain Mushtaq	not out	101
Waqar Younis	c Parore b Tuffey	12
Fazal-e-Akber	not out	0
Mohammad Sami		
Extras	(B 5, LB 8, NB 6)	19
Total	(8 wickets declared)	**571**

PAKISTAN	O	M	R	W		O	M	R	W
Waqar Younis	34	6	114	3		8	1	18	0
Mohammad Sami	36	4	107	0		11	3	32	0
Fazal-e-Akber	32	6	87	3		7	0	26	0
Saqlain Mushtaq	48	11	134	3		24	5	44	0
Younis Khan	6	1	15	0		21	6	47	1
Yousuf Youhana						1	0	3	0
Faisal Iqbal						1	0	7	0

NEW ZEALAND	O	M	R	W
Tuffey	49	13	152	2
Martin	41	9	153	2
Drum	8	1	21	1
Bradburn	42	10	124	1
McMillan	31	13	47	1
Astle	30	12	45	0
Richardson	9	0	16	0

FALL OF WICKETS

	NZ	P	NZ
Wkt	1st	1st	2nd
1st	102	5	69
2nd	163	25	–
3rd	248	157	–
4th	276	259	–
5th	282	260	–
6th	327	304	–
7th	428	552	–
8th	449	569	–
9th	468	–	–
10th	476	–	–

Umpires: D.J.Harper (*Australia*) (11) and D.M.Quested (5).
Referee: R.S.Madugalle (*Sri Lanka*) (34).   **Test No. 1537/41 (NZ287/P275)**

NEW ZEALAND v PAKISTAN (3rd Test)

At Seddon Park, Hamilton, on 27, 28 (*no play*), 29, 30 March 2001.
Toss: New Zealand. Result: **NEW ZEALAND** won by an innings and 185 runs.
Debuts: Pakistan – Humayun Farhat.

PAKISTAN

Imran Farhat	c Astle b Martin	24	c McMillan b Tuffey		1
Ijaz Ahmed	c Parore b Martin	5	c Parore b Franklin		17
Faisal Iqbal	c Bell b Martin	0	c Bradburn b Tuffey		5
*Inzamam-ul-Haq	lbw b Martin	5	c Tuffey b Franklin		20
Yousuf Youhana	c Parore b Tuffey	0	c Parore b Martin		16
Younis Khan	c Richardson b Tuffey	36	c Astle b Tuffey		4
†Humayun Farhat	c Parore b Tuffey	28	c Bradburn b Martin		26
Saqlain Mushtaq	run out	0	c Martin b Franklin		14
Waqar Younis	c Fleming b Franklin	0	c Parore b McMillan		4
Fazal-e-Akber	c Parore b Tuffey	0	not out		0
Mohammad Akram	not out	1	c and b Franklin		4
Extras	(LB 3, NB 2)	5	(LB 2, NB 5)		7
Total		**104**			**118**

NEW ZEALAND

M.H.Richardson	c Imran b Fazal	106
M.D.Bell	lbw b Waqar	105
M.S.Sinclair	c Waqar b Fazal	27
C.D.McMillan	c Waqar b Fazal	98
*S.P.Fleming	not out	51
N.J.Astle		
†A.C.Parore		
G.E.Bradburn		
J.E.C.Franklin		
D.R.Tuffey		
C.S.Martin		
Extras	(LB 10, NB 10)	20
Total	(4 wickets declared)	**407**

NEW ZEALAND	O	M	R	W	O	M	R	W		FALL OF WICKETS		
Tuffey	10.5	2	39	4	19	5	38	3			P	NZ	P
Martin	10	3	52	4	15	2	48	2		*Wkt*	*1st*	*1st*	*2nd*
Franklin	6	2	10	1	9.5	3	26	4		1st	28	181	10
McMillan					5	3	2	1		2nd	28	239	20
Astle					1	0	2	0		3rd	29	260	43
										4th	34	407	54
PAKISTAN										5th	38	–	69
Waqar Younis	31	2	98	1						6th	89	–	71
Fazal-e-Akber	27.2	6	85	3						7th	89	–	97
Mohammad Akram	22	1	106	0						8th	91	–	114
Saqlain Mushtaq	31	6	82	0						9th	103	–	114
Younis Khan	1	0	26	0						10th	104	–	118

Umpires: R.A.Dunne (38) and D.J.Harper (*Australia*) (12).
Referee: R.S.Madugalle (*Sri Lanka*) (35).   **Test No. 1538/42 (NZ288/P276)**

229

NEW ZEALAND v PAKISTAN 2000-01

NEW ZEALAND – BATTING AND FIELDING

	M	I	NO	HS	Runs	Avge	100	50	Ct/St
M.S.Sinclair	3	5	2	204*	325	108.33	1	1	1
A.C.Parore	3	3	2	46	78	78.00	–	–	16
M.H.Richardson	3	5	1	106	285	71.25	1	2	2
S.P.Fleming	3	4	–	86	174	58.00	–	2	5
M.D.Bell	3	5	–	105	248	49.60	1	1	1
C.D.McMillan	3	4	–	98	172	43.00	–	2	2
D.R.Tuffey	3	3	–	13	15	5.00	–	–	1
N.J.Astle	3	3	–	6	7	2.33	–	–	3
C.S.Martin	3	3	–	0	0	0.00	–	–	2
J.E.C.Franklin	2	2	–	0	0	0.00	–	–	1
G.E.Bradburn	2	1	–	0	0	0.00	–	–	2

Played in one Test: C.J.Drum 4 (1 ct); P.J.Wiseman 9, 8 (2 ct).

NEW ZEALAND – BOWLING

	O	M	R	W	Avge	Best	5wI	10wM
J.E.C.Franklin	54.5	13	150	7	21.42	4-26	–	–
D.R.Tuffey	129.5	36	368	16	23.00	4-39	–	–
C.S.Martin	100	17	424	12	35.33	4-52	–	–
C.D.McMillan	57	21	110	3	36.66	1- 2	–	–

Also bowled: N.J.Astle 52-21-83-0; G.E.Bradburn 42-10-124-1; C.J.Drum 8-1-21-1; M.H.Richardson 9-0-16-1; P.J.Wiseman 43-6-142-1.

PAKISTAN – BATTING AND FIELDING

	M	I	NO	HS	Runs	Avge	100	50	Ct/St
Younis Khan	3	5	1	149*	280	70.00	1	1	2
Yousuf Youhana	3	5	–	203	312	62.40	1	1	1
Inzamam-ul-Haq	2	3	–	130	155	51.66	1	–	–
Faisal Iqbal	3	5	1	63	162	40.50	–	2	1
Moin Khan	2	2	–	47	75	37.50	–	–	3
Saqlain Mushtaq	3	5	1	101*	119	29.75	1	–	1
Imran Farhat	3	5	–	63	115	23.00	–	1	4
Ijaz Ahmed	2	3	–	17	33	11.00	–	–	–
Waqar Younis	3	4	–	12	20	5.00	–	–	2
Fazal-e-Akber	2	3	2	0*	0	0.00	–	–	–
Mohammad Sami	2	1	1	0*	0	–			

Played in one Test: Humayun Farhat 28, 26; Misbah-ul-Haq 28, 10; Mohammad Akram 1*, 4; Mushtaq Ahmed 19; Salim Elahi 24, 7.

PAKISTAN – BOWLING

	O	M	R	W	Avge	Best	5wI	10wM
Saqlain Mushtaq	148.4	37	332	11	30.18	4- 24	–	–
Mohammad Sami	93.4	22	245	8	30.62	5- 36	1	–
Fazal-e-Akber	66.2	12	198	6	33.00	3- 85	–	–
Waqar Younis	106	19	305	6	50.83	3-114	–	–

Also bowled: Faisal Iqbal 1-0-7-0; Mohammad Akram 22-1-106-0; Mushtaq Ahmed 31-10-83-1; Younis Khan 28-7-88-1; Yousuf Youhana 1-0-3-0.

WEST INDIES v SOUTH AFRICA (1st Test)

At Bourda, Georgetown, Guyana, on 9, 10, 11, 12, 13 March 2001.
Toss: West Indies. Result: **MATCH DRAWN**.
Debuts: None.

WEST INDIES

W.W.Hinds	c Boje b Pollock	13	c Boucher b Donald		14
C.H.Gayle	c Boucher b Kallis	81	c Boucher b Boje		44
M.N.Samuels	b Boje	40	b Kallis		51
B.C.Lara	c Donald b Klusener	47	c Pollock b Ntini		45
R.R.Sarwan	b Donald	7	run out		91
*C.L.Hooper	c Klusener b Boje	69	c Cullinan b Boje		35
†R.D.Jacobs	lbw b Donald	0	not out		18
N.A.M.McLean	b Klusener	6	lbw b Boje		0
D.Ramnarine	run out	5			
M.Dillon	c Cullinan b Ntini	9			
C.A.Walsh	not out	2			
Extras	(B 2, LB 12, W 2, NB 9)	25	(B 10, LB 10, W 2, NB 8, P 5)		35
Total		**304**	(7 wickets declared)		**333**

SOUTH AFRICA

G.Kirsten	c Jacobs b Walsh	150	c Hinds b Ramnarine		24
H.H.Gibbs	b Dillon	8	not out		83
J.H.Kallis	lbw b McLean	50	lbw b McLean		30
D.J.Cullinan	c Jacobs b Ramnarine	7	not out		4
N.D.McKenzie	b Ramnarine	4			
†M.V.Boucher	lbw b Walsh	52			
L.Klusener	lbw b McLean	5			
N.Boje	c Hinds b Dillon	15			
*S.M.Pollock	not out	17			
A.A.Donald	c Lara b Ramnarine	2			
M.Ntini	c Jacobs b Dillon	11			
Extras	(B 4, LB 5, NB 2)	11	(B 1)		1
Total		**332**	(2 wickets)		**142**

SOUTH AFRICA	O	M	R	W		O	M	R	W
Donald	23	9	43	2		20	8	51	1
Pollock	18	2	54	1		17	4	51	0
Ntini	12	2	48	1	(5)	20	5	50	1
Kallis	17	2	33	1	(3)	15	2	36	1
Klusener	35	14	56	2	(6)	8	1	27	0
Boje	19.1	6	56	2	(4)	37	13	93	2
WEST INDIES									
Walsh	28	7	56	2		10	3	19	0
Dillon	27	5	64	3		5	1	21	0
McLean	22	0	75	2	(4)	10	3	25	1
Ramnarine	41	9	105	3	(3)	27.3	14	46	1
Hooper	8	0	21	0		14	8	23	0
Samuels	1	0	2	0	(7)	2	0	3	0
Sarwan					(6)	1	0	4	0

FALL OF WICKETS				
	WI	SA	WI	SA
Wkt	1st	1st	2nd	2nd
1st	43	25	51	66
2nd	131	171	78	134
3rd	165	186	147	–
4th	206	198	210	–
5th	221	274	299	–
6th	221	285	333	–
7th	228	287	333	–
8th	238	310	–	–
9th	300	315	–	–
10th	304	332	–	–

Umpires: J.H.Hampshire (*England*) (16) and E.A.Nicholls (14).
Referee: M.H.Denness (*England*) (6).   **Test No. 1539/7 (WI370/SA252)**

WEST INDIES v SOUTH AFRICA (2nd Test)

At Queen's Park Oval, Port-of-Spain, Trinidad, on 17, 18, 19, 20, 21 March 2001.
Toss: South Africa. Result: **SOUTH AFRICA** won by 69 runs.
Debuts: None.

SOUTH AFRICA

H.H.Gibbs	b Walsh	34	c sub (S.Chanderpaul) b Walsh		87
G.Kirsten	c Hooper b McLean	23	c Jacobs b Walsh		22
J.H.Kallis	c and b Hinds	53	lbw b Walsh		0
D.J.Cullinan	c Dillon b Ramnarine	103	c Lara b Ramnarine		73
N.D.McKenzie	c Gayle b Walsh	9	c Jacobs b Dillon		25
†M.V.Boucher	c Hooper b Hinds	16	(7) b Dillon		38
L.Klusener	c Jacobs b Ramnarine	15	(6) c Gayle b Dillon		5
N.Boje	c Jacobs b Ramnarine	3	c Jacobs b Walsh		9
*S.M.Pollock	not out	15	b Walsh		8
A.A.Donald	c Jacobs b McLean	0	lbw b Walsh		1
M.Ntini	c and b McLean	7	not out		5
Extras	(NB 8)	8	(B 1, LB 4, NB 9)		14
Total		**286**			**287**

WEST INDIES

W.W.Hinds	c Boucher b Donald	56	lbw b Kallis		2
C.H.Gayle	lbw b Pollock	10	c Boucher b Pollock		23
M.N.Samuels	c Klusener b Donald	35	(4) c Kallis b Donald		9
B.C.Lara	c Kallis b Ntini	12	(5) lbw b Ntini		0
R.R.Sarwan	c Cullinan b Donald	34	(6) c Boje b Kallis		39
*C.L.Hooper	lbw b Donald	53	(7) not out		54
†R.D.Jacobs	not out	93	(8) run out		4
N.A.M.McLean	c Ntini b Pollock	3	(9) c Gibbs b Kallis		0
D.Ramnarine	b Pollock	2	(3) c Kallis b Donald		11
M.Dillon	b Ntini	21	lbw b Kallis		0
C.A.Walsh	run out	0	b Pollock		0
Extras	(B 9, LB 4, W 3, NB 7)	23	(B 7, LB 4, NB 7)		18
Total		**342**			**162**

WEST INDIES	O	M	R	W		O	M	R	W
Walsh	21	5	47	2		36.4	13	61	6
Dillon	17	2	74	0	(3)	28	8	58	3
McLean	16.5	2	60	3	(2)	18	1	76	0
Ramnarine	18	6	57	3		35	8	64	1
Hooper	9	1	25	0		13	4	23	0
Hinds	5	0	23	2					

SOUTH AFRICA	O	M	R	W		O	M	R	W
Donald	30	6	91	4		15	4	32	2
Pollock	28	11	55	3		23.1	8	35	2
Ntini	16	4	56	2	(4)	16	4	22	1
Kallis	21	10	44	0	(3)	16	6	40	4
Boje	19	2	65	0					
Klusener	11	5	18	0	(5)	10	5	22	0

FALL OF WICKETS

	SA	WI	SA	WI
Wkt	1st	1st	2nd	2nd
1st	62	24	38	20
2nd	62	94	38	35
3rd	161	118	187	50
4th	189	123	198	50
5th	221	198	204	51
6th	256	235	253	143
7th	264	242	264	150
8th	265	250	276	159
9th	266	321	278	159
10th	286	342	287	162

Umpires: B.R.Doctrove (2) and D.B.Hair (*Australia*) (36).
Referee: M.H.Denness (*England*) (7).　　　　**Test No. 1540/8 (WI371/SA253)**

WEST INDIES v SOUTH AFRICA (3rd Test)

At Kensington Oval, Bridgetown, Barbados, on 29, 30, 31 March, 1, 2 April 2001.
Toss: West Indies. Result: **MATCH DRAWN**.
Debuts: None.

SOUTH AFRICA

G.Kirsten	c Gayle b Walsh	0	(2)	c Samuels b Cuffy	0
H.H.Gibbs	c Hooper b Dillon	34	(1)	c Sarwan b Hooper	19
J.H.Kallis	c Jacobs b Dillon	11	(5)	c Sarwan b Hooper	20
D.J.Cullinan	c and b Dillon	134		c Lara b Ramnarine	82
N.D.McKenzie	c Dillon b Hinds	72	(3)	c Jacobs b Ramnarine	12
†M.V.Boucher	c Jacobs b Cuffy	3	(7)	c Jacobs b Ramnarine	0
N.Boje	c Ramnarine b Dillon	34	(9)	not out	9
L.Klusener	b Walsh	1	(6)	c Cuffy b Ramnarine	4
*S.M.Pollock	not out	106	(8)	c Hooper b Walsh	40
A.A.Donald	c Hooper b Walsh	37		lbw b Ramnarine	0
M.Ntini	c and b Ramnarine	0			
Extras	(B 6, LB 4, W 2, NB 10)	22		(LB 3, NB 8)	11
Total		**454**		(9 wickets declared)	**197**

WEST INDIES

W.W.Hinds	c Boucher b Kallis	2	(2)	c Cullinan b Boje	8
C.H.Gayle	c Cullinan b Ntini	40	(1)	c Boucher b Kallis	48
M.N.Samuels	c McKenzie b Kallis	6		c Cullinan b Boje	3
B.C.Lara	c Boje b Kallis	83		b Klusener	8
R.R.Sarwan	c Gibbs b Ntini	16		b Kallis	0
*C.L.Hooper	c Boucher b Kallis	74		c Boucher b Boje	5
†R.D.Jacobs	not out	113		c McKenzie b Boje	1
M.Dillon	b Boje	14		not out	2
D.Ramnarine	lbw b Boje	6		not out	0
C.E.Cuffy	lbw b Kallis	4			
C.A.Walsh	b Kallis	4			
Extras	(B 4, LB 9, NB 12)	25		(B 8, LB 1, NB 4)	13
Total		**387**		(7 wickets)	**88**

WEST INDIES	O	M	R	W	O	M	R	W
Walsh	45	15	87	3	14	3	28	1
Dillon	34	1	147	4	(4) 4	2	7	0
Cuffy	30	7	71	1	(2) 10	4	28	1
Ramnarine	33.1	6	86	1	(5) 31.5	10	78	5
Hooper	18	5	31	0	(3) 34	12	49	2
Hinds	10	5	13	1				
Samuels	2	0	6	0	(6) 2	1	4	0
Gayle	1	0	3	0				

SOUTH AFRICA	O	M	R	W	O	M	R	W
Donald	14	7	30	0				
Pollock	35	11	84	0	(1) 5	0	25	0
Kallis	36	17	67	6	(2) 8	1	34	2
Ntini	28	7	93	2				
Boje	28	7	67	2	(3) 16.4	10	17	4
Klusener	10	3	33	0	(4) 9	3	9	0

FALL OF WICKETS

	SA	WI	SA	WI
Wkt	1st	1st	2nd	2nd
1st	0	37	0	2
2nd	53	49	31	59
3rd	58	57	36	64
4th	207	102	80	64
5th	230	218	95	72
6th	306	252	97	82
7th	307	316	167	82
8th	315	353	197	–
9th	447	381	197	–
10th	454	387	–	–

Umpires: S.A.Bucknor (55) and D.B.Hair (*Australia*) (37).
Referee: M.H.Denness (*England*) (8).

Test No. 1541/9 (WI372/SA254)

WEST INDIES v SOUTH AFRICA (4th Test)

At Recreation Ground, St John's, Antigua, on 6, 7, 8, 9, 10 April 2001.
Toss: West Indies. Result: **SOUTH AFRICA** won by 82 runs.
Debuts: West Indies – N.C.McGarrell.

SOUTH AFRICA

G.Kirsten	c Dillon b McGarrell	8	(2) c Sarwan b Walsh		9
H.H.Gibbs	c Jacobs b Hooper	85	(1) c Gayle b Ramnarine		45
J.H.Kallis	b Dillon	5	(6) not out		30
D.J.Cullinan	c Lara b Ramnarine	4	(5) c Gayle b McGarrell		28
N.D.McKenzie	c Jacobs b McGarrell	35	(3) b Walsh		44
L.Klusener	lbw b McGarrell	0	(7) c Hinds b Walsh		1
†M.V.Boucher	c Gayle b McGarrell	1	(8) c Jacobs b Walsh		3
*S.M.Pollock	not out	48	(9) not out		41
N.Boje	lbw b Walsh	36	(4) c sub (S.C.Joseph) b Hooper		0
J.M.Kemp	b Dillon	16			
M.Ntini	b Dillon	0			
Extras	(B 2, LB 5, NB 2)	9	(B 6, LB 3, W 4, NB 1)		14
Total		**247**	(7 wickets declared)		**215**

WEST INDIES

C.H.Gayle	c Pollock b Kallis	11	c McKenzie b Boje		12
W.W.Hinds	c Boucher b Pollock	9	c Kirsten b Boje		29
S.Chanderpaul	c Cullinan b Kemp	40	lbw b Boje		16
B.C.Lara	c McKenzie b Kemp	19	(5) c McKenzie b Kallis		91
R.R.Sarwan	c Boje b Kallis	25	(6) c Boucher b Pollock		26
*C.L.Hooper	c Kirsten b Klusener	17	(4) c McKenzie b Klusener		21
M.Dillon	b Klusener	0	(9) c Cullinan b Boje		1
†R.D.Jacobs	not out	3	(7) c Kirsten b Pollock		0
N.C.McGarrell	lbw b Klusener	1	(8) c Kemp b Pollock		6
D.Ramnarine	run out	2	c Kirsten b Kallis		9
C.A.Walsh	lbw b Pollock	4	not out		4
Extras	(B 3, LB 3, NB 4)	10	(B 18, LB 3, NB 4)		25
Total		**140**			**240**

WEST INDIES	O	M	R	W		O	M	R	W
Walsh	31	14	45	1		38	13	56	4
Dillon	18.2	4	47	3		0.3	0	3	0
McGarrell	43	19	72	4	(4)	15	3	41	1
Ramnarine	20	6	45	1	(6)	42	24	55	1
Hooper	10	2	31	.1		24	7	37	1
Hinds					(3)	3.3	0	14	0

SOUTH AFRICA									
Pollock	22.1	11	25	2		19	5	41	3
Kallis	17	8	24	2		15.4	6	23	2
Ntini	6	2	27	0					
Kemp	8	2	17	2		6	3	7	0
Boje	12	4	26	0	(3)	45	9	118	4
Klusener	11	4	15	3	(5)	14	6	30	1

FALL OF WICKETS				
	SA	WI	SA	WI
Wkt	1st	1st	2nd	2nd
1st	29	13	17	36
2nd	35	21	95	56
3rd	53	50	96	86
4th	120	88	123	89
5th	126	126	135	138
6th	136	127	146	138
7th	148	132	156	155
8th	223	134	–	176
9th	247	136	–	229
10th	247	140	–	240

Umpires: E.A.Nicholls (15) and S.Venkataraghavan (*India*) (44).
Referee: M.H.Denness (*England*) (9).   **Test No. 1542/10 (WI373/SA255)**

WEST INDIES v SOUTH AFRICA (5th Test)

At Sabina Park, Kingston, Jamaica, on 19, 20, 21, 22, 23 April 2001.
Toss: West Indies. Result: **WEST INDIES** won by 130 runs.
Debuts: West Indies – L.V.Garrick.

WEST INDIES

L.V.Garrick	c Pollock b Donald	0	c Boucher b Donald	27
C.H.Gayle	c Kemp b Donald	25	b Pollock	32
S.Chanderpaul	c Boucher b Kallis	7	c Cullinan b Kemp	7
B.C.Lara	c Kallis b Pollock	81	b Adams	14
M.N.Samuels	c Boucher b Pollock	3	b Pollock	59
*C.L.Hooper	c Kirsten b Pollock	25	c Pollock b Kallis	5
†R.D.Jacobs	c Boucher b Pollock	0	c McKenzie b Klusener	85
M.Dillon	c Boucher b Donald	24	c Gibbs b Pollock	13
D.Ramnarine	not out	35	c Cullinan b Pollock	9
C.E.Cuffy	c Boucher b Pollock	3	not out	13
C.A.Walsh	c Adams b Pollock	4	c Kirsten b Adams	3
Extras	(B 4, LB 12, W 2)	18	(B 14, LB 13, W 4, NB 3)	34
Total		**225**		**301**

SOUTH AFRICA

H.H.Gibbs	c Jacobs b Cuffy	18	(2) b Hooper	51
G.Kirsten	c Gayle b Walsh	0	(1) c Jacobs b Dillon	14
J.H.Kallis	c and b Dillon	17	(5) b Ramnarine	51
D.J.Cullinan	c Lara b Cuffy	6	lbw b Walsh	18
N.D.McKenzie	lbw b Ramnarine	45	(3) c Garrick b Ramnarine	55
L.Klusener	b Walsh	13	not out	31
†M.V.Boucher	c Garrick b Walsh	13	c Jacobs b Ramnarine	0
*S.M.Pollock	c Jacobs b Dillon	24	c Jacobs b Dillon	3
J.M.Kemp	c Walsh b Dillon	0	lbw b Walsh	10
A.A.Donald	not out	1	b Walsh	10
P.R.Adams	c Hooper b Dillon	3	c Samuels b Dillon	4
Extras	(W 1)	1	(B 4, LB 13, NB 1)	18
Total		**141**		**255**

SOUTH AFRICA	O	M	R	W	O	M	R	W
Donald	25	5	54	4	20	8	54	1
Pollock	26.5	17	28	5	34	8	66	4
Kallis	16	5	38	1	28	10	56	1
Kemp	16	3	45	0	(5) 18	9	30	1
Adams	11	1	43	0	(4) 21.5	7	54	2
Klusener	2	1	1	0	3	1	14	1

WEST INDIES	O	M	R	W	O	M	R	W
Walsh	18	8	31	3	22	6	62	3
Cuffy	17	6	58	2	10	3	13	0
Dillon	15.1	5	32	4	19	3	59	3
Ramnarine	11	4	20	1	31	6	61	3
Hooper					28	8	43	1

FALL OF WICKETS

	WI	SA	WI	SA
Wkt	1st	1st	2nd	2nd
1st	0	9	47	37
2nd	21	24	55	102
3rd	50	35	77	124
4th	54	51	103	190
5th	107	77	126	209
6th	113	97	184	209
7th	167	137	229	235
8th	188	137	255	236
9th	203	137	287	250
10th	225	141	301	255

Umpires: S.A.Bucknor (56) and S.Venkataraghavan (*India*) (45).
Referee: M.H.Denness (*England*) (10).   Test No. 1543/11 (WI374/SA256)

WEST INDIES v SOUTH AFRICA 2000-01

WEST INDIES – BATTING AND FIELDING

	M	I	NO	HS	Runs	Avge	100	50	Ct/St
R.D.Jacobs	5	10	4	113*	317	52.83	1	2	21
B.C.Lara	5	10	–	91	400	40.00	–	3	5
C.L.Hooper	5	10	1	74	358	39.77	–	4	6
C.H.Gayle	5	10	–	81	326	32.60	–	1	7
R.R.Sarwan	4	8	–	91	238	29.75	–	1	3
M.N.Samuels	4	8	–	59	206	25.75	–	2	2
S.Chanderpaul	2	4	–	40	70	17.50	–	–	–
W.W.Hinds	4	8	–	56	133	16.62	–	1	4
D.Ramnarine	5	9	2	35*	79	11.28	–	–	2
M.Dillon	5	9	1	24	84	10.50	–	–	5
C.E.Cuffy	2	3	1	13*	20	10.00	–	–	1
C.A.Walsh	5	8	2	4*	21	3.50	–	–	1
N.A.M.McLean	2	4	–	6	11	2.75	–	–	1

Played in one Test: L.V.Garrick 0, 27 (2 ct); N.C.McGarrell 0, 6.

WEST INDIES – BOWLING

	O	M	R	W	Avge	Best	5wI	10wM
C.A.Walsh	263.4	87	492	25	19.68	6-61	1	–
N.C.McGarrell	58	22	113	5	22.60	4-72	–	–
M.Dillon	168	31	512	20	25.60	4-32	–	–
D.Ramnarine	290.3	93	617	20	30.85	5-78	1	–
N.A.M.McLean	66.5	6	236	6	39.33	3-60	–	–
C.E.Cuffy	67	20	170	4	42.50	2-58	–	–
C.L.Hooper	158	47	283	5	56.60	2-49	–	–

Also bowled: C.H.Gayle 1-0-3-0; W.W.Hinds 18.3-5-50-3; M.N.Samuels 7-1-15-0; R.R.Sarwan 1-0-4-0.

SOUTH AFRICA – BATTING AND FIELDING

	M	I	NO	HS	Runs	Avge	100	50	Ct/St
S.M.Pollock	5	9	5	106*	302	75.50	1	–	4
H.H.Gibbs	5	10	1	87	464	51.55	–	4	3
D.J.Cullinan	5	10	1	134	459	51.00	2	2	10
N.D.McKenzie	5	9	–	72	301	33.44	–	2	7
J.H.Kallis	5	10	1	53	267	29.66	–	3	4
G.Kirsten	5	10	–	150	250	25.00	1	–	6
N.Boje	4	7	1	36	106	17.66	–	–	4
M.V.Boucher	5	9	–	52	126	14.00	–	1	17
L.Klusener	5	9	1	31*	75	9.37	–	–	1
A.A.Donald	4	7	1	37	51	8.50	–	–	1
M.Ntini	4	5	1	11	23	5.75	–	–	1
J.M.Kemp	2	3	–	16	16	5.33	–	–	2

Played in one Test: P.R.Adams 3, 4 (1 ct).

SOUTH AFRICA – BOWLING

	O	M	R	W	Avge	Best	5wI	10wM
J.H.Kallis	189.4	67	395	20	19.75	6-67	1	–
S.M.Pollock	228.1	77	464	20	23.20	5-28	1	–
A.A.Donald	147	47	355	14	25.35	4-54	–	–
L.Klusener	118	49	219	8	27.37	3-15	–	–
N.Boje	176.5	51	442	15	29.46	4-17	–	–
M.Ntini	98	24	296	7	42.28	2-56	–	–

Also bowled: P.R.Adams 32.5-8-97-2; J.M.Kemp 48-17-99-3.

ZIMBABWE v BANGLADESH (1st Test)

At Queens Sports Club, Bulawayo, on 19, 20, 21, 22 April 2001.
Toss: Zimbabwe. Result: **ZIMBABWE** won by an innings and 32 runs.
Debuts: Zimbabwe – A.M.Blignaut, D.D.Ebrahim, B.T.Watambwa; Bangladesh –
Javed Omar, Manjural Islam, Mohammed Sharif, Mushfiqur Rahman.

BANGLADESH

Javed Omar	c Ebrahim b Murphy	62		not out	85
Mehrab Hossain	c Whittall b Blignaut	16		b Streak	0
Habibul Bashar	c Murphy b Blignaut	0		c Murphy b Watambwa	24
Aminul Islam	c A.Flower b Blignaut	84		c Ebrahim b Streak	11
Akram Khan	run out	21		c Ebrahim b Blignaut	8
*Naimur Rahman	c Blignaut b Watambwa	22		c and b Nkala	6
†Khaled Masud	c A.Flower b Streak	30		absent hurt	–
Mushfiqur Rahman	c Streak b Blignaut	4	(7)	c Nkala b Watambwa	2
Hasibul Hussain	lbw b Streak	1	(8)	c G.W.Flower b Streak	5
Mohammed Sharif	c Campbell b Blignaut	0	(9)	c Whittall b Blignaut	8
Manjural Islam	not out	1	(10)	c and b Blignaut	6
Extras	(LB 1, W 6, NB 9)	16		(LB 2, W 6, NB 4)	12
Total		**257**			**168**

ZIMBABWE

G.J.Whittall	c Sharif b Hasibul	119
D.D.Ebrahim	c Masud b Manjural	2
S.V.Carlisle	b Manjural	3
A.D.R.Campbell	c Masud b Sharif	19
†A.Flower	c Naimur b Manjural	73
G.W.Flower	c Sharif b Hasibul	68
*H.H.Streak	c sub (Mohd Rafique) b Manjural	67
A.M.Blignaut	c and b Manjural	0
M.L.Nkala	c Mehrab b Manjural	47
B.A.Murphy	c Habibul b Naimur	30
B.T.Watambwa	not out	4
Extras	(B 2, LB 10, W 1, NB 12)	25
Total		**457**

ZIMBABWE	O	M	R	W		O	M	R	W
Streak	21	7	47	2		19	5	42	3
Blignaut	23.3	5	73	5		13.3	4	37	3
Watambwa	17	4	38	1	(4)	13	3	44	2
Nkala	13	2	45	0	(3)	9	0	34	1
Murphy	17	2	53	1		4	1	9	0

BANGLADESH	O	M	R	W
Hasibul Hussain	30	7	125	2
Manjural Islam	35	12	81	6
Mohammed Sharif	29	3	112	1
Mushfiqur Rahman	20	5	53	0
Naimur Rahman	24.4	7	74	1

FALL OF WICKETS			
	B	Z	B
Wkt	1st	1st	2nd
1st	26	18	6
2nd	30	27	61
3rd	114	66	105
4th	149	215	116
5th	194	233	129
6th	226	353	138
7th	253	353	149
8th	256	389	160
9th	256	445	168
10th	257	457	–

Umpires: K.C.Barbour (2) and R.E.Koertzen (*South Africa*) (25).
Referee: B.Warnapura (*Sri Lanka*) (1). **Test No. 1544/1 (Z49/B2)**

ZIMBABWE v BANGLADESH (2nd Test)

At Harare Sports Club on 26, 27, 28, 29, 30 April 2001.
Toss: Zimbabwe. Result: **ZIMBABWE** won by eight wickets.
Debuts: Bangladesh – Enamul Haque.

BANGLADESH

Javed Omar	c Blignaut b Streak	1	c G.W.Flower b Price		43
†Mehrab Hossain	c Carlisle b Price	71	c Blignaut b Watambwa		0
Al Sahariar	c G.W.Flower b Streak	11	c Streak b Watambwa		68
Aminul Islam	c Campbell b Price	12	lbw b Price		2
Habibul Bashar	st A.Flower b Price	64	c A.Flower b Streak		76
Akram Khan	c Campbell b Streak	44	c Campbell b Price		31
*Naimur Rahman	lbw b Price	16	run out		36
Mushfiqur Rahman	c A.Flower b Streak	2	(9) not out		2
Enamul Haque	not out	20	(8) c A.Flower b Watambwa		3
Mohammed Sharif	c Carlisle b Watambwa	0	c Carlisle b Streak		0
Manjural Islam	c Campbell b Watambwa	0	c A.Flower b Watambwa		0
Extras	(LB 8, W 3, NB 2)	13	(LB 2, W 1, NB 2)		5
Total		**254**			**266**

ZIMBABWE

G.J.Whittall	run out	59	b Enamul		60
D.D.Ebrahim	c Akram Khan b Naimur	39	run out		10
S.V.Carlisle	c Habibul b Sharif	21	not out		29
A.D.R.Campbell	c Mushfiqur b Naimur	73	not out		0
†A.Flower	run out	23			
G.W.Flower	c Sharif b Enamul	84			
*H.H.Streak	c Mehrab b Sharif	87			
A.M.Blignaut	run out	15			
M.L.Nkala	c Mushfiqur b Enamul	7			
R.W.Price	not out	0			
B.T.Watambwa					
Extras	(B 7, LB 6)	13	(LB 1)		1
Total	(9 wickets declared)	**421**	(2 wickets)		**100**

ZIMBABWE	O	M	R	W		O	M	R	W		FALL OF WICKETS			
Blignaut	27	6	67	0	(3)	15	6	27	0				B	Z	Z
Streak	30	12	38	4	(1)	21	7	47	2		Wkt	1st	1st	2nd	2nd
Watambwa	14.5	3	48	2	(2)	21.5	5	64	4		1st	1	90	2	35
Nkala	19	11	22	0	(6)	6	0	19	0		2nd	23	104	97	92
Price	30	9	71	4	(4)	30	9	94	3		3rd	48	164	99	–
G.W.Flower					(5)	6	0	13	0		4th	162	210	127	–
											5th	171	244	203	–
BANGLADESH											6th	196	377	246	–
Manjural Islam	34	9	113	0		9	2	21	0		7th	207	397	264	–
Mohammed Sharif	28.4	6	108	2		6	0	36	0		8th	253	419	264	–
Enamul Haque	46	15	94	2		3	0	8	1		9th	254	421	265	–
Mushfiqur Rahman	11	1	33	0		6	1	26	0		10th	254	–	266	–
Naimur Rahman	28	12	60	2		0.3	0	8	0						

Umpires: D.B.Cowie (21) and R.B.Tiffin (*Zimbabwe*) (19).
Referee: B.Warnapura (*Sri Lanka*) (2).

Test No. 1545/2 (Z50/B3)

238

ENGLAND v PAKISTAN (1st Test)

At Lord's, London, on 17 (*no play*), 18, 19, 20 May 2001.
Toss: Pakistan. Result: **ENGLAND** won by an innings and 9 runs.
Debuts: England – R.J.Sidebottom, I.J.Ward.

ENGLAND

M.A.Atherton	b Azhar	42
M.E.Trescothick	c Azhar b Razzaq	36
M.P.Vaughan	c Rashid b Azhar	32
*N.Hussain	c Rashid b Azhar	64
G.P.Thorpe	c Razzaq b Waqar	80
R.J.Sidebottom	c Inzamam b Wasim	4
†A.J.Stewart	lbw b Shoaib	44
I.J.Ward	c Razzaq b Waqar	39
D.G.Cork	c Younis Khan b Wasim	25
A.R.Caddick	b Azhar	5
D.Gough	not out	5
Extras	(B 1, LB 5, W 1, NB 8)	15
Total		**391**

PAKISTAN

Saeed Anwar	c Atherton b Gough	12	c Thorpe b Caddick	8
Salim Elahi	c Atherton b Caddick	0	c Thorpe b Caddick	0
Abdul Razzaq	c Stewart b Caddick	22	c Atherton b Caddick	53
Inzamam-ul-Haq	c Stewart b Caddick	13	c Stewart b Cork	20
Yousuf Youhana	lbw b Gough	26	c Vaughan b Gough	6
Younis Khan	b Cork	58	lbw b Cork	1
Azhar Mahmood	c Trescothick b Caddick	14	c Stewart b Caddick	24
†Rashid Latif	c Stewart b Gough	18	c Stewart b Gough	20
Wasim Akram	not out	19	c Thorpe b Gough	12
*Waqar Younis	c Thorpe b Gough	0	c Stewart b Cork	21
Shoaib Akhtar	b Gough	0	not out	2
Extras	(B 1, LB 7, NB 13)	21	(LB 6, NB 6)	12
Total		**203**		**179**

PAKISTAN	O	M	R	W	O	M	R	W
Wasim Akram	34	9	99	2				
Waqar Younis	25	5	77	2				
Shoaib Akhtar	19	4	64	1				
Abdul Razzaq	21	2	68	1				
Younis Khan	5	0	27	0				
Azhar Mahmood	26	12	50	4				

ENGLAND	O	M	R	W	O	M	R	W
Gough	16	5	61	5	16	4	40	3
Caddick	17	3	52	4	18	3	54	4
Sidebottom	11	0	38	0	9	2	26	0
Cork	11	3	42	1	15.3	3	41	3
Trescothick	2	1	2	0				
Vaughan					(5) 1	0	12	0

FALL OF WICKETS

		E	P	P
Wkt	1st	1st	2nd	
1st	60	4	2	
2nd	105	21	30	
3rd	114	37	67	
4th	246	60	84	
5th	254	116	87	
6th	307	153	121	
7th	317	167	122	
8th	365	203	147	
9th	385	203	167	
10th	391	203	179	

Umpires: D.B Hair (*Australia*) (38) and P.Willey (23).
Referee: B.F.Hastings (*New Zealand*) (7).

Test No. 1546/59 (E780/P277)

ENGLAND v PAKISTAN (2nd Test)

At Old Trafford, Manchester, on 31 May, 1, 2, 3, 4 June 2001.
Toss: Pakistan. Result: **PAKISTAN** won by 108 runs.
Debuts: None.

PAKISTAN

Saeed Anwar	c Atherton b Caddick	29	c Thorpe b Gough		12
Abdul Razzaq	b Caddick	1	c Cork b Hoggard		22
Faisal Iqbal	c Vaughan b Gough	16	c Stewart b Caddick		14
Inzamam-ul-Haq	c Ward b Hoggard	114	c Trescothick b Hoggard		85
Yousuf Youhana	c Knight b Caddick	4	c Atherton b Caddick		49
Younis Khan	lbw b Hoggard	65	lbw b Cork		17
Azhar Mahmood	c Knight b Hoggard	37	b Caddick		14
†Rashid Latif	run out	71	c Atherton b Hoggard		25
Wasim Akram	c Stewart b Gough	16	b Gough		36
Saqlain Mushtaq	not out	21	c Stewart b Gough		5
*Waqar Younis	lbw b Gough	5	not out		14
Extras	(LB 9, NB 15)	24	(LB 11, NB 19)		30
Total		**403**			**323**

ENGLAND

M.A.Atherton	c Rashid b Waqar	5	b Waqar		51
M.E.Trescothick	b Wasim	10	c Rashid b Wasim		117
M.P.Vaughan	c Rashid b Waqar	120	c Rashid b Razzaq		14
G.P.Thorpe	run out	138	b Waqar		10
*†A.J.Stewart	not out	39	lbw b Saqlain		19
I.J.Ward	run out	12	c Rashid b Saqlain		10
N.V.Knight	c Rashid b Razzaq	15	lbw b Wasim		0
D.G.Cork	c Saeed b Razzaq	2	lbw b Saqlain		4
A.R.Caddick	c Rashid b Saqlain	1	b Saqlain		0
D.Gough	b Razzaq	0	c sub (Imran Nazir) b Waqar		23
M.J.Hoggard	b Saqlain	0	not out		0
Extras	(LB 5, W 2, NB 8)	15	(B 6, LB 4, W 1, NB 2)		13
Total		**357**			**261**

ENGLAND	O	M	R	W	O	M	R	W
Gough	23.4	2	94	3	22.5	2	85	3
Caddick	28	2	111	3	22	4	92	3
Hoggard	19	4	79	3	29	4	93	3
Cork	21	2	75	0	25	9	42	1
Trescothick	3	0	14	0				
Vaughan	2	0	21	0				
PAKISTAN								
Wasim Akram	30	7	89	1	23	4	59	2
Waqar Younis	24	3	87	2	22.1	3	85	3
Azhar Mahmood	8	0	35	0				
Saqlain Mushtaq	30.2	7	80	2	(3) 47	20	74	4
Abdul Razzaq	19	2	61	3	(4) 13	5	33	1

FALL OF WICKETS				
	P	E	P	E
Wkt	1st	1st	2nd	2nd
1st	6	15	24	146
2nd	39	15	41	174
3rd	86	282	63	201
4th	92	283	204	213
5th	233	309	208	229
6th	255	348	232	230
7th	308	353	241	230
8th	357	354	300	230
9th	380	356	306	261
10th	403	357	323	261

Umpires: E.A.Nicholls (*West Indies*) (16) and D.R.Shepherd (56).
Referee: B.F.Hastings (*New Zealand*) (8).   **Test No. 1547/60 (E781/P278)**

ENGLAND v PAKISTAN 2001

ENGLAND – BATTING AND FIELDING

	M	I	NO	HS	Runs	Avge	100	50	Ct/St
G.P.Thorpe	2	3	–	138	228	76.00	1	1	5
N.Hussain	1	1	–	64	64	64.00	–	1	–
M.P.Vaughan	2	3	–	120	166	55.33	1	–	2
M.E.Trescothick	2	3	–	117	163	54.33	1	–	2
A.J.Stewart	2	3	1	44	102	51.00	–	–	10
M.A.Atherton	2	3	–	51	98	32.66	–	1	6
I.J.Ward	2	3	–	39	61	20.33	–	–	1
D.Gough	2	3	1	23	28	14.00	–	–	–
D.G.Cork	2	3	–	25	31	10.33	–	–	1
N.V.Knight	1	2	–	15	15	7.50	–	–	2
R.J.Sidebottom	1	1	–	4	4	4.00	–	–	–
A.R.Caddick	2	3	–	5	6	2.00	–	–	–
M.J.Hoggard	1	2	1	0*	0	0.00	–	–	–

ENGLAND – BOWLING

	O	M	R	W	Avge	Best	5wI	10wM
D.Gough	78.3	13	280	14	20.00	5-61	1	–
A.R.Caddick	85	12	309	14	22.07	4-52	–	–
M.J.Hoggard	48	8	172	6	28.66	3-79	–	–
D.G.Cork	72.3	17	200	5	40.00	3-41	–	–

Also bowled: R.J.Sidebottom 20-2-64-0; M.E.Trescothick 5-1-16-0; M.P.Vaughan 3-0-33-0.

PAKISTAN – BATTING AND FIELDING

	M	I	NO	HS	Runs	Avge	100	50	Ct/St
Inzamam-ul-Haq	2	4	–	114	232	58.00	1	1	1
Younis Khan	2	4	–	65	141	35.25	–	2	1
Rashid Latif	2	4	–	71	134	33.50	–	1	9
Wasim Akram	2	4	1	36	83	27.66	–	–	–
Saqlain Mushtaq	1	2	1	21*	26	26.00	–	–	–
Abdul Razzaq	2	4	–	53	98	24.50	–	1	2
Azhar Mahmood	2	4	–	37	89	22.25	–	–	1
Yousuf Youhana	2	4	–	49	85	21.25	–	–	–
Saeed Anwar	2	4	–	29	61	15.25	–	–	1
Faisal Iqbal	1	2	–	16	30	15.00	–	–	–
Waqar Younis	2	4	1	21	40	13.33	–	–	–
Shoaib Akhtar	1	2	1	2*	2	2.00	–	–	–
Salim Elahi	1	2	–	0	0	0.00	–	–	–

PAKISTAN – BOWLING

	O	M	R	W	Avge	Best	5wI	10wM
Azhar Mahmood	34	12	85	4	21.25	4-50	–	–
Saqlain Mushtaq	77.2	27	154	6	25.66	4-74	–	–
Abdul Razzaq	53	9	162	5	32.40	3-61	–	–
Waqar Younis	71.1	11	249	7	35.57	3-85	–	–
Wasim Akram	87	20	247	5	49.40	2-59	–	–
Shoaib Akhtar	19	4	64	1	64.00	1-64	–	–

Also bowled: Younis Khan 5-0-27-0.

ZIMBABWE v INDIA (1st Test)

At Queens Sports Club, Bulawayo, on 7, 8, 9, 10 June 2001.
Toss: Zimbabwe. Result: **INDIA** won by eight wickets.
Debuts: None.

ZIMBABWE

G.J.Whittall	b Nehra	6		c Ramesh b Srinath	20
D.D.Ebrahim	run out	12		c Dravid b Srinath	0
S.V.Carlisle	c Laxman b Khan	29		c Laxman b Nehra	52
A.D.R.Campbell	c Dighe b Harbhajan	21		c Das b Harbhajan	16
†A.Flower	c Das b Nehra	51	(6)	c Ramesh b Nehra	83
G.W.Flower	c Dighe b Srinath	5	(7)	run out	71
*H.H.Streak	run out	16	(8)	lbw b Khan	14
A.M.Blignaut	lbw b Nehra	0	(9)	not out	32
B.A.Murphy	c Dravid b Khan	7	(5)	c Das b Khan	10
H.K.Olonga	c Dighe b Harbhajan	16		b Srinath	0
B.T.Watamwba	not out	0		run out	0
Extras	(LB 4, NB 6)	10		(B 1, LB 17, W 2, NB 10)	30
Total		**173**			**328**

INDIA

S.S.Das	c Ebrahim b Murphy	30		not out	82
S.Ramesh	b Watamwba	2		c Carlisle b Blignaut	17
V.V.S.Laxman	c Whittall b Olonga	28		c and b G.W.Flower	38
S.R.Tendulkar	c Carlisle b Blignaut	74		not out	36
J.Srinath	c Whittall b Watamwba	1			
*S.C.Ganguly	c A.Flower b Streak	5			
R.Dravid	c A.Flower b Blignaut	44			
†S.S.Dighe	c A.Flower b Streak	47			
Harbhajan Singh	c Whittall b Watamwba	66			
Z.Khan	b Streak	0			
A.Nehra	not out	9			
Extras	(LB 4, W 1, NB 7)	12		(B 4, W 1, NB 6)	11
Total		**318**		**(2 wickets)**	**184**

INDIA	O	M	R	W		O	M	R	W	FALL OF WICKETS			
Srinath	15	5	47	1		32.2	11	71	3		Z	I	Z	I
Nehra	12	1	23	3		26.4	4	77	2	*Wkt*	*1st*	*1st*	*2nd*	*2nd*
Khan	11	1	54	2	(4)	22	6	44	2	1st	9	2	14	71
Harbhajan Singh	20.5	6	45	2	(3)	37.5	8	92	1	2nd	46	54	34	132
Tendulkar						6	0	23	0	3rd	65	81	63	—
Ganguly						1	0	3	0	4th	89	83	86	—
										5th	97	98	134	—
ZIMBABWE										6th	137	178	235	—
Streak	24	7	63	3						7th	139	208	273	—
Watamwba	25.5	6	94	3	(1)	15	4	54	0	8th	154	280	308	—
Blignaut	16	2	68	2	(2)	12	3	25	1	9th	165	280	312	—
Olonga	8	1	35	1						10th	173	318	328	—
Murphy	16	3	54	1	(3)	18.4	1	78	0					
G.W.Flower					(4)	8	0	23	1					

Umpires: D.J.Harper (*Australia*) (13) and R.B.Tiffin (20).
Referee: D.T.Lindsay (*South Africa*) (1).

Test No. 1548/6 (Z51/I341)

ZIMBABWE v INDIA (2nd Test)

At Harare Sports Club on 15, 16, 17, 18 June 2001.
Toss: India. Result: **ZIMBABWE** won by four wickets.
Debuts: Zimbabwe – T.J.Friend; India – H.K.Badani.

INDIA

S.S.Das	c A.Flower b Blignaut	57	lbw b Streak		70
H.K.Badani	lbw b Watambwa	2	(7) not out		16
V.V.S.Laxman	c Blignaut b Streak	15	c Murphy b Friend		20
S.R.Tendulkar	b Streak	20	c G.W.Flower b Streak		69
*S.C.Ganguly	c Blignaut b Streak	9	(6) lbw b Blignaut		0
R.Dravid	not out	68	(5) c A.Flower b Blignaut		26
†S.S.Dighe	c G.W.Flower b Friend	20	(2) c A.Flower b Blignaut		4
A.B.Agarkar	c Blignaut b Friend	6	c A.Flower b Streak		0
Harbhajan Singh	b Murphy	31	c Ebrahim b Blignaut		5
J.Srinath	run out	0	c A.Flower b Streak		3
A.Nehra	c sub (P.A.Strang) b Murphy	0	b Blignaut		0
Extras	(LB 2, W 6, NB 1)	9	(LB 9, W 12)		21
Total		**237**			**234**

ZIMBABWE

G.J.Whittall	c Dravid b Nehra	0	c Dravid b Srinath		10
D.D.Ebrahim	lbw b Harbhajan	49	c Badani b Harbhajan		20
S.V.Carlisle	c Badani b Nehra	3	not out		62
A.D.R.Campbell	b Nehra	8	lbw b Nehra		13
†A.Flower	c Das b Harbhajan	45	(8) not out		8
G.W.Flower	c Laxman b Srinath	86	(5) c Laxman b Agarkar		3
*H.H.Streak	b Tendulkar	40	(6) c Dighe b Srinath		8
A.M.Blignaut	st Dighe b Harbhajan	35	(7) b Nehra		16
T.J.Friend	b Nehra	15			
B.A.Murphy	b Harbhajan	17			
B.T.Watambwa	not out	2			
Extras	(B 4, LB 5, W 2, NB 4)	15	(B 1, LB 11, NB 5)		17
Total		**315**	(6 wickets)		**157**

ZIMBABWE	O	M	R	W		O	M	R	W
Watambwa	3.4	0	14	1					
Streak	20	4	69	3	(1)	27	12	46	4
Friend	20.2	4	48	2		22	4	47	1
Blignaut	20	1	84	1	(2)	31.5	14	74	5
Murphy	9.2	3	17	2		10	1	42	0
G.W.Flower	1	0	3	0		1	0	1	0
Whittall					(4)	7	4	15	0
INDIA									
Srinath	29.3	7	82	1	(2)	13	1	46	2
Nehra	24	6	72	4	(1)	13	0	45	2
Agarkar	24	7	62	0	(4)	8	3	22	1
Harbhajan Singh	26	5	71	4	(3)	19	6	25	1
Tendulkar	4	0	19	1		1	0	1	0

FALL OF WICKETS

	I	Z	I	Z
Wkt	1st	1st	2nd	2nd
1st	7	5	8	25
2nd	45	9	32	45
3rd	90	18	150	71
4th	103	105	197	89
5th	122	110	199	119
6th	165	175	202	144
7th	172	242	202	–
8th	228	271	207	–
9th	237	301	226	–
10th	237	315	234	–

Umpires: E.A.R.de Silva (*Sri Lanka*) (3) and I.D.Robinson (25).
Referee: D.T.Lindsay (*South Africa*) (2).

Test No. 1549/7 (Z52/I342)

ENGLAND v AUSTRALIA (1st Test)

At Edgbaston, Birmingham, on 5, 6, 7, 8 July 2001.
Toss: Australia. Result: **AUSTRALIA** won by an innings and 118 runs.
Debuts: England – U.Afzaal.

ENGLAND

M.A.Atherton	c M.E.Waugh b Gillespie	57	c M.E.Waugh b McGrath		4
M.E.Trescothick	c Warne b Gillespie	0	c M.E.Waugh b Warne		76
M.A.Butcher	c Ponting b Warne	38	c Gilchrist b Lee		41
*N.Hussain	lbw b McGrath	13	retired hurt		9
I.J.Ward	b McGrath	23	b Lee		3
†A.J.Stewart	lbw b McGrath	65	c Warne b Gillespie		5
U.Afzaal	b Warne	4	lbw b Gillespie		2
C.White	lbw b Warne	4	b Gillespie		0
A.F.Giles	c Gilchrist b Warne	7	c M.E.Waugh b Warne		0
D.Gough	c Gillespie b Warne	0	lbw b Warne		0
A.R.Caddick	not out	49	not out		6
Extras	(B 10, LB 8, NB 16)	34	(B 1, LB 5, NB 12)		18
Total		**294**			**164**

AUSTRALIA

M.J.Slater	b Gough	77
M.L.Hayden	c White b Giles	35
R.T.Ponting	lbw b Gough	11
M.E.Waugh	c Stewart b Caddick	49
*S.R.Waugh	lbw b Gough	105
D.R.Martyn	c Trescothick b Butcher	105
†A.C.Gilchrist	c Caddick b White	152
S.K.Warne	c Atherton b Butcher	8
B.Lee	c Atherton b Butcher	0
J.N.Gillespie	lbw b Butcher	0
G.D.McGrath	not out	1
Extras	(B 3, LB 7, NB 23)	33
Total		**576**

AUSTRALIA	O	M	R	W		O	M	R	W
McGrath	17.3	2	67	3		13	5	34	1
Gillespie	17	3	67	2		11	2	52	3
Lee	12	2	71	0	(5)	7	0	37	2
Warne	19	4	71	5	(3)	10.1	4	29	3
M.E.Waugh					(4)	1	0	6	0

ENGLAND	O	M	R	W
Gough	33	6	152	3
Caddick	36	0	163	1
White	26.4	5	101	1
Giles	25	0	108	1
Butcher	9	3	42	4

FALL OF WICKETS			
	E	A	E
Wkt	1st	1st	2nd
1st	2	98	4
2nd	106	130	99
3rd	123	134	142
4th	136	267	148
5th	159	336	150
6th	170	496	154
7th	174	511	155
8th	191	513	155
9th	191	513	164
10th	294	576	–

Umpires: S.A Bucknor (*West Indies*) (57) and G.Sharp (14).
Referee: Talat Ali (*Pakistan*) (6).   **Test No. 1550/297 (E782/A615)**

ENGLAND v AUSTRALIA (2nd Test)

At Lord's, London, on 19, 20, 21, 22 July 2001.
Toss: Australia. Result: **AUSTRALIA** won by eight wickets.
Debuts: None.

ENGLAND

*M.A.Atherton	lbw b McGrath	37	b Warne		20
M.E.Trescothick	c Gilchrist b Gillespie	15	c Gilchrist b Gillespie		3
M.A.Butcher	c M.E.Waugh b McGrath	21	c Gilchrist b Gillespie		83
G.P.Thorpe	c Gilchrist b McGrath	20	lbw b Lee		2
M.R.Ramprakash	b Lee	14	lbw b Gillespie		40
†A.J.Stewart	c Gilchrist b McGrath	0	lbw b McGrath		28
I.J.Ward	not out	23	c Ponting b McGrath		0
C.White	c Hayden b McGrath	0	not out		27
D.G.Cork	c Ponting b Gillespie	24	c Warne b McGrath		2
A.R.Caddick	b Warne	0	c Gilchrist b Gillespie		7
D.Gough	b Warne	5	c M.E.Waugh b Gillespie		1
Extras	(B 7, LB 8, W 2, NB 11)	28	(LB 3, W 2, NB 9)		14
Total		**187**			**227**

AUSTRALIA

M.J.Slater	c Stewart b Caddick	25	(2) c Butcher b Caddick		4
M.L.Hayden	c Butcher b Caddick	0	(1) not out		6
R.T.Ponting	c Thorpe b Gough	14	lbw b Gough		4
M.E.Waugh	run out	108	not out		0
*S.R.Waugh	c Stewart b Cork	45			
D.R.Martyn	c Stewart b Caddick	52			
†A.C.Gilchrist	c Stewart b Gough	90			
S.K.Warne	c Stewart b Caddick	5			
B.Lee	b Caddick	20			
J.N.Gillespie	b Gough	9			
G.D.McGrath	not out	0			
Extras	(LB 9, W 1, NB 23)	33			
Total		**401**	(2 wickets)		**14**

AUSTRALIA	O	M	R	W	O	M	R	W	FALL OF WICKETS				
McGrath	24	9	54	5	19	4	60	3		E	A	E	A
Gillespie	18	6	56	2	16	4	53	5	*Wkt*	*1st*	*1st*	*2nd*	*2nd*
Lee	16	3	46	1	9	1	41	1	1st	33	5	8	6
Warne	5.3	0	16	2	20	4	58	1	2nd	75	27	47	13
M.E.Waugh					2	1	12	0	3rd	96	105	50	–
									4th	121	212	146	–
ENGLAND									5th	126	230	188	–
Gough	25	3	115	3	2	0	5	1	6th	129	308	188	–
Caddick	32.1	4	101	5	1.1	0	9	1	7th	131	322	188	–
White	18	1	80	0					8th	178	387	193	–
Cork	23	3	84	1					9th	181	401	225	–
Butcher	3	1	12	0					10th	187	401	227	–

Umpires: S.A.Bucknor (*West Indies*) (58) and J.W.Holder (11).
Referee: Talat Ali (*Pakistan*) (7). **Test No. 1551/298 (E783/A616)**

ENGLAND v AUSTRALIA (3rd Test)

At Trent Bridge, Nottingham, on 2, 3, 4 August 2001.
Toss: England. Result: **AUSTRALIA** won by seven wickets.
Debuts: None.

ENGLAND

*M.A.Atherton	c M.E.Waugh b McGrath	0	c Gilchrist b Warne	51
M.E.Trescothick	c Gilchrist b Gillespie	69	c Gilchrist b Warne	32
M.A.Butcher	c Ponting b McGrath	13	lbw b Lee	1
M.R.Ramprakash	c Gilchrist b Gillespie	14	st Gilchrist b Warne	26
†A.J.Stewart	c M.E.Waugh b McGrath	46	b Warne	0
I.J.Ward	c Gilchrist b McGrath	6	lbw b Gillespie	13
C.White	c Hayden b McGrath	0	c S.R.Waugh b Warne	7
A.J.Tudor	lbw b Warne	3	c Ponting b Warne	9
R.D.B.Croft	c Ponting b Warne	3	b Gillespie	0
A.R.Caddick	b Lee	13	c Gilchrist b Gillespie	4
D.Gough	not out	0	not out	5
Extras	(B 1, LB 9, W 1, NB 7)	18	(B 4, LB 3, NB 7)	14
Total		**185**		**162**

AUSTRALIA

M.J.Slater	b Gough	15	(2) c Trescothick b Caddick	12
M.L.Hayden	lbw b Tudor	33	(1) lbw b Tudor	42
R.T.Ponting	c Stewart b Gough	14	c Stewart b Croft	17
M.E.Waugh	c Atherton b Tudor	15	not out	42
*S.R.Waugh	c Atherton b Caddick	13	retired hurt	1
D.R.Martyn	c Stewart b Caddick	4	not out	33
†A.C.Gilchrist	c Atherton b Tudor	54		
S.K.Warne	lbw b Caddick	0		
B.Lee	c Butcher b Tudor	4		
J.N.Gillespie	not out	27		
G.D.McGrath	c Butcher b Tudor	2		
Extras	(LB 3, W 1, NB 5)	9	(LB 4, NB 7)	11
Total		**190**	(3 wickets)	**158**

AUSTRALIA	O	M	R	W	O	M	R	W
McGrath	18	4	49	5	11	3	31	0
Lee	6.5	0	30	1	(3) 8	1	30	1
Gillespie	12	1	59	2	(2) 20	8	61	3
Warne	16	4	37	2	18	5	33	6

ENGLAND	O	M	R	W	O	M	R	W
Gough	15	3	63	2	9	1	38	0
Caddick	20	4	70	3	12.2	1	71	1
Tudor	15.5	4	44	5	7	0	37	1
White	2	1	8	0				
Croft	2	0	2	0	(4) 1	0	8	1

FALL OF WICKETS

	E	A	E	A
Wkt	1st	1st	2nd	2nd
1st	0	48	57	36
2nd	30	56	59	72
3rd	63	69	115	88
4th	117	82	115	–
5th	142	94	126	–
6th	147	102	144	–
7th	158	102	144	–
8th	168	122	146	–
9th	180	188	156	–
10th	185	190	162	–

Umpires: J.H.Hampshire (17) and S.Venkataraghavan (*India*) (46).
Referee: Talat Ali (*Pakistan*) (8).   Test No. 1552/299 (**E784/A617**)

ENGLAND v AUSTRALIA (4th Test)

At Headingley, Leeds, on 16, 17, 18, 19, 20 August 2001.
Toss: Australia. Result: **ENGLAND** won by six wickets.
Debuts: Australia – S.M.Katich.

AUSTRALIA

M.J.Slater	lbw b Caddick	21	(2) b Gough		16
M.L.Hayden	lbw b Caddick	15	(1) c Stewart b Mullally		35
R.T.Ponting	c Stewart b Tudor	144	lbw b Gough		72
M.E.Waugh	c Ramprakash b Caddick	72	not out		24
D.R.Martyn	c Stewart b Gough	118	lbw b Caddick		6
S.M.Katich	b Gough	15	not out		0
*†A.C.Gilchrist	c Trescothick b Gough	19			
S.K.Warne	c Stewart b Gough	0			
B.Lee	c Ramprakash b Mullally	0			
J.N.Gillespie	c Atherton b Gough	5			
G.D.McGrath	not out	8			
Extras	(B 5, LB 15, W 1, NB 9)	30	(B 5, LB 7, NB 11)		23
Total		**447**	(4 wickets declared)		**176**

ENGLAND

M.A.Atherton	c Gilchrist b McGrath	22	c Gilchrist b McGrath		8
M.E.Trescothick	c Gilchrist b McGrath	37	c Hayden b Gillespie		10
M.A.Butcher	run out	47	not out		173
*N.Hussain	lbw b McGrath	46	c Gilchrist b Gillespie		55
M.R.Ramprakash	c Gilchrist b Lee	40	c Waugh b Warne		32
U.Afzaal	c Warne b McGrath	14	not out		4
†A.J.Stewart	not out	76			
A.J.Tudor	c Gilchrist b McGrath	2			
A.R.Caddick	c Gilchrist b Lee	5			
D.Gough	c Slater b McGrath	8			
A.D.Mullally	c Katich b McGrath	0			
Extras	(B 2, LB 3, NB 7)	12	(B 14, LB 16, NB 3)		33
Total		**309**	(4 wickets)		**315**

ENGLAND	O	M	R	W		O	M	R	W
Gough	25.1	4	103	5		17	3	68	2
Caddick	29	4	143	3		11	2	45	1
Mullally	23	8	65	1	(4)	7.3	2	34	1
Tudor	18	1	97	1	(3)	4	1	17	0
Butcher	1	0	7	0					
Ramprakash	4	0	12	0					

AUSTRALIA									
McGrath	30.2	9	76	7		16	3	61	1
Gillespie	26	6	76	0		22	4	94	2
Lee	22	3	103	2	(4)	16	4	65	0
Warne	16	2	49	0	(3)	18.2	3	58	1
Waugh						1	0	7	0

	FALL OF WICKETS				
		A	E	A	E
Wkt	1st	1st	2nd	2nd	
1st	39	50	25	8	
2nd	42	67	129	33	
3rd	263	158	141	214	
4th	288	158	171	289	
5th	355	174	–	–	
6th	396	252	–	–	
7th	412	267	–	–	
8th	422	289	–	–	
9th	438	299	–	–	
10th	447	309	–	–	

Umpires: D.R.Shepherd (57) and S.Venkataraghavan (*India*) (47).
Referee: Talat Ali (*Pakistan*) (9).   **Test No. 1553/300 (E785/A618)**

ENGLAND v AUSTRALIA (5th Test)

At Kennington Oval, London, on 23, 24, 25, 26, 27 August 2001.
Toss: Australia. Result: **AUSTRALIA** won by an innings and 25 runs.
Debuts: England – J.Ormond.

AUSTRALIA

M.L.Hayden	c Trescothick b Tufnell	68
J.L.Langer	retired hurt	102
R.T.Ponting	c Atherton b Ormond	62
M.E.Waugh	b Gough	120
*S.R.Waugh	not out	157
†A.C.Gilchrist	c Ramprakash b Afzaal	25
D.R.Martyn	not out	64
S.K.Warne		
B.Lee		
J.N.Gillespie		
G.D.McGrath		
Extras	(B 10, LB 13, W 1, NB 19)	43
Total	**(4 wickets declared)**	**641**

ENGLAND

M.A.Atherton	b Warne	13	c Warne b McGrath	9
M.E.Trescothick	b Warne	55	c and b McGrath	24
M.A.Butcher	c Langer b Warne	25	c S.R.Waugh b Warne	14
*N.Hussain	b M.E.Waugh	52	lbw b Warne	2
M.R.Ramprakash	c Gilchrist b McGrath	133	c Hayden b Warne	19
U.Afzaal	c Gillespie b McGrath	54	c Ponting b McGrath	5
†A.J.Stewart	c Gilchrist b Warne	29	b Warne	34
A.R.Caddick	lbw b Warne	0	b Lee	17
J.Ormond	b Warne	18	c Gilchrist b McGrath	17
D.Gough	st Gilchrist b Warne	24	not out	39
P.C.R.Tufnell	not out	7	c Warne b McGrath	0
Extras	(B 3, LB 13, W 1, NB 5)	22	(LB 2, NB 2)	4
Total		**432**		**184**

ENGLAND	O	M	R	W	O	M	R	W		FALL OF WICKETS		
											A	E	E
Gough	29	4	113	1						*Wkt*	*1st*	*1st*	*2nd*
Caddick	36	9	146	0						1st	158	58	17
Ormond	34	4	115	1						2nd	292	85	46
Tufnell	39	2	174	1						3rd	489	104	48
Butcher	1	0	2	0						4th	534	166	50
Ramprakash	4	0	19	0						5th	–	255	55
Afzaal	9	0	49	1						6th	–	313	95
										7th	–	313	126
AUSTRALIA										8th	–	350	126
McGrath	30	11	67	2	(2) 15.3	6	43	5		9th	–	424	184
Gillespie	20	3	96	0	(5) 12	5	38	0		10th	–	432	184
Warne	44.2	7	165	7	28	8	64	4					
Lee	14	1	43	0	(1) 10	3	30	1					
Ponting	2	0	5	0	(4) 2	0	3	0					
M.E.Waugh	8	0	40	1	1	0	4	0					

Umpires: R.E Koertzen (*South Africa*) (26) and P.Willey (24).
Referee: Talat Ali (*Pakistan*) (10).   **Test No. 1554/301 (E786/A619)**

ENGLAND v AUSTRALIA 2001

ENGLAND – BATTING AND FIELDING

	M	I	NO	HS	Runs	Avge	100	50	Ct/St
M.A.Butcher	5	10	1	173*	456	50.66	1	1	4
M.R.Ramprakash	4	8	–	133	318	39.75	1	–	3
N.Hussain	3	6	1	55	177	35.40	–	2	–
A.J.Stewart	5	9	1	76*	283	35.37	–	2	13
M.E.Trescothick	5	10	–	76	321	32.10	–	3	4
M.A.Atherton	5	10	–	57	221	22.10	–	2	7
U.Afzaal	3	6	1	54	83	16.60	–	1	–
A.R.Caddick	5	9	2	49*	101	14.42	–	–	1
D.Gough	5	9	3	39*	82	13.66	–	–	–
I.J.Ward	3	6	1	23*	68	13.60	–	–	1
C.White	3	6	1	27*	38	7.60	–	–	1
A.J.Tudor	2	3	–	9	14	4.66	–	–	–

Played in one Test: D.G.Cork 24, 2; R.D.B.Croft 3, 0; A.F.Giles 7, 0; A.D.Mullally 0; J.Ormond 18, 17; G.P.Thorpe 20, 2 (1 ct); P.C.R.Tufnell 7*, 0.

ENGLAND – BOWLING

	O	M	R	W	Avge	Best	5wI	10wM
M.A.Butcher	14	4	63	4	15.75	4- 42	–	–
A.J.Tudor	44.5	7	195	7	27.85	5- 44	1	–
D.Gough	155.1	24	657	17	38.64	5-103	1	–
A.D.Mullally	30.3	10	99	2	49.50	1- 34	–	–
A.R.Caddick	177.4	24	748	15	49.86	5-101	1	–

Also bowled: U.Afzaal 9-0-49-1; D.G.Cork 23-3-84-1; R.D.B.Croft 3-0-10-1; A.F.Giles 25-0-108-1; J.Ormond 34-4-115-1; M.R.Ramprakash 8-0-31-0; P.C.R.Tufnell 39-2-174-1; C.White 46.4-7-189-1.

AUSTRALIA – BATTING AND FIELDING

	M	I	NO	HS	Runs	Avge	100	50	Ct/St
S.R.Waugh	4	5	2	157*	321	107.00	2	–	2
M.E.Waugh	5	8	3	120	430	86.00	2	1	9
D.R.Martyn	5	7	2	118	382	76.40	2	2	–
A.C.Gilchrist	5	5	–	152	340	68.00	1	2	24/2
R.T.Ponting	5	8	–	144	338	42.25	1	2	7
M.L.Hayden	5	8	1	68	234	33.42	–	1	4
M.J.Slater	4	7	–	77	170	24.28	–	1	1
J.N.Gillespie	5	4	1	27*	41	13.66	–	–	2
G.D.McGrath	5	4	3	8*	11	11.00	–	–	1
B.Lee	5	4	–	20	24	6.00	–	–	–
S.K.Warne	5	4	–	13	13	3.25	–	–	6

Played in one Test: S.M.Katich 15, 0* (1 ct); J.L.Langer 102* (1 ct).

AUSTRALIA – BOWLING

	O	M	R	W	Avge	Best	5wI	10wM
G.D.McGrath	194.2	56	542	32	16.93	7- 76	4	–
S.K.Warne	195.2	41	580	31	18.70	7-165	3	1
J.N.Gillespie	174	42	652	19	34.31	5- 53	1	–
B.Lee	120.5	18	496	9	55.11	2- 37	–	–

Also bowled: R.T.Ponting 4-0-8-0; M.E.Waugh 13-1-69-1.

ENGLAND v PAKISTAN and AUSTRALIA 2001

BATTING AND FIELDING

† ECB Central Contract 2001

	M	I	NO	HS	Runs	Avge	100	50	Ct/St
†M.P.Vaughan	2	3	–	120	166	55.33	1	–	2
M.A.Butcher	5	10	1	173*	456	50.66	1	1	4
†G.P.Thorpe	3	5	–	138	250	50.00	1	1	6
†N.Hussain	4	7	1	64	241	40.16	–	3	–
M.R.Ramprakash	4	8	–	133	318	39.75	1	–	3
†A.J.Stewart	7	12	2	76*	385	38.50	–	2	23
†M.E.Trescothick	7	13	–	117	484	37.23	1	3	6
†M.A.Atherton	7	13	–	57	319	24.53	–	3	13
J.Ormond	1	2	–	18	35	17.50	–	–	–
U.Afzaal	3	6	1	54	83	16.60	–	1	–
I.J.Ward	5	9	1	39	129	16.12	–	1	1
†D.Gough	7	12	4	39*	110	13.75	–	–	1
†D.G.Cork	3	5	–	25	57	11.40	–	–	1
†A.R.Caddick	7	12	2	49*	107	10.70	–	–	1
†C.White	3	6	1	27*	38	7.60	–	–	1
N.V.Knight	1	2	–	15	15	7.50	–	–	2
P.C.R.Tufnell	1	2	1	7*	7	7.00	–	–	–
A.J.Tudor	2	3	–	9	14	4.66	–	–	–
R.J.Sidebottom	1	1	–	4	4	4.00	–	–	–
†A.F.Giles	1	2	–	7	7	3.50	–	–	1
R.D.B.Croft	1	2	–	3	3	1.50	–	–	–
A.D.Mullally	1	1	–	0	0	0.00	–	–	–
†M.J.Hoggard	1	2	1	0*	0	0.00	–	–	–

BOWLING

	O	M	R	W	Avge	Best	5wI	10wM
R.D.B.Croft	3	–	10	1	10.00	1- 8	–	–
M.A.Butcher	14	4	63	4	15.75	4- 42	–	–
A.J.Tudor	44.5	7	195	7	27.85	5- 44	1	–
†M.J.Hoggard	48	8	172	6	28.66	3- 79	–	–
†D.Gough	233.4	37	937	31	30.22	5- 61	2	–
†A.R.Caddick	262.4	36	1057	29	36.44	5-101	1	–
†D.G.Cork	95.3	20	284	6	47.33	3- 41	–	–
U.Afzaal	9	–	49	1	49.00	1- 49	–	–
A.D.Mullally	30.3	10	99	2	49.50	1- 34	–	–
†A.F.Giles	25	–	108	1	108.00	1-108	–	–
J.Ormond	34	4	115	1	115.00	1-115	–	–
P.C.R.Tufnell	39	2	174	1	174.00	1-174	–	–
†C.White	46.4	7	189	1	189.00	1-101	–	–

Also bowled: M.R.Ramprakash 8-0-31-0; R.J.Sidebottom 20-2-64-0; †M.E.Trescothick 5-1-16-0; †M.P.Vaughan 3-0-33-0.

ZIMBABWE v WEST INDIES (1st Test)

At Queens Sports Club, Bulawayo, on 19, 20, 21, 22 July 2001.
Toss: Zimbabwe. Result: **WEST INDIES** won by an innings and 176 runs.
Debuts: Zimbabwe – T.Taibu.

ZIMBABWE

D.D.Ebrahim	lbw b Collins	0	lbw b Stuart		71
A.D.R.Campbell	c Jacobs b King	21	lbw b McGarrell		103
S.V.Carlisle	c Hooper b Collins	10	absent hurt		–
C.B.Wishart	c Chanderpaul b Stuart	36	lbw b Stuart		4
G.J.Whittall	c Gayle b Stuart	42	not out		10
G.W.Flower	c Jacobs b King	6	c Gayle b McGarrell		2
*H.H.Streak	c Chanderpaul b McGarrell	5	c Sarwan b McGarrell		2
A.M.Blignaut	c Gayle b King	21	c and b McGarrell		9
†T.Taibu	c Sarwan b Stuart	6	(3) lbw b Stuart		4
B.C.Strang	not out	0	(9) c sub (L.V.Garrick) b King		7
R.W.Price	lbw b King	0	(10) c sub (L.V.Garrick) b King		4
Extras	(LB 3, NB 5)	8	(LB 8, NB 4)		12
Total		**155**			**228**

WEST INDIES

D.Ganga	c and b Price	89
C.H.Gayle	c Price b Streak	175
S.Chanderpaul	c Whittall b Streak	7
R.R.Sarwan	c Blignaut b Strang	58
*C.L.Hooper	c Taibu b Strang	149
M.N.Samuels	b Price	42
†R.D.Jacobs	not out	19
N.C.McGarrell	not out	8
C.E.L.Stuart		
P.T.Collins		
R.D.King		
Extras	(B 1, LB 10, NB 1)	12
Total	(6 wickets declared	**559**

WEST INDIES	O	M	R	W	O	M	R	W	FALL OF WICKETS			
King	17	4	51	4	23.4	9	47	2		Z	WI	Z
Collins	13.3	4	29	2	13	1	47	0	Wkt	1st	1st	2nd
Stuart	15.3	3	45	3	(4) 19	5	45	3	1st	1	214	164
McGarrell	12	5	22	1	(3) 24	9	38	4	2nd	31	261	170
Hooper	1	0	5	0	21	6	38	0	3rd	31	289	187
Samuels					1	0	5	0	4th	80	420	193
									5th	105	520	195
ZIMBABWE									6th	119	538	197
Streak	35	8	110	2					7th	139	–	211
Blignaut	30	6	116	0					8th	155	–	218
Strang	45	15	111	2					9th	155	–	228
Price	44	6	157	2					10th	155	–	–
Flower	13	1	52	0								
Whittall	1	0	2	0								

Umpires: Riazuddin (*Pakistan*) (10) and I.D.Robinson (26).
Referee: D.T.Lindsay (*South Africa*) (3). **Test No. 1555/3 (Z53/WI375)**

ZIMBABWE v WEST INDIES (2nd Test)

At Harare Sports Club on 27, 28, 29, 30, 31 July 2001.
Toss: West Indies. Result: **MATCH DRAWN**.
Debuts: Zimbabwe – H.Masakadza.

ZIMBABWE

D.D.Ebrahim	c Browne b King	19	c Browne b Stuart		12
A.D.R.Campbell	lbw b Stuart	13	c Gayle b Hooper		65
H.Masakadza	b Stuart	9	c Hooper b McGarrell		119
C.B.Wishart	lbw b McGarrell	8	run out		93
G.J.Whittall	c Ganga b Black	43	lbw b McGarrell		12
G.W.Flower	c Browne b McGarrell	0	c Chanderpaul b King		15
*H.H.Streak	lbw b McGarrell	6	not out		83
A.M.Blignaut	c Browne b McGarrell	0	b Stuart		92
†T.Taibu	c King b Stuart	9	b Stuart		10
B.C.Strang	c Sarwan b Black	20	c Gayle b McGarrell		13
R.W.Price	not out	0			
Extras	(LB 1, W 2, NB 1)	4	(B 11, LB 21, NB 17)		49
Total		**131**	(9 wickets declared)		**563**

WEST INDIES

D.Ganga	c Taibu b Blignaut	43	c Strang b Streak		5
C.H.Gayle	lbw b Strang	6	not out		52
S.Chanderpaul	c Taibu b Streak	74			
R.R.Sarwan	run out	86	(3) not out		31
*C.L.Hooper	c Streak b Strang	39			
M.N.Samuels	c Campbell b Price	39			
†C.O.Browne	c Taibu b Blignaut	13			
N.C.McGarrell	c sub (T.J.Friend) b Strang	33			
C.E.L.Stuart	lbw b Strang	1			
M.I.Black	b Price	6			
R.D.King	not out	2			
Extras	(LB 2, W 2, NB 1)	5	(B 4, LB 5, W 1)		10
Total		**347**	(1 wicket)		**98**

WEST INDIES	O	M	R	W	O	M	R	W
King	16	6	39	1	27	7	80	1
Black	11.1	2	35	2	17	1	93	0
Stuart	13	2	33	3	(4) 32	9	99	3
McGarrell	17	7	23	4	(3) 60	19	162	3
Hooper					28	7	86	1
Samuels					3	0	11	0
ZIMBABWE								
Streak	22	6	75	1	15.2	4	34	1
Strang	32	13	83	4	(3) 14	8	19	0
Blignaut	16	2	92	2	(2) 8	3	24	0
Price	35.2	13	81	2	8	3	9	0
Flower	6	3	14	0				
Masakadza					(5) 1	0	3	0

FALL OF WICKETS

	Z	WI	Z	WI
Wkt	1st	1st	2nd	2nd
1st	20	14	27	25
2nd	42	114	118	
3rd	43	126	287	
4th	62	180	324	
5th	62	259	333	
6th	62	283	367	
7th	72	333	521	
8th	85	338	535	
9th	116	345	563	
10th	131	347		

Umpires: K.C.Barbour (3) and A.V.Jayaprakash (*India*) (10).
Referee: D.T.Lindsay (*South Africa*) (4). **Test No. 1556/4 (Z54/WI376)**

SRI LANKA v INDIA (1st Test)

At Galle International Stadium on 14, 15, 16, 17 August 2001.
Toss: Sri Lanka. Result: **SRI LANKA** won by ten wickets.
Debuts: None.

INDIA

S.S.Das	c Jayasuriya b Vaas	40	c A.S.A.Perera b P.D.R.L.Perera	23
S.Ramesh	c Jayasuriya b Muralitharan	42	b P.D.R.L.Perera	2
M.Kaif	b Fernando	37	c Tillekeratne b Muralitharan	14
R.Dravid	c Arnold b Muralitharan	12	not out	61
*S.C.Ganguly	c Sangakkara b Fernando	15	b Fernando	4
H.K.Badani	c Sangakkara b Fernando	6	c Sangakkara b Muralitharan	4
†S.S.Dighe	c Sangakkara b Fernando	9	c Arnold b Muralitharan	3
J.Srinath	retired hurt	0	absent hurt	
Harbhajan Singh	b Fernando	4	(8) c and b Muralitharan	12
Z.Khan	not out	2	(9) c Arnold b Jayasuriya	3
B.K.V.Prasad	b Muralitharan	0	(10) lbw b Muralitharan	20
Extras	(B 4, LB 3, W 2, NB 13)	22	(B 12, LB 8, NB 13)	33
Total		**187**		**180**

SRI LANKA

M.S.Atapattu	c Badani b Harbhajan	33	not out	0
*S.T.Jayasuriya	c Dravid b Khan	111	not out	6
†K.Sangakkara	not out	105		
D.P.M.deS.Jayawardena	c Dighe b Srinath	28		
R.P.Arnold	c Ramesh b Prasad	20		
H.P.Tillekeratne	lbw b Srinath	11		
A.S.A.Perera	lbw b Srinath	1		
W.P.U.C.J.Vaas	c Ramesh b Khan	13		
C.R.D.Fernando	c Srinath b Khan	3		
P.D.R.L.Perera	c Dighe b Srinath	0		
M.Muralitharan	c Kaif b Srinath	8		
Extras	(B 1, LB 6, W 8, NB 14)	29		
Total		**362**	(0 wickets)	**6**

SRI LANKA	O	M	R	W	O	M	R	W
Vaas	22	10	38	1	16	2	45	0
Fernando	25	9	42	5	17	4	35	1
P.D.R.L.Perera	12	4	25	0	8	1	21	2
Muralitharan	24.3	8	41	3	26.5	10	49	5
A.S.A.Perera	12	0	34	0				
Jayasuriya					(5) 7	3	10	1
INDIA								
Srinath	24.5	5	114	5	1	1	0	0
Prasad	24	4	83	1				
Khan	26	3	89	3	(2) 0.5	0	6	0
Harbhajan Singh	33	12	69	1				

FALL OF WICKETS	I	SL	I	SL
Wkt	1st	1st	2nd	2nd
1st	79	101	15	–
2nd	105	171	37	–
3rd	124	211	53	–
4th	155	274	64	–
5th	161	292	73	–
6th	176	296	81	–
7th	181	316	104	–
8th	185	340	120	–
9th	187	342	180	–
10th	–	362	–	–

Umpires: S.A.Bucknor (*West Indies*) (59) and E.A.R.de Silva (4).
Referee: C.W.Smith (*West Indies*) (34).   **Test No. 1557/21 (SL112/I342)**

SRI LANKA v INDIA (2nd Test)

At Asgiriya Stadium, Kandy, on 22, 23, 24, 25 August 2001.
Toss: India. Result: **INDIA** won by seven wickets.
Debuts: None.

SRI LANKA

M.S.Atapattu	b Khan	39	c Dighe b Prasad		45
*S.T.Jayasuriya	run out	3	b Khan		6
†K.Sangakkara	c Ramesh b Ganguly	31	c Dighe b Khan		13
D.P.M.deS.Jayawardena	c Dighe b Prasad	104	c Badani b Khan		25
R.P.Arnold	c Dravid b Khan	5	(6) lbw b Khan		4
H.P.Tillekeratne	c Dighe b Prasad	10	(5) lbw b Prasad		16
A.S.A.Perera	lbw b Ganguly	18	c Badani b Prasad		15
W.P.U.C.J.Vaas	b Harvinder Singh	42	lbw b Prasad		4
M.Muralitharan	b Harvinder Singh	5	c Ramesh b Harbhajan		67
C.R.D.Fernando	c Dighe b Khan	4	b Prasad		4
P.D.R.L.Perera	not out	0	not out		6
Extras	(LB 7, W 1, NB 5)	13	(B 4, LB 7, NB 5)		16
Total		**274**			**221**

INDIA

S.S.Das	lbw b Vaas	8	b Muralitharan		19
S.Ramesh	c Sangakkara b Fernando	47	c Jayasuriya b Fernando		31
R.Dravid	lbw b Vaas	15	c Arnold b Muralitharan		75
*S.C.Ganguly	c Tillekeratne b P.D.R.L.Perera	18	not out		98
M.Kaif	c Atapattu b Fernando	17	not out		19
H.K.Badani	c Fernando b P.D.R.L.Perera	16			
†S.S.Dighe	lbw b Vaas	28			
Harbhajan Singh	b Vaas	44			
Z.Khan	c Tillekeratne b Muralitharan	0			
B.K.V.Prasad	not out	1			
Harvinder Singh	b Muralitharan	6			
Extras	(LB 7, W 2, NB 23)	32	(B 4, LB 2, NB 16)		22
Total		**232**	(3 wickets)		**264**

INDIA	O	M	R	W		O	M	R	W
Khan	22	6	62	3		23	4	76	4
Harvinder Singh	14.3	1	62	2		8	1	25	0
Prasad	18	4	52	2		21	7	72	5
Ganguly	17	5	69	2		10	4	21	0
Harbhajan Singh	7	1	22	0		4.3	2	16	1
SRI LANKA									
Vaas	21	3	65	4		20.4	9	42	0
Fernando	14	2	66	2		16	4	64	1
P.D.R.L.Perera	7	2	23	2		9	2	26	0
Muralitharan	20.1	5	62	2		25	2	96	2
A.S.A.Perera	2	0	9	0	(6)	3	0	11	0
Jayasuriya					(5)	3	0	12	0
Arnold						2	0	7	0

FALL OF WICKETS

Wkt	SL 1st	I 1st	SL 2nd	I 2nd
1st	18	11	20	42
2nd	78	36	52	103
3rd	82	68	84	194
4th	101	120	108	–
5th	138	123	116	–
6th	189	154	137	–
7th	232	218	140	–
8th	245	223	157	–
9th	274	223	157	–
10th	274	232	221	–

Umpires: S.A.Bucknor (*West Indies*) (60) and T.H.Wijewardene (1).
Referee: C.W.Smith (*West Indies*) (35).

Test No. 1558/22 (SL113/I343)

SRI LANKA v INDIA (3rd Test)

At Sinhalese Sports Club, Colombo, on 29, 30, 31 August, 1, 2 September 2001.
Toss: India. Result: **SRI LANKA** won by an innings and 77 runs.
Debuts: Sri Lanka – T.T.Samaraweera.

INDIA

S.S.Das	b Muralitharan	59	c Tillekeratne b Muralitharan		68
S.Ramesh	c Jayawardena b Muralitharan	46	b Muralitharan		55
R.Dravid	c Tillekeratne b Muralitharan	36	run out		36
*S.C.Ganguly	lbw b Muralitharan	1	c Jayawardena b Samaraweera		30
M.Kaif	c Sangakkara b Vaas	14	run out		5
H.K.Badani	c Tillekeratne b Muralitharan	38	lbw b Vaas		11
†S.S.Dighe	lbw b Muralitharan	0	(8) run out		4
S.V.Bahutule	st Sangakkara b Muralitharan	18	(7) b Jayasuriya		0
Harbhajan Singh	lbw b Vaas	2	c Atapattu b Vaas		17
Z.Khan	c Jayawardena b Muralitharan	0	c Atapattu b Muralitharan		45
B.K.V.Prasad	not out	10	not out		4
Extras	(B 2, LB 3, W 2, NB 3)	10	(B 8, LB 5, W 2, NB 9)		24
Total		**234**			**299**

SRI LANKA

M.S.Atapattu	c Das b Harbhajan	108
*S.T.Jayasuriya	b Prasad	30
†S.Sangakkara	c Badani b Prasad	47
D.P.M.deS.Jayawardena	lbw b Bahutule	139
R.P.Arnold	b Prasad	31
D.K.Liyanage	c Dighe b Harbhajan	3
H.P.Tillekeratne	not out	136
T.T.Samaraweera	not out	103
W.P.U.C.J.Vaas		
C.R.D.Fernando		
M.Muralitharan		
Extras	(LB 4, W 4, NB 5)	13
Total	(6 wickets declared)	**610**

SRI LANKA	O	M	R	W	O	M	R	W
Vaas	24	7	60	2	27	9	62	2
Liyanage	9	2	32	0	(5) 5	0	12	0
Fernando	12	2	38	0	(2) 17	3	59	0
Muralitharan	34.1	9	87	8	(3) 46.5	17	109	3
Samaraweera	2	0	12	0	(6) 8	4	10	1
Jayasuriya					(4) 21	10	34	1

INDIA	O	M	R	W
Khan	27	3	134	0
Prasad	34	8	101	3
Harbhajan Singh	53.3	6	185	2
Ganguly	12.3	3	44	0
Bahutule	31	5	101	1
Badani	8	2	17	0
Ramesh	5	0	24	0

FALL OF WICKETS			
	I	SL	I
Wkt	1st	1st	2nd
1st	97	47	107
2nd	115	119	147
3rd	119	252	186
4th	146	310	196
5th	192	321	210
6th	192	416	211
7th	207	–	221
8th	210	–	221
9th	213	–	269
10th	234	–	299

Umpires: E.A.R.de Silva (5) and D.L.Orchard (*South Africa*) (24).
Referee: C.W.Smith (*West Indies*) (36).   **Test No. 1559/23 (SL114/I344)**

SRI LANKA v INDIA 2001

SRI LANKA – BATTING AND FIELDING

	M	I	NO	HS	Runs	Avge	100	50	Ct/St
D.P.M.deS.Jayawardena	3	4	–	139	296	74.00	2	–	3
K.Sangakkara	3	4	1	105*	196	65.33	1	–	6/1
H.P.Tillekeratne	3	4	1	136*	173	57.66	1	–	6
M.S.Atapattu	3	5	1	108	225	56.25	1	–	3
S.T.Jayasuriya	3	5	1	111	156	39.00	1	–	3
M.Muralitharan	3	3	–	67	80	26.66	–	1	1
W.P.U.C.J.Vaas	3	3	–	42	59	19.66	–	–	–
R.P.Arnold	3	4	–	31	60	15.00	–	–	4
A.S.A.Perera	2	3	–	18	34	11.33	–	–	1
P.D.R.L.Perera	2	3	2	6*	6	6.00	–	–	–
C.R.D.Fernando	3	3	–	4	11	3.66	–	–	1

Played in one Test: D.K.Liyanage 3; T.T.Samaraweera 103*.

SRI LANKA – BOWLING

	O	M	R	W	Avge	Best	5wI	10wM
M.Muralitharan	177.3	51	444	23	19.30	8-87	2	1
P.D.R.L.Perera	36	9	95	4	23.75	2-21	–	–
S.T.Jayasuriya	31	13	56	2	28.00	1-10	–	–
C.R.D.Fernando	101	24	304	9	33.77	5-42	1	–
W.P.U.C.J.Vaas	130.4	40	312	9	34.66	4-65	–	–

Also bowled: R.P.Arnold 2-0-7-0; A.S.A.Perera 17-0-54-0; D.K.Liyanage 14-2-44-0; T.T.Samaraweera 10-4-22-1.

INDIA – BATTING AND FIELDING

	M	I	NO	HS	Runs	Avge	100	50	Ct/St
R.Dravid	3	6	1	75	235	47.00	–	2	2
S.Ramesh	3	6	–	55	223	37.16	–	1	4
S.S.Das	3	6	–	68	217	36.16	–	2	1
S.C.Ganguly	3	6	1	98*	166	33.20	–	1	–
M.Kaif	3	6	1	37	106	21.20	–	–	1
B.K.V.Prasad	3	5	3	20	35	17.50	–	–	–
Harbhajan Singh	3	5	–	44	79	15.80	–	–	–
H.K.Badani	3	5	–	38	76	15.20	–	–	4
Z.Khan	3	5	1	45	48	12.00	–	–	–
S.S.Dighe	3	5	–	28	44	8.80	–	–	8

Played in one Test: S.V.Bahutule 18, 0; Harvinder Singh 6; J.Srinath 0* (1 ct).

INDIA – BOWLING

	O	M	R	W	Avge	Best	5wI	10wM
J.Srinath	25.5	6	114	5	22.80	5-114	1	–
B.K.V.Prasad	97	23	308	11	28.00	5- 72	1	–
Z.Khan	98.5	16	367	10	36.70	4- 76	–	–
Harvinder Singh	22.3	2	87	2	43.50	2- 62	–	–
S.C.Ganguly	39.3	12	134	2	67.00	2- 69	–	–
Harbhajan Singh	98	21	292	4	73.00	2-185	–	–

Also bowled: H.K.Badani 8-2-17-0; S.V.Bahutule 31-5-101-1; S.Ramesh 5-0-24-0.

PAKISTAN v BANGLADESH
(Asian Test Championship – 1st Match)

At Multan Cricket Stadium on 29, 30, 31 August 2001.
Toss: Bangladesh. Result: **PAKISTAN** won by an innings and 264 runs.
Pakistan 24 points, Bangladesh 0.
Debuts: Pakistan – Shoaib Malik, Taufiq Umar.

BANGLADESH

Batsman	Dismissal 1		Dismissal 2	
Javed Omar	c Shoaib b Waqar	12	c Abdul b Waqar	4
Mehrab Hossain	c Faisal b Kaneria	19	c Rashid b Waqar	9
Habibul Bashar	c Rashid b Waqar	13	not out	56
Aminul Islam	b Shoaib	10	c sub (Younis Khan) b Kaneria	18
Akram Khan	c Youhana b Kaneria	12	c sub (Younis Khan) b Kaneria	8
*Naimur Rahman	c Faisal b Kaneria	8	c sub (Younis Khan) b Kaneria	4
†Khaled Masud	lbw b Kaneria	4	c and b Kaneria	0
Enamul Haque	c Waqar b Kaneria	14	c Youhana b Kaneria	7
Hasibul Hossain	c Taufiq b Kaneria	18	c sub (Younis Khan) b Kaneria	31
Mohammed Sharif	b Shoaib	13	c Rashid b Waqar	3
Manjural Islam	not out	0	b Waqar	2
Extras	(LB 5, W 1, NB 5)	11	(LB 3, NB 3)	6
Total		**134**		**148**

PAKISTAN

Saeed Anwar	c Hasibul b Sharif	101
Taufiq Umar	c Masud b Hasibul	104
Faisal Iqbal	b Sharif	9
Inzamam-ul-Haq	retired ill	105
Yousuf Youhana	not out	102
Abdul Razzaq	not out	110
†Rashid Latif		
Wasim Akram		
*Waqar Younis		
Shoaib Malik		
Danish Kaneria		
Extras	(B 1, LB 3, W 3, NB 8)	15
Total	(3 wickets declared)	**546**

PAKISTAN	O	M	R	W	O	M	R	W
Wasim Akram	10	2	17	0	9	1	32	0
Waqar Younis	6	0	25	2	7.1	1	19	4
Abdul Razzaq	8	1	27	0	8	0	34	0
Danish Kaneria	13	3	42	6	15	3	52	6
Shoaib Malik	4.1	0	18	2	2	0	8	0

BANGLADESH	O	M	R	W
Manjural Islam	19	2	103	0
Mohammed Sharif	24.5	4	110	2
Hasibul Hossain	31	5	145	1
Naimur Rahman	19	1	77	0
Enamul Haque	16	1	78	0
Aminul Islam	4	0	17	0
Javed Omar	1	0	12	0

FALL OF WICKETS			
	B	P	B
Wkt	1st	1st	2nd
1st	20	168	5
2nd	50	178	22
3rd	55	258	52
4th	67	–	72
5th	76	–	84
6th	83	–	84
7th	101	–	96
8th	107	–	141
9th	134	–	144
10th	134	–	148

Umpires: D.B.Hair (*Australia*) (39) and P.T.Manuel (*Sri Lanka*) (9).
Referee: J.R.Reid (*New Zealand*) (48).

Test No. 1560/1 (P279/B4)

SRI LANKA v BANGLADESH
(Asian Test Championship – 2nd Match)

At Sinhalese Sports Club, Colombo, on 6, 7, 8 September 2001.
Toss: Sri Lanka. Result: **SRI LANKA** won by an innings and 137 runs.
Sri Lanka 24 points, Bangladesh 0.
Debuts: Sri Lanka – M.G.Vandort; Bangladesh – Mohammed Ashraful.

BANGLADESH

Javed Omar	c Jayasuriya b Vaas	7		lbw b Muralitharan	40
Mehrab Hossain	run out	23		lbw b Muralitharan	4
Habibul Bashar	c Vaas	4	(5)	c Jayawardena b Muralitharan	19
Aminul Islam	c Sangakkara b Perera	6		b Jayasuriya	56
Al Sahariar	c Sangakkara b Muralitharan	16	(3)	lbw b Samaraweera	7
*Naimur Rahman	b Muralitharan	0	(7)	c Atapattu b Perera	48
Mohammed Ashraful	c Jayasuriya b Muralitharan	26	(6)	c and b Perera	114
†Khaled Masud	b Muralitharan	0		lbw b Muralitharan	3
Hasibul Hossain	b Muralitharan	2		c Sangakkara b Perera	0
Mohammed Sharif	c Vandort b Vaas	1		c and b Muralitharan	19
Manjural Islam	not out	3		not out	1
Extras	(LB 1, NB 1)	2		(B 5, LB 5, NB 7)	17
Total		**90**			**328**

SRI LANKA

M.S.Atapattu	retired	201
*S.T.Jayasuriya	lbw b Naimur	89
†K.Sangakkara	c Aminul b Hasibul	54
D.P.M.deS.Jayawardena	retired	150
M.G.Vandort	c Manjural b Naimur	36
H.P.Tillekeratne	not out	10
T.T.Samaraweera		
M.Muralitharan		
K.R.Pushpakumara		
W.P.U.C.J.Vaas		
P.D.R.L.Perera		
Extras	(LB 5, W 2, NB 8)	15
Total	(5 wickets declared)	**555**

SRI LANKA	O	M	R	W		O	M	R	W
Vaas	14.2	2	47	3		16	2	71	0
Pushpakumara	7	4	9	0		8	5	15	0
Perera	5	1	17	1	(4)	13	3	40	3
Muralitharan	9.4	4	13	5	(3)	35.3	6	98	5
Samaraweera	1	0	3	0		13	2	42	1
Jayasuriya						16	2	52	1

FALL OF WICKETS			
	B	SL	B
Wkt	1st	1st	2nd
1st	10	144	31
2nd	16	269	54
3rd	29	440	54
4th	57	530	81
5th	58	555	207
6th	61	–	303
7th	61	–	308
8th	67	–	308
9th	72	–	314
10th	90	–	328

BANGLADESH	O	M	R	W
Manjural Islam	18	1	94	0
Mohammed Sharif	17	0	120	0
Hasibul Hossain	23	6	122	1
Naimur Rahman	30.3	8	117	2
Mohammed Ashraful	10	0	63	0
Habibul Bashar	5	0	34	0

Umpires: R.E.Koertzen (*South Africa*) (27) and Mian Mohammad Aslam (*Pakistan*) (7).
Referee: J.R.Reid (*New Zealand*) (49). **Test No. 1561/1 (SL115/B5)**

ZIMBABWE v SOUTH AFRICA (1st Test)

At Harare Sports Club on 7, 8, 9, 10, 11 September 2001.
Toss: South Africa. Result: **SOUTH AFRICA** won by nine wickets.
Debuts: Zimbabwe – D.T.Hondo; South Africa – C.W.Henderson, A.Nel.

SOUTH AFRICA

H.H.Gibbs	b Friend	147		
G.Kirsten	c A.Flower b Hondo	220	not out	31
J.H.Kallis	not out	157	not out	42
N.D.McKenzie	c Hondo b Friend	52		
L.Klusener	not out	8		
H.H.Dippenaar			(1) lbw b Friend	0
†M.V.Boucher				
*S.M.Pollock				
C.W.Henderson				
M.Ntini				
A.Nel				
Extras	(LB 2, W 6, NB 8)	16	(B 5, LB 1)	6
Total	(3 wickets declared)	**600**	(1 wicket)	**79**

ZIMBABWE

D.D.Ebrahim	st Boucher b Henderson	71	lbw b Pollock	0
A.D.R.Campbell	c Boucher b Nel	0	b Kallis	7
H.Masakadza	run out	13	c Dippenaar b Henderson	85
C.B.Wishart	c Klusener b Kallis	0	c Klusener b Pollock	6
†A.Flower	lbw b Pollock	142	not out	199
R.W.Price	c Kirsten b Nel	0	(10) c McKenzie b Klusener	4
G.W.Flower	c Dippenaar b Nel	0	(6) c Dippenaar b Ntini	16
G.J.Whittall	b Kallis	16	(7) lbw b Henderson	3
*H.H.Streak	lbw b Henderson	7	(8) c Kallis b Pollock	19
T.J.Friend	c Pollock b Nel	30	(9) b Klusener	17
D.T.Hondo	not out	1	lbw b Nel	6
Extras	(B 4, NB 2)	6	(B 10, LB 9, NB 10)	29
Total		**286**		**391**

ZIMBABWE	O	M	R	W		O	M	R	W
Streak	34	4	120	0	(2)	4	2	10	0
Friend	27	2	147	2	(1)	7	0	44	1
Hondo	18	0	87	1	(4)	1	1	0	0
Price	42	2	192	0	(3)	3.2	0	19	0
Whittall	12	2	34	0					
G.W.Flower	6	0	18	0					

SOUTH AFRICA	O	M	R	W		O	M	R	W
Pollock	22.3	5	62	1		29	6	67	3
Nel	16	6	53	4		14.5	5	33	1
Ntini	13	2	60	0	(5)	23	10	48	1
Kallis	12	1	39	2	(3)	21	4	52	1
Henderson	24	5	55	2	(4)	55	16	122	2
Klusener	3	0	13	0		29	9	50	2

FALL OF WICKETS

Wkt	1st SA	1st Z	2nd Z	2nd SA
1st	256	2	0	–
2nd	455	43	18	–
3rd	582	51	25	–
4th	–	133	211	–
5th	–	143	243	–
6th	–	143	260	–
7th	–	188	287	–
8th	–	207	326	–
9th	–	282	344	–
10th	–	286	391	–

Umpires: D.B.Hair (*Australia*) (40) and R.B.Tiffin (21).
Referee: Naushad Ali (*Pakistan*) (4).   **Test No. 1562/4 (Z55/SA257)**

ZIMBABWE v SOUTH AFRICA (2nd Test)

At Queens Sports Club, Bulawayo, on 14, 15 (*no play*), 16, 17, 18 September 2001.
Toss: Zimbabwe. Result: **MATCH DRAWN**.
Debuts: None.

ZIMBABWE

A.D.R.Campbell	c Gibbs b Klusener	77	c Dippenaar b Henderson		20
D.D.Ebrahim	c Pollock b Henderson	71	b Henderson		4
H.Masakadza	c Boucher b Nel	13	not out		42
S.V.Carlisle	lbw b Pollock	49	c Ntini b Henderson		4
†A.Flower	c McKenzie b Henderson	67	not out		14
G.W.Flower	run out	44			
G.J.Whittall	c Pollock b Henderson	16			
*H.H.Streak	c Klusener b Henderson	31			
P.A.Strang	not out	38			
T.J.Friend	b Pollock	4			
R.W.Price	not out	0			
Extras	(LB 8, NB 1)	9	(B 4, LB 4, NB 4)		12
Total	**(9 wickets declared)**	**419**	**(3 wickets)**		**96**

SOUTH AFRICA

H.H.Gibbs	c A.Flower b Price	74
G.Kirsten	st A.Flower b Price	65
J.H.Kallis	not out	189
N.D.McKenzie	lbw b Friend	88
H.H.Dippenaar	c G.W.Flower b Price	11
L.Klusener	c Campbell b Price	27
*S.M.Pollock	c Carlisle b Price	41
†M.V.Boucher	b Friend	14
C.W.Henderson	b Friend	0
M.Ntini		
A.Nel		
Extras	(B 3, LB 7)	10
Total	**(8 wickets declared)**	**519**

SOUTH AFRICA	O	M	R	W		O	M	R	W
Pollock	28	14	40	2		4	1	8	0
Nel	21	3	73	1		3	0	9	0
Ntini	25	9	68	0	(4)	3	0	11	0
Klusener	37	10	87	1	(5)	12	7	21	0
Henderson	67	24	143	4	(3)	18	11	33	3
Kirsten						2	1	6	0

ZIMBABWE	O	M	R	W
Streak	25	9	64	0
Friend	30.2	9	87	3
Strang	14.2	2	52	0
Price	79	19	181	5
Whittall	29.4	6	80	0
G.W.Flower	8	0	45	0

FALL OF WICKETS

	Z	SA	Z
Wkt	1st	1st	2nd
1st	152	117	21
2nd	154	162	38
3rd	175	343	58
4th	261	368	–
5th	327	418	–
6th	330	490	–
7th	377	513	–
8th	377	519	–
9th	406	–	–
10th	–	–	–

Umpires: K.C.Barbour (4) and J.H.Hampshire (*England*) (18).
Referee: Naushad Ali (*Pakistan*) (5).　　　　　　　Test No. 1563/5 (Z56/SA258)

SOUTH AFRICA v INDIA (1st Test)

At Springbok Park, Bloemfontein, on 3, 4, 5, 6 November.
Toss: South Africa. Result: **SOUTH AFRICA** won by nine wickets.
Debuts: India – D.Dasgupta, V.Sehwag.

INDIA

S.S.Das	b Hayward	9	c Boucher b Hayward	62
R.Dravid	c Kallis b Pollock	2	c Kirsten b Pollock	11
V.V.S.Laxman	c Boucher b Hayward	32	c Kallis b Pollock	29
S.R.Tendulkar	c McKenzie b Ntini	155	c Gibbs b Kallis	15
*S.C.Ganguly	c Kirsten b Kallis	14	c Boucher b Ntini	30
V.Sehwag	b Pollock	105	b Pollock	31
†D.Dasgupta	c Boucher b Pollock	34	c Boucher b Pollock	4
A.Kumble	c Boucher b Kallis	6	lbw b Hayward	4
J.Srinath	c Gibbs b Hayward	1	c McKenzie b Pollock	16
Z.Khan	c Boucher b Pollock	0	c Boucher b Pollock	0
A.Nehra	not out	0	not out	17
Extras	(LB 7, W 7, NB 7)	21	(B 4, LB 8, NB 6)	18
Total		**379**		**237**

SOUTH AFRICA

H.H.Gibbs	c Khan b Srinath	107	lbw b Kumble	1
G.Kirsten	b Kumble	73	not out	30
J.H.Kallis	c Laxman b Nehra	68	not out	21
N.D.McKenzie	lbw b Kumble	68		
H.H.Dippenaar	b Srinath	20		
L.Klusener	c and b Kumble	108		
*S.M.Pollock	c Das b Srinath	0		
†M.V.Boucher	c Dravid b Srinath	47		
N.Boje	c Dasgupta b Nehra	6		
M.Ntini	c Dasgupta b Srinath	23		
M.Hayward	not out	0		
Extras	(B 12, LB 6, W 4, NB 16, P 5)	43	(NB 2)	2
Total		**563**	(1 wicket)	**54**

SOUTH AFRICA	O	M	R	W		O	M	R	W	FALL OF WICKETS				
Pollock	27	8	91	4		21.4	10	56	6		I	SA	I	SA
Hayward	20.3	5	70	3		23	8	74	2	Wkt	1st	1st	2nd	2nd
Kallis	22	6	87	2		15	3	56	1	1st	7	189	29	6
Ntini	14.4	2	71	1		10	3	39	1	2nd	43	197	108	–
Klusener	6	1	32	0						3rd	51	327	108	–
Boje	5	1	21	0						4th	68	359	154	–
										5th	288	377	188	–
INDIA										6th	351	377	195	–
Srinath	33	6	140	5		5	1	13	0	7th	372	498	202	–
Nehra	22	3	121	2	(3)	3	0	9	0	8th	378	517	206	–
Khan	26	7	98	0	(4)	2.4	0	9	0	9th	379	548	206	–
Kumble	50	12	132	3	(2)	4	0	23	1	10th	379	563	237	–
Tendulkar	7	0	27	0										
Sehwag	5	0	22	0										

Umpires: E.A.R.de Silva (*Sri Lanka*) (6) and D.L.Orchard (25).
Referee: M.H.Denness (*England*) (11).   **Test No. 1564/13 (SA259/I345)**

SOUTH AFRICA v INDIA (2nd Test)

At St George's Park, Port Elizabeth, on 16, 17, 18, 19, 20 November.
Toss: India. Result: **MATCH DRAWN**.
Debuts: None.

SOUTH AFRICA

H.H.Gibbs	c Sehwag b Tendulkar	196	b Agarkar		12
G.Kirsten	c Laxman b Srinath	4	c Laxman b Srinath		5
J.H.Kallis	b Srinath	24	not out		89
N.D.McKenzie	b Harbhajan	12	c Dasgupta b Srinath		2
H.H.Dippenaar	c Dasgupta b Agarkar	29	c Sehwag b Harbhajan		28
L.Klusener	c Laxman b Srinath	9	c Sehwag b Harbhajan		29
*S.M.Pollock	c Harbhajan b Srinath	3	not out		55
†M.V.Boucher	not out	68			
N.Boje	lbw b Kumble	1			
M.Ntini	c Das b Srinath	10			
M.Hayward	b Srinath	0			
Extras	(LB 2, NB 4)	6	(B 3, LB 3, NB 7)		13
Total		**362**	(5 wickets declared)		**233**

INDIA

S.S.Das	lbw b Pollock	1	c Boucher b Pollock		0
†D.Dasgupta	b Ntini	13	c Kallis b Hayward		63
R.Dravid	b Pollock	2	c Boucher b Hayward		87
S.R.Tendulkar	c Klusener b Pollock	1	not out		22
*S.C.Ganguly	b Pollock	42	not out		4
V.V.S.Laxman	lbw b Pollock	89			
V.Sehwag	c Kirsten b Kallis	13			
A.B.Agarkar	c Boucher b Kallis	1			
Harbhajan Singh	run out	0			
A.Kumble	c Kirsten b Hayward	28			
J.Srinath	not out	0			
Extras	(LB 3, W 2, NB 6)	11	(B 10, LB 7, W 1, NB 12)		30
Total		**201**	(3 wickets)		**206**

INDIA	O	M	R	W		O	M	R	W		FALL OF WICKETS				
												SA	I	SA	I
Srinath	30	6	76	6		17	9	28	2		Wkt	1st	1st	2nd	2nd
Agarkar	22	2	85	1		23	3	71	1		1st	17	5	14	0
Ganguly	2	0	21	0		5	0	17	0		2nd	87	13	22	171
Kumble	29	10	67	1	(6)	9	0	22	0		3rd	116	15	26	184
Harbhajan Singh	34	6	89	1		20	2	79	2		4th	221	47	91	—
Tendulkar	4	0	22	1	(4)	4	0	10	0		5th	230	69	139	—
											6th	244	111	—	—
SOUTH AFRICA											7th	324	119	—	—
Pollock	16	3	40	5		26	11	39	1		8th	325	119	—	—
Hayward	17	5	45	1		25	6	58	2		9th	353	199	—	—
Ntini	14	3	49	1	(4)	12	4	25	0		10th	362	201	—	—
Kallis	10	2	50	2	(3)	11.2	5	15	0						
Boje	4	2	8	0		14	4	33	0						
Klusener	1	0	6	0		7	3	15	0						
McKenzie						1	0	4	0						

Umpires: I.L.Howell (2) and R.B.Tiffin (*Zimbabwe*) (22).
Referee: M.H.Denness (*England*) (12).   **Test No. 1565/14 (SA260/I346)**

AUSTRALIA v NEW ZEALAND (1st Test)

At Woolloongabba, Brisbane, on 8, 9, 10, 11, 12 November.
Toss: New Zealand. Result: **MATCH DRAWN**.
Debuts: None.

AUSTRALIA

J.L.Langer	c Vettori b McMillan	104	(4) not out		18
M.L.Hayden	c Richardson b Cairns	136	run out		13
R.T.Ponting	c Vettori b Cairns	5	not out		32
M.E.Waugh	lbw b Astle	0			
*S.R.Waugh	c Parore b McMillan	3			
D.R.Martyn	c Vettori b McMillan	4			
†A.C.Gilchrist	c sub (L.Vincent) b Cairns	118	(1) b Cairns		20
S.K.Warne	c Sinclair b Cairns	22			
B.Lee	c Parore b Cairns	61			
J.N.Gillespie	not out	20			
G.D.McGrath					
Extras	(LB 4, W 1, NB 8)	13	(NB 1)		1
Total	**(9 wickets declared)**	**486**	**(2 wickets declared)**		**84**

NEW ZEALAND

M.H.Richardson	lbw b Gillespie	26	lbw b Warne		57
M.D.Bell	c Ponting b Gillespie	6	lbw b McGrath		5
M.S.Sinclair	c Ponting b Lee	3	st Gilchrist b Warne		23
*S.P.Fleming	c Gilchrist b Gillespie	0	run out		57
N.J.Astle	c Gilchrist b Lee	66	c Gillespie b Warne		49
C.D.McMillan	c Warne b Lee	45	(7) not out		23
C.L.Cairns	c S.R.Waugh b Lee	61	(6) c Ponting b Lee		43
†A.C.Parore	c S.R.Waugh b Lee	11	not out		3
D.J.Nash	not out	25			
D.L.Vettori	not out	3			
S.B.O'Connor					
Extras	(LB 15, NB 26)	41	(B 1, LB 9, W 1, NB 3)		14
Total	**(8 wickets declared)**	**287**	**(6 wickets)**		**274**

NEW ZEALAND	O	M	R	W		O	M	R	W
Cairns	37	8	146	5		5	1	29	1
Nash	30	6	93	0					
O'Connor	17.2	4	67	0					
Vettori	13.4	0	65	0	(3)	2	0	8	0
Astle	19	7	46	1					
McMillan	14	1	65	3	(2)	7	0	47	0
AUSTRALIA									
McGrath	26	6	80	0	(3)	20	4	66	1
Gillespie	18.4	6	54	3		8	0	48	0
Lee	23	6	67	5	(1)	10	0	53	1
Warne	18	2	61	0		18	2	89	3
Ponting	3	0	8	0					
M.E.Waugh					(5)	1	0	8	0

FALL OF WICKETS				
	A	NZ	A	NZ
Wkt	1st	1st	2nd	2nd
1st	224	36	30	33
2nd	233	51	39	89
3rd	235	51	–	90
4th	256	55	–	190
5th	260	147	–	213
6th	263	242	–	264
7th	302	243	–	–
8th	437	271	–	–
9th	486	–	–	–
10th	–	–	–	–

Umpires: S.A.Bucknor (*West Indies*) (61) and D.J.Harper (14).
Referee: J.L.Hendriks (*West Indies*) (14).   **Test No. 1566/39 (A620/NZ289)**

AUSTRALIA v NEW ZEALAND (2nd Test)

At Bellerive Oval, Hobart, on 22, 23, 24, 25, 26 November.
Toss: New Zealand. Result: **MATCH DRAWN.**
Debut: New Zealand – S.E.Bond.

AUSTRALIA

J.L.Langer	c Vettori b Cairns	123
M.L.Hayden	c Bond b Vettori	91
R.T.Ponting	not out	157
M.E.Waugh	b Vettori	12
*S.R.Waugh	lbw b Bond	0
D.R.Martyn	lbw b Vettori	0
†A.C.Gilchrist	b Vettori	39
S.K.Warne	b Astle	70
B.Lee	c McMillan b Vettori	41
J.N.Gillespie		
G.D.McGrath		
Extras	(B 3, LB 5, W 2, NB 15)	25
Total	(8 wickets declared)	**558**

NEW ZEALAND

M.H.Richardson	lbw b Gillespie	30
M.D.Bell	c Gilchrist b Warne	4
M.S.Sinclair	b Gillespie	23
*S.P.Fleming	lbw b McGrath	71
N.J.Astle	c Warne b M.E.Waugh	11
C.D.McMillan	b Gillespie	55
C.L.Cairns	c Gilchrist b McGrath	20
†A.C.Parore	not out	10
D.L.Vettori	not out	10
D.R.Tuffey		
S.E.Bond		
Extras	(LB 1, NB 8)	9
Total	(7 wickets)	**243**

NEW ZEALAND	O	M	R	W
Cairns	28	3	122	1
Tuffey	15	1	74	0
Bond	28	0	135	1
Vettori	36	5	138	5
McMillan	8	0	51	0
Astle	9	0	30	1
AUSTRALIA				
McGrath	27	12	46	2
Gillespie	28	14	45	3
Warne	24.2	3	70	1
Lee	19	5	51	0
M.E.Waugh	7	1	30	1

FALL OF WICKETS

	A	NZ
Wkt	1st	1st
1st	223	11
2nd	238	53
3rd	253	76
4th	266	100
5th	267	197
6th	336	219
7th	481	223
8th	558	–
9th	–	–
10th	–	–

Umpires: S.A.Bucknor (*West Indies*) (62) and S.J.Davis (5).
Referee: J.L.Hendriks (*West Indies*) (15).   **Test No. 1567/40 (A621/NZ290)**

AUSTRALIA v NEW ZEALAND (3rd Test)

At W.A.C.A. Ground, Perth, on 30 November, 1, 2, 3, 4 December.
Toss: New Zealand. Result: **MATCH DRAWN.**
Debut: New Zealand – L.Vincent.

NEW ZEALAND

M.H.Richardson	b Gillespie	9		run out	30
L.Vincent	c M.E.Waugh b Warne	104		c M.E.Waugh b Lee	54
M.S.Sinclair	lbw b McGrath	2		c Gilchrist b McGrath	29
*S.P.Fleming	lbw b Lee	105	(5)	b Warne	4
N.J.Astle	not out	156	(6)	c Langer b Gillespie	40
C.D.McMillan	lbw b Gillespie	4	(7)	c Warne b Gillespie	19
D.L.Vettori	c Martyn b Gillespie	2	(9)	c S.R.Waugh b Lee	3
C.L.Cairns	c Gilchrist b Lee	8	(4)	c Warne b Lee	42
†A.C.Parore	c McGrath b Lee	110	(8)	not out	16
S.E.Bond	b Lee	0		b Lee	8
C.S.Martin					
Extras	(B 4, LB 15, W 2, NB 13)	34		(B 1, LB 6, NB 4)	11
Total	(9 wickets declared)	**534**		(9 wickets declared)	**256**

AUSTRALIA

J.L.Langer	c Parore b Cairns	75		c Vettori b Bond	0
M.L.Hayden	c Vincent b Bond	0		c Sinclair b Vettori	57
R.T.Ponting	c Parore b Martin	31		b Cairns	26
M.E.Waugh	c Bond b Vettori	42		b McMillan	86
*S.R.Waugh	c Parore b Vettori	8		run out	67
D.R.Martyn	c Fleming b Cairns	60		b Vettori	30
†A.C.Gilchrist	c Richardson b Vettori	0		not out	83
S.K.Warne	c Richardson b Vettori	99		run out	10
B.Lee	c McMillan b Vettori	17			
J.N.Gillespie	c Parore b Vettori	0	(10)	not out	1
G.D.McGrath	not out	0			
Extras	(LB 2, W 1, NB 16)	19		(LB 3, W 2, NB 16)	21
Total		**351**		(7 wickets)	**381**

AUSTRALIA	O	M	R	W		O	M	R	W
McGrath	27	11	72	1		17	4	63	1
Gillespie	40	7	112	3		17	0	55	2
Lee	32.5	5	125	4		16	3	56	4
Warne	43	9	135	1		21	3	75	1

NEW ZEALAND	O	M	R	W		O	M	R	W
Cairns	23	5	86	2	(4)	15	2	72	1
Bond	18	2	74	1	(1)	21	3	80	1
Martin	23	4	88	1	(2)	12	0	51	0
Vettori	34.4	7	87	6	(3)	45	11	142	2
Astle	5	1	14	0		12	5	18	0
McMillan						5	2	15	1

FALL OF WICKETS

	NZ	A	NZ	A
Wkt	1st	1st	2nd	2nd
1st	12	3	77	1
2nd	19	61	90	52
3rd	218	122	128	130
4th	264	137	151	195
5th	269	191	199	244
6th	272	192	208	339
7th	281	270	241	355
8th	534	342	246	–
9th	534	346	256	–
10th	–	351	–	–

Umpires: D.B.Hair (41) and I.D.Robinson (*Zimbabwe*) (27).
Referee: J.L.Hendriks (*West Indies*) (16).   **Test No. 1568/41 (A622/NZ291)**

265

AUSTRALIA v NEW ZEALAND 2001-02

AUSTRALIA – BATTING AND FIELDING

	M	I	NO	HS	Runs	Avge	100	50	Ct/St
R.T.Ponting	3	5	2	157*	251	83.66	1	–	3
J.L.Langer	3	5	1	123	320	80.00	2	1	1
A.C.Gilchrist	3	5	1	118	260	65.00	1	–	6/1
M.L.Hayden	3	5	–	136	297	59.40	1	2	–
S.K.Warne	3	4	–	99	201	50.25	–	2	4
B.Lee	3	3	–	61	119	39.66	–	1	–
M.E.Waugh	3	4	–	86	140	35.00	–	1	2
D.R.Martyn	3	4	–	60	94	23.50	–	1	1
J.N.Gillespie	3	3	2	20*	21	21.00	–	–	1
S.R.Waugh	3	4	–	67	78	19.50	–	1	3
G.D.McGrath	3	1	1	0*	0	0.00	–	–	1

AUSTRALIA – BOWLING

	O	M	R	W	Avge	Best	5wI	10wM
B.Lee	100.5	19	352	14	25.14	5-67	1	–
J.N.Gillespie	111.4	27	316	11	28.72	3-45	–	–
G.D.McGrath	117	37	327	5	65.40	2-46	–	–
S.K.Warne	124.2	19	430	6	71.66	3-89	–	–

Also bowled: D.R.Martyn 10-0-44-0; R.T.Ponting 7-3-9-0; M.E.Waugh 14-2-64-1.

NEW ZEALAND – BATTING AND FIELDING

	M	I	NO	HS	Runs	Avge	100	50	Ct/St
N.J.Astle	3	5	1	156*	322	80.50	1	1	–
A.C.Parore	3	5	3	110	150	75.00	1	–	6
S.P.Fleming	3	5	–	105	237	47.40	1	2	1
C.D.McMillan	3	5	1	55	146	36.50	–	1	2
C.L.Cairns	3	5	–	61	174	34.80	–	1	–
M.H.Richardson	3	5	–	57	152	30.40	–	1	3
M.S.Sinclair	3	5	–	29	80	16.00	–	–	2
D.L.Vettori	3	4	2	10*	18	9.00	–	–	5
M.D.Bell	2	3	–	6	15	5.00	–	–	–
S.E.Bond	2	2	–	8	8	4.00	–	–	2

Played in one Test: D.J.Nash 25; L.Vincent 104, 54 (1 ct). S.B.O'Connor, D.R.Tuffey and C.S.Martin did not bat.*

NEW ZEALAND – BOWLING

	O	M	R	W	Avge	Best	5wI	10wM
D.L.Vettori	131.2	23	440	13	33.84	6- 87	2	–
C.D.McMillan	34	3	178	4	44.50	3- 65	–	–
C.L.Cairns	108	19	455	10	45.50	5-146	1	–
N.J.Astle	45	13	108	2	54.00	1- 30	–	–
S.E.Bond	67	5	289	3	96.33	1- 74	–	–

Also bowled: C.S.Martin 35-4-139-1; D.J.Nash 30-6-93-0; S.B.O'Connor 17.2-4-67-0; D.R.Tuffey 15-1-74-0.

BANGLADESH v ZIMBABWE (1st Test)

At Bangabandhu National Stadium, Dhaka, on 8, 9, 10, 11 (*no play*), 12 November.
Toss: Zimbabwe. Result: **MATCH DRAWN.**
Debuts: Bangladesh – Khaled Mahmud, Mashrafe Bin Mortaza.

BANGLADESH

Javed Omar	b Streak	3	c Olonga b Marillier	35
Al Sahariar	lbw b Friend	4	c G.W.Flower b Friend	5
Habibul Bashar	c A.Flower b Friend	0	c Murphy b Friend	65
Aminul Islam	lbw b Olonga	12	not out	6
Mohammed Ashraful	c Wishart b Olonga	0	not out	0
Khaled Mahmud	c Gripper b Friend	6		
*Naimur Rahman	b Friend	13		
†Khaled Masud	c Carlisle b Friend	6		
Mashrafe Bin Mortaza	c A.Flower b Streak	8		
Enamul Haque	not out	24		
Manjural Islam	c Gripper b Olonga	9		
Extras	(B 3, LB 3, W 1, NB 15)	22	(B 3, LB 1, NB 10)	14
Total		**107**	(3 wickets)	**125**

ZIMBABWE

D.D.Ebrahim	lbw b Manjural	3
T.R.Gripper	c Omar b Manjural	0
S.V.Carlisle	c Masud b Mashrafe	33
G.W.Flower	c Al Sahariar b Mashrafe	10
†A.Flower	b Enamul	28
C.B.Wishart	run out	94
D.A.Marillier	lbw b Enamul	73
H.H.Streak	c Masud b Mashrafe	65
T.J.Friend	b Enamul	81
*B.A.Murphy	c Habibul b Mashrafe	25
H.K.Olonga	not out	2
Extras	(B 4, LB 7, W 4, NB 2)	17
Total		**431**

ZIMBABWE	O	M	R	W	O	M	R	W
Streak	18	8	30	2	11	4	25	0
Friend	18	7	31	5	11.4	2	26	2
Olonga	6.2	0	18	3	5	1	17	0
Murphy	6	1	22	0	12	4	37	0
Marillier					7	2	16	1

BANGLADESH	O	M	R	W
Manjural Islam	26	5	74	2
Mashrafe Bin Mortaza	32	8	106	4
Khaled Mahmud	15	2	59	0
Enamul Haque	43	13	74	3
Naimur Rahman	18	1	56	0
Mohammed Ashraful	15	3	49	0
Aminul Islam	1	0	2	0

FALL OF WICKETS			
	B	Z	B
Wkt	1st	1st	2nd
1st	6	3	6
2nd	6	4	108
3rd	11	31	120
4th	13	60	–
5th	30	89	–
6th	38	226	–
7th	49	259	–
8th	56	367	–
9th	84	417	–
10th	107	431	–

Umpires: Akhtaruddin Sahin (1) and Mian Mohammed Aslam (*Pakistan*) (8).
Referee: Hanumant Singh (*India*) (8).   Test No. 1569/3 (B6/Z57)

BANGLADESH v ZIMBABWE (2nd Test)

At Chittagong Stadium on 15, 16, 17, 18, 19 November.
Toss: Bangladesh. Result: **ZIMBABWE** won by eight wickets.
Debuts: None.

ZIMBABWE

D.D.Ebrahim	b Mashrafe	41	b Mashrafe		0
T.R.Gripper	run out	112	not out		11
*S.V.Carlisle	lbw b Enamul	14	c Akram Khan b Mashrafe		0
G.W.Flower	c Naimur b Enamul	33	not out		0
†A.Flower	not out	114			
G.B.Brent	c Habibul b Mashrafe	25			
C.B.Wishart	c Sharif b Ashraful	114			
D.A.Marillier	c Habibul b Aminul	52			
H.H.Streak	not out	16			
T.J.Friend					
H.K.Olonga					
Extras	(B 2, LB 5, W 2, NB 12)	21			
Total	(7 wickets declared)	**542**	(2 wickets)		**11**

BANGLADESH

Javed Omar	c A.Flower b Streak	8	lbw b Friend		80
Al Sahariar	lbw b Streak	29	lbw b Olonga		40
Habibul Bashar	b G.W.Flower	108	c sub (S.M.Ervine) b G.W.Flower		76
Aminul Islam	c and b Marillier	21	c Gripper b G.W.Flower		1
Akram Khan	lbw b Marillier	6	b G.W.Flower		2
Mohammed Ashraful	c Ebrahim b G.W.Flower	33	c sub (P.A.Strang) b Marillier		10
*Naimur Rahman	lbw b Streak	5	lbw b Marillier		28
†Khaled Masud	b G.W.Flower	8	c Ebrahim b G.W.Flower		12
Enamul Haque	not out	12	c and b Marillier		0
Mashrafe Bin Mortaza	lbw b Brent	1	st A.Flower b Marillier		0
Mohammed Sharif	c Brent b G.W.Flower	3	not out		24
Extras	(B 3, LB 3, W 2, NB 9)	17	(B 2, LB 16, W 1, NB 9)		28
Total		**251**			**301**

BANGLADESH	O	M	R	W	O	M	R	W
Mashrafe Bin Mortaza	28	4	101	2	1.4	1	10	2
Mohammed Sharif	29	7	118	0				
Enamul Haque	54	12	134	2	(2) 1	0	1	0
Naimur Rahman	15	2	54	0				
Mohammed Ashraful	17	0	62	1				
Aminul Islam	17	1	66	1				
ZIMBABWE								
Friend	16	3	63	0	25	7	53	1
Streak	19	6	32	2				
Olonga	12	0	40	1	(4) 15	5	31	1
Marillier	15	6	39	2	(5) 19	4	57	4
Brent	17	9	30	1	(2) 25	6	58	0
G.W.Flower	15.3	3	41	4	(3) 38.4	18	63	4
Gripper					(6) 4	2	21	0

FALL OF WICKETS

Wkt	1st	1st	2nd	2nd
	Z	B	B	Z
1st	108	15	73	0
2nd	145	80	195	0
3rd	210	135	201	–
4th	214	146	203	–
5th	280	204	227	–
6th	469	217	264	–
7th	496	226	267	–
8th	–	235	267	–
9th	–	244	267	–
10th	–	251	301	–

Umpires: S.R.Chinu (1) and E.A.R.de Silva (*Sri Lanka*) (7).
Referee: Hanumant Singh (*India*) (9).

Test No. 1570/4 (B7/Z58)

SRI LANKA v WEST INDIES (1st Test)

At Galle International Stadium on 13, 14, 15, 16, 17 November.
Toss: West Indies. Result: **SRI LANKA** won by ten wickets.
Debut: Sri Lanka – T.C.B.Fernando.

WEST INDIES

D.Ganga	c Jayawardena b Vaas	47	c Tillekeratne b Bandaratilake	33
C.H.Gayle	c Sangakkara b Vaas	9	c Muralitharan b Vaas	1
R.R.Sarwan	b Muralitharan	88	c Arnold b Muralitharan	30
B.C.Lara	c Sangakkara b Muralitharan	178	c Muralitharan b Samaraweera	40
*C.L.Hooper	c and b Muralitharan	69	c Jayasuriya b Bandaratilake	6
M.N.Samuels	b Muralitharan	16	lbw b Muralitharan	2
†R.D.Jacobs	c Sangakkara b Vaas	8	b Muralitharan	9
N.C.McGarrell	c Arnold b Muralitharan	4	not out	10
M.Dillon	c Jayasuriya b Vaas	5	lbw b Muralitharan	0
D.Ramnarine	not out	0	b Vaas	0
C.E.L.Stuart	b Muralitharan	0	c Vaas b Muralitharan	2
Extras	(B 8, LB 6, NB 5, P5)	24	(B 2, LB 2, NB 7)	11
Total		**448**		**144**

SRI LANKA

M.S.Atapattu	c Lara b Ramnarine	61	(2) not out	0
*S.T.Jayasuriya	c McGarrell b Dillon	25	(1) not out	6
†K.Sangakkara	run out	140		
D.P.M.deS.Jayawardena	run out	99		
R.P.Arnold	lbw b Ramnarine	33		
H.P.Tillekeratne	not out	105		
T.T.Samaraweera	c Jacobs b Stuart	77		
W.P.U.C.J.Vaas	c Samuels b Dillon	7		
M.R.C.N.Bandaratilake	c Jacobs b Ramnarine	4		
M.Muralitharan	lbw b Stuart	14		
T.C.B.Fernando				
Extras	(B 1, LB 13, W 4, NB 7)	25		
Total	(9 wickets declared)	**590**	(0 wickets)	**6**

SRI LANKA	O	M	R	W		O	M	R	W	FALL OF WICKETS				
											WI	SL	WI	SL
Vaas	31	6	95	4		17	8	20	2	*Wkt*	*1st*	*1st*	*2nd*	*2nd*
Fernando	18	2	80	0	(4)	2	0	10	0	1st	15	37	3	–
Muralitharan	53.4	11	126	6		31.3	10	44	5	2nd	95	146	70	–
Bandaratilake	22	3	76	0	(2)	19	6	46	2	3rd	240	308	70	–
Jayasuriya	9	3	24	0		5	0	13	0	4th	393	358	83	–
Samaraweera	6	0	24	0		4	1	7	1	5th	423	395	93	–
Arnold	2	1	4	0						6th	434	549	131	–
										7th	440	562	135	–
WEST INDIES										8th	448	567	138	–
Dillon	51	11	121	2						9th	448	590	139	–
Stuart	37.4	7	138	2	(1)	0.4	0	6	0	10th	448	–	144	–
McGarrell	31	3	95	0										
Ramnarine	58	12	158	3										
Hooper	24	3	59	0										
Samuels	1	0	5	0										

Umpires: J.H.Hampshire (*England*) (19) and P.T.Manuel (10).
Referee: R.Subba Row (*England*) (37). **Test No. 1571/4 (SL116/WI377)**

SRI LANKA v WEST INDIES (2nd Test)

At Asgiriya Stadium, Kandy, on 21, 22, 23, 24, 25 November.
Toss: Sri Lanka. Result: **SRI LANKA** won by 131 runs.
Debuts: None.

SRI LANKA

M.S.Atapattu	lbw b Dillon	0	st Jacobs b Ramnarine		84
*S.T.Jayasuriya	c Gayle b Collins	16	c Gayle b Ramnarine		55
†K.Sangakkara	b Ramnarine	15	c Ramnarine b Dillon		45
D.P.M.deS.Jayawardena	c and b Ramnarine	88	c Stuart b Dillon		16
R.P.Arnold	b Ramnarine	4	c Dillon b Ramnarine		1
H.P.Tillekeratne	b Collins	87	not out		7
T.T.Samaraweera	c Jacobs b Dillon	29	(8) not out		3
W.P.U.C.J.Vaas	c Hooper b Collins	0	(7) c Ganga b Ramnarine		0
M.R.C.N.Bandaratilake	not out	12			
D.N.T.Zoysa	b Collins	23			
M.Muralitharan	c Stuart b Dillon	4			
Extras	(LB 6, NB 4)	10	(B 3, LB 6, W 2, NB 2)		13
Total		**288**	(6 wickets declared)		**224**

WEST INDIES

C.H.Gayle	b Zoysa	44	(2) c Sangakkara b Vaas		0
D.Ganga	c Jayawardena b Zoysa	0	(1) b Muralitharan		8
R.R.Sarwan	b Muralitharan	17	c Arnold b Muralitharan		48
B.C.Lara	lbw b Muralitharan	74	c Tillekeratne b Bandaratilake		45
*C.L.Hooper	lbw b Muralitharan	23	lbw b Bandaratilake		4
M.N.Samuels	c Sangakkara b Muralitharan	4	lbw b Muralitharan		54
†R.D.Jacobs	b Vaas	24	c Sangakkara b Vaas		5
M.Dillon	c Sangakkara b Vaas	0	b Muralitharan		19
D.Ramnarine	lbw b Vaas	0	not out		0
P.T.Collins	lbw b Vaas	0	b Muralitharan		0
C.E.L.Stuart	not out	0	b Muralitharan		0
Extras	(LB 5, NB 4)	9	(B 3, LB 2, NB 2)		7
Total		**191**			**190**

WEST INDIES	O	M	R	W		O	M	R	W
Dillon	20	4	55	3		19	2	60	2
Collins	27	7	78	4		11	0	52	0
Stuart	0.1	0	2	0	(4)	8	1	21	0
Gayle	0.3	0	4	0					
Hooper	21	6	44	0		4	1	16	0
Ramnarine	25	6	81	3	(3)	16	2	66	4
Samuels	3	0	18	0					

SRI LANKA	O	M	R	W		O	M	R	W
Vaas	22	8	56	4		13	2	39	2
Zoysa	13	3	34	2		8	4	13	0
Muralitharan	23.4	5	54	4		35.5	16	81	6
Bandaratilake	4	0	25	0		15	7	39	2
Samaraweera	4	1	17	0		5	2	9	0
Jayasuriya						5	2	13	0
Tillekeratne						2	1	1	0

FALL OF WICKETS

	SL	WI	SL	WI
Wkt	1st	1st	2nd	2nd
1st	1	8	89	3
2nd	27	51	176	25
3rd	49	72	204	83
4th	53	126	206	107
5th	169	126	215	110
6th	249	167	215	126
7th	249	173	–	185
8th	249	173	–	190
9th	281	181	–	190
10th	288	191	–	190

Umpires: J.H.Hampshire (*England*) (20) and M.G.Silva (2).
Referee: R.Subba Row (*England*) (38). **Test No. 1572/5 SL117/WI378**

SRI LANKA v WEST INDIES (3rd Test)

At Sinhalese Sports Club, Colombo, on 29, 30 November, 1, 2, 3 December.
Toss: West Indies. Result: **SRI LANKA** won by ten wickets.
Debuts: None.

WEST INDIES

D.Ganga	lbw b Vaas	6	lbw b Vaas	10
C.H.Gayle	c Sangakkara b Vaas	0	c Jayawardena b Vaas	0
R.R.Sarwan	run out	69	c Sangakkara b Vaas	66
B.C.Lara	b Vaas	221	b Zoysa	130
*C.L.Hooper	lbw b Vaas	56	st Sangakkara b Muralitharan	9
M.N.Samuels	lbw b Vaas	4	c Jayawardena b Muralitharan	9
†R.D.Jacobs	b Zoysa	2	not out	31
M.Dillon	lbw b Vaas	2	c sub (U.D.U.Chandana) b Vaas	8
D.Ramnarine	c Jayawardena b Muralitharan	0	lbw b Vaas	0
P.T.Collins	c Samaraweera b Vaas	4	lbw b Vaas	0
M.I.Black	not out	0	lbw b Vaas	0
Extras	(B 5, LB 7, NB 14)	26	(B 4, LB 1, NB 3)	8
Total		**390**		**262**

SRI LANKA

M.S.Atapattu	c Gayle b Collins	4	not out	19
*S.T.Jayasuriya	c Ramnarine b Black	85	not out	8
†K.Sangakkara	c Gayle b Dillon	55		
D.P.M.deS.Jayawardena	lbw b Dillon	39		
R.P.Arnold	c Jacobs b Hooper	65		
H.P.Tillekeratne	not out	204		
T.T.Samaraweera	run out	87		
W.P.U.C.J.Vaas	c Samuels b Collins	23		
D.N.T.Zoysa	b Hooper	10		
M.R.C.N.Bandaratilake	c Jacobs b Collins	25		
M.Muralitharan	not out	0		
Extras	(B 5, LB 14, W 2, NB 5)	26		
Total	(9 wickets declared)	**627**	(0 wickets)	**27**

SRI LANKA	O	M	R	W		O	M	R	W		FALL OF WICKETS			
Vaas	32.2	5	120	7		25	3	71	7			WI	SL	WI	SL
Zoysa	20	4	55	1		11	1	45	1		Wkt	1st	1st	2nd	2nd
Samaraweera	8	0	31	0	(4)	8	2	23	0		1st	2	5	1	–
Bandaratilake	9	2	37	0	(5)	2	0	2	0		2nd	17	104	20	–
Muralitharan	37	6	115	1	(3)	36	5	116	2		3rd	211	179	161	–
Jayasuriya	3	0	11	0							4th	347	204	203	–
Arnold	3	0	8	0							5th	359	345	203	–
Tillekeratne	1	0	1	0							6th	368	510	240	–
											7th	376	550	258	–
WEST INDIES											8th	385	569	258	–
Dillon	46	9	131	2		3	0	12	0		9th	389	611	262	–
Collins	47	4	156	3		2.3	0	15	0		10th	390	–	262	–
Black	32	6	123	1											
Ramnarine	17	3	51	0											
Hooper	43	7	112	2											
Gayle	10	1	28	0											
Sarwan	2	0	7	0											

Umpires: E.A.R.de Silva (8) and R.B.Tiffin (*Zimbabwe*) (23).
Referee: R.Subba Row (*England*) (39).   **Test No. 1573/6 (SL118/WI379)**

SRI LANKA v WEST INDIES 2001-02

SRI LANKA – BATTING AND FIELDING

	M	I	NO	HS	Runs	Avge	100	50	Ct/St
H.P.Tillekeratne	3	4	3	204*	403	403.00	2	1	2
T.T.Samaraweera	3	4	1	87	196	65.33	–	2	1
K.Sangakkara	3	4	–	140	255	63.75	1	1	9/1
D.P.M.deS.Jayawardena	3	4	–	99	242	60.50	–	2	5
S.T.Jayasuriya	3	6	2	85	195	48.75	–	2	2
M.S.Atapattu	3	6	2	84	168	42.00	–	2	–
R.P.Arnold	3	4	–	65	103	25.75	–	1	3
M.R.C.N.Bandaratilake	3	3	1	25	41	20.50	–	–	–
D.N.T.Zoysa	2	2	–	23	33	16.50	–	–	–
M.Muralitharan	3	3	1	14	22	11.00	–	–	3
W.P.U.C.J.Vaas	3	4	–	23	30	7.50	–	–	1

Played in one Test: T.C.B.Fernando did not bat.

SRI LANKA – BOWLING

	O	M	R	W	Avge	Best	5wI	10wM
W.P.U.C.J.Vaas	140.2	32	401	26	15.42	7-71	2	1
M.Muralitharan	217.4	53	536	24	22.33	6-81	3	2
D.N.T.Zoysa	52	12	147	4	36.75	2-34	–	
M.R.C.N.Bandaratilake	71	18	215	4	53.75	2-29	–	

Also bowled: R.P.Arnold 5-1-12-0; T.C.B.Fernando 20-2-90-0; S.T.Jayasuriya 22-4-61-0; T.T.Samaraweera 35-6-111-1; H.P.Tillekeratne 3-1-2-0.

WEST INDIES – BATTING AND FIELDING

	M	I	NO	HS	Runs	Avge	100	50	Ct/St
B.C.Lara	3	6	–	221	688	114.66	3	1	3
R.R.Sarwan	3	6	–	88	318	53.00	–	3	–
C.L.Hooper	3	6	–	69	167	27.83	–	2	1
D.Ganga	3	6	–	47	104	17.33	–	–	1
R.D.Jacobs	3	6	1	31*	79	15.80	–	–	5/1
M.N.Samuels	3	6	–	54	76	12.66	–	1	2
C.H.Gayle	3	6	–	44	54	9.00	–	–	4
M.Dillon	3	6	–	19	34	5.66	–	–	1
P.T.Collins	2	4	–	4	4	1.00	–	–	–
C.E.L.Stuart	2	4	1	2	2	0.66	–	–	2
D.Ramnarine	3	6	2	0*	0	0.00	–	–	3

Played in one Test: M.I.Black 0, 0; N.C.McGarrell 4, 10*, (1 ct).*

WEST INDIES – BOWLING

	O	M	R	W	Avge	Best	5wI	10wM
D.Ramnarine	116	23	356	10	35.60	4- 66		
M.Dillon	139	26	379	9	42.11	3- 55		
P.T.Collins	87.3	11	301	7	43.00	4- 78		
C.E.L.Stuart	46.3	8	167	2	83.50	2-138		
C.L.Hooper	101	20	231	2	115.50	2-112		

Also bowled: M.I.Black 32-6-123-1; C.H.Gayle 10.3-1-32-0; N.C.McGarrell 31-3-95-0; M.N.Samuels 4-0-23-0; R.R.Sarwan 2-0-7-0.

INDIA v ENGLAND (1st Test)

At Punjab C.A. Stadium, Mohali, Chandigarh, on 3, 4, 5, 6 December.
Toss: India. Result: **INDIA** won by ten wickets.
Debuts: India – S.B.Bangar, I.R.Siddiqui, T.Yohannan; England – R.K.J.Dawson, J.S.Foster.

ENGLAND

M.A.Butcher	c Laxman b Yohannan	4	c sub (J.J.Martin) b Yohannan	18
M.E.Trescothick	b Yohannan	66	c Siddiqui b Yohannan	46
*N.Hussain	c Laxman b Kumble	85	b Kumble	12
G.P.Thorpe	c Laxman b Siddiqui	23	c and b Kumble	62
M.R.Ramprakash	c Das b Harbhajan	17	lbw b Kumble	28
A.Flintoff	c Kumble b Harbhajan	18	c Ganguly b Kumble	4
C.White	c Dravid b Kumble	5	c Dasgupta b Harbhajan	22
†J.S.Foster	lbw b Harbhajan	0	lbw b Harbhajan	5
J.Ormond	not out	3	b Kumble	0
R.K.J.Dawson	c Laxman b Harbhajan	5	b Kumble	11
M.J.Hoggard	c sub (C.C.Williams) b Harbhajan	0	not out	0
Extras	(LB 7, NB 5)	12	(B 10, LB 13, W 1, NB 3)	27
Total		**238**		**235**

INDIA

S.S.Das	b Butcher	2		
†D.Dasgupta	b White	100	not out	0
A.Kumble	c Foster b Dawson	37		
R.Dravid	lbw b Ormond	86		
S.R.Tendulkar	c Foster b Hoggard	88		
*S.C.Ganguly	c Thorpe b Hoggard	47		
V.V.S.Laxman	c Hussain b Dawson	28		
S.B.Bangar	c and b Dawson	36		
Harbhajan Singh	lbw b Dawson	1		
I.R.Siddiqui	b Hoggard	24	(1) not out	5
T.Yohannan	not out	2		
Extras	(LB 12, W 2, NB 4)	18		
Total		**469**	(0 wickets)	**5**

INDIA	O	M	R	W	O	M	R	W	FALL OF WICKETS				
										E	I	E	I
Yohannan	18	3	75	2	17	3	56	2	Wkt	1st	1st	2nd	2nd
Siddiqui	11	2	32	1	8	3	16	0	1st	4	23	68	
Bangar	5	2	17	0					2nd	129	76	82	
Kumble	19	6	52	2	(3) 28.4	6	81	6	3rd	172	212	87	
Tendulkar	4	3	4	0					4th	200	290	159	
Harbhajan Singh	19.3	4	51	5	(4) 24	9	59	2	5th	224	370	163	
									6th	227	378	196	
ENGLAND									7th	229	430	206	
Hoggard	32	9	98	3	0.2	0	5	0	8th	229	436	207	
Ormond	28	8	70	1					9th	238	449	224	
Butcher	7	1	19	1					10th	238	469	235	
Flintoff	34	11	80	0									
White	25	8	56	1									
Dawson	43	6	134	4									

Umpires: S.A.Bucknor (*West Indies*) (63) and S.Venkataraghavan (48).
Referee: D.T.Lindsay (*South Africa*) (5).   Test No. 1574/85 (I347/E787)

INDIA v ENGLAND (2nd Test)

At Sardar Patel (Gujarat) Stadium, Motera, Ahmedabad, on 11, 12, 13, 14, 15 December.
Toss: England. Result: **MATCH DRAWN**.
Debuts: None.

ENGLAND

M.A.Butcher	c Dasgupta b Kumble	51	c Dravid b Harbhajan		92
M.E.Trescothick	c Dasgupta b Kumble	99	c Das b Srinath		12
*N.Hussain	lbw b Kumble	1	c Sehwag b Harbhajan		50
M.P.Vaughan	c Sehwag b Kumble	11	not out	(7)	31
M.R.Ramprakash	b Tendulkar	37	c Tendulkar b Harbhajan	(4)	19
A.Flintoff	c Laxman b Kumble	0	b Kumble	(5)	4
C.White	b Harbhajan	121	run out	(6)	18
†J.S.Foster	c Tendulkar b Kumble	40	c Yohannan b Kumble		3
A.F.Giles	b Kumble	7	c Das b Harbhajan		8
R.K.J.Dawson	c Dasgupta b Srinath	9	c Tendulkar b Kumble		2
M.J.Hoggard	not out	4	c Das b Harbhajan		1
Extras	(B 6, LB 15, W 1, NB 5)	27	(B 6, LB 8, NB 3)		17
Total		**407**			**257**

INDIA

S.S.Das	c Butcher b Flintoff	41	run out		58
†D.Dasgupta	c Hussain b Giles	17	c Butcher b Dawson		60
R.Dravid	c Foster b Hoggard	7	not out		26
S.R.Tendulkar	c Hussain b Hoggard	103	c Vaughan b Dawson		26
*S.C.Ganguly	c sub (M.C.J.Ball) b Flintoff	5	not out		16
V.V.S.Laxman	c Butcher b Giles	75			
V.Sehwag	lbw b White	20			
A.Kumble	b Giles	5			
Harbhajan Singh	c Flintoff b Giles	0			
J.Srinath	c Butcher b Giles	0			
T.Yohannan	not out	3			
Extras	(B 6, LB 5, W 1, NB 3)	15	(B 12)		12
Total		**291**	(3 wickets)		**198**

INDIA	O	M	R	W	O	M	R	W	FALL OF WICKETS
Srinath	29	7	105	1	9	2	24	1					
Yohannan	17	2	57	0	4	0	25	0					
Harbhajan Singh	35.3	9	78	1	(4) 30.2	6	71	5					
Kumble	51	13	115	7	(3) 38	5	118	3					
Tendulkar	10	0	27	1									
Sehwag	2	1	4	0	(5) 2	0	5	0					

									FALL OF WICKETS
									E	I	E	I
									Wkt	*1st*	*1st*	*2nd*	*2nd*
ENGLAND	O	M	R	W	O	M	R	W	1st	124	54	21	119
Hoggard	28	7	65	2	17	6	33	0	2nd	144	64	133	124
Flintoff	22	7	42	2	(4) 8	4	17	0	3rd	172	86	178	168
Giles	43.3	16	67	5	(2) 31	12	57	0	4th	176	93	183	—
Dawson	15	0	73	0	(3) 32	9	72	2	5th	180	211	183	—
White	12	2	33	1	9	5	7	0	6th	239	248	225	—
									7th	344	268	231	—
									8th	360	272	247	—
									9th	391	274	253	—
									10th	407	291	257	—

Umpires: A.V.Jayaprakash (11) and I.D.Robinson (*Zimbabwe*) (28).
Referee: D.T.Lindsay (*South Africa*) (6). Test No. 1575/86 (I348/E788)

INDIA v ENGLAND (3rd Test)

At Chinnaswamy Stadium, Bangalore, on 19, 20, 21, 22, 23 (*no play*) December.
Toss: England. Result: **MATCH DRAWN**.
Debuts: None.

ENGLAND

M.A.Butcher	run out	27	not out	23
M.E.Trescothick	c Laxman b Srinath	8	not out	9
*N.Hussain	c Dasgupta b Srinath	43		
M.P.Vaughan	handled the ball	64		
M.R.Ramprakash	c Dravid b Sarandeep	58		
A.Flintoff	c Tendulkar b Sarandeep	0		
C.White	c Das b Srinath	39		
†J.S.Foster	c Dasgupta b Srinath	48		
A.F.Giles	lbw b Sarandeep	28		
R.K.J.Dawson	not out	0		
M.J.Hoggard	lbw b Kumble	1		
Extras	(B 8, LB 9, NB 3)	20	(B 1)	1
Total		**336**	(1 wicket)	**33**

INDIA

S.S.Das	b Flintoff	28
†D.Dasgupta	c Trescothick b Flintoff	0
V.V.S.Laxman	b Flintoff	12
S.R.Tendulkar	st Foster b Giles	90
R.Dravid	c Foster b Hoggard	3
*S.C.Ganguly	c Butcher b Hoggard	0
V.Sehwag	c Foster b Hoggard	66
A.Kumble	c Trescothick b Flintoff	14
Harbhajan Singh	c Hussain b Hoggard	8
Sarandeep Singh	run out	4
J.Srinath	not out	2
Extras	(B 4, LB 4, NB 3)	11
Total		**238**

INDIA	O	M	R	W		O	M	R	W
Srinath	29	9	73	4		4	0	19	0
Ganguly	13	3	39	0		3	0	12	0
Kumble	29.3	6	74	1					
Harbhajan Singh	27	7	59	0	(3)	0.1	0	1	0
Sarandeep Singh	21	5	54	3					
Tendulkar	3	0	19	0					
Sehwag	1	0	1	0					

ENGLAND	O	M	R	W
Hoggard	24.3	7	80	4
Flintoff	28	9	50	4
Giles	34	18	74	1
White	8	2	26	0

FALL OF WICKETS

	E	I	E
Wkt	1st	1st	2nd
1st	21	8	–
2nd	68	22	–
3rd	93	88	–
4th	206	121	–
5th	206	121	–
6th	219	173	–
7th	271	218	–
8th	334	228	–
9th	334	235	–
10th	336	238	–

Umpires: E.A.R.de Silva (*Sri Lanka*) (9) and A.V.Jayaprakash (12).
Referee: D.T.Lindsay (*South Africa*) (7).   **Test No. 1576/87 (I349/E789)**

INDIA v ENGLAND 2001-02

INDIA – BATTING AND FIELDING

	M	I	NO	HS	Runs	Avge	100	50	Ct/St
S.R.Tendulkar	3	4	–	103	307	76.75	1	2	4
D.Dasgupta	3	5	1	100	177	44.25	1	1	6
V.Sehwag	2	2	–	66	86	43.00	–	1	2
R.Dravid	3	4	1	86	122	40.66	–	1	3
V.V.S.Laxman	3	3	–	75	115	38.33	–	1	6
S.S.Das	3	4	–	58	129	32.25	–	1	5
S.C.Ganguly	3	4	1	47	68	22.66	–	–	1
A.Kumble	3	3	–	37	56	18.66	–	–	2
Harbhajan Singh	3	3	–	8	9	3.00	–	–	–
J.Srinath	2	2	1	2*	2	2.00	–	–	–
T.Yohannan	2	2	2	3*	5	–	–	–	1

Played in one Test: S.B.Bangar 36; Sarandeep Singh 4; I.R.Siddiqui 24, 5* (1 ct).

INDIA – BOWLING

	O	M	R	W	Avge	Best	5wI	10wM
Sarandeep Singh	21	5	54	3	18.00	3- 54	–	–
A.Kumble	166.1	36	440	19	23.15	7-115	2	1
Harbhajan Singh	136.3	35	319	13	24.53	5- 51	2	–
J.Srinath	71	18	221	6	36.83	4- 73	–	–
T.Yohannan	56	8	213	4	53.25	2- 56	–	–

Also bowled: S.B.Bangar 5-2-17-0; S.C.Ganguly 16-3-51-0; V.Sehwag 5-1-10-0; I.R.Siddiqui 19-5-48-1; S.R.Tendulkar 17-3-50-1.

ENGLAND – BATTING AND FIELDING

	M	I	NO	HS	Runs	Avge	100	50	Ct/St
M.P.Vaughan	2	3	1	64	106	53.00	–	1	1
M.E.Trescothick	3	6	1	99	240	48.00	–	2	2
M.A.Butcher	3	6	1	92	215	43.00	–	2	5
C.White	3	5	–	121	205	41.00	1	–	–
N.Hussain	3	5	–	85	191	38.20	–	2	4
M.R.Ramprakash	3	5	–	58	159	31.80	–	1	–
J.S.Foster	3	5	–	48	96	19.20	–	–	5/1
A.F.Giles	2	3	–	28	43	14.33	–	–	–
R.K.J.Dawson	3	5	1	11	27	6.75	–	–	1
A.Flintoff	3	5	–	18	26	5.20	–	–	1
M.J.Hoggard	3	5	2	4*	6	2.00	–	–	–

Played in one Test: J.Ormond 3*, 0; G.P.Thorpe 23, 62 (1 ct).

ENGLAND – BOWLING

	O	M	R	W	Avge	Best	5wI	10wM
M.J.Hoggard	101.5	29	281	9	31.22	4- 80	–	–
A.Flintoff	92	31	189	6	31.50	4- 50	–	–
A.F.Giles	108.3	46	198	6	33.00	5- 67	1	–
R.K.J.Dawson	90	15	279	6	46.50	4-134	–	–

Also bowled: M.A.Butcher 7-1-19-1; J.Ormond 28-8-70-1; C.White 54-17-122-2.

AUSTRALIA v SOUTH AFRICA (1st Test)

At Adelaide Oval on 14, 15, 16, 17, 18 December.
Toss: Australia. Result: **AUSTRALIA** won by 246 runs.
Debuts: None.

AUSTRALIA

J.L.Langer	c Pollock b Henderson	116		c Boucher b Pollock	1
M.L.Hayden	c Ntini b Klusener	31		b Kallis	131
R.T.Ponting	run out	54		lbw b Kallis	25
M.E.Waugh	c Boucher b Hayward	2		c Boucher b Henderson	74
*S.R.Waugh	c McKenzie b Henderson	8	(6)	c Pollock b Henderson	13
D.R.Martyn	not out	124	(7)	not out	6
†A.C.Gilchrist	c Kallis b Henderson	7	(5)	c McKenzie b Kallis	22
S.K.Warne	b Klusener	41		b Henderson	6
B.Lee	c McKenzie b Hayward	32			
J.N.Gillespie	c Boucher b Henderson	3			
G.D.McGrath	b Hayward	5			
Extras	(LB 6, NB 10)	16		(B 8, LB 16, NB 7)	31
Total		**439**		**(7 wickets declared)**	**309**

SOUTH AFRICA

H.H.Gibbs	st Gilchrist b Warne	78		c Langer b McGrath	9
G.Kirsten	lbw b McGrath	47		c Ponting b Warne	7
H.H.Dippenaar	c Ponting b McGrath	4		c Warne b McGrath	0
C.W.Henderson	run out	30	(9)	c Ponting b Warne	3
J.H.Kallis	lbw b McGrath	5	(4)	not out	65
N.D.McKenzie	lbw b Martyn	87	(5)	lbw b McGrath	0
L.Klusener	b Warne	64	(6)	c Warne b Gillespie	18
†M.V.Boucher	c Langer b Warne	64	(7)	c Gilchrist b Gillespie	0
*S.M.Pollock	c Gilchrist b Warne	0	(8)	c Ponting b Warne	1
M.Ntini	c Ponting b Warne	9		b Lee	4
M.Hayward	not out	0		c Gilchrist b Lee	12
Extras	(B 8, LB 9, NB 11)	28		(B 4, LB 1, W 1, NB 3)	9
Total		**374**			**128**

SOUTH AFRICA	O	M	R	W		O	M	R	W
Pollock	28	8	64	0		12	4	38	1
Hayward	31	5	108	3		10	0	32	0
Ntini	19	7	64	0	(5)	8	3	13	0
Kallis	16	1	37	0		15	2	45	3
Klusener	14	4	44	2	(6)	4	0	27	0
Henderson	33	4	116	4	(3)	29.1	1	130	3

AUSTRALIA	O	M	R	W		O	M	R	W
McGrath	33	10	94	3		14	8	13	3
Gillespie	23	7	57	0		11	4	23	2
Warne	39.4	9	113	5		29	7	57	3
Lee	19	2	81	0		12	3	29	2
M.E.Waugh	3	0	9	0					
Martyn	4	2	3	1	(5)	1	0	1	0

	FALL OF WICKETS			
	A	SA	A	SA
Wkt	1st	1st	2nd	2nd
1st	80	87	8	12
2nd	182	93	66	17
3rd	199	155	247	21
4th	211	178	273	21
5th	238	178	291	54
6th	248	214	303	58
7th	332	355	309	67
8th	409	356	–	74
9th	434	365	–	113
10th	439	374	–	128

Umpires: S.J.A.Taufel (2) and S.Venkataraghavan (*India*) (49).
Referee: R.S.Madugalle (*Sri Lanka*) (36). **Test No. 1577/66 (A623/SA261)**

AUSTRALIA v SOUTH AFRICA (2nd Test)

At Melbourne Cricket Ground on 26, 27, 28, 29 December.
Toss: Australia. Result: **AUSTRALIA** won by nine wickets.
Debuts: None.

SOUTH AFRICA

H.H.Gibbs	c Ponting b McGrath	14	c Gilchrist b Lee		21
G.Kirsten	b McGrath	10	c Ponting b Lee		10
H.H.Dippenaar	c Hayden b Lee	26	c Hayden b Warne		23
J.H.Kallis	c Gilchrist b Bichel	38	run out		99
N.D.McKenzie	lbw b Lee	67	c Gilchrist b Warne		12
L.Klusener	c and b Bichel	0	lbw b McGrath		7
†M.V.Boucher	c Bichel b M.E.Waugh	43	c M.E.Waugh b Warne		0
*S.M.Pollock	not out	42	run out		18
C.W.Henderson	run out	5	c M.E.Waugh b McGrath		16
A.A.Donald	c Ponting b Lee	0	b Bichel		7
M.Hayward	c M.E.Waugh b Bichel	14	not out		0
Extras	(B 1, LB 10, NB 7)	18	(B 4, NB 2)		6
Total		**277**			**219**

AUSTRALIA

J.L.Langer	c Klusener b Donald	85	c Henderson b Pollock		7
M.L.Hayden	c Donald b Henderson	138	not out		3
R.T.Ponting	c Kallis b Hayward	22	not out		0
M.E.Waugh	b Donald	34			
*S.R.Waugh	run out	90			
D.R.Martyn	c Kallis b Pollock	52			
†A.C.Gilchrist	not out	30			
S.K.Warne	c Kirsten b Donald	1			
B.Lee	c McKenzie b Hayward	3			
A.J.Bichel	c Boucher b Pollock	5			
G.D.McGrath	lbw b Pollock	0			
Extras	(LB 17, W 1, NB 9)	27			
Total		**487**	(1 wicket)		**10**

AUSTRALIA	O	M	R	W		O	M	R	W		FALL OF WICKETS			
											SA	A	SA	A
McGrath	26	8	70	2		21	6	43	2	*Wkt*	*1st*	*1st*	*2nd*	*2nd*
Lee	31	10	77	3		18	5	52	2	1st	24	202	24	7
Bichel	19.5	6	44	3	(4)	12.1	0	52	1	2nd	36	267	37	
Warne	19	3	56	0	(3)	24	3	68	3	3rd	59	267	74	
M.E.Waugh	8	1	19	1						4th	131	348	107	
										5th	131	429	120	
SOUTH AFRICA										6th	198	462	121	
Donald	29	5	103	3		2	0	4	0	7th	220	463	157	
Pollock	31	3	84	3		1	0	6	1	8th	225	470	192	
Hayward	26	1	109	2						9th	233	475	215	
Kallis	17	3	55	0						10th	277	487	219	
Henderson	29	3	108	1										
Klusener	7	1	11	0										

Umpires: D.B.Hair (41) and E.A.Nicholls (*West Indies*) (17).
Referee: R.S.Madugalle (*Sri Lanka*) (37).   Test No. 1578/67 (A624/SA262)

AUSTRALIA v SOUTH AFRICA (3rd Test)

At Sydney Cricket Ground on 2, 3, 4, 5 January.
Toss: Australia. Result: **AUSTRALIA** won by ten wickets.
Debuts: South Africa – J.L.Ontong.

AUSTRALIA

J.L.Langer	c McKenzie b Boje	126	not out	30
M.L.Hayden	c Kallis b Pollock	105	not out	21
R.T.Ponting	run out	14		
M.E.Waugh	c Boucher b Donald	19		
*S.R.Waugh	b Pollock	30		
D.R.Martyn	c McKenzie b Boje	117		
†A.C.Gilchrist	c Boucher b Kallis	34		
S.K.Warne	b Pollock	37		
B.Lee	b Boje	29		
S.C.G.MacGill	c Henderson b Boje	20		
G.D.McGrath	not out	1		
Extras	(B 4, LB 8, W 1, NB 9)	22	(LB 2, NB 1)	3
Total		**554**	(0 wickets)	**54**

SOUTH AFRICA

H.H.Gibbs	c M.E.Waugh b MacGill	32	b Lee	10
G.Kirsten	c Ponting b McGrath	18	b MacGill	153
H.H.Dippenaar	b McGrath	3	c Ponting b MacGill	74
J.H.Kallis	c Gilchrist b MacGill	4	c Gilchrist b Warne	34
N.D.McKenzie	b Warne	20	c MacGill b Lee	38
J.L.Ontong	lbw b Warne	9	lbw b Warne	32
†M.V.Boucher	c Ponting b Warne	35	c Gilchrist b McGrath	27
*S.M.Pollock	c Martyn b McGrath	6	not out	61
N.Boje	run out	7	b MacGill	1
C.W.Henderson	c McGrath b MacGill	9	b MacGill	2
A.A.Donald	not out	2	c Lee b Warne	2
Extras	(LB 8, NB 1)	9	(B 8, LB 7, NB 3)	18
Total		**154**		**452**

SOUTH AFRICA	O	M	R	W		O	M	R	W
Donald	31	6	119	1		3	0	12	0
Pollock	37	11	109	3		3	1	11	0
Kallis	22	1	129	1					
Henderson	27	3	112	0		2	0	14	0
Boje	25.2	6	63	4	(3)	2.1	0	15	0
Ontong	2	0	10	0					
AUSTRALIA									
McGrath	17	6	35	3		28	5	95	1
Lee	6	2	13	0	(3)	19	5	62	2
MacGill	20.2	6	51	3	(4)	45	13	123	4
Warne	19	5	47	3	(2)	42.5	8	132	3
M.E.Waugh						6	1	14	0
Ponting						1	0	11	0

FALL OF WICKETS				
	A	SA	SA	A
Wkt	1st	1st	2nd	2nd
1st	219	37	17	–
2nd	247	43	166	–
3rd	253	56	211	–
4th	302	77	282	–
5th	308	93	356	–
6th	356	98	372	–
7th	439	111	392	–
8th	502	121	393	–
9th	542	148	403	–
10th	554	154	452	–

Umpires: D.J.Harper (16) and D.R.Shepherd (*England*) (58).
Referee: R.S.Madugalle (*Sri Lanka*) (38).   Test No. 1579/68 (A625/SA263)

AUSTRALIA v SOUTH AFRICA 2001-02

AUSTRALIA – BATTING AND FIELDING

	M	I	NO	HS	Runs	Avge	100	50	Ct/St
D.R.Martyn	3	4	2	124*	299	149.50	2	1	1
M.L.Hayden	3	6	–	138	429	107.25	3	–	2
J.L.Langer	3	6	1	126	365	73.00	2	1	2
S.R.Waugh	3	4	–	90	141	35.25	–	1	–
M.E.Waugh	3	4	–	74	129	32.25	–	1	4
A.C.Gilchrist	3	4	1	34	93	31.00	–	–	9/1
R.T.Ponting	3	5	1	54	115	28.75	–	1	11
B.Lee	3	3	–	32	64	21.33	–	–	1
S.K.Warne	3	4	–	41	85	21.25	–	–	2
G.D.McGrath	3	3	1	5	6	3.00	–	–	1

Played in one Test: A.J.Bichel 5 (2 ct); J.N.Gillespie 3; S.C.G.MacGill 20 (1 ct).

AUSTRALIA – BOWLING

	O	M	R	W	Avge	Best	5wI	10wM
A.J.Bichel	32	6	96	4	24.00	3- 44	–	–
S.C.G.MacGill	65.2	19	174	7	24.85	4-123	–	–
G.D.McGrath	139	43	350	14	25.00	3- 13	–	–
S.K.Warne	173.3	27	473	17	27.82	5-113	1	–
B.Lee	105	27	314	9	34.88	3- 77	–	–
J.N.Gillespie	34	11	80	2	40.00	2- 23	–	–

Also bowled: D.R.Martyn 5-2-4-1; R.T.Ponting 1-0-11-0; M.E.Waugh 17-2-42-1.

SOUTH AFRICA – BATTING AND FIELDING

	M	I	NO	HS	Runs	Avge	100	50	Ct/St
J.H.Kallis	3	6	1	99	245	49.00	–	2	4
G.Kirsten	3	6	–	153	245	40.83	1	–	1
N.D.McKenzie	3	6	–	87	224	37.33	–	2	6
S.M.Pollock	3	6	2	61*	128	32.00	–	1	2
M.V.Boucher	3	6	–	64	169	28.16	–	1	7
H.H.Gibbs	3	6	–	78	164	27.33	–	1	–
H.H.Dippenaar	3	6	–	74	130	21.66	–	1	1
M.Hayward	2	4	2	14	26	13.00	–	–	–
L.Klusener	2	4	–	22	47	11.75	–	–	1
C.W.Henderson	3	6	–	30	65	10.83	–	–	2
A.A.Donald	2	4	1	7	11	3.66	–	–	1

Played in one Test: N.Boje 7, 1; M.Ntini 9, 4 (1 ct); J.L.Ontong 9, 32.

SOUTH AFRICA – BOWLING

	O	M	R	W	Avge	Best	5wI	10wM
N.Boje	27.3	6	78	4	19.50	4- 63	–	–
S.M.Pollock	112	27	312	8	39.00	3- 84	–	–
L.Klusener	25	6	82	2	41.00	2- 44	–	–
M.Hayward	67	6	249	5	49.80	3-108	–	–
A.A.Donald	65	11	238	4	59.50	3-103	–	–
C.W.Henderson	120.1	11	480	8	60.00	4-116	–	–
J.H.Kallis	70	7	266	4	66.50	3- 45	–	–

Also bowled: M.Ntini 27-10-77-0; J.L.Ontong 2-0-10-0.

NEW ZEALAND v BANGLADESH (1st Test)

At Seddon Park, Hamilton, on 18, 19, 20, 21, 22 December.
Toss: Bangladesh. Result: **NEW ZEALAND** won by an innings and 52 runs.
Debuts: Bangladesh – Sanwar Hossain.

NEW ZEALAND

M.H.Richardson	c and b Sharif	143
L.Vincent	c and b Mashrafe	0
M.S.Sinclair	c Masud b Manjural	7
*S.P.Fleming	c Masud b Mashrafe	4
N.J.Astle	c Al Sahariar b Manjural	5
C.D.McMillan	c Manjural b Mashrafe	106
C.L.Cairns	b Sharif	48
†A.C.Parore	b Sharif	20
D.L.Vettori	lbw b Mahmud	0
S.E.Bond	not out	4
C.S.Martin		
Extras	(B 2, LB 18, W 5, NB 3)	28
Total	(9 wickets declared)	**365**

BANGLADESH

Javed Omar	c Richardson b Cairns	9	lbw b Martin		15
Al Sahariar	c Sinclair b Bond	15	c Parore b Cairns		53
Habibul Bashar	c Martin b Vettori	61	c Parore b Cairns		1
Aminul Islam	c Parore b Bond	14	b Cairns		0
Mohammed Ashraful	c Sinclair b Vettori	1	c sub (C.J.Drum) b Bond		6
Sanwar Hossain	c Vincent b McMillan	45	b Bond		12
*†Khaled Masud	c Bond b McMillan	6	c Fleming b Cairns		6
Khaled Mahmud	c Richardson b Bond	45	c Sinclair b Cairns		0
Mohammed Sharif	b Martin	3	not out		4
Mashrafe Bin Mortaza	lbw b Bond	3	c Vincent b Cairns		2
Manjural Islam	not out	0	c Fleming b Cairns		1
Extras	(LB 1, NB 5)	6	(LB 4, NB 4)		8
Total		**205**			**108**

BANGLADESH	O	M	R	W	O	M	R	W
Mashrafe Bin Mortaza	27	3	100	3				
Manjural Islam	18	5	66	2				
Mohammed Sharif	20.1	2	114	3				
Khaled Mahmud	9	0	40	1				
Mohammed Ashraful	3	0	25	0				

NEW ZEALAND	O	M	R	W	O	M	R	W
Cairns	11	0	55	1	18.2	2	53	7
Bond	13.1	2	47	4	15	4	28	2
Martin	11	4	38	1	4	1	6	1
McMillan	8	1	39	2				
Vettori	15	4	25	(4)	9	4	17	0

FALL OF WICKETS

	NZ	B	B
Wkt	1st	1st	2nd
1st	1	24	39
2nd	19	32	42
3rd	29	92	42
4th	51	95	68
5th	241	121	90
6th	330	146	98
7th	357	155	98
8th	359	156	104
9th	365	204	107
10th	–	205	108

Umpires: A.L.Hill (1) and D.L.Orchard (*South Africa*) (26).
Referee: B.N.Jarman (*Australia*) (24).

Test No. 1580/1 (NZ292/B8)

NEW ZEALAND v BANGLADESH (2nd Test)

At Basin Reserve, Wellington, on 26, 27, 28, 29 December.
Toss: New Zealand. Result: **NEW ZEALAND** won by an innings and 74 runs.
Debuts: None.

BANGLADESH

Javed Omar	c Vincent b Cairns	0	lbw b Bond		12
Al Sahariar	c Bond b Vettori	18	c Horne b Bond		0
Habibul Bashar	c Sinclair b Cairns	6	lbw b Drum		32
Aminul Islam	c Vincent b Bond	42	c Vettori b Bond		4
Mohammed Ashraful	c Fleming b Cairns	11	lbw b Vettori	,	10
Sanwar Hossain	run out	10	b Bond		7
Khaled Mahmud	c Parore b Drum	10	run out		4
*†Khaled Masud	not out	10	not out		19
Hasibul Hossain	c Vincent b Drum	4	c Parore b Vettori		7
Manjural Islam	b Vettori	0	(11) c Sinclair b Cairns		5
Mashrafe Bin Mortaza	run out	8	(10) b Cairns		29
Extras	(LB 4, W 1, NB 8)	13	(LB 7, W 1, NB 3)		11
Total		**132**			**135**

NEW ZEALAND

M.H.Richardson	c Mashrafe b Hasibul	83
M.J.Horne	c Masud b Manjural	38
L.Vincent	c Masud b Mashrafe	23
*S.P.Fleming	c Masud b Manjural	61
C.D.McMillan	run out	70
M.S.Sinclair	not out	19
C.L.Cairns	c Habibul b Manjural	36
†A.C.Parore		
D.L.Vettori		
S.E.Bond		
C.J.Drum		
Extras	(B 1, LB 6, W 1, NB 3)	11
Total	(6 wickets declared)	**341**

NEW ZEALAND	O	M	R	W		O	M	R	W
Cairns	15	7	24	3		6	1	27	2
Bond	13	4	21	1		15	5	54	4
Drum	11	1	26	2	(4)	3	0	9	1
Vettori	25	6	57	2	(3)	17	8	38	2

BANGLADESH	O	M	R	W
Mashrafe Bin Mortaza	16	1	57	1
Manjural Islam	29	5	99	3
Hasibul Hossain	21	3	88	1
Aminul Islam	7	0	37	0
Khaled Mahmud	12	2	42	0
Mohammed Ashraful	3	0	11	0

FALL OF WICKETS

	B	NZ	B
Wkt	1st	1st	2nd
1st	0	104	5
2nd	6	148	28
3rd	49	153	41
4th	81	283	62
5th	92	285	64
6th	108	341	75
7th	114	–	79
8th	118	–	86
9th	119	–	135
10th	132	–	135

Umpires: B.F.Bowden (2) and D.J.Harper (*Australia*) (15).
Referee: B.N.Jarman (*Australia*) (25).

Test No. 1581/2 (NZ293/B9)

SRI LANKA v ZIMBABWE (1st Test)

At Sinhalese Sports Club, Colombo, on 27, 28, 29, 31 December.
Toss: Zimbabwe. Result: **SRI LANKA** won by an innings and 166 runs.
Debuts: None.

SRI LANKA

M.S.Atapattu	c A.Flower b Streak	25
*S.T.Jayasuriya	c A.Flower b Gripper	92
†K.Sangakkara	c Wishart b Brent	128
D.P.M.deS.Jayawardena	c Carlisle b Gripper	18
R.P.Arnold	lbw b Streak	13
H.P.Tillekeratne	c A.Flower b Streak	96
T.T.Samaraweera	not out	123
W.P.U.C.J.Vaas	not out	74
D.N.T.Zoysa		
T.C.B.Fernando		
M.Muralitharan		
Extras	(B 2, LB 4, W 3, NB 8)	17
Total	**(6 wickets declared)**	**586**

ZIMBABWE

H.Masakadza	c Tillekeratne b Zoysa	3		c Atapattu b Muralitharan	28
T.R.Gripper	c Jayawardena b Muralitharan	30		c Sangakkara b Muralitharan	10
*S.V.Carlisle	c Jayasuriya b Vaas	10		c Sangakkara b Fernando	32
G.J.Rennie	lbw b Muralitharan	35	(5)	c Jayawardena b Fernando	4
†A.Flower	b Samaraweera	42	(6)	lbw b Zoysa	10
G.W.Flower	c Tillekeratne b Muralitharan	0	(7)	c Tillekeratne b Muralitharan	18
C.B.Wishart	c Tillekeratne b Zoysa	21	(8)	c Tillekeratne b Samaraweera	27
H.H.Streak	not out	26	(9)	not out	36
T.J.Friend	lbw b Vaas	6	(4)	b Muralitharan	44
G.B.Brent	b Muralitharan	0		c Jayasuriya b Zoysa	7
H.K.Olonga	lbw b Fernando	4		c Sangakkara b Vaas	0
Extras	(LB 1, NB 6)	7		(B 4, LB 7, NB 9)	20
Total		**184**			**236**

ZIMBABWE	O	M	R	W	O	M	R	W
Streak	34	5	113	3				
Friend	27	5	102	0				
Olonga	23	3	103	0				
Brent	33	5	82	1				
Gripper	22	3	91	2				
G.W.Flower	22	3	89	0				
SRI LANKA								
Vaas	24	6	63	2	21.2	6	76	1
Zoysa	14	6	24	2	15	4	34	2
Muralitharan	26	8	53	4	(4) 36	17	35	4
Jayasuriya	1	0	4	0	(5) 7	3	22	0
Fernando	9.5	0	32	1	(3) 15	3	48	2
Samaraweera	5	1	7	1	7	2	10	1

FALL OF WICKETS

	SL	Z	Z
Wkt	1st	1st	2nd
1st	78	3	40
2nd	150	29	58
3rd	170	60	93
4th	249	89	105
5th	320	105	127
6th	450	146	145
7th	–	146	165
8th	–	166	197
9th	–	167	235
10th	–	184	236

Umpires: P.T.Manuel (11) and Riazuddin (*Pakistan*) (11).
Referee: C.W.Smith (*West Indies*) (37).

Test No. 1582/11 (SL119/Z59)

SRI LANKA v ZIMBABWE (2nd Test)

At Asgiriya Stadium, Kandy, on 4, 5, 6, 7 January.
Toss: Zimbabwe. Result: **SRI LANKA** won by an innings and 94 runs.
Debuts: None.

ZIMBABWE

H.Masakadza	b Muralitharan	10	b Vaas		0
T.R.Gripper	c Jayawardena b Muralitharan	20	lbw b Muralitharan		21
*S.V.Carlisle	lbw b Muralitharan	20	c Atapattu b Vaas		9
G.J.Rennie	st Sangakkara b Muralitharan	0	lbw b Fernando		68
†A.Flower	c Sangakkara b Muralitharan	8	lbw b Fernando		11
G.W.Flower	b Muralitharan	72	c Sangakkara b Fernando		21
C.B.Wishart	lbw b Muralitharan	26	c Jayasuriya b Muralitharan		3
H.H.Streak	b Muralitharan	1	not out		14
D.A.Marillier	b Muralitharan	8	lbw b Muralitharan		9
T.J.Friend	not out	29	b Fernando		0
H.K.Olonga	c Sangakkara b Vaas	18	c Samaraweera b Muralitharan		1
Extras	(B 3, LB 7, NB 14)	24	(LB 6, NB 12)		18
Total		**236**			**175**

SRI LANKA

M.S.Atapattu	lbw b Friend	9
*S.T.Jayasuriya	c Gripper b G.W.Flower	139
†K.Sangakkara	hit wicket b Friend	42
D.P.M.deS.Jayawardena	lbw b G.W.Flower	56
R.P.Arnold	c Wishart b G.W.Flower	71
H.P.Tillekeratne	lbw b Streak	37
T.T.Samaraweera	c A.Flower b Friend	17
W.P.U.C.J.Vaas	not out	72
T.C.B.Fernando	c Friend b Masakadza	45
D.N.T.Zoysa	run out	4
M.Muralitharan	b Streak	1
Extras	(B 3, LB 1, W 1, NB 7)	12
Total		**505**

SRI LANKA	O	M	R	W	O	M	R	W
Vaas	17	4	58	1	18	5	35	2
Zoysa	15	2	44	0	10	1	30	0
Muralitharan	40	19	51	9	26.4	7	64	4
Fernando	5	2	13	0	(7) 12	2	27	4
Samaraweera	8	2	33	0	(4) 2	2	0	0
Jayasuriya	12	3	27	0	1	0	3	0
Tillekeratne					(5) 1	0	8	0

ZIMBABWE	O	M	R	W
Streak	32.5	7	85	2
Friend	26	4	97	3
Olonga	24	2	131	0
Marillier	21	4	75	0
G.W.Flower	28	4	66	3
Gripper	14	3	38	0
Masakadza	3	0	9	1

FALL OF WICKETS

	Z	SL	Z
Wkt	1st	1st	2nd
1st	39	11	0
2nd	45	82	16
3rd	51	202	51
4th	67	273	109
5th	83	336	134
6th	137	365	138
7th	140	388	160
8th	166	499	173
9th	201	503	174
10th	236	505	175

Umpires: E.A.R.de Silva (10) and S.Venkataraghavan (*India*) (50).
Referee: C.W.Smith (*West Indies*) (38). **Test No. 1583/12 (SL120/Z60)**

SRI LANKA v ZIMBABWE (3rd Test)

At Galle International Stadium on 12, 13, 14, 15 January.
Toss: Sri Lanka. Result: **SRI LANKA** won by 315 runs.
Debuts: None.

SRI LANKA

M.S.Atapattu	c Rennie b G.W.Flower	50	not out	100
*S.T.Jayasuriya	b Friend	28	c Wishart b Olonga	36
†K.Sangakkara	b Marillier	29	c Gripper b Friend	56
D.P.M.deS.Jayawardena	c and b G.W.Flower	76	not out	17
R.P.Arnold	c A.Flower b Streak	40		
H.P.Tillekeratne	c A.Flower b Marillier	3		
T.T.Samaraweera	run out	76		
W.P.U.C.J.Vaas	lbw b Streak	8		
U.D.U.Chandana	c Carlisle b Marillier	92		
T.C.B.Fernando	b Marillier	1		
M.Muralitharan	not out	5		
Extras	(B 2, LB 5, NB 3)	10	(LB 1, NB 2)	3
Total		**418**	(2 wickets declared)	**212**

ZIMBABWE

*S.V.Carlisle	lbw b Muralitharan	64	lbw b Jayasuriya	28
T.R.Gripper	st Sangakkara b Jayasuriya	83	lbw b Jayasuriya	3
C.B.Wishart	lbw b Jayasuriya	1	c Samaraweera b Muralitharan	7
G.J.Rennie	c Sangakkara b Jayasuriya	7	c Arnold b Muralitharan	6
†A.Flower	c Tillekeratne b Muralitharan	6	c Jayawardena b Jayasuriya	3
G.W.Flower	lbw b Muralitharan	19	lbw b Jayasuriya	0
H.H.Streak	b Jayasuriya	33	c Jayasuriya b Muralitharan	7
D.D.Ebrahim	c Arnold b Jayasuriya	1	not out	15
D.A.Marillier	not out	0	c and b Muralitharan	3
T.J.Friend	b Muralitharan	1	lbw b Vaas	3
H.K.Olonga	b Muralitharan	0	c Fernando b Vaas	0
Extras	(B 11 LB 8, NB 2)	21	(LB 1, NB 1)	2
Total		**236**		**79**

ZIMBABWE	O	M	R	W		O	M	R	W	FALL OF WICKETS			
											SL	Z	SL	Z
Streak	32	11	70	2		11	1	35	0	Wkt	1st	1st	2nd	2nd
Friend	26	7	58	1		7	0	39	1	1st	50	153	75	17
Olonga	18	6	52	0	(5)	7	0	56	1	2nd	107	155	170	30
G.W.Flower	39	7	89	2	(3)	9	0	38	0	3rd	125	161	–	38
Marillier	34.4	5	101	4	(4)	6	0	34	0	4th	222	171	–	45
Gripper	9	0	41	0						5th	229	171	–	45
Rennie					(6)	1	0	9	0	6th	236	232	–	54
										7th	254	234	–	56
SRI LANKA										8th	400	235	–	72
Vaas	19	7	36	0		7.3	2	17	2	9th	413	236	–	79
Fernando	11	1	33	0		2	0	6	0	10th	418	236	–	79
Muralitharan	58.3	26	67	5	(4)	16	7	24	4					
Jayasuriya	29	10	43	5	(3)	18	5	31	4					
Chandana	12	4	24	0										
Samaraweera	5	1	14	0										

Umpires: D.R.Shepherd (*England*) (59) and T.H.Wijewardene (2).
Referee: C.W.Smith (*West Indies*) (39).   **Test No. 1584/13 (SL121/Z61)**

SRI LANKA v ZIMBABWE 2001-02

SRI LANKA – BATTING AND FIELDING

	M	I	NO	HS	Runs	Avge	100	50	Ct/St
W.P.U.C.J.Vaas	3	3	2	74*	154	154.00	–	2	–
T.T.Samaraweera	3	3	1	123*	216	108.00	1	1	2
S.T.Jayasuriya	3	4	–	139	295	73.75	1	1	4
K.Sangakkara	3	4	–	128	255	63.75	1	1	7/2
M.S.Atapattu	3	4	1	100*	184	61.33	1	1	2
D.P.M.deS.Jayawardena	3	4	–	76	167	55.66	–	2	4
H.P.Tillekeratne	3	3	–	96	136	45.33	–	1	6
R.P.Arnold	3	3	–	71	124	41.33	–	1	2
T.C.B.Fernando	3	2	–	45	46	23.00	–	–	1
M.Muralitharan	3	2	1	5*	6	6.00	–	–	1
D.N.T.Zoysa	2	1	–	4	4	4.00	–	–	–

Played in one Test: U.D.U.Chandana 92.

SRI LANKA – BOWLING

	O	M	R	W	Avge	Best	5wI	10wM
M.Muralitharan	203.1	84	294	30	9.80	9-51	2	1
S.T.Jayasuriya	68	21	130	9	14.44	5-43	1	–
T.C.B.Fernando	54.5	8	159	7	22.71	4-27	–	–
D.N.T.Zoysa	54	13	132	4	33.00	2-24	–	–
T.T.Samaraweera	29	8	66	2	33.00	1- 7	–	–
W.P.U.C.J.Vaas	106.5	30	285	8	35.62	2-17	–	–

Also bowled: U.D.U.Chandana 12-4-24-0; H.P.Tillekeratne 1-0-8-0.

ZIMBABWE – BATTING AND FIELDING

	M	I	NO	HS	Runs	Avge	100	50	Ct/St
H.H.Streak	3	6	3	36*	117	39.00	–	–	–
T.R.Gripper	3	6	–	83	167	27.83	–	1	2
S.V.Carlisle	3	6	–	64	163	27.16	–	1	2
G.W.Flower	3	6	–	72	130	21.66	–	1	1
G.J.Rennie	3	6	–	68	120	20.00	–	1	–
T.J.Friend	3	6	1	44	83	16.60	–	–	1
C.B.Wishart	3	6	–	27	85	14.16	–	–	3
A.Flower	3	6	–	42	80	13.33	–	–	6
D.A.Marillier	2	4	1	15	32	10.66	–	–	–
H.Masakadza	2	4	–	28	41	10.25	–	–	–
H.K.Olonga	3	6	–	18	23	3.83	–	–	–

Played in one Test: G.B.Brent 0, 7; D.D.Ebrahim 1, 5*.

ZIMBABWE – BOWLING

	O	M	R	W	Avge	Best	5wI	10wM
H.H.Streak	109.5	24	303	7	43.28	3-113	–	–
D.A.Marillier	61.4	9	210	4	52.50	4-101	–	–
G.W.Flower	98	14	282	5	56.40	3- 66	–	–
T.J.Friend	86	16	296	5	59.20	3- 97	–	–
T.R.Gripper	45	6	170	2	85.00	2- 91	–	–

Also bowled: G.B.Brent 33-5-82-1; H.Masakadza 3-0-9-1; H.K.Olonga 72-11-342-1; G.J.Rennie 1-0-9-0.

BANGLADESH v PAKISTAN (1st Test)

At Bangabandhu National Stadium, Dhaka, on 9, 10, 11 January.
Toss: Pakistan. Result: **PAKISTAN** won by an innings and 178 runs.
Debuts: Bangladesh – Fahim Muntasir.

BANGLADESH

Al Sahariar	lbw b Razzaq	18	(7)	lbw b Waqar	21
Mehrab Hossain	c Shadab b Razzaq	11	(1)	c Inzamam b Danish	19
Mohammed Ashraful	c Youhana b Danish	27	(2)	c Younis Khan b Razzaq	22
Habibul Bashar	c Danish b Waqar	53	(3)	c Waqar b Danish	0
Aminul Islam	lbw b Danish	25	(4)	lbw b Razzaq	11
Sanwar Hossain	c Inzamam b Waqar	3	(5)	c Shadab b Danish	1
*†Khaled Masud	lbw b Waqar	0	(6)	c Waqar b Danish	5
Enamul Haque	c Inzamam b Waqar	12		b Danish	19
Fahim Muntasir	b Waqar	0		c sub (Mohd Sami) b Danish	33
Mohammed Sharif	b Waqar	0		c Waqar b Danish	11
Manjural Islam	not out	0		not out	2
Extras	(LB 8, W 1, NB 2)	11		(LB 5, NB 3)	8
Total		**160**			**152**

PAKISTAN

Taufiq Umar	lbw b Sharif	53
Shadab Kabir	b Enamul	55
Younis Khan	c Masud b Enamul	0
Yousuf Youhana	run out	72
Saqlain Mushtaq	lbw b Enamul	9
Abdul Razzaq	c Aminul b Manjural	134
†Rashid Latif	c Al Sahariar b Sharif	94
Inzamam-ul-Haq	c Mehrab b Enamul	43
*Waqar Younis	c Al Sahariar b Manjural	8
Danish Kaneria	not out	3
Wasim Akram		
Extras	(LB 13, W 2, NB 4)	19
Total	(9 wickets declared)	**490**

PAKISTAN	O	M	R	W		O	M	R	W
Wasim Akram	2.4	1	5	0					
Waqar Younis	16.2	2	55	6	(1)	9	3	27	1
Abdul Razzaq	8.2	2	42	2	(2)	10	2	29	2
Danish Kaneria	19	5	36	2	(3)	19.4	4	77	7
Saqlain Mushtaq	7	2	14	0	(4)	5	1	14	0
BANGLADESH									
Manjural Islam	33	4	124	2					
Mohammed Sharif	35	9	95	2					
Fahim Muntasir	32	6	109	0					
Enamul Haque	39.4	9	136	4					
Mohammed Ashraful	1	0	13	0					

FALL OF WICKETS

	B	P	B
Wkt	*1st*	*1st*	*2nd*
1st	30	100	38
2nd	45	100	38
3rd	77	116	49
4th	140	162	52
5th	146	221	64
6th	146	396	86
7th	147	463	90
8th	147	471	112
9th	151	490	139
10th	160	–	152

Umpires: Akhtaruddin Sahin (2) and J.H.Hampshire (*England*) (21).
Referee: B.F.Hastings (*New Zealand*) (9). **Test No. 1585/2 (B10/P280)**

BANGLADESH v PAKISTAN (2nd Test)

At Chittagong Stadium on 16, 17, 18, 19, 20 January.
Toss: Bangladesh. Result: **PAKISTAN** won by an innings and 169 runs.
Debuts: None.

BANGLADESH

Javed Omar	c Shadab b Saqlain	17		c Rashid b Waqar	0
Al Sahariar	c Rashid b Waqar	13		c Rashid b Waqar	8
Mehrab Hossain	b Danish	16		c Rashid b Waqar	14
Habibul Bashar	c Shadab b Saqlain	2	(5)	c Shadab b Saqlain	51
Aminul Islam	c Youhana b Danish	25	(4)	b Shoaib	0
Sanwar Hossain	lbw b Saqlain	11		c Younis Khan b Saqlain	30
Enamul Haque	c Shadab b Danish	0	(8)	b Shoaib	9
*†Khaled Masud	c Taufiq b Saqlain	28	(7)	not out	15
Fahim Muntasir	c Inzamam b Danish	9		b Shoaib	2
Mohammed Sharif	st Rashid b Saqlain	0		b Shoaib	0
Manjural Islam	not out	4		c Shadab b Waqar	0
Extras	(B 5, LB 9, NB 9)	23		(B 8, LB 1, NB 8)	17
Total		**148**			**148**

PAKISTAN

Taufiq Umar	c Aminul b Sharif	47
Shadab Kabir	c Masud b Sharif	4
Younis Khan	c Mehrab b Fahim	119
Inzamam-ul-Haq	c Aminul b Fahim	30
Yousuf Youhana	not out	204
Abdul Razzaq	b Sharif	18
†Rashid Latif	lbw b Manjural	15
*Waqar Younis	c Mehrab b Fahim	10
Saqlain Mushtaq	c Aminul b Sharif	7
Shoaib Akhtar	c Sanwar b Manjural	2
Danish Kaneria	not out	4
Extras	(W 1, NB 4)	5
Total	(9 wickets declared)	**465**

PAKISTAN	O	M	R	W		O	M	R	W
Waqar Younis	7	2	19	1		8.5	0	36	4
Shoaib Akhtar	6	2	15	0		11	1	48	4
Danish Kaneria	22	6	62	4	(5)	6	3	9	0
Abdul Razzaq	5	2	3	0		2	0	12	0
Saqlain Mushtaq	16.4	3	35	5	(3)	11	3	34	2

BANGLADESH	O	M	R	W
Manjural Islam	35	9	95	2
Mohammed Sharif	35.5	10	98	4
Enamul Haque	33	6	114	0
Fahim Muntasir	27	3	131	3
Aminul Islam	4	0	27	0

FALL OF WICKETS

	B	P	B
Wkt	1st	1st	2nd
1st	21	12	0
2nd	57	99	23
3rd	60	166	24
4th	65	236	41
5th	84	274	110
6th	85	315	128
7th	112	339	144
8th	126	438	147
9th	127	447	147
10th	148	–	148

Umpires: Mahbubur Rahman (1) and R.B.Tiffin (*Zimbabwe*) (24).
Referee: B.F.Hastings (*New Zealand*) (10).   **Test No. 1586/3 (B11/P281)**

TEST MATCH CHAMPIONSHIP SCHEDULE

2002

Apr	South Africa host Bangladesh
	West Indies host India
	Zimbabwe host Australia
May	England host Sri Lanka
Jun	West Indies host New Zealand
Jul	England host India
	Sri Lanka host Bangladesh
Sep	Pakistan host Australia
Oct	India host West Indies
	South Africa host Sri Lanka
Nov	Australia host England
	Zimbabwe host Pakistan
Dec	Australia host Sri Lanka
	New Zealand host India
	South Africa host Pakistan
	Bangladesh host West Indies

2003

Jan	Australia host England
Feb	*World Cup in South Africa*
Apr	Pakistan host India
	West Indies host Australia
May	England host Zimbabwe
	Sri Lanka host New Zealand
Jul	England host South Africa
	West Indies host Sri Lanka
Sep	Pakistan host Bangladesh
Oct	India host New Zealand
	Pakistan host South Africa
	Zimbabwe host West Indies
	Bangladesh host Australia
Nov	Australia host Zimbabwe
	Sri Lanka host England
Dec	Australia host India
	New Zealand host Pakistan
	South Africa host West Indies
	Bangladesh host England

2004

Jan	Australia host India
	Bangladesh host Zimbabwe
Feb	India host Pakistan
	New Zealand host South Africa
	Sri Lanka host Australia
	West Indies host England
Apr	Zimbabwe host Sri Lanka
	Bangladesh host India
May	England host New Zealand
	West Indies host Bangladesh
Jul	England host West Indies
Aug	Sri Lanka host South Africa
Sep	India host Australia
Oct	Pakistan host Zimbabwe
	Bangladesh host New Zealand
Nov	Australia host West Indies
	India host South Africa
	Zimbabwe host England
	Bangladesh host Sri Lanka
Dec	Australia host Pakistan
	New Zealand host Sri Lanka
	South Africa host England

2005

Jan	South Africa host England
Feb	New Zealand host Australia
	Pakistan host India
	South Africa host Zimbabwe
Mar	Pakistan host Sri Lanka
	West Indies host South Africa
Apr	India host Bangladesh
May	England host Bangladesh
	West Indies host Pakistan
Jun	England host Australia
Jul	Sri Lanka host West Indies
Sep	Australia host Bangladesh
	Zimbabwe host New Zealand
Oct	South Africa host New Zealand
	Zimbabwe host India
Nov	India host Sri Lanka
	Pakistan host England
Dec	Australia host South Africa
	New Zealand host West Indies

2006

Jan	India host Pakistan
	New Zealand host West Indies
Feb	India host England
	New Zealand host Zimbabwe
	South Africa host Australia
Mar	Sri Lanka host Pakistan
Apr	West Indies host Zimbabwe
May	England host Sri Lanka
	West Indies host India
Jul	England host Pakistan
Aug	Zimbabwe host South Africa
Sep	Zimbabwe host Australia
Oct	Pakistan host Zimbabwe
	Sri Lanka host South Africa
Nov	Australia host New Zealand
Dec	Australia host England
	Pakistan host West Indies
	South Africa host India

2007

Feb	New Zealand host India
	South Africa host Pakistan
	Sri Lanka host Zimbabwe
	West Indies host Australia
Apr	*World Cup in West Indies*
Jun	England host India
Aug	Sri Lanka host New Zealand
Sep	Zimbabwe host Pakistan
Oct	India host Zimbabwe
	Pakistan host South Africa
	Sri Lanka host England
Nov	Australia host Sri Lanka
Dec	Australia host India
	New Zealand host Sri Lanka
	South Africa host West Indies

SECOND XI FIXTURES 2002

No symbol	Second XI Championship	3 days
*	Second XI Championship	4 days
†	Second XI Trophy	1 day

APRIL

23–26	Bristol	*Glos v Warwks
24–26	Chester-le-St (R)	Durham v Yorks
	Kidderminster	Worcs v Northants

MAY

1–3	Hinckley	Leics v Kent
	Uxbridge (Vine L)	Middx v Sussex
	Chesterfield	Derbys v Surrey
7	Bradford & Bingley	†Yorks v Derbys
7–10	Manchester (OT)	*Lancs v Notts
	Pontarddulais	*Glam v Glos
8–10	Maidstone	Kent v Essex
	Moseley CC	Warwks v Northants
	Stamford Bridge	Yorks v Derbys
	North Perrott	Somerset v Worcs
14–16	Leicester	Leics v Glam
	Crosby	Lancs v Northants
14–17	The Oval	*Surrey v Hants
	Unity Casuals CC	*Notts v Derbys
	Hove	*Sussex v Kent
15–17	Chester-le-St CC	Durham v Middx
	Barnt Green	Worcs v Yorks
20	Southampton (WE)	†Hants v Glam
20–22	Coventry & N Wwk	Warwks v Durham
20–23	Liverpool	*Lancs v Yorks
21–24	Hinckley	*Leics v Derbys
22–24	Cheam	Surrey v Notts
	North Perrott	Somerset v Northants
27	Southampton (WE)	†Hants v Somerset
27–29	Milton Keynes	Northants v Kent
28–30	Southgate	Middx v Essex
28–31	Hove	*Sussex v Glos
	Stockton	*Durham v Lancs
	Taunton	*Somerset v Glam
29	Southampton (WE)	†Hants v Worcs
29–31	Nottingham (TB)	Notts v Leics

JUNE

3	Southampton (WE)	†Hants v Glos
4–6	Hartlepool	Durham v Worcs
	Nottingham (Boots)	Notts v Warwks
4–7	Scarborough	*Yorks v Lancs
5	Sutton	†Surrey v MCC YC
5–7	Dunstall CC	Derbys v Leics
	Uxbridge CC	Middx v Glos
	Abergavenny	Glam v Northants
	Halstead	Essex v Sussex

JUNE

10	Nottingham (TB)	†Notts v Yorks
10–12	Grappenhall CC	Lancs v Durham
10–13	Bristol	*Glos v Somerset
11–14	Southampton (WE)	*Hants v Essex
	Hinckley	*Leics v Notts
	Cardiff	*Glam v Yorks
12–14	Canterbury	Kent v Surrey
	Northampton	Northants v Warwks
17	Sutton	†Surrey v Kent
18–20	Southampton (WE)	Hants v Middx
18–21	Denby CC	*Derbys v Notts
	Ombersley	*Worcs v Warwks
	Blackpool	*Lancs v Somerset
20	Beckenham	†Kent v Surrey
	Hinckley	†Leics v Minor C
	Bishop's Stortford	†Essex v Sussex
24	Leeds (H)	†Yorks v Notts
	Stratford-u-Avon	*Warwks v Middx
	O Brentwoods	†Essex v Surrey
	Uxbridge (Vine L)	†MCC YC v Sussex
	Southport	†Lancs v Derbys
	Taunton	†Somerset v Worcs
25	Milton Keynes	†Northants v Leics
	Tynemouth	†Durham v Notts
	Bristol	†Glos v Somerset
26	Canterbury	†Kent v MCC YC
	Sutton	†Surrey v Sussex
	Wellington CC	Minor C v Warwks
	Bristol	†Glos v Worcs
	Castleford	†Yorks v Lancs
	Taunton	†Somerset v Glam
27	Hinckley	†Leics v Middx
	Sutton Valence	†Kent v Sussex
	Sunderland	†Durham v Lancs
28	Bristol	†Glos v Hants
	Banstead	†Surrey v Essex
	Darlington	†Durham v Yorks
	Usk	†Glam v Worcs

JULY

1	Taunton	†Somerset v Hants
	Ilkeston	†Derbys v Notts
	Uxbridge CC	†Middx v Northants
	Wormsley	†MCC YC v Surrey
	Hove	†Sussex v Essex

	Worcester	†Worcs v Glos
	Nelson CC	†Lancs v Durham
2	Unity Casuals CC	†Notts v Durham
	Studley	†Warwks v Northants
	Wigan	†Lancs v Yorks
3	Neath CC	*Glam v Glos
	Oakham S	†Leics v Warwks
	Hove	†Sussex v Kent
	Glossop	†Derbys v Yorks
4	Hove	†Sussex v Surrey
	Studley	†Warwks v Minor C
5	Canterbury	†Kent v Essex
	Newport	†Glam v Hants
	Finchley	†Middx v Leics
	Hove	†Sussex v MCC YC
	Chesterfield	†Derbys v Lancs
	Worcester	†Worcs v Somerset
	York CC	†Yorks v Durham
	Isham	†Northants v Minor C
8	Harborne	†Warwks v Leics
	Welbeck	†Notts v Derbys
	Northampton	†Northants v Middx
9	Taunton	†Somerset v Glos
9–11	Coggleshall	Essex v Notts
9–12	Southampton (WE)	*Hants v Surrey
	Sandiacre CC	*Derbys v Warwks
	Worcester	*Worcs v Glam
	Northampton	*Northants v Sussex
10–12	Taunton	Somerset v Glos
11	Uxbridge (Vine L)	†MCC YC v Kent
	High Wycombe CC	†Minor C v Middx
12	Milton Keynes	†Minor C v Leics
	Coggleshall	†Essex v Kent
15	Uxbridge (Vine L)	†MCC YC v Essex
	Oakham S	†Leics v Northants
	Richmond CC	†Middx v Warwks
	Dunstall CC	†Derbys v Durham
16	Old Hill CC	†Worcs v Hants
	Farnsfield CC	†Notts v Lancs
16–19	Stirlands CC	*Sussex v Surrey
17	Uxbridge (Vine L)	†Middx v Minor C
	Old Hill CC	†Worcs v Glam
17–19	Nottingham (Boots)	Notts v Yorks
	Knowle & Dorridge	Warwks v Somerset
18	Cheltenham/Bristol	†Glos v Glam
	(venue depends on CGT draw)	
	South Shields	†Durham v Derbys
	Luton	†Minor C v Northants
19	Billericay	†Essex v MCC YC
22	Manchester (OT)	†Lancs v Notts
	Northampton	†Northants v Warwks
	Cardiff	†Glam v Somerset
23–25	Oakham S	Leics v Essex

23–26	Hove	*Sussex v Hants
	Nottingham (TB)	*Notts v Durham
	Usk	*Glam v Somerset
24–26	Canterbury	Kent v Middx
	Todmorden	Yorks v Surrey
	Bristol	Glos v Worcs
	Repton S	Derbys v Lancs
30–1 Aug	Seaton Carew	Durham v Northants
30–2 Aug	Bristol U	*Glos v Hants
	Banstead	*Surrey v Sussex
31–2 Aug	Merchant Taylors S	Middx v Kent
	Worksop C	Notts v Lancs
	Walmley	Warwks v Essex

AUGUST

6–9	Northampton	*Northants v Hants
	Chelmsford	*Essex v Kent
	Stratford-u-Avon	*Warwks v Worcs
7–9	The Oval	Surrey v Lancs
	S Northumberland	Durham v Derbys
	Taunton	Somerset v Yorks
	Horsham	Sussex v Glam
12 (13)	tbc	†Trophy Semi-Finals
13–15	Hastings	Sussex v Northants
13–16	Denby CC	*Derbys v Hants
14–16	Harrogate	Yorks v Leics
	Ealing	Middx v Notts
	Whitgift S	Surrey v Durham
19–21	Bristol	Glos v Leics
20–22	Wimbledon	Surrey v Middx
	Worcester	Worcs v Lancs
20–23	Southampton (WE)	*Hants v Notts
	Panteg	*Glam v Warwks
21–23	Beckenham	Kent v Somerset
	Stowe S	Northants v Derbys
26–28	Northampton	Northants v Worcs
27–29	Canterbury	Kent v Hants
	Kenilworth Wardens	Warwks v Leics
27–30	Nottingham (TB)	*Notts v Sussex
	Chelmsford	*Essex v Middx
	Bristol U	*Glos v Glam
	Middlesbrough	*Yorks v Durham
28–30	Manchester (OT)	Lancs v Surrey

SEPTEMBER

2–4	Stamford Bridge	Yorks v Notts
3–5	Halesowen	Worcs v Leics
	Abergavenny	Glam v Lancs
4–6	Southampton (WE)	Hants v Sussex
	Shenley	Middx v Derbys
	Colchester	Essex v Surrey
	Northampton	Northants v Glos
9 (10)	tbc	† Trophy Final
11–13	Hinckley	Leics v Northants

MINOR COUNTIES CHAMPIONSHIP
FIXTURES 2002

3-day matches. † Noon start

	Venue	Div	Match		Venue	Div	Match
JUNE				**JULY**			
2–4	Dunstable	E	Beds v Cambs		Finchampstead	W	Berks v Herefords
	†Falkland	W	Berks v Cornwall		Marlow	E	Bucks v Cambs
	Ascott Park	E	Bucks v Norfolk		Dean Park	W	Dorset v Devon
	Cheadle Hulme	W	Cheshire v Oxon		Long Marston	E	Herts v Cumb
	Exmouth	W	Devon v Salop		Horsford	E	Norfolk v Suffolk
	†Colwall	W	Herefords v Wales MC		Thame	W	Oxon v Wilts
	Grantham	E	Lincs v Staffs		Stone	E	Staffs v Northumb
	Corsham	W	Wilts v Dorset		†Swansea	W	Wales MC v Salop
4–6	†Carlisle	E	Cumb v Northumb	29–31	Alderley Edge	W	Cheshire v Cornwall
23–25	Hertford	E	Herts v Norfolk	**AUGUST**			
	Jesmond	E	Northumb v Suffolk	4–6	Luton Town	E	Beds v Suffolk
	Challow	W	Oxon v Berks		Reading CC	W	Berks v Wilts
	Shrewsbury	W	Salop v Wilts		Beaconsfield	E	Bucks v Staffs
30–2 Jul	Dean Park	W	Dorset v Cornwall		Fenners	E	Cambs v Northumb
	Luctonians	W	Herefords v Cheshire		Oxton	W	Cheshire v Wales MC
	Welwyn Gdn City	E	Herts v Cambs		Luctonians	E	Herefords v Dorset
	Grantham	E	Lincs v Bucks		Grantham	E	Lincs v Herts
	Tamworth	E	Staffs v Beds		Banbury	E	Oxon v Devon
	†Lamphey	W	Wales MC v Berks	5–7	St Austell	W	Cornwall v Salop
	South Wilts	W	Wilts v Devon		Horsford	E	Norfolk v Cumb
				18–20	March	E	Cambs v Lincs
JULY					†Truro	E	Cornwall v Herefords
1–3	Bury St Edmunds	E	Suffolk v Cumb		Netherfield	E	Cumb v Beds
14–16	March	E	Cambs v Staffs		Torquay	W	Devon v Berks
	Falmouth	W	Cornwall v Wales MC		Jesmond	E	Northumb v Norfolk
	Sidmouth	W	Devon v Cheshire		Whitchurch	W	Salop v Oxon
	Dean Park	W	Dorset v Oxon		Walsall	E	Staffs v Herts
	Jesmond	E	Northumb v Lincs		Mildenhall	E	Suffolk v Bucks
	Shifnal	W	Salop v Herts		†Abergavenny	W	Wales MC v Dorset
	Ransomes	E	Suffolk v Herts		Westbury	W	Wilts v Cheshire
15–17	Barrow	E	Cumb v Bucks	**SEPTEMBER**			
21–23	Horsford	W	Norfolk v Beds	8–10	tba	W	**CHAMPIONSHIP FINAL**
28–30	Bedford Town	E	Beds v Lincs				

ECB 38-COUNTY CUP
FIXTURES 2002

† Noon start.

	Venue	Gp	Match
MAY			
Sun 5	Chippenham	1	Wilts v Somerset
	Bishop's Stortford	3	Herts v Suffolk
	Slough	4	Berks v Middx
	Bristol U	5	Glos v Worcs
	N'ham (Boots)	7	Notts v Hunts
Thu 9	York CC	8	Yorks v Northumb
Sun 19	St Just	1	Cornwall v Wilts
	Bovey Tracey	1	Devon v Dorset
	Southampton (WE)	2	Hants v Channel Is
	Harpenden	3	Herts v Essex
	March	3	Cambs v Beds
	Thatcham	4	Berks v Oxon
	Ascott Park	4	Bucks v Northants
	†Pontarddulais	5	Wales MC v Worcs
	Stratford-u-Avon	5	Warwks v Glos
	Oswestry	6	Salop v Cheshire
	Longton	6	Staffs v Lancs
	Hinckley	7	Leics v Norfolk
	N'ham (Boots)	7	Notts v Lincs
	South Shields	8	Durham v Northumb
Tue 21	Millom	8	Cumb v Yorks
Sun 26	Taunton	1	Somerset v Devon
	Exning	3	Suffolk v Cambs
Thu 30	Imber Court	2	Surrey v Sussex
JUNE			
Tue 4	Imber Court	2	Surrey v Kent
Sun 9	Camborne	1	Cornwall v Devon
	Bournemouth (DP)	1	Dorset v Somerset
	Jersey (St Saviours)	2	Channel Is v Sussex
	Southill Park	3	Beds v Herts
	Chelmsford	3	Essex v Suffolk
	Challow	4	Oxon v Bucks
	Stowe S	4	Northants v Berks
	†Leominster (Dales)	5	Herefords v Wales MC
	Kidderminster	5	Worcs v Warwks
	Lullington	6	Derbys v Salop
	Horsford	7	Norfolk v Notts
	tba	7	Hunts v Lincs
	S Northumberland	8	Northumb v Cumb
Wed 12	Ealing	4	Middx v Bucks
Thu 13	†Blackpool	6	Lancs v Cheshire
	Stamford Bridge	8	Yorks v Durham
Sun 16	N Perrott	1	Somerset v Cornwall
	Swindon	1	Wilts v Dorset
	Havant Park	2	Hants v Surrey
	Hastings	2	Sussex v Kent

	Venue	Gp	Match
JUNE			
	Flitwick	3	Beds v Essex
	Banbury	4	Oxon v Northants
	Coventry & N Wk	5	Warwks v Wales MC
	Bristol U	5	Glos v Herefords
	Nantwich	6	Cheshire v Staffs
	Wellington	6	Salop v Lancs
	Lincoln Lindum	7	Lincs v Norfolk
	Hinckley	7	Leics v Notts
	Tynemouth	8	Northumb v Yorks
Tue 18	Hartlepool	8	Durham v Cumb
Sun 23	Stirlands	2	Sussex v Hants
	Ashford	2	Kent v Channel Is
	Chelmsford	3	Essex v Cambs
	O Northamptonians	4	Northants v Middx
	Kidderminster	5	Worcs v Herefords
	Alvaston & Boulton	6	Derbys v Staffs
	tba	7	Hunts v Leics
Tue 25	New Brighton	6	Cheshire v Derbys
Thu 27	Middleton	6	Lancs v Derbys
JULY			
Wed 3	Richmond	4	Middx v Oxon
Sun 7	Torquay	1	Devon v Wilts
	Bournemouth SC	1	Dorset v Cornwall
	Jersey (St Saviours)	2	Channel Is v Surrey
	Ashford	2	Kent v Hants
	Wisbech	3	Cambs v Herts
	Woodbridge S	3	Suffolk v Beds
	Wormsley	4	Bucks v Berks
	†Penarth	5	Wales MC v Glos
	Brockhampton	5	Herefords v Warwks
	Porthill Park	6	Staffs v Salop
	Horsford	7	Norfolk v Hunts
	Cleethorpes	7	Lincs v Leics
Tue 9	Furness	8	Cumb v Durham

AUGUST

Thu 1	QUARTER-FINALS (*No reserve day*)	
	Match A	(*Winner #1 v Winner #4*)
	Match B	(*Winner #6 v Winner #8*)
	Match C	(*Winner #5 v Winner #7*)
	Match D	(*Winner #3 v Winner #2*)
Thu 15	SEMI-FINALS (*Reserve 16 August*)	
	Match E	(*Winner #D v Winner #A*)
	Match F	(*Winner #B v Winner #C*)

SEPTEMBER

Tue 3	FINAL (Lord's) (*Reserve 4 September*)

PRINCIPAL FIXTURES 2002

BHC   Benson and Hedges Cup
CC1   County Championship (1st Division)
CC2   County Championship (2nd Division)
CGT   Cheltenham & Gloucester Trophy
F   Floodlit
FCF   First-Class Friendly

LOI   NatWest Limited-Overs International
NL1   NU National League (1st Division)
NL2   NU National League (2nd Division)
TM   npower Test Match
UCCE   Univ Centre of Cricketing Excellence
*   *Match to be confirmed*

Sat 13 – Mon 15 April
FCF	Cambridge	Cambridge UCCE v Middx
FCF	Chester-le-St	Durham v Durham UCCE
	Canterbury	Kent v Loughborough UCCE
	Leicester	Leics v Brad/Leeds UCCE
FCF	Oxford	Oxford UCCE v Worcs
	Millfield S	Somerset v Cardiff UCCE

Thurs 18 – Sat 20 April
FCF	Oxford	Oxford UCCE v Northants

Fri 19 – Mon 22 April
CC2	Chester-le-St	Durham v Middlesex
CC2	Cardiff	Glamorgan v Derbyshire
CC1	Canterbury	Kent v Hampshire
CC2	Lord's	Middlesex v Worcs
CC1	Manchester	Lancashire v Leics
CC1	The Oval	Surrey v Sussex
CC2	Worcester	Worcs v Glos

Sat 20 – Mon 22 April
	Cambridge	Cambridge UCCE v Essex
	Nottingham	Notts v Durham UCCE
	Birmingham	Warwks v Cardiff UCCE
	Leeds	Yorks v Brad/Leeds UCCE

Weds 24 – Sat 27 April
CC2	Derby	Derbyshire v Durham
CC2	Chelmsford	Essex v Glos
CC1	Southampton	Hampshire v Leics
CC2	Lord's	Middlesex v Notts
CC2	Northampton	Northants v Worcs
CC1	Hove	Sussex v Somerset
CC1	Birmingham	Warwks v Lancashire
CC1	Leeds	Yorks v Surrey

Weds 24 – Fri 26 April
	Cardiff	Glam v Cardiff UCCE

Fri 26 – Sun 28 April
FCF	Canterbury	Kent v Sri Lankans

Sun 28 April
BHC	Derby	Derbyshire v Lancashire
BHC	Chelmsford	Essex v Sussex
BHC	Lord's	Middlesex v Surrey
BHC	Northampton	Northants v Glamorgan
BHC	Nottingham	Notts v Yorkshire
BHC	Birmingham	Warwks v Somerset

Mon 29 April
BHC	Southampton	Hampshire v Kent
BHC	Leicester	Leics v Durham
BHC	Worcester	Worcs v Glos

Tues 30 April
BHC	Lord's	Middlesex v Essex
BHC	Nottingham	Notts v Derbyshire
BHC	Taunton	Somerset v Glamorgan

Weds 1 May
BHC	Chester-le-St	Durham v Lancashire
BHC	Bristol	Glos v Warwks
BHC	Canterbury	Kent v Sussex
BHC	Northampton	Northants v Worcs
BHC	The Oval	Surrey v Hampshire
BHC	Leeds	Yorkshire v Leics

Thurs 2 – Sat 4 May
FCF	Northampton	British U v Sri Lankans

Thurs 2 May
BHC	Chester-le-St	Durham v Yorkshire
BHC	Chelmsford	Essex v Surrey
BHC	Canterbury	Kent v Middlesex

Fri 3 May
BHC	Derby	Derbyshire v Leics
BHC	Cardiff	Glamorgan v Glos
BHC	Manchester	Lancashire v Notts
BHC	Taunton	Somerset v Northants
BHC	Hove	Sussex v Hampshire
BHC	Birmingham	Warwks v Worcs

Sat 4 May
BHC	Derby	Derbyshire v Yorkshire
BHC	Nottingham	Notts v Durham
BHC	The Oval	Surrey v Kent

Sun 5 May
BHC	Chelmsford	Essex v Hampshire
BHC	Bristol	Glos v Somerset
BHC	Manchester	Lancashire v Leics
BHC	Lord's	Middlesex v Sussex
BHC	Birmingham	Warwks v Northants
BHC	Worcester	Worcs v Glamorgan

Mon 6 May
BHC	Chester-le-St	Durham v Derbyshire
BHC	Cardiff	Glamorgan v Warwks
BHC	Southampton	Hampshire v Middlesex

BHC	Canterbury	Kent v Essex
BHC	Leicester	Leics v Warwks
BHC	Northampton	Northants v Glos
BHC	Taunton	Somerset v Worcs
BHC	Hove	Sussex v Surrey
BHC	Leeds	Yorkshire v Lancashire

Tues 7 – Thurs 9 May
FCF	Chester-le-St	Durham v Sri Lankans

Weds 8 – Sat 11 May
CC2	Derby	Derbyshire v Northants
CC1	Southampton	Hampshire v Kent
CC1	Leicester	Leics v Warwks
CC2	Nottingham	Notts v Essex
CC1	Taunton	Somerset v Yorkshire
CC1	The Oval	Surrey v Lancashire
CC2	Worcester	Worcs v Glamorgan

Weds 8 – Fri 10 May
	Hastings	Sussex v Brad/Leeds UCCE
FCF	Oxford	Oxford UCCE v Glos

Sat 11 – Mon 13 May
FCF	Shenley	Middlesex v Sri Lankans

Sun 12 May
NL2	Derby	Derbyshire v Sussex
NL1	Chester-le-St	Durham v Warwks
NL2	Southampton	Hampshire v Glos
NL1	Leicester	Leics v Notts
NL1	Taunton	Somerset v Yorkshire
NL2	The Oval	Surrey v Lancashire

Weds 15 – Sat 18 May
CC2	Cardiff	Glamorgan v Durham
CC2	Bristol	Glos v Notts
CC1	Canterbury	Kent v Yorkshire
CC1	Manchester	Lancashire v Sussex
CC2	Northampton	Northants v Middlesex
CC1	Taunton	Somerset v Leics
CC1	Birmingham	Warwks v Hampshire
CC2	Worcester	Worcs v Essex

Weds 15 – Fri 17 May
FCF	Cambridge	Cambridge UCCE v Surrey
	Derby	Derbys v Loughborough UCCE

Thurs 16 – Mon 20 May
TM1	Lord's	England v Sri Lanka

Sun 19 May
NL2	Chelmsford	Essex v Derbyshire
NL1	Cardiff	Glamorgan v Durham
NL2	Bristol	Glos v Surrey
NL1	Canterbury	Kent v Yorkshire
NL2	Manchester	Lancashire v Sussex
NL2	Northampton	Northants v Middlesex
NL1	Nottingham	Notts v Warwks
NL1	Worcester	Worcs v Somerset

Tues 21 May
BHC	Quarter-Final #1 (*Reserve 22 May*)

Weds 22 May
BHC	Quarter-Finals #2, 3, 4 (*Reserve 23 May*)

Thurs 23 – Sun 26 May
FCF	Cardiff	Glamorgan v Sri Lankans

Fri 24 – Mon 27 May
CC2	Chester-le-St	Durham v Glos
CC2	Nottingham	Notts v Northants
CC1	The Oval	Surrey v Somerset
CC1	Horsham	Sussex v Leics
CC1	Leeds	Yorkshire v Hampshire

Fri 24 May
CGT	Round 3 (*part – see p 300; reserve 25 May*)

Sun 26 – Weds 29 May
CC2	Chelmsford	Essex v Derbyshire

Sun 26 May
NL2	Manchester	Lancs v Middlesex

Weds 29 May
CGT	Round 3 (*part – see p 300; reserve 30 May*)

Thurs 30 May – Mon 3 June
TM2	Birmingham	England v Sri Lanka

Fri 31 May – Mon 3 June
CC2	Derby	Derbys v Glamorgan
CC2	Bristol	Glos v Worcs
CC1	Southampton	Hampshire v Warwks
CC1	Tunbridge W	Kent v Sussex
CC1	Manchester	Lancashire v Surrey
CC1	Leicester	Leics v Yorkshire
CC2	Lord's	Middlesex v Durham
CC2	Northampton	Northants v Essex

Tues 4 June
NL1	Tunbridge W	Kent v Notts
NL2	Manchester	Lancashire v Glos
NL1	Leicester	Leics v Glamorgan
NL2	Lord's	Middlesex v Hampshire
NL2	Northampton	Northants v Surrey
NL2	Horsham	Sussex v Essex
NL1	Birmingham	Warwks v Durham
NL1	Leeds	Yorkshire v Worcs

Thurs 6 – Sun 9 June
FCF	Chesterfield	MCC v Sri Lankans

Thurs 6 June
BHC	SEMI-FINAL #1 (*reserve 7, 8 June*)

Fri 7 June
BHC	SEMI-FINAL #2 (*reserve 8 June*)

Sun 9 June

NL1	Cardiff	Glamorgan v Kent
NL1	Oakham S	Leics v Worcs
NL2	Southampton	Hampshire v Derbyshire
NL2	Lord's	Middlesex v Sussex
NL2	Northampton	Northants v Glos
NL1	Nottingham	Notts v Yorks
NL1	Birmingham	Warwks v Somerset

Weds 12 – Sat 15 June

CC2	Chester-le-St	Durham v Worcs
CC2	Ilford (tbc)	Essex v Northants
CC2	Lord's	Middlesex v Glamorgan
CC2	Nottingham	Notts v Derbyshire
CC1	Bath	Somerset v Hampshire
CC1	The Oval	Surrey v Kent
CC1	Birmingham	Warwks v Leics
CC1	Leeds	Yorkshire v Sussex

Weds 12 – Fri 14 June

FCF	Durham	Durham UCCE v Lancashire

Thurs 13 – Mon 17 June

TM3	Manchester	England v Sri Lanka

Sun 16 June

NL2	Derby	Derbyshire v Northants
NL1	Chester-le-St	Durham v Worcs
NL2	Ilford (tbc)	Essex v Lancashire
NL2	Bristol	Glos v Middlesex
NL2	Southampton	Hampshire v Surrey
NL1	Nottingham	Notts v Kent
NL1	Bath	Somerset v Leics
NL1	Leeds	Yorkshire v Warwks

Mon 17 June

	Oxford	British U v W Indies A

Tues/Weds 18, 19 June

CGT	Round 4 (see p 300; reserve 19, 20 June)	

Weds 19 June

FHove	Sri Lankans v W Indies A	

Fri 21 June

	Hove/Chelms/	†Sussex/Essex/Surrey v
	The Oval	West Indies A
	Taunton/Card/	†Somerset/Glamorgan/
	Bristol	Glos v Sri Lankans

Sat 22 June

BHC	Lord's	FINAL (Reserve 23 June)
	FHove/So'ton/	*†Sussex/Hampshire/Kent
	Canterbury	v Indians

Sun 23 June

NL2‡	Derby	Derbyshire v Lancashire
NL1‡	Chester-le-St	Durham v Yorkshire
NL2‡	The Oval	Surrey v Sussex
NL1‡	Worcester	Worcs v Warwks
	Cant/So'ton/	†Kent/Hampshire/Essex
	Chelmsford	v West Indies A

	Bristol/Taunt/	†Glos/Somerset/Glamorgan
	Cardiff	v Sri Lankans

† Tourist's opponents in order of priority – BHC
  Finalists not available.

‡ If in BHC Final, matches will be played on Mon
  24 June.

Mon 24 June

	Cardiff	Wales v England
	Canterbury	*Kent v Indians
	Northampton	Northants v Sri Lankans

Tues 25 – Thurs 27 June

	Southampton	Hampshire v
		Loughborough UCCE

Tues 25 June

	Lord's	Cambridge U v Oxford U

Weds 26 – Sat 29 June

FCF	Oxford	Oxford U v Cambridge U
FCF	Derby	Derbyshire v W Indies A
CC2	Cardiff	Glamorgan v Middlesex
CC2	Gloucester	Glos v Essex
CC1	Liverpool	Lancashire v Kent
CC2	Northampton	Northants v Notts
CC1	Arundel	Sussex v Yorkshire
CC1	Birmingham	Warwks v Somerset
CC2	Worcester	Worcs v Durham

Weds 26 June

	Leicester	*Leics v Indians

Thurs 27 June

LOI	FNottingham	England v Sri Lanka

Sat 29 June

LOI	Lord's	England v India

Sun 30 June

LOI	The Oval	India v Sri Lanka
NL2	Gloucester	Glos v Essex
NL2	Manchester	Lancashire v Surrey
NL1	Nottingham	Notts v Leics
NL1	Taunton	Somerset v Glamorgan
NL2	Arundel	Sussex v Middlesex
NL1	Birmingham	Warwks v Kent
NL1	Worcester	Worcs v Durham

Tues 2 July

LOI	Leeds	England v Sri Lanka
	Lord's	UCCE Challenge Final

Weds 3 – Sat 6 July

CC2	Derby	Derbyshire v Glos
CC2	Swansea	Glamorgan v Essex
CC1	Southampton	Hampshire v Sussex
CC1	Maidstone	Kent v Warwks
CC1	Leicester	Leics v Lancashire
CC2	Lord's	Middlesex v Worcs
CC2	Northampton	Northants v Durham

FCF	Nottingham	Notts v West Indies A
CC1	Taunton	Somerset v Surrey

Thurs 4 July
LOI	^FChester-le-St	England v India

Sat 6 July
LOI	Birmingham	India v Sri Lanka

Sun 7 July
LOI	Manchester	England v Sri Lanka
NL2	Derby	Derbyshire v Glos
NL1	Swansea	Glamorgan v Leics
NL2	Southampton	Hampshire v Sussex
NL1	Maidstone	Kent v Durham
NL2	Southgate	Middlesex v Surrey
NL2	Northampton	Northants v Lancashire
NL1	Taunton	Somerset v Worcs
	Leeds	Yorkshire v W Indies A

Tues 9 July
LOI	The Oval	England v India

Weds 10 – Sat 13 July
CC2	Darlington	Durham v Derbyshire
CC2	Southend	Essex v Worcs
FCF	Liverpool	Lancashire v W Indies A
CC1	Leicester	Leics v Hampshire
CC2	Southgate	Middlesex v Glos
CC2	Nottingham	Notts v Glamorgan
CC1	The Oval	Surrey v Warwks
CC1	Hove	Sussex v Kent
CC1	Scarborough	Yorkshire v Somerset

Thurs 11 July
LOI	^FBristol	India v Sri Lanka

Sat 13 July
LOI	Lord's	FINAL (Reserve 14 July)

Sun 14 July
NL2	Southend	Essex v Hampshire
NL1	Canterbury	Kent v Worcs
NL1	Leicester	Leics v Warwks
NL2	Southgate	Middlesex v Glos
NL1	Nottingham	Notts v Glamorgan
NL2	Hove	Sussex v Northants
NL1	Scarborough	Yorkshire v Somerset

Mon 15 July
NL2	^FManchester	Lancashire v Derbyshire

Tues 16 July
CGT	Quarter-Finals #1, 2 (Reserve 17/18 July)	
	Arundel (tbc)	*Indians v West Indies A

Weds 17 July
CGT	Quarter-Finals #3, 4 (Reserve 18 July)	

Thurs 18 – Sun 21 July
CC2	Southgate	Middlesex v Essex

Thurs 18 July
NL2	Cheltenham	Glos v Hampshire

Fri 19 – Mon 22 July
CC2	Derby	Derbyshire v Notts
CC2	Cheltenham	Glos v Glamorgan
CC1	Canterbury	Kent v Surrey
CC1	Taunton	Somerset v Sussex
CC2	Worcester	Worcs v Northants
CC1	Leeds	Yorkshire v Lancashire

Sat 20 – Mon 22 July
FCF	Southampton	*Hampshire v Indians
FCF	Birmingham	Warwks v West Indies A

Sun 21 July
NL1	Chester-le-St	Durham v Leics

Mon 22 July
NL2	^FChelmsford	Essex v Middlesex

Tues 23 July
NL2	^FSouthampton	Hampshire v Lancashire

Weds 24 – Sat 27 June
CC2	Chester-le-St	Durham v Notts
CC2	Chelmsford	Essex v Glamorgan
CC2	Cheltenham	Glos v Middlesex
CC1	Leicester	Leics v Kent
FCF	Taunton	Somerset v West Indies A
CC1	Guildford	Surrey v Yorkshire
CC1	Birmingham	Warwks v Sussex

Weds 24 July
NL2	^FNorthampton	Northants v Derbyshire

Thurs 25 – Mon 29 July
TM1	Lord's	England v India

Thurs 25 – Sun 28 July
CC1	Southampton	Hampshire v Lancashire
CC2	Northampton	Northants v Derbyshire

Sun 28 July
NL1	Chester-le-St	Durham v Notts
NL2	Cheltenham	Glos v Sussex
NL1	Leicester	Leics v Kent
NL2	Guildford	Surrey v Essex
NL1	Birmingham	Warwks v Glamorgan
NL1	Worcester	Worcs v Yorkshire

Mon 29 July
	Cheltenham	Glos v West Indies A

Tues 30 July
NL1	^FCanterbury	Kent v Warwks

Weds 31 – Sat 3 August
FCF	Worcs/Leics/	*†Worcs/Leics/Sussex
	Hove	v Indians

† Tourist's opponents in order of priority – CGT
Semi-Finalists not available.

Weds 31 July
CGT   Semi-Final #1 (*Reserve 1, 2 August*)

Thurs 1 August
CGT   Semi-Final #2 (*Reserve 2 August*)

Sat 3 August
NL2	Derby	Derbyshire v Hampshire
NL1	Chester-le-St	Durham v Kent
NL1	Cardiff	Glamorgan v Somerset
NL2	Bristol	Glos v Lancashire
NL2	Whitgift S	Surrey v Northants
NL1	Leeds	Yorkshire v Notts

Sun 4 August
NL2	Lord's	Middlesex v Essex
NL2	Northampton	Northants v Hampshire
NL1	Birmingham	Warwks v Leics
NL1	Worcester	Worcs v Glamorgan

Mon 5 August
| NL2 | FHove | Sussex v Glos |
| NL1 | FLeeds | Yorkshire v Durham |

Tues 6 August
| NL2 | FManchester | Lancashire v Hampshire |
| NL2 | Whitgift S | Surrey v Middlesex |

Weds 7 – Sat 10 August
CC2	Derby	Derbyshire v Essex
CC2	Cardiff	Glamorgan v Glos
CC1	Canterbury	Kent v Somerset
CC2	Lord's	Middlesex v Northants
CC1	Leeds	Yorkshire v Warwks

Weds 7 August
| NL2 | FHove | Sussex v Surrey |
| NL1 | Worcester | Worcs v Notts |

Thurs 8 – Mon 12 August
TM2   Nottingham   England v India

Thurs 8 – Sun 11 August
CC1	Manchester	Lancashire v Hampshire
CC1	Hove	Sussex v Surrey
CC2	Kidderminster	Worcs v Notts

Sun 11 August
NL2	Derby	Derbyshire v Essex
NL1	Cardiff	Glamorgan v Yorkshire
NL1	Canterbury	Kent v Somerset
NL1	Leicester	Leics v Durham
NL2	Lord's	Middlesex v Northants

Tues 13 August
| NL2 | FBristol | Glos v Northants |

Weds 14 – Sat 17 August
CC2	Derby	Derbyshire v Worcs
FCF	Chelmsford	*Essex v Indians
CC1	Southampton	Hampshire v Somerset
CC1	Manchester	Lancashire v Yorkshire
CC1	Leicester	Leics v Surrey

CC2 Nottingham   Notts v Middlesex
CC1 Birmingham   Warwks v Kent

Weds 14 August
| NL1 | FChester-le-St | Durham v Glamorgan |

Thurs 15 – Sun 18 August
| CC2 | Bristol | Glos v Northants |

Fri 16 – Mon 19 August
| CC2 | Chester-le-St | Durham v Glamorgan |

Sun 18 August
NL2	Southampton	Hampshire v Essex
NL1	Leicester	Leics v Yorkshire
NL1	Nottingham	Notts v Somerset
NL2	The Oval	Surrey v Derbyshire

Mon 19 August
| NL1 | FTaunton | Somerset v Notts |
| NL1 | FBirmingham | Warwks v Worcs |

Tues 20 August
| NL2 | FHove | Sussex v Lancashire |

Weds 21 – Sat 24 August
CC2	Colchester	Essex v Durham
CC2	Lord's	Middlesex v Derbyshire
CC2	Northampton	Northants v Glamorgan
CC2	Nottingham	Notts v Glos
CC1	Taunton	Somerset v Warwks

Weds 21 August
| NL1 | FCanterbury | Kent v Leics |
| NL2 | FThe Oval | Surrey v Hampshire |

Thurs 22 – Mon 26 August
TM3   Leeds   England v India

Thurs 22 – Sun 25 August
CC1	Canterbury	Kent v Leics
CC1	The Oval	Surrey v Hampshire
CC1	Hove	Sussex v Lancashire

Sun 25 August
NL2	Colchester	Essex v Northants
NL2	Lord's	Middlesex v Derbyshire
NL1	Taunton	Somerset v Warwks

Mon 26 August
| NL1 | Colwyn Bay | Glamorgan v Notts |

Tues 27 – Fri 30 August
CC2	Chester-le-St	Durham v Northants
CC2	Colwyn Bay	Glamorgan v Notts
CC1	Southampton	Hampshire v Yorkshire
CC1	Blackpool	Lancashire v Somerset
CC1	Leicester	Leics v Sussex
CC1	Birmingham	Warwks v Surrey
CC2	Worcester	Worcs v Middlesex

Tues 27 August
| NL2 | FColchester | Essex v Glos |

Weds 28 – Fri 30 August
FCF Derby   Derbyshire v Indians

Thurs 29 August
CGT Round 1 (2003) *(see p 300; reserve 30 August)*

Sat 31 August
CGT Lord's   FINAL *(Reserve 1 September)*

Sun 1 September
NL1‡ Chester-le-St   Durham v Somerset
NL2‡ Southampton   Hampshire v Middlesex
NL2‡ Manchester   Lancashire v Essex
NL2‡ Northampton   Northants v Sussex
NL1‡ Birmingham   Warwks v Notts
NL1‡ Worcester   Worcs v Kent
NL1‡ Leeds   Yorkshire v Glamorgan
‡ *Depending on CGT Finalists*

Mon 2 September
NL2 ^FDerby   Derbyshire v Surrey

Tues 3 September
NL1 ^FCardiff   Glamorgan v Worcs
NL2 ^FHove   Sussex v Hampshire

Weds 4 – Sat 7 September
CC2 Chelmsford   Essex v Middlesex
CC2 Bristol   Glos v Derbyshire
CC1 Manchester   Lancashire v Warwks
CC1 Taunton   Somerset v Kent
CC1 Scarborough   Yorkshire v Leics

Weds 4 September
NL1 ^FNottingham   Notts v Durham

Thurs 5 – Mon 9 September
TM4 The Oval   England v India

Thurs 5 – Sun 8 September
CC2 Cardiff   Glamorgan v Worcs
CC1 Hove   Sussex v Hampshire

Fri 6 – Mon 9 September
CC2 Nottingham   Notts v Durham

Sun 8 September
NL2 Chelmsford   Essex v Surrey
NL2 Bristol   Glos v Derbyshire
NL2 Manchester   Lancashire v Northants
NL1 Taunton   Somerset v Kent
NL1 Scarborough   Yorkshire v Leics

Tues 10 September
NL1 ^FBirmingham   Warwks v Yorkshire

Weds 11 – Sat 14 September
CC2 Derby   Derbyshire v Middlesex
CC2 Chester-le-St   Durham v Essex
CC1 Southampton   Hampshire v Surrey
CC1 Canterbury   Kent v Lancashire
CC2 Northampton   Northants v Glos
CC2 Nottingham   Notts v Worcs

Weds 11 September
NL1 ^FLeicester   Leics v Somerset

Thurs 12 – Sun 15 September
CC1 Leicester   Leics v Somerset
CC1 Birmingham   Warwks v Yorkshire

Thurs 12 September
CGT Round 2 (2003) *(see p 300; reserve 13 September)*

Sun 15 September
NL1 Canterbury   Kent v Glamorgan
NL2 Shenley   Middlesex v Lancashire
NL2 Northampton   Northants v Essex
NL1 Nottingham   Notts v Worcs
NL2 Hove   Sussex v Derbyshire

Weds 18 – Sat 21 September
CC2 Chelmsford   Essex v Notts
CC2 Cardiff   Glamorgan v Northants
CC2 Bristol   Glos v Durham
CC1 Taunton   Somerset v Lancashire
CC1 The Oval   Surrey v Leics
CC1 Hove   Sussex v Warwks
CC2 Worcester   Worcs v Derbyshire
CC1 Leeds   Yorkshire v Kent

Sun 22 September
NL2 Derby   Derbyshire v Middlesex
NL2 Chelmsford   Essex v Sussex
NL1 Cardiff   Glamorgan v Warwks
NL2 Southampton   Hampshire v Northants
NL1 Taunton   Somerset v Durham
NL2 The Oval   Surrey v Glos
NL1 Worcester   Worcs v Leics
NL1 Leeds   Yorkshire v Kent

WOMEN'S TRIANGULAR SERIES
Jul 10 Grainville, Jersey England v India
Jul 11 Grainville, Jersey New Zealand v India
Jul 12 Grainville, Jersey England v New Zealand
Jul 16 Chester-le-St   New Zealand v India
Jul 17 Chester-le-St   England v New Zealand
Jul 19 Chester-le-St   England v India
Jul 20 Chester-le-St   FINAL

WOMEN'S TEST MATCH SERIES – England v India
TM1 Shenley   Thurs 8 – Sun 11 August
TM2 Taunton   Weds 14 – Sat 17 August

ENGLAND U-19 v INDIA
TM1 Cardiff   Sat 27 – Tues 30 July
TM2 Southampton   Weds 7 – Sat 10 August
TM3 Northampton   Tues 13 – Fri 16 August
LOI Bristol   Tues 27 August
LOI Taunton   Thurs 29 August
LOI Taunton   Fri 30 August

CHELTENHAM & GLOUCESTER TROPHY FIXTURES 2002

Round 3 – Weds 29 May (reserve 30 May)

29	Exmouth	Devon v YORKS
30	Bury St E	Suffolk v NORTHANTS
31	Telford	Salop v GLOS
32	Beaconsfield	Bucks v SUSSEX
33	Horsford	Norfolk v KENT
34	Sleaford	Lincs v GLAM
35	Cov/N Wa	Warwks CB v LEICS
36	Clontarf	Ireland v NOTTS
37	Stone	Staffs v WARWKS
38	St Austell	Cornwall v WORCS
39	Edinburg	Scot v SURREY
40	Scarboro'	Yorks CB v SOMERSET
41	Folkestone	Kent CB v HANTS
42	Cardiff	Wales MC v DURHAM
43	Manchester	†LANCS v DERBYS
44	Chelmsford	†ESSEX v MIDDX

† to be played on 24 (25) May.

Round 4 – Tues/Weds 18, 19 June
(reserve 19, 20 June)

45	Winner # 36	v	Winner # 38
46	Winner # 33	v	Winner # 37
47	Winner # 40	v	Winner # 41
48	Winner # 30	v	Winner # 29
49	Winner # 44	v	Winner # 43
50	Winner # 35	v	Winner # 32
51	Winner # 31	v	Winner # 42
52	Winner # 39	v	Winner # 34

Quarter-Finals 16, 17 July
Semi-Finals 31 July, 1 August
Final 31 August

C & G TROPHY QUALIFICATION
FOR 2003

Round 1 – Thurs 29 Aug 2002 (prov. reserve day 30 Aug)

1	Banbury	Oxon v Lancs CB
2	Finchampst'd	Berks v Ireland
3	Kidderminster	Worcs CB v Dorset
4	Ratcliffe U	†Denmark v Leics CB
5	Camborne	Cornwall v Som CB
6	Southgate	Middx CB v Derbys CB
7	Cov/N Wa	Warwks CB v Herefords
8	Bristol	Glos CB v Surrey CB
9	Dinton	Bucks v Suffolk
10	Hursley Pk	Hants CB v Wilts
11	Luton	Beds v Herts
12	Keswick	Cumb v Notts CB
13	tba	Cheshire v Hunts
14	Northampton	Northants CB v Yorks CB

Round 2 – Thurs 12 Sep 2002 (prov. reserve day 13 Sep)

15	Scotland	v	Winner # 1
16	Winner # 2	v	Norfolk
17	Winner # 3	v	Sussex CB
18	Kent CB	v	Winner # 4
19	Wales MC	v	Winner # 5
20	Winner # 6	v	Cambridgeshire
21	Durham CB	v	Winner # 7
22	Essex CB	v	Winner # 8
23	Winner # 9	v	Shropshire
24	Winner # 10	v	Staffordshire
25	Winner # 11	v	Holland
26	Devon	v	Winner # 12
27	Winner # 13	v	Lincolnshire
28	Northumberland	v	Winner # 14

† Leicestershire will play at home as Denmark's pitch has not yet been approved for CGT matches.

FIRST ROUND BYES (14): 2001 County Competition Quarter-Finalists (Devon, Durham CB, Essex CB, Kent CB, Lincolnshire, Norfolk, Shropshire, Sussex CB) and six free draws (Cambridgeshire, Holland, Northumberland, Scotland, Staffordshire, Wales CB). First-class counties enter in Round 3.
CB Cricket Board 'recreational team'.

2003 WORLD CUP FIXTURES

The eighth World Cup (the first to be staged in Africa) will be played over 43 days in February and March 2003. Its record tally of 54 matches has been divided among 12 venues in South Africa, two in Zimbabwe and one in Kenya. Because of the dew factor only ten of the games will be floodlit day/night affairs (†), five apiece at Newlands and Kingsmead.

Match	Pool	Feb	Venue	
PRELIMINARY ROUNDS				
1	B	Sun 9	†Cape Town	South Africa v West Indies
2	B	Mon 10	Bloemfontein	Sri Lanka v New Zealand
3	A	Mon 10	Harare	Zimbabwe v Namibia
4	A	Tue 11	Johannesburg	Australia v Pakistan
5	B	Tue 11	†Durban	Bangladesh v Canada
6	B	Wed 12	Potchefstroom	South Africa v Kenya
7	A	Wed 12	Paarl	India v Holland
8	B	Thu 13	Port Elizabeth	West Indies v New Zealand
9	A	Thu 13	Harare	Zimbabwe v England
10	B	Fri 14	Pietermaritzburg	Sri Lanka v Bangladesh
11	B	Sat 15	†Cape Town	Kenya v Canada
12	A	Sat 15	Pretoria	Australia v India
13	B	Sun 16	Johannesburg	South Africa v New Zealand
14	A	Sun 16	East London	England v Holland
15	A	Sun 16	Kimberley	Pakistan v Namibia
16	B	Tue 18	Benoni	West Indies v Bangladesh
17	A	Wed 19	Port Elizabeth	England v Namibia
18	B	Wed 19	Paarl	Sri Lanka v Canada
19	A	Wed 19	Harare	Zimbabwe v India
20	A	Thu 20	Potchefstroom	Australia v Holland
21	B	Fri 21	Nairobi	Kenya v New Zealand
22	A	Sat 22	†Cape Town	England v Pakistan
23	B	Sat 22	Bloemfontein	South Africa v Bangladesh
24	B	Sun 23	Pretoria	West Indies v Canada
25	A	Sun 23	Pietermaritzburg	India v Namibia
26	A	Mon 24	Bulawayo	Zimbabwe v Australia
27	B	Mon 24	Nairobi	Kenya v Sri Lanka
28	A	Tue 25	Paarl	Pakistan v Holland
29	A	Wed 26	†Durban	England v India
30	B	Wed 26	Kimberley	New Zealand v Bangladesh
31	B	Thu 27	East London	South Africa v Canada
32	A	Thu 27	Potchefstroom	Australia v Namibia
33	B	Fri 28	†Cape Town	Sri Lanka v West Indies
34	A	Fri 28	Bulawayo	Zimbabwe v Holland
		Mar		
35	B	Sat 1	Johannesburg	Kenya v Bangladesh
36	A	Sat 1	Pretoria	Pakistan v India
37	A	Sun 2	Port Elizabeth	Australia v England
38	B	Mon 3	Benoni	New Zealand v Canada
39	B	Mon 3	†Durban	South Africa v Sri Lanka
40	A	Mon 3	Bloemfontein	Namibia v Holland
41	B	Tue 4	Kimberley	West Indies v Kenya
42	A	Tue 4	Bulawayo	Zimbabwe v Pakistan

SUPER SIX

43	Fri	Mar	7	Pretoria	Pool A – 1st v Pool B – 1st
44	Fri	Mar	7	†Cape Town	Pool A – 2nd v Pool B – 2nd
45	Sat	Mar	8	Bloemfontein	Pool A – 3rd v Pool B – 3rd
46	Mon	Mar	10	Johannesburg	Pool A – 2nd v Pool B – 1st
47	Tue	Mar	11	Port Elizabeth	Pool A – 1st v Pool B – 3rd
48	Wed	Mar	12	Bloemfontein	Pool A – 3rd v Pool B – 2nd
49	Fri	Mar	14	Pretoria	Pool A – 2nd v Pool B – 3rd
50	Sat	Mar	15	East London	Pool A – 3rd v Pool B – 1st
51	Sat	Mar	15	†Durban	Pool A – 1st v Pool B – 2nd

SEMI-FINALS

52	Tue	Mar	18	Port Elizabeth	Super 6 – 1st v Super 6 – 4th
53	Thu	Mar	20	†Durban	Super 6 – 2nd v Super 6 – 3rd

FINAL

54	Sun	Mar	23	Johannesburg

PREVIOUS WORLD CUP FINALS

1975	WEST INDIES (291-8) beat Australia (274) by 17 runs	Lord's
1979	WEST INDIES (286-9) beat England (194) by 92 runs	Lord's
1983	INDIA (183) beat West Indies (140) by 43 runs	Lord's
1987-88	AUSTRALIA (253-5) beat England (246-8) by 7 runs	Calcutta
1991-92	PAKISTAN (249-6) beat England (227) by 22 runs	Melbourne
1995-96	SRI LANKA (245-3) beat Australia (241-7) by 7 wickets	Lahore
1999	AUSTRALIA (133-2) beat Pakistan (132) by 8 wickets	Lord's

SCORING OF EXTRAS 2002

The variable penalties involved in scoring no-balls and wides in our international and county cricket remain unchanged from last season:

COMPETITION	NO-BALL PENALTY	WIDE PENALTY
Test Matches Limited-Overs Internationals }	1 + other runs scored	1 + other runs scored
County Championship Second XI Championship }	2 + other runs scored	2 + other runs scored
Tourist Matches (First-Class) Tourist Matches (Limited-Overs) Benson & Hedges Cup C & G Trophy Second XI Trophy }	2 + other runs scored	1 + other runs scored
NU National League }	2 + other runs scored + a free hit next ball	1 + other runs scored

FIELDING CHART

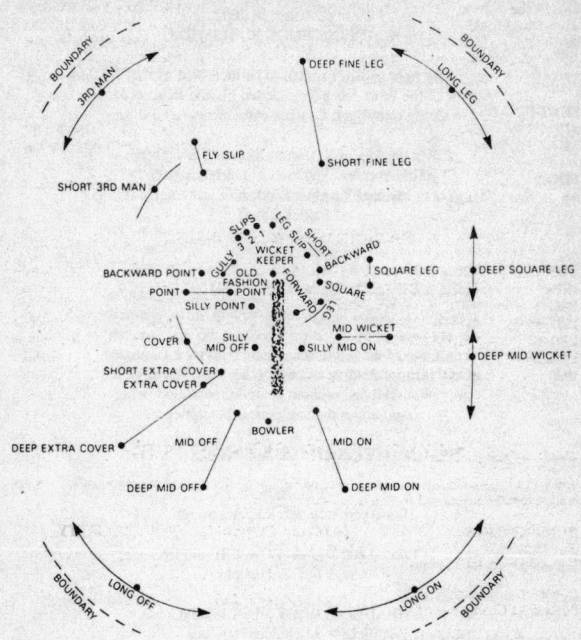

First published in 2002
by HEADLINE BOOK PUBLISHING

The right of Bill Frindall to be identified as the
Author of the Work has been asserted by him in accordance
with the Copyright, Designs and Patents Act 1988.

Cover photographs: (*Front*) Marcus Trescothick
(Somerset and England) © Patrick Eagar;
(*back*) Michael Vaughan (Yorkshire and England)
© Patrick Eagar.

10 9 8 7 6 5 4 3 2 1

ISBN 0 7553 1039 X

Typeset by
Letterpart Limited, Reigate, Surrey

Printed and bound in Great Britain by
Clays Ltd, St Ives plc.

HEADLINE BOOK PUBLISHING
A division of Hodder Headline
338 Euston Road
London NW1 3BH

www.headline.co.uk
www.hodderheadline.com